Building Powerful Platforms with Windows CE®

Building Powerful Platforms with Windows CE®

James Y. Wilson
Aspi Havewala

ADDISON–WESLEY

Boston • San Francisco • New York • Toronto • Montreal
London • Munich • Paris • Madrid
Capetown • Sydney • Tokyo • Singapore • Mexico City

The publisher offers discounts on this book when ordered in quantity for special sales. For more information, please contact:

Pearson Education Corporate Sales Division
201 W. 103rd Street
Indianapolis, IN 46290
(800) 428-5331
corpsales@pearsoned.com

Visit AW on the Web: www.awl.com/cseng/

Library of Congress Cataloging-in-Publication Data

Wilson, James Y.
Building powerful platforms with Windows CE® / James Y. Wilson, Aspi Havawala.
p. cm.
Includes bibliographical references and index.
ISBN 0-201-61636-X
1. Microsoft Windows (Computer file) 2. Operating systems (Computers)
I. Havewala, Aspi. II. Title.
QA76.76O63W5615 2001
005.4'469—dc21
00–054835

Text printed on recycled and acid-free paper.
ISBN 020161636X
3 4 5 6 7 8 MA 06 05 04 03
3rd Printing December 2003

For additional copyright information, please see p. vi.

This book is dedicated to you the reader, for without you it would be nothing more than the remnants of a tree whose fall went unheard. The printed word, like the sound without a listener, is nothing until it occupies the mind of its reader. Only then does it spring to life, full of possibilities.

For my wife Denise, who sacrificed countless weekends to the many hours of writing and research required to author a technical book; my friend and coauthor Aspi, truly a member of my extended family; and my fur children Monte and Coffee, whose dedication to the simple art of lap warming never failed to comfort.

James Y. Wilson

For my wife Mudita, my son Romil, my parents Jimmy and Arnawaz, my friend Jim, and Robocop.

Aspi Havewala

Contents

Preface

Introduction

Throughout the 1980s and 1990s, technological advances that gave rise to the Internet and wireless communications began to mount a serious challenge to the limited role of a *personal* computer (PC). Initially visualized as a more *personalized* extension for large mainframe computers, concealed in mysterious rooms with raised floors and noisy air conditioners, the personal computer soon became the center of home and office computing. Today we are witnessing the emergence of yet another type of computer: portable information appliances, offering even more personalized computing than the personal computer anchored to one's desktop. These devices are made more powerful not by ever increasing CPU speed and available storage, but by their ability to function as a distributed computer, accessing the world's most powerful asset, information.

Digital cable and digitized music, voice, and video are some examples of this information, which is made more valuable by access through portable information appliances. Just imagine what would happen if televisions, music entertainment systems, telephones, and camcorders could all work together. New usage models would appear, effectively creating a scenario in which the functionality of these systems acting collectively would exceed their usefulness when acting individually. For example, entire movies could be shot, edited, and produced via an array of interconnected, portable information appliances that worked together to provide online distribution, without the need for physical media. When usage models such as these become reality, they will challenge traditional ways of doing business.

The technological objectives in the engineering of a portable information appliance are quite different from those of a desktop PC. Portable information appliances must be compact, lightweight, and economical, and they must provide a slew of new features—most importantly, connectivity with other information appliances. Established operating systems like Windows, UNIX, MacOS, and Linux, designed for desktops with ever increasing processing and storage capabilities, are often unsuitable for such appliances. A smaller, lightweight, and highly flexible operating system is required.

Microsoft's solution in this space is the Windows CE operating system. Designed and implemented for devices with limited computing and storage resources, it offers a variety of features that make it possible to create highly specialized, portable information appliances. A small sample of such devices would include industrial controllers, phones, music players, televisions, game consoles, camcorders, organizers, and even compact laptops.

Using Windows CE to create a custom platform is a process that we call *Building Powerful Platforms with Windows CE.* Microsoft's premier tool for building custom platforms is aptly called Windows CE Platform Builder. This book takes a focused look at the use of this tool and, in exploring its features, outlines the process by which CE is modified to support your platform's distinguishing features.

We would like to think that this book has something for everyone, and though this may be true, you will undoubtedly find it most useful if you are an engineer working to adapt CE to function on a custom platform. If you are a software engineer dedicated to writing software for a particular device, traditionally known as embedded-systems engineering, your job will be to get CE up and running as soon as possible. Our prime directive in writing this book is to accelerate this process, by giving you an understanding of CE from the perspective of an embedded-systems software engineer. If we are successful, you will be as familiar with CE as you are with your custom platform, and you will be well equipped to avoid any unexpected gotchas.

We have taken great pains to go beyond simply documenting the use of Platform Builder. We treat Platform Builder as a tool that you can use effectively only if you're equipped with an understanding of certain principles and practices. To this end we have created a set of 12 chapters that will provide you with expertise in a particular principle or practice. Chapter 1 introduces Windows CE—its motivation, goals, architecture, design, and implementation. In Chapter 2 we discuss the often ignored project management aspects of creating a custom platform with Windows CE. This chapter walks the technical lead and/or project manager through the discrete steps involved in completing a CE custom platform project.

Chapter 3 introduces Windows CE Platform Builder. It describes how to use Platform Builder to quickly create a custom build of the Windows CE kernel. In Chapter 4 we demystify the more challenging aspects of creating and debugging a boot loader by analyzing the Platform Builder sample boot loader source code and the various options available for debugging boot loader code. Development of the OEM Adaptation Layer (OAL), the mechanism used by CE to access the hardware of your custom platform, is covered in Chapter 5. Chapters 6 through 9 dissect how to design, implement, and debug Windows CE device drivers.

To put it all together, Windows CE uses a complex and powerful process to build the operating system. This build process is explored in Chapters 10 and 11. In Chapter 12 we detail a little-used feature of Windows CE, the Device Driver Test Kit (DDTK), which can be used to implement automated testing and can be of significant value in the manufacturing process for your custom device.

Four different appendices are provided for additional background on topics of interest to CE developers. Appendix A lists the CE modules that help to document how the functionality of the overall operating system has been partitioned. Appendix B provides a primer on the use of the Nmake tool and the creation of the files needed to manage the build process for any software project. Appendix C provides a list of resources that are helpful in jump-starting the process of making CE operational on your custom platform. This appendix is referenced at various places throughout the book. Appendix D provides an excellent overview of the process of creating CE display drivers.

Document Conventions

Upload versus *Download*

The terms *upload* and *download* are used throughout this book. The Microsoft documentation that accompanies the Windows CE Platform Builder (CEPB) does not distinguish between the uploading and downloading of data and uses these terms interchangeably. In this book we have opted to use both the terms *upload* and *download* to describe more accurately what is happening when data is flowing from one location to another. To minimize any confusion on this matter, we will explain how these terms are used in the context of this book.

At times the location of data may correspond to a development workstation, while at other times the device (or target platform) is the focus of your CE development efforts. Consider for a moment that we are describing the flow of data with respect to your development workstation. If data is being sent *to* your CE device, it is flowing away (upstream) from its source (the development workstation), so it is said to be *uploading*. In contrast, if data is being received *from* its source (the CE device), it is flowing into your development workstation (downstream), so it is said to be *downloading*. The key to remembering the difference is to realize that you can only upload *to* and download *from*.

Text Conventions

The following table describes the typographic conventions used throughout the book. These conventions do not apply to listings or figures.

Convention	Main Purpose(s)	Examples
`Monospace` font	To format all listings and to refer to a particular element (i.e., function name, variable, macro, etc.) of a listing, as well as to path and file names.	(1) Beginning of the SHx StartUp routine... (2) `.\PLATFORM\ODO\EBOOT\EBOOT\SHX`
Boldface type	To refer to menu items, window names, and new terms.	(1) **File | New** menu item (2) **New Platform** window (3) A **component** is a particular functionality...
Italic type	To refer to words as words, to emphasize an important point, and to identify on-screen messages.	(1) The word *project* in this case... (2) It is best to follow the dictum, *Do not add files you do not own.* (3) The message *Copying Platform header files...* is displayed...
Angle brackets: < >	To refer to the name of an item or symbol. When you see this notation in a syntax statement,	If you see <CE Version>\PLATFORM\<Platform Name>\KERNEL\HAL\

(continued)

Convention	Main Purpose(s)	Examples
	substitute the item or symbol with the data it references, but do not type the angle brackets. If angle brackets appear without surrounding square brackets or braces (described below), the associated data is required.	debug.c and the name of your platform is Sherry and you're using CEPB version 3.0, you might type "WINCE30\PLATFORM\SHERRY\KERNEL\HAL\debug.c".
Square brackets: [ ]	To refer to optional arguments or parameters for commands. You may omit optional arguments and parameters in any command.	If you see CESH [-p <CESH configuration saved in the registry>], you might type "CESH –p CEPC" or "CESH".
Braces: { }	To indicate a choice of arguments or parameters for commands. If the arguments appear separated by a vertical line—{ | }—you must select *one*.	If you see .\PLATFORM\ODO\BOOTLOAD\{SHX|MIPS}, you might type ".\PLATFORM\ODO\BOOTLOAD\SHX".

Web References

The Addison-Wesley Web site at http://www.aw.com/cseng will provide an updated list of any scheduled appearances by this book's authors, along with scheduled trade shows for Addison-Wesley and references to book reviews for this book as they become available. The Addison-Wesley Web site specifically dedicated to this book, at http://www.aw.com/cseng/titles/0-201-61636-X, will provide additional information on this book's content and an errata section for errors discovered after publication. The same page will include a link to the authors' Web site, providing general references for Windows CE software development and updates to the book's accompanying software.

Acknowledgments

Various people helped us in creating this text to make it adhere to our high standards. We are grateful to all of them, but some are worth special mention to acknowledge their "discretionary" efforts.

No amount of thanks is sufficient to express our gratitude to Regis Bridon, at Microsoft. Simply stated, without his help this book would not have been possible. He encouraged us along the way and helped us to present early versions of our work to audiences at Microsoft development conferences. As one of those people who manages to work on many tasks simultaneously, he is always very busy. Somehow he found the time to add just one more task whenever we needed help.

Our copy editor, Stephanie Hiebert, is to be congratulated for single-handedly conducting a masterful transformation of our prose. We would no doubt be sounding less articulate, less consistent, and less accurate, were it not for the wonder of her watchful eye. Her ability to spot errors both grammatical and technical is truly amazing.

Karen Gettman convinced us we should do the book with Addison-Wesley, and this has been a decision we have never regretted. Gary Clarke worked closely with us during most of the content development, and his input and encouragement kept us going. In addition, we want to acknowledge the inputs and help extended to us from Addison-Wesley by Mary Hart, Meera Ramchandran, Rebecca Bence, Emily Frey, and Mamata Reddy. We are also indebted to our reviewers: Bill Craun, Jeffery R. Galinovsky, Paula Tomlinson, Monika Weikel, and Michael Whitley.

This book has seen us through several transitions in our lives. We changed jobs, houses, cities, and perspectives. Our family and friends remained the same, and we believe they had much to do with us finishing our book and making it the best text on Windows CE that we could possibly make it.

About the Authors

James (Jim) Y. Wilson graduated with a B.S. in Information Systems from California State University, Long Beach. He has accumulated eight software patents for various algorithms used in data communcations and mobile device technology. He currently resides in Atlanta with his wife and two fur children, Monte and Coffee.

Jim began his software career writing Windows applications in the early days of its evolution with version 2.11. From there, he progressed to Windows device drivers and embedded systems programming for specialized consumer electronic devices. He has contributed to the development of various technology standards such as PCMCIA and USB. He was also a member of the development team producing one of the first wireless Windows Based Terminals called CruisePAD, based on Windows CE 2.01. Jim works as an independent software consultant for Quantum Computing, Inc. and may be reached at james_y_wilson@acm.org or jywilson99@hotmail.com. Please check this book's Web site for the most current contact information.

Jim's research interests focus on evolutionary algorithms for robotic control and learning. He is currently working on an open source project called the Open Robot SDK (ORSDK) that will provide a platform independent software library for robotics research and development. It is scheduled for release at *http://www.openrobot.org* sometime in the middle of 2001.

Aspi Havewala has extensive experience developing products for different markets. His experience includes managing software projects, consulting, and designing and developing device drivers, desktop, and web applications. He also writes technical articles on programming, process, and management for journals and online content providers.

Aspi has a master's degree in computer science from Texas Tech University in Lubbock, Texas, and a bachelor's degee in computer science from M.S. University in Vadodara, India. He lives in Arlington Heights, Ill., with his wife Dr. Mudita Rastogi and two-year-old son Romil and makes frequent trips back home to fulfill his urge for home-cooked Indian cuisine. His spare time is often devoted to discussing the state of the world with his wife, playing with his son, the pursuit of art, and catching up on cricket scores from around the world.

1 Windows CE Architecture

Traditional desktop operating systems developed by Microsoft benefit from running on well-defined, if not strictly standardized, hardware. Operating systems like Windows 98, NT, and 2000 contain kernel code and drivers that are written for the IBM-compatible PC platforms. Moreover, the evolution of desktop PCs permits the use of ever increasing hardware resources like processor speed, RAM, persistent storage, and so on. The operating system is relatively free to make assumptions about what is available in terms of minimum memory, speed and type of processor, and hard disk space.

Windows CE, on the other hand, is targeted to the consumer electronics space. In this world of embedded systems, hardware architectures come in garden varieties, and nothing can be assumed. Devices are also typically constrained by resources. They include processors, but not with the traditional muscle associated with desktop processors. In contrast, embedded processors focus on reducing power consumption. Memory is available but is typically minimal because of cost limitations. Hard drives are usually absent because they are not rugged enough to withstand the shocks and jolts of a mobile environment (rugged hard drives that are capable of operating in such environments come at a significant price premium). Displays are small because many consumer devices are portable. Most of the hardware components are optimized first for size, power consumption, and cost, and only then for speed. Think of the conundrum contained in the words *smaller, smarter, cheaper, faster.* They reflect the directive for the design of most consumer electronic devices.

The architecture of Windows CE reflects the hardware the operating system was designed to support. To fully explain all aspects of the architecture would take a book in its entirety. We will make the best use of a single chapter to cover the most important aspects of the Windows CE operating system. We will eschew explaining CE internals unless they are critical to the understanding of the component.

Whenever relevant, we will briefly introduce the API used to accomplish specific tasks related to the module being discussed. The fleeting API primer serves as a quick reference. It should always be supplemented with the Windows CE Platform Builder documentation. (Chapter 3 will explain Platform Builder in detail.) For example, we talk about the functions that perform certain tasks, but we don't necessarily explain their parameters or give examples. This material is available in the Platform Builder documentation and doesn't need to be reproduced here.

Cross-Processor Support

Windows CE can be used to operate a variety of devices. These devices might be designed to serve different markets and hence will vary significantly in hardware architecture. One such difference in hardware is the microprocessor itself. To accommodate such variations, Windows CE supports a variety of processors.

Windows CE is written to be as portable as possible across processors. However, because of fundamental differences in microprocessor design, portions of the operating system must contain specific knowledge about a processor. This makes these portions processor-specific. Windows CE isolates this processor-specific code in three sections. One is a portion of the kernel, which is provided by Microsoft. The second is called the OEM Adaptation Layer (OAL), which is typically written by the device manufacturer (OEM stands for *original equipment manufacturer*). The third is called the boot loader, which is also provided by the device manufacturer. Chapter 4 examines the boot loader; Chapter 5 provides details on the OAL. The boot loader is responsible for booting the system by correctly configuring the processor and peripheral chips. The OAL contains code specific to a particular platform that is built through the use of a given microprocessor, and it is responsible for abstracting and managing hardware resources of the processor.

A third-party vendor, also called a Windows CE system integrator, may provide an OAL and bundle it with the processor-specific kernel. Commonly referred to as a board support package (BSP), such a software bundle also has device drivers for any devices that are platform specific. BSPs can be purchased from a system integrator or created by a device vendor.

You can access processor-specific information on Windows CE by calling the system function `CeGetSystemInfo`. This function returns information such as processor type, addressable memory, and page size.

Page Size

One important factor to understand when considering processor-specific code is the page size. Processors address memory by groups of bytes called pages in order to optimize access and subsequent manipulation of chunks of memory. Page sizes vary among processors. Windows CE processors support two page sizes: 1K and 4K. For instance, the Hitachi SuperH processors use a 1K page size, while Intel, AMD, and Motorola PowerPC processors use a 4K page size. Why is page size important to a developer? Because memory will be allocated in chunks equal to page sizes whenever you request it, even if it is only a single byte you need. Optimization of memory usage is very critical because the devices on which the processor is likely to run usually have small memory footprints.

Common Executable Format

When compiling software for Windows CE, you must consider the processor on which the software will execute. In other words, if an application is expected to run on a variety of Windows

CE systems (like the Pocket PC), it must be compiled for all the different processors that are supported by the device. The Windows CE SDK ships with processor-specific compilers for every processor or family of supported processors. When compiling an application for a particular processor, you must invoke the corresponding compiler. This procedure is simplified if you are using Visual C++ configurations. **Configurations** are groups of instructions that are used to build an application. Invoking processor-specific compilers and setting their options correctly are operations that are automatically provided in different configurations by the Visual C++ wizards for Windows CE. However, the deployment of the application remains an issue when multiple copies of the application must be shipped as part of a single installation.

To address this problem, Windows CE for Visual C++, also called eMbedded Visual C++, provides an executable format called Common Executable Format (CEF). CEF allows application vendors to produce processor-independent executables. CEF must eventually be translated into the native code for the given processor. This conversion can take place in two different ways: It can occur during the installation process after the processor type of the device is known to the installer or at runtime when the CEF application is being executed.

For components such as ActiveX controls, CEF offers significant advantages. Normally, when an ActiveX control is downloaded via a browser on a user's device, the browser must first identify the type of processor on the device. Then the appropriate processor-specific binary of the ActiveX component is downloaded. If the device contains a processor that was added later to the list of those supported by Windows CE and the appropriate binary for the ActiveX component is not available, the user is out of luck.

CEF resolves all these issues. An ActiveX component compiled into a CEF executable can be safely downloaded to any device with casual disregard for the processor on the device. Processors added later are not a concern as long as the device knows how to convert a CEF file into native code. The only caveat is that CEF files, although processor independent, are still platform specific. Thus, a separate CEF file must be created for each specific device on which the application can execute.

When a CEF file is translated on the fly, Microsoft's internal benchmarks indicate that code runs between 3 and 20 percent slower than in a native executable. Executables translated from CEF files at install time also tend to be 10 to 20 percent larger than native executables, and this increased size causes an additional slowdown in execution. The benefits of using CEF files must be weighed against the disadvantages. The best way to do this is to run the CEF executable on several different devices and then compare the results to a processor-specific version of the executable. If multiple classes of devices are supported by the application, the fact that separate CEF files must be produced for each class of device must also be considered. Although not a comprehensive solution, CEF files can be a major help during development and deployment.

Processes and Threads

A **process** is an instance of a program in Windows CE. A program becomes an instance when it is loaded in executable memory by the CE loader. A process consumes no other resources except the memory footprint it occupies. Thus, it has no context. The memory of a process is isolated from that of other processes by the virtual memory implementation in Windows CE. Each process sees a unique memory address space. In other words, a certain address in the address space of a process could contain a value that is not visible from another process.

Handles allocated by a process for files, memory buffers, and CE objects are invalid in another process. This form of protection is necessary to create a robust runtime environment for an operating system. Malicious or otherwise, processes cannot overwrite the memory of a process and thus do untold damage. When a process terminates, the operating system kernel simply deallocates the virtual address space of that process.

Up to 32 processes can be running at any given time in Windows CE. However, only the available resources—namely, the system's available memory—limit the number of threads that each process can have in the system.

Threads are the smallest unit of execution in Windows CE. The CE scheduler, which allows all programs to execute in parallel, recognizes and schedules only threads. What if a process never creates a thread? How does the scheduler execute it? Each process gets a default, or **primary**, thread automatically, even if it never explicitly creates a thread. A thread occupies more resources than just memory. For example, it uses processor registers and requires a stack. Together these resources constitute the context of a thread. When threads are stopped from executing on the processor by the scheduler, the thread is **swapped**, a procedure in which the kernel saves the context information of the thread and starts executing the next thread in the system. When the thread resumes execution, its context is restored first so that the thread continues to execute from where it left off.

Threads can run in either **kernel mode** or **user mode**. In kernel mode, they have full access to all the resources of the operating system. The ability to run in kernel mode is restricted under Windows CE. The operating system threads and interrupt service routines (ISRs), for example, run in kernel mode. Applications and device drivers (except for the portion that executes in the ISR) run in user mode. Having full access to the entire system means that crashing a kernel mode thread can have devastating consequences on the operating system. The gain in this case is increased performance because the kernel bypasses security checkpoints when its thread accesses a resource. User mode threads, while slower in execution, offer a more protected operating environment. For example, crashing the display driver on Windows CE will not render the operating system unusable, so debugging can continue on a responding system over, say, a serial port.

The behavior by which all operating system threads run in kernel mode is called **full kernel mode** and can be changed by the OEM of the device. When changed, the threads run in user mode, allowing development of a device that is open to running programs from third-party vendors.

Creating Processes and Threads

Processes are created with the `CreateProcess` function. The name of an executable is passed as one of `CreateProcess`'s many arguments. The entire path name of the executable can be passed to this function. If the path is not known, Windows CE looks in the Windows directory (`\WINDOWS`), then in the root directory (`\`), then in directories specified by the OEM as the search path, and finally in the directory of an OEM-defined shell if one exists (`\PPSHELL`). If a process is being created from within another process, Windows CE looks in the current process's launch directory before going to the Windows directory. An OEM can specify a search path by adding a registry key under `HKEY_LOCAL_MACHINE` called `Loader` that contains the value `SystemPath`. `SystemPath` is a multistring value that contains each directory in the search path as a separate string. For more information on registry keys and values, see the section titled Manipulating the Registry later in this chapter.

CE Version Memo

Versions of Windows CE prior to 3.0 do not look in the process's current directory.

Amid other information, `CreateProcess` returns a handle to the created process (if the call was successful) and the ID of the process. The handle can be passed to other process management calls, such as `OpenProcess` and `TerminateProcess`, to identify the process.

A thread is created via the `CreateThread` function. The entry point of a thread is typically a function. The address of this function is passed to `CreateThread`, which creates a thread, starting its execution at the first line of the function. Although the signature of the function that can be used as a thread entry point is fixed, its one argument is a pointer to void data. This data is passed to the function via a parameter to the `CreateThread` call. The pointer can be a structure that holds all the information that needs to be passed to the thread by its creator. Because a pointer to the structure is passed, it is the creator's responsibility to ensure that the memory allocated to hold the structure is valid until the thread finishes using the values passed in the structure.

A thread may be created in a suspended state. Resources are allocated to such a thread, and the thread is then immediately put in the suspended queue by the kernel. A suspended thread may be resumed later via the `ResumeThread` function.

`CreateThread` returns a handle to the newly minted thread, as well as the thread's ID. The thread handle can be used in thread management calls such as `TerminateThread`, `GetExitCodeThread`, and `GetThreadPriority`, to name a few, in order to identify the thread.

A thread terminates when it returns from its function. The value that is returned by the thread can be obtained by another thread by a call to `GetExitCodeThread`. This function allows a thread to return its status to other threads. After termination<K>, <K>a thread's handle must be passed to `CloseHandle` to ensure that the thread's resources are released back to the operating system.

The Scheduler

The CE scheduler is preemptive and uses a priority-based time slice scheme to execute threads. Each thread gets a default time slice, or **thread quantum**, of 100 milliseconds. The OEM can configure this value during kernel initialization. The quantum allocated to a thread can be obtained at runtime by a call to the `CeGetThreadQuantum` function. A handle to a thread is required as a parameter to this call. If multiple threads are contending for execution time, the scheduler uses a simple round-robin mechanism to determine which thread runs first. However, CE also allows a thread to have up to 256 priorities, 0 being the highest priority and 255 the lowest.

CE Version Memo

`CeGetThreadQuantum` is supported only in Windows CE 3.0 and later versions.

CE Version Memo

1. The default thread quantum in Windows CE 2.12 and earlier versions is 25 milliseconds.
2. Windows CE 2.12 and earlier versions support only eight priorities.

Threads with higher priority run before threads with lower priority. The highest priority that a thread can obtain under CE is the **Time Critical Priority**. This priority is typically used by routines that process interrupt service routine (ISR) requests. An ISR itself is the only piece of executable code that can preempt a thread running at Time Critical Priority. We'll say more on this when we look at device drivers (Chapters 6 through 9). The priority of a thread is returned by the function `CeGetThreadPriority`, which accepts a handle to a thread.

CE Version Memo

CeGetThreadPriority is supported only in Windows CE 3.0 and later versions.

A thread normally uses its entire allocated time slice. However, a thread may voluntarily give up its time slice by making a `Sleep(0)` call. This call tells the thread to sleep for zero seconds, in effect passing control back to the scheduler, which swaps out the thread and looks for the next eligible thread to schedule. A thread may also decide to wait for some resources that may become available soon. It does so by calling the function `WaitForSingleObject` or `WaitForMultipleObjects`. This call also causes the thread to relinquish its time slice because the scheduler swaps out the thread and marks it in sleep state.

This last scenario can give rise to an interesting problem. Referred to as **priority inversion**, this problem occurs when a lower-priority thread is holding a resource that is required by a thread of higher priority. In this situation, the higher-priority thread waits for a resource that never becomes available because the lower-priority thread that is holding it is never scheduled to run. The result is **deadlock**. The scheduler detects the deadlock and boosts the priority of the lower-priority thread to at least that of the higher-priority thread, thereby forcing the lower-priority thread to run and release the resource. After the resource is released, the scheduler bumps the lower-priority thread back to its original priority.

Since only threads are visible to the scheduler, processes can get more CPU time simply by spinning more threads. For example, if process A has a single thread and process B has five threads, process B will get five out of every six time slices allocated to both processes. Creating more threads per process to accomplish tasks is always more resource friendly than creating multiple processes and passing messages back and forth. Threads are a more lightweight mechanism and can easily share information.

Synchronization

Threads often need to synchronize their operations. Windows CE provides several objects for this purpose: mutexes, semaphores, events, and critical sections. All of these objects, except critical sections, can have two states: signaled and nonsignaled. The nonsignaled state represents the ownership of the object by a particular thread or threads, and its nonavailability to other (waiting) threads. When an object becomes signaled, objects waiting for its availability are notified and scheduled to run, thereby enabling a lockstep operation between threads—the basis for synchronization.

Synchronization objects are represented, like all other objects in Windows, by a handle: a 32-bit pointer to a structure that points to the data used to identify the object. Windows CE provides a set of functions, collectively referred to as a **wait function**, which allows a thread to gain access to a resource. The wait function comes in two flavors: `WaitForSingleObject` allows a thread to wait for a single synchronization object, and `WaitForMultipleObjects` is used to wait for multiple synchronization objects.

Mutexes

A **mutex** is a mutual exclusion object. A thread can take ownership of this object to indicate that it is not available to any other thread. Subsequent threads that decide to acquire this mutex must wait for the first thread to signal its availability. Ownership can pass from thread to thread in the order in which the threads issued the wait call.

Mutexes can be used to synchronize access to a resource that can be used by only a single thread at a given time. Mutexes know about the thread that owns them. In other words, if a thread that owns a mutex decides to wait for it later in the code, the call will succeed immediately. This provision prevents the thread from accidentally deadlocking itself—a feature that is unique to a mutex and not available with the other synchronization objects.

Semaphores

It is most useful to think of a **semaphore** as a mutex with a count associated with it. If a semaphore has a count of *n,* then *n* threads can acquire the semaphore before additional threads are blocked. This restriction is useful for allowing access to a resource that can be used with only a fixed number of threads.

On creation (through the function `CreateSemaphore`), a semaphore's count is set to its maximum value. A thread acquires a semaphore by calling one of the Windows CE wait functions. When the wait function returns, the count of the semaphore is decremented by 1. When the semaphore's count is decremented to 0, subsequent threads calling the wait functions are blocked. A semaphore's count is incremented when a thread calls the `ReleaseSemaphore` function. Semaphores do not retain thread information. A thread that has acquired a semaphore can call the wait function again and block itself. As an alternative, the thread may decrement a semaphore's count by calling the wait function multiple times. With semaphores, care must be taken that this does not happen unless by design.

Semaphores are created with an initial count that can be any value held by a 32-bit variable. A new count can be associated with the semaphore after its creation. New counts can be specified after creation any time a semaphore is released by a thread. This feature can be used to model a resource that supports a dynamic number of threads.

An existing semaphore can be obtained by the `OpenSemaphore` function.

Events

To inform another thread that an event has occurred, a thread can use an event object. The first thread must signal the event. A thread interested in this notification typically calls one of the wait functions with the handle of the event. If the event has not been signaled by the first thread, subsequent threads block on the wait function.

A thread signals an event by calling `SetEvent`. An event can be put in nonsignaled state by a call to `ResetEvent`. Both actions are encapsulated by a single call to `PulseEvent`, which calls `SetEvent` and `ResetEvent`, releasing a thread waiting for the event and then putting the event back in nonsignaled state. Note the terminology "releasing *a* thread." This is the caveat to using `PulseEvent`: Only a single thread waiting for the event is released. If multiple threads are waiting for an event to be signaled, only the first one to call a wait function is released.

Critical Sections

If serial access needs to be provided to a resource in source code, a critical section can be used. A critical section is used to guard the source code that manipulates the resource. A thread claims ownership of a critical section by entering the section after calling `EnterCriticalSection`. A thread executing the same code tries to execute the call and blocks, thereby preventing more than one thread from manipulating the protected resource. A thread gives up the critical section by calling `LeaveCriticalSection`, which allows the blocked thread to enter the section and manipulate the resource.

Using Synchronization Objects

When a synchronization object is created, a handle is passed back to the caller. This handle can be used to identify the object in the wait function and other functions that operate on the object. The handle to the object can be passed between threads either by being put in a global object or by being passed to each thread on creation by the parent thread. All threads can then refer to the same synchronization object.

An alternative to this approach is to create a named object. Synchronization objects can be named. All threads can then create this object by name. The first thread to make the create call creates the object. Subsequent create calls simply return the handle to the already existing object. Thus, all threads refer to the same object. The only overhead you incur is in making the create call multiple times. You must make sure that the object is named uniquely as well. The name of the synchronization object must be unique regardless of its type. You cannot have a mutex and a semaphore of the same name without running into trouble.

Blocking on Threads and Interrupts

It is worth noting that a thread itself can function as a synchronization object. It may be passed as a parameter to any of the wait functions. When a thread terminates, either normally or abnormally, it acts like a synchronization object that has become available, thereby allowing a thread to block on another thread.

Windows CE allows threads to block on interrupts. This behavior is achieved through events. An interrupt service routine sets an event. A worker thread, which performs further service for this interrupt (also called a **deferred procedure call**) waits on this event. When the event is signaled, the worker thread finishes servicing the interrupt. We'll say more on this later in the book when we delve into the world of Windows CE device drivers (Chapters 6 through 9).

Communicating between Processes

Windows Messaging has long been the means by which processes communicate with each other (see the section titled Windows Messaging later in this chapter for additional details). Processes call the `RegisterWindowMessage` function, which returns a message ID that is guaranteed to be unique in the entire system. This message can safely be sent to windows or threads in other processes. The reason these messages need to be unique is to ensure that they do not conflict with a predefined message.

Windows messages can be used for communication between processes when the data that needs to be passed between processes can be packed into the well-known `wParam` and `lParam` members of a message. Both of these members are unsigned long integers (`DWORD`), so the amount of data that may be passed is limited to eight bytes. When more data needs to be passed, a structure can be used to hold the data and a pointer to the structure can be packed into `lParam` and sent to another process. However, the separate address space feature provided by virtual memory means that data allocated at a particular address for one process will contain a completely different set of values when the next process is executed. To bypass this limitation, Windows provides the predefined message `WM_COPYDATA`. The `lParam` member of this message is set to a structure of type `COPYDATASTRUCT`. A pointer to data to be passed to another process along with its size can be specified in this structure. The message *must* be sent by a call to `SendMessage`. This function gives the message management code an opportunity to copy the data into the recipient's address space before delivering the message.

Microsoft Message Queue

Windows messages can be delivered only to windows and threads that reside on the same workstation. When a message is being sent across a network, delivery must account for recipient identification, network transport, and systems that may be offline. The technology that allows for this form of message delivery is called Microsoft Message Queue (MSMQ). Unlike Windows Messaging, MSMQ provides guaranteed delivery based on message priority. The fact that messages may be delivered to offline processes makes MSMQ ideal for use when the client and server may not necessarily run at the same time.

Central to the concept of MSMQ is the **queue manager**, a component that manages messages sent to and received by applications. Queues are identified by name and have the format *<MachineName>\{PUBLIC|PRIVATE}$\<QueueName>*. The queue manager can manage multiple queues independently of the applications, thus providing the ability for either the client or the server to be offline at any time.

MSMQ supports three types of applications: MSMQ servers, independent clients, and dependent clients. An MSMQ server and an independent client both contain a queue manager. The MSMQ server, however, has the ability to route messages from the queues to other queues in the system. Independent clients cannot route messages from one queue to another; in this case a message in the queue must be consumed by another application. Dependent clients do not contain a queue manager and hence must always be connected to an MSMQ server. Queues created by independent clients are denoted as **private queues**; MSMQ servers create **public queues**.

MSMQ applications in Windows CE are independent clients. These applications can create only private queues, and only direct-format queue names are supported. **Direct-format** queue names are queues with the machine name specified as part of the queue name. Direct-format queues require the devices on which applications reside to be connected at all times. Since CE devices may not be connected to each other all the time, a routing server is required to route messages between intermittently connected devices. A separate queue called OutFRS (outgoing Falcon Routine Server) is implemented in CE. Messages are sent from an independent client to an OutFRS queue, in which messages contain the name of the desktop machine that implements the OutFRS server. When a device connects to the desktop, the messages held in the OutFRS queue are moved to the desktop and routed to the receiving device when the latter connects to the desktop.

The implementation of MSMQ on CE does not support transactions except for single message transactions, which guarantee a single delivery of a message.

A queue is created by a call to `MQCreateQueue` and deleted by a call to `MQDeleteQueue`. An existing queue can be opened via `MQOpenQueue` and closed via `MQCloseQueue`. Once a queue has been opened, it is referred to by the queue handle that is returned by the create or open calls. Messages are sent to the queue via `MQSendMessage` and received from it via `MQReceiveMessage`.

Memory Architecture

On a Windows CE system, memory can be provided via RAM, ROM, or flash memory. RAM is used in the traditional sense to run applications and provide buffers for application data. Many Windows CE devices, such as Handheld PCs, break from tradition by providing battery-backed RAM. Battery backup allows the contents of RAM to be saved even after the device has been turned off. Thus, an application in RAM remains until battery backup is exhausted or the system is manually reset. This feature is responsible for executing the instant-on capability of such devices. Although this capability is mainly a hardware feature, the operating system does provide support for it.

ROM in Windows CE devices may be used to hold programs. Its contents are persistent, and it can be compared to a hard disk in traditional PCs, without, of course, the moving parts. ROM typically contains the CE image, files that make up the operating system. For the operating system to be upgraded, a new ROM chip must be programmed and physically inserted into the device. This upgrade procedure protects the operating system from accidental overwrites, an essential feature in the creation of low-maintenance consumer devices. When a program is being run from ROM, it may be copied into RAM, where it is then executed. Windows CE supports execute-in-place (XIP) ROM that allows programs to be run directly from ROM memory itself. Running directly from ROM saves the RAM normally required to make a copy of the application. However, it also prevents the application in ROM from being compressed because decompressing it would require it to be loaded in RAM again. We discuss this in more detail in Chapter 10.

XIP functionality requires the use of memory where locations can be addressed individually. Thus, block mode devices such as memory that emulates hard disks cannot be used for XIP functionality. Another limitation of XIP is that because Windows CE itself uses XIP mode, the address space for XIP operation *must* be the address space in which the CE kernel is loaded. Only processes that load in this address space can use XIP mode.

An alternative to ROM is flash memory. Flash memory can be reprogrammed so that operating system images can be modified. Upgrades are thus possible. During upgrading, however, the entire image of the operating system must be burned in byte for byte. An ATA (Advanced Technology Attachment) flash card uses hardware components to simulate an ATA-style hard disk. However, linear flash cards can also be used with a software driver to emulate a hard disk under Windows CE. When the cards are used in this way, it is possible to upgrade portions of the operating system because flash memory can be addressed nonlinearly. For XIP functionality, linear flash memory is required.

Virtual Memory

A flat address space of 32 bits is supported. This means that processes can address up to 4GB of memory. Out of this, only the lower 2GB is available for use by the process. Allocations made by the process return memory in the lower 2GB of address space. The upper 2GB is used by the system for various purposes, which we will discuss shortly. The 4GB address space is supported by a page-based mechanism that implements virtual memory. Because a hard disk is not available, however, there is no place for the memory manager to swap out pages to accommodate additional requests in RAM. The memory requirements on such devices are very stringent and must be considered by all processes that utilize memory buffers.

Although it is possible to attach hard drives to CE devices, the operating system was designed for devices that used solid-state memory. Thus, CE does not swap pages in RAM to disk to sustain the illusion of having more memory than available RAM. However, virtual memory is a critical component of CE. It maps program requests for memory to physical memory and allows the system to address a 4GB address space. This total RAM is addressable in Windows CE. In reality, the available RAM in a device is much less. Thanks to virtual memory, however, an application does not have to worry about that. It can safely use the 4GB address space. Memory will be allocated and mapped from this 4GB space to whatever RAM is available on the device. When all available RAM on the device is used up, the allocations will fail.

Slot Architecture

Windows CE makes the virtual address space below 2GB available to programs. The lower 1GB of memory is divided into 33 slots of 32MB each. Each slot is further divided into 512 blocks of 64K each. Each process that is executing (whose threads are in the pool of schedulable threads) gets one slot to map its program and data space. Up to 32 processes can be running in the system at any given time. The thirty-third slot, or slot 0, as designated by CE, is used for the currently active process—essentially the process whose thread is being executed. Although the number of processes is limited to 32, only available RAM limits the number of threads that can be running in the system.

The next 1GB is used by the operating system for large memory allocations (Figure 1.1), including memory-mapped files. The address space from 2GB to 4GB is used exclusively by the system to store its own data and is considered off-limits for direct manipulation by applications.

When loading a process, the loader assigns it the next available slot in RAM. DLLs (dynamic link libraries) are loaded at the lowest address in the slot, followed by the stack, then the default process heap, and finally the executable. Whenever a process's thread is scheduled to run, it is copied from its slot into slot 0. Windows CE processes like the kernel, file system, windowing system, and so on all run in their own slots. This scheme greatly simplifies the need for memory management across multiple processes that interact.

If a process allocates memory, it gets an address that corresponds to slot 0. When inactive, the allocated memory must be mapped back to the original slot allocated to the process. This scenario is complicated when interprocess calls are made and pointers to data in slot 0 are passed to another process. Let's say that process A running in slot 4 is active (in slot 0) and allocates a buffer. It passes this buffer in a call to process B, which is running in slot 5. When process B is made active in slot 0, the buffer must be mapped to the actual data buffer in slot 4 because slot 0 is cleaned out and replaced with program and data information for process B and

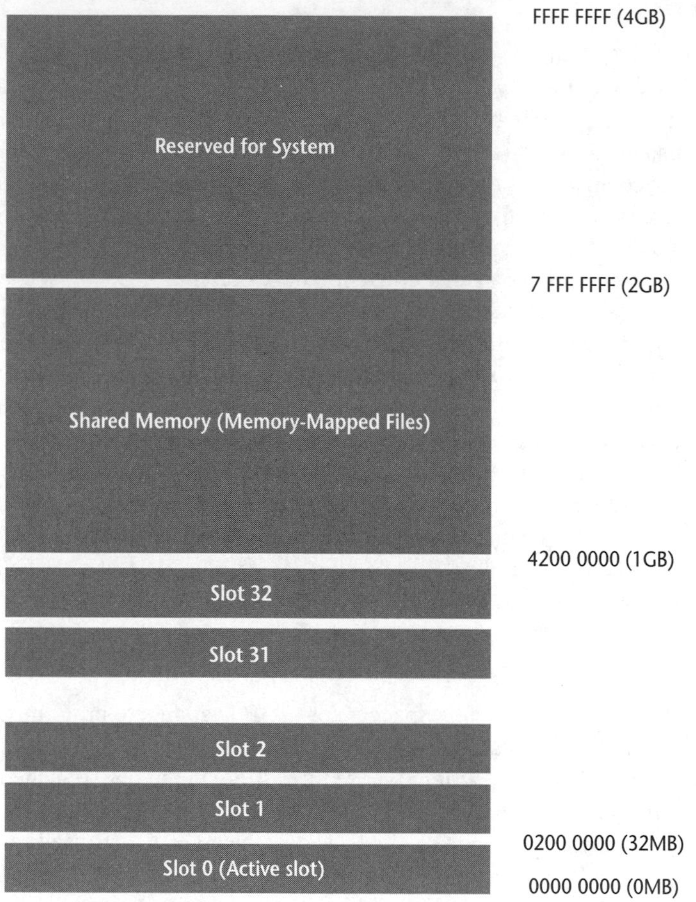

FFFF FFFF (4GB)

Reserved for System

7 FFF FFFF (2GB)

Shared Memory (Memory-Mapped Files)

4200 0000 (1GB)

Slot 32

Slot 31

Slot 2

Slot 1

0200 0000 (32MB)

Slot 0 (Active slot)

0000 0000 (0MB)

Figure 1.1 Memory layout in Windows CE

process A's data ceases to exist in slot 0. As an optimization, the kernel first checks to see if any call to another process has a pointer that maps to slot 0. If this is the case, the kernel first maps the data to its actual home in the appropriate process slot and then completes the call. Now when the process that processes the call is made active in slot 0, the buffer passed to it points to the correct data.

The Politics of Slot 0

If each process has its own slot, why have a special slot 0 for the active process and incur the overhead of moving a process across a slot? The answer is in the way Windows programs are structured. Windows programs are rarely stand-alone executables. Most of them have modular code structured in DLLs. In any given program there is plenty of traffic between the executable and one or more DLLs. When an executable process initializes a DLL, an instance of the DLL is created in the address space of the process. In the case of multiple processes, each process gets its own copy of the DLL.

Note
In process ActiveX servers and ActiveX controls are also DLLs.

When loading the code that belongs to the DLL, the loader makes sure that all instances of the DLLs, across multiple processes, are mapped to the same physical page of memory. This is a safe optimization because code is read-only memory and will not be modified. It can thus safely be shared. The data that is used by the DLL, however, is unique to each process and cannot be shared. Each process gets its own instance of the DLL data. Here, then, is the problem that is responsible for the existence of slot 0. The instance data for each DLL is in the slot that is occupied by the corresponding process that loaded the DLL.

How does the shared code know the slot in which it must access the instance data? The answer is that the shared code is always fixed up by the loader to use the instance data in slot 0. This makes sense because the DLL accesses the data only when its owning process is active and hence the data has already been copied into slot 0. Now the shared code can access instance data in a generic fashion. The overhead of housekeeping for slot 0 is justified when you consider the significant number of DLLs that are used across processes.

Protected Server Libraries

This brings us to an interesting, obscure question: If the address spaces of processes are separated from each other, how can a buffer allocated by one process be meaningful to another process? This is where the 33-slot model of Windows CE comes in handy: It implements isolated address spaces with workarounds in which a process can access the memory of another process simply because the process is mapped to a different region of the same 2GB of memory. The kernel, of course, can see all the memory available to all processes and can make these translations. This mechanism is used only internally by trusted system processes and is unavailable for use by any other processes.

When a process calls another process via an API, the thread that executes the API is running in the context of the called process. This mechanism allows one thread to easily cause a sibling process to crash. A common technique for isolating processes from one another is to trap a call made by the client process and copy the parameters to a thread running in the server process. After the server process is done processing the call, it returns control to the kernel, which then copies the results back into the client thread. This allows threads to run in their proper process context. This mechanism, however, requires significant overhead for resource-constrained systems. Threads require stack space and memory to manage. To optimize this precious commodity, Windows CE uses a mechanism called **protected server libraries** (**PSLs**). PSLs are threads that can register an API with the kernel. The kernel stores the function signature and traps any calls made to that function by other processes. The kernel then takes the client thread and modifies it to run in the process space of the server. This saves the overhead of creating an additional thread to process the call on the server side.

All threads have a special access token that gains them entry into PSLs. When a client thread enters a PSL, it is automatically given access to the PSL and its address space by the kernel. The thread behaves like any other thread in the PSL itself. When the thread leaves the PSL, the access is removed. Each 64K block of memory inside every slot has a set of access permissions. Before any operation is performed on this block, the kernel checks that the thread requesting the operation has access to that block. Thus, if a thread in a process is not executing inside a PSL, its access token prevents it from modifying memory that belongs to another process.

PSLs are used internally by Windows CE and are not available to users or OEMs.

Manipulating Memory

Processes can allocate memory in two forms: reserved and committed. The `VirtualAlloc` function must be used to allocate memory and specify its attributes. Reserved memory simply reserves address space for the application without actually mapping the virtual page to a physical page. When the memory is committed by the application, either during allocation or later (also by `VirtualAlloc`), the virtual page is mapped to a physical page in RAM and marked in use by the process. This allows processes to reserve memory and commit it only as needed. A process that requires 8K of memory may use only 2K at runtime. In this case only 8K of physical memory would be reserved, but only 2K would be mapped, thus freeing up the remainder for use elsewhere. Allocating reserved memory is very efficient and considerably faster than allocating committed memory.

The drawback of this scheme is that reserved memory is not guaranteed to be available when it needs to be committed. Additional calls must be made to commit memory when required. As an alternative, the autocommit flag (`MEM_AUTO_COMMIT`) can be passed when reserved pages of memory are being created. This flag will cause the system to automatically commit any previously reserved memory when the memory is accessed. Just as a request to commit a reserved page can fail because of low memory conditions, so can an access to memory allocated using the autocommit flag. Failed access attempts must be wrapped in a try/catch block to handle the failure.

Allocated virtual memory can be released back to the system by a call to the `VirtualFree` function. Using the `VirtualProtect` function can change the permissions of previously committed memory. `VirtualProtect` takes a starting address and the size of the memory whose attributes need to be changed. The function converts the addresses into corresponding pages and changes the permission of those pages. Note this important caveat: By calling this function, you may end up changing the permission of a page you do not intend to change.

The virtual memory functions also provide for a way to access specific physical memory locations. Why would one need such specific access? Usually device driver developers require such access to manipulate memory-mapped devices, which map their register space in a certain region of memory. To do this, first virtual memory must be reserved by a call to the `VirtualAlloc` function. Then a function called `VirtualCopy` must be called with the handle to the memory reserved and the physical location to which it wishes the virtual memory to be mapped. Other arguments accepted by the `VirtualCopy` function are the size of the physical memory that needs to be mapped and the permissions to be set on the corresponding pages. Since the underlying pages exist, the memory is considered committed.

To find out if memory is reserved or committed, the `VirtualQuery` function must be called with the base address of the memory being queried. Among other pieces of information in a structure called `MEMORY_BASIC_INFORMATION`, `VirtualQuery` also returns the protection attributes of the pages and the size of the allocated buffer.

Heap Memory

A process also has access to the local heap under Windows CE. The local heap is memory that can be allocated on a four- or eight-byte basis, as opposed to a page basis using the virtual memory functions. Although underneath a request for bytes may be a page allocation, using the heap functions at least isolates a process from the page size supported by the processor. The heap functions figure out how many pages must be allocated to satisfy a request for a certain number of bytes of heap memory.

Heaps are referenced by handles in Windows CE. All processes are allocated a default heap by the kernel. The handle to this heap can be obtained by a call to the `GetProcessHeap` function. There is no limit to the amount of memory available in the heap. Windows CE simply allocates memory as needed by the process. An initial amount of 192K is reserved by CE when a process starts up. If a process requires more memory, Windows CE allocates additional memory for the heap using the virtual memory functions. This behavior tends to fragment memory over a period of time because subsequently allocated memory probably will not be contiguous with the previous chunk of memory allocated for the heap. This must be a consideration for application developers, as must be the careful freeing of heap memory. Since the heap is built on top of the virtual memory functions, memory freed by the heap will not necessarily be reclaimed by the system until an entire page is freed.

CE Version Memo

In Windows CE 1.0 and 1.1, there is a limit of 1MB per heap.

Once a handle to a heap has been obtained, it can be used to allocate (`HeapAlloc`), reallocate (`HeapReAlloc`), or free (`HeapFree`) heap memory. `HeapAlloc` always returns at least the number of bytes requested if it succeeds. To adjust page sizes, however, the kernel may allocate more bytes than requested. The `HeapSize` function should be called on newly allocated memory to determine its actual size. Memory allocated from the heap can be passed into the `HeapSize` function to obtain the size of the buffer.

Processes can create heaps in addition to the default heap. The function that does this is called `HeapCreate`. `HeapCreate` takcs an initial size and a maximum size as arguments. The maximum size is supposed to specify the number of bytes that the system will reserve for the heap. The initial size specifies the number of bytes actually committed. Windows CE doesn't support the maximum size. The initial size specified is used, and the heap grows as necessary.

`HeapCreate` takes a third argument (actually its first argument when you make the call): A double word variable holds a series of flags. Windows CE supports only one such flag: `HEAP_NO_SERIALIZE`. If this flag is *not* specified, access to the heap will be serialized, thereby preventing multiple threads within a process from accessing the heap simultaneously and resulting in potentially corrupted data. Specifying `HEAP_NO_SERIALIZE` then should be thought of as an optimization to be used if serialization is not needed because of the way the program behaves or if another means of serialization is provided by the program.

A created heap is destroyed by a call to the `HeapDestroy` function. Memory allocated on the heap is not movable. Since the Windows CE memory manager cannot reorganize this memory, it tends to become fragmented with increasing use of the heap space.

Win32 developers should note that Windows CE does not differentiate between a local heap and a global heap. For this reason the functions `LocalAlloc`, `LocalSize`, and `LocalFree` all map to their Heap counterparts.

Stack Memory

Windows CE preallocates 60K of stack space per thread in a process. Of this space, 58K is available for use by the program, and Windows CE uses 2K for guarding against stack overflows. Stack space is used when a call frame is being created for a function to save the arguments to the function and its return address. Variables declared inside functions are also allocated on the stack. Take special care when using recursion in your functions because you could hit the stack space limit. Threads that do so will cause a system violation, which in turn will cause the program to be shut down.

Even if your thread is requesting stack space well under the 58K limit, it might not get the memory it is looking for. Since the scenario might be a temporary low memory condition, Windows CE simply suspends the thread that makes the request in the hope that memory will free up later. CE itself goes around reclaiming unused stack space from other threads until enough memory frees up to satisfy the thread's request or low memory conditions bring CE to a screeching halt (CE does offer the user some storage space to use as program RAM to keep applications running).

The memory allocated for a thread's stack is reclaimed whenever the thread terminates. A thread terminates by either calling the `ExitThread` function or simply returning from the function that implements the thread.

Handling Low Memory Conditions with WM_HIBERNATE

The instant-on feature of Windows CE uses battery-backed RAM. This means that a program may never leave RAM once loaded unless the device is reset under unusual circumstances. Consumption of significant amounts of memory by a program depletes system resources. When multiple programs are running, the system may run out of memory. In such a situation the system sends out a `WM_HIBERNATE` message to all top-level windows in their reverse Z order. A program must respond to this message by freeing as much memory as possible. After all programs have returned from processing `WM_HIBERNATE`, Windows CE retries allocating the memory it requires to fulfill any outstanding requests.

Graphics, Windowing, and Events Subsystem

The Graphics, Windowing, and Events Subsystem (GWES) in Windows CE provides the following basic services: a Graphical Device Interface, window and dialog management, user input, Windows Messaging, and power management.

Graphical Device Interface

The Graphical Device Interface (GDI) is the module that provides rendering for text and graphics. GDI makes heavy use of a concept in Windows called a **device context**, which is realized in

Windows CE as a data structure that stores certain rendering attributes. Device contexts contain information such as the target device, a pen for rendering lines, a brush for drawing and filling, a font for text, a palette that defines available colors, and a clipping region used to define the visible area of the display. When text or graphics are rendered on a device context, these attributes are used. Device contexts get default values for all these attributes, which are subsequently customizable by the user.

The word *context* in *device context* refers to the fact that the device context is an abstraction of an area on which text or graphics can be rendered. The target device could be any device that supports the rendering. Device contexts can be defined for the video display, printer, plotter, and even memory. This critical abstraction creates device-independent graphics output, reducing headaches for scores of developers who want to draw, print, and paint without having to worry about the underlying device.

Window and Dialog Management

GDI routines can be used to create windows, dialogs, and controls that interact with a user. Since the need for a program to create these elements is fundamental, Windows CE provides standard functions for these tasks. In doing so, it also allows programs to create a unified and integrated look for their user interface.

User Input

Devices often need to accept information from users. The users can choose to input the information using a variety of mechanisms—for example, keyboard, mouse, touch panel, or customized devices such as wheels. The processing of input from these devices is unified under GWES, which notifies programs when input is accepted from the user.

The input support provided by GWES also includes internationalization components such as the Input Method Manager (IMM), which is responsible for channeling input from the user to the Input Method Editor (IME). The IME is a component that translates keyboard characters into non-Roman character input. IMEs are heavily used for Asian languages that have complex scripts.

Windows Messaging

At the heart of Windows CE lies the messaging system, its **event system**. Note that these events are distinguished from the interprocess communication event objects.

Windows are constantly notified of activities such as user input, power management, and significant events in the operating system via Windows messages. GWES places messages addressed to a particular window in a queue dedicated to that window. At the heart of virtually every Windows program is a **message pump**, a portion of code that asks Windows for the next message in the queue. The placement of this component into GWES is a reflection of the tight integration between input and the way in which Windows CE notifies programs of the input: messages. Programs process these messages by registering a callback with Windows for every window it creates. The callback is called once for each message in the program's queue. This is an approximate working scenario; there are exceptions. However, since these exceptions are extraneous to our discussion here, we will bypass them.

Although we have said that a message queue is associated with a window, the reality is a bit different. Queues are associated with a thread. Every thread in Windows CE is given its own message queue. Messages can be addressed to a thread or a window. In the latter case, the message is sent to the message queue of the thread that created the window. Messages that come off the message queue are passed to the thread and serialized by the system. In other words, the messaging system makes sure that the thread's message procedure is not reentered.

Sending Messages

Messages are sent by calls to one of two functions: `PostMessage` or `SendMessage`.

`PostMessage` packages its arguments into a message and puts the message in the queue of the target thread. The call returns immediately. This is the preferred way of sending messages to another thread when the sending thread cannot afford to wait for the time required to process the message. Another scenario for making use of this call is when the sender cannot call certain Windows functions. In this case the sender cannot rely on what calls the recipient may make and thus simply plays it safe by posting the message and returning. Sending a message from an interrupt service routine is an example of such a scenario. When executing in an ISR, it is not prudent to make Windows calls that are likely to generate additional interrupts (e.g., disk access).

`SendMessage` is a synchronous version of `PostMessage`. When the sender calls `SendMessage`, the call does not return until the recipient thread has finished processing the message. `SendMessage` packages its arguments into a message and puts the message in the queue of the recipient thread. It then waits for the recipient to finish processing the message by waiting on an internal Windows interprocessor event. If the message is sent across a thread, a thread switch occurs before the message can be processed. Windows CE provides another flavor of this function called `SendNotifyMessage`, which behaves like `SendMessage` if the sending and recipient threads are the same. `SendNotifyMessage` behaves like `PostMessage` if the sending and recipient threads are distinguished.

Since threads are the ones that own a message queue, Windows CE provides a call to send a message directly to the thread. This function (`SendThreadMessage`) requires that the thread already have a message queue created. In an effort to keep thread creation lightweight and in the event that the thread might never use one, Windows CE does not automatically create a message queue for every thread. A thread will get a message queue when it invokes the calls that make up the message pump. The function in the pump that creates the message queue for the thread is called `GetMessage`, which also retrieves the first message from the message queue. This is a blocking call. In other words, `GetMessage` won't return until a message is available for processing. A nonblocking version of `GetMessage`, called `PeekMessage`, can be used to create a message queue and continue processing before blocking at a message pump. `PeekMessage` simply states whether a message is in the queue and gives its particulars. The message can be retrieved later by the `GetMessage` function.

Power Management

Like many other Windows CE modules, the power management module is optional. However, the nature of CE target devices makes it very critical to include power management. Note that this discussion is limited to power management of the device itself. Any peripherals attached to the device may manage power independently. Their power state may not necessarily correspond to that of the device itself, although the device will always be in a state that consumes more or equal power to that consumed by the state of any of its peripherals.

No Power

Ground zero is defined as the No Power state. In this state the device is receiving no power from any power source, including AC outlet, battery, and backup battery. No programs are loaded in RAM, and the device has not yet been configured. When Windows CE starts from a state of no power, the system registry is initialized from scratch. During normal operation, persistent information is stored in the registry. This includes but is not limited to program settings, user information, date/time, and communications settings.

As an example, the first Windows CE devices, such as Handheld PCs, required users to enter their information and calibrate their touch panel when starting from a No Power state. When a device is subsequently turned off, it is not put in a No Power state and the user does not have to go through the entire cycle of configuration again because the backup battery always refreshes the RAM and hence keeps the system registry intact.

On

The On state is a state of full power to the device. All peripherals have all the power available to them, and the CPU is consuming maximum power. Most devices are considered to be in an On state during normal operation.

Idle

When the device is on but is not used for a configurable period of time, it enters the Idle state. In this state peripherals like the display, PCMCIA cards, modems, network cards, and so on are shut down. The CPU continues to function in a low power state. This state is ideal to enter after short bursts of inactivity because the power savings gained from shutting down peripherals can be significant. However, since the CPU is still functioning at full power, resumption from this state takes very little time.

Suspend

In this state the peripherals and CPU are turned off. The Suspend state corresponds to the lowest power consumption of the device. If capable of doing so, the device can continue to receive enough power to refresh RAM so that its settings and programs are not lost. Windows CE suspends the device in a graceful way by providing notification to programs and device drivers, which take appropriate action. The Suspend state is entered in response to four major events:

1. The device manufacturer may provide an **Off** button on the device. If the user presses the **Off** button, the device appears to turn itself off by entering the Suspend state. When the **On** button is pressed, the device wakes up the CPU, restores power to the device, and continues normal operations—a feature called **instant on**.
2. If the device enters a configurable period of sustained inactivity, the Suspend state may be entered. The assumption here is that the user has quit operating the device and it is prudent to save power.
3. The Suspend state may also be entered under low battery conditions. In this case, the device attempts to save power by putting the device in Suspend state without

waiting for the inactivity time-out or for the user to press the **Off** button. The device manufacturer must then provide a message to the user regarding the low battery condition.

4. Finally, the user may initiate a Suspend sequence by selecting the **Suspend** menu choice from the **Start** menu. This is effectively like pressing the **Off** button.

Critical Off

The Critical Off state is like the Suspend state: It stops the CPU and cuts power to the peripherals. The difference is in the condition that creates the transition to the Critical Off state. Critical Off is reached when the device reaches a low battery condition that makes it impossible for the device to continue normal operation and creates a danger of RAM data being lost. In this case, Windows CE does not notify any programs or device drivers but simply cuts power to the peripherals and stops the CPU. The device does not make the transition out of this state until it receives appropriate power.

During this state a RAM refresh voltage is continually supplied so that the device does not lose its state. As an example, on a Handheld PC the Critical Off state is reached when the replaceable or rechargeable batteries run out of power and the backup battery is called into service to refresh RAM.

Power Management Transitions

While Windows CE defines the states, the device manufacturer (OEM) controls the state *transitions.* For example, the OEM can specify that the device enter the Suspend state when the user explicitly asks an OEM-provided software utility to do so.

Table 1.1 shows how various power states can make the transition to one another. The state diagram in Figure 1.2 depicts the transitions visually.

Table 1.1 Conditions That Lead to Power State Transitions

FROM \ TO	No Power	On	Idle	Suspend	Critical Off
No Power		If the device undergoes (1) a cold boot, in which RAM contents are cleared, including the file system, system registry, and all programs loaded in RAM (this is the case when power is applied for the first time to the device) or (2) a warm boot, in which all programs loaded in RAM are cleared, but the file system and system registry are retained (this is the case when the user explicitly resets the device).			
On	If the device is explicitly reset by the user (warm boot) or all power to the device is removed immediately (cold boot).		In response to a previously configured inactivity time-out.	In response to a prolonged inactivity time-out, if the user turns the device off, or if a program requests entry into this state.	If power supplied to the device reaches a critical low, making it impossible for the device to function normally.
Idle		In response to user activity on the device, usually by means of some input.		In response to a prolonged inactivity time-out.	If power supplied to the device reaches a critical low, making it impossible for the device to function normally.
Suspend		If the user turns off the device or a program requests entry into this state.			If power supplied to the device reaches a critical low, making it impossible for the device to function normally.
Critical Off	If the device runs out of all power, including battery backup.	If sufficient power is applied to the device.		If sufficient power is applied to the device.	

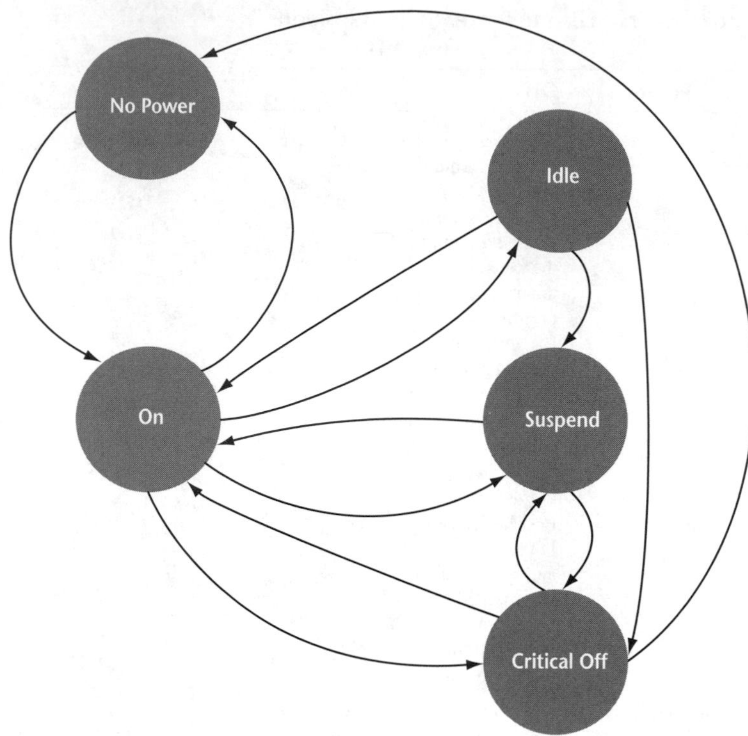

Figure 1.2 Power state transitions

Programs in Windows CE can get power information, including battery level, by calling `GetSystemPowerStatusEx`. However, GWES does not notify programs of any transitions in power states. Programs can be written to be impervious to power transitions. The only issue about which developers need to be scrupulous is following proper application guidelines and allowing the message pump or the wait functions to block their threads at appropriate times. If a program had a loop that ran continuously and performed its own scheduling, the system would be unable to make the transition to a low power state because technically the program was never idle, and the battery life of the device would thus be decreased.

If a program needs to be aware of power on and off transitions, a companion device driver can be written that notifies the program when the changes occur. Device drivers get power on and off notifications from GWES.

File System

Like any other file system, the Windows CE file system allows users to create files and folders. The underlying implementation, however, is significantly different from that of other file systems and bears mention in a discussion of CE architecture. The file system's job is to allow users to access data stored in ROM, flash memory, RAM, and any other media attached to the device in a uniform way—namely, as files and folders. Abstractions are built on top of these two basic primitives.

The ROM and flash memory are used to store program files. In RAM, however, things are a bit different. RAM can hold program files, data files, and the system registry. In addition, an object store is maintained in RAM. CE splits the RAM address space into an area for loading programs and data, and an area for the object store.

Object Store

The object store is used to create databases that provide basic features such as compression and transaction-oriented access. Compression and transaction-oriented access are always provided with databases. On battery-powered mobile devices, these features are crucial. Compression helps save precious memory on memory-constrained devices. Transaction-oriented access keeps the data in a consistent state in case the device loses its power source. If the device loses power during an access or a series of accesses, designated as a **transaction**, the entire transaction is rolled back and the database is restored to its previous state.

Each database in the object store is placed in a separate file of a particular format, referred to as a **database volume**. Data is stored as a series of records in each database. The object store and database volume have upper size limits: 256MB and 16MB, respectively.

CE Version Memo

In Windows CE 2.0 and earlier versions, files in RAM cannot be more than 4MB in size.

Storage Media

Windows CE supports a file system based on file allocation tables (FATs). The FAT driver works with any external storage cards that can be plugged into the device, such as Advanced Technology Attachment (ATA) and linear flash cards. Most such cards are PCMCIA cards; the device itself is not restricted from providing alternative hardware for interfacing with non-PCMCIA storage media.

A file system can exist on the storage cards. Cards can be partitioned into sections. Each section is then mounted as a FAT **volume** and placed under a special folder in the CE root directory. The device driver associated with the card provides the name of the mounted folder. If a name is not provided, CE uses the default label *Storage Card* to mount the file system. The file system can now be used to hold folders, files, and databases, although the database is not considered part of the object store. Such a file system is referred to as an **installable file system**. An installable file system device *must* support FAT for it to work with Windows CE.

CE Version Memo

Installable file systems are supported in Windows CE 2.10 and later versions.

If the FAT file system does not fit an OEM's needs, all is not lost. There is the option of developing your own file system driver (FSD). A driver for a storage card can request CE to load a specific FSD that provides support for any new features that may be inaccessible via FAT. An FSD is simply a DLL that provides predefined entry points. These entry points map to well-known Windows CE file system functions. When a call is made to a volume, the module called the FSD Manager looks for the FSD associated with the mounted volume being accessed and calls the appropriate entry point in the FSD DLL.

Besides providing this mapping, the FSD Manager provides calls that isolate an FSD from operating system details. For example, when a program tries to create a file, the FSD Manager calls the appropriate FSD entry point, which creates the file and passes back a file handle to the program. The file handle is an operating system object, and hence the FSD Manager provides a call to create such a handle. The FSD will simply call the FSD Manager, obtain this handle, and then pass it back to the calling program.

Manipulating Files

A file's attributes can be obtained by a call to the `GetFileAttributesEx` function. This function can also be used to check for directories. A file that has the attribute `FILE_ATTRIBUTE_DIRECTORY` is a directory. A file with the attribute `FILE_ATTRIBUTE_ROMMODULE` is a file that is stored in ROM; this is an important attribute. `GetFileAttributesEx` also returns file creation and modification time, as well as the size of the file, in a `WIN32_FILE_ATTRIBUTE_DATA` structure.

CE Version Memo

In Windows CE 2.12 and earlier versions, this function is called `GetFileAttributes` and returns only file attributes. To get creation and modification time and the size of the file, you must make additional calls to `GetFileTime` and `GetFileSize`.

Files stored in ROM cannot technically be altered for content or attributes in any way. However, some files stored in ROM are required to be modified. For example, configuration files in the `\WINDOWS` directory need to be modified by the operating system itself. In this case a copy of the file is created in RAM in the same directory. Windows CE hides the ROM version of the file and shows only the RAM version to the user. This is how files may be *modified* in ROM. When the file in RAM is deleted, the ROM file shows up again. In effect, if a file is in ROM, you cannot delete it. But you can modify its contents. Deleting it reverts the file to its original content.

This *RAM shadowing* also applies to DLLs. A DLL in ROM can be replaced by a newer DLL with the same signature as the previous one in RAM. The newer DLL will be used in place of the older one even if a program is statically linked to the older DLL.

Files can be either created or opened by name with `CreateFile`. This function can be instructed to create a file only if one by the same name doesn't already exist in the folder. In this case if a file exists, `CreateFile` will simply open the file. This handy feature allows you to create a file or open an existing file with just one call. If a new file must be created every time `CreateFile` is called, the flag `CREATE_NEW` can be passed in the flags argument of the call. The return value is the handle to the file. If the operation fails, the handle is not set to `NULL` as one might expect. Instead, the handle is set to the predefined value `INVALID_HANDLE_VALUE`. Recall that `CreateFile` will not work in a directory in ROM that does not have an existing file with the same name.

Once opened, the handle to the file obtained via `CreateFile` can be passed to the `ReadFile` and `WriteFile` functions to read a buffer from and write a buffer to the file, respectively. To be able to read from a file, you must pass the `GENERIC_READ` flag to `CreateFile`. To support writes to a file, `CreateFile` must be given the `GENERIC_WRITE` flag. These flags can be OR'd together when passed as an argument. To close a file, you must call the `CloseHandle` function with the file handle as a parameter. Write operations on files are buffered by the operating system. Although CE will periodically flush the buffers to the file, it is good practice to flush these buffers directly if the file is open for long periods of time and is gathering data. The function to call in this case is `FlushFileBuffers`.

Some operations that can be performed on a file do not require a file handle. The functions `CopyFile` and `MoveFile` copy and move a file to a new location, respectively. An important caveat is that `MoveFile` returns failure if you attempt to move a file across a mounted volume. While `MoveFile` moves a file across folders, the function `DeleteAndRenameFile` may be used to move a file and change its name simultaneously. The function `DeleteFile` removes a file identified by name.

To search for a file by specifying its name or a filter with wild-card letters (like * or ?), you must invoke the function `FindFirstFile`. This function returns a handle that serves to identify the search. `FindFirstFile` returns information about the first file that meets the search criteria. Subsequently, you must call `FindNextFile` with the same search handle to obtain information on additional files that meet the criteria.

Manipulating Folders

Although a folder is a file with the `FILE_ATTRIBUTE_DIRECTORY` attribute set, `CreateFile` cannot be used to create the directory. For this purpose, you must use `CreateDirectory`. To delete a directory, you should use `RemoveDirectory`.

Note that the well-known computing concept of a current working directory does not exist on Windows CE.

To determine the amount of used and available storage space in the file system, you can use the `GetDiskSpaceFreeEx` function. The file system probably will not exist on a disk, and the function derives its name from its Win32 counterpart. To get the corresponding information for an object store, you must call the function `GetStoreInformation`.

Manipulating Databases

The object store is a dense programming topic, and the full API set cannot possibly be covered here. Nevertheless, we will describe some interesting calls to get you started. A sample database hierarchy is shown in Figure 1.3.

Before a database in the object store can be used, the database volume must be mounted by a call to `CeMountDbVol`. The database can then be opened by `CeOpenDatabaseEx`. A brand-new database can be created with `CeCreateDatabaseEx`. `CeCreateDatabaseEx` allows you to specify up to four sort orders in the database. You can specify functions or predefined sorting orders on any property in the database. The default sort order is alphabetically ascending

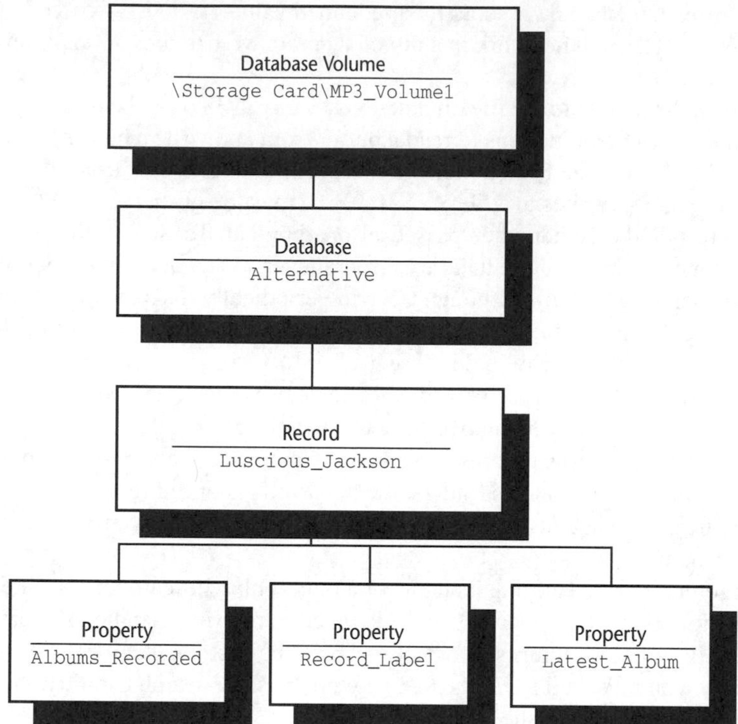

Figure 1.3 Database hierarchy

and case insensitive. You can change these stipulations when you specify the sort order. `CeOpenDatabaseEx` allows you to specify one property (database field) as a primary sorting key, which cannot be changed. It also allows you to set up notifications when other threads modify the database. The notifications are delivered to a window specified in the open call and arrive in the form of `WM_DBNOTIFICATION` messages. These messages are accompanied by structures of type `CENOTIFICATION` that describe the type of operation performed on the database. These structures are allocated on a heap either specified when notifications are being set up or assigned to the process by default. Upon receipt of a `WM_DBNOTIFICATION` message, this allocated structure must be freed to free heap space. The function used to perform this operation is called `CeFreeNotification`.

To modify an existing record in a database, you must locate the record by calling the `CeSeekDatabase` function. Once a record is located, it must be read via the `CeReadRecordProps` function. Either the record is read into a user-supplied buffer, or a buffer can be allocated by the function itself on the default process heap. A variant of this function, called `CeReadRecordPropsEx`, takes an additional handle to a heap other than the default heap, from which the buffer is then allocated. Records can be written by a call to `CeWriteRecordProps`. If it is passed an appropriate flag, `CeWriteRecordProps` can also be made to delete properties in a database.

The transaction feature of databases also requires space on the heap. Remember that your heap will be used a lot if you are generating heavy traffic in and out of a database.

A record can be deleted by a call to `CeDeleteRecord`, an entire database by a call to `CeDeleteDatabaseEx`.

Manipulating the Registry

The Windows CE registry is a repository for information. The operating system and its modules, device drivers, and applications can use it. Although the registry can be used to store information that is temporal for the duration of a single invocation of the program, it is traditionally used to hold information that must be persisted after the program has been unloaded from memory.

A program typically stores configuration information in the registry during its operation and before it exits. On startup, the program retrieves these values and reconfigures itself. A simple example could be an application that interacts with the user via a window. The user might move and resize the window to organize desktop space. The application could obtain the location and size of its window and store this information in the registry before exiting. Then on startup, it could retrieve these values and position and size its window accordingly.

Since potentially hundreds of programs can store information in the registry, its structure is organized to allow programs to store and retrieve information from consistent locations. Information is stored as name-value pairs referred to as registry **items**. Each piece of information or value must be named. The value is then stored along with its name. The name must then be used to retrieve the value. Values can be grouped together into **keys**. For example, a program may organize its window size and location information as follows:

Key: Position
- **Name:** Top **Value:** 100
- **Name:** Left **Value:** 100

Key: Size
- **Name:** Width **Value:** 450
- **Name:** Height **Value:** 300

Registry items can be strings, double words (unsigned long integers), or binary data.

The registry structure is organized as a tree hierarchy with four roots. A sequence of registry keys (see Table 1.2) separated by a slash (\) forms a registry **path**. CE supports up to 16 levels of nesting in the path hierarchy. Each registry key or name is limited to 255 characters. Item data can be up to 4K in size.

To read or write to a registry item, you must first open the registry key. A registry key is opened by a call to the `RegOpenKeyEx` function with the path name of the key passed in. The root key under which to find this path must also be specified as an argument. The handle passed back by this call is used in subsequent calls that operate on this key. A new key can be created by a call to `RegCreateKeyEx`. Permissions for the new key being created must be specified when you make this call. If the key being created already exists, `RegCreateKeyEx` will inform you via an output parameter.

The function `RegQueryValueEx` should be used to read an item value. An item value can be changed by the function `RegSetValueEx`. A value can be deleted via `RegDeleteValue;`

Table 1.2 Top-Level Registry Keys

Key	Contents
HKEY_LOCAL_MACHINE	Configuration data for the device. For example, hardware information about different peripherals like ports, mounted volumes, and so on is stored here. Applications store data that applies to all users that access the device.
HKEY_USERS	User-specific configuration data.
HKEY_CURRENT_USERS	Configuration data for the user currently logged in to the device. This root entry points to the relevant key for the user under HKEY_USERS. Thus, changes made to this root will automatically be made in the user's key under HKEY_USERS. The convention followed by applications is to drill down into the registry hierarchy and store software items under \HKEY_USERS\SOFTWARE\<Company Name>\<Product Name>.
HKEY_CLASSES_ROOT	Configuration data that establishes associations between file types and programs. These associations are used to automatically launch the associated program when the user chooses to open a file. This root also serves as a repository for registered COM components.

an entire key can be deleted via RegDeleteKey. Once all registry operations are performed, the handle to the registry key should be closed via the RegCloseKey function.

Two more functions are useful when you're working with the registry. RegEnumKeyEx is used to enumerate all the subkeys under a previously open key. Its counterpart, RegEnumValue, can be used to enumerate all items under a previously open key. Remember that any key can contain a mix of subkeys and items.

Like file writes, registry modifications are cached by the operating system. The cached information is saved periodically, when the user calls RegCloseKey or, in CE 2.10 and later, manually decides to flush the modifications by calling RegFlushKey.

Although registry keys have permissions associated with them that restrict access, certain keys are off-limits to any program that is considered *not trusted* (see Table 1.3). A trusted program is one that has registered itself with the OEM Adaptation Layer (OAL) via a call to OEMCertifyModule. In general, programs that come bundled with the device (part of the build image) are considered trusted because they have been tested by the OEM, as opposed to programs installed on the device after market. More information on the OAL will be available in Chapter 5, and Chapter 10 will cover build images in more detail. The trust level at which a program is executing can be determined by a call to CeGetCurrentTrust.

CE Version Memo

A trust relation between a program and registry keys is supported in Windows CE 3.0 and later versions.

Table 1.3 Protected Registry Keys

Key	Contents
HKEY_LOCAL_MACHINE\Comm	Network configuration for the device, including available adapters and protocols.
HKEY_LOCAL_MACHINE\Drivers	Device drivers that are loaded at device boot.
HKEY_LOCAL_MACHINE\Hardware	Hardware configuration of the device.
HKEY_LOCAL_MACHINE\System	System configuration settings such as power, time and date format, and so on.
HKEY_LOCAL_MACHINE\Init	Programs that must be started with the operating system. The shell is an example of such a program.
HKEY_LOCAL_MACHINE\WDMDrivers	List of Windows Driver Model device drivers that are loaded at device boot.

Communications

Windows CE provides communications over a variety of transports—namely, serial port, modem, network interface card (NIC), and infrared port. This section provides a quick tour of the major players in the world of CE networking, which are diagrammed in Figure 1.4.

Serial

A standard serial device driver at the data link layer (see Figure 1.4) is capable of handling communications over a serial port or an infrared port, which looks, acts, and feels like a serial port. The serial and infrared ports are accessed via the Windows CE serial port API.

COM and infrared ports are listed under the HKEY_LOCAL_MACHINE\Comm registry key. The regular file functions can be used to open, close, read from, and write to a serial port. Additional control is provided by functions that follow a naming convention of *<Action>Comm<Object>*. For example, the functions GetCommState and SetCommState are used to retrieve and set configuration information for the port. The function EscapeCommFunction is commonly used to set a serial port to infrared mode.

You can also use a serial port to provide a networking connection via TCP/IP by making use of the SLIP/PPP protocol provided by Windows CE for this specific purpose.

TAPI

A modem could be connected to the serial port or be available as a PCMCIA card. Modems are configured under the registry key HKEY_LOCAL_MACHINE\Drivers\PCMCIA because they are expected to be PC cards. Windows CE provides the Telephony API (TAPI) at the data link layer (see Figure 1.4). TAPI is a set of calls that a program can make to operate a configured modem. The API abstracts the details of programming the modem from the developer. Think of TAPI as an API-based AT command set for modems. TAPI allows dynamic feature discovery for any configured modem. Additional features, such as answering and placing calls, conference calling,

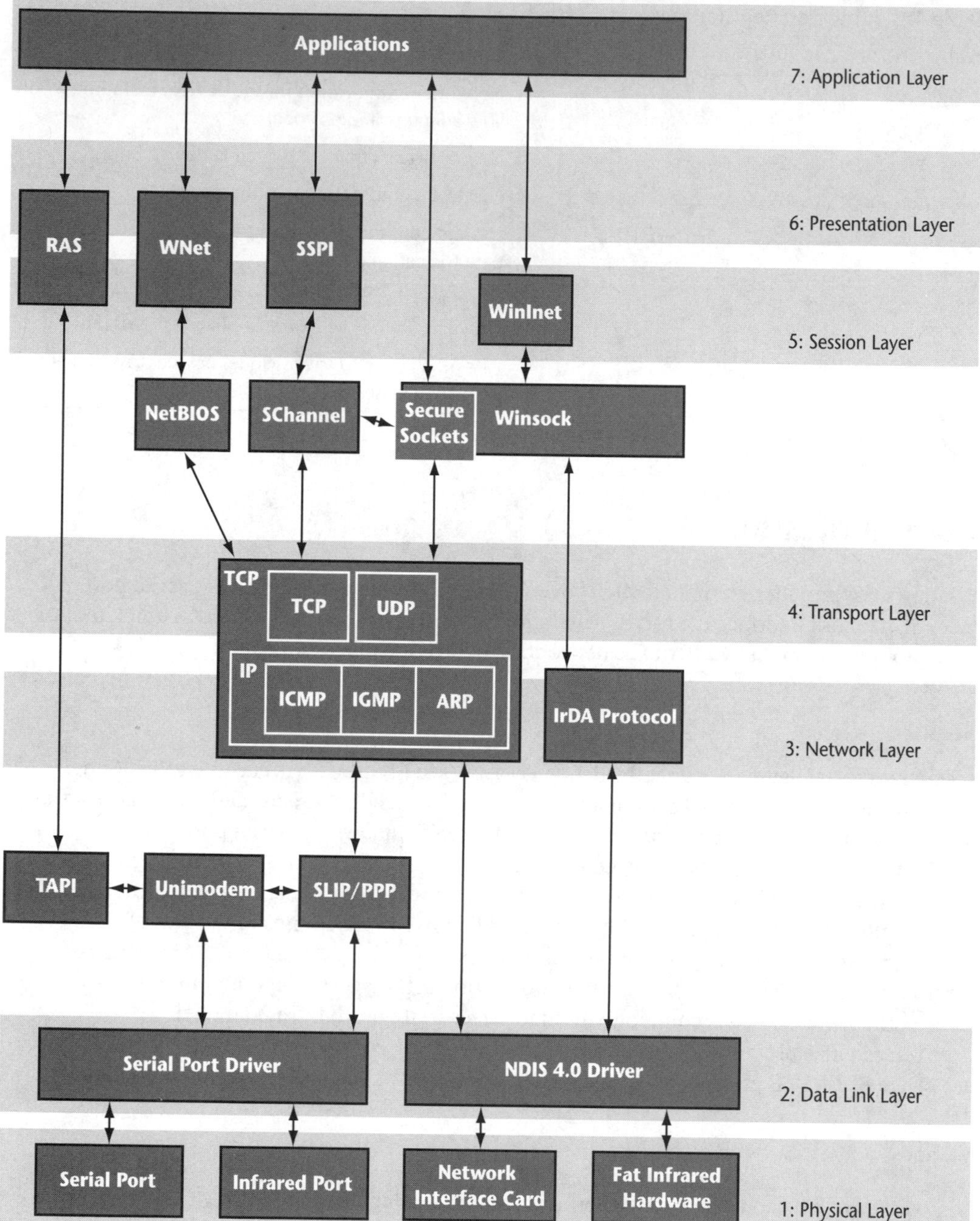

Figure 1.4 Windows CE networking architecture

caller ID, call forwarding, call hold, and configuring and monitoring status, are provided for the telephone line. The functions that realize this feature set are called **line services**. TAPI also allows the monitoring and configuration of the phone attached to a modem or other line device. These functions form a set called **phone services**.

To support TAPI, a modem manufacturer must provide the device driver for the modem along with the TAPI Service Provider Interface (TSPI) DLL. TSPI is a module that provides well-defined entry points to support TAPI. Windows CE provides a generic TSPI called Unimodem that provides TAPI support with most modems.

TAPI line services are of the format *line<Action><Object>*. For example, the function `lineAnswer` will answer an inbound call. TAPI phone services are of the format *phone<Action><Object>*.

CE Version Memo

Windows CE 2.10 and earlier versions supported only outgoing calls. Inbound calls are supported starting with Windows CE 2.12.

RAS

Windows CE supports Remote Access Services (RAS), a set of modules that allow a CE device to connect to a Windows server over an IP connection. RAS is used primarily via either a direct serial connection to the server or a dial-up connection. Once connected to the server, the CE device can be authenticated on the domain and participate in the network just like any other workstation. Thus, RAS allows remote users to access a corporate network in a seamless way.

RAS uses the Point-to-Point Protocol (PPP) to manage the serial or dial-up connection. A well-known example of RAS over the serial connection is Windows CE Services, which allows a device to connect to the user's primary desktop and synchronize information between the desktop and the device. Users of the Handheld PC, Palm-size PC, and Pocket PC devices use Windows CE Services extensively.

ActiveSync

Windows CE Services is built on top of a technology called ActiveSync. ActiveSync allows the synchronization of data between a CE device and a Windows-based desktop. Windows CE comes bundled with synchronization for Microsoft Outlook data and the Microsoft Office documents like Word, PowerPoint, Excel, and Access files. OEMs can add synchronization for their other information by creating ActiveSync components that are responsible for converting information into a byte stream for transferring. At the other end, the ActiveSync component converts the stream into the information required by the OEM application.

SLIP/PPP

Point-to-Point Protocol (PPP) and Serial Line Internet Protocol (SLIP) allow the transmission of IP packets over a serial line, essentially enabling dial-up connections to TCP/IP networks. Windows CE comes with Microsoft's implementation of the PPP stack. Although this implementation is not designed for replacement, in theory a third-party vendor could choose to replace it with a custom implementation as long as all the entry points of a PPP stack were supported.

TCP/IP

Microsoft Windows CE ships with a TCP/IP stack. TCP/IP is a connectionless protocol that does not guarantee delivery. It does guarantee that packets fragmented for transmission are assembled in the correct order when received on the remote side. The TCP/IP stack was not designed for replacement by a third-party vendor. It is the only transport protocol supported on Windows CE. TCP/IP has several components, which are described in the following subsections.

TCP

Transmission Control Protocol (TCP) is a connection-oriented protocol that guarantees delivery of packets to its intended destination. The sequence of packets delivered to the destination is also guaranteed to be the same as that generated at the source. TCP achieves this reliability via two mechanisms. It uses an acknowledgment message (ACK) from the recipient to confirm the delivery of bytes. If an ACK is not received, the bytes are retransmitted until an ACK is received or the connection is timed out. TCP also provides a sequence number for each packet transmitted. The server negotiates the starting number in the sequence as part of TCP's three-way handshake.

TCP packets are always directed to a numbered port. **Ports** are a software abstraction that logically segment a physical connection into multiple channels. Each available channel can then be used by an application to send and receive TCP data. Multiple applications can thus open and use ports without having to deal with synchronizing access over the single available physical connection. The server and client open a prespecified port to exchange data. HTTP, for example, uses TCP as a transport mechanism over port 80. An HTTP client opens port 80 to send or receive data. Correspondingly, an HTTP server listens on port 80 for any client requests. Similarly, FTP uses ports 20 and 21 as data and command channels, respectively.

UDP

User Datagram Protocol (UDP) is a connectionless protocol that does not guarantee delivery of packets to its intended destination. Moreover, unlike TCP, it does not guarantee that the sequence of packets delivered at the destination will match the sequence in which the packets were sent from the source. These limitations define the usefulness of UDP as an IP protocol.

For one, UDP is lightweight compared to TCP because sequencing or error recovery is not required. When small pieces of data are being sent, UDP may be preferred over TCP. Moreover, during broadcasting or multicasting, the establishing of a connection between two network resources is not meaningful. As a connectionless protocol, UDP fits the bill.

Examples of UDP are Simple Network Management Protocol (SNMP), Trivial File Transfer Protocol (TFTP), and Domain Name System (DNS) queries.

ICMP

Internet Control Message Protocol (ICMP) is a protocol that implements the Packet Internet Groper (PING) protocol. PING messages are packets of data sent by a device to another device to confirm its existence on the network. ICMP also provides diagnostic functions and error reporting for packet delivery. Its functionality is available as part of the Winsock API in the form of functions that bear the prefix *Icmp*.

IGMP

Internet Group Management Protocol (IGMP) is used to support IP multicasting, which allows a server to broadcast data to multiple clients simultaneously. Multicasting requires support from routers that need to be configured for multicast support. Devices that require a multicast transmission register themselves with a multicast router. IGMP is the protocol that is used by devices to register them. We use IGMP by setting certain options in Winsock calls.

ARP

The Address Resolution Protocol (ARP) maps IP addresses into Ethernet hardware addresses. In effect, it enables an application to tie an IP address to a device. There are no Winsock calls for ARP. ARP is transparent to applications.

Winsock

Winsock is a networking protocol–independent implementation of sockets that allows developers to produce client-server applications independent of the protocol stack running on the device. Winsock applications communicate over **software sockets**, which allow multiple applications to share a single physical port. The Winsock API is extensively documented and has been supported since the days of Windows CE 1.0. Asynchronous socket support was added in Windows CE 2.0, when Windows-based terminals required their implementation to be in the base operating system.

A section of Winsock, called infrared socket support (IrSock), provides a socket-based abstraction of the IrDA (Infrared Data Association) infrared protocol. The IrSock API is identical to Winsock except for some areas that express the unique features of infrared communications. These differences focus on the fact that infrared connections are not static and devices may come in and go out of range. In addition, a relatively small number of devices are expected to network with infrared.

Secure Sockets

Secure Sockets Layer (SSL) protocols 2.0 and 3.0 are supported via the SChannel module. Data transmitted over the network is encrypted transparently when a secure connection is established. SSL is accessed via Winsock calls. In most cases, parameters passed to Winsock calls indicate that a secure connection is being established. The most significant difference a Winsock application must undergo when supporting secure sockets is in the authentication process. SSL uses certificate authority (CA) to verify the identity of the socket client before establishing a connection. A client implements a callback that provides its certificate to the caller. This certificate, handed out by established CAs, who validate the business and its applications, is compared with CE's own internal database of trusted certificates. If a match is found, the secure socket is established. Without a match, the client requesting the secure connection is out of luck.

Winsock applications can also switch from nonsecure mode to secure mode by calling the Winsock input/output control entry point (NetBIOS). This process is called **deferred handshake**. The client application's certificate is validated (or not) when the call is made.

NetBIOS

Network Basic Input/Output System (NetBIOS) is a session layer interface (see Figure 1.4). A developer can use this interface to build transport-independent applications. NetBIOS consists of an API and a session management layer. It allows resources to be named on the network, establishes a session between the named resources, and then supports data transfer between them. Transports provide NetBIOS compatibility for applications via mapping layers. TCP/IP implements its NetBIOS compatibility via a mapping layer called NetBIOS over TCP/IP (NetBT).

All NetBIOS functionality can be accessed via the Winsock API, which is the preferred way to develop network applications.

WNet

WNet is a session and presentation layer module (see Figure 1.4) that allows the sharing of drives and printers. WNet supports only Microsoft as a network provider. Files available on shares provided by other vendors, like Novell or IBM, cannot be accessed through WNet on Windows CE. Like Winsock, WNet is network independent and isolates developers from transport-specific details.

CE Version Memo

WNet support is provided in Windows CE 2.0 and later versions. Printer sharing is supported in Windows CE 2.10 and later versions.

WinInet

WinInet is an API designed specifically to allow developers to build Internet support into applications easily. WinInet allows an application to use HTTP or FTP (Gopher is not supported on Windows CE) without having to open a socket. Although built on top of Winsock itself, it hides developers from the gritty details of sockets programming. WinInet is powerful and simple to use. It can be called from multiple threads. It performs synchronization and allows the Internet session to be shared among threads. A feature of WinInet is that the set of functionality that can be obtained by the API is achieved via function calls that perform the same task regardless of the underlying Internet protocol being used. For example, a file can be downloaded via HTTP or FTP by a call to `InternetReadFile`.

The underlying Internet protocol is used in the creation of an Internet connection. WinInet must be initialized by a call to `InternetOpen`, and `InternetConnect` can then be invoked to establish a session with a named server, with a specified protocol, on a specified port. Since the time taken to complete some WinInet calls is inherently dependent on the performance on the network, a mechanism to register callbacks is provided via the `InternetSetStatusCallback` function. The callback can then be used to monitor the status of a blocking call.

Specific servers can be directly addressed by construction of a Uniform Resource Locator (URL) through calls to construction functions such as `InternetCanonicalizeURL` and `InternetCombineURL`, followed by a call to `InternetOpenURL`. The opened URL can be used to process data via either HTTP or FTP. WinInet also supports secure HTTP (HTTPS), which transfers encrypted data. HTTPS can be specified as the underlying protocol in the `InternetOpen` call. It requires the Windows CE device to include Secure Sockets Layer (SSL) support.

WinInet comes with its own dial-up component that allows a dial-up connection to be established when a request is made to create a session.

Web Server

The need for CE devices, particularly appliances, to communicate with each other has prompted Microsoft to add a Web server of minimal footprint that can include Active Server Pages (ASP). This allows development of ASP-based server applications on the CE device. Without the ASP interpreter, the device can still host simplified Web pages. As an example, a printer that uses Windows CE can have an embedded Web server. You can access the printer's interface by using a browser and typing in the printer's IP address. The printer's Web page can then allow a user to list the spool queue, submit print requests, cancel pending requests, or run diagnostics on the printer.

The Web server component in Windows CE is loaded like a device driver, although it really doesn't process any interrupts. This allows the Web server to be loaded as part of the boot process. A user interface application is also provided that allows the Web server to be started and stopped dynamically for development and debugging purposes.

The server supports a subset of HTTP 1.0 and additional features, albeit also stripped down from their desktop counterparts. Features such as ASP, ISAPI (Internet Server API) extensions, ISAPI filters, and authentication can be added if space is available on the device.

ASP is a server-based environment that can be used to glue together Web pages, COM components, and scripts. ASP pages can be requested directly from the Web server, just like HTML pages but with an *.asp* extension. The ASP page executes scripts entirely on the server side and sends a resulting Web page back to the server to send to the client. Because ASP, including its components, is executed on the server, cross-platform issues can be sidestepped. Components and scripts, for example, do not have to run on a variety of client-side operating systems.

ASP allows the development of server-side scripts. ISAPI extensions can be used to create DLLs that can be plugged into the Web server to extend its functionality. ISAPI extensions are a replacement for Common Gateway Interface (CGI) scripts, which were traditionally used to provide a Web page with access to operating system functionality.

ISAPI filters are DLLs that are notified of critical events that occur while the Web server is processing requests from clients. For example, a filter can receive notification when a client authenticates itself with a server, after a data request, and during subsequent processing of data.

RAPI

An important feature of Windows CE is the ability to establish connectivity between the CE device and a Windows-based desktop computer. Such connectivity allows desktops to exchange information such as contacts, e-mails, and task lists with the device. ActiveSync, formerly called Windows CE Services, is one such synchronization application that allows users to exchange information between Microsoft Outlook and the Windows CE Inbox. Files can also be synchronized in the same way.

On the development side, desktop applications can query data from the device for display. For example, an application can display the processes and threads executing on the CE device. Another application can be used to read and manipulate the registry on the device. These applications run on the desktop and use an API designed for such connectivity called Remote Access

Programming Interface (RAPI). Applications that use RAPI and run on the desktop are considered clients, and the remote device itself is the RAPI server.

The function `CeRapiInit` establishes connectivity with a CE device. An asynchronous version of `CeRapiInit`, called `CeRapiInitEx`, uses an event to notify the calling thread when a connection has been established. Making a call to `CeRapiUninit` terminates a connection between the desktop and the device.

RAPI function signatures resemble their desktop counterparts with the exception that the letters *Ce* are added as a prefix to the name. A variety of device information can be queried via RAPI calls. For example, the function `CeGetSystemMetrics`, the remote equivalent of `GetSystemMetrics`, can be used to obtain information regarding a variety of user interface elements and to determine whether a network, mouse, or low-end processor is present on the device. `CeGetVersionEx` returns the version of the operating system running on the device. `CeGetSystemInfo` obtains processor and application address space information.

RAPI equivalents exist for file, database, and registry manipulation (discussed in the section titled File System earlier in the chapter). In addition, RAPI provides some shell and window manipulation functions. Shell functions are prefixed on the desktop by *SH.* The RAPI equivalent is thus prefixed by *CeSH.* `CeSHCreateShortcut` is used to create a shortcut to an application or a file. To find an existing target's shortcut, you can use the function `CeSHGetShortcutTarget`.

RAPI window management functions include `CeGetWindow`, which returns a given window's child window or Z-order siblings, ancestors, and children. `CeGetWindowLong` returns information associated with a window. The information is usually kept in the window data structure, the same chunk of memory to which the handle of the window points. `CeGetWindowLong` can be used to subclass a window, a technique by which a window's procedure is replaced so that messages directed to the window can be redirected to another procedure. Finally, `CeGetWindowText` returns the title of a window with a border or the contents of borderless windows such as text boxes, and `CeGetClassName` returns the class name of a window.

A couple of powerful functions in RAPI allow a desktop to execute code on the remote device. `CeCreateProcess` launches an executable on the remote device. The more complex `CeRapiInvoke` can execute a function on the remote device. `CeRapiInvoke` operates in synchronous and asynchronous modes, with data being exchanged between client and server via an `IStream` interface.

Summary

In this chapter we've taken a whirlwind tour of the Windows CE architecture that we hope has served its purpose as an introduction to this operating system built from the ground up for embedded systems. Although it belongs to the Win32 family of operating systems from Microsoft, and in spite of borrowing many architectural details from its desktop brethren, Windows CE is substantially different in its implementation. The differences affect all aspects of development and subsequent use of the devices that use this operating system.

In the following chapters it will become clear how many of the modules discussed in this chapter can be optionally included in the operating system. Although we briefly mentioned the API for using these modules, we will now focus on how to combine these modules and create a specific version of Windows CE for a given device.

2 Road Map to Managing a Windows CE Project

Welcome to the world of managing embedded projects using Windows CE. As with any other project, your career in this area will be lined with challenges. You will need to improvise or learn quickly how to delegate, train, cajole, coax, throw a fit or two, and whatever else it takes to get a quality product out the door.

In many respects, an embedded project that uses Windows CE is not much different from one that uses a different off-the-shelf real-time operating system. Yet each technology creates certain unique (but predictable) situations in the life of a project. When we looked closer, we found several aspects of a Windows CE project that were unique. We looked for repeatable patterns and categorized them. Then we devised best practices that produced the most leverage.

In this chapter we present a road map for the journey you will undertake from the moment your company commits to building a Windows CE product all the way to that Holy Grail, First Customer Ship (FCS). Even if you're not a project lead, you will find the material in this chapter implicitly useful. Every developer should be aware of how a project is structured. This knowledge creates a team in which each member understands his role in the big picture and plays it accordingly.

Orbiter: A Windows-Based Terminal

We promise not to inundate you with best practices and techniques that look great on paper. Instead, we will use a sample product to illustrate our points. Our efforts are to map this example to real-world situations that you are likely to encounter as you move along in your project. We also pledge to eschew overly complicated terminology. We'll even minimize that modern-day monster that will surely find its way into a Steven Spielberg film soon: Acronyms.

Orbiter is a Windows-based terminal. This embedded terminal is used to host a session running on a remote server using Windows NT Terminal Server (WTS). WTS goes a step beyond

NT Server and allows *simultaneous* multiple users to work on the system. Sometimes the term *interactive users* is used to describe the same functionality. A session on WTS is established by a client provided by Microsoft as part of the WTS software. We will plan to use the Windows CE client for WTS. In effect, we will create a tablet device that embeds a Windows CE client. This device will allow us to log in to WTS, establish a session, and run applications on it.

The following list summarizes the features of Orbiter:

- AMD Elan SC400 processor
- 1024_768 display resolution, using Chips & Technologies CT65550 display controller and an 11-inch LCD panel
- Touch panel interface
- Wireless networking via PCMCIA
- Detachable PS/2 keyboard
- Serial port
- Enhanced parallel port
- Eight-bit audio support
- Power management

Is Windows CE the Right Choice?

Chances are that someone has already presented you with the question, Is Windows CE the right choice for our project? Moreover, they probably expected an answer out of you within ten minutes. Unfortunately, quite a bit of work is required to make an informed decision. Anyone who answers this question without performing the work required probably has a stake in stating one choice or the other. Such an answer must be treated with the suspicion it deserves. We encourage you to conduct your own research into the appropriateness of Windows CE for your project. And in this section, we will show you how to plan and execute such a small research project.

One of the first items on your activity list for determining if you should use Windows CE for your project is to make a list of requirements for the operating system. Does your device require multitasking? Does it need to provide hard real-time response? Does your device require development of an extensive user interface? Such questions can be laid down to create the list of requirements. As a guide, we provide the following sample list of requirements for Project Orbiter:

- Choice of processor
- Licensing
- Soft real-time capabilities
- Multitasking
- Interprocess communication

- Graphical user interface (not extensive)
- Wireless networking capability
- Ability to network with a PC
- Ability to network with a variety of devices in the home
- Ability to perform software upgrades
- Kernel-level debugger
- Well-defined driver model
- Emulation environment for developing applications
- GUI-based development environment

When formulating these requirements, include critical features first. It is important to spend some time thinking about what kind of a development environment will be optimal for developing under the operating system. Most operating systems offer a rich set of development tools that can be leveraged to shorten the project schedule. Expecting more out of the operating system in this regard is not unwarranted.

A compelling reason to use Windows CE is an extensive user interface. Because it is Win32 compatible, your platform can support a large number of third-party applications. This support for applications might be a critical feature for your product line. Allowing a variety of vendors to develop competing applications on your platform will create competition and benefit your customers. In this aspect Windows CE is a clear winner. As desktop technologies are created, the Windows CE team ports these in part to the embedded platform, thereby giving developers access to the latest desktop technologies and facilitating the porting of applications to the embedded world.

Several available operating systems ship with a source code license, which is particularly useful if you want to make extensions at the operating system (OS) level for your product. Such licenses may involve purchasing a one-time source code license or paying a runtime fee for each OS license that you use (even after you modify it). In some cases, the OS vendor has the right of ownership to any extensions you may have made. If this scenario is what you expect for your product, Windows CE is not an option for you. Microsoft does not allow source code licenses. For products that don't really benefit from OS-level changes, this constraint is not much of a concern.

You can develop a spreadsheet for evaluating the project requirements in which the requirements themselves are listed in the first column and each operating system you plan to consider is allocated an additional column. Filling out this spreadsheet is the best way to make an informed decision about the operating system that is best for you.

Platform Requirements

Windows CE supports an array of processors. When working with Windows CE, you will need to select a processor from the certified list. And some additional initial requirements are important to bear in mind when you're starting a project.

Windows CE RAM is restricted to 1GB, but in reality you will end up using much less RAM on the target platform. For a debug version of the platform, however, you should plan to add RAM of at least an order of magnitude beyond what you think you need. You should also plan for either ROM or flash memory for nonvolatile storage.

CE Version Memo

Windows CE 2.11 can use from 350K of ROM for a minimal configuration to 5MB for a configuration packed with goodies.

In CE debugging, an image is uploaded to the target platform and debug information is collected over another transport. Uploads in early versions of CE took place over a bidirectional parallel port. In 2.10 and later versions, Ethernet support was added. This addition sped up the uploading process considerably. However, if your device uses the Ethernet transport, it will not be available for debugging. You will need to consider building a special development version of your platform that has two Ethernet interfaces on it, one of which is then reserved for debugging. A serial port is used by the CE kernel to communicate debugging information to the kernel debugger running on a workstation. It should be a design priority to facilitate debugging. Make sure at an early stage that the hardware design will accommodate at least a parallel and a serial port on the development platform, and preferably an Ethernet port as well.

Windows CE Licensing and Development Model

The Windows CE licensing model is quite different from the traditional embedded OS model. Microsoft has several categories of *helper* organizations that perform specific tasks.

Distributors are responsible for reselling Windows CE. When declaring your intention to use Windows CE for your product, you will need to size your estimate for the volume shipment of the resulting device. On the basis of this estimate, you will buy CE licenses from either the distributor or Microsoft. Your project volume sales must reach a certain number (20,000 at last count) before Microsoft will sell you licenses directly. Distributors are also responsible for selling the Windows CE development tools.

Windows CE licenses are split into three levels. The **full operating system license** comes with all available components in Windows CE: the kernel, file system, communications, connectivity, device driver support, events and messages, graphics, keyboard and touch screen, window management, and common controls. It is important to understand which components Microsoft does not include in the base operating system. Applications like Pocket Word, Pocket Excel, and so on that are standard issue on a Handheld PC are *not* regarded as part of the CE operating system. Also not included are the Handheld PC shell and Pocket Internet Explorer. The online help system is also missing from these components.

The **limited operating system license** is structured for devices without heavy-duty user interface requirements. The components that are bundled with this license come with GUI support but exclude sophisticated controls. Missing in action are window and dialog management, buttons, menus, and message boxes.

A third licensing option, called the **kernel operating system license**, is also available for devices with no display requirements at all (headless devices). All GUI support is eliminated from this license. You get some text-only components, the file system, communications, connectivity, and keyboard support.

Most OS vendors develop board support packages that allow the OS to be used on different processors. Microsoft off-loads this task to system integrators. If you need specific processor support in the form of a board support package, you will need to buy the package from any one of the system integrators listed on Microsoft's Web site (http://www.microsoft.com/windows/embedded/ce/partners/si.asp). System integrators often provide services such as consulting and value add-ons to Windows CE in the form of driver models or applications that can be bundled with target hardware. If you plan to develop all the software for your target hardware yourself, you will probably *not* need the services of a system integrator. A hybrid approach can also be used in which critical pieces like the boot loader and Hardware Abstraction Layer are purchased from the system integrator before more development is done in-house. When you're purchasing the initial board support package to jump-start your project, it is advisable that you sign up for some support from the integrator to fully leverage the advantage you're seeking.

Development Environment

A powerful development environment should always be a factor in the operating system that is selected. In this section we will discuss the different tools in the Windows CE development environment and how these tools are packaged because the terminology can be quite confusing.

CE Toolkits

Microsoft provides separate Windows CE development support in the form of toolkits. For versions 2.10 and below, these toolkits were available in several incarnations. The operating system and tools for embedded development were packaged as the embedded toolkit (ETK), also sometimes referred to as the embedded development kit (EDK). This package was used by OEMs to customize Windows CE for target hardware.

A software development kit (SDK) was available for developers who wished to develop applications for the Handheld PC. It was referred to as the Windows CE Platform SDK. The Platform SDK contained cross-compilers for the Handheld PC processors in use at that time: MIPS and Hitachi SH3. It also contained header files and libraries for Windows CE.

Yet another toolkit, specifically catered toward application developers, was called Windows CE Toolkit for Visual C++ 5.0. This toolkit plugged into the Visual C++ integrated development environment (IDE) and contained the Platform SDK and an emulation environment that allowed the prototyping of applications and some device drivers.

Meanwhile, Microsoft started working on gearing Windows CE for custom platform categories like the AutoPC (Windows CE in an automobile) and WBTs (Windows-based terminals). This task required each group to take the base OS toolkit and structure it separately for the target platform. In turn, each group created its own toolkit specifically tailored for a category of devices. More toolkits were created. Some categories, like the AutoPC, required SDKs of their own.

The need to provide a plug-in for Visual C++ took its toll on the development process in the Windows CE group. Several inconsistencies and incompatibilities in the way the pieces of software worked together and in the release schedules of the different groups proved detrimental to the schedules of either product. Ultimately, Microsoft decided to provide a stand-alone Visual C++ IDE that used the existing Visual C++ 6.0 source code but was developed and maintained separately by the Windows CE group. The Windows CE Platform Builder was born! Application development is now supported by eMbedded Visual C++, part of the eMbedded Visual Tools for Windows CE. A corresponding toolkit also exists for Visual Basic developers called eMbedded Visual Basic.

The Windows CE Platform Builder is the replacement for the ETK. However, it includes everything you need in order to develop applications for the embedded device: stand-alone Visual Studio look-alike IDE, headers, libraries, and cross-compilers for supported processors. Not included is the emulator, which still ships with the device-specific SDK because emulation can be different for different devices.

So what do you need as a developer? If you are developing an embedded solution using Windows CE, Platform Builder and Platform SDK should take care of all your needs. If you are an application developer, you will need the Platform SDK. If you use MFC (Microsoft Foundation Classes) or ATL (Active Template Library), the eMbedded toolkit for Visual C++ or Visual Basic is required.

But there's more! Although the Platform Builder contains all the pieces required to construct a custom platform using a supported processor, Microsoft also provides a few enhanced versions of the Platform Builder to service CE devices in markets that are of strategic importance. Platform Builder versions are available for the Pocket PC, Handheld PC, Palm-size PC, and AutoPC. These kits include Platform Builder components and add enhancements in the form of canned configurations, utilities, and system software specific to the target platform. You can purchase any of these toolkits in lieu of Platform Builder.

Other toolkits, such as the Windows-based terminal (WBT) kit, come in the form of an add-on to Platform Builder. In other words, you must buy Platform Builder, install it, and then purchase and install the WBT kit separately. Although it means a more time-consuming process, the add-on model makes for fewer headaches during ongoing maintenance, which calls for version management. In effect, if a market segment grows enough to warrant a special toolkit, Microsoft might be inclined to produce one.

Development Tools

Windows CE development tools can be split into two separate categories: application development tools and embedded development tools. The embedded tools can be used with facility to develop applications, but they are not optimal.

The preferred application development tool is the stand-alone Visual C++ IDE that ships with the Platform Builder. Like its desktop counterpart, this IDE contains wizards to automate the task of building boilerplate applications. The wizards are integrated with MFC and ATL, so if applications use these frameworks, they benefit from working with this IDE. The IDE also contains a debugger that can be used for source code debugging of applications on your target. When you are developing applications, the IDE calls a utility to upload your newly built code to the target platform using the communication facilities built into Windows CE services. You can execute, debug, and terminate the application on your target entirely from the IDE. In addition, several remote monitoring utilities ship with the Platform SDK that can be used to determine the condition of the target hardware. You can view and modify the registry, view the process space, and examine the target memory by launching utilities from the IDE. Debug traces emitted from your application end up in the output window of the IDE. Throughout the process, the desktop communicates with the target hardware using Windows CE services, which communicate through the serial port.

Embedded development requires another set of tools. Drivers and system modules are usually built by a command-line utility (see Chapter 10 for details). When finished, the modules are bundled into the final Windows CE image, which is then uploaded into flash memory or RAM. A utility called CESH (CE Shell, formerly called Parallel Port Shell, or PPSH) uses the parallel port to upload the image to the target hardware. CE 2.11 and upward can also use an Ethernet port for faster uploads. Debugging is done via the kernel mode debugger WinDbg. The debug kernel in Windows CE sends all debug traces to the serial port that is monitored by WinDbg. The final output appears in the trace window of WinDbg. WinDbg also provides an array of powerful debugging facilities such as source code debugging, single steps, breakpoints, memory dumps, and so on.

CESH also provides some very useful commands for debugging. One command supports zone debugging. **Zone debugging** is the notion that traces and debug conditions can be categorized by zones, which can then be dynamically enabled or disabled via the CESH command line. This provides a trace filtering capability for the debugger. The implication in all of this is that your target hardware should optimally have a serial port and either an IEEE 1284 bidirectional parallel port or an Ethernet port. When debugging serial port drivers, you will need an additional serial port. If the final retail version of the hardware doesn't have space for either of these options, building a special development version of the target hardware can save hours of time during development.

These two sets of tools can present a problem. Developers have to learn two different interfaces and potentially switch between them. However, the embedded set of tools can be used with applications, thereby alleviating the problem somewhat. Your team may also consist of two distinct groups—application and embedded developers—who each use a particular set of tools and never switch.

Training Your Team

Windows CE is a 32-bit operating system that brings some of the new exciting desktop technologies to the embedded world. The first line of attack in getting a development team ready is to create excitement about working with CE. Although CE's Win32 compatibility is touted in the marketing documents, familiarity with Win32 is not a prerequisite when you're working with this operating system. Given Microsoft's standing with the developer community, you also stand to exploit a huge Hawthorne effect with Windows CE.

Note

Steve McConnell describes the Hawthorne effect in *Rapid Development: Taming Wild Software Schedules* (Microsoft Press, 1996, page 263).

A growing developer community for CE is staking out quite a bit of territory on the Internet. Put your team members in touch with these resources. A regular scan of the Usenet newsgroups can yield important information. Usenet newsgroups and mailing lists are a great place to have your questions answered. Most newsgroups have their own FAQ (frequently asked questions) document. Ask for one before submitting questions to keep redundant discussions from creeping into the newsgroup.

The best place to ask CE questions, including preliminary ones, is the windowsce-dev mailing list. Usenet newsgroups also yield quick answers of good quality. Appendix C provides a comprehensive list of resources for Windows CE development.

Getting Started

One of the first documents that should be produced is an installation document outlining the software packages required. Acquiring the software always has a lag time associated with it. While the team digs into preliminary research, it is best to begin the software acquisition process in the background. When the documentation arrives, your installation document should be updated to describe the installation process. A certain sequence may need to be followed during installation. For example, service packs may need to be installed in a certain order. Windows CE software comes with tools for all certified processors. Installing the entire contents of the CDs will eat up hard disk space faster than you can say, "I wonder why my disk is spinning so much." The installation document should mention the installation options that need to be selected. By facilitating a standard development environment in this manner, you will reduce the frustration of tracking down errors that are caused by differences in installations (which occur all the time!).

A good way to jump-start the project is to do something concrete with the operating system. Windows CE comes with a custom version (named CEPC) designed to be executed on a PC (which may itself be referred to as a CEPC). The Platform Builder CDs contain the specification for building this PC. This specification is never physically installed on your hard disk when you install Platform Builder. It is also not readily available on the Microsoft Web site. The specification describes the hardware requirements for a PC that will run Windows CE out of the box.

This is an excellent opportunity to have your team start working with Windows CE before the target hardware arrives. All you need to do is dig up some 486 or even Pentium-class machines (P90s are a particularly good choice because usually they are orphans required by no one and confined to a storage room somewhere in your office). Getting the PC to boot with CE is not a trivial task. Making different peripherals functional also takes some time and understanding. You can take advantage of these facts to hand out small assignments to the team. Such assignments create milestones and deadlines that are useful in guiding the research process. Let's look at some examples of small CEPC-related projects.

Build the DEMO1 project for CEPC (which is found on the Platform Builder CD) and upload it to a CEPC. To do so, you must build the parallel port driver required to connect the parallel port between the CEPC and the development workstation. A debug image will allow a developer to get a good feel for how debugging will work on the final platform. The team member(s) assigned this task will also get a feel for how the build process works. Booting the operating system on a target is also an important emotional milestone that you can use to energize your team. It "legitimizes" this new technology and creates a willingness to work with it.

The CEPC platform contains a boot loader to boot the PC from DOS. The source code for this boot loader is available with Platform Builder. This is one of the first modules that will need to be produced when the target hardware is available. After the boot loader has been debugged and is functional on the target hardware, the rest of the team can join the act and develop or port their portions. Because this is a critical module that is the root of many dependencies in the schedule, one task for which you should set aside time is to read and understand the CEPC boot loader source.

Next, get the keyboard and mouse peripherals working. Modify the keyboard driver to accept a sequence of keys and pop up a message box in response. You will gain a good understanding of CE device drivers from this assignment.

CEPC contains drivers for a selection of networking cards. A modular assignment is to purchase such a card, install it, and get it working on the CEPC. Adding networking capability to Windows CE is an excellent learning exercise in how to customize the operating system. Additional capabilities like DHCP (Dynamic Host Configuration Protocol), hard-coded IP address, and so on can be tested.

A sample application is quick and easy to generate. The Windows CE emulator can be used to prototype one while the CEPC is being primed for development. When ready, the application can be ported to the target hardware. Such porting attempts are always a fair indication of the amount of effort you will expend in moving source code from the emulator to a target platform. If certain drivers require testing, you can add these capabilities in the application to make it interesting.

These sample assignments will enable the team to attack the learning curve. At best, your team members will experience the Hawthorne effect and be excited to work with new technology. If you hear your team complaining about features that don't work correctly, about a lack of features, or about the development environment, address those complaints swiftly by providing a forum for team members to vent their frustration. If the frustration is allowed to build, your team members will feel forced to work with a technology that doesn't meet their needs.

An excellent way to provide a forum for discussion is to create discussion groups. You can create discussion groups on the company intranet or use groupware packages to create them. Such vehicles provide an active, nondisruptive, and engaging forum for discussion and venting. If e-mail begins to fly around, you can moderate the exchange and move it over to the discussion group. Discussion groups also have inherent, instant archiving capability. All messages, or posts, to the group are always available. Conversation threads are thus easy to follow at any given time. This arrangement can be exploited to create an archive on the project's technical issues that will grow into a useful source of reference material as the project progresses. Encourage team members to share snippets of information, tips, and technical discoveries on the discussion list. Such exchange can be powerful motivation for developers to attack the learning curve and establish personal technical expertise.

Identifying Prototyping Opportunities

Dogs have been pushed down the list; an evaluation board is now a developer's best friend. Evaluation boards present an opportunity to prototype software that can be leveraged to attack the schedule. Depending on the target hardware being designed—the choice of processor, peripherals, and so on—an evaluation board can be selected as the project's prototyping environment.

Table 2.1 lists the certified processors for all versions of Windows CE and evaluation boards that can be used with each. Evaluation boards are sometimes called reference boards.

Table 2.1 Windows CE Evaluation Boards

Manufacturer	CPU	Evaluation Board	Source for More Information
AMD	Elan SC400, Elan SC410	μforCE Demonstration System	http://www.amd.com/products/epd/processors/4.32bitcont/32bitcont/index.html
AMD	K6-2, K6E		
ARM	720T	ARM Development Kit	http://www.arm.com/sitearchitek/devtools.ns4/html/dev_tools?opendocument&style=dev_tools
Cyrix	Media-GX	MediaGXm 5530 Unicorn board	1-800-777-9988
Hitachi	SH-3	D9000, C1, and CP09 reference platforms	http://semiconductor.hitachi.com/developers/toolsbriefs/refplats.pdf
Hitachi	SH-4	S1 reference platform	http://semiconductor.hitachi.com/developers/toolsbriefs/d9000.pdf
IBM	PPC403GC	Odo board	http://www.chips.ibm.com/products/powerpc/tools/ek.html
Intel	Pentium	CEPC	
Intel	StrongARM 1100	SA-1100 Evaluation Platform	http://developer.intel.com/design/edk/product/strongarm_edk.htm
Intel	X486	EV486ULP Evaluation Board	http://amber.intel.com/scripts-toolcat/listtools.asp?pid=4649&cid=647
Motorola	PPC850, PPC860, PPC821, PPC823	The MPC82x Family Application Development System (MPC8xxFADS motherboard and a daughter board for the MPC821, MPC860, or MPC832)	http://www.mot.com/sps/powerpc/solutions/windowsce/hardware.html
NEC	VR4102		
NEC	VR4111, VR4111A	DDB-VR4111U	http://www.necel.com/home.nsf/main?readformµprocessors
NEC	VR4121	DDB-VR4121U	http://www.necel.com/home.nsf/main?readformµprocessors
NEC	VR4300, VR4310	DDB-VRC4373	http://www.necel.com/home.nsf/main?readformµprocessors
Phillips	Poseidon v1.0, v1.5	TwoChipHCG Development Kit	http://www.semiconductors.philips.com/acrobat/literature/9397/75003247.pdf
QED	RM5230	P-4032	http://www.algor.co.uk/algor/info/p4032-benefits.html
QED	RM5260	P-5064	http://www.algor.co.uk/algor/info/p5064-benefits.html
ST Microelectronics	STPC Client	Gloria	http://www.st.com/stonline/products/support/stpc/eval/index.htm
Toshiba	TX3912, TX3922		

The list of certified processors differs for different versions of CE. You should confirm that the processor you're considering is supported for the version of Windows CE you plan to deploy.

If you are working with multiple processors, the D9000 Odo development platform is best suited for your needs. This is the platform that was used to develop the early versions of Windows CE at Microsoft. The development board itself supports a variety of processors via plug-in modules . The entire system is expensive, but for special multiprocessor development needs it is the best value for the money. Platform Builder comes with drivers for the Odo board.

A newer version of a development board that supports multiple processors is widely referred to in the industry as a HARP (Hardware Architecture Reference Platform) board . A HARP board is capable of supporting multiple processors within a standard board framework. Besides providing a common reference platform for different processors, this board also significantly eases the test environment that Microsoft has to produce for testing certified processors.

If you aren't convinced of the need for a sophisticated development board like that specified by HARP, consider the multitude of iterations that can be created with a modular, customizable operating system like Windows CE. Now multiply that by the number of processors currently certified. Each processor must be tested on specialized hardware, a process that involves setting up different connectors and cables in the lab. Then each test must be run across the entire matrix of possible configurations versus available processors. In other words, this is a test engineer's nightmare. A standard development board like HARP can significantly ease the hardware requirements of the testing lab.

If you cannot use an evaluation board, look for a Windows CE device available in the market that can serve as a development platform for the project. You might be able to glean development opportunities, albeit severely limited, from these devices. At the start of your project, measure the investment of a few hundred dollars in one of these devices against the idle time that your team members will spend waiting for the target hardware to be available.

The CEPC platform may also present some unusual prototyping opportunities. While developing a display driver for a Chips & Technologies CT65550 display controller, a developer on our team once built an 80486 PC with a VESA (Video Electronics Standards Association) bus and ordered a version of the CT65550 on a VESA bus card, which he then used to prototype the display driver on the PC itself, giving himself a tremendous head start.

Architecture and Design

The architecture and design of the software for the product together form a process that is best started in parallel with the training of staff. As the knowledge base for Windows CE grows, your team will be ready to apply this newfound information to a product design. A draft of the hardware design is assumed to be available. You will need this to begin preliminary software design.

Also on your list of required information is a product road map. Although future iterations of a product may be furthest from your mind, referring to the road map can often make some design choices straightforward. From the product road map, you will be able to extrapolate the iterations of the current product. Any significant variations of the product must also be considered. If you are a vendor that sells boards to OEMs, your product road map will differ from that of a vendor who sells its product directly to customers. An ideal product specification contains a detailed list of features for the first version of the product and an overview of features for the following two versions. If you have this information, consider yourself lucky and use all of it to design the software.

We propose discovering (i.e., identifying) all the software that must be written for the project in two distinct stages. In the first stage, focus on determining hardware-related software components that must be created. In the second stage, turn your attention to all system and application software. In the Windows CE world, hardware-related software is categorized as a **platform**. System and application software that is independent of the hardware is classified as either **platform independent** or **public**. Mapping our stages to Windows CE terminology, we call the first stage platform task discovery and the second stage public task discovery.

Platform Task Discovery

An essential document for this stage is the hardware specification. Again, a preliminary hardware specification is all that is required to kick off this stage. Task discovery must be revisited every time the hardware specification changes. However, the output from your task discovery may not necessarily change as a result of a change in the hardware specification.

Platform discovery means understanding a feature related to the platform and determining what corresponding piece of software must be developed. Looking at the high-level hardware components will give you a good idea of which device drivers are required. A few additional components, like the boot loader and hardware diagnostics, are standard issue. You'll need to quickly focus on the specifics of the boot loader, and a good set of diagnostics take a long time to refine, so getting started on both of these tasks first is a good idea.

If you pick a prototyping platform that is fairly close to the final piece of hardware you'll be producing, accept the freebies gracefully. Start by getting the prototype drivers working. You might even need to debug and optimize them a bit to get them into shape. The next step is to integrate the platform-specific software with the target hardware when it becomes available. This integration will save you the effort of producing a driver from scratch. If a prototype driver is available for a particular piece of hardware, use it as a point on your checklist when comparing hardware options

During this phase you should determine any communication that your drivers might carry out with applications or even with each other. For example, your network driver may want to update the LED driver directly to notify the user of network activity. Instead of letting applications synchronize this activity by communicating with each driver, you can have the drivers talk directly to each other for quicker response. Device drivers in Windows CE are user mode DLLs, so you can use any mode of interprocess communication that is available to a Win32 application. Interprocess communication primitives such as events, semaphores, and mutexes (see Chapter 1) are available. Shared memory can be used to pass data between processes readily. You can even use the registry to pass static data between drivers.

Power management should be a consideration in this phase. If your device requires power management, you need to determine the level of management required. Different devices have different requirements depending on their usage scenarios. In contrast to a stationary terminal that is plugged into a power outlet, a wireless, mobile terminal needs sophisticated power management. Ask the following questions of each device driver in your platform task discovery:

- Does this device require power management?
- What will the state of the device be during each stage of power management?

At the end of this phase you should have a task list of platform-dependent software. For Orbiter, a sample task list jotted down at the end of this phase might be as follows:

- Boot loader
- OEM Abstraction Layer
- Serial port driver
- Parallel port driver
- Display driver
- Flash I/O (input/output) driver
- PS/2 keyboard
- PS/2 mouse
- Audio driver
- LED driver
- Power button driver
- PCMCIA driver
- Wireless radio driver
- TCP/IP
- Diagnostics
- Migrate remote control software to platform

Public Task Discovery

Public task discovery doesn't necessarily follow platform task discovery. Generally both happen in parallel. As you discover each task, you can decide the phase in which it belongs. Public tasks are tasks that are not platform dependent. It is important to identify them as such because this categorization will affect how you design and implement the software module that accompanies the task. Platform-independent modules can be used across different platforms or incremental iterations of your platform if your product warrants such treatment.

Any user interface that a custom device may have is a likely candidate for a public task. Applications can be platform independent if care is taken during design and implementation. Applications should communicate with drivers that are guaranteed to be present on all platforms. If a driver may not exist on a particular platform, you should give the application the ability to handle that condition gracefully and continue to perform its duties. Another issue to watch out for is display metrics. Different devices may have different display sizes depending on their form factor. Your application should be able to adjust its interface according to the screen resolution.

Applications are not the only modules that can be public. Note that a device driver in Windows CE doesn't always have to be associated with a piece of hardware. A driver can function as an independent software-only module that is loaded by `device.exe` like a driver. An example is a module that monitors and synchronizes power management on the platform. Another example is a module that interprets events from a touch panel that provides quick-access function keys. Such modules should be part of your public task discovery phase.

For Orbiter, we enumerate the following public tasks:

- User interface for setting configuration parameters
- User interface agent to communicate settings via device drivers
- Universal wireless radio driver Interface

If you plan to qualify for the *Powered by Windows CE* logo, you need to enroll in the logo program and promptly propagate the requirements to all your team members. Tasks related to enrollment should be included in the schedule.

Specifying the System

You've warmed up enough by now to start specifying the system. In this phase you will customize Windows CE to meet the needs of your platform. Recall that you can pick and choose components from Windows CE to include in your final image. Once you have gone through the public and platform task discovery phases, you can customize the Windows CE system.

Customizing the Windows CE system is a matter of selecting the components and modules that will be included in your image. For example, if you are producing a network driver for your hardware, which presumably has an Ethernet interface, you will need to add a networking stack (or two) to the system. If TCP/IP is your protocol of choice, add the TCP/IP module to the list of modules in the system. You must carry out this process until you get an operating system that will provide all the interfaces and features required by your target hardware.

Once you have a list of essential components required for your device, you can start sizing your memory requirements. Make a list of all components and modules that includes their estimated sizes. You can check the size of a module by simply looking at the size of the file itself. Components are a bit trickier. Components add up to a module. The best way to determine the memory requirements of a component is to build the Windows CE system and look at the size of the resultant module. The completed list will give you a fair idea of the size that the Windows CE system will occupy. Of course, you won't have a good idea of what the drivers and applications are going to need, but you'll have something to work with. By looking up similar drivers on your prototype environment, if one is available, you can make additional estimates. You will at least have a ballpark idea that will allow you to make sure the RAM and ROM requirements of your hardware are not completely off the mark.

Creating a Technical Specification

The effort expended on the architecture and design of the software should be captured in a technical specification, which you should use to communicate expectations to every member on the team. A specification is also a great way to introduce the team to the effort involved in making the project happen. If your team members are sufficiently primed, expect them to start stating their preferences for tasks right after the specification is made public.

When you're presenting an overview of the modules to be developed, we suggest that you start with the Windows CE diagram found in the CE documentation (Figure 2.1). This diagram provides a recognized starting point for your team members, who are becoming familiar with CE and probably have come across that diagram.

In addition, your specification should have the following essential elements:

- All the platform and public tasks in the project. Identify device drivers, applications, and modes of communication between modules.
- Resource assignments (IRQ, DMA, memory ports, and so on) for all devices on the hardware
- All selected system components and modules of Windows CE
- A memory map for the system

The technical specification will remain a live document until your product ships. Acknowledging this fact and managing the changes to the specification promptly and after due deliberation will help you control the architecture of the product. In the next section we will describe a task discovery process that will enable you to list all the components and modules that will be part of the product. At the end of this process you will be able to create the block diagram for Orbiter (Figure 2.2). This diagram serves several purposes. It provides an overview of the software. If you are ever pitching the architecture of your product outside of engineering, this is an excellent diagram to initiate the technical discussion. Within engineering, this overview also helps the team understand how all the parts of the system will come together and fit in with the entire operating system.

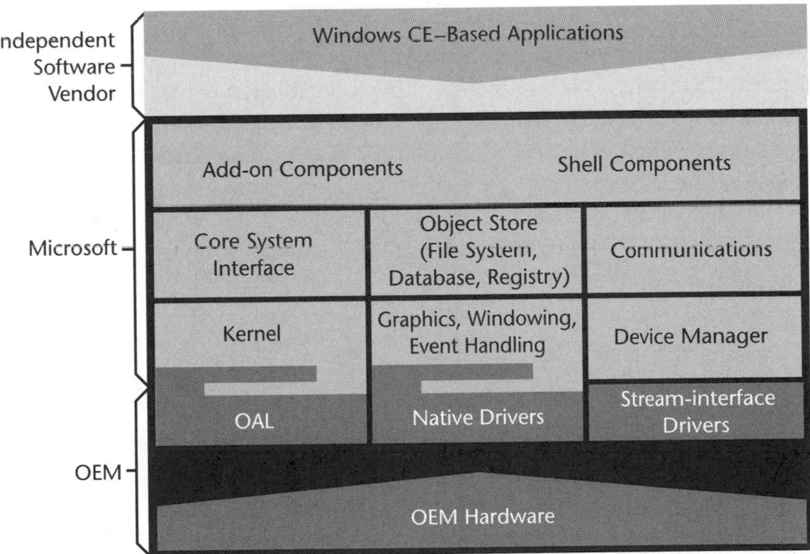

Figure 2.1 Block diagram of Windows CE (adapted from Microsoft Windows CE Books Online)

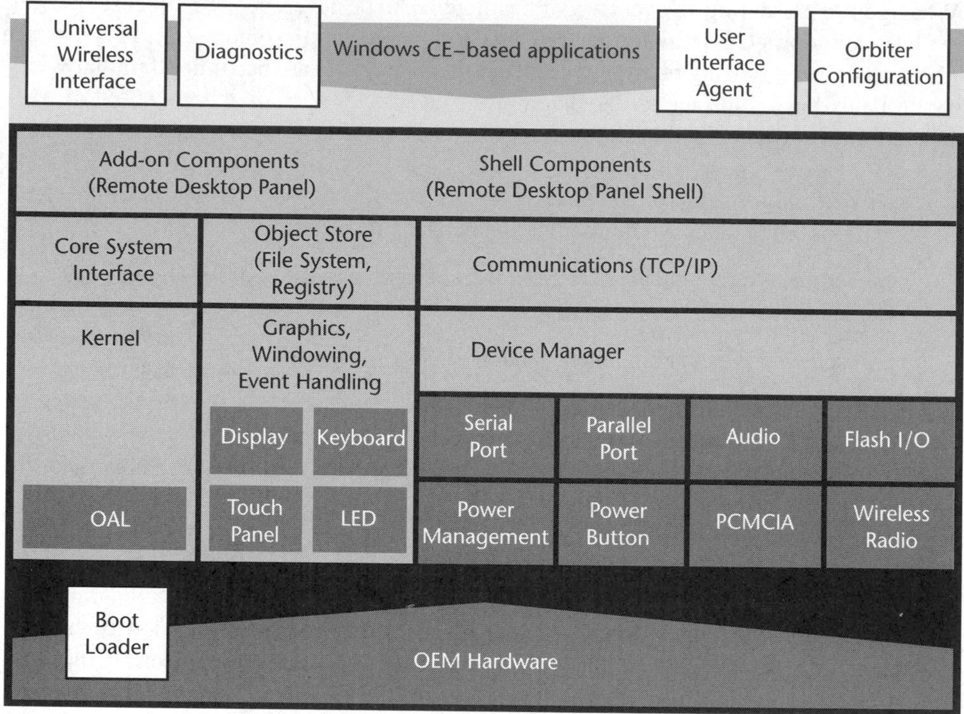

Figure 2.2 Block diagram of Orbiter

Creating a Schedule

In this section we leave the realm of science and technology and delve into the world of art. We need to create a schedule for our project. When creating a schedule, most project managers try to keep things simple. Simple project plans are easy to communicate to upper management and easy for team members to follow. They certainly are very easy to maintain. However, we would like to propose an alternate approach. A project schedule should be made as complex as is warranted by its dependencies. Don't be afraid of specifying complex dependencies that reflect reality in your project. In fact, initially, this is all you should do when creating a schedule. The first two things you should focus on are

1. Creating a list of tasks and subtasks
2. Specifying the dependencies between tasks

Contrary to popular belief, project schedules don't have to be understood completely by everyone in the company. It is your obligation to know the entire schedule like the back of your hand. Even individual developers on your team don't have to be able to read and understand the complete schedule. If someone has trouble understanding the schedule, you can always explain bits and pieces of it. When you are faced with the choice of creating a complex schedule that reflects reality or creating a schedule that is simple enough for everyone to understand, we recommend the former.

Creating and Allocating Tasks

Once you have your task list mapped out, assign tasks to different members of your team. By this point the developers on the team should have reviewed the specification enough to state preferences for tasks. We encourage project managers to accommodate as many preferences as possible, even when they seem to go against a developer's area of expertise. The short-term liability you will incur while the developer trains himself will be more than made up for when a happy developer decides to be part of your team for the next five projects.

As a project manager, take note of one particular implication of this process: You will have to come up with the initial task list and dependencies by yourself. This is an excellent exercise if you plan to lead the project. Not only will you get an excellent overall picture of the project, but you will also win the respect and confidence of your developers by being able to absorb any technical conversation you may have regarding a particular task. Don't worry too much about details. If you include the touch panel driver as a task in your schedule and you don't know enough about a touch panel driver to break it down into subtasks, don't be concerned. The details will be fleshed out later.

Once the assignments are made, ask for help. In other words, have all developers look over their tasks on the schedule. All you need to do at this time is check if the given task list is accurate. More importantly, have your developers verify dependencies as much as they can at this stage. In trying to verify dependencies, developers will stray from verifying their tasks into inspecting the task lists of other developers. Such cross-inspection is quite useful in validating the big picture.

Allocate some time with each developer to walk through each task allocated to him or her. Look for things that might fall through the cracks. If a developer has a task called *Test keyboard driver on CEPC,* make sure that related tasks—such as *Obtain and set up CEPC, Successfully boot Windows CE on the CEPC,* and *Upload an image to the CEPC*—have been defined. It is the project manager's responsibility to identify tasks that developers may miss.

Adding Big-Picture Tasks

When you are done tending to the needs of each developer, add big-picture tasks to your schedule. Big-picture tasks are those that don't necessarily fall cleanly into a particular developer's plate. Usually these tasks involve everyone on the team. Some big-picture tasks are identified in the list that follows and discussed in more detail later in this chapter.

- Generating automated builds
- Creating a version control database and policies
- Integrating upcoming releases of Windows CE
- Integrating software with each revision of the target hardware
- Integrating and testing the project
- Planning and executing a beta program
- System testing

We are ready to take a crack at creating a schedule framework. Table 2.2 shows the framework for a schedule for Project Orbiter. The framework simply lists tasks down to a reasonable level of detail and attempts to capture the dependencies among tasks. A Gantt chart corresponding to Table 2.2 is available on the CD that accompanies this book.

Note that we set up a prototyping environment early in the life of the project, thereby allowing training of the team to begin. We also get started on licensing early in the process. Note that the boot loader and OAL are the roots of the dependencies of most development tasks. This level of importance puts them on the critical path for your project. Staff these tasks first with your most capable engineers.

In addition to the boot loader, the display driver and wireless radio drivers are critical components. Although they don't act as predecessors for as many tasks as their aforementioned colleagues, they affect the performance of the WBT singularly. It is best to tackle these tasks early because you will spend quite a bit of time benchmarking and optimizing these drivers. As part of our design, we will use the PCMCIA form factor as a generic interface for wireless radio drivers. This form factor allows us to remain independent of wireless hardware vendors. You will probably end up pruning the cost of the final product significantly by integrating an OEM version of the radio. For our example, we'll stick with flexibility rather than cost (a decision that in real life has caused much grief for more than one aspiring company).

Before the display driver becomes functional, you can develop and test various components on a "headless" device. However, the completion of the display driver is essential to tasks like applications that require a GUI. You can mitigate this dependency to some extent by prototyping the applications, especially their GUIs, on the Windows CE emulator or the prototype platform. Whenever a task is on the critical path of other tasks, look for creative ways to reduce dependencies. By reducing dependencies even for small portions of a task, you will reduce your schedule risk incrementally, and sometimes exponentially. Often you can split a task into smaller subtasks, some of which have no predecessors. Tasks that deal with the research, design, and specification of a component are ideal candidates for such splits. You can then clear them of dependencies, leaving your schedule open to leveling optimizations.

One of our first big milestones in Project Orbiter is what we call the "Hello" CE system. Platform Builder ships with a sample program called `hello.exe`, which simply emits a greeting to the debug output (serial port). This simple application requires a minimal CE configuration to execute. The "Hello" CE system benefits from the fact that it can operate entirely on a headless device. Thus, we can leave out a large percentage of OS features related to display and GUI. This capability makes `hello.exe` a prime candidate to work with in the early stages of verifying the hardware. Because of its uncomplicated nature, you can rest assured that there are not too many cooks around to spoil the broth.

Table 2.2 identifies milestones in the schedule. External milestones are added so that dependencies can be constructed on the basis of these dates. Remember that milestones are an excellent way of demonstrating progress inside and outside of engineering. Decide which milestones you would like to publish externally. Make sure these milestones are spread as evenly as possible across the life of the project. Regularly scheduled milestones convey the impression that you are firmly in control. In the event that your schedule is complicated and not easy to understand by someone outside of engineering (or someone besides you), the list of milestones is an ample substitute.

The corresponding Gantt chart is available in a Microsoft Project file on the CD that accompanies this book.

Table 2.2 Orbiter Schedule Framework

ID[a]	Milestone	Task[b]	Predecessors[c]
1		**External software milestones**	
2	♦	Beta 1 of Windows CE version x	
3	♦	Beta 2 of Windows CE version x	2
4	♦	Release candidate of Windows CE version x	3
5	♦	FCS of Windows CE version x	4
6	♦	Beta 1 of wireless radio driver	
7	♦	Release of wireless radio driver	6
8		**Development setup**	**2**
9		**Tools**	
10		Purchase and install	
11		Create installation document	10
12		Build Windows CE for CEPC	11
13		**Prototype platform (CEPC)**	
14		Obtain and configure CEPC systems	
15		Upload and boot CE	14, 12
16		Test debugging environment	15
17	♦	Prototyping environment available	16
18		**CE licensing**	
19		Microsoft	
20		System integrator?	
21		Network card vendor	
22		Display vendor	
23		Any other vendors who offer source code	
24	♦	CE licensing complete	23, 22, 21, 20, 19
25		**System design**	
26		Develop Orbiter design and architecture	
27		List required CE system modules and components	26
28	♦	Initial memory map available	27
29	♦	Orbiter technical specification available	26
30		**Hardware and electrical milestones**	
31	♦	Revision 0 of boards available	
32	♦	Revision 1 of boards available	31
33	♦	Submit platform for FCC (Federal Communications Commission) tests	32, 148
34		**Development** (see Figure 2.2)	**17**
35		**Windows CE build**	
36		Modify `cesysgen.bat` to include system components	27
37		Create platform and public directories for project	
38		Build CE image using system components and `hello.exe`	37, 36
39	♦	"Hello" CE image available	38
40		Create WBT build for Windows CE	39
41	♦	WBT image available	40
42		**Boot loader**	**31**
43		Configure hardware	

(continued)

Table 2.2 *Continued.*

ID[a]	Milestone	Task[b]	Predecessors[c]
44		Create and run hardware tests to verify board functionality	43
45		Initialize operating system	44
46		Integrate with serial driver to support downloads	45
47	♦	Boot loader available	46
48		**OEM Abstraction Layer**	
49		Provide hardware abstraction in CE DDK (Windows CE Device Driver Kit) library	
50		Hook and test interrupts	49
51	♦	OAL available	50
52		Upload and test `hello.exe`	51, 47, 39
53	♦	"Hello" CE system ready and verified	52
54		**Display driver**	**53**
55		Create a CE build image with the polygons sample application in Platform Builder	
56		Initialize display	
57		Adapt existing display driver to Orbiter	56
58		Add support for TFT (thin film transistor) and DSTN (double-layer supertwist nematic) LCD displays	57
59		Test display driver using Polygons sample	58
60	♦	Basic display driver available	59
61	♦	Orbiter with display available	60
62		Add hardware acceleration	60
63		Create test plug-in for Tux (a client-server application discussed later in this chapter)	62
64		**Serial port driver**	
65		Test and modify on CEPC	17
66		Migrate to Orbiter	65, 53
67		Create test plug-in for Tux	66
68		**Parallel port driver**	
69		Test and modify on CEPC	17
70		Migrate to Orbiter	69, 53
71		Create test plug-in for Tux	70
72		**Keyboard driver**	
73		Test and modify on CEPC	17
74		Migrate to Orbiter	73, 53
75		Create test plug-in for Tux	74
76		**Touch panel driver**	
77		Test and modify on CEPC	17
78		Migrate to Orbiter	77, 53
79		Create test plug-in for Tux	78
80		**Flash driver**	
81		Implement flash I/O driver	17
82		Migrate to Orbiter	81, 53
83		Create test plug-in for Tux	82
84		**Audio driver**	**53**
85		Port existing audio driver to Orbiter	

Table 2.2 *Continued.*

ID[a]	Milestone	Task[b]	Predecessors[c]
86		Create test plug-in for Tux	85
87		**LED driver**	**53**
88		Implement LED driver	
89		Test LED driver via published API	88
90		Create test plug-in for Tux	89
91		**Power button driver**	**53**
92		Implement power button driver	
93		Provide support for software shutdown	92
94		Create test plug-in for Tux	93
95		**TCP/IP**	**53**
96		Configure and test TCP/IP on Orbiter	
97		**PCMCIA Driver**	**53**
98		Port to Orbiter	
99	♦	PCMCIA driver available	98
100		**Universal wireless radio interface**	
101		Specify universal interface	
102		Implement	101, 99
103		Create test plug-in for Tux	102
104		**Wireless radio driver**	**53**
105		Port radio driver to Orbiter	96, 6
106	♦	Radio driver available	105
107		Run preliminary stress test for radio driver using RDP (Remote Desktop Protocol)	123, 106
108		Create test plug-in for Tux	107
109		Integrate release version of radio driver	108, 7
110		**Power management**	
111		Create power management interface and specify	
112	♦	Power management specification available	111
113		Implement OEM functions	112, 53
114		Implement Suspend and state change notification	113
115		Implement inactivity timeout	114
116		Integrate and test changes with all device drivers	115, 97, 91, 84, 80, 76, 72, 68, 64, 54
117		Run stress test for power management	116
118		**RDP client**	**61, 53**
119		Set up WTS server	
120		Test with Win32 client for connection	119
121		Benchmark Win32 client	120
122		Test with CE client for connection	121, 106
123	♦	RDP client for CE functional	122
124		Benchmark CE client	123
125	♦	Benchmark results available	124
126		**Diagnostics**	**53**
127		Study diagnostics requirements and design	
128	♦	Diagnostics specification available	127

(continued)

Table 2.2 *Continued.*

ID[a]	Milestone	Task[b]	Predecessors[c]
129		Implement diagnostics	128
130		Create test plug-in for Tux	129
131		Integrate diagnostics on all development units and test	130
132		**User interface agent**	**61**
133		Specify user interface agent interface with device drivers	
134		Design and implement user interface agent	133
135		Test operation with each communicating driver	134
136		**Orbiter configuration**	
137		Specify configuration settings	
138		Design and prototype user interface	137
139		Port to Orbiter	138, 61
140		Interface with user interface agent	139, 134
141		Create test plug-in for Tux	140
142		**Intermediate integrations**	
143		**Integration stage 1**	**32, 2**
144		Integrate CE into build	
145		Test integration of operating system	144
146		Call for check-in of working source and checkpoint	145
147		Integrate all software modules	146
148	◆	Software build available	147
149		**Integration stage 2**	**143, 3**
150		Integrate CE into build	
151		Test integration of operating system	150
152		Call for check-in of working source and checkpoint	151
153		Integrate all software modules	152
154	◆	Software build available	153
155		**Version control**	**39**
156		Identify source code that will be put under version control	
157		Set up version control and automated builds server if required	156
158		Create version control database on server	157
159		Identify and create users and permissions	158
160	◆	Version control database online	159
161		**Automated builds**	**160, 39**
162		Create and test makefile for building CE image	41
163		Create and test file sweeper assistant	162
164		Automate creation of Orbiter-related directories from scratch	163
165		Automate refresh of source code from version control	164, 160
166		Schedule automated builds at desired intervals	165
167		Test automated builds	166
168	◆	Development complete	161, 155, 149, 136, 132, 126, 118, 104, 91, 87, 84, 80, 76, 72, 68

Table 2.2 *Continued.*

ID[a]	Milestone	Task[b]	Predecessors[c]
169		**Final integration**	**168, 7, 5**
170		Integrate CE into build	
171		Test integration of operating system	170
172		Call for check-in of working source and checkpoint	171
173		Integrate all software modules	172
174		Run benchmarks	173
175		Roll out software build	174
176	♦	Alpha release	175
177		**Testing**	**176**
178		Create test plan for user and automated testing	
179		Set up Tux server and test with sample module	
180		Create automated Tux scripts	179
181		Do a dry run of user and automated testing	180
182	♦	Testing environment set up	181, 178, 176
183		Conduct user testing	182
184		Conduct automated testing	182
185	♦	First beta available	183
186		Conduct user testing	185
187		Conduct automated testing	185
188	♦	Release candidate available	187, 186

[a] Boldface represents a task that has subtasks.
[b] Indentation indicates relative levels of tasks.
[c] This column identifies the other tasks upon which a given task depends. Boldface identifies predecessors for a task that has subtasks, thus indicating a significant dependency.

Adding Duration to Tasks

Once you have completed a detailed task and dependencies list, most of your work is done. Creating a detailed task list forces you to understand each task thoroughly. Specifying dependencies gives you an excellent idea of the forces of interaction between modules. When you are done with this exercise, estimating the duration of each task is easy.

Once your project chart contains timelines, we suggest you run them by your developers one more time. This will be the second and final pass of the schedule through your team. These passes are extremely essential in creating "buy-in" from your team. If all team members feel involved in the decision making, they will be likely to stand by the choices they helped you make and feel a personal responsibility toward making the schedule a reality.

Using Milestones to Create a Visible Schedule

One of the first signs that your project might be canceled—a phenomenon you may already have experienced—is a sudden lack of interest from upper management. Such a change in attitude usually is an indication that your project doesn't command the attention it used to and that the company might be refocusing. As a project manager, you need to track the corporate phenomenon of changing management attention span, staying alert to its constant vagaries.

One great way to track the interest of management is to create a visible schedule—that is, one that is extremely easy to track. This suggestion does not mean that we're retracting the advice we gave earlier; we still believe that you should create a complex schedule that potentially no one but you will understand. A schedule can be complex and yet easy to track. The feature that bridges the gap the **milestone**. By peppering your project schedule with milestones, you will create a *measurable* schedule, a prime requisite toward creating a visible schedule. When presenting your schedule at program reviews, you can simply present the list of milestones. No one needs to see your Gantt charts (does anyone really, anyway? ☺). A visible schedule holds management attention like nothing else. If the engineering manager, sales department, and marketing team can all see tasks being mowed down one by one, the interest level in your project will remain healthy.

Maintaining a Live Schedule

So now we have a schedule, and we need to track it. Tracking a schedule means tracking the progress of each task and determining if each milestone is being met. On an ideal project, with each update you will simply increase the completed percentage for each task. Tasks will never be completed late, and you won't have to make a single adjustment. As we all know, however, few projects of reasonable complexity—certainly any project in which we are building a custom Windows CE device—progresses this smoothly. In reality, a particularly difficult technical problem may wreak havoc with a task, a developer may find the learning curve a bit too steep to climb, or you may simply have grossly underestimated a task's duration.

You should always be ready to adjust a schedule. Don't bother fussing around whenever a task's order, priority, or resource assignment needs to be changed. Provided that you are convinced the change is for the better, make it quickly and move on. When you're done, you will probably not recognize the original schedule. This is not necessarily a bad thing, particularly if this is the first project of its kind for you.

Something you should keep in mind is that a project in which tasks are shifting constantly makes outside observers nervous. You can address this problem by creating an external milestone list. **External milestones** are milestones that are established for the sake of observers of your project. Make sure you pick a fairly extensive list of immutable milestones. Milestones like *Prototype platform development complete, Integration with first revision of hardware complete, First alpha available, First beta available,* and so on are good examples of sturdy external milestones. The idea behind external milestones is that even if your project is being continually adjusted internally, you can take care to make sure the external milestones don't necessarily change. Sometimes they will, but for quite a few internal adjustments you may find that the external milestones don't have to be rescheduled. If the external milestones are static, observers tend to have a good feeling about your project. Your internal milestones are your own, on the other hand, and you can change them all you want.

What about estimating the percentage completed for each task? Different formats for collecting this information work best for different teams. Some project leads prefer to visit each developer in turn and get a feel for how far along they are with their tasks. Others prefer the much dreaded weekly meeting. A weekly meeting works fine as long as the lead makes sure it doesn't exceed a reasonable amount of time. For our project, we kept the weekly meetings to one hour.

Getting a developer to estimate what percentage of a task is completed is easier said than done. For one thing, how is the completed percentage measured? There is no easy or known method. It varies tremendously according to the type of task, the complexity of the task, the working style of the developer, and other, unknown variables. How, then, can one reasonably estimate the percentage completed? The only answer we can provide is, "By practice."

Encourage your developers to come up with a ballpark figure, no matter how wild it is initially. Refine the percentage each week. Finally, compare the estimated progress with actual progress and, if necessary, help the developer analyze what went wrong. Over a period of time, a developer will learn how to anticipate work on a task. She will also learn how her working patterns affect progress. In addition, she'll be able to anticipate some, although not all, of the unforeseen problems. This "gut feel" isn't a spiritual thing. Rather it is developed and fine-tuned by the best of developers gradually. If your team members practice estimating the percentage completed on each task, they will improve with time. Toward the end of the project, don't be surprised to find some developers nailing down their percentages accurately.

Task-Complete Demos

One curious phenomenon is that sometimes developers mark a task 100 percent complete by Friday but do not actually finish it until the weekend. As long as the task is finished over the weekend, this is not a problem. If the task is not completed, however, you may end up with incomplete tasks on a developer's plate, which eat into his next task. Being late on a task is not such a bad thing, but being late on one while falsely appearing to be late on another gives a distorted impression of the project and its tasks.

One way to work around these "pseudo-completions" is to ask the developer to set up a demo of the module that has just been completed. Demos often are not possible, especially if the developer is working on an internal system module. If a test harness must be produced for the module, however, this can be used in a demo. The demo does not have to be fancy—just functional. Besides allowing you to visually verify the completion of a task, demos provide an opportunity for the developer to shine in front of the whole team. If the demo is visually pleasing, we suggest you make a meal out of it and invite key players from management, sales, and marketing to observe. Not only do such demos significantly boost the pride quotient for the developer and motivate him, but they also give concrete indication of progress to external observers.

Strategies for Version Control and Automated Builds

Source code version control is an increasingly essential component of any serious project. Version control allows team members to share source code and provides the capability of archiving changes made to each source file. Advanced features such as branching allow multiple projects to progress in parallel. A fair bit of source code can be shared for an embedded Windows CE project. The reason you need to plan for version control up front is that the need for it will arise suddenly. It is best not to wait until developers start working on private copies of the same file that should have been shared from the beginning. In this section we will discuss strategies for version control and show which files should be placed in version control and which should not.

Windows CE Platform Builder creates an extensive directory tree on your hard disk. Your modules are made within this tree. When you're adding files to be maintained under version control, it is best to follow the dictum, *Do not add files you do not own.* In other words, if Platform

Builder contains files that you will never modify for any purpose, do not add them to version control. Add only the files that your team will modify and maintain. This practice significantly simplifies ongoing version control maintenance.

So which files should you change? The Platform Builder directory tree is formatted as a top-level hierarchy (see Figure 2.3). The PLATFORM and PUBLIC directories are under the Platform Builder installation root (referred to by the environment variable _WINCEROOT). These are the only directories that an OEM is required to modify. PLATFORM holds platform-dependent files. PUBLIC holds platform-independent files. Refer to Chapter 10 for a more detailed explanation of each directory and its contents in the installation. Under PUBLIC, you will find a directory called COMMON. The OEM should not modify this directory unless it is reselling Platform Builder after enhancements. COMMON holds components that are owned by Microsoft (and third-party vendors) and are shipped as standard components with Platform Builder. Modified files in this directory will be overwritten when upgrades of Platform Builder are installed.

You will end up creating directories under PLATFORM and PUBLIC for your custom hardware. Let's revisit the Orbiter project. We can create a directory called ORBITER in this case under PLATFORM. Similarly, platform-independent files will be collected under a new subdirectory in the PUBLIC directory called WBT to denote the fact that we are creating a Windows-based terminal. Our new directory hierarchy looks like the one shown in Figure 2.4.

Copying a directory tree that closely resembles your platform can set up this hierarchy. The copied directory should then be renamed. New source code produced for Orbiter should be added to the ORBITER tree if it is platform dependent. Separate directories like DRIVERS and KERNEL under ORBITER that should be used to categorize the source being produced. If the new source is platform independent, put it under the WBT tree. The WBT tree really does not have any organization for new source code. Older versions of Platform Builder, a.k.a. the ETK, used a directory called OAK\SRC to hold OEM source code. You can essentially set up your own hierarchy here under the OAK directory.

If you are programming in C or C++, as you probably will be for Windows CE, you will produce header files. Some header files may be shared across modules. The best place to put

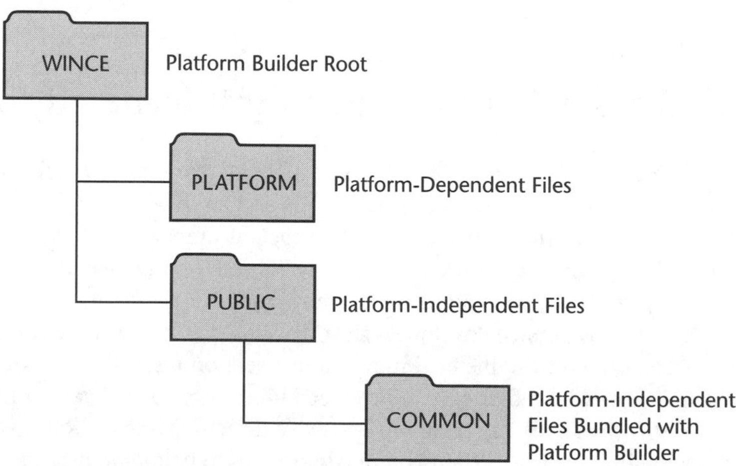

Figure 2.3 Directory hierarchy of Platform Builder

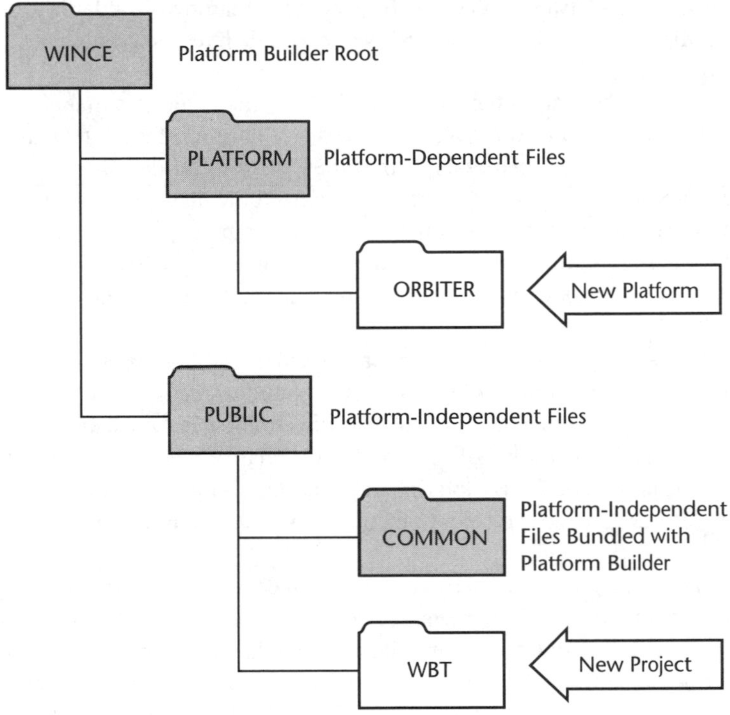

Figure 2.4 Directory hierarchy of the Orbiter project

shared header files that are platform dependent is `\WINCE\PLATFORM\ORBITER\INC` or, to be more generic, `_TARGETPLATROOT\INC`. Shared header files that are platform independent can be placed in a similar directory of your own creation. When you're setting up `INCLUDE` paths for building source code, be sure to include these directories for all modules so that the correct header files can be shared.

The header files that you author will not be the only files used by modules. Windows header files are collected in the `\WINCE\PUBLIC\WBT\CESYSGEN\OAK\INC` (`_PROJECTROOT\CESYSGEN\OAK\INC`) directory. This should be the directory from which you will include header files. You will likely find similar header files in other directories. These header files are filtered for your target platform before being copied into the `CESYSGEN` path. These filtered header files are customized to reflect the components and modules selected for your platform. In turn, they reflect the system services available to modules running on that platform. Make sure this path is in your `INCLUDE` path for any standard header files.

The files that you will put under version control should be the files that you own, including all files in the `ORBITER` and `WBT` directory trees. Everything else should be left alone. When setting up a workstation for development, you must install Platform Builder first. If you chose to make a copy of an existing platform or project to start the tree for your own project, you will need to do that. Then rename the copied directories and refresh the source code from version control over your new installation. These steps should set up the directories with the correct source code, and you will then be ready to build. We recommend that the working folders that you set up in your version control software reflect the folders in the Platform Builder installation. This configuration simplifies refreshes considerably because each refreshed file goes directly into its correct location.

The entire process described here should be automated from a batch file or a makefile. Most version control packages support a command-line interface. This interface can be used in the makefile to produce an automated script that primes the Platform Builder installation for your project. In Chapter 11 we show you how to produce a makefile that can be completely automated to produce builds from an existing installation. When combined, these makefiles can be used to set up an automated build solution that can be scheduled to run overnight. Overnight runs of the build are extremely useful in detecting incompatible updates to version control.

Often a developer updates a file or two in version control and the build breaks. Broken builds should be caught as soon as possible, and the automated build takes the grunt work out of detecting such problems. Insist that developers fix broken builds immediately because they usually hold up all other developers from building. Fortunately, it is relatively easy to identify the developer responsible for the broken build. By looking at the build error and checking the update log of the file that refuses to build, you can track down the accountable team member quite accurately.

When the first revision of hardware becomes available, each developer will spend some time migrating software from the prototype to the target. You should start integrating pieces as soon as they have been migrated. Integration will involve running the migrated pieces on the target hardware to check for incompatibilities. Modules that are added to the target image are controlled by the binary image builder (BIB) and registry (REG) files. When a module has been migrated and tested, it should be added to the integrated list by modification of the BIB and REG files. The developer who performs this integration should refresh all the source code and test her changes before checking the source into version control.

We recommend that you encourage all team members to refresh source code frequently. Often developers work on source code and are reluctant to refresh it because they are apprehensive of introducing new bugs and incompatibilities that will slow them down. This is a valid concern. Nevertheless, the long-term collective disadvantages of avoiding source code refreshes far outweigh the short-term individual benefits. Integration should be a constant process for Windows CE projects. If this phase is left to the very end of the project, the number of problems you encounter may be overwhelming. If the software starts crashing to kingdom come once it is all put together, the morale of your team may take a dive. Unstable software generates fast-flying rumors within a company, creating lack of confidence. As a result, concerned members of the nontechnical staff might stop by to "see what's going on."

Include in your schedule some official time for such integration phases. Although integration should be constant, the time you schedule should be used as a checkpoint to make sure that modules are functioning together. If issues need to be addressed, you should use this scheduled time to do so. You might be working with a version of Windows CE that is in the beta stage. It is worthwhile to determine how many beta cycles of Windows CE are being planned. You can then schedule your integration phases around these scheduled releases, thus attacking two issues at the same time. If you are lucky (or really adept) and you have no issues at all, you can fold this time into a task that is dragging along.

Managing New Projects

No project planning is complete without some thought devoted to how iterations of the existing product or new products will be integrated into the current scheme of things. For example, your company may plan to create a line of Windows-based terminals with different configuration options that affect price. Mobile WBTs might be created in various form factors for different applications. All of these iterations must be accommodated by the system software.

Recall that Windows CE Platform Builder allows for one project and one platform directory. Any iterations of the current product should be added to the existing project and platform structure. This structure implies that for each new platform designed and rolled out, a new platform directory must be created. If a platform does not change but a new product release requires platform-independent software to change or the *composition* of the platform to change, then a new project directory must be created. By *changing the composition of the platform,* we mean that the platform remains the same but is packaged differently for a new product. For example, the WBT might remain the same except that a TFT display is used instead of a DSTN. Alternatively, the PCMCIA interface for the wireless radio card might be replaced with a more integrated OEM-based interface offered by the radio vendor that would result in lower costs.

Platform Builder allows for the existence of multiple processors under a given platform. It stores binaries under processor-specific directories for a given platform. The implication here is that if you use different processors for the same platform—say, an SH3 and a PPC821 for different WBTs—you can reuse the platform directory. Because the trend is toward highly integrated processors, your platform will probably change with the choice of a processor significantly enough to warrant a new platform directory.

We present the following guide to expanding your project road map under the Platform Builder structure.

A Brand-New Product

Create a new platform and a new project directory. This is the process outlined earlier in this chapter.

Feature Enhancements to an Existing Product

Reuse the platform and project directories and label your source code for different versions under version control. Feature enhancements are usually made to existing modules. In the event that new modules need to be created, simply add them to the appropriate location in the directory hierarchy.

A New Product with Platform-Specific Changes

An example of this type of iteration would be a Windows-based terminal (WBT) with a different form factor (maybe a wearable WBT). Create a new platform directory. If the product is essentially the same, you may find yourself using a significant amount of source code from the original platform directory. We recommend not copying this source code over to the new platform directory. Instead, you can share it dynamically by continuing to build source code from the original platform directory and copying it into the binary section of the new platform directory.

An alternative to this approach is to create a common platform directory. Let's see how this works. The idea is to move code that is shared between two platforms in a common directory under the `PLATFORM` directory. As an example, we will add a platform similar to Orbiter but with a wearable form factor that includes a heads-up display, realized by supporting a smaller display on a visor.

After a passionate meeting in which several *Star Trek* and *Babylon 5* specific names are debated, the developers decide to simply call the platform Heads Up. Figure 2.5 shows how this arrangement is mapped into the directory structure of Platform Builder. A directory called `HEADSUP` is created under the `PLATFORM` hierarchy. This directory will be home to the modules and components specific to the Heads Up platform. For example, a different display controller may be used to meet the specialized demands of a heads-up display that in turn will require a different display driver. The touch panel may be replaced with a touchpad that is positioned on the user's belt, allowing manipulation of a cursor. The result will be a different driver for each platform.

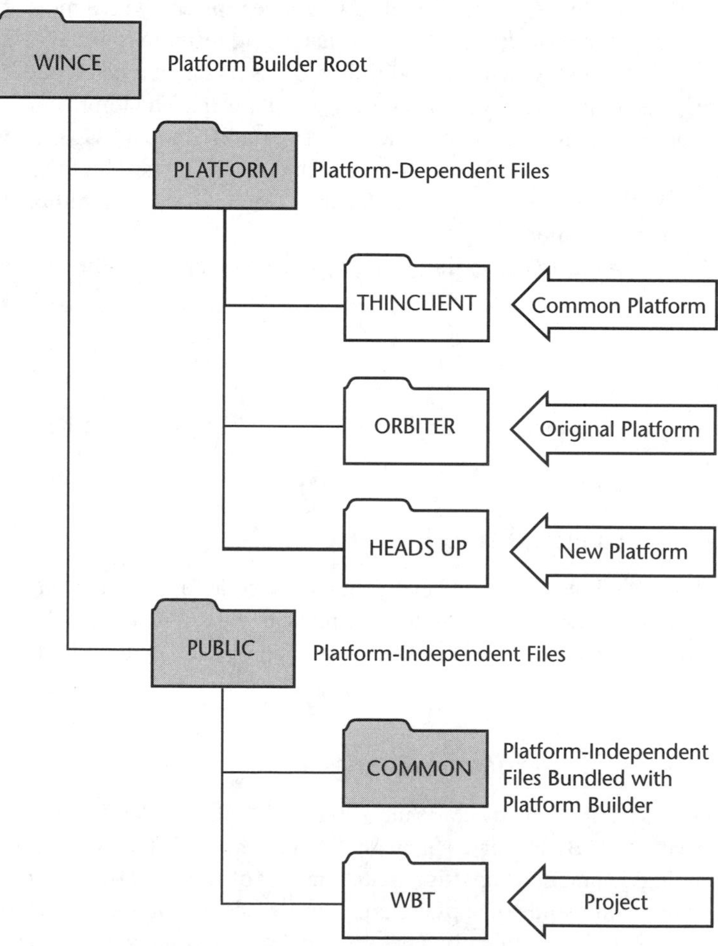

Figure 2.5 Common platform directory structure

On the other hand, the boot loader, OAL, serial port driver, flash driver, and other modules may all be shared across both platforms. The source code relevant to these shared modules can be moved into a separate directory that is created under the `PLATFORM` hierarchy called `THINCLIENT`. This directory will be home to source code shared across thin-client platforms. `ORBITER` and `HEADSUP` can both reference and actively use the source code in this directory. The way this is done is trivial. You will need to modify your build script to find the directories that contain shared code in the `THINCLIENT` tree and build each one. The Windows CE build process automatically places built modules in the appropriate platform tree. In other words, if your platform is set to `HEADSUP` and you build the audio driver in the `THINCLIENT` directory, the resulting binary is automatically copied in the repository for the `HEADSUP` platform.

Testing

Finally we come to the neglected child that everyone talks about and insists is vital to the quality of the product. For all its vaunted importance, testing is one of the most ill organized aspects of a project. Becase it is usually scheduled at the end of the project, when all development is coming to a close, it also is a prime candidate for schedule and budget cuts. It is not uncommon for a project lead to reduce testing time significantly in order to meet a project deadline.

We recommend that testing be folded into development as much as possible. Under this scheme, each developer working on a particular module is responsible for specifying how the module must be tested. Attempts at automating unit testing are extremely beneficial. In such cases, the developer must be expected to specify the tests that can be operated on the module in an automated fashion. This is not to say that the developer needs to write detailed test plans or even develop the test harness herself. A test engineer could perform either of those tasks. But including test plans in the development schedule will not only give testing the up-front time it deserves, but also will minimize back-end slicing and dicing of the testing schedule.

Windows CE Device Driver Test Kit

Windows CE provides support for automated and user testing in the form of the Device Driver Test Kit (DDTK). We discuss the DDTK in detail in Chapter 12, but we'll provide enough of an explanation here that you can plan to use it.

The DDTK provides a client-server application called Tux for running automated tests. The Tux client is a test harness with well-defined entry points and callback messages. The client expects a user mode DLL that can interface with these entry points and messages. Any user mode DLL that provides this interface and registers with the Tux client can be tested via Tux. Since device drivers in Windows CE are user mode DLLs, Tux can be used as a test harness for drivers. The Tux server can be run from a workstation and controls one or more Tux clients.

The Tux server provides an interface that can be used to look at the tests available on each Windows CE device. These tests can be selected, executed, and automated via the server interface. Given this arrangement, a developer can produce a set of tests and add them to the device driver DLL along with the required Tux interface. If a testing engineer is involved, he can consult with the developer and reuse portions of code to create those tests himself. The Tux interface is then produced entirely by the test engineer.

The functionality of Tux can be extended by another tool in the DDTK, called Kato. Kato is a logging engine that can grab the results of a test and send them to a garden variety of output devices. Plug-ins can be written that communicate with output devices of your choice. This ability enables Kato to page you, for instance, if a certain percentage of tests fail. Alternatively, Kato can play "Bermuda, Here I Come" over the intercom if all your tests pass.

When configuring a server for version control and automated builds, you should set up a Tux server as well. For good reason, project managers prefer their testing servers to be separate machines, often confined to a subnet where any havoc the servers may potentially wreak can be restricted. The implication here is that your budget should include the cost of a high-end test server.

Benchmarking the Device

Although not necessarily categorized as testing, benchmarking the device is essential, especially because customers will be comparing Orbiter to their desktops. If you have a testing department in your company, you can leverage that resource by having the department run benchmarks for your project. Benchmarking consumes lots of time. It works best for your development schedule if you off-load that task to a set of resources other than your team of developers.

When running a benchmark, consider the main areas of bottleneck on your platform. For the WBT, we can identify the wireless radio driver and the display as two such problem areas. The radio driver is responsible for pushing display and I/O information between client and server. This component directly affects how responsive the WBT will be to the user. The display driver also represents a centerpiece of functionality. Its performance when you're viewing information is critical. Benchmarking these two components separately will indicate more precisely where the critical bottleneck lies.

Perceived areas of bottleneck should not be the only subjects of benchmarking. Often what you don't think of can surprise you. Make sure you come up with good benchmark tests that test the performance of your device thoroughly. Again, the key is to plan for this activity up front and allocate time on the schedule for it. The best time to begin these tasks is as soon as functional beta versions of the required pieces of software are available *and integrated.* If the display driver and radio driver are performing adequately, start the benchmark process. Keep it in place for the lifetime of your project because you will find reason to visit it repeatedly.

Summary

In this chapter we have looked at the essential aspects of executing a Windows CE project. We focused on using the Platform Builder to create a device based on a custom platform. We analyzed techniques to help speed up the project. Using a platform to prototype modules can provide a huge head start. Attacking critical tasks like the boot loader and the OAL early in the process mitigates schedule risk because they are predecessors for a majority of tasks.

We looked at ongoing ways to keep tight control of the project, including maintaining a live schedule, using version control, and conducting automated builds. Because planning for the growth of your project is also important, we also discussed some project and directory layouts to help extend the project to cover iterations of the product.

3 Platform Builder Basics

The goal for Windows CE is to be able to run in a variety of devices and appliances. If you stop and think for a moment, you will realize that the world of consumer electronics is home to an array of devices that have wildly fluctuating hardware architectures. It would be hazardous to make assumptions about the processor, processor speed, available RAM, and storage medium on any given device. Can a tiny handheld digital telephone make room for a Pentium processor? Does it make sense for a refrigerator to have a hard disk? What's an operating system to do?

Microsoft has attempted to resolve these issues by making Windows CE a component-based operating system. A few of the basic OS functions are mandatory and must be supported by any hardware device that intends to use Windows CE. Everything else is up for grabs; you can add it to your operating system, or you can leave it out.

What exactly are these components? A **component** is a particular functionality that can be integrated into or left out of Windows CE. Components are available in the form of drivers, static or dynamic libraries, and executables. Windows CE can be built with selected components that are appropriate to the platform being developed. The tool that is used to build modified versions of Windows CE is called Platform Builder. Platform Builder is a set of CDs that contain utilities, files, and the components of Windows CE. Components can be platform dependent or platform independent. An example of a platform-dependent component is the kernel for an x86 PC. A component that allows the user to calibrate the touch panel and saves the coordinates is an example of a component that is platform independent. In addition, a component usually has a distinct resulting build target—either an executable or an object module library.

Let's look at the concept of a module. Several components can be linked together to form a module. A **module** is an executable or library file that performs a set of well-defined operations and exports a well-defined API. A module is divided into components according to areas of functionality, although such division is historically restricted by how the code was written. Microsoft has done its best to separate the modules into components in such a way that OEMs can select only the functionality they need for their platform. On value-priced consumer devices with multiple form factors, this is a critical feature. However, not all modules can be broken down into components.

Exploring Components in Platform Builder

Now that we have an idea of what components are, let's look at the real situation in the Platform Builder IDE. If you start Platform Builder and wait for it to open its main window, you will see all components collected in a **Catalog** window (Figure 3.1).

Platform Builder Catalog

The **Catalog** window in Platform Builder lists all the components that are available for inclusion in your build of the operating system. To create a custom version of Windows CE, also referred to as a build, you must create a **project** in Platform Builder. Note that Platform Builder terminology dictates that a component in the **Catalog** window is referred to as an **implementation**. When the implementation is included in a project, it becomes a component. An implementation is depicted by the icon shown in Figure 3.2. Implementations are grouped together by functionality into categories, or **types**. Types are depicted by the icon shown in Figure 3.3. An example of a type is `display`, which groups together available display drivers in a platform.

The types can be traversed and viewed just like a folder hierarchy. The implementations contained in the types and folders of the default catalog (see Figure 3.1) opened by Platform

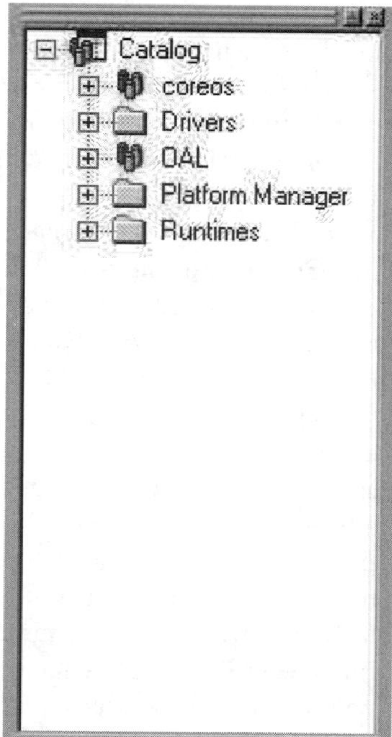

Figure 3.1 **Catalog** window in Platform Builder

Figure 3.2 Implementation icon

Figure 3.3 Type icon

Builder are presented in Table 3.1. You can extend the default catalog view by adding components of your own. We'll say more about that later in the chapter.

Table 3.1 Types and Implementations in the Default Catalog

Folder	Configuration	Type	Implementation	Description
coreos				A folder that contains sample configurations of the operating system.
	IESAMPLE			A sample configuration that includes almost all available components and adds the Internet Explorer Web browser control. Full localization is supported, and the Input Method Manager (IMM) is also included.
	MAXALL			A sample configuration that includes almost all available components, including the shell and Pocket applications.
	MINCOMM			A sample configuration that includes a minimal set of components and adds serial communications and networking.
	MINGDI			A sample configuration that includes a minimal set of components that can support the Graphical Device Interface (GDI). No window support is provided, but you can use GDI calls to create a minimal user interface if required.
	MININPUT			A sample configuration that includes a minimal set of components that can support user input via the keyboard. A display

(continued)

Table 3.1 *Continued.*

Folder	Configuration	Type	Implementation	Description
				driver is included, but GDI is not supported.
	MINKERN			A sample configuration that contains the operating system kernel and a "Hello World!" application that outputs text to the debug serial port. This is a good first configuration to use when you're booting a platform with Windows CE.
	MINSHELL			A sample configuration that is very much like MAXALL without the Pocket applications.
	MINWMGR			A sample configuration that includes components that can support the window manager. Full networking support is included.
Drivers				A folder that contains platform-specific device drivers.
	CEPC			A folder that contains device drivers for the CEPC platform, which supports the x86 family of processors.
		display		Display drivers type.
			Ddi_ct	Display driver for Chips & Technologies CT6555x chip set.
			Ddi_364	Display driver for the S3 Trio64 chip set.
			Ddi_s3v	Display driver for the S3 ViRGE chip set.
			Ddi_vga8	A simple VGA display driver for eight-bits-per-pixel displays. A good first choice when testing a display adapter on a CEPC or any other platform that supports a VGA-compatible display.
		kbdms		Keyboard and mouse drivers type.
			Kbdmsengus1	Driver for U.S. English keyboards.

Table 3.1 *Continued.*

Folder	Configuration	Type	Implementation	Description
			Kbdmsjpn1, Kbdmsjpn2	Drivers for Japanese keyboards.
		nscirda		Infrared driver.
		ohci		Universal Serial Bus (USB) host controller interface driver.
		pc_ddk		Hardware Abstraction Library (HAL).
			Ddk_bus	Implementation of routines to abstract bus I/O (input/output).
			Ddk_map	Implementation of routines to abstract memory I/O.
		pcmcia		PCMCIA driver.
		serial		Serial port driver.
		sermouse		Serial mouse driver.
		wavedev		SoundBlaster AWE64 PNP ISA driver.
		eboot		Ethernet debugging library and helper routines for creating an Ethernet boot loader.
	ODO			Device drivers for the Hitachi D9000 (Odo) platform, which supports multiple processors.
OAL				OEM Abstraction Layer type. This is a platform-specific layer of code that is created by the OEM.
	CEPC			OAL for the CEPC.
	ODO			OAL for the D9000.
Platform Manager				A folder that contains Platform Manager client components. These components are used to provide a communication channel between Platform Builder and the operating system being developed on the platform.
	Cemgrc			Platform Manager client. This component manages high-level communication between the Platform Builder (cemgr.exe) and the operating system running on the platform.

(continued)

Table 3.1 *Continued.*

Folder	Configuration	Type	Implementation	Description
	Transport			Transport component type. A transport component is the protocol to be used between Platform Builder and the Platform Manager client.
		pm_ppp		PPP protocol used as transport.
		pm_tcpip		TCP/IP protocol used as transport.
		pm_cesrv		Windows CE services transport.
Runtimes				A folder that contains runtime environments for Windows CE application development.
	Adoce			A configuration that contains ActiveX data objects for Windows CE.
	VB			A configuration that contains components for Visual Basic runtime support.
		vbeng		Visual Basic runtime engine.
		vbforms		Support for forms.
		controls		Visual Basic controls.
			MSCEComDlg	Common dialog control.
			MSCEComm	Support for common controls.
			MSCECommandBar	Command bar control.
			MSCEFile	File I/O control.
			MSCEGrid	Grid control.
			MSCEImage	Image control.
			MSCEImageList	Image list control.
			MSCEListView	List view control.
			MSCEPicture	Picture control.
			MSCETabStrip	Tab control.
			MSCETreeView	Tree view control.
			MSCEWinSock	A control that supports the Windows Socket API.
	VC			A folder that contains components for Visual C++ runtime support.

Table 3.1 *Continued.*

Folder	Configuration	Type	Implementation	Description
		`mfc`		Runtime component for Microsoft Foundation Classes.
		`atl`		Runtime component for Active Template Library.

Now that we have these components in a catalog, what can we do with them? Components are reusable objects and can be added to any project. The best way to illustrate the use of the catalog is to create a sample project. As we discussed in Chapter 2, the best place to start is to run Windows CE on a PC. For our first Windows CE build, we'll create a special build of the CEPC based on `MAXALL` called Adam. A special build of Windows CE is referred to as a **platform**.

Creating a New Platform with the Platform Wizard

To create a new platform, select the **File | New** menu item in the Platform Builder IDE. This selection invokes the **New Platform** window of the Platform Wizard (Figure 3.4).

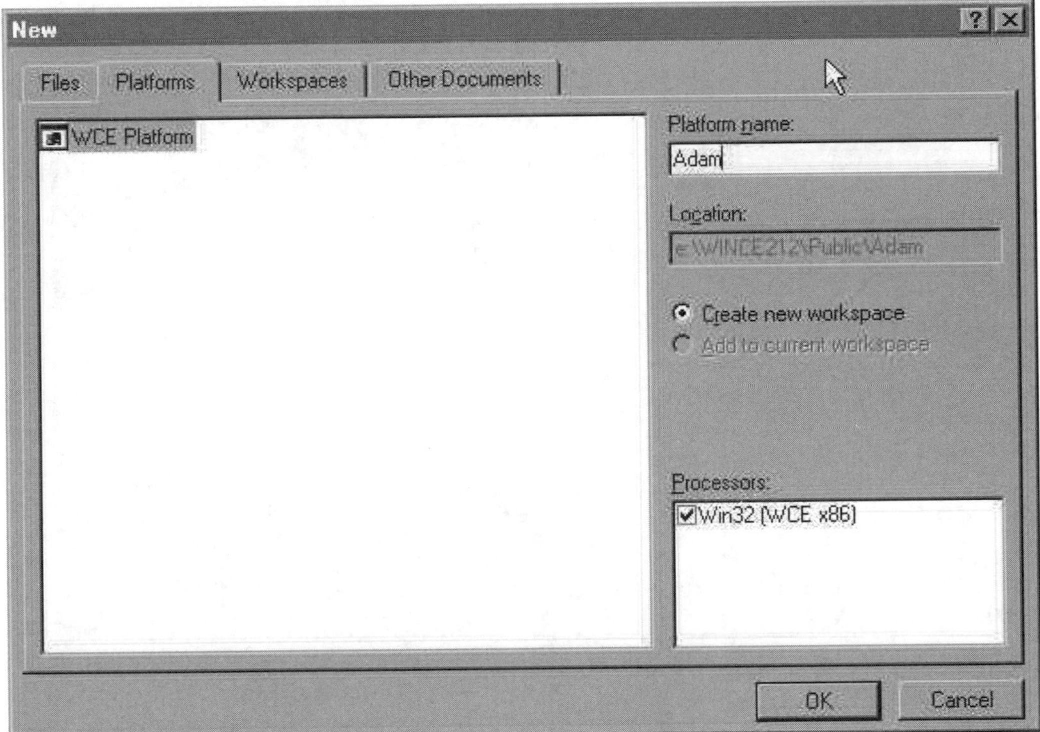

Figure 3.4 Platform Wizard

Platform Wizard gives you just one choice—a Windows CE (WCE) platform. When you type in a platform name, the wizard automatically constructs the location folder for the platform. This location is under the subdirectory `PUBLIC` in the `Platform Builder` folder. In theory you cannot modify this location. However, as we plumb the depths of the build process in Chapter 10, you will see that there is nothing magical about this folder location; it can easily be changed, although there may be no compelling reason to do so. The **Processors** list box contains choices for processor types supported by the Platform Wizard. In Figure 3.4, the only available choice is Win32 for Windows CE on an x86 processor. Additional processor types are added to this window if you select the processor choices when you install Platform Builder on your workstation.

Clicking on **OK** in the **New Platform** window activates the wizard by opening the first of two dialog boxes. This first dialog box gives you an opportunity to select a board support package for the platform being created (Figure 3.5). A **board support package** (BSP) is a set of basic, hardware-dependent components that have been created for a particular platform. These components support a particular processor type and hardware configuration. Platform Builder includes two preconfigured BSPs. The CEPC BSP is the package for an x86 PC. The Odo BSP is for the Hitachi D9000 platform. We will select **CEPC** (see Figure 3.5) because this BSP runs on an x86 PC.

We could have made two other choices. The option **My BSP** allows you to create your own BSP. This option is useful when you are working with a board that is not supported by Windows

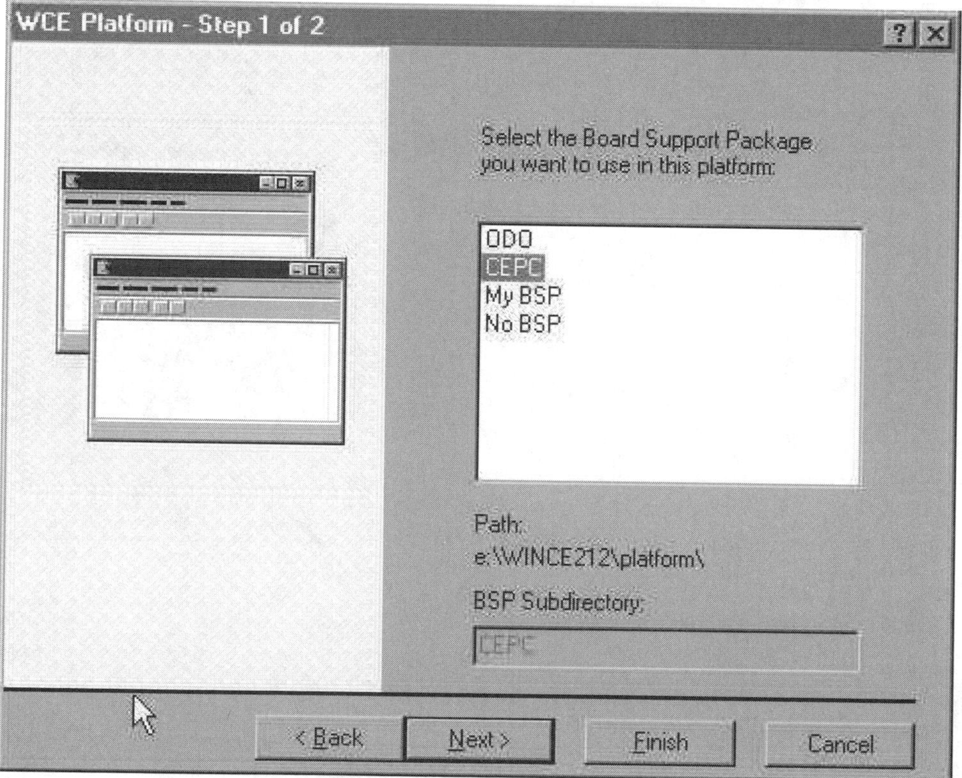

Figure 3.5 Selecting a BSP for your project

CE out of the box. After you create your own BSP, the board support list box in this dialog will list your BSP by name.

Selecting **No BSP** allows you to create a platform without a board support package. In this case, you have to create a BSP and add it to your platform later, which you do using the **My BSP** choice just described. We will cover this aspect in detail later in the chapter.

Note that the wizard automatically fills in the path of the BSP. BSPs are generally found under the `PLATFORM` subdirectory of Platform Builder.

The second and final dialog box allows you to select the type of platform you are creating (Figure 3.6). In essence, you are selecting one of the sample configurations that come in Platform Builder and that were listed under the `coreos` type described in Table 3.1. You can modify this choice in finer detail after the platform has been created. However, selecting the best option here will minimize the effort you spend later in fine-tuning the components in your platform. The default choice is `MAXALL`. Clicking on the **Finish** button brings up one final dialog box, which informs you of the choices you have made so far. When you have confirmed your choices, Platform Builder proceeds to build the new platform.

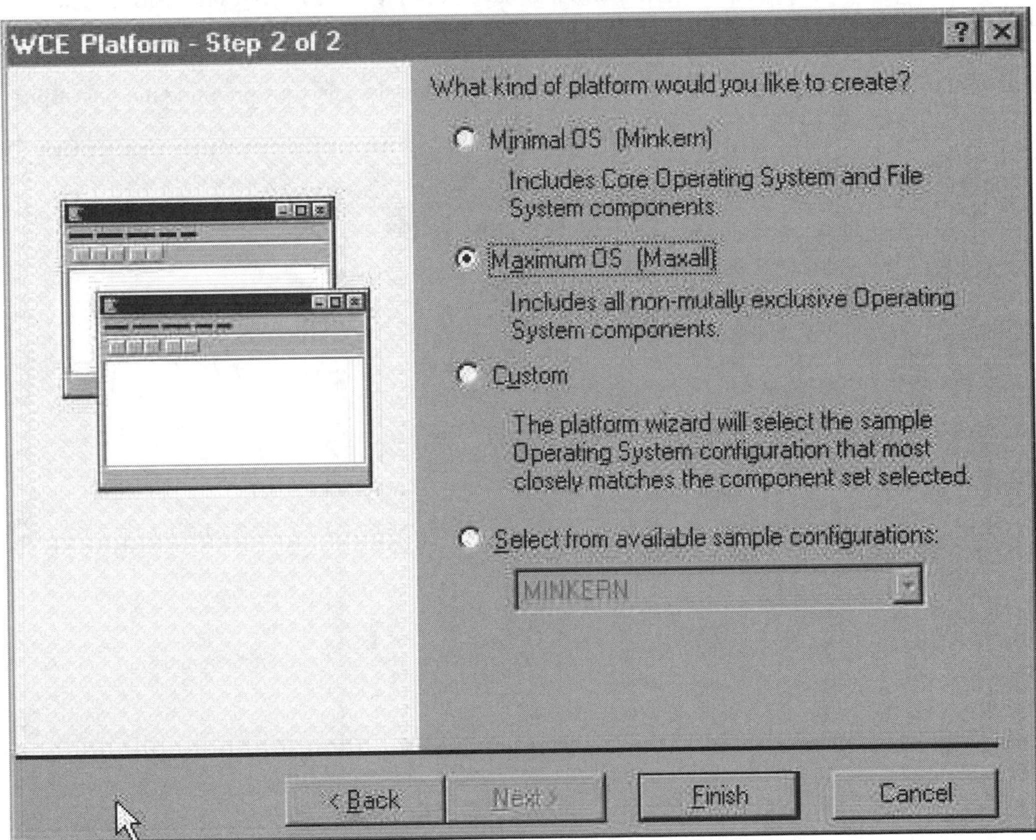

Figure 3.6 Selecting a platform for your project

Building and Executing the Platform

Once Adam is created, Platform Builder shows the components included in the project in its **Workspace** window (Figure 3.7). The **Workspace** window has two tabs: **Components** and **Parameters**. The component view shows that several essential components have been included in Adam for us by the Project Wizard. Of particular interest is the component called `MAXALL`.

Recall that we selected `Maximum OS (MAXALL)` by default as the kind of platform we wanted to create. `MAXALL` has several subfolders, each of which corresponds to a module (see Table 3.2). Recall that a module is a set of components that have a common basis of functionality. By including a module, you can pull in all or selected components of related functionality into your project. The modules included in Adam are inherited from `MAXALL`.

Building Adam will build all the components and modules that are part of the platform. Select **Build | Build Platform . . .** from the menu to build the platform. The Platform Builder IDE shows the results of the build in the **Output** window under the **Build** tab. You will notice a series of messages that correspond to important sequences undertaken by the CE build process. Since we will dissect these sequences in Chapter 10, let's look at them just briefly for now.

The first message you see is *Building Platform header files. . . .* The process of building platform header files is also called **building the system**. This phase is responsible for building the Windows CE components and modules that have been included in your platform. During this process, header files specific to your platform are generated. When creating code for your platform, you must include these header files because they will contain only information that is relevant to components that are part of your platform. These header files preclude the possibility

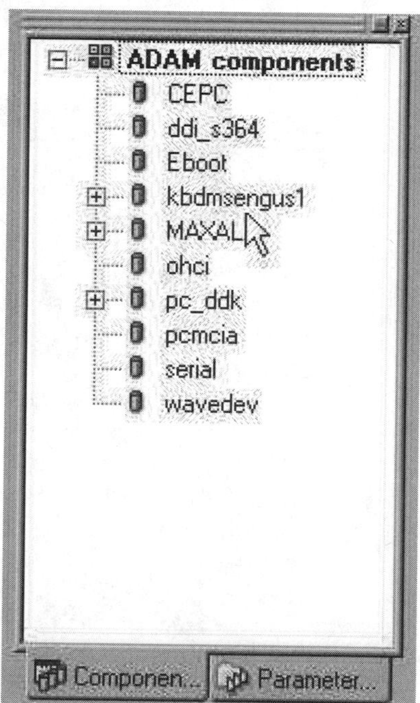

Figure 3.7 The new project's **Workspace** window

Table 3.2 Modules Inherited from MAXALL

Module	Description	Examples
CE_MODULES	Operating system components	filesys (the file system), GWES, tcpstk (TCP/IP), and so on
IE_MODULES	Internet Explorer components	wininet (the WinInet API)
WCEAPPS_MODULES	Windows CE application components	msgstore (the message store), office (Pocket Office applications)
WCESHELL_MODULES	Windows CE shell components	ctlpnl (control panel), explorer, webview (an HTML Web control)

that a platform-specific module will compile and link but fail at runtime because of a failure to locate the component. What follows is a series of messages emitted by Cebuild and its helper utilities.

The next step in the build process is accompanied by the message *Building. . . .* This message marks the process of compiling and linking source code from the BSP and platform-specific drivers, libraries, and applications. The verbiage that follows this message comes from the build process as it attempts to build the libraries, drivers, and applications in the platform.

The message *Copying Platform header files . . .* is displayed to indicate the phase in which all the binaries and configuration files generated by the previous stages of the build are copied into a folder, which acts as a repository for the final phase. The final phase takes all the files copied into the repository and creates the image of the Windows CE operating system. This image will conform to the specifications laid out by your platform. It includes the components you specified and will support the processor and board you selected via the wizard. This final phase is preceded by the message *Creating kernel image. . . .* On completion of a successful build, you should see the message *Adam – 0 error(s), 0 warning(s).* We are now ready to create an application!

Creating Applications for Your Platform

A famous software developer once said, "With every platform must come applications." OK, we made that up. However, the fact is obvious: After you're done developing the OAL, drivers, and related libraries for your platform, you will have to turn your attention to delivering applications on your platform that your customers can use to accomplish tasks. Let's start by creating an application called Welcome for our platform Adam.

We create an application using a process similar to the one we use to create a new platform. Select **File | New** from the menu, which eventually launches Project Wizard (Figure 3.8). From that screen, follow the steps we've already outlined for creating a new platform.

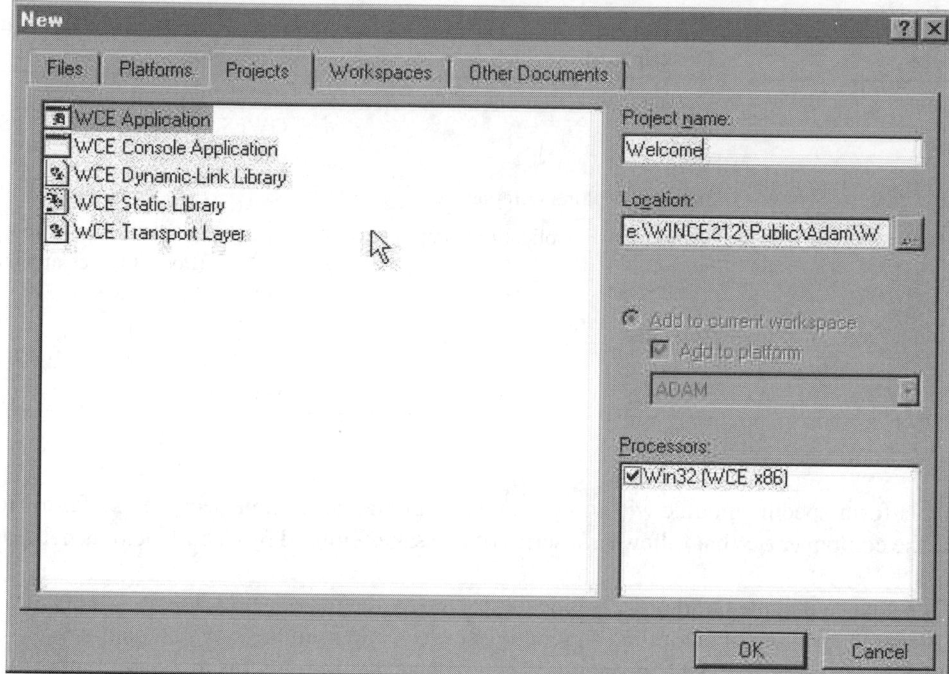

Figure 3.8 Project Wizard

Windows CE Project Wizard

Since a platform already exists in your current workspace, Platform Builder automatically adds a **Projects** tab to the initial **New** dialog box (Figure 3.8). The **Projects** tab allows you to select the type of application you would like to create. You can choose to create a Windows CE executable, a console executable (no windowing support), a Windows CE dynamic link library (DLL), a static library, or a transport layer (which is a DLL with special entry points). For our sample Welcome application, we will choose to create a Windows CE executable. Note that when you type in the name of the application you're creating, the **Location** field is updated to point to a subdirectory under the platform directory for Adam.

Clicking on **OK** launches the Windows CE (WCE) Application Wizard. This simple wizard displays a single dialog box (Figure 3.9). It allows you to select a template for your application. The choice **An empty project** simply allows you to insert a project into your workspace that doesn't contain any files. This option is useful when you have an existing application that you would like to integrate into your platform. In this case you would then insert the files of the existing application into the empty project created by the wizard.

The second option, **A simple Windows CE application**, creates a project with files that compile into an application that has a `winmain` entry point. Windows applications are started at `winmain`. However, the wizard-created `winmain` does nothing except return immediately. This option allows you to insert code into the entry point and start building your application.

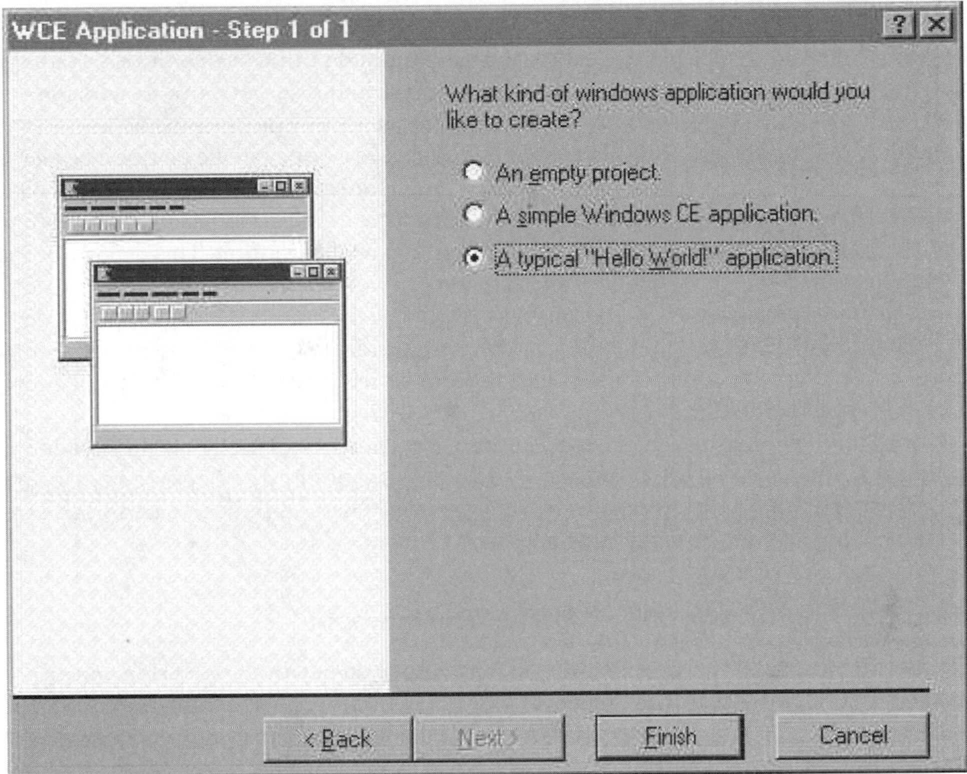

Figure 3.9 Selecting the type of application to create

Finally, the option **A typical "Hello World!" application** creates a complete application that displays "Hello World!" in a dialog box. We'll choose this option so that we have a complete sample application to run on our platform.

When you click on the **Finish** button, the wizard shows you a single dialog box displaying the type of application it will generate. The application Welcome is then inserted into your project workspace.

Applications arc always inserted in Platform Builder's project workspace. Platform Builder now has two views: a platform view, which contains Adam, and a project view, which contains Welcome. The platform view contains a view of the platform under development. The project view displays applications being developed for the platform. You can toggle between the project view and the platform view from the Platform Builder toolbar using the buttons shown in Figure 3.10. These buttons are mutually exclusive. When one is depressed the other is not, and vice versa; you can view only either your platform or your project at any given time. This separation is provided to facilitate the development of both platform software and applications for that platform.

Figure 3.10 Switching between platform and project views

Building the Application

To build `welcome.exe`, you must select the menu item **Build | Build Welcome.exe**. Platform Builder first attempts to build the platform. If the platform builds successfully, then Platform Builder builds `welcome.exe`. You can make this selection also by pressing the **F7** key. Before attempting to build `welcome.exe`, the build process checks to see if all the platform header files have been generated since the last time the project was modified. Recall that the platform build process has generated header files on the basis of the selected configuration. These header files are to be used by any applications or drivers that must run on the platform. This dependency is built into the project file generated for `welcome.exe`.

Another dependency added explicitly to the IDE when the project is generated is for the platform build. The platform build for Adam will now attempt to build `welcome.exe` after the platform build completes successfully. You can check this new dependency by selecting **Platform | Dependencies...** .

Successfully building `welcome.exe`, however, does not automatically include it in the operating system image that will be uploaded to the target platform. The steps required to do so must be performed manually. Alternatively, you can set up Platform Builder to perform these for you automatically. We will take the latter approach.

Testing the Application during Rapid Development

While still developing the application, we will make use of an interesting CESH feature to shorten our development and debugging cycle. CESH transfers an image from the workstation to the target and then continues to monitor the kernel on the target using an undocumented API. If the kernel attempts to load a module that does not exist in the operating system image, it asks CESH for a copy of the module. If CESH finds the module in its working directory, it uploads a copy of the module to the target platform, where the kernel copies it into RAM. This process causes the module to be executed on the target platform. Once the module is done executing, it is unloaded from RAM and its copy is discarded.

This feature allows us to create an application and simply copy it into the release directory without including it in the operating system image. Thus, when we modify the application, we simply copy a new version to the release directory and execute the application on the target platform. On execution, the kernel asks CESH to load the module because it is unable to locate it in the image. CESH obliges by sending the kernel a fresh copy of the module. Once the application is terminated, we can repeat the entire cycle with a new copy of the module.

If we chose to include the application in the operating system image, we would have to create a new copy of the image for every change in the application. The new copy would then have to be uploaded to the target. The entire image of the operating system takes considerably longer than just a single executable to upload to the target.

After a successful build, the build process for the project copies the output file into the release directory for the platform. The variable `_FLATRELEASEDIR`, defined by the Windows CE build process, contains the value of the release directory. The variable is set up for each platform, and for Adam it is set to `\WINCE212\PUBLIC\ADAM\RELDIR\X86_DEBUG` for the debug build of the platform.

Once we have our custom build step in place, `welcome.exe` will be copied, after every successful build, into the release directory. From here, it will initially be uploaded *on demand* by

CESH to the target platform. Later, we will integrate it directly into the operating system image. First, though, we need to figure out how to upload the operating system to the target platform and run it there.

Running Windows CE on a CEPC

Running Windows CE is not as straightforward as creating a new platform and project. This task requires two separate operations. The final build of Windows CE, also referred to as the **image**, must be uploaded to the target platform first. Next, the kernel debugger built into the Platform Builder IDE must connect with the debug kernel on the target. There are several ways to upload an image and debug it. For starters, we will focus on uploading via the parallel port and debugging over the serial port. These methods are supported on all versions of Windows CE, including those that use the early version of Platform Builder called the Embedded Development Kit (EDK).

How does one upload the image to that target platform? You'll need a bidirectional enhanced parallel port (EPP) on both sides of the equation: the workstation and the platform. It is a good idea to make sure that the parallel port is in EPP mode by checking the settings in the system BIOS. The parallel port cable itself must be tweaked a bit. First you'll need a male DB25 connector at both ends. Next, the cable itself must be wired as shown in Table 3.3. You can order such a cable from a variety of vendors, but it's not difficult to make one yourself. Start with a regular parallel port cable and add an expansion box with the appropriate pins soldered to meet the requirements in Table 3.3. If you don't have an EPP-compatible port on the workstation or the CEPC target, you can buy a plug-in ISA card that supports an EPP-compatible port. The EPP-compatible port is jumper configurable on these cards. Be sure to avoid conflicts with your regular parallel port in the workstation or CEPC.

The serial connection used to debug the kernel is fortunately quite straightforward, simply requiring a serial cable. Once both connections have been set up, you are ready to upload.

An upload is carried out via the Windows CE Debug Shell Tool (CESH). CESH is capable of uploading images to the target via several transports, including serial and Ethernet. For the exercise we are conducting, we have already decided to use CESH's parallel port capabilities.

To use CESH to upload the image, we must first start a command prompt. Platform Builder provides a convenient way to create a command prompt and change directory to the release directory for the platform under development with a few simple mouse clicks. From the **Build** menu, select **Open Build Release Directory**. This selection will launch a command prompt in the release directory of the platform. The release directory of a platform refers to the repository for the final phase, `\WINCE212\PUBLIC\ADAM\RELDIR\X86_DEBUG`. This directory contains the final Windows CE image to be uploaded to the target. The image is called `nk.bin` and must be sent to the target in its entirety. This is accomplished by the following command:

```
Cesh -p CEPC Nk.bin
```

Table 3.3 CESH Parallel Port Cable Pin Connections

Pin	**1**	**2**	**3**	**4**	**5**	**6**	**7**	**8**	**9**	**10**	**11**	**12**	**13**	**14**	**15**	**16**	**17**	**18**	**19**	**20**	**21**	**22**	**23**	**24**	**25**
Pin	10	2	3	4	5	6	7	8	9	1	14	16	17	11	—	12	13	18	19	20	21	22	23	24	25

The `-p` option of CESH indicates the profile that CESH must use. In this case, the profile is called CEPC. Profiles for CESH are set up in the registry by the Platform Builder installation procedure. The CEPC profile urges CESH to use the parallel port with some predefined settings that configure the parallel port protocol. When using this profile, CESH starts passing `nk.bin`, chunk by chunk, to the parallel port. The parallel port base address and interrupt level are assumed to be the default values for LPT1 (base address `0x378` and IRQ 7). Should this change on your workstation, you must edit the CEPC profile directly to reflect the changed parallel port settings. To change these settings, you must change the registry values shown in Listing 3.1.

Listing 3.1 CESH registry settings

```
HKEY_LOCAL_MACHINE\SYSTEM\CurrentControlSet\Services\ppsh\CEPC:
InterruptLevel   = REG_DWORD 7
InterruptMode    = REG_DWORD 1
InterruptVector  = REG_DWORD 7
PortAddress      = REG_DWORD 0x378
```

On a CEPC, at the other end, a tool called Loadcepc communicates with CESH to receive pieces of the operating system image and then loads and boots the operating system. You must start by creating a bootable floppy, preferably with MS-DOS 6.22, and put `loadcepc.exe` on it. This floppy disk should be used to boot the CEPC. Loadcepc is available in Platform Builder, and its source code is in the CEPC platform directory. Once the two utilities start to communicate, a progress bar indicates the portion of the image that has been transferred successfully between the workstation and the CEPC (Figure 3.11). After the entire image has been uploaded, Windows CE will boot on the CEPC.

Kernel Debugging

The Platform Builder IDE has a built-in kernel debugger. You can launch this debugger by selecting the **Build | Start Debug | Go** menu item or by hitting the **F5** key. The kernel debugger displays its output in the IDE output window under the **Debug** tab. You can view the output window by selecting the **View | Output** menu item. Then select the **Debug** tab.

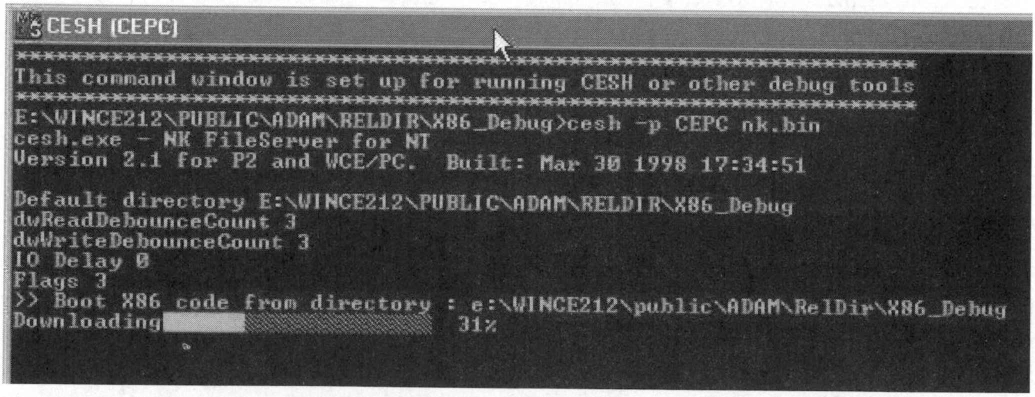

```
CESH (CEPC)
*********************************************************************
This command window is set up for running CESH or other debug tools
*********************************************************************
E:\WINCE212\PUBLIC\ADAM\RELDIR\X86_Debug>cesh -p CEPC nk.bin
cesh.exe - NK FileServer for NT
Version 2.1 for P2 and WCE/PC.  Built: Mar 30 1998 17:34:51

Default directory E:\WINCE212\PUBLIC\ADAM\RELDIR\X86_Debug
dwReadDebounceCount 3
dwWriteDebounceCount 3
IO Delay 0
Flags 3
>> Boot X86 code from directory : e:\WINCE212\public\ADAM\RelDir\X86_Debug
Downloading                       31%
```

Figure 3.11 Uploading an image using CESH

Like downloading, debugging can occur over an Ethernet connection. It can also occur over the serial port. We'll choose the latter because it is easy to set up and use. A simple serial cable (not null modem) will do the trick. You can improve the debugger throughput by increasing the speed at which the debugger and target platform communicate over the serial port. On the workstation, select **Build | Debugger | Remote Connection** to view the **Remote Connection** dialog box. In the **Connection** list box, you must select **Kernel Debugger Port** and then click on **Settings...** (see Figure 3.12).

At the other end, the change in the default speed of the serial connection must be passed on Loadcepc. This is accomplished with the `/B:115200` option. In addition, if you are using the S3 display drivers that are bundled with the CEPC, you must instruct Loadcepc to initialize the display adapter in 640_480 mode. This is done via the `/D:2` option. Finally, Loadcepc must be told to expect the image to come down the parallel port, with the `/P` option.

```
Loadcepc /B:115200 /D:2 /P
```

You can request Loadcepc to use the serial port to download the binary image, provided that you set up CESH to do the same on the workstation. In this case, you specify the `/Q` option. The COM port to be used by Loadcepc is identified with an additional option, `/C:{1 | 2}`.

After you initiate the kernel debugger, the first messages in the debug window announce the handshaking between the debugger and the target:

Kernel debugger waiting to connect on com1 at 115200 baud
Host and target systems resynchronizing . . .

When the debugger is started, you may get the erroneous error message shown in Figure 3.13. You can safely ignore this message. The IDE is simply trying to find an updated copy of

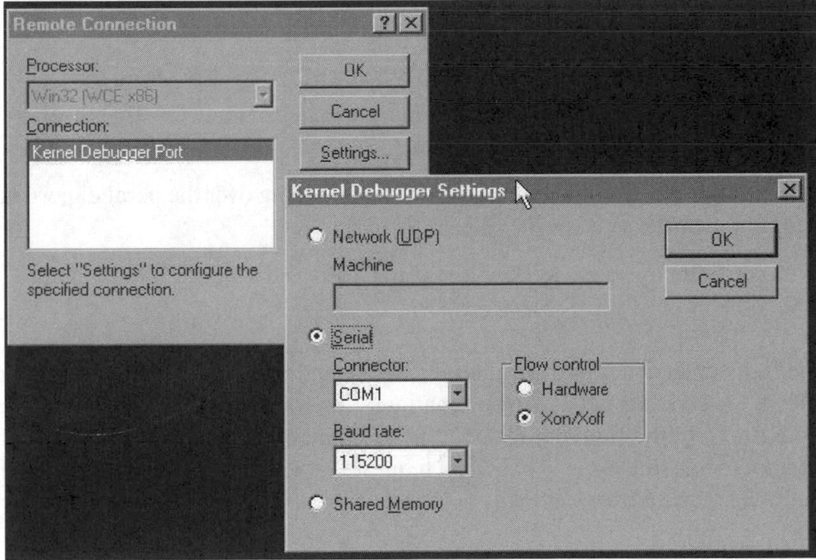

Figure 3.12 Setting the kernel debugger port's speed

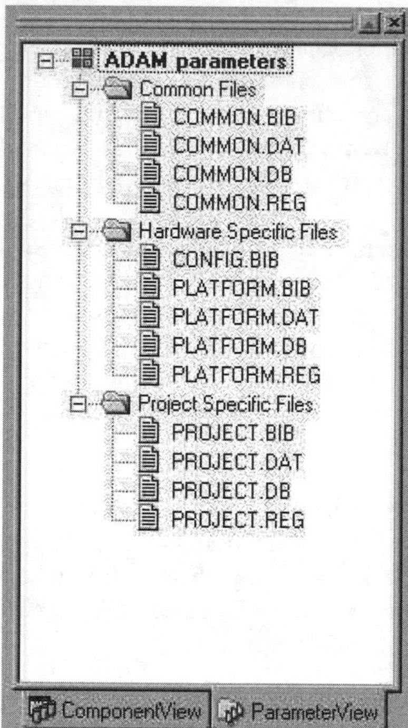

Figure 3.13 Error message when the debugger is started

`welcome.exe` in the wrong release directory, a throwback from the days of the Embedded Development Kit (EDK).

Let's review what we've done so far:

1. Created a new platform, Adam, based on the `MAXALL` configuration
2. Created a simple new application for Adam called `welcome.exe` that displays a "Hello World!" message in a dialog box
3. Connected the workstation and CEPC for downloading over the parallel port and debugging over the serial port
4. Downloaded the operating system image to CEPC and watched it boot on the CEPC

After the last step is completed, you should see a Handheld PC–like shell pop up, complete with a Windows CE task bar. Let's take our configuration for a spin. Select the **Start** button and then click on **Run...** . In the **Run** dialog box, type in "welcome.exe" and then click on **OK**. The shell will attempt to execute `welcome.exe`, a request that will be translated in the inner layers of the kernel into a request from CESH to load `welcome.exe` from the release directory on the workstation:

```
KernelLoader: Using PPFS to load file welcome.exe
```

PPFS stands for Portable Parallel File System, which supports loading on demand. On the target platform, you should see `welcome.exe` running and greeting the world in a dialog box. You can close `welcome.exe` by right-clicking on its icon in the task bar and selecting **Close**.

You can try out our rapid development technique by stopping the debugger, making a change to the string displayed by Welcome, and then building the project, restarting the debugger and executing `welcome.exe` from the **Run** dialog box on the target.

Debugging Capabilities of CESH

CESH is more than just a downloading utility. It is called the Windows CE Debug Shell Tool for a reason. After the download is over, CESH gives you a command prompt. You can type in a variety of commands at the prompt to get useful information from the kernel running on the target platform. Typing "?" retrieves a list of all the commands supported by CESH (see Table 3.4).

Table 3.4 Commands Supported by CESH

Command	Options	Function
`break`		Stops the kernel at the current line of execution. This command can be used to halt the kernel and set a new breakpoint.
`dd`	`addr [<size>]`	Displays the contents of `addr`. The optional size argument tells the command how many bytes to display.
`df`	`filename addr [<size>]`	Writes contents of `addr` to the file specified by `filename`. The optional size argument tells the command how many bytes to display.
`dis`		Tells the virtual memory manager to mark all discardable memory as available.
`gi`	`proc`	Lists all the processes running on the target. Processes are created from executables by the operating system.
	`thrd`	Lists all the threads running on the target. A process may have multiple threads.
	`mod`	Lists all the modules loaded on the target. Modules are DLLs that are loaded by executables. Device drivers are DLLs loaded by `device.exe` (mostly); as such, they appear under the modules' listing.
	`all`	Lists processes, threads, and modules. This is the default value for the `gi` command.
`kp`	`pid`	Kills the process with process ID `pid`.
`mi`	`kernel`	Displays detailed information on memory used by the kernel.
	`full`	Displays memory maps used by all processes and modules in the system.
`run`	`filename`	Runs the file specified by `filename` in batch mode.
`s`	`process`	Starts a new process. This command is useful when you don't have a user interface on the target platform that can be used to start a process. The `s` command can also be used for rapid development because it supports load on demand via PPFS.
`zo`		Displays and modifies debug zones for a process or module. This command is discussed in more detail in Chapter 9.

After booting Adam successfully on a CEPC, you can run the `gi` command from the CESH command prompt and observe output similar to that shown in Listing 3.2. When executing `welcome.exe`, you will notice it listed as a process. The `gi` command prints out information that is used not just for debugging, but also for indexing other commands. For example, the process or module index, a number prefixed by either *P* or *M*, is passed to the `zo` command to identify the entity whose debug zone is being displayed or modified. Debug messages emitted by the kernel are prefixed with the address of the line that originated the message. You can map these addresses by looking at the `pModule` field of a module in the output of `gi`.

Listing 3.2 shows the processes running on the target platform. The file `nk.exe` is the Windows CE kernel process, `filesys.exe` manages the CE file system, the debug shell that communicates with CESH is `shell.exe`, `device.exe` loads and manages all the device drivers on the target platform, `gwes.exe` is responsible for creating and managing windows and messages, and finally, `explorer.exe` is the Handheld PC–like shell included in our image.

Listing 3.2 Running the `gi` command in CESH

```
Windows CE>gi
PROC: Name            hProcess: CurAKY :dwVMBase:CurZone
THRD: State :hCurThrd:hCurProc: CurAKY :Cp:Bp:CPU Time
 P00: NK.EXE          00ffefe2 00000001 02000000 00000100
 T    Blockd 00ffdefe 00ffefe2 00000001  3  3 00:00:00.000
 T    Blockd 00ffe012 00ffefe2 00000001  7  7 00:00:00.082
 T    Blockd 00ffe31e 00ffefe2 ffffffff  2  2 00:00:00.005
 T    Blockd 00ffef1a 00ffefe2 00000001  1  1 00:00:00.063
 P01: filesys.exe     00ffdaf6 00000002 04000000 00000000
 T    Blockd 00ffdb16 00ffdaf6 00000003  3  3 00:00:01.491
 P02: shell.exe       00ffbd42 00000004 06000000 00000001
 T    Runing c0ffc942 00ffbd42 ffffffff  1  1 00:00:02.965
 P03: device.exe      00ffb70a 00000008 08000000 00000000
 T    Sl/Blk 00eb5366 00ffb70a 00000009  2  2 00:00:00.081
 T    Blockd 00ff517e 00ffb70a 00000009  3  3 00:00:00.001
 T    Blockd 00ff551a 00ffb70a 00000009  3  3 00:00:00.004
 T    Sl/Blk 00ff7d56 00ffb70a 00000009  2  2 00:00:00.001
 T    Sl/Blk 20ff98ce 00ffb70a 00000009  2  2 00:00:00.132
 T    Blockd 20ff98ee 00ffb70a 00000009  2  2 00:00:00.000
 T    Blockd 00ffb72a 00ffb70a 00000009  3  3 00:00:03.026
 P04: gwes.exe        00fd626e 00000010 0a000000 00000040
 T    Blockd 00f60e02 00fd626e 00000011  3  3 00:00:00.029
 T    Blockd 00f6200a 00fd626e 00000011  3  3 00:00:00.014
 T    Blockd 00f6230e 00fd626e 00000011  1  1 00:00:00.000
 T    Blockd 00f625f2 00fd626e 00000011  1  1 00:00:00.004
 T    Blockd 00f62a56 00fd626e 00000011  1  1 00:00:00.193
 T    Blockd 00f62b6a 00fd626e 00000011  1  1 00:00:00.046
 T    Sl/Blk a0f74386 00fd626e 00000011  1  1 00:00:00.291
 T    Sl/Blk 00fd628e 00fd626e 00000011  3  3 00:00:01.029
 P05: explorer.exe    00f60c5a 00000020 0c000000 00000000
 T    Blockd 40ea6c02 00fd626e 00000031  3  3 00:00:01.769
 T    Blockd 00eb572a 00fd626e 00000031  3  3 00:00:04.446
 T    Blockd 00f60c7a 00f60c5a 00000021  3  3 00:00:00.430
 MOD: Name            pModule :dwInUSE :dwVMBase:CurZone
 M00: unimodem.dll    80eb5584 00000008 01160000 0000c000
```

```
 M01: TAPI.DLL          80eb5ec0 00000008 01180000 0000c000
 M02: SHLWAPI.dll       80f4e640 00000020 01060000 00000000
 M03: IECEEXT.dll       80f4e810 00000020 01090000 00000000
 M04: WININET.dll       80f4ed40 00000020 00f70000 0000c000
 M05: imgdecmp.DLL      80f4ef44 00000020 00ed0000 00000000
 M06: webview.dll       80f493ec 00000020 00e20000 00000000
 M07: commctrl.dll      80f49c28 00000020 01520000 00000000
 M08: CEShell.DLL       80f49ef8 00000020 00ef0000 00000000
 M09: OLEAUT32.dll      80f60358 00000020 01390000 00000000
 M10: ASForm.dll        80f627c8 00000020 00f50000 00000000
 M11: kbdmouse.dll      80f62d78 00000010 00d20000 00000000
 M12: DDI.DLL           80fd6b80 00000010 00d30000 00000003
 M13: Redir.dll         80ff50c0 00000008 01110000 0000c001
 M14: irdastk.dll       80ff6b78 00000008 011a0000 00008000
 M15: netbios.dll       80ff76ec 00000008 010f0000 0000c000
 M16: dhcp.dll          80ff7840 00000008 01220000 0000ffff
 M17: arp.dll           80ff7a20 00000008 01290000 00000001
 M18: tcpstk.dll        80ff8250 00000008 011d0000 00000001
 M19: ppp.dll           80ff8800 00000008 01340000 00000000
 M20: CXPORT.dll        80ff89a0 00000008 01330000 0000c000
 M21: AFD.Dll           80ff8c88 00000008 012a0000 00000000
 M22: ole32.dll         80ff8f88 00000028 013d0000 00000000
 M23: softkb.DLL        80ff9320 00000008 01500000 00000000
 M24: WINSOCK.dll       80ff95a0 00000028 01310000 0000c000
 M25: IRCOMM.DLL        80ff971c 00000008 01320000 0000c003
 M26: irsir.dll         80ff9e74 00000008 00ce0000 0000c000
 M27: NDIS.Dll          80ffa6bc 00000008 01270000 00000000
 M28: msfilter.dll      80ffa810 00000008 00cb0000 00000000
 M29: CEDDK.dll         80ffaef0 00000018 00da0000 00000000
 M30: Serial.Dll        80ffb020 00000008 00cf0000 00000000
 M31: toolhelp.dll      80ffbf68 00000004 015a0000 00000000
 M32: coredll.dll       80ffe690 0000003f 015e0000 00000000
Windows CE>
```

Integrating New Components into the Image

We can use the rapid development scenario described in earlier sections until we finish all basic development of `welcome.exe`. We made changes to the Welcome application so that it displays a message greeting on startup. We also added a caption and a system menu so that the window can be conveniently closed. The text now appropriately welcomes users to the first Windows CE platform in this book. Welcome will be started every time Adam boots so that the welcome message is the first message users see. Let's see how to add this somewhat concocted example to the image and automatically start Welcome on startup.

To add `welcome.exe` to the operating system image, we will need to modify a file in the parameter view of the platform workspace. Figure 3.14 shows the parameters view window for Adam. The files displayed in this window are used to specify how the operating system image will be built.

We'll delve into the specifics of each file elsewhere throughout the book, so a brief overview will suffice for now. The parameter view is organized into a set of files in three different

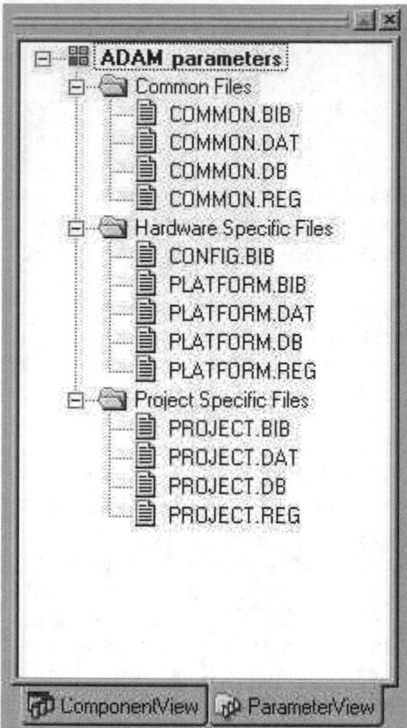

Figure 3.14 Parameter view

categories. The option **Common Files** refers to files that are provided by Microsoft to specify how the operating system must be built with Microsoft-supplied components. You should not modify these files. Any modifications you make will affect *all* platforms and projects you create.

Different types of files contain different types of information:

- **BIB files** contain information about which files, executables, and libraries should be included in the operating system image.
- **DAT files** contain a directory map for the file system on Windows CE.
- **DB files** contain information on how the Windows CE database should be initialized.
- **REG files** contain a map of the system registry on startup.

The option **Hardware Specific Files** refers to files that specify configuration and initialization when you're building the platform.

Files specified by the option **Project Specific Files** contain additional information in each of these categories that is specific to the project being created. The word *project* in this case does not refer to Welcome, although that's what we've been telling you all along. Here the term *project* is a confusing throwback to the old days of the EDK. Under the terminology used then (and still reflected in the Platform Builder directory and file structure), CEPC is our platform and

Adam is our project. This clarifies the role of these categories. Platform-specific files typically contain information regarding platform-specific drivers and modules. Project-specific files contain information about platform-independent modules. All the files are used by the set of Windows CE build tools when the image is being created.

If you have been following along closely, you might have already identified the BIB file as the one we must modify to integrate `welcome.exe` in the final operating system image. The first question, of course, is, To which BIB file should we add `welcome.exe`? The answer is simple enough: Since `welcome.exe` is platform-independent, it should be added to the BIB file `project.bib` in the Project Specific Files category.

Listing 3.3 shows the line that needs to be added to the BIB file to integrate the executable in the image. This line instructs the appropriate build tool to add the file `$(_FLATRELEASEDIR)\welcome.exe` to the image, where it will be called `welcome.exe`. The file must be loaded into the `NK` section of memory in ROM and must be uncompressed (type `U`). Sections of memory are set up in the file `config.bib`. We'll say more about this later in the book. Leaving the executable uncompressed gives the operating system the option of running the program in place in ROM. This avoids the work that the loader would normally do of uncompressing a file from ROM into RAM before executing it. In addition to the time gained because the file does not need to be uncompressed, precious RAM is made available for other programs.

Listing 3.3 Adding `welcome.exe` to `project.bib`

```
MODULES
;  Name            Path                                          Memory Type
;  --------------  --------------------------------------------  -----------
   welcome.exe     $(_FLATRELEASEDIR)\Welcome.exe                NK     U
```

Now that Welcome is part of the operating system image, it will be transferred to the target platform by CESH. PPFS will no longer be required to load it on demand because the loader will find the file in the local file system on the target platform.

We still need to make Welcome execute automatically on startup. The kernel looks for a special registry entry after starting the file system to look for modules to load during startup. Since the REG file allows us to specify the contents of the system registry when the target platform is initialized, we can zero in on the platform-independent registry file `project.reg`. To automatically execute Welcome on startup, we must add the following lines to the registry initialization file `project.reg`:

```
[HKEY_LOCAL_MACHINE]\Init
"Launch80"="Welcome.exe"
"Depends80"=hex:1E,00
```

The `Launch80` registry entry tells the kernel to launch the program `welcome.exe`. The function performed by the `Depends80` line is not immediately obvious. This registry entry lists a hex number (`001E`) as its value. To discover the significance of this number, we must take a peek at the common registry file, `common.reg`. This file has its own `init` section that is used to specify programs to launch on startup. An excerpt of this file is shown in Listing 3.4.

Listing 3.4 The `init` registry key in `common.reg`

```
 [HKEY_LOCAL_MACHINE\init]
; @CESYSGEN IF CE_MODULES_SHELL
      "Launch10"="shell.exe"
; @CESYSGEN ENDIF
; @CESYSGEN IF CE_MODULES_DEVICE
      'Launch20"="device.exe"
; @CESYSGEN ENDIF
; @CESYSGEN IF CE_MODULES_GWES
IF NOGUI !
      "Launch30"="gwes.exe"
      "Depend30"=hex:14,00
ENDIF
; @CESYSGEN ENDIF
```

The hex number 001E corresponds to 30. The `Launch30` registry item in the listing is the module `gwes.exe`. The entries related to `gwes.exe` instruct the kernel to launch `gwes.exe` on startup. The `Depends80` line simply tells the kernel to wait until `gwes.exe` has been launched before launching `welcome.exe`, because `welcome.exe` uses the windows and message support made available by `gwes.exe`. Finally, the number 80 was chosen at random from among numbers higher than 30. This number indicates the sequence in which the registry entries must be processed. We need a number higher than that corresponding to the last entry in the `common.reg` file.

However, this dependency only synchronizes the launch sequence of different modules. It does not guarantee that `gwes.exe` will have fully initialized its services before `welcome.exe` is executed. To make sure that the window manager is available, Welcome must call `IsAPIReady` with its lone argument set to the constant `SH_WMGR`.

```
...
#include "windev.h"
...
While (!IsAPIReady (SH_WMGR))
       Sleep (1000);
```

The `IsAPIReady` call will return a value of `TRUE` if the API specified by the constant is available. If a value of `FALSE` is returned, the API is not yet ready for use and Welcome must wait in a loop for the API to initialize before it executes the remainder of its code.

Note the inclusion of the header file `windev.h`. This file contains the function prototype for `IsAPIReady`. Welcome loops and checks the value returned by this call to see if the window manager API is available. If the API is not available, Welcome sleeps for one second before checking again.

Now that we are ready with all the changes, we can test out the build by selecting the **Platform | Build | Build Platform** menu item after switching to the platform view. To confirm that `welcome.exe` has been included in the image, sift through the final output of the build process that lists all the files included in the image. The entry for `welcome.exe`, if included in the image, should look like Listing 3.5.

Note:
To make sure that the compiler can find the file `windev.h`, you must add the include path in the `CESYSGEN` directory of Adam to the list of additional include directories in which the compiler may find included header files. `CESYSGEN` is the directory in which header files generated for the specific platform are placed. To add this directory to the include path for the compiler, you must click on the **Project | Settings...** menu item and then click on the **C/C++** tab. Next, select **Preprocessor** in the **Category:** combobox. In the **Additional include directories:** edit box, type in "$(_WINCEROOT)\PUBLIC\ADAM\CESYSGEN\OAK\INC". This directory path will be passed to the compiler with the `/I` flag, which instructs the compiler to search the specified directory for the include path after looking in the standard include paths.

Listing 3.5 Output from the build process

```
MODULES Section
Module        Section  Start     Length  psize   vsize   Filler
------------ -------- --------- ------- ------- ------- ------
...
welcome.exe  .text    80a6f000h    8192    5632    5508 o32_rva=1000h
welcome.exe  .rdata   80a71000h    4096     512     289 o32_rva=3000h
welcome.exe  .idata   80a72000h    4096    1024     565 o32_rva=5000h
welcome.exe  .rsrc    80a73000h    4096    2560    2254 o32_rva=6000h
...
welcome.exe  .data    8024ffdbh       0       0    2584 FILLER
...
welcome.exe  E32      8052b55ch     100                 FILLER
welcome.exe  O32      8052b5c0h     120                 FILLER
```

The next time you download the new image and boot the CEPC, Welcome should pop up as it did before on startup, welcoming the user to our new platform, Adam.

Customizing the Build Using Environment Variables

Once a Platform has been defined, you can use it to produce builds of the operating system that vary slightly in flavor without having to change the underlying definition of the platform. For example, you could choose to build Adam with a different display driver (either an S3 ViRGE or a Chips & Technologies CT65555) or choose to omit support for audio altogether. Such modifications to a platform are made dynamically through environment variables.

You can set environment variables in Platform Builder by selecting the **Platform | Settings...** menu item and then clicking on the **Environment** tab. Most, although not all, of the environment variables carry the prefix *IMG*. This prefix is short for *image,* which refers to the binary image of the operating system. *IMG* variables modify the way in which the image is built. The variables available in the **Environment** tab are listed in Table 3.5. To take effect, these variables must be defined. You can set up the definition by simply setting the variable to 1. Most variables work in a negative fashion. When set, they have the effect of *not* including a component or module. These variables have the word *NO* in their names and can be particularly confusing to use.

Table 3.5 Environment Variables Used by Platform Builder

Environment Variable	Usage	Description
FBBPP	Sets the number of bits per pixel on the display supported by the platform. This value is usually set to FB16BPP to indicate a display of 16 bits per pixel.	When FBBPP is set, the display drivers in the CEPC platform display drivers (S3 ViRGE, S3 Trio64, CT65555x, and so on) compile themselves for a pixel depth of 16; otherwise the default depth of 8 bits per pixel is used.
IME	Selects the type of Input Method Manager (IME) bundled with the platform. If the value of this variable is PIME, the Pocket IME version is added to the image. Pocket IME does not contain a user interface. If the value of this variable is TESTTIME, support that allows you to create your own IME is added to the image. The default value is IME98, which adds an IME with a user interface that mimics the full-blown Win32 API IME.	The value of IME is checked for the configuration file common.bib, and depending on its value, corresponding modules are added to the image.
IMGACMSAMPLES	Adds the sample codec driver (cegsm.dll) and the sample filter driver (msfilter.dll) to the image.	The value of IMGACMSAMPLES is checked in the project-specific configuration file project.bib. If the value is defined, the corresponding sample drivers are added to the image. However, the only project in Platform Builder 2.12 that supports this behavior is the MINSHELL project. Changing this value in our sample platform Adam will have no effect because it is derived from MAXALL.
IMGBIGFLASH	Configures the image to utilize a larger area of flash memory (an additional 8MB of flash is assumed).	IMGBIGFLASH is used in config.bib as a conditional to lay out the image to use the additional 8MB. This conditional is used only for the Odo platform. Hence, it doesn't affect Adam because Adam is derived from the CEPC platform.
IMGCOM2	Configures COM2 on the platform at 0x3E8.	IMGCOM2 is used in platform.reg, which initializes the system registry with platform-specific information.
IMGCOM3	Configures COM3 on the platform at 0x2E8.	IMGCOM3 is used in platform.reg, which initializes the system registry with platform-specific information.
IMGCOMMDEMOS	Adds two sample communication programs—ping.exe and ipconfig.exe—to the image.	IMGCOMMDEMOS is used in common.bib, which specifies the CE system files included in the operating system image.

Table 3.5 *Continued.*

Environment Variable	Usage	Description
IMGCTLPNL_G	Unknown	
IMGDUB	Leaves additional space in the image layout to include the CE dial-up boot loader (DUB). The DUB is a component that can be used to upgrade the operating system image.	IMGDUB is used in config.bib to make space for the DUB file in the image layout. It is used only in the config.bib file for the Odo platform; hence, it doesn't affect Adam because Adam is derived from CEPC.
IMGEBOOT	Adds support for Ethernet debugging by bundling the Ethernet boot loader in the image.	IMGEBOOT is used in config.bib to make space for Ethernet debugger modules. It is used only in the config.bib file for the Odo platform.
IMGFLASH	Lays out the image in flash memory as opposed to RAM.	IMGFLASH is used in config.bib to make space for Ethernet debugger modules. It is used only in the config.bib file for the Odo platform.
IMGICONPOSITIONS	Allows explicit positioning of icons on the desktop as opposed to automatic positioning set by the shell.	Not used.
IMGMOREAPPS	Allows additional applications to be added to the image.	Not used.
IMGMORERAM	Lays out the image to simulate less area for ROM and release it for use as RAM area.	IMGMORERAM is used in config.bib to allocate more space to the RAM section. Use this setting if your image is relatively small (less than 6MB). The total memory assumed in the system is 32MB.
IMGMOREROM	Lays out the image to simulate less area for R<K>AM <K>and release it for use as ROM area.	IMGMOREROM is used in config.bib to allocate more space to the ROM section. Set this variable if your image is large (more than 6MB but less than 20MB). The total memory assumed in the system is 32MB.
IMGMOREROM16	Used just like IMGMOREROM, but when total memory in the system is assumed to be 16MB.	
IMGNOBROWSER	Excludes Internet browser components in the operating system. Since Windows CE Help uses browser components, also disables Help. We are now in *NO* territory, so note that not defining this variable causes components	IMGNOBROWSER is used (1) in wceshell.bib to add the Pocket Internet Explorer files iexplore.exe, webview.dll, and imgdecmp.dll; (2) in wceshell.reg to specify browser proxy, start and search pages, and file associations; and (3) in wceapps.bib to

(continued)

Table 3.5 *Continued.*

Environment Variable	Usage	Description
	to be added. The same goes for the *NO* variables that follow.	ensure that browser components are bundled before Help is added.
IMGNOCEDDK	Excludes the CE DDK library in the image. The CE DDK library provides a processor-independent interface to the kernel, memory, and I/O to device drivers.	`IMGNOCEDDK` is used (1) in `common.bib` to include `ceddk.dll` in the image, and (2) in `platform.bib` for the CEPC platform to include the file `pc_ddk.dll` and rename it as `ceddk.dll`. The latter directive overrides the former when the image is being built.
IMGNOCOMM	Excludes all communications components in the image.	`IMGNOCOMM` is used in `common.bib` to include communication-specific components in the image.
IMGNOCONN	Excludes the components `repllog.exe` and `rapisrv.exe`, which communicate with Windows CE Services, which provide connectivity to a server (referred to as a *desktop*). An example of such an application is ActiveSync.	`IMGNOCONN` is used (1) in `common.bib` to include the components, and (2) in `common.reg`, where it is used to set up a registry entry that specifies the version of the modules. You must successfully negotiate this version number when you're communicating with a desktop.
IMGNOCONSOLE	Excludes the console support component `console.dll` and the console command language processor `cmd.exe` in the image.	`IMGNOCONSOLE` is used in `common.bib` to include the components.
IMGNOCTLPNL	Excludes the control panel and all applicable control panel applets in the image.	`IMGNOCTLPNL` is used in `wceshell.bib` to include the components. It is used in `wceshell.reg` to set up registry entries that describe the control panel color scheme and specify default settings for the various control panel applets.
IMGNODEBUGGER	Builds an image with a kernel debugger. Kernel debugging enables the kernel on the target to communicate with the kernel-debugging tool in Platform Builder. Extensive traces are also displayed by the kernel debugger.	`IMGNODEBUGGER` is used in `common.bib` to include either the kernel with debugging (`nk.exe`) or the kernel without debugging (`nknodbg.exe`) in the image.
IMGNODRIVERS	Excludes certain common drivers from the image.	`IMGNODRIVERS` is used in `common.bib` to include the parallel port and printer drivers (`prnport.dll`, `prnerr.dll`, `pcl.dll`), PC card ATA and IDE driver (`atadisk.dll`), PC card static RAM

Table 3.5 *Continued.*

Environment Variable	Usage	Description
		(SRAM) driver (sramdisk.dll), PC card linear flash driver (trueffs.dll), dual serial driver (dualio.dll) and waveform audio driver (waveapi.dll).
IMGNOETHER	Includes Ethernet support in the image.	IMGNOETHER is used in common.bib to include Address Resolution Protocol driver (arp.dll), NDIS driver (ndis.dll), NE2000-compatible card driver (ne2000.dll), Proxim RangeLAN PC card driver (proxim.dll), Xircom PC card driver (xircce2.dll), and Dynamic Host Configuration Protocol driver (dhcp.dll).
IMGNOFILES	Excludes certain files depending on context.	IMGNOFILES is used (1) in wceshell.bib to include desktop shortcuts (LNK files) and help files for shell components that have been included in the image, (2) in project.bib for the project MAXALL to include WAV files for system sounds, and (3) in wceapps.bib to include the shortcuts and help files for applications that have been included in the image.
IMGNOFLTDDK	See IMGNOCEDDK.	
IMGNOHELP	Excludes Windows CE Help in the operating system.	IMGNOHELP is used (1) in wceshell.bib to include help components (part of the shell), (2) in wceshell.reg to include registry entries that set up help file associations with the appropriate modules, (3) in wceapps.bib to include help for components included in the image, and (4) in wceapps.reg to include registry entries in a manner similar to wceshell.reg.
IMGNOIDE	Not used.	
IMGNOIE	Excludes Pocket Internet Explorer and support components.	IMGNOIE is used in ie.bib to exclude localization support for Internet Explorer (mlang.dll), ieceext.dll, shlwapi.dll, WinInet API (wininet.dll), URL and Moniker support (urlmon.dll), HTML support (mshtml.dll), HTML frames support (shdocvw.dll), limited XML support (msxml.dll), and mmefx.dll.

(continued)

Table 3.5 *Continued.*

Environment Variable	Usage	Description
IMGNOJAVA	Excludes Java support from the operating system.	IMGNOJAVA is used in common.bib to exclude the Java modules cejvm.dll, jview.dll, ce_awt.dll, ce_local.dll, ce_math.dll, ce_irda.dll, ce_zip.dll, ce_net.dll, jcls.dll, and verifier.dll.
IMGNOJSCRIPT	Excludes JavaScript support from the operating system.	IMGNOJSCRIPT is used (1) in common.bib to exclude jscript.dll, and (2) in common.reg to set up OLE IDs for the JScript component in the system registry.
IMGNOLOC	Not used. Localization support is not optional.	
IMGNOMAIL	Excludes Pocket Mail, Internet Message Access Protocol (IMAP), and Simple Mail Transport Protocol (SMTP) support.	IMGNOMAIL is used (1) in wceapps.bib to exclude pmail.exe, imap4.dll, smtp.dll, msgstore.dll, tnefutil.dll, mailutil.dll, labledit.dll, uicom.dll, and pimprint.dll; and (2) in wceapps.reg to set up registry entries for Pocket Mail.
IMGNOMLANG	Excludes localization support from Pocket Internet Explorer.	IMGNOMLANG is used in ie.bib to exclude mlang.dll.
IMGNOMSHTML	Excludes HTML support from the operating system.	IMGNOMSHTML is used in ie.bib to exclude mshtml.dll.
IMGNONETUI	Excludes the network user interface from the operating system. The network user interface allows manipulation of the configuration properties of the network via the Communication control panel applet.	IMGNONETUI is used in common.bib to exclude netui.dll.
IMGNOOLE32	Disables OLE support in the operating system.	IMGNOOLE32 is used in common.bib to exclude the OLE support components ole32.dll and oleaut32.dll.
IMGNOPCMCIA	Disables PC card support in the operating system. This entry doesn't exclude PC card support in the operating system. It includes it but disables it at runtime. To exclude PC card support, you must exclude the file pcmcia.dll from the image (see ODO_NOPCMCIA).	IMGNOPCMCIA is used in common.reg to exclude registry entries for all supported PC cards.

Table 3.5 *Continued.*

Environment Variable	Usage	Description
IMGNOPWORD	Excludes Pocket Word from the operating system.	IMGNOPWORD is used (1) in wceapps.bib to exclude office.dll, pwd_res.dll, pwwiff.dll, and pword.exe; and (2) in wceapps.reg to set up registry entries that define OLE IDs and file associations for Pocket Word.
IMGNOREDIR	Excludes network redirector support from the operating system.	IMGNOREDIR is used in common.bib to exclude the redirector components redir.dll and netbios.dll.
IMGNOSECURITY	Excludes security components from the operating system.	IMGNOSECURITY is used in common.bib to exclude the digital signature and data certificates (rsabase.dll) and the corresponding 128-bit version (rsaenh.dll).
IMGNOSERVERS	Excludes all servers from the operating system. If you plan to ship two different versions of your OS build (à la NT workstation and server), you can use this variable to switch between the versions.	IMGNOSERVERS is used in msmq.bib to exclude Microsoft Message Queue components msmqd.dll, netregd.dll, mqoa.dll, msmqadm.exe, and msmqrt.dll.
IMGNOSHDOCVW	Excludes HTML frames support from Pocket Internet Explorer.	IMGNOSHDOCVW is used in ie.bib to exclude shdocvw.dll.
IMGNOSHELL	Excludes the Windows CE shell and related components, shortcuts, and help files from the operating system. Excluding shell components automatically excludes the browser and CE Help.	IMGNOSHELL is used (1) in wceshell.bib to exclude the task manager (taskman.exe), asform.dll, the CE shell support component (ceshell.dll), and the explorer shell (explorer.exe); (2) in wceshell.reg to create registry entries that automatically launch the task manager and explorer shell on startup; (3) in wceapps.bib to exclude browser and help files if set; and (4) in wceapps.reg in the same way as in wceshell.reg.
IMGNOTXTSHELL	Excludes the CE shell from the operating system. The CE shell communicates with a designated desktop for debugging and synchronization services.	IMGNOTXTSHELL is used in common.bib to exclude the CE shell components cesh.dll and toolhelp.dll.
IMGNOURLMON	Excludes URL and Moniker support from the browser.	IMGNOURLMON is used in ie.bib to exclude urlmon.dll.
IMGNOWININET	Excludes WinInet API support from the operating system.	IMGNOWININET is used in ie.bib to exclude wininet.dll.

(continued)

Table 3.5 *Continued.*

Environment Variable	Usage	Description
IMGNSCFIR	Includes the National Security Council Fast Infrared driver.	IMGNSCFIR is used in platform.bib for the CEPC platform to include nscirda.dll (if not set, the regular IrDA driver irsir.dll is included), and (2) in platform.reg to set up registry entries for the appropriate IrDA driver included in the operating system.
IMGPROFILER	Builds a profile-enabled kernel in the operating system.	IMGPROFILER is used (1) in common.bib to include the profile-enabled kernel nkprof.exe in the image, and (2) in config.bib for the CEPC and Odo platform to instruct the OS build tool that profiling has been enabled in the kernel (PROFILE=ON).
IMGSTRICTLOC	Not used.	
IMGTINY	Builds a special bare-bones version of the operating system.	IMGTINY is used in common.bib, wceshell.bib, wceapps.bib, wceapps.bib, and the platform.bib files for the CEPC and Odo platforms.
IMGTINYFSRAM	Uses a (relatively) tiny percent of RAM for the file system. By default, CE uses the RAM for file system storage.	IMGTINYFSRAM is used in config.bib to set another variable, FSRAMPERCENT, to the hex value of 80. This number instructs CE to use only 50 percent of the *first* 1MB of RAM for the file system.
IMGUSB	Adds USB support to the operating system.	IMGUSB is used in platform.bib for the CEPC platform to include the USB support components Open Host Controller Interface driver (ohci.dll), USB driver (usbd.dll), and USB mouse driver (usbmouse.dll).
IMGUSEPROXY	Enables the use of a proxy server for HTTP.	IMGUSEPROXY is used in wceshell.reg to add lines to the system registry that instruct the browser to use a proxy server called itg-proxy for HTTP access on port 80. Edit these settings to configure your own proxy server by name if you turn on this variable.
INITNOCOMM	Disables the NDIS and auxiliary function driver (AFD) protocol manager at runtime.	INITNOCOMM is used in common.reg to disable the registry settings for the NDIS and AFD components. Note that this setting does not remove ndis.dll and afd.dll from the image. It allows the components to be part of the image but simply disables them at runtime.

Table 3.5 *Continued.*

Environment Variable	Usage	Description
SCHEDLOG	Includes the scheduler log functions in the operating system.	Scheduler log functions are implemented in schedlog.dll and are used as helper functions when thread and process logging are being implemented in the kernel. SCHEDLOG is used in the Sources file for the kernel modules in CEPC and Odo platforms to link the kernel with schedlog.lib. In the Sources file for the Hardware Abstraction Layer (HAL), this variable is used to pass -D SCHEDLOG to the compiler. This flag is used to conditionally add a HAL IOCTL (I/O control) code that enables scheduler logging.
TESTSIP	Includes the Software Input Panel (SIP) control panel applet in the operating system. The applet is used to configure the SIP, a keyboard implemented in software for devices that do not have a keyboard (e.g., the Palm-size PC).	TESTSIP is used (1) in common.bib to include the SIP control panel applet (msim.dll), and (2) in common.reg to specify default values for SIP configuration (manipulated by msim.dll).
WINCEPROFILE	Builds a version of the kernel that supports profiling.	WINCEPROFILE is used in the HAL Sources file for the CEPC platform to pass the -D PROFILE flag to the compiler. This flag is not really used by the HAL, since a kernel with profile information is always built (nkprof.exe). However, you can use conditional compiling around the constant PROFILE to add any profile-specific code to the HAL.

Environment variables also find use in customization of the base platform chosen to build a new platform. For example, we chose MAXALL to build Adam. Now we can modify the MAXALL configuration for use in Adam by changing the value of these environment variables appropriately.

These variables can also be put to good use during development and debugging. It may not be necessary for every developer on the project to include all components of the operating system. A developer working on writing a PC card driver for a bar code scanner may not need to include any of the Pocket applications like Explorer and Mail, the serial port driver, or communication components. Such choices can help reduce the size of the operating system image being built, which is instrumental in shorter download times to the hardware platform, resulting in a more rapid development cycle.

Of course, when the driver is finally ready, the developer must test it with the full build of the operating system that is expected to run on the hardware platform.

Extending the Platform Builder Catalog

The Platform Builder catalog isn't for components that ship with Windows CE. Components can be added to the catalog so that they become available as standard components for a given platform. When you're adding a component, the principal pieces of information you must supply are its name, a method to build the component, the group to which this component belongs (this could be a new group or an existing one in the catalog), and a unique ID. A multitude of other information, which we will discuss shortly, must also be supplied.

Let's start by introducing the unique ID. This ID must be unique across any component ever created for Windows CE. A globally unique identifier (GUID), also referred to as a universally unique identifier (UUID), is a 128-bit value that uniquely identifies a component. You can generate a unique number on demand by using the Microsoft utility `guidgen.exe`. You can then use this number to identify a component that must be added to the catalog. If a GUID is not supplied, Platform Builder generates one for the component when adding it to the catalog. However, providing a GUID for each component is recommended because it must be supplied when modifications are made to the component in the catalog.

Guidgen will generate a new GUID and allow you to copy it to Clipboard so that you can paste it into any other application. One of four formats can be selected. For a format suitable for our purposes, select **Registry Format**. Then click on the **Copy** button. Now the GUID can be pasted in via the editor being used to create the component that will be added to the catalog.

Components to be imported into a catalog must be specified by a special syntax and placed in a file with a *.cec* extension. Files with the *.cec* extension are called **component files**.

Component Files in Depth

Component files have a format for laying out information about a component. The best way to start is by example. Recall that we built an application called `welcome.exe` for our project Adam. This simple welcome application can be included as a standard component in the catalog. A CEC file must be used to describe this component before it can be imported into the catalog.

CECInfo Block

Every component file starts with the `CECInfo` block (Listing 3.6), a structure that contains information about the component file itself. Note that any text following the characters "//" up to the end of the line is considered to be a comment.

Listing 3.6 Sample component file header

```
CECInfo (
    Name(New.cec)
    CECVersion (3.00)
    // GUID() - left blank
    Vendor ("Windows CE Unlimited")
    Description ("A sample Cec file")
)
```

The fields of the CECInfo block are specified as follows:

- Name is an optional field that identifies the name of the component file.
- CECVersion is a mandatory field that can have a value of either 2.12 or 3.00. It identifies the version of Windows CE for which the component file was written.
- GUID is an optional field containing a number that uniquely identifies the component file. If it is left blank, a GUID will automatically be generated for the component file when it is used to import the component.
- Vendor is an optional field identifying the vendor that is distributing this component as part of the catalog.
- Description is an optional field that describes the component file.

ComponentType Block

The component itself is described by a ComponentType block. Consider the sample shown in Listing 3.7, which describes welcome.exe as a component.

Listing 3.7 Sample component file

```
ComponentType (
  Name( Welcome )
  GUID( {232FBCF4-72DD-4208-A40F-686A42FFE8B3} )
  Description( "Welcome application" )
  Group( "\Standard Applications" )
  Implementations(
    Implementation(
       Name(Welcome)
       GUID( {2A8D35B5-F6BC-485c-867B-8352826D27CF} )
       Description( "Welcome application" )
       Vendor("Windows CE Book")
       Date(05/05/2000)
       BuildMethods(
            BuildMethod(
                 Step( buildrel )
                 GUID( {A3CED1C5-617E-4065-A784-8551FA00A249} )
                 CPU( x86 )
                 InputFiles(  )
                 OutputFiles(  )
                 Action( "#COPY( "$(_PROJECTROOT\Welcome\Obj\Welcome.exe",
$(_FLATRELEASEDIR)" )))
                 Setting( '#CHM( "Welcome.chm" )' )
                 Setting( '#CHM( "Welcome.chi" )' )
                 Setting('#INPUT("Include Welcome", INCLUDE_WELCOME, 1, 0,
"")')
            )
       )
    )
  )
)
```

The fields of the `ComponentType` block are specified as follows:

- `Name` specifies the name of the component. The name of the component in Listing 3.7 is Welcome.
- `GUID` is an optional field containing a number that uniquely identifies the component. In this case we have assigned a GUID to the component so that we can specify it later to modify this component.
- `Description` is an optional field that describes this component. It is displayed when the properties for a component are viewed in Platform Builder.
- `Group` is an optional field that refers to the organization hierarchy displayed in the catalog. If you specify *\Standard Applications* in the sample, this component will be added to a new group in the catalog at the root level called Standard Applications. Welcome will be added as a component to this group. You can add a component to an existing component simply by specifying its name. Group names in a group hierarchy can be separated by a backslash (\). If no other option is specified, the component is added directly to the root of the catalog.
- `Vendor` identifies the vendor of the component. The value of this field is displayed when the properties for the component are viewed (right-click on the component in the catalog and select **Properties** from the pop-up menu).

Implementation Block

Each `ComponentType` block must have an embedded `Implementations` block (see Listing 3.7). The `Implementations` block can consist of one or more `Implementation` blocks that describe how the component has been implemented.

The fields of the `Implementation` block are specified as follows:

- `Name` is a mandatory field that identifies the `Implementation` block in other `Implementation` blocks.
- `GUID` contains the unique identifier for the `Implementation` block. This field is optional, but if specified, it must be unique for each block. An implementation may be referred to by name or by GUID. If this field is left blank, Platform Builder automatically generates and applies a GUID to this block.
- `Description` is an optional field that describes the implementation.
- `Vendor` is an optional field that identifies the vendor of the implementation and is optional.
- `Children` is an optional field that lists any children of an implementation. This field can be used to specify any dependent implementations. A child implementation must be described earlier in the component file. Implementations may be identified by name or GUID in this field.
- `Date` is an optional field that specifies the date of implementation in MM/DD/YY format. This date can be set to the date the component was built or to the date it was included in the catalog.

BuildMethods Block

The `BuildMethods` block, along with the `Name` field, is required in the `Implementation` block. The `BuildMethods` block is followed by one or more `BuildMethod` blocks, each of which specifies a method for building the component (see Listing 3.7).

The fields of the `BuildMethod` block are specified as follows:

- `Step` and `Action` are mandatory fields that form the heart of the `BuildMethod` block. Together these fields specify how this particular implementation of the component will be built. The following list gives the different keywords that can be specified in these fields. For a more thorough treatment of how each of these keywords operates, refer to Chapter 10. The command specified in the `Action` field depends on the keyword specified in the `Step` field (see Table 3.6).

  The `Action` field can contain the commands specified in the list that follows. In each case the entire command must be enclosed in quotation marks for it to be executed—that is, `Action ("<command>")`.

  - `#COPY("SrcPath", "TargetDir")` copies a file with a fully qualified path name into the target directory. Use this command to copy files during the system generation or build-release phases. For example, this command can be used to copy a component to the final target directory from which the operating system image is constructed.
  - `#ENV("Variable", "Value")` sets an environment variable to a specific value. For a more detailed explanation of how environment variables can affect a build, refer to the section titled Customizing the Build Using Environment Variables earlier in this chapter and to Chapter 10.

Table 3.6 Build Actions

`Step` **Keyword**	**Phase of Build**	`Action` **Command**
`CESYSGEN`	System generation phase. The Microsoft modules and third-party vendor components that make up the Windows CE system are combined to create a core operating system. Components supplied by the system integrator are added to this build to create the final image.	`#COPY`
`BSP`	Core build phase. During this phase of the build process, each component that is part of the Windows CE image is built individually.	`#ENV`
		`#BUILD`
		`#CUSTOM`
`BUILDREL`	Build-release phase. In this phase, all the output files are collected in a predetermined location in a mass copy operation.	`#COPY`
		`#CUSTOM`
`MAKEIMG`	Make-image phase. The final operating system image is built from the collected files.	`#ENV`

- `#BUILD(Dirs | Sources, "Directory")` tells the build process to build either a `Dirs` file or a `Sources` file to be found in the directory specified in `Directory`. `Dirs` and `Sources` files specify commands for building one or more components. A more thorough treatment of these files can be found in Chapter 11.
- `#BUILD(MAK, "Directory", "Makefile")` is an alternative flavor of the `BUILD` command that can be used to build a component with a custom makefile. A custom makefile would be used in lieu of a sources file for better control of the build process. This command can also be helpful in porting components to Windows CE, where you can use a fully tested makefile instead of converting it into a sources file. For a quick primer on how makefiles work, refer to Appendix B.
- `#CUSTOM("WorkingDirectory", "CustomCommand")` can be used to execute a command specified by `CustomCommand`. This command is executed from the directory specified by `WorkingDirectory`. It can be used to execute scripts like batch files that perform tasks that either cannot be performed by a makefile or would be extremely tedious to port to a makefile. Again, legacy components that are built by scripts can be accommodated by this command.

• `GUID` contains the unique identifier for the `Implementation` block. This field is optional, but if specified, it must be unique for each block. An implementation may be referred to by name or by GUID. If the field is left blank or not specified, Platform Builder automatically generates and applies a GUID to this block.

• `CPU` is a mandatory field that indicates if the implementation is CPU specific. Current CPU values that can be specified in this field are SH3, SH4, SA1100, ARM720, ARM720T, R3912, R4102, R4111.16, R4111.32, R4300, PPC403, PPC821, and x86 for Windows CE 3.0. This list, supported by Microsoft, may grow in the future as more processors are supported by Windows CE. Processors may also be dropped from this list. The value of the CPU field must be enclosed in quotation marks. The value `default` indicates that the implementation is for the default list of processors for the operating system. The default list is the list supported by Microsoft.

• `Setting` is an optional field that supports three different operations:

1. `#INPUT( "Sysgen setting", EnvironmentVariable, 1 | 0, InitialValue, BspValue)`. Each `BuildMethod` block is allowed to specify a setting during the system generation phase, referred to as `Cesysgen` or `Sysgen`. In the Platform Builder IDE, you can select or deselect `Sysgen` by selecting **Build** and then **Settings**, and finally clicking on the **Sysgen** tab in the **Platform Settings** dialog box.

   Each setting sets an environment variable. The `#INPUT` operation allows such a setting to be made visible in the **Sysgen** tab of the **Platform Settings** dialog box. The string *Sysgen setting* is displayed in the tab. The environment variable specified by `EnvironmentVariable` is either set or unset depending on its value: either 1 or 0. If the value is 1, then the environment variable will be set to `TRUE` when the setting is selected. A value of 0 specifies that the variable be set to `FALSE` when the setting is selected. Finally, `InitialValue` specifies the initial value of the environment variable and hence the default selection of the setting in the tab. `BspValue` is a string that is set to the name or GUID of the board support package that allows this setting.

2. `#OUTPUT(Output)` allows the selection of a particular module in the image. `Output` is usually an environment variable that is read by the `cesysgen.bat` file during the system generation phase (we'll give more details in Chapter 10).
3. `#CHM("HelpOrHelpIndexFile")` associates an HTML help file (.chm extension) or a help index file (.chi extension) with the component. When an SDK is exported, the component's help files specified by this operation are automatically included in the SDK by Platform Builder.

- `InputFiles` is an optional field that is used to specify a list of files, separated by spaces, required to perform the build for this component.
- `OutputFiles` is an optional field that is used to specify a list of files, separated by spaces, output by the build.

Adding a Component to the Catalog

One global catalog is used by Platform Builder to store components and can be reused across projects. To add a component to the catalog, you must create the component. Component files have a *.cec* extension. To import the component, select **Manage Platform Builder Components...** in the **File** menu. The resulting dialog box lists all the components that have already been imported (Figure 3.15). Click on **Import New...** and browse for the component file that has been created for the new component.

As an example, save Listing 3.6 to a file called `new.cec` and import it into the catalog. Welcome will show up as a member of the catalog under the folder `Standard Applications`. After Welcome has been added to the catalog (Figure 3.16), it is available for inclusion in all new platforms.

The dialog box to manage platform builder components is a front end to the `pbcec.exe` utility that comes with Platform Builder. Pbcec imports components into the catalog. To import a component, we call Pbcec with the component file name as its argument. For example, to import the Welcome component into the CEPC catalog via the command line, we would have invoked Pbcec in the following way:

```
Pbcec New.cec
```

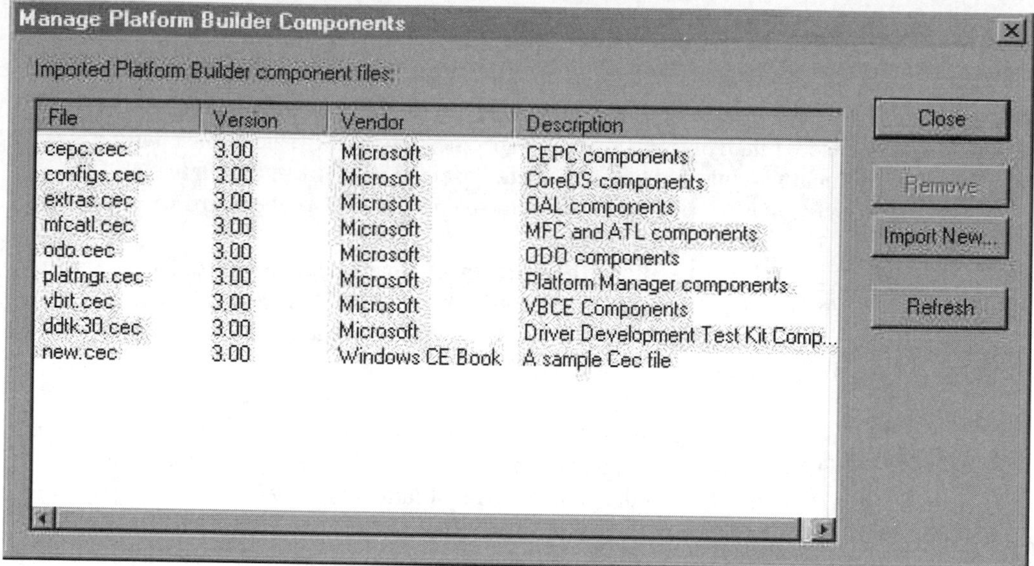

Figure 3.15 Adding Welcome to the catalog

Figure 3.16 The catalog after Welcome has been added

Calling Pbcec with the `/list` argument lists the components in the catalog. A sample run yielded the following output:

```
Microsoft (R) Platform Builder 3.00 Catalog Utility
Copyright (C) Microsoft Corp 2000.  All rights reserved.
CEC File                Description
========                ===========
cepc.cec                CEPC components
```

```
configs.cec              CoreOS components
extras.cec               OAL components
mfcatl.cec               MFC and ATL components
odo.cec                  Odo components
platmgr.cec              Platform Manager components
vbrt.cec                 VBCE Components
ddtk30.cec               Driver Development Test Kit Components
new.cec                  A sample Cec file
There are currently 9 cec files in the catalog.
```

When called with the `/r` option, Pbcec removes from the catalog the component that is specified in the file passed in as the Pbcec argument. The `/clean` option does exactly what it says: It clears out all components from the catalog.

Creating a New Board Support Package

Extending the catalog allows components to be used across platforms that use the same board support package. System integrators may want to create a new BSP for a new processor or for a significantly new platform for an existing processor. The key to creating a new BSP is to create a new BSP file. The BSP file contains a list of instructions for how to build the platform and which OEM components are required for the platform. Users of the BSP can then build the platform in the manner that is prescribed in the BSP. In other words, a BSP file contains directions for the build process, whereas component files define the components to be built.

Before a BSP can be created, all of its components must be imported into the catalog. Let's say we are creating a BSP called Appliances. Appliances will support the x86 CPU and will provide components typically used by kitchen appliances, such as coffee makers, refrigerators, and so on. We'll keep the Appliances BSP simple for illustration purposes.

The first step is to import all of the Appliances components. We take the CEPC component file and modify it for Appliances. Then we import it into the catalog. Before we do that, we adjust Appliances so that it has no display, no keyboard support, and no USB or infrared support because these are not needed for the type of BSP we are creating. All GUIDs in the file being copied must be created again via `guidgen.exe` because Platform Builder expects all of these new components to be exported into the catalog. Listing 3.8 shows the component file for Appliances after `cepc.cec` was copied and modified.

Listing 3.8 Component file for Appliances

```
//  appliances.cec - Appliances components

CECInfo (
    Name(Appliances)
    GUID({D1E60FE9-4370-4deb-B111-781D7CBAEA73})
    CECVersion(3.00)
    Vendor("Microsoft")
    Description("Appliances components")
)
```

```
//  type "OAL" and 2 implementations
//  Appliances
ComponentType (
    Name( OAL )
    GUID( {B3509B99-F1E4-11d2-85F6-004005365450} )
    Description( "OEM Adaptation Layer" )
    Implementations(

        Implementation(
            Name( Appliances )
            GUID( {E0A5CD0C-9D7D-4c4c-B4E7-17A6CACB3E3B} )
            Description( "Appliances OAL" )

            BuildMethods(
                BuildMethod(
                    Step( BSP )
                    GUID( {188258EE-AE2C-4013-8514-1D6EA325027C} )
                    CPU( "x86" )
                    Action( '#BUILD(DIRS, "$(_WINCEROOT)\platform\cepc\kernel")' )
                    Action( '#BUILD(DIRS, "$(_WINCEROOT)\platform\cepc\gwe")' )
                )
            )
        )
    )
)

//  child type "ddk_bus" and implementation
ComponentType (
    Name( ddk_bus )
    GUID( {4BB97298-47AC-43ef-BD2D-9E5B9FC3D1CA} )
    Description( "ddk_bus" )
    Implementations(
        Implementation(
            Name( ddk_bus )
            Description( "ddk_bus" )
            GUID( {C87FA2D3-8D13-49e4-91BD-A94C74DA6EE6} )

            BuildMethods(
                BuildMethod(
                    Step( BSP )
                    GUID( {84A08ED9-87A1-466a-A268-F9DEA522D2C1} )
                    CPU( "x86" )
                    OutputFiles( ddk_bus.LIB )
                    Action( '#BUILD(SOURCES,
"$(_WINCEROOT)\platform\Appliances\Drivers\CEDDK\DDK_BUS")' )
                )
            )
        )
    )
)
```

```
//  child type "ddk_map" and implementation
ComponentType (
    Name( ddk_map )
    GUID( {8886E23C-797C-4b19-A871-843AA949B866} )
    Description( "ddk_map" )
    Implementations(
        Implementation(
            Name( ddk_map )
            Description( "ddk_map" )
            GUID( {02A46E4A-1CDB-4504-B99C-470C27157015} )

            BuildMethods(
                BuildMethod(
                    Step( BSP )
                    GUID( {F07C875B-1D69-4cf0-A54B-D7486886627B} )
                    CPU( "x86" )
                    OutputFiles( ddk_map.LIB )
                    Action( '#BUILD(SOURCES,
"$(_WINCEROOT)\platform\Appliances\Drivers\CEDDK\DDK_MAP")' )
                )
            )
        )
    )
)


//  type "ceddk" and implementation
ComponentType (
    Name( ceddk )
    GUID( {8630294D-6B62-4422-9B72-2B2D29629AE5} )
    Description( "ceddk" )
    Group( "\Drivers\Appliances" )
    Implementations(
        Implementation(
            Name( ceddk )
            Description( "ceddk" )
            GUID( {BBD69EB7-AA85-440b-ADCC-8C8D1D8C34C0} )
            Children( ddk_bus ddk_map )

            BuildMethods(
                BuildMethod(
                    Step( BSP )
                    GUID( {D6907409-E7DB-4d98-8841-58AD8A25B75F} )
                    CPU( "x86" )
                    OutputFiles( pc_ddk.DLL )
                    Action( '#BUILD(SOURCES,
"$(_WINCEROOT)\platform\Appliances\Drivers\CEDDK\DLL")' )
                )

                BuildMethod(
                    Step( makeimg )
                    GUID( {C792A2F8-0419-49aa-8B1E-CEB62BA274F8} )
                    CPU( "x86" )
```

```
                    Action( '#ENV(IMGNOCEDDK, "")' )
                )
            )
        )
    )
)


//  type "serial" and 2 implementations
//  "serial", and "NewSerialMDD"
ComponentType (
    Name( serial )
    GUID ( {6401DC3D-E93A-4bfb-B58F-6818A0500E64} )
    Description( "serial" )
    Group( "\Drivers\Appliances" )
    Implementations(
        Implementation(
            Name( serial )
            Description( "serial" )
            GUID ( {81AA1070-3B88-4680-AD9D-E132F6773584} )

            BuildMethods(
                BuildMethod(
                    Step( BSP )
                    GUID( {4DAB8E7F-365B-4f51-B905-EE82FA242D14} )
                    CPU( "x86" )
                    OutputFiles( serial.DLL )
                    Action( '#ENV(ODO_NOSERIAL, "")' )
                    Action( '#BUILD(SOURCES,
"$(_WINCEROOT)\platform\Appliances\Drivers\SERIAL.PDD")' )
                )

                BuildMethod(
                    Step( makeimg )
                    GUID( {8D6179A9-0BD4-4387-A664-5A8C5D946714} )
                    CPU( "x86" )
                    Action( '#ENV(ODO_NOSERIAL, "")' )
                    Action( '#ENV(NEW_SERIAL_MDD, "") ')
                )
            )
        )

        Implementation(
            Name( NewSerialMDD )
            Description( "New Serial MDD" )
            GUID ( {52B0F538-8E24-4a07-BDE5-76A7259608BF} )

            BuildMethods(
                BuildMethod(
                    Step( BSP )
                    GUID( {2F65E925-A228-4875-841A-A1B456E2B23A} )
                    CPU( "x86" )
                    OutputFiles( com_card.dll com16550.dll )
                                   Action( '#ENV(ODO_NOSERIAL, "")' )
```

```
                    Action( '#BUILD(SOURCES,
"$(_WINCEROOT)\platform\Appliances\Drivers\COM_CARD")' )
                    Action( '#BUILD(SOURCES,
"$(_WINCEROOT)\platform\Appliances\Drivers\COM16550")' )
                )

                BuildMethod(
                    Step( makeimg )
                    GUID( {6CA564F3-178D-47ff-9D6B-D81378F1FC40} )
                    CPU( "x86" )
                    Action( '#ENV(ODO_NOSERIAL, "")' )
                    Action( '#ENV(NEW_SERIAL_MDD, 1)' )
                )
            )
        )
    )
)


//  type "wavedev" and implementation
ComponentType (
    Name( wavedev )
    GUID ( {E0B38875-FF8F-4685-99D4-9A591368609D} )
    Description( "wavedev" )
    Group( "\Drivers\Appliances" )
    Implementations(
        Implementation(
            Name( wavedev )
            Description( "wavedev" )
            GUID ( {0F132F1D-4AB8-4c57-853D-68935FDED1DF} )

            BuildMethods(
                BuildMethod(
                    Step( BSP )
                    GUID( {A0E49B67-614C-47bf-80D0-48C7E25C664B} )
                    CPU( "x86" )
                    OutputFiles( wavedev.DLL )
                    Action( '#ENV(ODO_NOAUDIO, "")' )
                    Action( '#BUILD(SOURCES,
"$(_WINCEROOT)\platform\Appliances\Drivers\WAVEDEV")' )
                )

                BuildMethod(
                    Step( makeimg )
                    GUID( {6DE00180-A0BD-4e74-87E7-4BD50AF5E158} )
                    CPU( "x86" )
                    Action( '#ENV(ODO_NOAUDIO, "")' )
                )
            )
        )
    )
)
```

```
//  type "EBOOT" and implementation
ComponentType (
    Name( EBOOT )
    GUID( {F02E3B9F-CD10-44a5-BED5-1EAE187A2AE6} )
    Description( "Appliances Eboot.bin" )
    Group( "\Drivers\Appliances" )
    Implementations(
        Implementation(
            Name( Eboot )
            Description( "Appliances Eboot.bin" )
            GUID( {086BA8F9-0788-4900-A48C-2D27F8AA8397} )

            BuildMethods(
                BuildMethod(
                    Step( BSP )
                    GUID( {C1450E38-C813-426f-BB98-6FDF40EC2216} )
                    CPU( "x86" )
                    Action( '#BUILD(SOURCES,
"$(_WINCEROOT)\platform\Appliances\EBOOT")' )
                )
            )
        )
    )
)
```

When the component file shown in Listing 3.8 is imported into the catalog, the catalog shows the addition of an OAL component, Appliances, and the drivers that are part of the Appliances BSP (Figure 3.17).

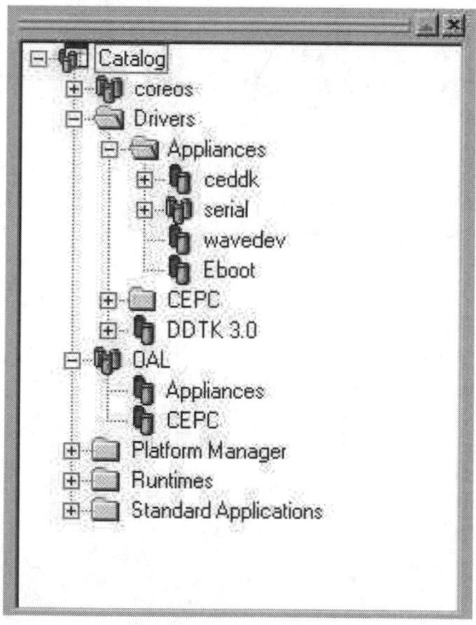

Figure 3.17 The catalog with imported Appliances components

Once the components for the BSP have been imported into the catalog, we need to create a new BSP. Platform Builder allows you to create a project with a placeholder for a BSP. To finish creating the BSP, you must expand the placeholder—a painstaking process that must be carried out by hand.

To create a placeholder for a BSP, click on the **File | New...** menu option in Platform Builder. Choose to create a WCE platform from the **Platforms** tab and type in the name of a sample platform when the WCE Platform Wizard launches its first dialog box. For example, to create a BSP for a category called Appliances, type in "Brewster." Brewster is a sample coffee maker that uses Windows CE. We will take a more intimate tour of Brewster later on in this book. For now, it makes a guest appearance for illustration purposes.

In the second dialog box (step 2) of the wizard, select **My BSP**. This option indicates to Platform Builder that you are trying to create a new board support package. Type in the name of the BSP subdirectory. In our example we chose the name *Appliances* (Figure 3.18).

You *must* create this directory before you can execute step 2. Platform Builder will not create it for you. Accepting the defaults in the ensuing wizard dialogs will lead to the creation of Brewster. Figure 3.19 shows the **Project** window after Brewster is created and loaded in Platform Builder.

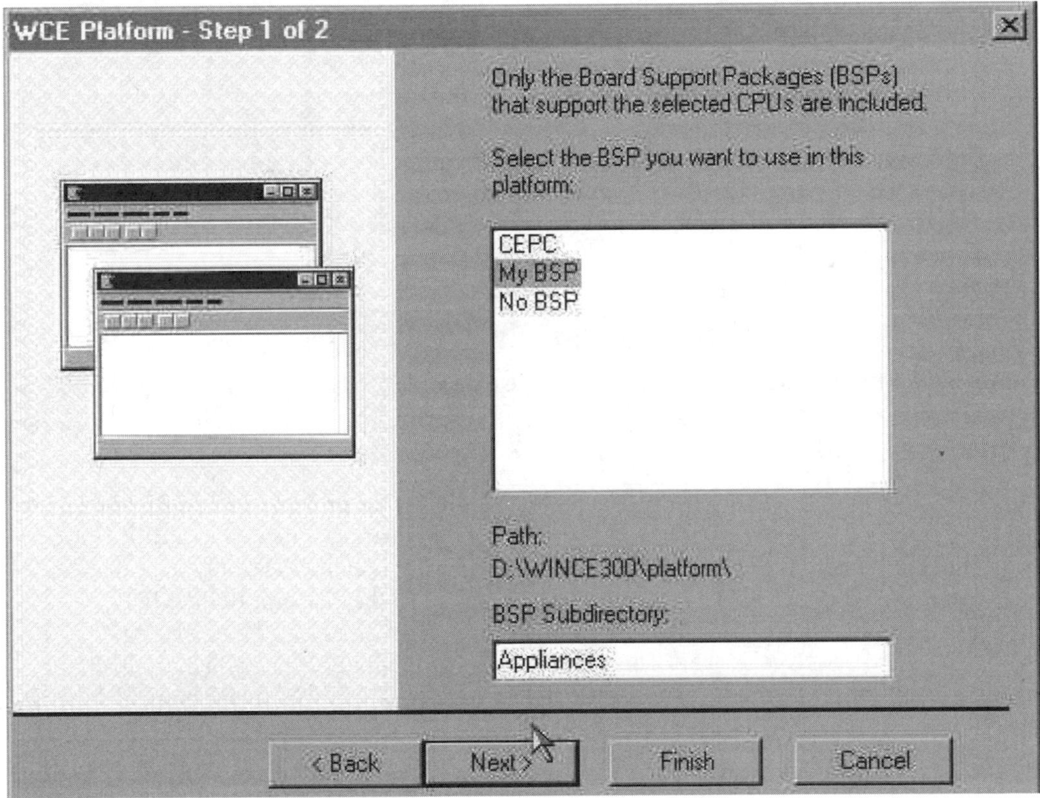

Figure 3.18 Creating a new BSP

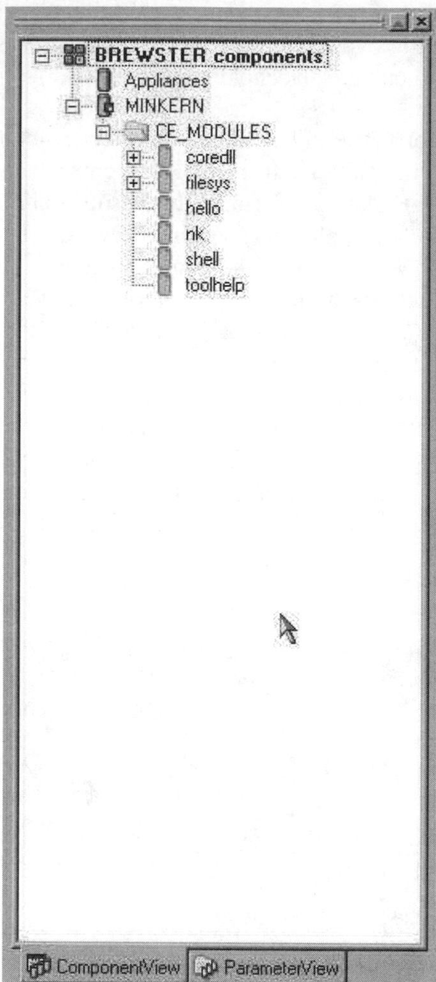

Figure 3.19 The Brewster platform used to create a new BSP

Note that Appliances shows up as an implementation in the project window. Right-clicking on it and selecting **Properties** will reveal that Platform Builder recognizes it as a BSP. However, there is nothing in the BSP yet. The directory created earlier is empty. The only trace that you have a new BSP is a file called `appliances.bsp` created in the Platform Builder IDE directory. For Windows CE 3.0, this directory is `\WINCE300\WINDOWS CE PLATFORM BUILDER\3.00\CEPB\BIN\IDE`. This file represents an empty BSP, and you must modify it by hand to complete the board support package. The `appliances.bsp` file is presented in Listing 3.9.

Listing 3.9 `Appliances.bsp`

```
//  *** Appliances ***

//  NOTE:  You will need to create an appliances.cec file
//  and import it into the catalog.  When you have done that,
//  you can delete the two #ADD_USER_OAL lines below.

//  *** Global components (for all the configs) ***

#ADD_USER_OAL_BUILD_METHOD ('#BUILD(dirs, "$(_WINCEROOT)\platform\
Appliances")')

#ADD_USER_OAL_COMPONENT ("{2367C526-2821-4CEF-94A2-7286D5152E6F}",
"Appliances")

//  *** CoreOS-specific components ***
#IF ("COREOS","MINKERN")
#ENDIF
#IF ("COREOS","MAXALL")
#ENDIF
#IF ("COREOS","MINCOMM")
#ENDIF
#IF ("COREOS","MINGDI")
#ENDIF
#IF ("COREOS","MININPUT")
#ENDIF
#IF ("COREOS","MINSHELL")
#ENDIF
#IF ('COREOS","MINWMGR")
#ENDIF
#IF ("COREOS","IESAMPLE")
#ENDIF
```

The BSP file contains placeholders for adding CoreOS-specific components. *CoreOS* refers to a configuration that represents a specific type of build of the operating system. Familiar configurations like `MINKERN`, `MAXALL`, and `MINCOMM` have already been added to this file. The directives required to build your custom platform should be inserted in this file as the final step to creating a board support package.

BSP File Directives

Before we add directives to the file, let's look at the types of directives that can be added to a BSP file. BSP file directives all start with the pound sign (#). Text that follows "//" is considered to be comment to the end of the line.

- `#ADD_COMPONENT_BY_GUID_TO_ROOT ("guid")`. This directive is used to add a component implementation to the BSP. The component is identified by its GUID. Recall that right-clicking on a component and selecting **Properties** from the pop-up menu will reveal its GUID. To add the serial port driver to the BSP, you would add the following line within a CoreOS conditional:

```
#ADD_COMPONENT_BY_GUID_TO_ROOT ("{35E70441-EEA9-11D2-A092-
0060085C1833}")
```

- `#ADD_FOLDER_TO_ROOT ("Folder")`. You can organize the components by creating folders under the root. This directive is used to create a folder.
- `#ADD_COMPONENT_BY_GUID_TO_FOLDER ("guid", "Folder")`. You can add a component to a specific folder using this directive.
- `#ADD_FOLDER_TO_FOLDER ("SubFolder", "Folder")`. You can create deeper hierarchies by creating subfolders with this directive.
- `#ADD_TYPE_BY_GUID_TO_ROOT ("guid")`. You can add a component type to the root via this directive.
- `#ADD_TYPE_BY_GUID_TO_FOLDER ("guid","Folder")`. Using this directive, you can also add a component type under a folder, just as you would a component.
- `#ADD_ENV_VAR ("Variable","Value")`. You can define an environment variable and set it to a specific value using this directive. Environment variables are like settings for the platform. They are used to communicate values between different utilities that build the operating system (Chapter 10 shows exactly how this works).

Note the two directives in `appliances.bsp` (see Listing 3.9). These lines are added by Platform Builder to an empty BSP file to support the creation of a new BSP. After you have populated the BSP file with components using the directives discussed, you must delete these lines. The lines provide a placeholder for the empty BSP and specify how to build the BSP.

Notice also from the same listing that the BSP files support conditional directives. Conditionals are used in the sample listing to specify which CoreOS is being built.

Finishing the New BSP: Appliances

After the required directives have been added to the BSP file (Listing 3.10), all of the physical implementation of all the components that are part of this new BSP must be copied under the newly created BSP directory. This means copying source code, libraries, and so on. The CEPC and Odo directories are examples of what a BSP directory should look like.

Listing 3.10 Modified `appliances.bsp`

```
//  *** Appliances ***

//  NOTE:  You will need to create an appliances.cec file
//  and import it into the catalog.  When you have done that,
//  you can delete the two #ADD_USER_OAL lines below.

//  *** Global components (for all the configs) ***
```

```
// #ADD_USER_OAL_BUILD_METHOD ('#BUILD(dirs, "$(_WINCEROOT)\platform\
Appliances")')

// #ADD_USER_OAL_COMPONENT ("{2367C526-2821-4CEF-94A2-7286D5152E6F}",
"Appliances")

//  Appliances

#ADD_COMPONENT_BY_GUID_TO_ROOT ("{B3509B99-F1E4-11D2-85F6-004005365450}")

// EBOOT.BIN
#ADD_COMPONENT_BY_GUID_TO_ROOT ("{B4569ABC-F1E4-11D2-85F6-123405365450}")

//  *** CoreOS-specific components ***

//  *** MAXALL ***
#IF ("COREOS","MAXALL")
      //  pc_ddk
      #ADD_COMPONENT_BY_GUID_TO_ROOT ("{B3509B75-F1E4-11D2-85F6-
      004005365450}")

      //  ddi_flat
      #ADD_COMPONENT_BY_GUID_TO_ROOT ("{E2B049C8-F7DC-45d3-8204-
      0AA54FB4D4CC}")

      //  wavedev
      #ADD_COMPONENT_BY_GUID_TO_ROOT ("{35E7043C-EEA9-11D2-A092-
      0060085C1833}")

      //  serial
      #ADD_COMPONENT_BY_GUID_TO_ROOT ("{35E70441-EEA9-11D2-A092-
      0060085C1833}")

#ENDIF

//  *** MINKERN ***
#IF ("COREOS","MINKERN")
      //  pc_ddk
      #ADD_COMPONENT_BY_GUID_TO_ROOT ("{B3509B75-F1E4-11D2-85F6-
      004005365450}")
#ENDIF

//  *** IESAMPLE ***
#IF ("COREOS","IESAMPLE")
      //  pc_ddk
      #ADD_COMPONENT_BY_GUID_TO_ROOT ("{B3509B75-F1E4-11D2-85F6-
      004005365450}")

      //  ddi_flat
      #ADD_COMPONENT_BY_GUID_TO_ROOT ("{E2B049C8-F7DC-45d3-8204-
      0AA54FB4D4CC}")

      //  serial
      #ADD_COMPONENT_BY_GUID_TO_ROOT ("{35E70441-EEA9-11D2-A092-
      0060085C1833}")
```

```
#ENDIF

//  *** MINSHELL ***
#IF ("COREOS","MINSHELL")
      //  pc_ddk
      #ADD_COMPONENT_BY_GUID_TO_ROOT ("{B3509B75-F1E4-11D2-85F6-
      004005365450}")

      //  ddi_flat
      #ADD_COMPONENT_BY_GUID_TO_ROOT ("{E2B049C8-F7DC-45d3-8204-
      0AA54FB4D4CC}")

      //  serial
      #ADD_COMPONENT_BY_GUID_TO_ROOT ("{35E70441-EEA9-11D2-A092-
      0060085C1833}")

      //  wavedev
      #ADD_COMPONENT_BY_GUID_TO_ROOT ("{35E7043C-EEA9-11D2-A092-
      0060085C1833}")

#ENDIF

//  *** MINWMGR ***
#IF ("COREOS","MINWMGR")
      //  pc_ddk
      #ADD_COMPONENT_BY_GUID_TO_ROOT ("{B3509B75-F1E4-11D2-85F6-
      004005365450}")

      //  ddi_flat
      #ADD_COMPONENT_BY_GUID_TO_ROOT ("{E2B049C8-F7DC-45d3-8204-
      0AA54FB4D4CC}")

      //  wavedev
      #ADD_COMPONENT_BY_GUID_TO_ROOT ("{35E7043C-EEA9-11D2-A092-
      0060085C1833}")

      //  serial
      #ADD_COMPONENT_BY_GUID_TO_ROOT ("{35E70441-EEA9-11D2-A092-
      0060085C1833}")

#ENDIF

//  *** MINGDI ***
#IF (“COREOS”,"MINGDI")
```

```
        //  pc_ddk
        #ADD_COMPONENT_BY_GUID_TO_ROOT ("{B3509B75-F1E4-11D2-85F6-
        004005365450}")

        //  ddi_flat
        #ADD_COMPONENT_BY_GUID_TO_ROOT ("{E2B049C8-F7DC-45d3-8204-
        0AA54FB4D4CC}")

        //  wavedev
        #ADD_COMPONENT_BY_GUID_TO_ROOT ("{35E7043C-EEA9-11D2-A092-
        0060085C1833}")

#ENDIF

//  *** MINCOMM ***
#IF ("COREOS","MINCOMM")
        //  pc_ddk
        #ADD_COMPONENT_BY_GUID_TO_ROOT ("{B3509B75-F1E4-11D2-85F6-
        004005365450}")

        //  serial
        #ADD_COMPONENT_BY_GUID_TO_ROOT ("{35E70441-EEA9-11D2-A092-
        0060085C1833}")

#ENDIF

//  *** MININPUT ***
#IF ("COREOS","MININPUT")
        //  pc_ddk
        #ADD_COMPONENT_BY_GUID_TO_ROOT ("{B3509B75-F1E4-11D2-85F6-
        004005365450}")

#ENDIF

//  end of appliances.bsp file
```

We are now done creating a new BSP. The next time the WCE Platform Wizard is run, Appliances will appear as a choice in the **Select BSP** list box (Figure 3.20). Platform Builder filters the BSPs you can choose on the basis of the CPU you have chosen in the preceding dialog box. Since the Appliances BSP is valid only for x86, this CPU must be checked.

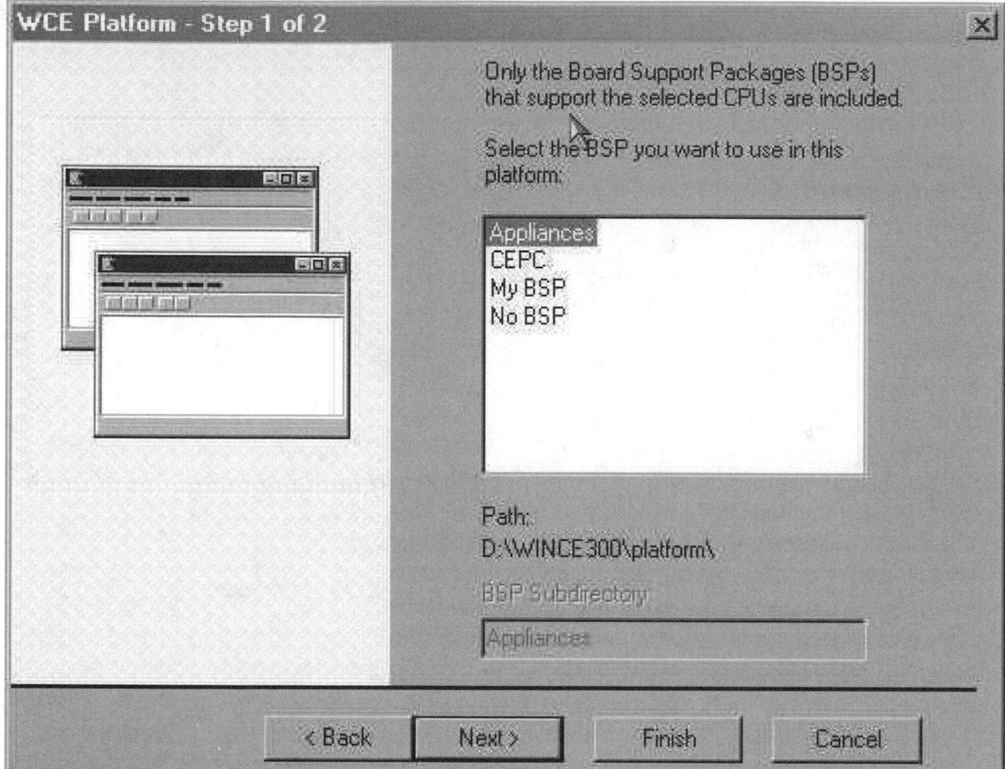

Figure 3.20 The new BSP added to an existing list

Summary

The Windows CE Platform Builder is used to customize Windows CE and tailor the operating system to a particular hardware platform. Platform Builder comes with an IDE in the style of Visual C++ that provides wizards to help create a platform. A project can also be created that contains applications and platform-independent modules that will execute on the platform.

In this chapter we looked at how environment variables can be used to further customize a build for a particular platform. The Platform Builder can be extended, and a completely new board support package can be created. In Chapter 10 we will take a closer look at the fascinating process used by Platform Builder to build the Windows CE operating system.

4 The Windows CE Boot Loader

If you are reading this chapter, you undoubtedly need to get your custom hardware, the culmination of a supreme hardware engineering effort, up and running with Windows CE. The software that will make this happen is called the **boot loader** and is the subject of this chapter.

The boot loader is the beginning of the beginning, and it quite probably represents the first lines of code to run in any system, embedded or not. Perhaps one of the most difficult parts of running CE on custom hardware is adapting it to boot your board. This is true for most commercial off-the-shelf (COTS) embedded operating systems because everyone's hardware is different in some way. You are, after all, trying to distinguish your product from the competition. Even if your board is using a well-known CPU, at a minimum you will still be required to modify a reference boot loader to properly initialize your board. This task can be especially difficult when the board has recently been developed and is not fully tested. The boot loader in this case serves double duty, acting also as a hardware debugging tool to isolate and verify problems.

To make matters worse, debugging with the boot loader code is particularly trying because you are flying blind, so to speak. Windows CE 2.12 provides few tools to support boot loader debugging and does not support the use of the built-in hardware debugging capabilities of some processors. CE 3.0, however, has added support for a hardware debugging interface called EXDI, but as of this writing, support for EXDI by hardware debugging tools vendors (those who develop emulators, probe boards, and interface adapters) is limited. Ultimately you might be forced to use passive debugging techniques that require you to emit some kind of output to determine how far your code has progressed.

This chapter will attempt to make the job of writing and customizing a Windows CE boot loader much easier. It will be different from other chapters in that a specific example, providing a step-by-step prescription of success, will not be presented. Because a boot loader requires direct hardware access to your custom platform, no single example could meet the requirements of all custom platforms with varying hardware designs. We will, however, identify common practices and minimum requirements for bringing the CE kernel to life. We will also demonstrate debugging techniques that will equip you to get your nonbooting boot loader working.

Note:
Sample boot loaders from both versions 2.12 and 3.0 of the Windows CE Platform Builder (CEPB) are analyzed in this chapter. Where possible, any reference to a sample in CEPB 2.12 has been cross-referenced to the same or similar sample in CEPB 3.0, and vice versa. In CEPB 3.0, however, the boot loader for the Odo platform that supports downloads of the kernel image through a parallel port (in the `BOOTLOAD` subdirectory) has been merged with the one for Ethernet downloads (in the `EBOOT` subdirectory). If you have an old copy of CEPB 2.12 available, we strongly recommend that you refer to this `BOOTLOAD` sample source code as you read this chapter. Considering that it supports only a parallel port, it represents a simpler example than that offered in CEPB 3.0. If the CEPB 2.12 sample source is unavailable, fear not. Sufficient narrative and references to CEPB 3.0 are provided to make the principles presented quite comprehensible.

Occasionally the CEPB online documentation will be referenced to provide more information on a particular topic. This documentation is provided on your hard disk during the installation of CEPB, and it may be activated from the **Help** menu of the CEPB integrated development environment (IDE).

Windows CE Boot Loaders

Being first is not always best, and being the boot loader in a custom platform is a significant burden. It is the boot loader's job to set the stage for starting what is the heart of most devices: the system software (at least from a software engineer's perspective). In some cases the system software may contain a full-blown operating system, equipped with a file system, kernel, and assortment of device drivers. It is not uncommon, however, for this software to contain simply a minimal microkernel that provides basic multitasking and synchronization services. Fortunately, being able to control which modules are included in the build of the CE image (discussed in more detail in Chapter 3) makes it possible to use the CEPB to create a configuration approaching a middle ground between these two extremes.

Note:
In this book the term *system software* is used to refer to a specific type of software that is directly involved in providing an abstraction of a hardware resource. Examples include a device driver that implements predefined read and write services, specialized functions that configure your custom platform, and the CE kernel itself, which supports (among other things) shared access to the processor's computing resources through time slicing.

Designing a CE Boot Loader

The two basic functions of the CE boot loader are platform initialization and kernel image download. Precisely what is meant by platform initialization in this context depends largely on your platform's design and configuration, but a few general practices will be the focus of this section. Kernel image download is the process by which the CE kernel build image, as opposed to the build image of the boot loader itself, which is discussed later in this section, is acquired. The key here is to get the kernel image into the memory of your custom platform as quickly as possible to minimize the duration of your compile/build/download/debug cycle. There are no restrictions on how you download the CE kernel, so any form of I/O (input/output) provided by your platform is fare game, ranging from a hard disk all the way up to an Ethernet port. Each solution requires varying degrees of effort and must be developed with no help from any of the CE kernel device drivers supplied with the Windows CE Platform Builder (CEPB) because these are, after all, the subject of our download.

Figure 4.1 depicts the sequence of events for most boot loaders, thus acting as an outline of what will be covered in this chapter. With extreme brevity, we will explain here what each step in the diagram means, and we will provide more detail in subsequent sections.

Beginning with code relocation, the boot loader often copies itself from one location in memory to another that provides better access times, perhaps copying from flash memory to RAM, or from uncached memory to cached memory. Next, we configure the platform memory in a manner appropriate to the needs of the boot loader, keeping in mind that some aspects of this configuration may be altered by the CE kernel's own startup code. The environment required for the execution of C source code is then initialized so that execution can continue from the `main` routine common to all boot loaders.

Once in the `main` routine, one of the first things we must do is get the data sections that are defined as writable by the compiler copied into RAM because the boot loader is typically running from read-only media. The next step requires that we initialize all ports used on this platform for debugging. By doing this early in the boot process, we can use a port for debugging the boot loader itself. At this point, because the platform is now minimally configured, it is not uncommon to initiate a Power-On Self-Test (POST). Because protected-mode memory has not yet been activated by the CE kernel, now is an ideal time to perform the abundant hardware accesses necessary for a self-test. Next, the status of the self-test is recorded, and if this is a debug build of the boot loader, the firmware monitor is loaded. The **firmware monitor** is an optional module you must supply that provides an interactive command-line debugger. Because the primary debugging tools available for CE drivers and applications cannot be used until after the CE kernel is activated, the firmware monitor can be particularly handy for debugging problems related to bringing up an unproven, custom platform.

If the firmware monitor is not loaded, then the download of the kernel image on the development workstation is initiated. Once the download is complete, the starting address is validated and the code jumps into the CE kernel. The precise address to which the code jumps depends on how the kernel was downloaded. The code could also jump into a copy of the CE kernel previously downloaded into ROM. The address of the entry point, however, must correspond to the address used in the `RAMIMAGE` entry in the `boot.bib` file, after the `ROMOFFSET` value is added. (This last statement will make more sense later in the chapter, when the building of the boot loader is explained.)

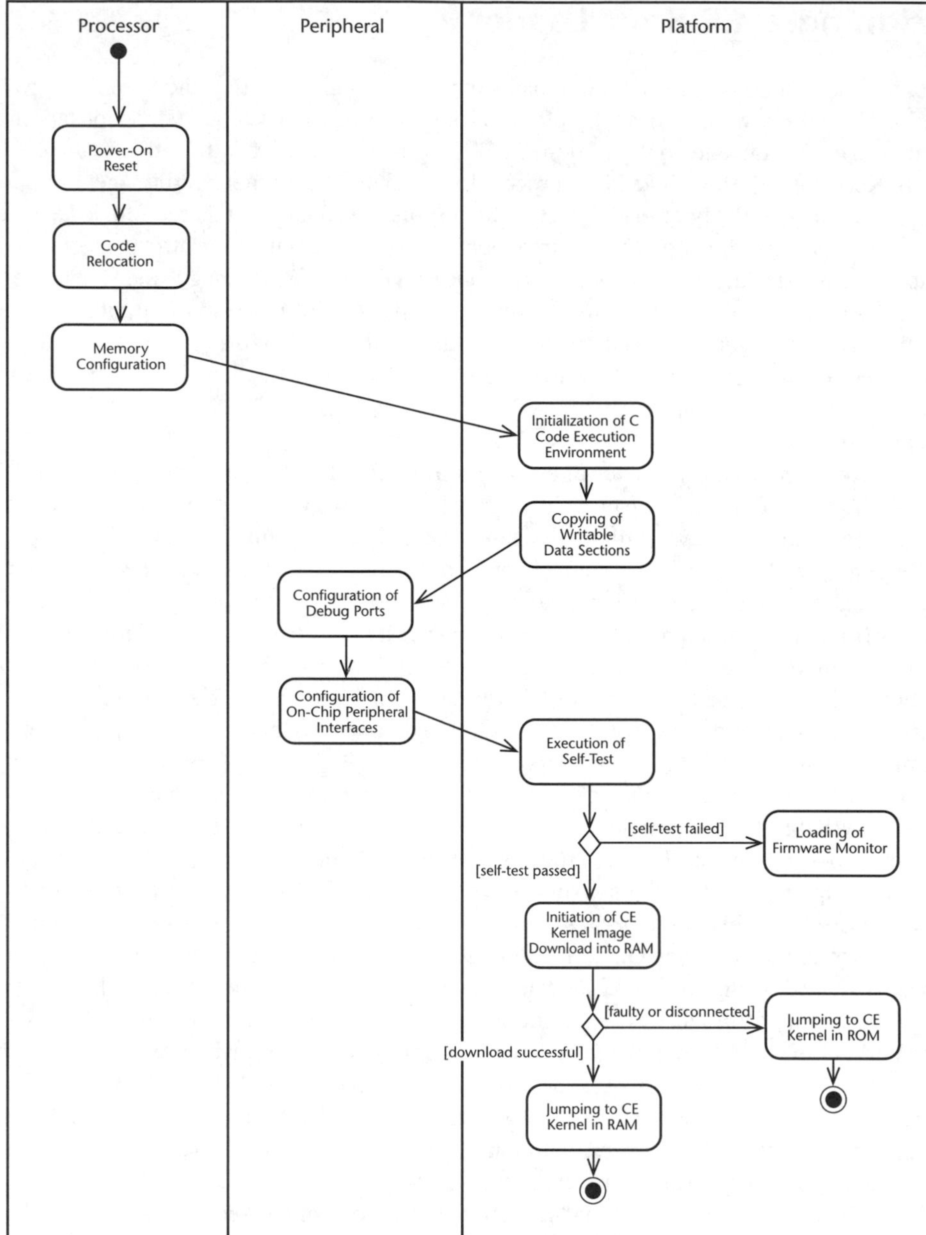

Figure 4.1 Activity diagram of the CE boot process

Decomposition/Analysis/Modification

Once given a large quantity of sample source code, as in the CEPB, you will be confronted with the task of adapting it to a custom platform. We will attempt to quantify this process in a repeatable method called **decomposition/analysis/modification** (**DAM**). DAM is typically used whenever existing source code is available and you must attempt to salvage it for use in a new product, as in this case for your CE custom platform. This method will certainly not constitute a dramatic breakthrough in software engineering. We are simply presenting what has been applied time and again by experienced software engineers in their daily exercise of "uncommon" sense. But it is our hope that if we elucidate a time-honored practice, new appreciation for its value will emerge and the reuse of existing code branded unusable might become possible.

Decomposition

We begin with decomposition. In this first step you are faced with a body of unexplored source code and the question of whether the time spent "mining" it for unspoken secrets is worthwhile. To answer this question, begin by creating a Visual Studio project with a name that reminds you of the purpose of the module under decomposition. Determine the name and location of all source files involved in the build of this module and categorize them by dragging each file icon into an appropriately named project subfolder. Remember that the names of the subfolders do not matter because they do not correspond to actual directories in your project's work space. If you find a source file, document file, or any other file of interest along the way that is used by this module, add it to the project and place it in a subfolder. At the end of this process you will have a list of files that can be instantly accessed as you traverse the source tree with a simple double click.

Do not underestimate the value of this task. We often find that we have lost track of the source file we're looking for and are forced to "remine" the source tree to locate the file again. Think of this Visual Studio project as your personal trail of bread crumbs that allows you to retrace the steps of your long journey through the realm of decomposition.

Analysis

Now the real work begins. Extending the mining metaphore, you have extracted your source gems during decomposition, and now it is time to examine them for purity using your trusty ocular. Your goal here is not to understand every facet of every gem, but instead to find the right gem well suited for setting in the jewelry you have designed. Translated, this means that you should look for the source that contains the functionality you want to provide in your custom platform. Once you have found it, try to make sense of what the original developer was trying to do and ask yourself again if this resembles the functionality you are planning to implement. If it does, then proceed to the modification step.

Modification

As you prepare to cut a new facet in this source gemstone, ask yourself another question: How might I change or add to the existing source code in a manner that will allow it to work with my platform, while retaining its capability to work on the original platform? This task might require the addition of another parameter to a particular function or the derivation of a new class that alters the behavior of a defined member function. The most conservative approach to modification begins with adding code rather than replacing it. The riskiest approach includes both the removal of code and the addition of new code with enhanced functionality. Either approach might also serve to enhance or clarify the existing design.

Wherever your approach falls into the spectrum of modification possibilities, begin by marking your modification with a comment that describes the untested nature of the modification and, if appropriate, a copy of the existing source code. This way, if things don't work as planned, you will be able to return to the working source and reconsider your modification. After each clearly commented modification, if feasible, rebuild and test the module to determine if your modification worked as intended. The message here is, do not implement too many modifications at once. Otherwise you may never know if your source code is malfunctioning as the result of complementary effects that exist only when the modifications collectively interact and would work correctly if the modifications existed independently. As you become more confident in your understanding of the original code, your modifications will naturally become riskier, representing larger and more complex source changes.

When finally the intended design of the original code is clear, you may be tempted to launch a grand effort to improve or discard the original source code in favor of your own. Taking this step would not only add the required functionality to support your custom platform, but might also bestow the favor of improved design and source quality (coherent design, improved readability, and/or enhanced performance) on those who might follow you with the same mission: to adapt your source code to yet another custom platform. One word of advice to you in this endeavor is, simply, wait.

Let us explain. You are undoubtedly confronted with enormous time-to-market pressures, so why not make the source code operational in its current form? Then immediately record a detailed specification of the modifications that you reluctantly withheld. Make certain that this specification is published in a common location that can be used by all developers to record other specifications of delayed modifications. As the project draws to a close, or a particularly visible milestone is achieved, take this list to the person maintaining the project schedule and begin your lobbying efforts to have an officially sanctioned maintenance period added for implementation of all or some of the items on the list. This approach has the added benefit of exposing your keen observations on the quality of the current source and will earn you the recognition you justly deserve.

Note:
A book called *Anti-patterns: Refactoring Software, Architectures, and Projects in Crisis* (Brown et al., 1998) covers the very subject of how to deal with the maintenance and salvage of existing code. It begins by describing the concept of an antipattern in the context of the design patterns movement (begun in 1995 by Gamma et al. in their book *Design Patterns: Elements of Reusable Object-Oriented Software*). The symptoms of various software antipatterns are characterized as the design patterns that exist in *unsuccessful* systems. For each of these antipatterns, a *refactored solution* is proposed to translate the antipattern into a bonafide design pattern.

We found this book quite inspiring, and we highly recommend it. It provided us with the tools for applying a keen eye to our own design practices and to the code we occasionally maintain, all from a perspective that we find memorable. The study of good design practices is indeed effective, but knowing how to identify the antipatterns that already exist in most software makes the corresponding design pattern (anti-antipattern) even more cogent.

Beginning with the Sample Code

The easiest way to start developing your boot loader code is to begin with the sample source code provided in the CEPB. The directories `.\PLATFORM\<Platform Name>\BOOTLOAD` (CEPB 2.12 only), `.\PLATFORM\<Platform Name>\EBOOT`, and `.\PLATFORM\<Platform`

Name>\DUB (CEPB 3.0 only) contain the sample boot loaders for specific platforms. The source for each platform appears in separate subdirectories under the .\PLATFORM directory, with each subdirectory named after the platform type. In the case of the Odo platform, many different processors are supported, so the .\PLATFORM\ODO\BOOTLOAD (CEPB 2.12) directory and the .\PLATFORM\ODO\EBOOT\EBOOT (CEPB 3.0) directory isolate the processor-dependent source code using more subdirectories, named after the CPU or CPU family.

Table 4.1 lists all of the sample boot loader directories and summarizes their contents. As we discuss the common aspects of all boot loaders in subsequent sections, we will reference these directories to illustrate certain concepts.

Table 4.1 Platform Directories Containing Sample Boot Loader Code

Path	Description
.\PLATFORM\ODO\BOOTLOAD (CEPB 2.12)	Contains the files required to build the boot loader for the Odo platform targeted to the specified processor. (See Chapter 10 for more information on how to build for specific target processors.)
.\PLATFORM\ODO\BOOTLOAD\COMMON (CEPB 2.12)	Contains the processor-independent boot loader code used in downloading the kernel image and configuring the Odo platform. The kernel image is downloaded via your platform's onboard parallel port and the host program CESH. The destination of the downloaded image is either RAM or flash memory, depending on the destination address encoded in the BIN file.
.\PLATFORM\ODO\BOOTLOAD\DOCS (CEPB 2.12)	Contains documentation on the setup options of the Odo platform, as well as a document describing how to download and debug an image using only an Ethernet port, instead of the combination of a parallel and serial port.
.\PLATFORM\ODO\BOOTLOAD\<CPU Type> (CEPB 2.12)	Contains the processor-dependent source code used to configure the target processor, to set up the stack for execution of the portion of the boot loader written in C, and to provide processor-dependent utility routines called by the boot loader source in the .\PLATFORM\ODO\BOOTLOAD\ subdirectory. The code in this directory is the first to run during power-on reset.
.\PLATFORM\ODO\EBOOT (CEPB 2.12), .\PLATFORM\ODO\EBOOT\EBOOT (CEPB 3.0)	Contains another type of boot loader for the Odo platform that provides support for downloading the kernel image using an Ethernet port, instead of the parallel port as in the boot loader under the BOOTLOAD directory. The contents of this

(continued)

Table 4.1 *Continued.*

Path	Description
	directory are slightly different from those of the `BOOTLOAD` directory. It contains the files required to build the boot loader, in addition to the processor-independent code.
`.\PLATFORM\ODO\EBOOT\<CPU Type>` (CEPB 2.12), `.\PLATFORM\ODO\EBOOT\EBOOT\<CPU Type>` (CEPB 3.0)	Contains another type of boot loader for the Odo Contains the processor-dependent source code used to configure the target processor. Also provides functionality similar to the processor-dependent source code in the `.\PLATFORM\ODO\BOOTLOAD\<CPU Type>` directory.
`.\PLATFORM\ODO\EBOOT\BOOT2RAM` (CEPB 2.12)	Contains a special boot loader that copies the kernel image into RAM. The kernel image itself is represented as a BIN file in the `FILES` section of the `boot.bib` file. The startup code determines the destination address in RAM of the kernel image by reading the image record header of the kernel image BIN file.
`.\PLATFORM\ODO\EBOOT\BOOT2RAM\<CPU Type>` (CEPB 2.12)	Contains the processor-dependent source code used in configuring the target processor, and provides functionality similar to the other processor-dependent source code directories presented in this table.
`.\PLATFORM\ODO<Model Number>\` (CEPB 2.12)	Acts as the parent directory to the sample boot loaders provided for other models of the Odo platform.
`.\PLATFORM\ODODUB\DUB` (CEBP 3.0)	Contains a dial-up boot loader (DUB) designed to download the kernel image from a remote host, connected via modem. This is also the parent directory for other directories that contain the host application source code and utilities, used by DUB to request a kernel image from the remote host.
`.\PLATFORM\ODODUB\DUB\BOOT` (CEBP 3.0)	Contains the dial-up boot loader source code for an Odo platform based on a StrongARM processor.

Startup Code

When a processor is first activated or, as it is more commonly described in hardware reference manuals, when it enters power-on reset mode, the program counter (the register in the processor that contains the address of the currently executing instruction) is set to an initial value. This value differs between processors and in some cases is determined by the address contained in a reserved memory location. In the latter case, the processor loads the initial value of the program counter from the reserved memory location. The CE startup code corresponds to the first code executed during power-on reset and has the responsibility to set the stage for the execution of subsequent boot loader code, in addition to that of the CE kernel.

Typically, the startup code is written in the assembly language of the target processor to allow the use of specialized op codes required for processor configuration during power-on reset mode. The startup code generally concludes by setting up a minimal environment for the execution of the `main` routine, which is written in C. The sample startup source code provided in the CEPB boot loaders for various processors generally conforms to the following sequence:

1. Initialization of internal timers
2. Configuration of the memory controller
3. Activation of the processor's onboard cache
4. Configuration of the processor's internal peripheral interfaces, such as that for a serial port
5. Relocation of the boot loader to cached memory for processors that initialize the program counter to an uncached address

The real focus of our efforts will be in determining how the CEPB sample startup source code provided for the processor on your custom platform needs to be changed. Using the SHx sample startup source code, we will begin our decomposition. When we reach a section of source code that should be analyzed for possible modification to support your custom platform, we will describe why the modification is required in the context of the SHx processor family. This same process of decomposition/analysis/modification (DAM) may be used on any of the startup sample source code provided in the CEPB.

Note:
Many third-party CE systems integrators now provide boot loaders tailor-made for certain reference platforms. These products are commonly referred to as board support packages (BSPs) or accelerator kits, and they are often installed over the CEPB directory tree, enabling you to produce a build of the CE boot loader and kernel image for the supported reference platform without changing any code. These reference platforms are typically made available by hardware manufacturers to show off the capabilities of their processor (or peripheral device) in the context of a complete working platform, and they are an excellent resource when your own custom hardware is still in development. See Appendix C for a list of CE system integrators.

Beginning with the file `init.src` located in the CEPB 2.12 directory `.\PLATFORM\ODO\EBOOT\SHX` or the CEPB 3.0 directory `.\PLATFORM\ODO\EBOOT\EBOOT\SHX`, find the `StartUp` routine, positioned just after a long list of equates. (The term *equates* is commonly used to refer to the constants defined in an assembly language source file and is synonymous with the *#define* syntax in C.) This routine is defined through the use of the `Sources` file (described in more detail later in this chapter) as the primary entry point into the boot loader. It is not the first code to execute during power-on reset of the SHx, however, because the first few bytes of the boot loader image file, produced as a product of the boot loader build, contain a jump instruction to the address of the `StartUp` routine. Certain entries in the `boot.bib` file control how execution passes to the `StartUp` routine; they are explained later in this chapter.

Certain sections of the file `init.src` are presented as the source code is decomposed, but you may want to refer to the CEPB for a complete copy of this file. We will not explore the intricacies of SHx assembly language, but you may be able to infer the syntax simply from the functional explanation of the code. If not, the Chipset Reference section of the CEPB online documentation provides programming guides for all CE-supported processors.

Listing 4.1 contains the first few lines of `StartUp` routine excerpted from `init.src` in CEPB 2.12. A comparable version of `init.src` can be found in CEPB 3.0 under the `.\PLA FORM\ODO\EBOOT\EBOOT\SHX` directory. The first line of code initializes the value of the `r8` register with the address of the LED port. This address is used by the `WRITE_LED` macro that displays a numeric value, acting as a limited `printf`-style function to report progress through the startup code. This is a key requirement for development of the `StartUp` routine because the Microsoft-supplied CE debugging tools are not yet loaded. Refer to the section titled Debugging the Boot Loader later in this chapter for more information on the use of hardware-assisted third-party debugging tools that support startup code debugging.

Listing 4.1 Beginning of the SHx `StartUp` routine in the `.\PLATFORM\ODO\BOOTLOAD\SHX` directory

```
; Beginning of code excerpted from .\PLATFORM\ODO\BOOTLOAD\SHX\INIT.SRC

...

        LEAF_ENTRY _StartUp

        mov       #0xA4040000,r8              ; Set up WRITE_LEDS macro

        WRITE_LEDS       0x01

...

; End of code excerpted from .\PLATFORM\ODO\BOOTLOAD\SHX\INIT.SRC
```

The startup code in Listing 4.1 will probably need to be modified for your custom platform. This code assumes that the LED may be accessed at address `0xA4040000`, which may not be true for your custom platform.

In each of the following sections we will continue to apply DAM to the remainder of the CEPB sample `StartUp` routine presented in Listing 4.1.

Processor Configuration Code

The first thing you must do in most boot loader code is configure the processor on your custom platform. As implied in the term *processor configuration,* the processor may not be fully functional until certain configuration steps are completed. It is difficult to describe precisely what those steps are for every processor because each processor varies in its capabilities and degree of integration. Most manufacturers today offer processors with an internal bus that connects what could have required discrete logic into a single package. Operations that are supported gluelessly (i.e., with the processor pinouts wired directly to the peripheral) include the memory interface, synchronous and asynchronous serial communications interfaces, and video controller and LCD panel interfaces.

Note:
We have found that one of the few downsides to this approach is that often more features are provided than we intend to support on our custom platform. Manufacturers have begun to address this concern by generating a plethora of processor spin-offs, each targeted to a specific market segment. These segments and their common feature sets are identified by the manufacturer, resulting in the birth of a new part number in the same processor family. If your business maps well to one of these identified segments, you're in good shape, and you will find a processor that has the potential to significantly reduce the size and cost of your bill of materials.

For many platform designs the sample processor configuration code provided in the CEPB is adequate, requiring few or no changes, except to reflect the correct memory map and configuration values required for your custom platform. Most processor manufacturers also offer sample configuration code on their Web sites to demonstrate processor configuration for a particular reference platform. Such sample code is an excellent starting point in the development of your own processor configuration code. The key point to remember is not to start from scratch. The processor configuration code, above all other code, can be quite troublesome and difficult to debug if developed from scratch. Though it is a small amount of code, it generally requires a specialized knowledge of the processor that takes time to acquire—time that projects rarely have in abundance.

So, assuming that you have found this sample code somewhere (refer to the section titled Beginning with the Sample Code earlier in this chapter for more information on where this sample code is located), we are ready to continue the DAM process started in the previous section using the SHx `StartUp` routine provided as a CEPB sample boot loader.

Listing 4.2 contains the next section of the file `init.src`, which is dedicated to SHx processor configuration. Each step in the configuration, as it applies to an SH3 processor, is described in the inline comments that appear in the listing. The configuration begins with the initialization of the status register `sr`. The value `TM_SR` places the processor in privileged mode, sets up the general registers, enables interrupts and exceptions, and defines the interrupt mask level to a value that allows all interrupts. A numeric LED is updated to let the outside world know how far we have progressed, just in case the processor locks up in subsequent instructions. Including a numeric LED is a good habit for debugging startup code and is discussed, along with other more advanced debugging techniques, in the section titled Debugging the Boot Loader later in this chapter.

The next step configures the SH3 on-chip timers, including both the watchdog timer and the crystal oscillator used to drive the CKIO (clock I/O) line from which other timed events, such as memory refresh, are driven. You should carefully examine this code to determine if the clock frequency is appropriate for your particular platform and processor.

The glueless memory interface of the SH3 is configured next. This is the area most likely to differ on your custom platform. The requirements of your application will determine the type and configuration of memory you use. The SH3, like other processors offering built-in memory controllers, supports many options, each offering their own cost and performance tradeoffs. With flexibility comes complexity, and the memory configuration code is no exception. After examining how the current code sets each bit in each memory register, modify the value of the initialization constants to reflect the differences in your configuration.

Configuring the processor's internal cache is the last step in the processor configuration. First, flush the cache to place it in a known state after power-on reset; then enable it in write-through mode. If your platform is SH4 based, you will want to consider modifying this code to configure the advanced cache options of the SH4 over the SH3. You may also want to delay activation of the cache while debugging the remaining platform configuration startup code. When more advanced debug tools are in use, such as those described in the section titled Debugging the Boot Loader later in this chapter, the instruction trace capabilities of the debugger may not function properly during execution of code directly from cache.

Other sample boot loaders provided in the CEPB continue processor configuration by initializing any other registers that configure the remaining built-in functions. Included are the PC card (PCMCIA) registers that configure the built-in PC card controller.

Listing 4.2 Sample SH3 processor configuration excerpted from the CEPB

```
; Code excerpted from .\PLATFORM\ODO\BOOTLOAD\SHX\INIT.SRC

...

; Initialization of the Status Register:
; privilege mode enabled, general registers assigned to bank 1,
; and all interrupts enabled.  JYW

    mov.l    TM_SR,r0
    ldc      r0,sr

    WRITE_LEDS       0x02

; -----------------------------------------------------
; TIMER CONFIGURATION:
; -----------------------------------------------------

; Initialize the Watchdog Control/Status Register:
; Disable the watchdog timer for now, but configure the
; clock input to the Watchdog Timer Counter register to
; the peripheral clock divided by 16.  JYW

    mov.l    #CPG_WTCSR,r2
    mov.w    #InitialWTCSR,r1
    mov.w    r1,@r2
    nop

; Initialize the Watchdog Timer Counter register to
; COUNT_INIT.  JYW
```

```
    mov.l   #CPG_WTCNT,r2
    mov.w   #COUNT_INIT,r1
    mov.w   r1,@r2
    nop

; Initialize the Frequency Control Register to configure
; the on-chip crystal oscillator:  Enable the internal
; PLL circuit, leaving it in standby mode, establish a
; PLL multiplication ratio of 4, and set the internal
; and peripheral clock frequency dividers to 1.  JYW

    mov.l   #CPG_FRQCR,r2
    mov.w   #InitialFRQCR,r1
    mov.w   r1,@r2
    nop

    WRITE_LEDS  0x03

; ------------------------------------------------------
; MEMORY INTERFACE CONFIGURATION:
; ------------------------------------------------------

; Configure the memory interface to support the memory
; technology in use on our custom platform.  This and the
; other memory-related registers may need to be modified
; in derivative products if the memory configuration
; changes.  Do not access memory outside external area 0
; until after all memory configuration steps are
; complete. JYW
;
; Initialize Bus Control Register 1: Physical memory
; areas 0, 1, 2, 4, and 5 are connected to normal
; ROM ("normal memory" in SHx parlance), physical memory
; area 3 is connected to DRAM, and physical memory area 6 is
; reserved for PCMCIA access .
; Note that areas 1 and 4 may be connected only to normal
; ROM. JYW

    mov.l   #BCN_BCR1,r2
    mov.l   #InitialBCR1,r1
    .aif SH_CPU eq h'40
    mov.l   r1,@r2
    .aelse
    mov.w   r1,@r2
    .aendi
    nop

; Configure the bus size for each memory area.  Like the
; configuration of BCR1, this code may need to be
; modified for derivative products.  JYW
;
; Intialize Bus Control Register 2: All physical memory
; areas with the exception of 6, which is reserved for
; PCMCIA access, are 32 bits wide.  Area 6 is 8 bits wide.
```

```
; Data lines 23 through 16 are not used as an 8-bit port.
; JYW

    mov.l    #BCN_BCR2,r2
    mov.w    #InitialBCR2,r1
    mov.w    r1,@r2
    nop

; Initialize the Memory Control Register for access to
; DRAM in physical memory area 3:  Enable high-speed page
; mode access to normal (non-EDO) DRAM, set the data bus
; size to 32 bits (takes precedence over this same
; setting in BCR2), enable address multiplexing for DRAM
; using a 12-bit column address product, enable "ordinary"
; refresh of DRAM.  The read/write precharge, RAS/CAS
; delay, and the refresh RAS assert time are set to their
; default values.  JYW

    WRITE_LEDS  0x04

    mov.l    #BCN_MCR,r2
    mov.l    #InitialMCR,r1
    .aif SH_CPU eq h'40
    mov.l    r1,@r2
    .aelse
    mov.w    r1,@r2
    .aendi
    nop

; Initialize the Refresh Timer Control/Status Register:
; Set the value of the CKIO divisor used to generate the
; the clock input to the Refresh Timer Counter register.
; Leave all other settings in this register to the
; default values.

    mov.l    #BCN_RTCSR,r2
    mov.w    #InitialRTCSR,r1
    mov.w    r1,@r2
    nop

; Initialize the Refresh Timer Counter register: Set the
; initial value of the counter to 0.

    mov.l    #BCN_RTCNT,r2
    mov.w    #InitialRTCNT,r1
    mov.w    r1,@r2
    nop

; Initialize the Refresh Timer Constant register: Set
; the value to 144 to cause a refresh to occur when the
; RTCNT register reaches this same value.  JYW

    mov.l    #BCN_RTCOR,r2
    mov.w    #InitialRTCOR,r1
```

```
    mov.w   r1,@r2
    nop

    WRITE_LEDS  0x05

; Initialize the value of Wait State Control
; register 1:  Specify the number of wait states to
; insert when access to one physical memory area is
; followed by subsequent access to another physical
; memory area: 0 wait states for DRAM in physical memory
; area 3; 1 wait state each for physical memory areas 1, 2, 4,
; 5, and 6; and 2 wait states for physical memory area 0.
; JYW

    mov.l   #BCN_WCR1,r2
    mov.l   #InitialWCR1,r1              ;
    .aif SH_CPU eq h'40
    mov.l   r1,@r2
    .aelse
    mov.w   r1,@r2
    .aendi
    nop

; Initialize the value of Wait State Control register
; 2:  Specify the number of wait states to insert in each
; memory cycle for each physical memory area: 0 wait
; states for physical memory areas 6, 5 and 3; 1 wait
; state for physical memory area 4; 2 wait states for
; physical memory area 0; and 3 wait states for physical
; memory area 2 (ROM).  JYW

    mov.l   #BCN_WCR2,r2
    mov.l   #InitialWCR2,r1
    .aif SH_CPU eq h'40
    mov.l   r1,@r2
    .aelse
    mov.w   r1,@r2
    .aendi
    nop

; Initialize the value of Wait State Control register
; 3: This register is unavailable on the SH3 processor,
; which is assumed in this example.  JYW

    .aif SH_CPU eq h'40
    mov.l   #BCN_WCR3,r2
    mov.l   #InitialWCR3,r1
    mov.l   r1,@r2
    nop
    .aendi

    WRITE_LEDS      0x06
```

```
; --------------------------------------------------------
; CACHE CONFIGURATION:
; --------------------------------------------------------

; Initialize the value of the Cache Control Register:
; First flush the cache, then enable the cache in write-
; through mode.   JYW

        mov         #CCN_CCR,r2
        mov         #FlushCCR,r1
        mov.l       r1,@r2

        mov         #EnableCCR, r1
        mov.l       r1,@r2
        nop
        nop
        nop

        WRITE_LEDS          0x07
...
```

Platform Configuration Code

As is true of the processor configuration code between processors, the platform configuration code varies between platforms. Note that platform variation occurs not when processors differ between platforms, but when a particular aspect of the platform configuration differs. In this context we are using the term *platform* to describe the entire device, with the exception of the device's processor. In this way we can differentiate between platform and processor dependencies. It is true that most platforms would require major modifications to support a different processor, but in many cases the selection of peripherals (Ethernet adapter, video controller, flash memory devices, and so on) on this platform could remain unchanged. The mechanism for the interface to these devices might change, but the methods for using them might not. In this section we will focus on the aspects of the platform configuration that are most common in all platforms. The sample boot loader in the `.\PLATFORM\ODO\BOOTLOAD` (CEPB 2.12) directory will continue to act as our primary example of how these common aspects are implemented.

Platform configuration, at least for the purposes of a CE boot loader, begins in the `main` routine, to which the code jumps from the `StartUp` routine. Figure 4.2 depicts the sequence of events for configuration of the Odo platform in the sample boot loader located in the `.\PLATFORM\ODO\BOOTLOAD` (CEPB 2.12) directory (a comparable file exists for CEPB 3.0 in the `.\WINCE300\PLATFORM\ODO\EBOOT\EBOOT` directory).

Before you can safely run any other C code in `main.c`, you must initialize the remainder of the C environment by calling the `KernelRelocate` function. This function is provided in source code form in the `main.c` file and should be copied directly to your boot loader's `main.c` file. It works by using the global variable `pTOC` (described in the section titled Romimage Build Tool later in this chapter) to access the beginning of the writable data section in the boot loader image. A `for` loop processes each copy entry in sequence by copying the values for initialized global variables into RAM and setting the uninitialized variables to 0.

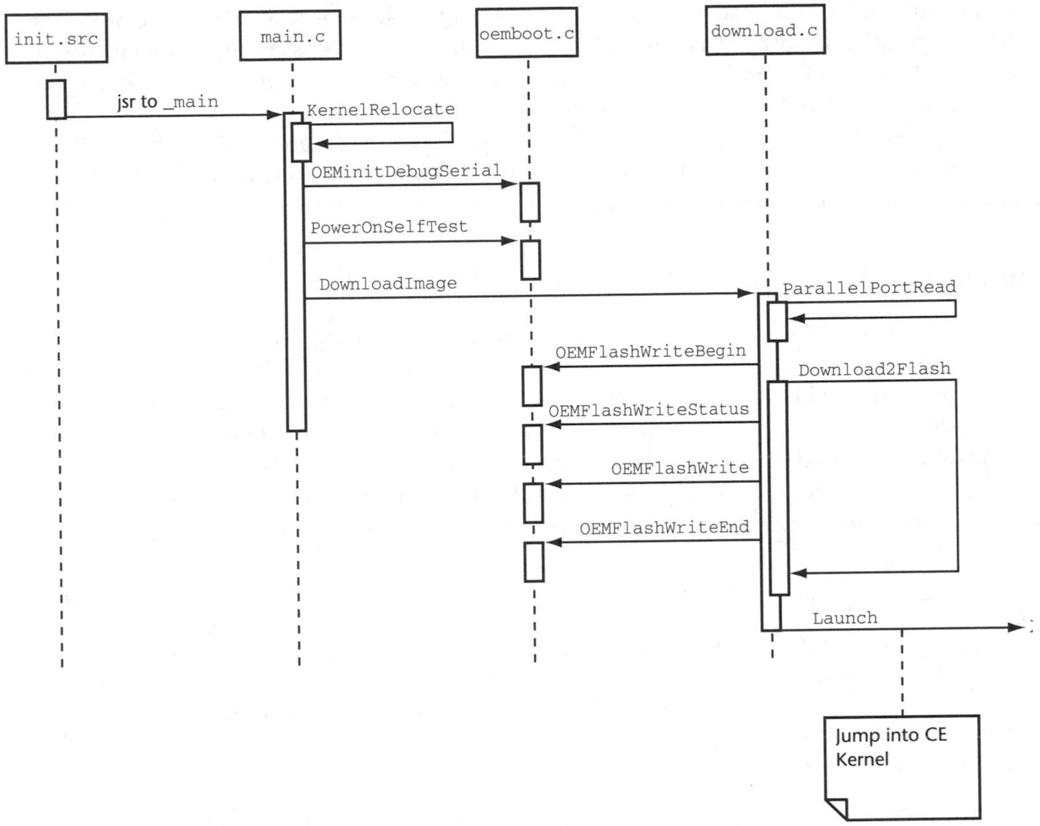

init.src
main.c
oemboot.c
download.c
jsr to _main
KernelRelocate
OEMinitDebugSerial
PowerOnSelfTest
DownloadImage
ParallelPortRead
OEMFlashWriteBegin
Download2Flash
OEMFlashWriteStatus
OEMFlashWrite
OEMFlashWriteEnd
Launch
Jump into CE Kernel

Figure 4.2 Sequence diagram for configuration of the Odo platform

In most cases the writable data section of a particular module is compressed and you may not process it by simply copying its contents into RAM, as was performed in the `KernelRelocate` function. Because the `boot.bib` file (used by the Romimage build tool to generate the boot loader image file) sets the `COMPRESSION` entry to `OFF`, this constraint is not a problem. We'll say more about the contents of a `boot.bib` file later in the chapter.

Note:
Romimage is a build utility that is run at the end of the build process to locate an EXE module to run at a particular address.

The next step uses an OEM function to initialize the serial port. This initialization is performed immediately after `KernelRelocate` is called so that the debug message macros can be used as soon as possible. At this point the Odo platform and processor are fully configured, and the real work of the boot loader may commence. As Figure 4.2 shows, the Power-On Self-Test (POST) operation is initiated, and if it succeeds, the download process for the kernel image is initiated. If the POST fails, a firmware monitor is started to provide a command-line debugging interface over the serial port. Note that in the sample code, the call to the `PowerOnSelfTest` function is commented out and is provided only as placeholder of a potential capability. These final steps in the platform configuration, including the Power-On Self-Test, are discussed in more detail in the next few sections.

Initializing the Contents of RAM

One step in your platform configuration that you may want to consider is the initialization of the entire contents of your custom platform's RAM. In standard, consumer-level CE devices, RAM is battery backed and is used to maintain the CE internal file system known as the object store. If your custom platform leaves the contents of RAM in an unknown state after a cold boot, RAM initialization is a good idea. Otherwise, when the CE kernel loads the object store driver, it may mistake the unintended contents of RAM as a valid object store. This mistake can, in some cases, cause an unhandled exception when the driver accesses invalid object store data.

Note:
During a warm boot (manual reset), RAM should not be initialized. This is true even if your custom platform does not provide battery-backed RAM because the contents of RAM are generally retained during a warm boot for both types of platforms.

The method used for initializing RAM may seem intuitively obvious: Simply write a whole lot of zeros to every location in RAM not currently in use by the boot loader. The following line of source code will do just that by clearing the RAM addresses referenced in the `ROMHDR` structure:

```
memset((LPVOID)RomHdr.ulRAMStart, 0, RomHdr.ulRAMEnd-RomHdr.ulRAMStart);
```

The address of the `ROMHDR` structure itself is contained in the reserved variable `pTOC` and is described in more detail in the section titled Romimage Build Tool later in this chapter. If your custom platform provides a large amount of RAM, this approach could significantly delay the overall duration of your platform's boot sequence. If such delay is a problem, there is an alternative.

Assuming that your only concern is to avoid a crash of the object store during initialization of the kernel image, you really just need a method of invalidating the accidental contents of RAM in a way that prevents the object store from considering it valid. One method for doing this is to search the location in RAM used by the object store for the character string *EKIM* (*MIKE* spelled backward) (Spurgat 1999), overwriting it with `NULL` values. The starting address of your search is contained in the `ulObjstoreStart` member of the ROM header (`ROMHDR`) structure. Note that this method of invalidating an existing object store is highly version dependent and may not be effective in future versions of CE.

Power-On Self-Test

The Power-On Self-Test (POST) is an operational mode in which the system software in your custom platform attempts to identify, and perhaps even diagnose, a hardware problem. The term *POST* is more commonly used to describe the boot sequence for PCs than for custom platforms with more limited functionality. Because Windows CE supports the construction of PC-like devices, it is a good idea to consider including POST code in the CE boot loader.

Before you decide whether to commit your precious programming resources to such a task, let's consider the advantages and disadvantages. The first and most obvious advantage is the early identification of defective hardware. A user who has been informed that his or her device is malfunctioning is more likely to seek the correct remedy than to attribute the problem to unreliable software while continuing to use the device with increasing levels of frustration. Taking a broader view, including POST code might also help in repair of the device if the POST code is capable of reporting which subsystem is faulty. This capability could very well be extended to the manufacturing process used to mass-produce your device.

If your device is sufficiently complex, your manufacturing process may include a burn-in test that repeatedly tests your device over a long period of time. This acts as a kind of stress test and is designed to simulate long-term usage compressed into a short time period. Your POST code could be used as the basis of the burn-in test and could operate over an extended period of time in a special burn-in test mode. You could even use a communications peripheral on your device to transmit test results to a PC acting as a test server that logs the collective test results of all devices in burn-in test mode.

That being said, let's look at the disadvantages. The use of POST code compromises one of the distinct advantages of embedded devices: the ability to frequently cycle power without the tedious startup delays common to desktop PCs. A long POST may frustrate users who expect instant-on behavior. You may be able to remedy this problem by limiting the execution of POST to a cold boot. Since cold boots occur less often, this would lengthen the startup sequence far less frequently.

Note:
A cold boot in this context can be defined as a startup sequence from an unpowered state, as when the device is completely powered off. A cold boot is therefore distinguished from a warm boot, which is a startup sequence from a low-power or Suspend state, and from a reset that is manually initiated by the end user. These power states are explained in more detail in Chapter 1.

Another option for the activation of POST is to allow it to be manually selected by the user through the device's user interface, possibly appearing as a dialog box of the type displayed in Figure 4.3. If the end user selected a particular test, the application would write a designated value into a reserved location in EPROM. This value would be read by the boot loader on reset, causing it to execute all or some of the POST operations as specified.

Let's assume for now that you have carefully considered these issues and you have decided to include POST code in your custom platform's boot loader. The next question is what hardware the POST code might actually test and how this test might be accomplished. As with the boot loader itself, it is difficult to provide one example that suits all platforms. We can, however,

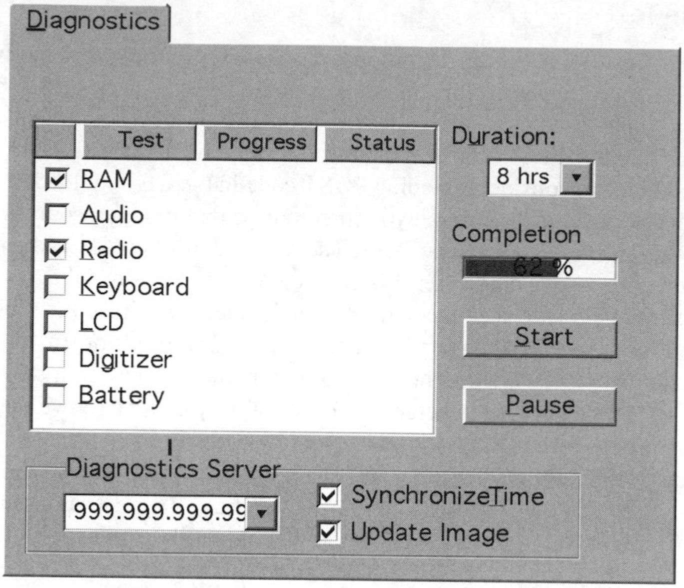

Figure 4.3 Possible user interface for end user control of POST

consider the general requirements of the POST code and where it might be added to the sample CEPB boot loaders. If, for example, your device conformed to the reference design of a Windows-based terminal, you would test the subsystems listed in Table 4.2.

Writing the test code for a particular subsystem is no small feat. It requires that the engineer have an understanding of nearly all of the subsystem's capabilities, including how they might fail. If the subsystem consists of a particular peripheral with a built-in self-test mode, the job is greatly simplified because the device itself does most of the work of determining its operational state. In either case, you might consider establishing a department-level design standard for the development of your CE device drivers that requires the inclusion of a specialized testing interface. This standard would then allow you to reuse the expertise acquired during development of these drivers, and possibly some amount of the actual driver code used in basic communications with the peripheral.

If you adopt this practice, keep in mind that *stream-interface drivers* exist as DLL modules. This implies that they may be loaded only after the CE kernel is loaded. Therefore, be certain that you also specify that the portion of the driver code dedicated to self-test operations exist as a modular add-on to the driver that can be statically linked into the boot loader image. Since *native drivers* (which will be explored in Chapter 7) often exist as object module libraries linked directly into the kernel, the requirement for static linkage with the boot loader should not be a problem.

The CEPB sample boot loaders make a minor reference to the need for Power-On Self-Test functionality by calling the `PowerOnSelfTest` function. Listing 4.3 contains the excerpt of the file `main.c` in the `.\PLATFORM\ODO\BOOTLOAD\COMMON` (CEPB 2.12) directory that calls this function. The `PowerOnSelfTest` function is called unconditionally, and if it is successful, the download process is initiated. Potential modifications to this code include checking a reserved

Table 4.2 POST Requirements of a Windows-Based Terminal

Subsystem under Test	Interactive[a]	Automatic[b]	Driver Support[c]	External Peripheral Device[d]
Battery		√		Battery pack
RAM		√	√	
EEPROM		√		
Flash EPROM		√	√	
PC card socket		√		
Radio		√		Wireless LAN PC card
RS-232		√	√	
Mouse	√	√		PS/2 mouse
Keyboard	√	√		PS/2 keyboard
LCD	√			LCD panel
Pen	√			Digitizer controller
Audio	√			Audio controller

[a] Indicates whether the test may be controlled manually through outside intervention, perhaps by a technician or assembly line worker.
[b] Indicates whether the test may be run in a mode requiring no outside intervention for completion of the test sequence.
[c] Indicates whether the CE drivers developed for this platform may be used to test the associated subsystem.
[d] Indicates the type of onboard peripheral required for the particular subsystem if one is required.

location in EPROM (as described earlier) for a designated value that indicates the type of self-test, if any, to run. If the Power-On Self-Test fails, you could take any number of actions, some of which have already been discussed. If the self-test were executing as part of a long-term burn-in, you could transmit the test results to the test server. You could also execute a ROM monitor program that provides an interface for communicating with the device from a PC serial terminal.

Listing 4.3 CEPB sample boot loader activation of Power-On Self-Test

```
...

if (PowerOnSelfTest()) {
    //
    // If Power-On Self-Test returns 0,
    // we'll jump to the debugger directly.
    // This doesn't mean the debugger will run (since the system fails
    // to pass the test).  However, since the failure is most likely in
    // an I/O device (hopefully not the monitor port),
    // which is not required for the debugger to successfully run,
    // it may still work.
    //
    DownloadImage(NULL, &vAddr, 1);
}

...
```

Loading the CE Image

One thing that you may immediately notice about Windows CE boot loaders is that, unlike PC-based operating systems, you do not have to load the operating system image into RAM before jumping to its starting address. Depending on the configuration of your platform, you may simply be required to jump to a certain address in ROM (or flash memory). If the CE image is stored on disk-based media of some kind, you first need to read it from the disk into a predetermined location in RAM. Your configuration may also require that you copy the writable data sections of the CE image from ROM into RAM. Figuring out what your configuration requires is the subject of the next few sections.

Downloading Code

In the "old days," what feels like yesterday to some of us, it was not uncommon to reprogram nonvolatile storage media, typically ultraviolet erasable ROM devices, every time a source code change was made and required testing. To remedy this situation, most of the sample CEPB boot loaders provide the capability for downloading the CE kernel from a remote host. In most cases you would probably designate your development workstation as your remote host because this is where the kernel image would reside upon completion of the build process.

Note:
Download in this context refers to the flow of data from the perspective of the CE platform. Data flows *down*stream from the remote host to the CE platform. If we were to use the term *upload,* we would be describing an *up*stream data flow from the CE platform to the remote host.

We mention this distinction just to eliminate any confusion that may arise as you read the online documentation in Platform Builder. The term *download* is incorrectly used to describe the flow of data to the CE platform from the perspective of the remote host. In this case the term *upload* would be more correct because data is being pushed upstream to the CE platform from the remote host.

The sample boot loaders use either the parallel port or an Ethernet port as the transport medium to connect to the remote host. The sample boot loaders for the platform designated in <*Platform Name*> in the `.\PLATFORM\<Platform Name>\BOOTLOAD` (CEPB 2.12) directory use a parallel port for downloading the kernel image, while the ones in the `.\PLATFORM\<Platform Name>\EBOOT` (CEPB 2.12 and CEPB 3.0) directory use an Ethernet port. The boot loader in the `.\PLATFORM\<Platform Name>\EBOOT\BOOT2RAM` (CEPB 2.12) directory provides support for booting a kernel image that is not really downloaded. The kernel image is actually included as a file in the build of the boot loader via an entry in the `FILES` section of the `boot.bib` file (described later in this chapter).

Note:

It is unclear to us why `BOOT2RAM` is a subdirectory under `EBOOT`. Upon careful examination, it does not use any of the code in `EBOOT`, the parent subdirectory, nor does it define a specific processor type as the other subdirectories under **`EBOOT`** do. In our installed copy of CEPB 2.12, we have opted to relocate the `BOOT2RAM` directory tree to the `.\PLATFORM\<Platform Name>\` parent directory so that its relationship to the `BOOTLOAD` and `EBOOT` boot loaders is clearly represented as a separate type of boot loader.

In theory, the boot loader for your custom hardware could incorporate elements of all three boot loaders, and even add support for downloading the kernel image over yet another transport medium, such as a serial port. It would be possible for this boot loader to systematically check each available transport medium, determining if the connection to the remote host was active, then initiating the download over the identified medium. If none of the transport mediums were active, you would determine if a kernel image were present in ROM or flash memory. If the image were valid, you would either jump to this address directly if the image were formatted as an NBx file (executable code), or copy the image into RAM if it were formatted as a BIN file. In the latter case, the same routines used to download the image through an active transport medium would be used to copy the image into the memory region designated in the BIN file records. Figure 4.4 presents a Harel state chart depicting this process.

Note:

Harel state chart notation was used as the basis of the behavioral models of the Unified Modeling Language (UML) and is based on finite-state machines. Harel state charts are more powerful than the more common Mealy-Moore state charts because they provide support for nesting of states, concurrency, guards on transitions, propagated transitions, actions on transitions, actions on state entry, actions on state exit, and actions that occur only while a state is active.

To create such a comprehensive boot loader, you'll need to learn a few more things. In particular, how is a valid kernel image identified, including BIN file record format processed in downloading a kernel image or copying it from ROM to RAM? These questions will be answered in the next few sections. The SHx sample boot loader will demonstrate some of these concepts. We do not, however, present an example of a boot loader that is as capable as the theoretical model just described. Even though we always dreaded reading college textbooks with the phrase *left to the reader as an exercise,* we too must now resort to the same escape.

Let's get down to the details. We'll begin by describing the download process relative to the SHx sample boot loader and returning to the decomposition/analysis/modification of `main.c` in the `.\PLATFORM\ODO\BOOTLOAD\COMMON` (CEPB 2.12) directory. Just after successful execution of the `PowerOnSelfTest` function, the `DownloadImage` function, which is located in the file `.\PLATFORM\ODO\BOOTLOAD\COMMON\download.c` and depicted in Figure 4.5, is called. This function sends a boot packet to the remote host through the parallel port. If the boot packet

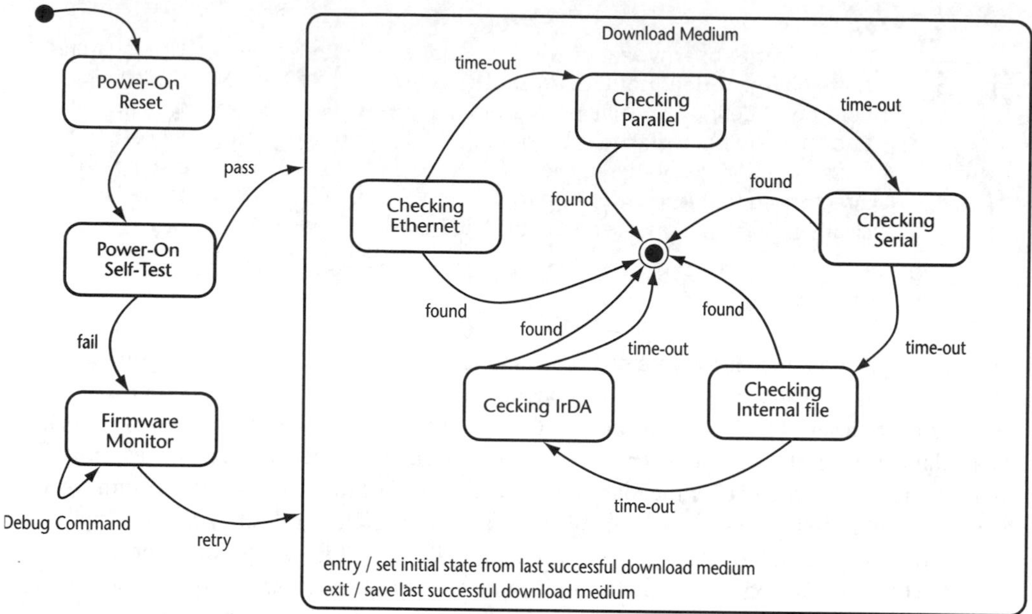

Figure 4.4 State chart of a multimedium boot loader

is properly acknowledged through a predefined byte sequence beginning with the character B, the next step in the download process begins.

> ***Note:***
> Only BIN files can be downloaded by this boot loader because only BIN files contain enough information to allow the download to proceed with no assumptions about the location of the downloaded data. The download of SRE files, however, would require that the starting address be hard-coded.

The next eight bytes retrieved describe the physical starting address and length of the kernel image. The starting address is then checked to determine if it corresponds to a flash ROM (since flash technology may be programmatically rewritten without the benefit of an external PROM programmer) or RAM address, resulting in a call to either `Download2Flash` or `Download2RAM`. The method used to determine if the address is a valid flash ROM address is simply to call the `OEMFlashWriteBegin` function (described in more detail in the section titled OEM Boot Loader Functions a little later in this chapter). If the address passed to this function is a valid address, the flash routines and the flash hardware will be configured, ultimately resulting in a call to the `Download2Flash` function. This process repeats for each received data record so that they may be written to separate blocks of flash memory. Note that if your `OEMFlashWriteBegin` function does not return a 0 value, indicating success, the download will occur as though the starting address corresponds to a RAM address and the `Download2RAM` function will be called. If there is any chance that your implementation of the

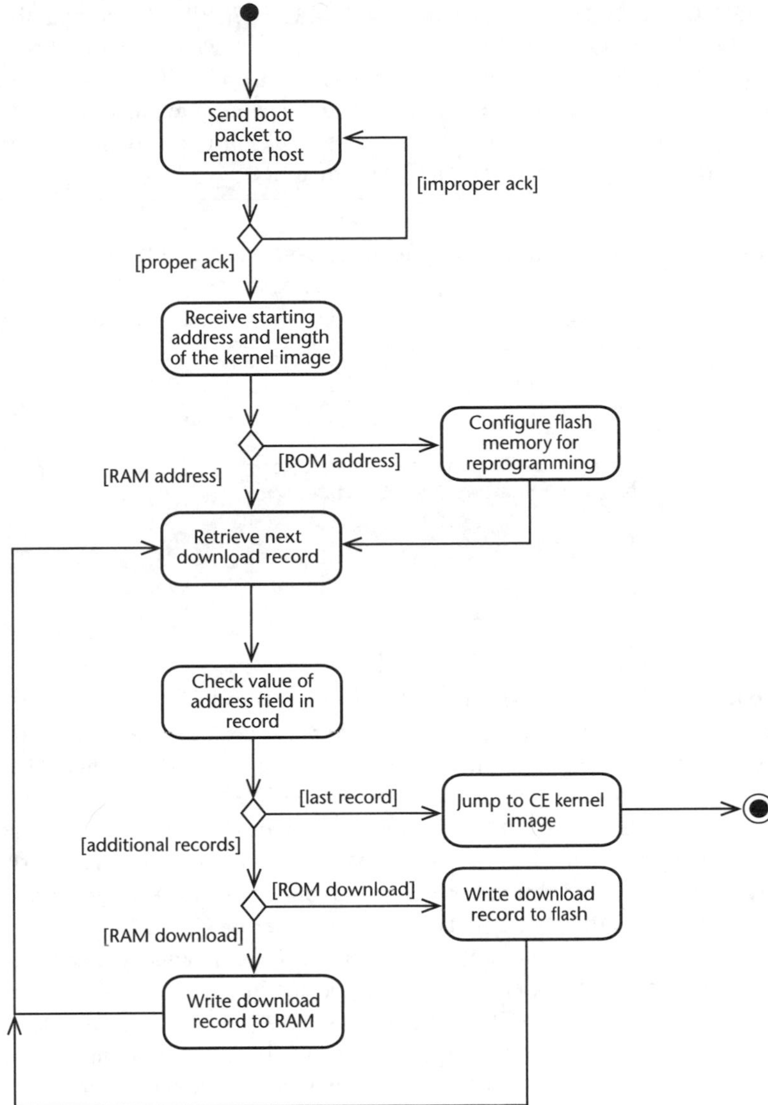

Figure 4.5 Activity diagram of the `DownloadImage` function

`OEMFlashWriteBegin` function could fail for any reason other than an invalid starting address parameter, you should modify the calling code in `main.c` to process additional return values.

Jumping into the CE Kernel Image

The last step in the kernel image download process requires that you jump to the starting address of the kernel image. The last 4 bytes received at the conclusion of the download correspond to the starting address. Let's look again at the function `Download2Flash` in the file

.\PLATFORM\ODO\BOOTLOAD\COMMON\download.c (CEPB 2.12, comparable to the CEPB 3.0 file .\PLATFORM\ODO\EBOOT\EBOOT\parallel.c), which is partially excerpted in Listing 4.4. If the Vaddr field of the record header has a value of 0, the starting address is assumed to be stored in the record size field cbRecord, and the value is retained for later use in the ulLaunch variable. The function Download2RAM works in basically the same manner, without the use of the buffer required for writing to flash memory.

Listing 4.4 Determining the starting address of the kernel image in the function Download2Flash

```
...

if (iHeaderBytes == 12) {
if (!header.fields.Vaddr) {
              iDone=1;
              // save launch address
              ulLaunch= header.fields.cbRecord;
}
}
...
```

The functions used in download.c (CEPB 2.12) and parallel.c (CEPB 3.0) for jumping to the kernel image starting address are Launch and LaunchExisting. These functions are implemented in the file init.*, where the asterisk represents a file extension that varies with the CPU type. This file, as you would expect, is located in the boot loader directories .\PLATFORM\<Platform Name>\BOOTLOAD\<CPU Family> (CEPB 2.12) and .\PLATFORM\ODO\EBOOT\EBOOT\<CPU Family> (CEPB 3.0) and is better known for its ability to perform processor initialization, as described in the section titled Startup Code earlier in this chapter. The function Launch is implemented with a simple jump instruction to the address passed in the pFunc parameter. The function LaunchExisting allows jumping into a kernel image that is already stored in ROM or flash memory. The implementation of this function in the MIPS-based init.s file, located in .\PLATFORM\<Platform Name>\ODO\BOOTLOAD\MIPS (CEPB 2.12) or .\PLATFORM\<Platform Name>\EBOOT\EBOOT\MIPS (CEPB 3.0) and excerpted in Listing 4.5, begins by reading the double word value from the memory location 0xBF800004 and storing the results in register t1.

Listing 4.5 MIPS implementation of LaunchExisting

```
...
      li            t0,0xBF800004
      lw            t1,0(t0)
      li            t2,0xFFFF0000
      and           t1,t1,t2
      li            t2,0x3C1A0000
      beq           t1,t2,26f
      nop
```

```
        li      t0,0xBF000004
26:
        j       t0
        nop

...
```

The lower word is masked with the value `0xFFFF0000` and then compared to the value `0x3C1A0000`. This comparison is attempting to verify that the entry point to the kernel image contains valid starting instructions and effectively determines that the kernel image does exist at this memory location. If the values are different, the starting address is changed from the ROM/flash address of `0xBF800004` to the RAM address of `0xBF000004` and is jumped to immediately. For better or worse, no additional validation of the kernel image is performed at this RAM address.

Now that the decomposition and analysis of this code are complete, let's discuss a possible modification. If your custom hardware is MIPS based, the hard-coded address in `LaunchExisting` will need to be modified to accommodate the starting address you have selected in your build of the kernel image. The address used in the example is based on the starting address defined in the `config.bib` file located in `.\PLATFORM\<Platform Name>\FILES`. The `MEMORY` entry `NK 9F800000 00800000 RAMIMAGE` tells `romimage.exe` that the kernel image it is building will run initially at the address `0x9F800000`, which is mapped (aliased) on a MIPS processor to the same external memory device as `0xBF800000`. The comparison in the function `LaunchExisting` occurs 4 bytes after this address to avoid comparison with the value of `nop` instructions generally located at the first 4 bytes of a kernel image.

Another possible starting address defined with conditional statements in the `config.bib` file is `0xBF000000`, which corresponds to the alternative starting address present in the `LaunchExisting` function. Note that because there is no `ROMOFFSET` entry for the MIPS processor, the `RAMIMAGE` address just mentioned represents both the address at which the kernel image will run and the address that the BIN file record headers contain for downloading and storing the kernel image. The use of `ROMOFFSET` is explained in the section titled Boot.bib later in this chapter.

In this boot loader example, if you build the MIPS kernel image for support of the R3000 target processor and the conditional `IMGBIGFLASH` is true, the starting address will be `0x9F400000` (aliased to `0xBF400000`). The `LaunchExisting` function will then need to be modified as in Listing 4.6. Note that the address has been offset by a value of 4 to be consistent with the current form of the comparison.

Listing 4.6 Sample modification of `LaunchExisting`

```
...
        li          t0,0xBF400004     ;Modified for the R3000 build
        lw          t1,0(t0)
        li          t2,0xFFFF0000
        and         t1,t1,t2
        li          t2,0x3C1A0000
```

```
        beq          t1,t2,26f
        nop
        li       t0,0xBF000004
26:
        j        t0
        nop
...
```

OEM Boot Loader Functions

A group of functions that carry the prefix *OEM* are implemented in the file `oemboot.c` in the directories `.\PLATFORM\<Platform Name>\BOOTLOAD\<CPU Type>` (CEPB 2.12) and `.\PLATFORM\<Platform Name>\EBOOT\<CPU Type>` (CEPB 3.00). The OEM functions implemented in the `BOOTLOAD` directory tree provide read/write access to the parallel port for downloading the kernel image from a remote PC host running CESH (see Chapter 9 for more information on the use of this tool). Functions are also provided for writing the downloaded kernel image into flash memory.

Another set of functions provide read/write access to the serial port and are used by the boot loader to send debug character strings out through the serial port to the remote PC host. One additional function is provided that initializes the display hardware, though this is not defined as an OEM function. The same functions that access the parallel port are also defined in the OEM Adaptation Layer (OAL) (described in Chapter 5). In fact, if a sample boot loader is unavailable, then the implementation of the parallel port functions in the OAL is a good starting point for your own implementation.

The OEM functions implemented in `oemboot.c`, located in the `EBOOT` (CEPB 2.12 and CEPB 3.0) directory tree, are quite different. Parallel port access is missing and is instead provided through the inclusion of the Hardware Abstraction Layer (HAL) source file `KERNEL\HAL\mdppfs.c` from within the source file `parallel.c`. Instead, functions that access the real-time clock are provided in the `EBOOT` file `oemboot.c`, and are called from `main.c` for timing access to the Ethernet port. The functions required to write the downloaded kernel image into flash memory are still available, but are instead implemented in the `ethdown.c` source file and are not prefixed with *OEM*. Table 4.3 lists the functions defined in `oemboot.c` for both the `BOOTLOAD` and `EBOOT` directory trees and comparable implementations in other source files.

Let's assume again that the processor in use on your platform is an SHx processor. In this case you would begin your analysis with the file `oemboot.c` in the directory `.\PLATFORM\ODO\BOOTLOAD\SHX` (CEPB 2.12) or `.\PLATFORM\ODO\EBOOT\EBOOT\SHX` (CEPB 3.0), copying it to the destination directory of your platform's boot loader directory `.\PLATFORM\<Your Platform>\BOOTLOAD\SHX`. At the top of the file you will notice a series of include statements, most of which are located in the `.\PLATFORM\ODO\INC` directory. The include files `windows.h`, `nkintr.h`, and `memory.h`, however, are general files located in directories common to all boot loader projects and will be found by the compiler within its include search path. Let's take a moment to decompose and analyze the remaining include files in the `.\PLATFORM\ODO\INC` directory to determine how they might apply to your custom platform.

Table 4.3 Functions Implemented in `Oemboot.c`

Function	BOOTLOAD (CEPB 2.12)	EBOOT (CEPB 3.0 and 2.12)	Description
`FlashClose`	No	Yes (in `ethdown.c`)	All pending write commands initiated through calls to the `FlashWrite` function are checked and compared against the cache image for consistency.
`FlashErase`	No	Yes (in `ethdown.c`)	The memory blocks specified are erased. If multiple blocks are specified, the erase commands are queued up and the status of pending erase requests is monitored. This function is specific to Intel 28F016SV.
`FlashError`	No	Yes (in `ethdown.c`)	The current error code is determined and the error condition is cleared. This code is specific to Intel 28F016SV.
`FlashPageWrite`	No	Yes (in `ethdown.c`)	The specified 256-byte block is written to flash memory via the internal buffers of the Intel 28F016SV.
`FlashWrite`	No	Yes (in `ethdown.c`)	The specified memory region is written to flash memory. This function uses the internal buffers of the Intel 28F016SV to avoid writing individual words.
`InitDisplay`	Yes	Yes	The display controller is initialized just enough to allow the display of a bitmap while the boot sequence is in progress.
`OEMFlashWrite`	Yes	No	A word is written to the specified address via CFI-compliant commands.
`OEMFlashWriteBegin`	Yes	No	If necessary, the flash device is initialized and the designated flash sector is erased through Common Flash Interface (CFI)–compliant commands. If your flash memory does not support CFI, this function will require modification.
`OEMFlashWriteEnd`	Yes	No	This function is a placeholder and is currently implemented with a single return statement.
`OEMFlashWriteStatus`	Yes	No	The status of the flash device is checked. This function must be called once for each block being written. The commands used are CFI compliant.

(continued)

Table 4.3 *Continued.*

Function	BOOTLOAD (CEPB 2.12)	EBOOT (CEPB 3.0 and 2.12)	Description
`OEMGetRealTime`	No	Yes	The current value in the real-time clock is loaded into a structure for later use in the implementation of *OEMEth* functions.
`OEMParallelPortGetByte`	Yes	Yes (through HAL functions)	If received data is available, the byte is returned immediately in the least significant bit (LSB) of the return value. Otherwise the function enters an endless loop waiting for the byte to arrive. The implementation of this function provided in `oemboot.c` of the sample boot loader does not use a time-out when waiting for the received data. One word of caution: Use this function only if the reception of data is absolutely certain.
`OEMParallelPortGetStatus`	Yes	Yes (through HAL functions)	If received data is available, the byte is returned in the LSB of the return value. Otherwise a value of –1 is returned, indicating that no data is available.
`OEMParallelPortSendByte`	Yes	Yes (through HAL functions)	The byte of data in the parameter `ch` is written to the parallel port only when the port status indicates that the port is ready to transmit another byte.
`OEMSetRealTime`	No	Yes	The real-time clock is initialized with the specified value.
`PowerOnSelfTest`	Yes	Yes	A self-test is initiated that verifies the operational state of the hardware.

The include file `sh3.h` contains constants for access to the interrupt and timer registers specific to the SH3 processor and should not require modification. The next two include files, `p2.h` and `p2debug.h`, contain constants that define register addresses and valid register values, along with a host of other constants defined for specific peripheral devices on the Odo platform. The only constants used are those for implementation of the parallel port functions and the `InitDisplay` function in `oemboot.c`, and these may need to be modified to support your custom platform. The include files `tchaud.h`, `drv_glob.h`, and `memory.h` (CEPB 2.12) are not really required for compilation of `oemboot.c` and were probably included as part of a cut-and-paste operation of a group of header files originally in a different boot loader file.

The include statement of the source file ..\..\KERNEL\HAL\bitmap.c provides a definition of a bitmap used as a type of splash screen, displayed while the kernel image is downloaded and initialized. This bitmap is statically defined in a byte array called bitmap that is referenced in the InitDisplay function. This function will initialize the display hardware and copy the bytes in the bitmap array to the frame buffer. As you might imagine, this function is highly platform specific, and you should carefully scrutinize it to determine if it will function with the graphics controller on your platform.

The functions implemented in oemboot.c (ethdown.c in CEPB 3.0) that are prefixed with *OEMFlash* allow you to change the contents of flash memory and are typically used to update the stored kernel image by writing the BIN file records as they are downloaded. These functions may need to be modified if either a different method is used to place the destination write address in write mode, or the flash manufacturer expects a different command set other than that defined in the Common Flash Interface (CFI) used in the CEPB example. In the latter case you should review the contents of the file f016sa.h (CEPB 2.12) in the .\BOOTLOAD\SHX directory to verify that the command code values match those of your flash manufacturer. Valid flash command codes are generally available with the user manual for your flash device.

Serial Port Input/Output Functions

Another group of functions that carry the prefix *OEM* are defined to provide basic serial port access, which is used in the development of the boot loader as a means of monitoring the progress of the executing code without the benefit of a single-stepping debugger. The functions are implemented with as little overhead as possible and do not return until the requested action is complete. In the transmit case, this implies that when a character string is being transmitted, a loop is used to transmit each character and the universal asynchronous receiver-transmitter (UART) is polled for a change in status indicating that it is ready for the next byte. This method is the simplest for accessing the UART, and it eliminates the need for queuing and synchronizing with the calling code. Because the transmission of a debug string effectively delays the execution of the boot loader, it is best not to use this function to debug time-critical boot loader code.

The file oemboot.c contains, in addition to the functions described in the previous section, the implementation of the serial port functions. The file debug.c contains the implementation of the serial port functions and is incorporated into oemboot.c via #include of the file debug.c located in the .\PLATFORM\<Platform Name>\KERNEL\HAL directory. These same serial port functions are also used by the kernel to send debug strings, and this shared use explains why they are located in the HAL directory tree. The address of the serial port is defined in the constant pCSRA or pCSRB, which in turn uses the constant DEBUG_SER_BASE defined in the file p2.h. As was true for oemboot.c, you should modify this constant to correspond to the actual address for your custom platform. Table 4.4 lists the OEM serial functions defined for use in the boot loader and the kernel and implemented in debug.c.

LED Function

Other than the firmware monitor and third-party debug tools, the software options for debugging the boot loader are limited. We discuss those options in the section titled Debugging the Boot Loader later in the chapter. One function that is implemented for the HAL in debug.c located

Table 4.4 Serial Debug Functions Implemented in `Debug.c`

Function	Description
`OEMClearDebugCommError`	The last error in the serial port hardware is cleared.
`OEMInitDebugSerial`	The serial port is initialized with the correct bit rate and data format.
`OEMReadDebugByte`	If a byte is available in the receive buffer register, it is copied and returned to the caller.
`OEMWriteDebugByte`	A single byte is written to the serial port, and an endless loop is entered until the status changes, indicating that the byte has been transmitted. The implementation of this function does not use a time-out. One word of caution: Unreliable serial port hardware may prevent the function from ever returning to the caller, thereby locking up the boot loader.
`OEMWriteDebugString`	The individual bytes of a character string are transmitted through repeated calls to the `OEMWriteDebugByte` function.

in the `.\PLATFORM\<Platform Name>\KERNEL\HAL` directory, but that is equally useful in the boot loader, is `OEMWriteDebugLED`, which provides the ability to write a double word value to an alphanumeric LED. The implementation of this function is highly platform dependent and will require, of course, that your platform be designed to include debug LEDs. You will also need to consider the mechanism for accessing those LEDs as you modify this function. Specifically how this function might be used in debugging the boot loader is discussed later in this chapter.

Ethernet Boot Loader Functions

An alternative of the parallel port as a means for uploading the kernel image to your custom platform is an Ethernet port. The advantage in the use of Ethernet is the obvious increase in the data rate between your custom platform and the remote host. This higher rate will noticeably reduce the time required for uploading the kernel image to your custom platform and will improve the performance of the debug tools that would otherwise use the serial and parallel ports.

Having your custom platform accessible in a LAN may also provide some ancillary benefits. If the custom hardware is assembled by hand, or if the parts are not yet available in large quantities, by offering accessibility via a LAN, you would allow other members of the engineering team access without having to relocate the board to a different remote PC host. Though it won't be possible for multiple engineers to simultaneously share the board, at least you will eliminate the need to move a delicate prototype board, possibly shrouded in a web of wire wrap.

When Ethernet debug services are available, PC host development tools are used slightly differently. We will not go into detail on these differences in this chapter; instead, see Chapter 9. We will, however, discuss the design of Ethernet debug services, and along the way you will gain an understanding of the modifications that may be required to accommodate your custom platform.

Your custom platform and the PC host communicate via a specialized protocol called TFTP. Like its predecessor FTP, TFTP defines a protocol specifically engineered for file transfer, but without the additional complexity inherent in the support of FTP's more advanced capabilities, such as user authentication and the determination of available directories. To ease its implementation and reduce the code size of the client and server TFTP implementations, User Datagram Protocol (UDP) is used as the underlying protocol. This could explain the decision to name the protocol TFTP, which stands for *Trivial File Transfer Protocol.*

In the context of TFTP, your custom platform performs the functions of a TFTP server, while the debug services that reside on the PC host are clients requesting access to your custom platform's resources. So, when you boot your custom platform, the same boot packet that was previously sent over the parallel port is sent to the PC host over Ethernet. The Eshell utility (or the CEPB 3.0 IDE) then responds by requesting a write link to your custom platform for uploading the kernel image. The majority of the code in the `EBOOT` directory tree is dedicated to processing these TFTP requests in the form of UDP packets. Refer to Figure 4.6 for more details on the overall architecture of the Ethernet debug services.

As depicted in Figure 4.6, the `main` function runs in an infinite loop calling `SMCGetFrame`. The type of the retrieved frame is identified, and a state transition is made on the basis of its value. ARP frames are handled separately from UDP frames, which are then processed as a DHCP message if an IP address is not yet assigned. If an IP address is already assigned, a state transition processes the frame as an administrative Ethernet services message or as a message to the TFTP server, depending on its contents.

In the latter case, a state transition occurs and the function `EbootTFtpReceiver` is called. This function acts as the main TFTP server routine to process incoming TFTP data, verifying and identifying the active link, causing another state transition to the function `TFtpStateMachine`. The `TFtpStateMachine` function in turn forwards the call to `TFtpCallBack`, which then selects the appropriate registered callback, in this case the `EthDown` function in the Ethernet boot loader `EBOOT`. Now that we have decomposed and analyzed the functional basics of booting over an Ethernet port, let's drill down into the sample Ethernet boot loader provided in the CEPB.

The `EBOOT` sample boot loader located in the `.\PLATFORM\<Platform Name>\EBOOT` directory is a specialized boot loader specifically designed to boot your custom platform using an Ethernet port, unlike the sample boot loader `BOOTLOAD` (located in the CEPB 2.12 `.\PLATFORM\<Platform Name>\EBOOT` directory), which is designed for a parallel port. `EBOOT` will be the subject of our decomposition/analysis/modification and will be discussed in some detail in this section. Let's first examine how `EBOOT` is built so that we understand its architecture and where it may require modifications.

`EBOOT` is built with the library modules located in the `.\PUBLIC\COMMON\OAK\DRIVERS\ETHDBG` directory. A subdirectory also called `EBOOT` exists under `ETHDBG`, not to be confused with the boot loader `EBOOT` directory mentioned earlier. `ETHDBG`'s `EBOOT` contains the implementation of the TFTP server that is accessed by the boot loader (and ultimately by the CE kernel after completion of the kernel image upload by the PC host). Note that this code is referenced in the boot loader's `Sources` file as `$(_COMMONOAKROOT)\lib\$(_CPUDEPPATH)\eboot.lib`.

Two other libraries exist in the `ETHDBG` directory tree: `NE2000` and `SMC9000`. The functions in these libraries provide basic access to SMC9000 and NE2000 Ethernet controllers. They are used primarily in the implementation of the functions prefixed with *OEMEth* and are defined in the section of the CEPB 2.12 online documentation entitled Implementing Windows CE Ethernet Debug Services on Your Target Platform (Platform Builder Reference in the CEPB 3.0 online documentation). If your custom platform does not possess either of these controllers, you will need to write a similar library of your own. It need not have the exact functions defined in either of these libraries because they are called only indirectly through the *OEMEth* functions. Note once again that this code is referenced in the boot loader's `Sources` file as

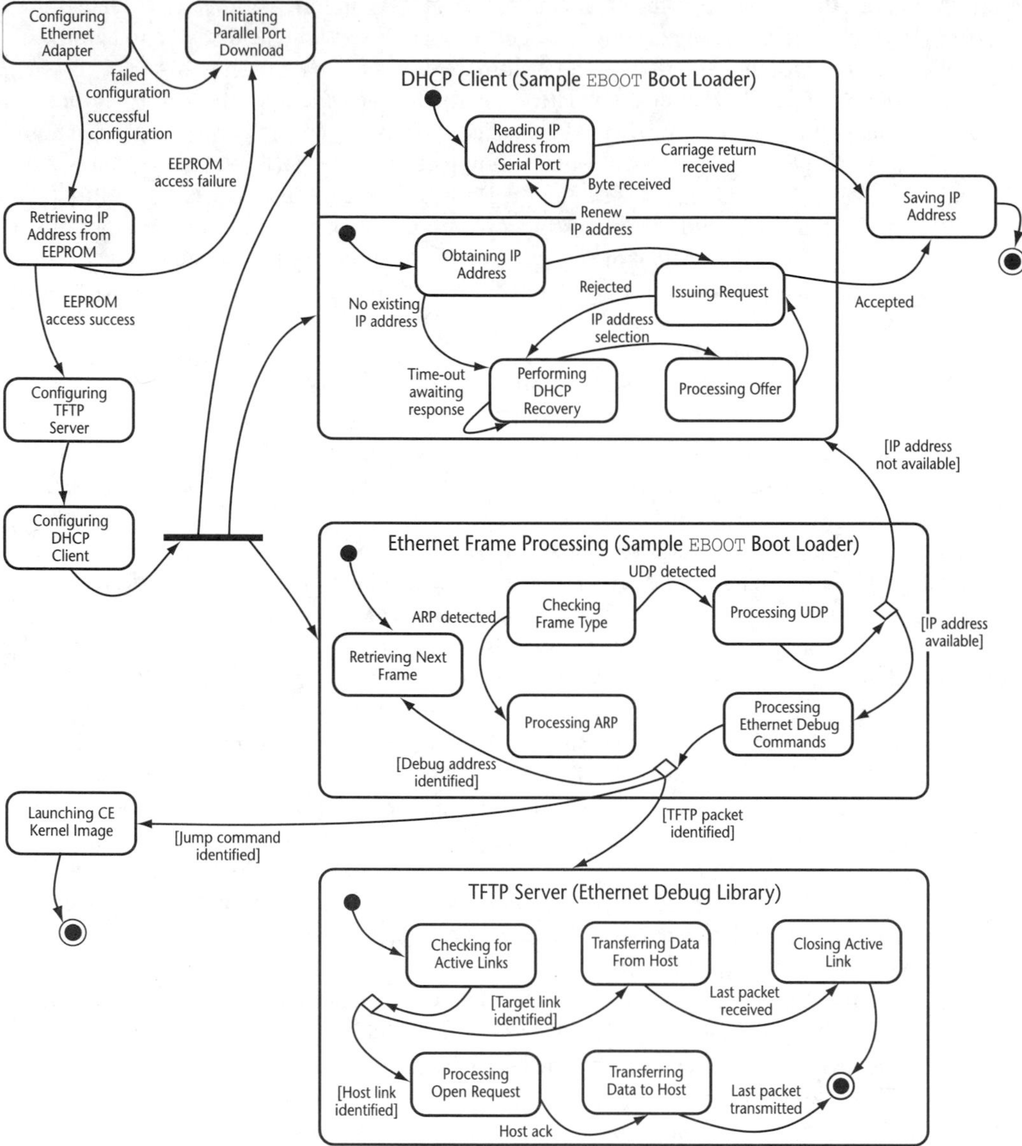

Figure 4.6 State chart for uploading a kernel image to the TFTP server in the CE boot loader

`$(_COMMONOAKROOT)\lib\$(_CPUDEPPATH)\smc9000.lib`, indicating that this boot loader example supports the SMC9000 Ethernet controller.

Now that we have decomposed and analyzed Ethernet debug functions, let's consider what might need modification in the sample source for your custom platform. Beginning with `main.c` located in the `.\PLATFORM\<Platform Name>\EBOOT` (CEPB 2.12) and `.\PLATFORM\<Platform Name>\EBOOT\EBOOT` (CEPB 3.0) directories, you will notice little similarity to the same file in the parallel port boot loader `BOOTLOAD` located in `.\PLATFORM\<Platform`

Name>\BOOTLOAD (CEPB 2.12). The list of included header files is similar, with the notable exception of ethdbg.h and ethdown.h. Ethdbg.h contains the declaration of the functions that facilitate communication with a debugging application running on the development workstation and need not be changed. The location of this file in the .\PUBLIC\COMMON\OAK\INC directory is a clear indication that it contains platform-independent constants and declarations.

The file ethdown.h contains the declarations and constants for writing the received kernel image to flash memory. This file should not require modification, but the source file ethdown.c located in the same directory most likely will. The implementation of the flash functions in this file must be reviewed carefully because they are written for an Intel 28F016SV flash chip that may not be compatible with the flash interface of the chips on your custom platform. Table 4.3 lists the flash functions used by the EBOOT Ethernet boot loader example.

Note:
Many manufacturers of flash memory now conform to the specification for the Common Flash Interface (CFI). This specification was intended to allow manufacturer-independent flash software that may simultaneously support the reading and writing of different flash technologies from different manufacturers. Thus, it is possible that all or some portion of the sample flash code in ethdown.c will work with your flash memory if it is also CFI compliant.

If you end up needing to make modifications to the file ethdown.c, consider replacing the functions prefixed with *Flash* that appear in Table 4.3 with the equivalent functions prefixed with *OEMFlash.* The *OEMFlash* functions are defined in the CEPB documentation and can be used in other modules, particularly the BOOTLOAD (CEPB 2.12) sample boot loader.

Let's return to the consideration of modifications to the file main.c located in the directory .\PLATFORM\<Platform Name>\EBOOT. We were just discussing the list of header files, focusing particularly on those unique to the Ethernet boot loader. The remaining header files will require modification only if you were planning on using the serial or parallel port in the boot loader, in addition to the Ethernet port. It might be useful to use the serial port when you're debugging the Ethernet port code itself. The specific nature of these modifications is described in the section titled OEM Boot Loader Functions earlier in this chapter.

As we continue our analysis of main.c, note the calls to the functions prefixed with *Eboot.* As described earlier, the *Eboot* functions are located in the ETHDBG directory tree and provide the functionality required for a TFTP server. These functions access the Ethernet port to transmit and receive data frames and will call the functions prefixed with *OEMEth* to access the Ethernet controller. The only platform-dependent aspect of this process is the access to the Ethernet controller through the *OEMEth* functions located in main.c. These should be reviewed carefully because they will be implemented for a specific Ethernet controller. The sample implementation in main.c calls the SMC9000 Ethernet functions located in an SMC9000 library under the ETHDBG directory tree. If you have a different Ethernet controller on your custom platform and you have created your own Ethernet controller library, you will need to modify these functions to call the functions in your library. Table 4.5 lists the *OEMEth* functions implemented in main.c.

Additional *OEMEth* functions are implemented in the file halether.c, located in the .\PLATFORM\<Platform Name>\KERNEL\HAL directory, but they are not included in

Table 4.5 *OEMEth* Functions Implemented in `Main.c`

Function	Description
`OEMEthGetFrame`	The `ETHDBG` function is called to determine if a frame has been received. If so, it is copied to the specified buffer.
`OEMEthGetSecs`	The number of seconds that have passed is determined by a call to `OEMGetRealTime`.
`OEMEthSendFrame`	The `ETHDBG` function is called to repeatedly attempt the sending of a frame.

Table 4.5 because they are used primarily in the implementation of Ethernet debug services provided by the CE kernel and are not required by the boot loader.

As you continue your examination of `main.c`, you may notice that certain functions of the Ethernet controller library in `.\PUBLIC\COMMON\OAK\DRIVERS\ETHDBG` are called directly. The functions `SMCInit` and `SMCGetFrame`, for example, are called, rather than the equivalent `OEMEthInit` and `OEMEthGetFrame`. The function `UpdateEEPROMData` updates the EEPROM on the Ethernet controller with new address information and calls `SMCWriteEEPROM`, and indirectly `SMCReadEEPROM`. If your custom platform uses a different Ethernet controller, the calls to these functions will need to be replaced with calls to your own Ethernet controller library.

If the `EBOOT` boot loader is unable to complete the kernel image download, and the last known jump address into the kernel image is invalid, a default jump address will be used. These addresses are hard-coded in `main.c` and will need to be modified if your custom platform stores the kernel image at a different address. The value of the address corresponds to the value of the `RAMIMAGE` entry for your custom platform in the `config.bib` file located in the `.\PLATFORM\<Platform Name>\FILES` directory. Refer to the section titled Building the Boot Loader later in this chapter for more information on the meaning of the `RAMIMAGE` entry.

Whether or Not to Ship the Boot Loader in Production Code

After you have gone to all the trouble of developing the boot loader for your custom platform, you may ask yourself how the boot loader will be used in the production (nondevelopment) version of the product. After all, a large percentage of the boot loader's functionality is dedicated to downloading the kernel image from the development workstation, which you may assume is of no use to your product's end users. This assumption may not be valid if you intend to offer your end users the option of upgrading their kernel image without requiring factory service or physical replacement of ROM chips. Because this sort of process is very similar to the one you go through when uploading a newly built kernel image into your custom platform for testing, you may want to retain some form of your boot loader.

Another possibility is that your boot loader contains advanced self-test code that conducts an overnight burn-in test and provides a specialized ROM monitor–like interface for entry of commands through the serial port. Upon successful completion of the burn-in test, the boot loader automatically downloads a production version of the kernel image. If the boot loader was running in RAM, it may then opt to write over its own image in flash memory with a kernel image that boots without a boot loader, thereby permanently removing the boot loader from flash memory.

Whether or not the boot loader you worked so hard on becomes a part of the production product depends entirely on how you wish to use it. As you make this decision, be certain that you have a clear understanding of the conceptual differences between booting CE with a boot loader and without a boot loader. The separation between the boot loader and the kernel exists more as the result of a build process that produces separate images, one for the boot loader and the other for the kernel. Because the HAL code is essentially a subset of the boot loader, nothing is stopping you from merging all or selected portions of your boot loader code into the kernel's HAL code (Chapter 5 covers HAL development). There is, however, a significant architectural advantage in keeping them separate, allowing the HAL and boot loader to be developed and maintained separately.

One sample boot loader that was not discussed in this chapter, but that illustrates the relationship between the boot loader code and HAL code, is the `BOOT2RAM` (CEPB 2.12) boot loader located in the `.\PLATFORM\<Platform Name>\EBOOT` directory.

Note:
`BOOT2RAM` has no functional association with the Ethernet boot loader `EBOOT`, though such an association is implied by its location under the `EBOOT` directory tree.

The platform-dependent source file `fwp2.s` in the `PPC` directory borrows directly from the file of the same name, using the include statement `#include "..\..\KERNEL\HAL\PPC\fwp2.s"`. This code is also used in the PowerPC HAL to boot the CE kernel and performs the same type of processor configuration as the `StartUp` function in the other sample boot loaders we have been analyzing. One distinct difference, however, is that this startup code will jump to `KernelStart` unless the assembler directive `BOOT_LOADER` is defined, in which case it will jump to the boot loader's `main` function. So, even though the HAL startup code has a lot in common with the boot loader startup code, you cannot use it without first performing the same decomposition/analysis/modification that has been used throughout this chapter for identifying possible modifications.

Building the Boot Loader

After you have gone to all the trouble of creating your CE boot loader for your custom hardware, you will need to build it to form a ROMable binary image for testing. The file that results from the build process may then be written to ROM or flash memory. In this section we will explore how to create the necessary build files to allow the CEPB command-line build tools to generate the binary image. Many options exist for directing the build tools to generate the image according to a certain format. For more information on these same build topics as they relate to the build of the CE kernel, see Chapter 10.

Note:
We have opted to use the command-line build tools rather than the CEPB IDE to build the boot loader. Because the IDE automatically executes certain tools required to build a CE kernel image that are not required for building a boot loader, it can extend the duration of the build process.

Sources File

The file `Sources` exists in the directories where there is source code to be built and is described in detail in Chapter 10. In this section we will focus on those `Sources` file entries that are less commonly used in other projects, but that are critical to building the boot loader. The best way to complete your own boot loader `Sources` file, as in many other parts of the boot loader, is to copy the `Sources` file from one of the CEPB sample boot loaders. You can then modify the entries as explained in the next few paragraphs.

As a matter of convention, the CEPB sample boot loaders use the name `StartUp` for the routine that contains the first code to be executed. The `Sources` file entry `EXEENTRY` is used to define the name of this routine in your own code and places it in the linker command-line parameter `-entry: <Routine Name>`. The address of this routine is particularly important for the boot loader that will use it as the address of the code to run upon reset. We'll say more about this when we discuss the `CONFIG` section of another build file, `boot.bib`, later in this chapter.

You should verify that two additional entries are present for the boot loader: `RELEASETYPE` and `WINCECPU`. The value of `RELEASETYPE` should be set to `PLATFORM` to indicate that the files produced during the build process (also described in this section as *build products*) should be placed in the `.\PLATFORM\ directory tree.` The value of `WINCECPU` should be set to 1 to indicate that the source code being built is placed in a subdirectory reserved for processor-dependent code. As it turns out in the CEPB, all build products are placed in processor-dependent subdirectories, whether or not this entry is used. It is still a good idea to use this entry, however, just in case future versions of the CEPB act differently.

If you have copied a `Sources` file from one of the sample boot loaders in CEPB 2.12, you may have a problem that will produce a linker error indicating that the library file `fulllibc.lib` cannot be found or built. This problem occurs because the path name used for `fulllibc.lib` in the `TARGETLIBS` entry is incorrect. Instead of `$(_PLATFORMROOT)\ODO\LIB\$(_CPUINDPATH)\fulllibc.lib`, as it appears in the sample `Sources` file, it should be `$(_COMMONOAKROOT)\LIB\$(_CPUDEPPATH)\fulllibc.lib`. Files that are located under the `$(_PLATFORMROOT)` directory tree are generally build products described in the `Sources` file. The object module library `fulllibc.lib`, however, is provided in the CEPB already compiled for your target processor and is not considered a build product.

The processor-dependent source code in the sample CEPB source code generally appears under a subdirectory named for the processor family. *SHx,* for example, is used to refer to processor-dependent source code for both the SH3 and SH4 processors. This is a wise convention because it avoids the unwieldy mess of the large number of complex assembly and compiler directives that is required when one source file simultaneously contains code for multiple processor families. For these source files, you must use the name of the processor family as a prefix to the `SOURCES` entry in the `Sources` file. This entry would appear as `SHX_SOURCES (<Processor Family>_SOURCES)` and `MIPS_SOURCES (<Processor Family>_SOURCES)` for the SHx and MIPS family processors, respectively.

Boot.bib

The `boot.bib` file is one of the most important files in the build process for the CE boot loader. Our discussion of its structure and content will be rather limited, however, focusing exclusively on the needs of the boot loader build. For a more general reference of how BIB files work in the overall CE build, refer to Chapter 10.

Boot.bib is a self-contained description of the memory map of your custom platform and is used by the linker to determine how to locate the relocatable object modules generated by the compiler. The term *locate* in this context refers to what the linker must do to produce a module that may be directly executed at a designated physical memory address (ROM or RAM). This means that the usual headers that appear at the beginning of an EXE file in Windows are not present and that the associated relocation table is not necessary. It is still possible, however, to generate EXE files that are relocatable, as is the case when the module is stored as a compressed file in the CE object store. The object store is not a requirement of the boot loader, so we will once again defer to Chapter 10 for a more detailed discussion of this topic.

The MEMORY Section

Boot.bib is divided into three distinct sections: MEMORY, CONFIG, and MODULES. The MEMORY section describes the layout of memory on your custom platform in terms of one of three predefined types: RAM, RAMIMAGE, and RESERVED. The RAM memory type, as the name implies, indicates that the memory is a read/write medium with direct byte-level read/write access. Though you may think of flash memory as a type of RAM with reduced access time because it provides read and write capabilities, it does not qualify as RAM because it requires the use of special commands to write and erase the required memory address. Moreover, erasure typically occurs within a predefined block size and is not possible for individual bytes.

Note:
The FILES section is used in the BOOT2RAM sample boot loader provided in CEPB 2.12. This is not a common practice, and was used only in BOOT2RAM to allow the CE kernel image to be included in the build of boot loader, without the need for downloading it from a remote host.

Considering that there is a RAM memory type, you might expect to find a ROM memory type as well to define memory as a read-only medium with direct byte-level access. This type is not defined per se, but it is functionally equivalent to the RAMIMAGE memory type. The name *RAMIMAGE* is used to imply that the memory at this location should be given a read-only attribute by the linker (and by the kernel for full builds of the CE kernel), and that it may physically reside in RAM or ROM. If it resides in RAM, it will be treated as a read-only region of memory. The actual memory technology (flash, EEPROM, ultraviolet erasable PROM) used in your custom platform's read-only memory is of concern only to the tool used to write the binary image.

The important thing to note about the RAMIMAGE memory type is how it is used to locate your boot loader at the address in memory that corresponds to the location of the power-on reset code of your platform's processor. It may also be used to locate your boot loader to the address that is contained in the power-on reset vector (location in memory from which the processor loads the initial value of the program counter). Choosing which memory address to use can be a bit tricky. If you know, for example, that your processor loads the program counter with an initial value of 0xA0000000 (as in the case for the SHx processor family), you may want to use this same address for the RAMIMAGE entry. If, however, you prefer to speed the execution of the boot loader code by executing it from cached RAM, you may use a corresponding address from your platform's memory map. In this example, you would still write the binary image to the address of the power-on reset code, but at some point your boot loader code would copy itself to the memory address in the RAMIMAGE entry. The code that copies the boot loader into the RAMIMAGE address would need to be location independent because it would be running at the defined location of the power-on reset code.

The CONFIG Section

As we eluded to in the previous paragraph, the memory address in the RAMIMAGE entry is affected by the way your custom platform's processor begins life when in power-on reset mode. Since the SHx program counter is initialized to 0xA0000000, the binary image produced by the boot loader build may be written directly to this address. The x86 CPU family requires the use of a jmp instruction to jump to the address of the boot loader. Still other processors require that the address of the boot loader code (rather than the actual boot loader code) be in a specific memory location so that it may be loaded directly into the program counter during power-on reset. Certain entries in the CONFIG section of the boot.bib file are designed to address (pun intended ☺) this issue. For a more complete, less boot loader–oriented description of these entries, refer to the CEPB online documentation.

X86BOOT, BOOTJUMP, and RESETVECTOR

X86BOOT, BOOTJUMP, and RESETVECTOR all describe how the processor for your custom platform behaves during power-on reset. If X86BOOT is set to a value of ON, the Romimage build tool (described later in this section) inserts an x86 jump instruction (0xE9) at the beginning of the binary image, after a series of nop instructions. The jump instruction generated jumps to the address of the startup routine specified in the Sources file.

BOOTJUMP is basically a processor-independent version of X86BOOT and accomplishes the same purpose. By default, a jump instruction appropriate for the target CPU is inserted at the beginning of the binary image. As in X86BOOT, the address for the jump instruction corresponds to the address of the StartUp routine defined in the Sources file. Using the statement BOOTJUMP=address, you can position the jump instruction at the address specified, rather than at the beginning of the binary image. The statement BOOTJUMP=NONE indicates that no jump instruction is necessary and that the StartUp routine should be located at the beginning of the binary image

RESETVECTOR provides the same options as BOOTJUMP without affecting the location of the binary image in memory. Thus, the jump instruction can be positioned anywhere inside the binary image, while the binary image itself is positioned at the beginning of the RAMIMAGE memory region.

There are few things you must do, however, to enable the Romimage build tool to alter the contents of the binary image in this way. First you must reserve a spot in the RAMIMAGE memory region to contain this address. For a RAMIMAGE entry of NK 9F800000 00800000 RAMIMAGE, the entry would be RESERVE 9FC00000 00001000 in the MEMORY section. This entry tells Romimage that as it generates the binary image file, it should not place anything (except, of course, the address of the StartUp routine) in the 4,096-byte page that begins at the location of the power-on reset vector at address 0x9FC0000. Note in this example that the address of the RESETVECTOR entry falls within the address range of the RAMIMAGE entry named *NK*.

ROMOFFSET

ROMOFFSET provides a means of specifying where the memory region defined by the RAMIMAGE entry in the MEMORY section is actually stored in physical memory. So when the Romimage build tool finds this entry, it adds this value to the address of each record of output files with the extension *.sre* or *.bin.* Refer to the CEPB online documentation for a specification of the format of SRE and BIN files.

`ROMOFFSET` is useful in situations in which you need to write the binary image to a particular ROM or flash address but you plan on running the code contained in this image at a different address. Such a scenario is common for the boot loader when you are required by the processor to write the image file to a particular address that is uncached and you're planning on copying your boot loader code to a different address that is cached for faster execution. A section of the SHx `boot.bib` file provided in the `.\PLATFORM\ODO\EBOOT\SHX` directory of the CEPB is excerpted in Listing 4.7 as an example of this use of `ROMOFFSET`.

Listing 4.7 Using `ROMOFFSET` for an SHx platform

```
;*******************************************************************************
; TITLE:          BOOT.BIB
;
; Odo Boot Loader Source Module
;
;*******************************************************************************
MEMORY
;    Name       Start      Size       Type
;    -------    -------    -------    ----
     BOOT       8C010000   00010000   RAMIMAGE
...
CONFIG
...
        ROMOFFSET=F3FF0000
...
```

In this example, the `BOOT` entry in the `MEMORY` section will direct the Romimage build tool to produce a binary image that may be run at address `0x8C010000`. If you check the *SHx Programming Manual,* you will notice that this address can be cached, which would allow the boot loader code to run faster. But because the SHx initializes the program counter register to address `0xA0000000`, the binary image must not be written to this address in flash or ROM. This is where the `ROMOFFSET` of `0xF3FF0000` comes in. When Romimage generates its output file, this value is added to address `0x8C010000`, producing records in the binary image that point to an address of `0x80000000` (an alias for `0xA0000000`). When the binary image is then written to ROM or flash memory, it will be written to `0x80000000`, while the code itself is run at address `0x8C010000`. Note that one of the first things the boot loader code running at `0x80000000` must do is copy itself to `0x8C010000` and jump to this address to continue execution from a cacheable address.

The use of `ROMOFFSET` in the `config.bib` file (explained in more detail in Chapter 10) is a bit different. `Config.bib` is used to describe the memory map of the CE kernel, unlike `boot.bib`, which describes the memory map for the boot loader. The CE kernel reserves the upper 2GB of its 4GB address space for hardware access, and all entries in the `MEMORY` section of `config.bib` are offset from a 2GB base address of `0x80000000`. You must decide what offset is needed to produce the address where the binary image will actually be written in ROM or flash memory. Then, as we mentioned for the boot loader, the Romimage build tool will produce an output file containing records pointing to the address of your custom platform's ROM or flash memory where the CE kernel will be stored. The ROMOFFSET value most commonly used in the sample CE kernel builds included with the CEPB is 0x80000000, indicating that the binary image should simply be written to the lower 2GB of your custom platform's address space.

ROMSIZE, ROMWIDTH, and ROMSTART

By now you might be asking what you need to do to tell the Romimage build tool how to construct the binary image in a manner suitable for writing directly to ROM or flash memory. The ROMSIZE, ROMWIDTH, and ROMSTART entries in the CONFIG section of boot.bib are used to generate separate files that contain raw data forming a mirror image of a particular ROM device (flash or EPROM device). The format of these files is referred to in the CEPB online documentation as the *Absolute Binary Data Format.*

The number of files generated corresponds to the number of ROM or flash devices on your platform. Each file has an extension of *.nb<x>,* where the value of *x* begins with 0 for the file to be written to the memory device at the lowest memory region and is incremented by 1 for the device at the next highest memory region. The rest of this section will focus on how to define the values for ROMSIZE, ROMWIDTH, and ROMSTART.

ROMSIZE, as the name implies, refers to the size of the read-only media where the binary image will be written. More specifically, it refers to the size in bytes of each individual device. So, let's say that your platform has four flash chips, each of which is capable of storing 1MB of data, for a total memory capacity of 4MB. The corresponding value of ROMSIZE would be 0x100000. Four binary files would be generated, with the extensions *.nb0, .nb1, .nb2,* and *.nb3.* The size of each file would be exactly 1,048,576 bytes, thus defining the value of each byte of each device to be programmed.

Note:
Note that the boot loader will most likely be smaller than the ROMSIZE value. In this case the NBx file(s) generated will be filled with zeros to produce a file equal to the size specified in ROMSIZE.

ROMWIDTH defines the width of the bus connected to each individual read-only memory device and supports values of 32, 16, and 8. For values of 16 or 8, the Romimage build tool divides the image file into separate files, each containing 16-bit or 8-bit values. For a value of 32, Romimage simply leaves the image in one file.

Assume for a moment that your custom platform's processor provides a 32-bit bus and the value of ROMWIDTH is set to 16. One group of 16-bit memory devices is then connected to 16 bits of the 32-bit bus, and the other group of 16-bit memory devices is connected to the remaining 16 bits. In this configuration, the processor fetches a byte contained in an even word (the even-numbered memory location when memory is counted in units of 16 bits) from one device, and bytes contained from odd words (the odd-numbered memory location when memory is counted in units of 16 bits) from the other device. To support this configuration, the Romimage build tool must create two corresponding sets of image files: one set with values contained in even words, and the other with values contained in odd words.

If your custom platform uses eight-bit memory devices and the value of ROMWIDTH is set to 8, your processor will fetch a byte each from four different groups of devices. So, if the value to be fetched is contained in the low byte of an even word, it will be fetched from one group, while the high byte of the same even word will be fetched from another group. The odd words work the same way, with the low and high bytes assigned to different groups of memory devices. Therefore, each byte of every double word is stored in a different device group. To support this configuration, the Romimage build tool must create four corresponding sets of image files, each set corresponding to different bytes within a double word.

To generate the image files properly, the Romimage build tool must also know the lowest address assigned to the read-only memory devices. The ROMSTART entry provides this capability and is assigned a value that corresponds to the lowest address before the addition of the ROMOFFSET (described in the previous section). So if the ROMSTART value were lower than the address in the RAMIMAGE entry of the MEMORY section, the image file would be padded with zeros up to the starting address of the RAMIMAGE entry.

Listing 4.8 presents an excerpt of a boot.bib file in which ROMSIZE, ROMWIDTH, and ROMSTART are being used to allow the generation of Absolute Binary Data Format files.

Listing 4.8 Sample CONFIG entries defining the geometry of your platform's read-only media

```
...
MEMORY

BOOT      00008000   00020000   RAMIMAGE
RAM       00400000   00100000   RAM
CONFIG
...
          ROMSIZE=80000
          ROMWIDTH=32
          ROMSTART=00008000
...
```

The value of ROMSIZE indicates that each nonvolatile memory device can store as much as 512K of data. The BOOT entry of the MEMORY section indicates that it is 0x20000 bytes, or 256K, long. Because this value is less than the value of ROMSIZE, only one binary image file will be generated. The ROMWIDTH value of 32 indicates that the image file need *not* be split between multiple files. The ROMSTART entry of 0x8000 indicates that the lowest address for all nonvolatile memory devices is 0x8000. Because this value is identical to the starting address of the BOOT entry, no zero fill is required at the beginning of the image file.

IMAGESTART

If you need the image file to begin somewhere within the address range defined by RAMIMAGE but not at the beginning of this range, use IMAGESTART. The image file will be produced by the Romimage build tool (to be described shortly) via the address assigned to IMAGESTART and will continue until it reaches the end of the address range. At this point the address used will wrap to the beginning of the address range defined in RAMIMAGE.

AUTOSIZE

If the image file produced by Romimage will only be located in RAM and will never be executed in place (XIP) from ROM, then the `AUTOSIZE` entry may be of interest. If `AUTOSIZE` is set to `ON`, all of the unused space of the address range defined in the `RAMIMAGE` entry will be combined with the address range defined in the RAM entry. The effective result is the automatic reduction of the size of `RAMIMAGE` to be just large enough to accommodate the image file produced by the Romimage build tool, together with an increase in the size of RAM by the same amount. For images that execute only from RAM, the `AUTOSIZE` entry can be quite handy because it means that the size of `RAMIMAGE` does not need to be changed every time code is added or removed from the build.

`AUTOSIZE` is generally not used in boot loader builds because the resulting image file must be located in nonvolatile memory such as EPROM or flash.

COMPRESSION

The sections of an image file that may be modified by executable code (writable data sections), are generally compressed. This compression saves space in the image file and therefore in the size of the required ROM device. Because to be modified, these sections must be copied from ROM into RAM, the decompression occurs as the initial data values of the section are being copied. By default, the value of the `COMPRESSION` entry is `ON`.

The CEPB sample boot loader source, for example, assumes that the writable data section in the boot loader image is uncompressed, and therefore sets the value of the `COMPRESSION` entry to `OFF` in the `boot.bib` file. At the beginning of the platform configuration in the boot loader source code, the contents of the writable data section are then copied into RAM without the need for decompression. This process reduces the complexity of the boot loader code, and because the overall size of the boot loader is usually quite small when compared to the kernel image, the amount of memory to be saved through compression is insignificant.

FSRAMPERCENT

A certain percentage of the address range defined in the RAM entry may be reserved for use by the CE file system. `FSRAMPERCENT` is set to a hex value, where each byte indicates the number of 4K blocks per megabyte. See the CEPB online documentation for more information on the use of this entry.

`FSRAMPERCENT` is not used in `boot.bib` because the CE file system is not yet loaded when the boot loader is active.

KERNELFIXUPS

As the Romimage build tool is producing the boot loader image file, it determines the RAM address for the writable data sections and makes the appropriate entry in the image file's table of contents. To make certain that these sections are located at the beginning of the RAM address range, you should set `KERNELFIXUPS` to `ON`. The CEPB boot loader and platform examples always set this value to `ON`.

OUTPUT

Unless directed otherwise, the Romimage build tool will place the resulting image file in the same directory as the first module file listed in the `MODULES` section of the `boot.bib` file. You can override this placement by setting `OUTPUT` to an alternative path where you want the image file to be written.

PROFILE

By default, the Romimage build tool does not include profiling structure and symbols in the resulting image file. You can override Romimage's default action by setting the value of the `PROFILE` entry to `ON`. Because the boot loader is not the type of code you would optimize, the `PROFILE` entry is generally not used in `boot.bib`.

ROMFLAGS

The `ROMFLAGS` entry allows you to add a double word value to an image file. Before you build the boot loader, you add the double word value to the `boot.bib` file by assigning it to `ROMFLAGS`. This value may then be read from the `ROMHDR` structure referenced in the `pTOC` global variable (which is described shortly, in the section titled Romimage Build Tool).

SRE

By assigning the `SRE` entry a value of `ON`, you can tell the Romimage build tool to generate both the BIN image file and an SRE image file. The latter is compliant with the Motorola 32-bit Binary Data Format (described in the CEPB online documentation) and is widely supported by most EPROM burners; the former is a relatively new Microsoft proprietary format. If you are using an EPROM burner to write the resulting image file to ROM, you will need to use this option to generate both BIN and SRE image files.

Romimage Build Tool

Near the end of the boot loader build process, the CEPB-supplied linker is run and a portable executable (PE) file is produced. Though this PE file contains executable code, it is not yet ready to be written to and run from ROM (a feature referred to as execute-in-place, or XIP, in the CEPB online documentation). A PE file contains headers and relocation information that allows the execution address to be decided by the operating system as it loads the program into RAM. Since the RAM of most desktop operating systems is highly dynamic, with multiple programs being simultaneously loaded and unloaded, this is a particularly important capability. The life of a PE file built for execution from ROM (XIP) is quite different, however.

Once written to ROM, the program will not be moved or unloaded. It is stuck at this one address and must always be run from this same address—thus the name *XIP*. The only way to change the execution address of a program written to ROM is to replace it, a change that would imply that it has been rebuilt and is no longer the same exact program. So, to confine a PE file to a single address and transform it to support XIP, you must remove its headers and process its relocation information, thus creating code that is executable only at its designated address. The CEPB build utility `romimage.exe` performs this transformation, which is often referred to as a *locate* in the phrase "link and locate."

Note:

We have both the CEPB and eMbedded Visual C++ (Windows CE Toolkit for Visual C++ in earlier versions of CE) installed on our systems. If we were to execute a search, we would find many copies of the file `link.exe`, all associated with different development products. In the course of experimentation, we have had an occasion to use different linkers for different projects. That is, to avoid altering the `PATH` environment variable, we have copied or renamed a given linker to force execution of another linker. In one case when an experiment was complete, we forgot to restore the linkers to their original locations and/or names. When we tried to run a build of our boot loader, we were quite disturbed to find that we were no longer able to successfully run Romimage. No amount of changes to the `boot.bib` file fixed the problem until we restored the CEPB `link.exe` file to its original location.

The lesson that we learned most painfully was that the only PE-compliant EXE files that Romimage can successfully process are those produced by the CEPB linker. So if ever you experience an unexpected error while executing Romimage, verify that the CEPB linker is being run during the build process, rather than another linker that happens to be referenced in your `PATH` variable.

To help you understand Romimage and what it does to produce an image capable of XIP, we will now explore how to read the large block of text generated by Romimage at the end of the build process.

Console Output

Figure 4.7 depicts the output from the execution of Romimage for a typical boot loader.

The first few lines contain two pieces of key information. First is the page size: 1,024 bytes. This value will be used to decide the alignment of the individual modules (PE files or DLL files) that are collected together into the resulting image file. Next is the value of something called `pTOC`.

`pTOC` is a reserved variable of type `ROMHDR` and should be declared and defined in your boot loader code as a global variable. Romimage will then initialize `pTOC` with the physical address in ROM of the image file's table of contents. You may then use this variable to gain access to certain values defining your platform configuration, such as the beginning and ending addresses of RAM, and the starting address of the writable data sections that must be copied to RAM. The structure `ROMHDR` is declared in various source files of CEPB's sample boot loaders and will need to be copied into one of your boot loader's source files. (Refer to the section titled Platform Configuration Code earlier in this chapter for more information on the use of `pTOC`.) Figure 4.7 also indicates that the `pTOC` global variable may be found at `0x0000750C`. This value represents the offset to the location of the `pTOC` variable from the start of RAM (`0x8C028000`) indicated at the end of Figure 4.7.

The `MODULES` section is next and contains a table providing a detailed description of the space used by each module in the boot loader image file. The name of the module appears first and is pulled directly from the `MODULES` section of the `boot.bib` file. In our example, the boot loader module is linked to form a PE file named `bootload.exe` but is associated with a module name of *nk.exe*. The convention used throughout all CEPB BIB files, including those used to

```
G:\Dev\Wince\PLATFORM\ODO\BOOTLOAD\SHX>romimage boot.bib
Windows CE ROM Image Builder  v1.0  Copyright Microsoft 1995.
Setting PageSize to 1024
DumpSymbols: pTOC found at 0000750C

MODULES Section
Module        Section   Start      Length  psize   vsize   Filler
------------ -------- --------- ------- ------- ------- ------
nk.exe        .text     8c010400h   35840   35840   35766 o32_rva=400h
nk.exe        .pdata    8c019000h    1024     512     288 o32_rva=9400h
nk.exe        .data     8c018fb8h       4       4      84 FILLER>8c028000h
nk.exe        E32       8c019120h     100                 FILLER
nk.exe        O32       8c019184h      72                 FILLER
nk.exe        FileName 8c018fbch        7                 FILLER
Unfilled ROM Holes (Address,Length):
8c0191cch       564 8c018fc3h        61
ROM Header                               8c019400  00000054h  (        84)
Modules Table of Contents                8c019454  00000020h  (        32)
Files Table of Contents                  8c019474  00000000h  (         0)
Kernel Data Copy Section                 8c019474  00000010h  (        16)

Starting ip= a0007c18h

First DLL Address:          02000000h
Last DLL Address:           02000000h
Physical Start Address:     8c010000h
Physical End Address:       8c019484h
Start RAM:                  8c028000h
Start of free RAM:          8c028400h
End of RAM:                 8c030000h
Number of Modules:          1
Number of Copy Sections:    1
Copy Section Offset:        8c019474h
Starting ip:                8c010004h
Raw files size:             00000000h
Compressed files size:      00000000h
FileSys 4K Chunks/Mbyte:    128 <2Mbyte  128 2-4Mbyte  128 4-6Mbyte  128 >6Mbyte
Total ROM size:             00009484h (     38020)
```

Figure 4.7 Sample console output from Romimage running on `boot.bib`

build the kernel image, is that the module containing the main entry point uses the module name of *nk.exe in the resulting image. Being the only module defined in* `boot.bib`, the main entry point is, of course, contained in `bootload.exe`.

Note:
The main entry point is the address of the first function to be run in the image file and is indicated by a special entry in the `Sources` file, which was described earlier in the chapter.

Before we continue with a definition of the columns describing each module entry, you need to know how Romimage processes BIB files. This is important because the definition of the column is slightly different depending on how far Romimage has progressed. Romimage processes BIB files in two stages. In the **alignment stage**, Romimage processes each entry in the `MODULES` section of the BIB file in the order presented and focuses primarily on alignment of these modules on a page boundary. In the **filling stage**, the focus turns to filling the unused space between modules in the image file, and therefore in memory, considering that the image file supports XIP. Romimage performs this filling stage by locating writable `.pdata` and `.data` sections in the unused space. Because these sections are not required to support XIP, they are also compressed, saving space in the image file while allowing the unused space to accommodate more writable `.pdata` and `.data` sections. In the next few paragraphs, we will see how this compression affects the definition of the each of the columns.

To the right of the module name is the section name that defines the type of data contained at this particular address. The only types defined in the CEPB online documentation are described in Table 4.6. Other than the section name *FileName,* whose data type is self-evident, the other section names are undocumented. The term *section* in this context is not to be confused with the reference to the `MODULES` section in the console output.

After the section name comes the starting address (`Start`) of the module named at the left. If the module is not identified as `FILLER` in the rightmost column, this address is aligned on the page according to the page size indicated at the top of the console output. The value of the starting address does *not* reflect the value of `ROMOFFSET` as defined in `boot.bib`. The address occurs within the range defined in the `RAMIMAGE` memory region and does not correspond to the location of the image file when written to ROM.

The `Length` column, which appears next, contains the number of bytes allocated for the module in the image file, including any additional bytes added for page alignment. As individual modules are processed in the alignment stage, Romimage rounds up the size of the `.text` and `.rsrc` sections within each module so that each adjacent address falls on an even page bound-

Table 4.6 Section Types Named in the Romimage Console Output

Section	Description
`.text`	Executable code.
`.rsrc`	Resource data.
`.pdata`	Debug and exception processing information for each function in the `.text` section. This section type is typically used in the filling stage to fill the gaps between page-aligned modules.
`.data`	Writable data section. This section type is also used in the filling stage.
`E32`	Undocumented as of this writing.
`O32`	Undocumented as of this writing.
`FileName`	Section containing the file name of one of the modules with a `.text` section.
`.CRT`	Code that must be executed before the module's startup routine is run.
`.KDATA`	Undocumented as of this writing.
`INIT`	Undocumented as of this writing.

ary. The `Length` column of the `.data` and `.pdata` entries in the filling stage, however, contains the number of bytes rounded up to the nearest double word. The reason for this will become clear when we discuss how Romimage fills the unused space caused by the page alignment in the alignment stage.

In the alignment stage, the `psize` column contains the actual size of the module entry rounded up to the nearest paragraph (512 bytes for the sample console output presented in Figure 4.7). In the filling stage, the `psize` column contains the actual size of the module entry, before any required rounding. The only alignment required in the filling stage is double word, and since Romimage positions filler entries only on double word–aligned addresses, no rounding is ever required. Consequently, in the filling stage, `Length` and `psize` are always identical.

In the alignment stage, the `vsize` column represents the actual size of the module entry before any rounding required for alignment. In the filling stage, the `vsize` column represents the actual size of the module entry before compression.

The `Filler` column is used to indicate simply whether the module list entry is being used to fill an available hole caused by page alignment. For our discussion, then, the entries that appear with the word *FILLER* in the `Filler` column, are generated in the filling stage of Romimage processing. Now that we've mentioned what Romimage does in each stage, let's consider the console output in Figure 4.7 and walk through each entry.

Since only one module is listed in the `MODULES` section of the `boot.bib` file, Romimage does not have much work to do. From the first entry in the `MODULES` section of the console output, we can see that the `.text` section of the `nk.exe` module is assigned to the address `0x8C010400`. This address is offset by `0x400` from the starting address of the `RAMIMAGE` entry in the `boot.bib` file. As a general rule, Romimage does not position any modules in the first page of the address space defined in `RAMIMAGE`. This arrangement allows `NULL` pointer errors to be more easily caught because no valid code or data occupies the first page of memory. The `Length` column indicates that 35,840 bytes were reserved for this module in the image file. This value, when added to the starting address for the module, produces a page-aligned address of `0x8C019000`, meeting the alignment requirement for first-stage processing. The `psize` value is identical because the `Length` value is also paragraph aligned. The `vsize` value is the actual size of the `.text` section of the `nk.exe` module.

The alignment stage continues until all relevant sections of the modules listed in the BIB file have been properly aligned. The sections processed are generally the `.text` and `.rsrc` sections; the exception is the `.pdata` section of the first module, which is also processed in the alignment stage. The filling stage begins with the processing of the `.data` section in the `nk.exe` module. Beginning with the first unused space of 74 bytes (`psize` – `vsize`) produced by the alignment of the `.text` section of the `nk.exe` module, the `.data` section of `nk.exe` is located at `0x8C018FB8`. This location is calculated by the addition of the `vsize` (actual size of the module) to its starting address of `0x8C100400`, producing an address of `0x8C018FB6`. An additional 2 bytes are added to this address to make it double word aligned on `0x8C018FB8`. The `Length` value of this entry indicates the number of bytes required in the image file, and the `psize` value is identical because no rounding is ever necessary for filler entries. Of particular interest is the comparatively large value (84) for `vsize`. This is the actual size of the entry before compression. Because this is a writable data section, it is compressed in the image file and decompressed when copied into RAM.

The filling stage continues until all remaining `.pdata` and `.data` sections are processed. If any one of these sections is too large to fit in any of the available unused spaces, it will be located just after the last entry processed in the alignment stage. The next section encountered that is too large to fill an unused space will be positioned just after this one. The Unfilled ROM Holes section of the console output lists the addresses and lengths of the unused spaces that could not be filled by a `.pdata` or `.data` section.

The next group of entries in the console output of Romimage provide some basic statistics on the content of the image file generated. The definitions of most of the entries are self-evident and are derived directly from the contents of the BIB file. A few, however, require further explanation. The first occurrence of *Starting ip* represents the address of the `StartUp` routine, relative to the value of the `BOOTJUMP` entry (in the `CONFIG` section of the `boot.bib` file). It is effectively the first executable instruction of the boot loader code. The second occurrence of *Starting ip* represents the address of the first executable instruction of the image file, which in this example contains a jump instruction to the address of the `StartUp` routine.

The *Raw files size:* entry in the sample console output represents the total size of the entries in the `FILES` section of the BIB file, before compression, while the *Compressed files size:* entry represents the size after compression. In the sample console output of Figure 4.7, these values are both 0 because `boot.bib` does not contain a `FILES` section.

Running the Build

Building the boot loader is slightly different from the build process for the CE kernel (which is covered in more detail in Chapter 10). Because the boot loader executable, `bootload.exe`, must be processed into an image file that is separate from the kernel image file, you cannot use the `blddemo.bat` batch file provided for building the CEPB demonstration platforms. `BLDDEMO` produces a single kernel image file and is unable to produce a separate boot loader image file. The CEPB IDE is also inappropriate for building the boot loader because it is designed to create a binary image file containing a CE kernel, something our boot loader lacks because the CE kernel is not yet booted. Considering how long it takes to complete a build of the CE kernel, this is probably for the best, at least during the initial development of the boot loader.

Once you have created the `Sources` and the `boot.bib` files, you are almost ready to build your boot loader. One additional file, `makefile`, is needed and may be copied from any of the CEPB example boot loaders. This file is usually the same in all source trees, and it is used to include a large and complex generic makefile that in turn includes your `Sources` file.

The first step in the boot loader build is to open a console window. The CE build environment must then be initialized by the `wince.bat` batch file located in the `.\PUBLIC\COMMON\OAK\MISC` directory. To simplify the execution of repeated builds, you may want to create a shortcut that executes this batch file in a console window. All that's required for building the boot loader is that you run `wince.bat` with the correct processor defined. The actual platform selected, such as `MINSHELL`, does not matter.

Once `wince.bat` has run with no error messages, you are ready for the next step. Run `blddemo.bat` with no parameters. Doing so will cause the target compiled header and library files provided in the CEPB to be copied to the `.\PUBLIC\<Platform Name>` directory tree. It is necessary to copy these files because the include path and library paths created by the makefiles will reference these directories. When your hard disk stops churning away, the appropriate files have been copied and you are ready to issue the build command.

The CEPB boot loader examples use two distinct types of source trees: One collects all of the common, processor-independent source code, in the `.\PLATFORM\<Platform`

Name>\BOOTLOAD\COMMON (CEPB 2.12) directory, and the other leaves them in the parent directory of the boot loader source tree, as in .\PLATFORM\<Platform Name>\EBOOT. If you have modeled your source tree on the latter structure, all you have to do is type "build" at the command line. If your tree is modeled after the former structure, you must first go to the COMMON subdirectory and type "build," and then return to the parent subdirectory and type "build" once again.

At this point you should be ready to generate the boot loader image file using the Romimage build tool. This tool will process the boot loader EXE file produced by the build command(s) (bootload.exe in the CEPB boot loader examples) into an image file ready to be written to the address specified in the RAMIMAGE entry of the boot.bib file. Go to the processor-dependent subdirectory just below the top-level boot loader source directory. For the CEPB 2.12 boot loader examples, this would be .\PLATFORM\ODO\BOOTLOAD\{SHX|MIPS}, and for the CEPB 3.0 boot loader examples, .\PLATFORM\ODO\EBOOT\EBOOT\{ARM|PPC|SHX|MIPS}. Type the command "ROMIMAGE <Name of the BIB File>". If the name of your BIB file were boot.bib, as in the CEPB boot loader examples, this command would be ROMIMAGE BOOT.BIB.

If the build is successful, a large amount of information will rapidly scroll by, describing in detail the space allocated by each module specified in boot.bib. Unless you specified otherwise using the OUTPUT entry in your BIB file, the image file(s) will be located in the same directory as the first module listed in the MODULES section of the BIB file. Precisely which image files are created depends on the entries appearing in the BIB file (see the section titled The CONFIG Section earlier in this chapter). Romimage can optionally generate Motorola S-record image files or raw image files that contain a byte-for-byte mapping of the data to be written to ROM. The BIN file image file is always generated but is supported only by the kernel image download program in the boot loader itself. Refer to the section titled ROM Emulator Products later in this chapter for a possible alternative to rewriting the boot loader into ROM each time it needs to be rebuilt and tested.

Note:
If you are familiar with using the Windows NT or Windows 2000 console window, you may already be familiar with the following: After you have created the console window used to build the boot loader (or any other CE build), click on the icon in the upper left corner and select the **Properties** option, then select the **Layout** tab. Notice the **Screen Buffer Size** group box. By increasing the size of the **Height** value beyond 25, you are creating an off-screen buffer that will allow you to scroll back though the informative output of such build tools as Romimage.

Debugging the Boot Loader

Because the boot loader is generally the first software to run after power-on reset, it lacks the benefit of the debug interface provided by the CE kernel for a connection to the development workstation. When debugging native and stream-interface device drivers, you may use the CEPB kernel debugger to control the execution of your driver. Debug commands are transmitted through the serial port or Ethernet port to a specialized module included in the build of the kernel image. The boot loader, however, precedes the loading of the kernel and is pretty much on its own for providing debug services to the development workstation.

Some of our hardware engineer friends occasionally remind us that they are "perfect" and do not require sophisticated debug tools because they do not make mistakes in the first place. We are not so gifted, however, and are forced to equip ourselves with any tool that we can find that may let us peer into the inner workings of our code creations. This section is dedicated to describing the tools and techniques that are useful in debugging a boot loader, or any other code for that matter that runs before the CE kernel is started. Certain tools require the purchase of some sort of device that connects directly to your custom platform or processor and communicates with a debugger running on the development workstation. Other tools are purely software based and are included in the build of the boot loader, in some cases communicating with an application also running on the development workstation. Other possibilities we will discuss require you to write your boot loader code in a particular manner that allows the custom platform itself to aid in the debugging process. If you qualify as a "perfect" engineer, like our hardware engineer friends, you may want to skip this section.

Output through LEDs and Sound

As you assemble your arsenal of debugging tools and techniques in preparation for debugging the boot loader, one of the most primitive mechanisms available might be an onboard speaker or LED. The term *primitive* in this context is not meant to be disparaging, but meant instead to refer to the fact that little or no extra code is required to initialize the speaker and LED ports. This feature makes these mechanisms inherently useful for attacking problems that can occur in the first few lines of your boot loader.

Note:
When designing your custom platform, you may want to consider including an alphanumeric LED, perhaps in a special debug version of the board. We realize that an extra device, such as an alphanumeric LED, can be problematic in designs that are particularly space constrained and that are not specified for an LED in the end user product. If you need to justify the extra effort this might require, we recommend using the argument that it will save far more engineering time than it will cost. This truism appears to apply to virtually all efforts expended to extend one's debugging options.

If your custom platform is x86 based, you might consider the use of port 80 for access to your LEDs. This port is generally considered the Manufacturing Diagnostics port and will avoid conflict with other reserved ports (Phoenix Technologies, 1991). Port 80 is also used by aftermarket developers of ISA bus, PC diagnostics cards to display Power-On Self-Test (POST) codes produced by the PC BIOS. Assuming that your custom platform has an ISA expansion bus (understandably a big assumption) and it is lacking LEDs or perhaps requires that they be removable, you can use one of these cards to add an LED alphanumeric display. Your LED debug statements, written to use port 80, would then be visible.

Another equally "primitive" debugging mechanism is an onboard speaker. The usefulness of this option depends on how your onboard speaker is controlled. If a tone may be generated in response to the value of certain bits in a register begin toggled, then the quantity and complexity of the code required will be low, making it a good candidate for debug output. This kind of speaker control is most common on PC platforms in which the speaker is manually modulated by the appropriate value being written to a particular register, successively turning the speaker on and off. This method is impractical when you're playing back prerecorded pulse code modulation (PCM) samples, as in a Windows WAV file, but it works well for debugging. If, on the other hand, your onboard speaker were controlled by an audio controller device, the quantity of code required to transfer PCM samples to the device would make the use of sound an unattractive option for debug output.

Let's assume that your speaker is controlled in a manner similar to that of a traditional onboard PC speaker. The next step requires that you establish a convention for how certain events will sound in terms of tone duration and pitch. If you're feeling particularly adventurous, you might want to use a well-known international standard we're sure you have heard of: Morse code. It defines at least 45 individual codes (including numbers and international characters) that may be used in combination to define an unlimited number of codes. It's a long way from the graphical user interface of the CEPB kernel debugger, but then you would probably resort to this method only when debugging the first few lines of startup code in your boot loader.

Serial Port and Parallel Port Output

Of the more primitive debug options, serial port and parallel port output are likely to be the most useful. With very little required code you can write character strings to a serial or parallel port and read the debug output on the development workstation connected to your custom platform. The serial port requires more code both to initialize and configure the UART controller and to write data to its transmit register. The parallel port, however, requires very little code for both initialization and transmission of data.

The sample boot loader code included in the CEPB generally uses the serial port for debug output and the parallel or Ethernet port for downloading the kernel image from the development workstation. The parallel port is generally used instead of the serial port for downloads because it has significantly higher data rates. If instead an Ethernet port is designated for downloads and you don't plan on using the parallel port as a fail-over mechanism, you might as well modify the sample boot loader to use the parallel port for debug output.

The category of debug functionality described in the CEPB online documentation as *Ethernet debug services* is not available when you're debugging the boot loader. Certain client registration functions that allow a process running on your custom platform to connect to a debugging application on the development workstation are available only after the CE kernel startup has been initiated. For boot loaders that provide Ethernet support, a large percentage of their code is dedicated to management of this transport medium. This means that a mechanism would still be required for debugging the Ethernet code itself, making the use of the Ethernet port as a primitive debug port impractical.

Display Output

Perhaps the simplest method for debugging the boot loader is to display an occasional character string to describe the current state of execution. What you include in your character string depends on the surrounding code and the problem being debugged. This is not unlike the use of `printf` calls when you're developing a *character mode* (or in Windows programming a *console mode*) application, but different in that `printf` calls will, in most cases, not be an option in the development of the boot loader. The implementation of `printf` offered by the CE standard runtime library is generally not defined for a boot loader build and is removed from the `stdlib.h` header file during preprocessing (see Chapter 10 for more information on the selective inclusion of APIs during the build process).

To use the screen output debugging option, you will need to create a function that directs the character string to whatever form of display device exists on your custom platform. You will also have to create another function that configures the display controller. You must call this configuration function as soon as possible to allow debugging of the boot loader code that occurs early in the boot sequence. Of course, you will be unable to debug the display code using the display hardware because it is the display code itself that enables this capability. The best strategy, then, is to make the display functions as simple as possible in the hope that they will work right the first time and require no debugging.

If your custom platform is PC based and contains a standard PC BIOS, software interrupts may be used to display a character string for debugging. In this case, the existence of a BIOS represents a kind of pre-boot loader, equipped with an impressive array of well-documented, standardized services. By the time the CE boot loader is executed, most of the primary onboard devices have already been configured and are available for access through any of the predefined software interrupts.

ROM Monitor

Another method exists that provides varying degrees of debugging capability for your boot loader code. ROM monitors, as a generic category of debugging software, represent a module of software that runs on a target processor and is used to provide remote debugging access from a development workstation. Just to give you some idea of how a ROM monitor would be used in debugging the boot loader, let's discuss a few implementations of a ROM monitor.

As you read through the CEPB documentation on how to develop a boot loader, you will find occasional mention of a firmware monitor. This module is functionally equivalent to a ROM monitor and is one example of a ROM monitor that may be used to debug your boot loader. Though this is not clearly stated in the documentation, the firmware monitor is actually not provided in the CEPB, but it is referenced in certain boot loader examples. The file `main.c` in the `.\PLATFORM\ODO\BOOTLOAD\COMMON` (CEPB 2.12) directory contains a line of code that calls the function `StartMonitor`, but it is commented out.

The firmware monitor provides a way to interact with your custom platform, through a command-line interface transmitted to the development workstation over an RS-232 null modem cable. It provides a limited degree of control for enabling such basic operations as searching memory, setting and retrieving register values, and specifying the name of the kernel image for download from the development workstation.

Some third-party suppliers of firmware monitors are specifically dedicated to certain reference platforms and processors. These firmware monitors are designed to be included in your boot loader's image file and are added to the boot loader build. In some cases the firmware monitor may be offered as a part of a larger product designed to aid in the integration of CE with your custom platform. Appendix C lists companies that offer firmware monitors, alone or as part of a larger offering.

A more advanced implementation of a ROM monitor is provided in certain graphical debugger products. The ROM monitor is used as the back end for a source-level debugger running on your development workstation, and it accepts commands to perform any required debugging operations, such as setting breakpoints, querying memory, and examining register values. The connection to the debugger is not limited to a serial cable, and it can include Ethernet and a specialized cable connected to an on-chip debugging port of the target platform (described in more detail shortly). After a connection is made to the ROM monitor, the boot loader is downloaded from the development workstation, and execution is initiated and continues until a breakpoint or another event you have defined with the debugger occurs. The ROM monitor provides the required control to modify the boot loader code at runtime, to halt execution of the code, and to notify the development workstation of the location in a source file for display when a breakpoint is detected. This control effectively allows single-stepping and supports any of the other features provided by the development workstation debugger.

This type of ROM monitor is generally developed by the same company that offers the debugger and must support your target processor. It is assumed that your custom platform is at least stable enough to run the ROM monitor, so this may not be the answer if your hardware is not yet proven. The more primitive debugging alternatives previously discussed, or the hardware-assisted debugging options discussed later in this section, would be better alternatives. To provide source-level debugging, the ROM monitor must also support the symbol table format produced by your boot loader build process. At the time of this writing, very few debugger companies offer support for the symbol tables generated by CE compilers, so this, too, could be a problem (see Appendix C). In the next section we will describe one possible method to work around the problem of symbol table support for ROM monitor debugging.

ROM Emulator Products

Simply stated, ROM emulators emulate memory. The kind of memory they emulate is not limited to ROM and in some cases will include flash, SDRAM, DRAM, SIMM (single inline memory module), and other forms of memory, depending on the product being considered. They work by replacing the memory chips on your custom platform with special connectors or adapters leading to a cable that forms a connection to the actual ROM emulator hardware. Exactly how this connection is established varies with the packaging and memory technology you're using. If you think you might want to use a ROM emulator (a decision that will be clarified by the end of this section), you should consult the manufacturer of the ROM emulator to determine if your memory configuration is supported, well before the design of your custom platform is finalized. Making this determination early will allow you enough time to consider possible changes to accommodate the use of a ROM emulator, such as changes in your layout to make room for an adapter.

You can use ROM emulators for debugging the boot loader code through a variety of mechanisms. Many ROM emulators are also equipped with their own form of specialized ROM monitor software to support a graphical debugger that runs remotely on the development workstation. As was true with the ROM monitor, however, the debugger may not support the symbol table format in use by CEPB compilers.

Note:
One alternative you should consider to get around the problem of CEPB symbol table support is the use of GNU tools. The symbol table format is widely supported by most, if not all, debugger products, and the list of supported processors is quite large. This support would allow you to debug the boot loader at the source level, and when all problems were resolved you could go back to using the standard CEPB build process. Assuming that no build- or compiler-dependent problems emerge when you're changing back to the CEPB build, this would remain your default build option for the boot loader until another problem was discussed or an enhancement was needed, at which time you would roll out your alternative GNU build.

Another way to use ROM emulators is through an area of reserved memory used by your code to write character strings just as it would to a serial port, but without requiring the resources of the onboard serial port. Some ROM emulator products can also provide an internal trace buffer that collects a list of addresses accessed. Not unlike a similar feature offered by much costlier processor emulators, this information can be used to determine which code was executed in real time. Being able to make this determination is absolutely essential for post-mortem debugging of your boot loader after it has crashed.

Perhaps the most significant feature in the use of a ROM emulator, particularly as it relates to boot loader development, is that you need not reprogram your EPROM devices every time you wish to test a modification in the boot loader code. Because the boot loader is the first code to run, there is no software to upload it into RAM or flash memory, as there is for the kernel image. This feature alone may justify the cost of the ROM emulator, even if none of its other, more advanced features are put to use.

Note:
One word of caution when you're using a ROM emulator: Be certain that you carefully read the documentation provided with the debugger product on the use of its monitor program. Certain assumptions are likely to be made concerning the target CPU configuration that may conflict with the configuration performed in the very boot loader code you are trying to debug.

On-Chip Debugging

The ultimate goal of any debugging solution is to allow control and interrogation of the target platform without requiring the use of any target resources, and therefore with little or no detectable intrusion in the normal execution of the code. Generally this goal must be achieved with some kind of hardware to "assist" in monitoring and controlling certain processor signals. The complexity of such hardware has grown over time as a function of the corresponding increase in the capabilities of the processor, and it is quite costly. To remedy this situation, many processor families are designed with an extra set of signals that may be used by remote debugging tools to control and monitor program execution without using any ROM monitor software (as described in the previous section). Because the processor provides breakpoint support internally, it is even possible to set breakpoints in code running from ROM. This is usually not possible for software-oriented breakpoints because XIP ROM code may not be modified with the additional instructions required for a breakpoint. Additional signals are also provided to allow the code to be uploaded directly into the target platform's RAM for execution and debugging.

This capability is generically referred to as on-chip debugging (OCD) and is known by various trade names. Perhaps the most popular OCD implementation is provided on the PowerPC processor family and is referred to as *background debug mode.* The term *JTAG* is used to describe the interface adapted from the IEEE 1149.1 specification for boundary-scan testing of chip- and board-level hardware and is commonly used by Texas Instruments in its DSP product lines.

If your processor offers OCD capability, your first step in using this capability to debug the boot loader is to acquire the debugging tools that support the OCD interface. For OCD to work, the debugging software running on the development workstation must communicate with your custom platform using the appropriate OCD protocol. This communication generally occurs via an adapter device that allows an existing port or installed adapter card on the development workstation to communicate with the target platform's OCD port.

Note:
The term *OCD adapter* as we have used it was invented for the purposes of this narrative. As you research this topic beyond this book, you may find that the term *wiggler* is used to describe the same device.

With the introduction of CEPB 3.0, OCD interfaces and protocols are supported through the use of an EXDI driver provided by the adapter device vendor. When installed, the EXDI driver can be selected as a type of transport in the CEPB 3.0 IDE for the specified debug services. As of this writing, EXDI was not yet supported by any adapter device vendors. This book's Web site will be updated with this information as we become aware of such support.

Logic Analyzer

All the tools described thus far in this chapter work well when you're debugging the boot loader on proven hardware. If your custom platform is not fully tested and you suspect that a particular problem with the boot loader is really the symptom of malfunctioning hardware, then software-assisted debugging such as that provided by the ROM monitor may not be the best option. OCD, acting as a hardware-assisted debugger, may help in isolating and demonstrating the problem without being affected by the occurence of a hardware problem.

One limitation in the implementation of most OCD adapters, however, is that the collection of a real-time trace of program or data accesses is usually not supported. When using a logic analyzer, however, you can assess what the processor was doing up to the moment it appeared to lock up (possibly because of an unhandled exception), by using a postmortem trace that displays past instruction and data accesses. You can also analyze any other digital signals that can be sampled with an external probe.

For specific debug scenarios, such as that just described, logic analyzers are the logical (no pun intended) choice. For general boot loader debugging, however, a logic analyzer quickly loses its appeal. Because a logic analyzer by its very nature is monitoring and interpreting signals, it cannot easily provide breakpoint functionality. You can, however, instrument the boot loader code with writes to or reads from uncached memory that can then be monitored by the logic analyzer, triggering a breakpoint when the specified condition is true.

This approach, of course, is less convenient than simply clicking on a line of source code on your graphical debugger. When the logic analyzer's trace buffer is examined, it may or may not be possible to view the instructions in their original source code form. In addition, if the processor's cache is enabled, you may not be able to view the instruction in the trace buffer if it was executed from the processor's internal cache without external memory being accessed. Upload of the boot loader code to your custom platform's RAM is also not possible, as it is with OCD and ROM emulators. And depending on the packaging technology used by the manufacturer of your custom platform's processor, it may be necessary to encase the processor in a special adapter that is then soldered to your board. This process can be both costly and time-consuming.

In-Circuit Emulator

An in-circuit emulator (ICE) is a device that acts as a complete replacement for the processor on your custom platform. The internal functional units of the processor and the signaling of the processor pinouts are emulated so precisely that communication with the emulated processor by surrounding components is compatible with that of the real target processor. This type of emulation gives ICE hardware complete visibility into the operation of the processor and can provide bus event detection and real-time trace functions similar to those available on many logic analyzers. Unlike logic analyzers, however, processor emulators possess an understanding of the processor architecture and are able to perform the level of processor control required for hardware breakpoints. Because the emulator hardware functions independently of the executing code, it is possible to query the state of the processor, even after the processor is in an unknown state. This is not possible when you're using a ROM monitor or emulator because it relies on the resources of the target processor to respond to the queries of the development workstation debugging tools.

As with the ROM monitor, the ROM emulator, and OCD, a remote debugger running on your development workstation is required for source-level debugging. The debugger interfaces to the ICE through a port on the development workstation, using a predefined command protocol. If the ICE vendor provides an EXDI driver, the CEPB 3.0 kernel debugger can act as the remote debugger and communicate with the ICE hardware through the designated port on the development workstation.

Attaching the emulator to your custom platform can be as difficult as attaching the probes required for a logic anlayzer. In fact, it may be necessary to alter the layout of your custom platform to allow room for the installation of this adapter. Depending on the packaging technology used by the processor manufacturer, installation of the adapter may be possible only during board fabrication. Because of the precision tooling required to manufacture an adapter for high-density, high–pin count processors, these adapters are generally quite expensive.

With this in mind, you should carefully consider the use of an ICE. The debugging alternatives already presented are sufficient to resolve most problems, but when your custom platform is unproven, using an ICE provides the highest degree of control with the lowest degree of intrusiveness. This allows debugging of problems related to the interaction of the hardware and software. So consider an ICE to be one of the biggest debugging weapons in your arsenal, to be activated only for the biggest problems.

Summary

If you have made it this far, you are now well-equipped to venture forth into the brave new world of CE boot loaders. We have discussed the functional requirements of a boot loader and how the DAM method can be used to adapt the sample boot loader code provided in the CEPB. Once you are ready to test your boot loader, you need a means of building it into an executable image, ready to execute at a particular reset address. This is where the CE build tools are used, and in this chapter we discussed the mechanism for configuring these tools specifically to build your boot loader image. Because the boot loader, by definition, runs before any other CE software, you may need to extend your debug arsenal to include tools outside of the CEPB tool chain. This is not an uncommon problem in the world of embedded system development, so there are many options to choose from, and we discussed the relative advantages and disadvantages of each.

Developing the CE boot loader can be one of the most difficult aspects of getting CE operational on your custom platform. By its very nature, it is on the critical path of everyone's software development schedule and should therefore be implemented as early as possible in the development process. The sample boot loaders provided in the CEPB and third-party boot loaders have the potential to reduce your development risk by providing a working template that matches, or nearly matches, your custom platform.

5 OAL Development

If you're developing a custom platform (meaning that you have designed or modified a board populated with peripheral devices and a CE-supported CPU), you will also need to develop a *custom* CE kernel. OAL development is the mechanism for customizing the CE kernel. You are required to implement certain OAL-defined functions, and the CE kernel calls these functions at various times to obtain access to the capabilities of your platform. Most of these functions carry the prefix *OEM* to indicate that they are associated with the hardware manufacturers developing custom CE platforms.

The base OAL directory structure (created during CEPB installation), the `<CE Version>\PLATFORM\<Platform Name>\KERNEL` directory, will be discussed later in this chapter. If you examine this directory further looking for an OAL directory that contains OAL code, you will not find one. The Hardware Abstraction Layer (HAL) directory is the primary repository of OAL code. It is best to think of the OAL as the accumulation of the functions that define a particular portion of the HAL implemented by you, the OEM. In the first section of this chapter (OAL Architecture), the HAL is depicted in relation to the OAL code.

After discussing OAL architecture, we will break down the OAL development process into three distinct phases:

1. **Phase 1.** Developing a minimal set of OAL functions required to successfully start the CE kernel
2. **Phase 2.** Expanding on the functionality of the first phase by adding remote debugging support and interrupt service routines (ISRs)
3. **Phase 3.** Adding features to provide module certification, power management, and a persistent registry

Note that many of the same development techniques applied to the Windows CE boot loader (see Chapter 4) are used in OAL development. You will find yourself with minimal debugging tools, perhaps limited to an LED of some sort to indicate the status of your running OAL code.

Because OAL development includes the code that is run at system startup, you may be able to copy many of the routines developed for the boot loader, for the implementation of certain OAL functions. We will indicate where this is the case as we progress through this chapter.

OAL Architecture

The architecture of the OAL can be compared to that of a PC BIOS. For most end users, the BIOS is the software they see when the system is first loaded, generally announcing the capabilities of their system, possibly alerting them to a recent system enhancement or malfunction that might require their attention. What they do not know is that the PC BIOS also provides a standard software interface for a range of services that expose the platform's capabilities in a standardized way. This is where the OAL and PC BIOS are quite similar.

The CE OAL is a collection of functions that may be accessed by the CE operating system to gain access to platform-specific features. The important point here is the use of the term *platform.* Because the CEPB provides a different set of binaries for each supported CPU, the OAL code does not attempt to resolve *CPU* dependencies, but instead focuses on *platform* dependencies. This focus allows the operating system to remain unchanged when running on custom platforms.

In Figure 5.1, the OAL is depicted in relationship to the whole of the CE operating system when functioning on a custom platform. Note that the OAL, like the boot loader, runs in kernel mode. This means that access to the physical resources of your platform (memory, base ports, and I/O [input/output] regions) may occur without a specifically allocated virtual memory address (allocated by the `VirtualAlloc`, `VirtualCopy`, and `MmMapIoSpace` functions, which are discussed in Chapter 8). Also note the overlap between the OAL and the boot loader. This overlap occurs because the code that must be developed for the boot loader may also be used in the implementation of certain OAL functions. The overlap does not extend to the loca-

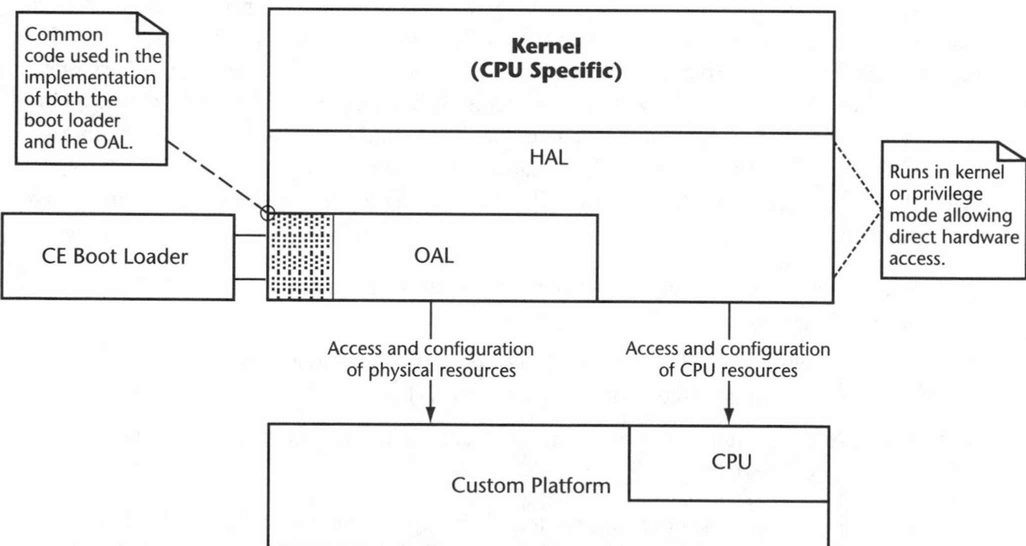

Figure 5.1 Block diagram of the OAL architecture on a custom platform

tion of the code in memory when the CE kernel image is being built. The boot loader is generally built as a stand-alone image, while the OAL functions are included in the kernel image.

Because the OAL is the first code to run in the CE kernel, it is also possible to produce a kernel image that does not require the presence of a boot loader. A portion (or all for that matter) of the actual boot loader code that executes at system startup would be included in the kernel image and positioned in memory to correspond to the location of the first instruction executed by the CPU. Because the boot loader often provides startup and configuration options developed separately from the OAL, it is often better to retain this separation. In addition, maintaining separate images makes it possible for the boot loader to update the kernel image in flash memory when a new version becomes available.

It is interesting to note that the sample OAL provided in the CEPB for CEPC platforms uses the PC BIOS for the implementation of many OAL functions. The program Loadcepc acts as a kind of boot loader and uses DOS calls to read the CE kernel image (containing the OAL code) from the disk, and copies it into RAM. This use of the PC BIOS for the implementation of certain CEPC OAL functions, and of DOS to support the implementation of the CEPC boot loader, is depicted in Figure 5.2.

Note:
You might be thinking of using a CEPC platform as your production platform, perhaps to leverage the tremendous economies of scale available in the production of PC platforms. One cost item that is not immediately apparent, however, consists of the licensing fees for the BIOS and DOS. These fees apply only if you use the CEPC platform support provided in the CEPB, with no changes. Possible changes to avoid these added licensing fees include the use of a true boot loader that is loaded from a disk's boot sector and/or an OAL implemented without PC BIOS calls.

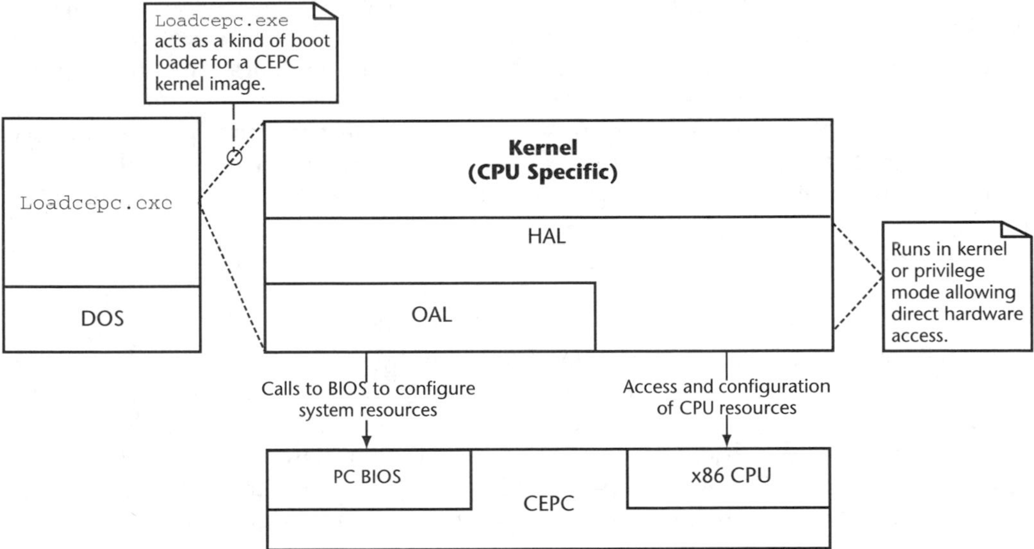

Figure 5.2 Block diagram of the OAL architecture on a CEPC

OAL Development: Phase 1

Our primary goal in OAL development phase 1 is to start execution of the CE kernel. In this section we will walk through the steps required for developing an OAL, with just enough functionality to start execution of the CE kernel. We will also discuss the directory structure of the OAL sample source code, which will help us better understand the build process run by CEPB. This will bring us to a discussion of the OAL modifications most likely required for your custom platform and will allow us to cover various debugging strategies available during OAL development. Because the OAL runs before the CE kernel, we cannot use the CE kernel debugger (discussed in Chapter 9) for debugging OAL code.

Sample OALs

Like so many other aspects of CE system development where we begin with a sample provided in the CEPB, the best way to begin OAL development is to determine which of the sample OAL implementations most closely matches your custom platform. The way to identify the most relevant sample OAL will become clear in the next section.

Sample OALs are provided in the CEPB for two different platforms: the Odo platform (used internally by Microsoft and available directly from Hitachi at www.hitachi-first.com), and the CEPC platform based on a standard 486/Pentium PC platform. The sample OAL code provided for the CEPC platform is specific to an x86 family CPU and will not be useful to you unless your custom platform is also x86 based. The sample OAL code for the Odo platform, however, supports a variety of CPU families: ARM, MIPS, PowerPC, and SHx.

To begin developing the OAL for your custom platform, you will need to identify which of the sample OALs most closely matches the configuration of your custom platform. You could simply match the CPU family of your custom platform to that of the OAL sample source. Another option would be to find a board support package (BSP) from your CPU vendor or third party (see Appendix C) with support for your CPU family. The route you take will probably depend on how closely your platform matches the one used in the development of the sample OAL (provided either by Microsoft or by a third party offering a BSP). In some cases the OAL might provide support for a specific onboard device included in your custom platform, such as an audio chip, digitizer controller, or network interface card (NIC) chip. In any case, you will be provided with OAL source code, and your first task will be to create a directory tree that mirrors the one used by the Microsoft sample OALs. This directory tree will support the building of your OAL and will be covered in more detail in the next section.

OAL sample code consists of a combination of assembly language and C source code. The assembly language is used where register access is needed, particularly in the code that initializes the CPU and its associated platform. Table 5.1 lists the directories used by the sample OAL code, including a description of the contents of each directory and how it is used in the OAL build process. The assembly language modules provided in the sample OAL are located in the `<CE Version>\PLATFORM\<Platform Name>\KERNEL\HAL\<CPU Family>` directory. In most cases the modules provided for your CPU family will not require modification. If modifications are required, they are usually identical to those required during development of the boot loader, which generally uses the same assembly language modules.

Table 5.1 OAL Sample Source Code Directory Structure

OAL Sample Source Code Path	Description
CE Version>\PLATFORM\<Platform Name>\KERNEL	The parent directory where the CE kernel image (nk.exe) is built from the source and object module libraries contained in the subdirectories listed in the Dirs file.
<CE Version>\PLATFORM\<Platform Name>\KERNEL\BUILDEXE	The parent directory of the subdirectories containing the Sources files for building each type of kernel image. Each type of kernel image is built into an executable module of a different name. Later in the build process, the common.bib file checks the values of certain environment variables to determine which executable module to use in forming the final ROM image file, nk.bin.
<CE Version>\PLATFORM\<Platform Name>\KERNEL\BUILDEXE\NOKD	Contains the Sources file used to build a kernel image (nk.exe) that contains no kernel debugging capability.
<CE Version>\PLATFORM\<Platform Name>\KERNEL\BUILDEXE\PROFILER	Contains the Sources file used to build the kernel image that provides profiling support, but without kernel debugging capability.
<CE Version>\PLATFORM\<Platform Name>\KERNEL\BUILDEXE\PROFKD	Contains the Sources file to build a kernel image with both profiling and kernel debugging support.
<CE Version>\PLATFORM\<Platform Name>\KERNEL\BUILDEXE\WITHKD	Contains the Sources file used to build the kernel image that contains support for kernel debugging.
<CE Version>\PLATFORM\<Platform Name>\KERNEL\HAL	Contains the CPU-independent code for the implementation of your custom platform's OAL functions. In practice, it is unlikely that a custom platform would be implemented with support for more than one CPU, but you should maintain this structure for consistency with the sample OAL source code. The majority of the OAL code you develop for your custom platform will be located in this directory. As a matter of necessity, all code in this directory is written in C to maintain CPU independence.
<CE Version>\PLATFORM\<Platform Name>\KERNEL\HAL\<CPU Family>	Contains the CPU-specific OAL code. At a minimum it contains an implementation of the system startup code (the code first run by the CPU on power-up). It may also contain initialization code for specific peripheral devices or interrupt service routines (ISRs).
<CE Version>\PLATFORM\<Platform Name>\KERNEL\Profiler\<CPU Family>	Contains the CPU-specific implementation of the OAL functions OEMProfileTimerDisable and OEMProfileTimerEnable, called by the CE kernel profiler code. If your CPU provides the capability for an additional timer, separate from the one used for the system tick, this directory will be used to maintain a separate profiling timer. It will also contain your implementation of the ISR for this timer.

Building the OAL

To begin debugging your newly developed (or adapted from a sample) OAL code, you must first be able to build the OAL using the CEPB. Building anything platform specific, such as an OAL or device drivers for an onboard device, requires that it appear in the component view of the CEPB IDE. Two specially formatted files are used by the CEPB to control this process, a CEC file and a BSP file. The CEC file defines each of the modules in your platform directory and provides instructions on how they must be built. The BSP file is used when the platform project is first created with the Platform Wizard (activated when you select the **New | Platforms | WCE Platforms** option), and it provides a list of the components in the component library that must be included for each platform configuration. If you are not using a third-party resource that supplies your drivers and OAL code (along with the associated CEC and BSP files), it is still possible to use the Platform Wizard to generate a template BSP file that will cause your OAL code to be built.

To begin, you must create a new platform project using the Platform Wizard tool. Before you do so, you must have already selected a sample OAL (described in the previous section) and copied it to your platform directory. The Platform Wizard tool is accessed through the **File | New | Platforms** menu option. A series of dialog boxes are displayed to define the properties of your platform, beginning with the name of the platform in the first dialog box. The second dialog box asks you to identify the BSP that applies to your platform. At a minimum, the two sample BSPs that accompany the CEPB—Odo and CEPC—will be displayed. If you have installed a third-party BSP, it should also be named in the same list box.

If your platform is not specifically mentioned by name, then the MyBSP platform is an effective alternative. It creates a CEPB project and template BSP file (located in the `Windows CE Platform Builder\3.00\CEPB\BIN\IDE` directory) that builds anything located under the `<CE Version>\PLATFORM\<Platform Name>` directory, specified in the **BSP Subdirectory** edit field. The `Dirs` file (described in Chapter 3) in this directory is used internally during the build process to specify which of the directories contain source code that must be built. The next and last step requires you to select one of five predefined operating system configurations.

Note:
The `WINCE300\<Platform Name>` directory, as the name implies, contains those components that are platform specific. Drivers, object module libraries containing platform-specific functions, and your OAL code all reside in this directory. Refer to Chapter 10 for more information on the organization of CEPB source code directories and for an explanation of the internal workings of the CEPB build process.

Selecting **MyBSP** in the Platform Wizard produces a project with just two components in the component view. The component in the component view with the same name as your platform represents the build of everything in the platform directory. The next component contains all of the modules organized by type that are associated with the predefined configuration selected in the Platform Wizard.

If you had selected a specific BSP in the Platform Wizard, the component view would contain separate entries for each of the modules located in the platform directory. A separate component would appear for the OAL itself, along with each driver module, thereby effectively breaking down the build of the platform directory into individual modules that may be built separately or deleted from the component view and removed from the build process. To accomplish the same level of build granularity in your own BSP, you would need to create a CEC file that listed each distinct module in your platform directory.

You could also modify the template BSP file for use when the Platform Wizard generated the next project. The modified template BSP file would be used by the Platform Wizard to select the components associated with the platform configuration selected by the end user in the last dialog box. Each of these components would then appear in the component view window immediately after generation of the project. Note, however, that you do not have to modify the template BSP file to allow components in the component library to appear in the component view for a particular platform project. After the platform project is generated, it is also possible to simply drag a component appearing in the component library window to the component view window. The BSP file just allows this process to occur automatically during generation of the platform project by the Platform Wizard. For more information on how to create a CEC file or how to modify your template BSP file, refer to Chapter 3, as well as to the component file and board support package file appendices in the Operating System Development section of the CEPB online documentation.

Once the platform project has been generated, building your OAL code is simply a matter of selecting the **CEPB Build | Build Platform** option. Doing so begins a process that will build not only the OAL code located in your platform's `<CE Version>\PLATFORM\<Platform Name>\KERNEL` directory, but all the drivers and modules associated with the platform configuration that you selected using the Platform Wizard. Refer to the section titled Sample OALs earlier in this chapter for more information on the organization of OAL source code directories.

Kernel Startup Routine and OEMWriteDebugLED

As we mentioned earlier, the OAL code is linked directly into `nk.exe`, the relocatable module containing the CE kernel. When your custom platform is cold-booted, the CPU begins running the boot loader code (located at a reserved address or at an address contained in a particular CPU register). The very last thing the boot loader must do is begin execution of the CE kernel, the address of which varies with CPU type, but which is controlled by the address of the `RAMIMAGE` memory region in your platform's BIB file, typically `config.bib` (located in the `<CE Version>\PLATFORM\<Platform Name>\FILES` directory of the sample OAL source code). To ensure that the CE kernel appears at the beginning of the `RAMIMAGE` memory, the relocatable kernel module `nk.exe` always appears as the first module named in the `MODULES` section for the memory type of `NK` (defined in the `config.bib` file as a memory region of type `RAMIMAGE`). BIB files are discussed in more detail in Chapter 4.

Note:
The `nk.exe` module is included in the ROM image file `nk.bin`. The last phase of the build process locates relocatable modules such as `nk.exe` to a specific ROM address, while allowing the other modules located in RAM to remain relocatable. This process is discussed in more detail in Chapter 10.

The name of the routine in `nk.exe` that represents its primary entry point (activated by the boot loader, as we just mentioned) is controlled by the value of the `EXEENTRY` macro in the `Sources` file (located in the `<CE Version>\PLATFORM\<Platform Name>\KERNEL\BUILDEXE\<Debug and Profile Kernel Type>` directory) used in the build of the CE kernel and indirectly the OAL code. Typically the name of this routine in the sample OAL source code is *StartUp*. The address of the `StartUp` routine is hard-coded in the boot loader to correspond to the beginning address for the `RAMIMAGE` memory region defined in `config.bib`.

Consider the sample OAL code `fwp2.src` located in the `<CE Version>\PLATFORM\ODO\KERNEL\HAL\SHX` directory. The startup routine `_StartUp`, copied from the boot loader `init.src` module as noted in the source code comments, initializes the memory controller, PCMCIA registers, and watchdog timer, among other things. Effectively this code places the CPU in a known state for the CE kernel. Any additional initialization unique to your platform typically is performed after the kernel is started by one of the OAL routines prefixed with *OEM*, which are described later in this chapter. In Figure 5.3, the order in which these *OEM* functions is called during system initialization is portrayed in a sequence diagram.

Note:
Undoubtedly, throughout most of your OAL code you will be accessing physical resources (memory, registers, I/O ports, and so on) of your platform. It should give you some comfort to know that you may do so with impunity, meaning that you need not map virtual to physical memory addresses by calling `MmMapIoSpace` or `VirtualAlloc` and `VirtualCopy` (as discussed in Chapter 8). Your OAL code runs in kernel mode (synonymous with *privilege mode*) and has direct access to the physical resources of your platform.

If a peripheral device is mapped to a particular physical address, be certain that this address is uncached. Depending on the CPU in use, it may be necessary to use the uncached alias of the address to your peripheral's physical resources. One example is in the SH3 processor on which addresses between `0xA000000` and `0xBFFFFFFF` act as an uncached alias to physical memory between addresses `0x00000000` and `0x1FFFFFFF`. The upper three bits effectively specify a memory region with predefined attributes.

The first step in this phase of OAL development is to make certain that the `StartUp` routine is functioning correctly. Considering that this code is run before the kernel is loaded, debug services are not yet available. In most cases this means that you are limited to the use of the platform itself to monitor the progress of your `StartUp` routine. If LEDs are present on your platform, this monitoring might be accomplished by toggling the state of the LED or, if you are lucky enough to have an alphanumeric LED available, displaying a different value. Just after a critical line of startup code, you would insert an additional line of code to toggle or alter the appearance of this hardware indication. The function `OEMWriteDebugLED` is defined in the OAL for just this purpose, and it should be implemented at the same time you implement the `StartUp` routine. Listing 5.1 contains an excerpt of a `StartUp` routine for an x86-based processor. Note the use of the `OEMWriteDebugLED` function to create a hardware indication for the beginning of the startup code.

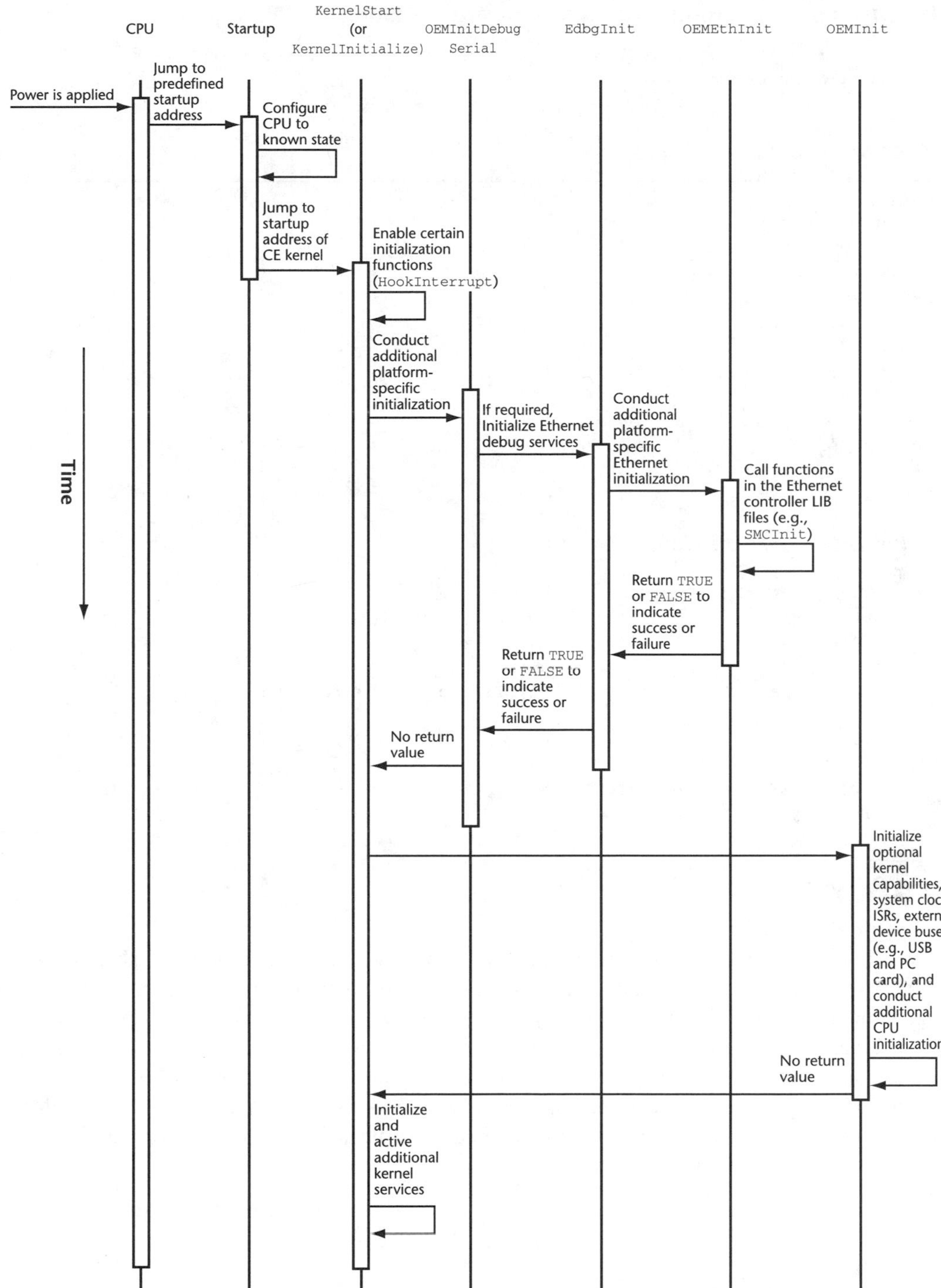

Figure 5.3 Sequence diagram for OAL startup

Listing 5.1 `StartUp` **routine using a hardware indication for debugging**

```
; Definition of port 80 codes used for hardware indications of the status of
; of the StartUp routine.
; ---------------------------------------------------------------------------
P80CODESTART=00h
P80ENABLESERIAL=01h
P80DETECTMEM=02h
P80PRESET=03h
P80COPYLOADER=04h
P80RAMJUMP=05h
P80INRAM=06h
P80SMIENABLE=07h
P80SMIADJUST=08h
P80SMIA000=09h
P80INPROT=0ah
P80INPOST=0bh
P80EXITPOST=0ch
P80PARALLELSET= 080h
P80PARDWNLOAD= 090h
P80SERIALMAN=0e0h

OEMWriteDebugLED PROTO C arg1:SBYTE

StartUp PROC NEAR C PUBLIC
    cli                           ; shut off any interrupts
; *** Disable NMI
    mov al, 080h                  ; set bit 7 of port 70
    out 70h, al                   ;   the cmos index location

    cld

    INVOKE OEMWriteDebugLED, P80CODESTART ; indicate that we are booting

    . . .

Startup ENDP
```

As in the sample OAL code for the Odo platform, in most cases you should be able to share much of the same platform initialization code developed for the boot loader. This code will already have been tested and debugged, by many of the same techniques described in this chapter. If you can assume that your boot loader will be present in the production version of your platform and that the boot loader will always be the code that causes execution of the `StartUp` routine, you might also be able to rely on the boot loader for most, if not all, of the functionality in the `StartUp` routine. The `StartUp` routine in the sample x86 OAL is a good example, having only two lines of code, as depicted in Listing 5.2.

Listing 5.2 Minimal startup routine that assumes prior initialization by the boot loader

```
Naked StartUp()
{
    __asm
    {
    cli
    jmp  KernelInitialize // equivalent to KernelStart for other CPU
families
    }
}
```

CE Version Memo

With the introduction of CE 3.0, it is now possible to use the CEPB integrated debugger for debugging OAL code. Debugging OAL code requires the use of hardware-assisted debugging, enabled through a probe device or through the built-in capabilities of your target board's CPU. CE 3.0 now supports hardware-assisted debugging through an interface known as EXDI. A driver, provided by the vendor of the debugging hardware, is used by the CEPB IDE to access and control the target platform with only the resources of the debugging hardware. No operating system or monitoring software need reside on the target platform, so the impact of the debugger on the software being debugged is minimized. Some debugging hardware products also allow you to upload new code to the flash memory or RAM on the target platform.

The EXDI interface becomes available only after installation of the vendor-supplied drivers for the debugging hardware. (At the time of this writing, CE support of EXDI is relatively recent, so be certain to contact the vendor that is providing hardware-assisted debugging for your target platform and CPU family, to determine if CE 3.0 EXDI support is provided.) The **Target | Configure Remote Services** option allows the EXDI interface to be selected over the other supported interface options (Ethernet, parallel, and serial).

For your information, hardware-assisted debugging is required to debug OAL code because the CE kernel debugger (implemented as a software module contained in the kernel itself) is not yet loaded during OAL initialization. The CE kernel debugger is also unable to debug code running in kernel (or privilege) mode, the mode in which the kernel debugger itself is running; it is limited to debugging user mode code (debugging options are discussed in more detail in Chapter 9.)

OEMInit

If your `StartUp` routine executes successfully, it then transfers control (through a jump or call instruction) to the CE entry point `KernelStart` (`KernelInitialize` for the x86 CE kernel). After minimal initialization of the CE kernel, the function `OEMInit` will be called. You must supply the implementation of this function in your platform's OAL. It is here that the major portion of your platform initialization should be completed, unlike the `StartUp` routine presented in the previous section, which focuses more on configuring the CPU to a known state.

Considering that the CE kernel has completed only minimal initialization, the only kernel service that you may call in `OEMInit` is `HookInterrupt`. The `HookInterrupt` function is called from `OEMInit` to set up the interrupt service routines (ISRs) for each of your platform's interrupt request (IRQ) lines. If a particular interrupt is not exposed to CE device drivers, then `HookInterrupt` need not be called, but then your code will be responsible for associating the interrupt with the address of the ISR, something `HookInterrupt` would do for you. Developing CE ISRs will be discussed in more detail in our discussion of phase 2 of OAL development later in this chapter. The implementation of the `OEMInit` function requires the following functionality:

- If building for module certification, assign global variables `pOEMLoadInit` and `pOEMLoadModule` the address of your `OEMCertifyModuleInit` and `OEMCertifyModule` functions, respectively. (These functions were introduced in CE 3.0.) *Delay development until phase 3.*
- Initialize the platform clock.
- Initialize shared (global) memory regions.
- Configure interrupts (leave disabled and clear pending interrupts).
- Associate ISRs with physical interrupts. *Partially delay development until phase 2.*
- Assign global variable `pKDIoControl` the address of the `OEMKDIoControl` function. (This variable was introduced in CE 3.0.) *Delay development until phase 3.*

Because we are still in phase 1 of OAL development, the implementation of `OEMInit` will be minimal. We will configure just enough of the platform to get the CE kernel to load successfully. Additional complexity will be added in subsequent phases, after successful completion of a prior phase, allowing us to grow the capabilities of the OAL, while minimizing the risk of errors. This is an effective strategy, particular for OAL code, which may be limited to debugging with hardware indications (i.e., LEDs and serial port output). When a failure occurs, you may then remove recently added features until the problem disappears, thus isolating the problem to the code associated with the new feature. (This may seem a bit archaic when compared to the CEBP graphical debugger, but like the boot process for an operating system, custom platform development is a process that must be "bootstrapped" to progressively higher levels of functionality.) The development tasks for `OEMInit` that may be delayed are indicated in the specification for its implementation (above).

Timer ISR

The most important task in the implementation of `OEMInit` is to initialize your platform's clock. The timer ISR, set up in `OEMInit`, is essential for operation of the CE scheduler and must be implemented in this phase. In most cases, the timer ISR provided in the sample OAL for your CPU family will work with few or no modifications. If your CPU family is not directly supported with a sample OAL, or if you need to make slight modifications, you will need to understand the functional requirements of the timer ISR and how it is used by the CE kernel. The subject of how to create an ISR for interrupts other than the timer will be covered in the section on phase 2 of OAL development.

In CEPB 3.0, the timer ISR received a major overhaul. The global variables `ticksleft` and `dwSleepMin` were created (linked in from `nk.lib`) to provide information on the status of the CE scheduler. These global variables are used in the implementation of `OEMIdle` (discussed in the section on phase 3 of OAL development) and provide a means to place the CPU in a low power state. The maximum time period that the CPU may remain suspended before it processes the next scheduled thread may be calculated from the value of these variables. Each global variable is listed in Table 5.2.

Table 5.2 CE 3.0 Timer-Related Global Variables

Variable	Applicable CE Versions	Description
`CurMSec`	2.10 and above	Indicates the number of milliseconds since the platform was booted. This value must be updated in the timer ISR for CE 2.1x and CE 3.0. In CE 3.0, the `OEMIdle` function (discussed in the section on phase 3) is used to vary the timer interval and extend the duration of the CPU's low power mode, thus saving battery life.
`DiffMsec`	2.10 and above	Indicates the number of milliseconds since the last time the CE scheduler examined its sleep queue. This value is used both when the system is about to enter a low power state (in the function `OEMIdle`) and to determine if the timer ISR should return the value `SYSINTR_RESCHED` to activate the CE scheduler. It is subtracted from `dwSleepMin` (see below) to produce a value representing the time remaining for the CPU to remain in low power mode.
`CurTicks`	2.10 and above	Indicates the number of system ticks (a CPU-specific value that varies with the frequency of the internal clock) since the platform was booted.
`ticksleft`	2.10 and above	Indicates the number of system ticks not yet processed by the CE scheduler's sleep queues. A nonzero value indicates that the CE scheduler needs to be activated, causing the timer ISR to return with a `SYSINTR_RESCHED` value and the `OEMIdle` function to return without placing the CPU in low power mode.
`dwSleepMin`	3.0 and above	Indicates the number of milliseconds remaining until the sleep period of a thread expires. This value is used in `OEMIdle` to determine the duration of time the CPU may be placed in low power mode, and the calculated value of the variable timer period. The timer ISR uses this value to determine if the CE scheduler should be activated by determining if it is less than or equal to `DiffMsec` (see above), causing the timer ISR to return `SYSINTR_RESCHED`. Because the value of `dwSleepMin` indicates the minimum time before another thread may run, the scheduler should not be inactive longer than this period of time (the duration of inactivity is indicated by `DiffMsec`).
`dwPreempt`	3.0 and above	Indicates the number of milliseconds remaining until the CE scheduler needs to preempt the execution of a thread. This value is compared to the value of `DiffMsec` to determine if the timer ISR should reactivate the CE scheduler by returning `SYSINTR_RESCHED`.

Your implementation of the timer ISR acts as the system heartbeat and is the primary mechanism for driving the scheduler. On each timer interrupt, the global variables are updated in your timer ISR as noted in Table 5.2. The timer ISR must also check the values of `ticksleft`, `dwSleepMin`, and `dwPreempt` to determine if the scheduler should run to resume any sleeping and preempted threads. A return value from the ISR of `SYSINTR_RESCHED` causes the CE kernel to activate the scheduler; a return value of `SYSINTR_NOP` causes it to ignore the timer interrupt. The timer ISRs provided in the CEPB sample OALs provide an example of this process. Essentially your timer ISR, most likely written in the assembly language of your platform's CPU, implements the logic depicted in Listing 5.3 as an expression written in C.

Listing 5.3 Timer ISR logic represented in C source code

```
if (ticksleft || (dwSleepMin && (DiffMSec >= dwSleepMin)) ||
     (dwPreempt && (DiffMSec >= dwPreempt)))
  return SYSINTR_RESCHED;
else
  return SYSINTR_NOP;
```

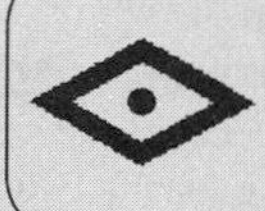

CE Version Memo

It is interesting that in CE 3.0, the timer is now programmed to one-millisecond intervals, while in CE 2.12 a 25-millisecond interval is generally used, and this interval can vary between hardware vendors. Consequently, in CE 2.12 it is not possible to know just how long a thread might sleep after the sleep function is called to request a sleep period of a particular number of milliseconds. The value depends on the rescheduling period selected by the hardware vendor when the vendor is writing its OAL timer ISR. If in CE 2.12 an application calls the sleep function with a particular number of milliseconds less than the vendor-selected rescheduling period, the thread resumes only after sleeping for a period of time equal to or less than the number of milliseconds in the vendor's rescheduling period. Because this time period varies between platforms in CE 2.12, the duration of the thread's sleep period can also vary.

One potential downside of a one-millisecond timer interval in CE 3.0 comes from the extra power consumption that occurs because a CPU in lower power mode must resume more frequently to process the increased frequency of timer interrupts. This problem is avoided in CE 3.0 through the use of variable timer intervals, which are implemented in the `OEMIdle` function (discussed in more detail in the section on phase 3 of OAL development). If the `OEMIdle` function determines that the duration of time before any threads need to be rescheduled (effectively the duration of time that the CE scheduler may remain inactive) exceeds the current timer period of one millisecond, it may temporarily reprogram the timer to interrupt just before the scheduler needs to be activated.

OEMInitDebugSerial, OEMWriteDebugByte, OEMWriteDebugString, OEMReadDebugByte, and OEMClearDebugCommError

Unless your platform supports hardware-assisted debugging, as described earlier, you will be limited to the use of hardware indications as a means of monitoring the progress of your OAL code. Flashing an LED or writing characters to an alphanumeric LED are the least intrusive hardware indications, but they provide very little information on the state of your code. If your platform has an extra I/O port (a serial port in the CEPB sample OAL code) that will not be required by application-level code, it may be used as another source of hardware indications. It is slightly more intrusive than LEDs but far less intrusive than an Ethernet port.

The functions `OEMWriteDebugByte` and `OEMWriteDebugString` may be called by your OAL to direct a single byte or a character string to a port, dedicated for debug use on your platform. The sample CEPB code demonstrates an implementation of these functions for a serial port, but there is nothing limiting you to the use of a serial port. You may notice, however, that a serial port bias has leaked into the naming of a few of the OEM APIs and their parameters. The `SetKernelCommDev` function for example, when called with the `KERNEL_COMM_SERIAL` parameter, assigns the global variables `lpWriteDebugByteFunc` and `lpReadDebugByteFunc` (available to code linked into the kernel executable module `nk.exe`) the address of `OEMWriteDebugByte` and `OEMReadDebugByte`, respectively. The CE kernel then calls these functions when an application calls the Win32 `OutputDebugString` function, or when the kernel debugging module KDSTUB needs to communicate with the CEPB debugger running on your development workstation. The function `OEMReadDebugByte` is called to receive debugger commands from the CEPB debugger. When an error is returned from either the write or read functions, the CE kernel ultimately calls the `OEMClearDebugCommError` function to clear the error condition.

Despite the appearance of the word *serial* in the name of the function `OEMInitDebugSerial`, this function is not limited to the initialization of serial ports used for debugging. It is called by the kernel just after your startup routine calls the `KernelStart` (`KernelInitialize` for x86 platforms) function, to initialize a debug port that may be used to communicate with the CEPB kernel debugger. As will be noted shortly, this function is even used to configure an Ethernet port for debugging if appropriate hardware is available and if such configuration is requested by the boot loader. The CEPB sample x86 OAL delays initialization of the Ethernet port until the execution of `OEMInit`, which is called immediately after `OEMInitDebugSerial`.

We recommend that the initial implementation of the `OEMInitDebugSerial` function be limited to the configuration of a debug port of simple design and high reliability, requiring very little supporting software (and therefore very little overhead). Ethernet hardware, though highly reliable (in some cases integrated with other highly reliable components), requires the coordination of a significant number of software modules and functions. The focus in phase 1 of OAL development should be getting the CE kernel successfully initialized. Ethernet debugging is used primarily to support the CEPB kernel debugger and can be delayed until phase 2. The implementation of `OEMInitDebugSerial` (delayed until phase 2) requires the following functionality:

- Initialize serial port (if present) for debugging.
- If Ethernet debugging is requested and is supported in hardware, initialize Ethernet debugging by calling `EdbgInit`. If your boot loader provides a user interface, you may need to check a reserved area of memory to determine if the user has requested Ethernet debugging. `EdbgInit` will in turn call the OAL functions prefixed with *OEMEth* to initialize your platform's Ethernet hardware. *Delay development until phase 2.*

- Continue Ethernet debugging configuration by calling `SetKernelCommDev` to associate kernel debug services with the Ethernet transport `KERNEL_COMM_ETHER`. *Delay development until phase 2.*
- Refer to the CEPB sample OAL file `<CE Version>\PLATFORM\<Platform Name>\KERNEL\HAL\debug.c` for a sample implementation of `OEMInitDebugSerial`.

OAL Development: Phase 2

If you successfully completed phase 1 of your OAL development project, then you have managed to start the CE kernel. In phase 2, we will add additional ISRs (beyond that developed in phase 1 for the timer) so that the unique capabilities of your custom platform can be supported through the development of native and stream-interface drivers (discussed in Chapters 6 and 7). We will also explore how ISRs can be made preemptable by higher-priority ISRs (nested interrupts), a new feature of CE 3.0. Finally, we will activate kernel debugging over an Ethernet connection and discuss the functional requirements of the associated code.

Ethernet Kernel Debugging Functions

By the time you have completed phase 1, you will long for the rapid upload speeds (*upload* in this context refers to the transfer of a newly built kernel image to the memory, flash or RAM, of your target platform) and snappy single-step debugging that only a high-speed debugging connection can provide. Hardware-assisted debugging generally requires a specialized connection between your development workstation and your target platform. This connection is generally the fastest debugging connection available, but the speed depends on the capabilities (quite often a function of cost) of the interface hardware between your target platform and development workstation.

Another, more software-oriented option for a high-speed connection to your target platform is to dedicate an available Ethernet port for use by the CE kernel to communicate with the CEPB kernel debugger (running on the development workstation). We mentioned this briefly in our discussion of phase 1, but we recommended that this feature be delayed because of the complexity of the software required to support an Ethernet device. In phase 2, however, you have achieved enough functionality to begin the development of Ethernet debugging capability. In this section we will discuss the OEM functions that you must provide for Ethernet debugging, and the CEPB resources that you may draw from to get started.

It is now time to revisit your implementation of the `OEMInitDebugSerial` function. In phase 2, we need to enhance its functionality to determine if Ethernet debugging was enabled (or requested by the end user through a boot loader menu) by the boot loader. If it was enabled, you will need to call the `SetKernelCommDev` function with the `KERNEL_SVC_KDBG` parameter to inform the CE kernel that it may call the *OEMEth* functions (discussed later in this section) to communicate with the remote kernel debugger over Ethernet. You would call the same function with the `KERNEL_SVC_DBGMSG` and `KERNEL_SVC_PPSH` parameters to cause both debug messages and the CE shell program to use the Ethernet port for communication with the development workstation. An example of the use of these functions may be found in the CEPB sample OAL file `<CE Version>\PLATFORM\<Platform Name>\KERNEL\HAL\debug.c`.

Once the SetKernelCommDev function is called, the CE kernel begins to use a series of OAL functions prefixed with *OEMEth* to send and receive data through the Ethernet port. You may think of these functions as a hardware-independent abstraction of the Ethernet hardware, much as OEMWriteDebugByte and OEMReadDebugByte are when the kernel uses the serial port for debugging. A list of the required *OEMEth* functions, including a brief description of each, is presented in Table 5.3.

Table 5.3 OEM Ethernet Functions

Function	Description
DWORD OEMEthISR(void)	This function is called by the kernel's interrupt service thread (IST) when the logical interrupt ID for the Ethernet controller is returned from your ISR. Its purpose is to check for any pending interrupts in the Ethernet controller and begin processing them. The logical ID Ethernet port interrupt is known to the kernel through the EDBG_ADAPTER structure, initialized in the OEMEthInit function.
BOOL OEMEthInit(EDBG_ADAPTER *pAdapter /* out */)	This function is called by the CE kernel during the call to the EdbgInit function from your OAL OEMInit or OEMInitDebugSerial function. As the name implies, its purpose is to initialize the Ethernet controller. It must also assign applicable values to the members of the EDBG_ADAPTER structure passed by the kernel in the pAdapter parameter. If your implementation of the OEMEthInit function assigns the SysIntrVal member (of the EDBG_ADAPTER structure) a value of EDBG_SYSINTR_NOINTR, the kernel uses the Ethernet controller in polling mode (with interrupts disabled).
void OEMEthEnableInts(void), void OEMEthDisableInts(void)	These functions are called to enable and disable interrupts from the Ethernet controller. The initial call to OEMEthEnableInts function occurs only when a valid logical interrupt ID is specified in the EDBG_ADAPTER structure passed to the OEMEthInit function.
BOOL OEMEthSendFrame (BYTE pData, /* in */ DWORD dwLength /* in */), OEMEthGetFrame(BYTE pData, /* out */ DWORD dwLength /* in/out */)	These functions are used to send and receive Ethernet frames to and from the Ethernet controller.
DWORD OEMEthGetSecs(void)	This function is used to check the value of the current tick count. It is used by the kernel when you're operating in polled mode (the mode used when interrupts are not enabled in the Ethernet controller)

(continued)

Table 5.3 *Continued.*

Function	Description
	to determine if a time-out has occurred. See the OEMEthInit function above for more details on polled mode.
BOOL OEMEthQueryClientInfo (UCHAR id, /* in */ EDBG_ADDR pPeerAdr, /* out */ PUCHAR pWindowSize, /* out */ PUCHAR ppBufferPool); / out */	This function is used by the kernel to determine certain configuration options for each type of kernel debug service, CE shell (EDBG_SVC_PPSH), kernel debugging (EDBG_SVC_KDBG), and debug messages (EDBG_SVC_DBGMSG). The address of the buffer used by the service specified in the id parameter is placed in ppBufferPool. The IP/Ethernet address of the remote development workstation associated with each service is placed in the pPeerAdr parameter.

Fortunately, you are not required to implement each of the functions in Table 5.3 from scratch. Source code is provided with the CEPB to support NE2000- and SMC9000-compatible Ethernet controllers and is located in the <CE Version>\PUBLIC\COMMON\OAK\DRIVERS\ETHDBG\NE2000 and <CE Version>\PUBLIC\COMMON\OAK\DRIVERS\ETHDBG\SMC9000 directories, respectively. During the build process the source is linked into an object module library that may in turn be linked with your OAL code by the TARGETLIBS macro in your Sources file. The *OEMEth* functions in the CEPB sample OALs use these functions as the basis of their implementation, in some cases simply passing the call to an equivalent function in the object module library.

Interrupt Service Routines

When a peripheral device generates an interrupt in CE, it causes a processor exception that is handled in the kernel. The kernel immediately runs the code previously registered for this interrupt. (The time from generation of the interrupt to the response by the kernel is referred to as *interrupt latency.*) This code, as we have already mentioned elsewhere in this chapter, is referred to as the interrupt service routine (ISR). If you're familiar with developing ISRs for other embedded operating systems, you may find that ISRs for CE are quite different.

Perhaps the most notable difference is that in CE, ISRs are really designed just to identify the peripheral device causing the interrupt and return the associated identifier for this peripheral device to the CE kernel. This identifier is then used to unblock a waiting interrupt service thread (IST, discussed in detail in Chapter 6) running in a CE device driver. The IST is what does all the real work to service the peripheral device, reading or writing data as necessary.

You may notice that some of the sample OALs included with CEPB provide ISRs written in assembly language, while most are written in C. The language you choose, either C or assembly language, may be constrained by the processor in use on your target platform. The ISR code for the SHx processor family, for example, may access only registers r0, r1, r2, r3, and r6—something that is far easier to do in assembly language. The file <CE Version>\PLATFORM\

<Platform Name>\KERNEL\HAL\SHX\p2isr.src contains a sample implementation of an ISR written in assembly language for the SHx processor family.

Creating Interrupt Identifiers

Each peripheral device on your platform that generates an interrupt must have an associated SYSINTR constant. These constants are located in a file you must create that is called oalintr.h and is generally located in the <CE Version>\PLATFORM\<Platform Name>\INC directory. The constants in this file are then made available to device driver source code as an include file and are referenced in the call to the function InterruptInitialize to associate an IST with an interrupt from the supported peripheral device.

Note:
The constants you place in the oalintr.h file may not necessarily exist in a one-to-one relationship with a particular interrupt generated by a peripheral device. You can also create arbitrary constants that are associated with the separate functions in a multifunction device. This device may generate only one interrupt, but as long as your ISR code can identify which function within the device requires servicing, it can return a designated identifier defined in the oalintr.h file. This ID allows the one physical interrupt to be exposed to device drivers as separate logical interrupts, each of which may be separately registered for servicing through the InterruptInitialize function.

The value of each of the constants in the file oalintr.h must be offset from the constant SYSINTR_FIRMWARE (defined in the file nkintr.h) and must not exceed the value SYSINTR_MAXIMUM (also defined in the file nkintr.h). Listing 5.4 contains an excerpt from the oalintr.h file provided in the sample OAL source for the Odo platform. The second part of Listing 5.4 contains an excerpt from the driver source code that calls InterruptInitialize to register its IST and associate it with the interrupt identifier.

Listing 5.4 Sample oalintr.h file and its use in driver source code

```
// Beginning of the excerpt of oalintr.h
#define SYSINTR_KEYBOARD     (SYSINTR_FIRMWARE+0)
#define SYSINTR_TOUCH        (SYSINTR_FIRMWARE+1)
#define SYSINTR_ADC          (SYSINTR_FIRMWARE+2)
#define SYSINTR_SERIAL       (SYSINTR_FIRMWARE+3)
#define SYSINTR_AUDIO        (SYSINTR_FIRMWARE+4)
#define SYSINTR_PCMCIA_STATE     (SYSINTR_FIRMWARE+5)
#define SYSINTR_PCMCIA_EDGE      (SYSINTR_FIRMWARE+6)
#define SYSINTR_PCMCIA_LEVEL     (SYSINTR_FIRMWARE+7)
#define SYSINTR_TOUCH_CHANGED    (SYSINTR_FIRMWARE+8)
#define SYSINTR_IR           (SYSINTR_FIRMWARE+9)
#define SYSINTR_ETHER        (SYSINTR_FIRMWARE+10)
// End of the excerpt of oalintr.h

// Sample of the use of a logical interrupt ID in a device driver.
m_hevInterrupt = CreateEvent(NULL, FALSE, FALSE, NULL);
```

```
if ( m_hevInterrupt == NULL)
{
    goto leave;
}

if ( !InterruptInitialize(SYSINTR_KEYBOARD, m_hevInterrupt, NULL, 0) )
{
    goto leave;
}
```

Creating and Registering the ISR

The HookInterrupt function is one of the few kernel services that may be called from OEMInit (discussed earlier in this chapter). This function is used to register your ISR with the kernel and associates the address of your ISR with a physical IRQ (interrupt request) line. Note that the number of the physical IRQ line is used to identify the interrupt handled by your ISR, *not* the logical interrupt identifiers defined in the file oalintr.h (discussed in the previous section).

The HookInterrupt function is often used to associate a single ISR with multiple physical IRQs. The inverse, in which a single physical IRQ causes the activation of multiple ISRs, is not possible, however. The use of a single ISR to service multiple physical IRQs is the favored approach to ISR development in CE. In some cases, it may be necessary to check the value of a particular register before the physical interrupt asserted can be identified, necessitating the use of a common routine from which multiple logical interrupt identifiers can be returned.

Listing 5.5 contains an excerpt of the ISR used in the sample CEPC OAL. It also contains an excerpt from the OEMInit function that calls HookInterrupt to associate this ISR with all 16 physical IRQ lines. The same ISR services the system timer interrupt, real-time clock interrupt, and all physical interrupts on the target PC platform. By analyzing the values in dwSleepMin and dwPreempt, you can determine if the duration of time since the CE scheduler was last activated exceeds the time for the next thread to be preempted or resumed from sleep. Note that if this is a physical interrupt associated with a peripheral device, the function PICEnableInterrupt is called with a FALSE value to leave the physical interrupt disabled. It is reenabled by the CE kernel after an IST (if one is associated with this interrupt) calls InterruptDone to indicate that it has completed servicing the interrupt. If no IST exists for this interrupt, it is simply reenabled by the CE kernel through a call to OEMInterruptDone.

Listing 5.5 Excerpt of the sample ISR from the CEPC 3.0 OAL (WINCE300\PLATFORM\CEPC\KERNEL\HAL\cfwpc.c)

```
ULONG PeRPISR(void)
{
    // Initialize with the default return value that causes this interrupt
    // to be ignored.
    ULONG ulRet = SYSINTR_NOP;
    UCHAR ucCurrentInterrupt;

    // Since this ISR is used to respond to all physical interrupts from this
    // platform, identify which IRQ was asserted.
    ucCurrentInterrupt = PICGetCurrentInterrupt();
```

```
// Determine if this was the system timer interrupt. If so, update the
// global variables used by the CE scheduler.
if (ucCurrentInterrupt == INTR_TIMER0)
{
    // Was the profiler timer enabled? If so, record profiler
    // information.
    if (PProfileInterrupt)
    {
       ulRet= PProfileInterrupt();
    }
    else
    {
        // Update the global variables used by the CE scheduler for
        // thread rescheduling.
        CurMSec += SYSTEM_TICK_MS;
        DiffMSec += SYSTEM_TICK_MS;
        CurTicks.QuadPart += TIMER_COUNT;

        // Determine if this interrupt is being timed.
        if (fIntrTime)
        {
            // CODE IN THIS SECTION REMOVED TO PRESERVE SPACE
        }
        else
        {
            // Determine if it is time to activate the CE scheduler
            // to run scheduled threads.
            if (ticksleft || (dwSleepMin && (dwSleepMin <= DiffMSec))
                          || (dwPreempt && (dwPreempt <= DiffMSec)))
            {
                // The time for the next thread to be scheduled has
                // arrived. Return SYSINTR_RESCHED to indicate that
                // the scheduler needs to be activated.
                ulRet = SYSINTR_RESCHED;
            }
        }
    }
    // Determine if a reboot was requested.
    // CODE IN THIS SECTION REMOVED TO PRESERVE SPACE
}
else
{
    // Determine if this is an interrupt from the real-time clock.
    if (ucCurrentInterrupt == INTR_RTC)
    {
        // CODE IN THIS SECTION REMOVED TO PERSERVE SPACE
    }
    else
    {
        // Determine if the interrupt was caused by a physical IRQ line.
        if (ucCurrentInterrupt <= INTR_MAXIMUM)
        {
            // Obtain the logical interrupt ID associated with this
            // physical interrupt.
```

```
                    ulRet = MapIntr2Sysintr[ucCurrentInterrupt];

                    // Determine if this physical interrupt has actually been
                    // mapped to a logical interrupt. If not, return
                    // SYSINTR_NOP to inform the kernel to ignore this interrupt.
                    // If it is, disable this interrupt in case it is
                    // to be processed by a driver's IST.
                    if (ulRet != 0xFF)
                    {
                        PICEnableInterrupt(ucCurrentInterrupt, FALSE);
                    }
                    else
                    {
                        ulRet = SYSINTR_NOP;
                    }
                }
            }
        }
        // Clear the physical interrupt in the PIC device.
        // CODE IN THIS SECTION REMOVED TO PRESERVE SPACE.

        // Return the SYSINTR value produced by the above code.
        return (ulRet);
}

// The following is an excerpt of the code called in the CEPC
// implementation of OEMInit to register the ISR with all of the PC's
// physical interrupts.
void OEMInit()
{

. . .

    for (i = 64; i < 80; i++)
    {
        HookInterrupt(i, (void *)PeRPISR);
    }

. . .

}
```

Device Input/Output Buffering

If your platform includes a peripheral device with small internal buffers, you may find that it generates interrupts at a high frequency. As the internal buffers become full with incoming data (or empty in the case of outgoing data), the device generates an interrupt to alert the host CPU of the need to read the accumulated data in the internal receive buffer. If the device's internal receive buffers are small, it will need to generate this interrupt more frequently to avoid the loss of data that occurs when newly received data overwrites the old data waiting to be read from the internal buffer. This increased interrupt frequency has the potential to significantly affect overall system performance.

One method to mitigate this problem is to create a specialized ISR that behaves as a kind of pseudo-DMA controller by sharing the work of servicing the interrupt with the IST running in a device driver. The ISR reads the data from the device and copies it into an area of reserved memory. The address of this reserved memory appears in the `MEMORY` section of your `config.bib` file (located in the `<CE Version>\PLATFORM\<Platform Name>\FILES` directory) and has the type `RESERVED`. After each interrupt, the ISR returns `SYSINTR_NOP` to prevent activation of the IST and eliminate the associated overhead. On a future interrupt, when the ISR detects that the reserved memory area is about to become full with received data, it then returns the logical interrupt ID for this device (instead of `SYINTR_NOP`). The result is that the IST becomes unblocked and can read the accumulated data in the reserved memory area. You would need to devise a mechanism by which the IST could indicate to the ISR that the received data in reserved memory area had already been read so that it could be overwritten by the ISR on the next interrupt from this device.

A similar technique can be used to support peripheral devices with small internal write buffers, which interrupt the host CPU to indicate readiness to process more outgoing data. The main difference in this case is that the ISR reads the data written into the reserved memory area by the IST in a previous interrupt and returns a logical interrupt ID to activate the IST only when the outgoing data in the reserved memory area is fully processed. Then when the IST is reactivated, it may overwrite the reserved memory area with the next batch of outgoing data to be processed.

Figure 5.4 portrays the relationship between the ISR and the IST when the ISR is buffering received data. Two receive buffers are designated—`RECEIVEBUFFER1` and `RECEIVEBUFFER2`—in the reserved memory area and are used in a "ping-pong" configuration. The `SYSINTR_NOP` return value is used instead of the logical interrupt ID until `RECEIVEBUFFER1` is filled. This substitution keeps the IST blocked and reduces the associated overhead. The logical interrupt ID `SYSINTR_SMALLBUFFERDEVICE` is returned when `RECEIVEBUFFER1` is full, causing the IST's event object (registered with the kernel's exception-handling code through the `InterruptInitialize` function) to be signaled by the kernel. The IST is then unblocked and immediately determines which buffer to read by checking the status bytes for `RECEIVEBUFFER1` and `RECEIVEBUFFER2` to determine which contains the larger value. The `PINGPONG` byte is assigned a value of 1 or 2 to indicate that `RECEIVEBUFFER1` or `RECEIVEBUFFER2`, respectively, is being read. The larger value in `RECEIVEBUFFER1` is then used to indicate the number of bytes that must be read from this buffer and copied into the IST's local buffer. When the data in `RECEIVEBUFFER1` has been transferred into the driver's local buffer, the value in the `RECEIVEBUFFER1` status byte is reset to zero to indicate that it has been fully processed and may be overwritten by the ISR with newly received data. The `PINGPONG` byte is also reset to zero to indicate that no receive buffers are currently being read.

Note that in a real-world scenario, you would need to provide a time-out for received data, meaning that if the device had not generated an interrupt for some period of time (calculated to be the maximum length of time required to fill a single receive buffer), the IST would need to be activated to read the data that had accumulated in the ISR's receive buffers, even though the receive buffers were not yet full. This time-out could be added to the IST by a call to `WaitForSingleObject` with the time-out period in the `dwMilliseconds` parameter. By checking for a return value of `WAIT_TIMEOUT`, the IST would know to check the receive buffer status bytes for a nonzero value. If it found a nonzero value, it would then begin normal processing of the received data as though its event object had been signaled.

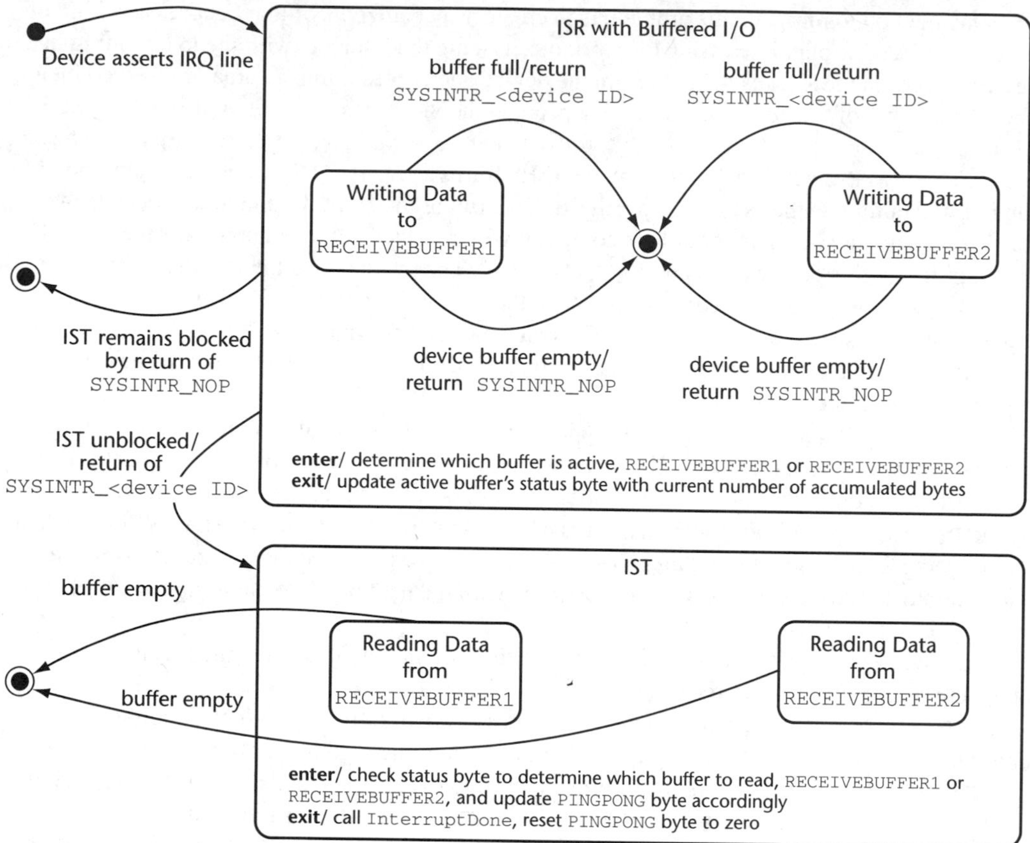

Figure 5.4 State chart for ISR ping-pong I/O buffers

OEM Interrupt Functions

Between the generation of the processor exception and the return from the IST in a device driver, certain OEM functions are called by the CE kernel to enable and disable the interrupt being serviced. These functions are named `OEMInterruptDone`, `OEMInterruptDisable`, and `OEMInterruptEnable`. Considering that the interrupt architecture for each CPU varies, these functions provide the necessary abstraction for the kernel to enable and disable interrupts. Each function is called at different points in the progression of the interrupt from kernel mode to user mode (see Chapter 8 for a sequence diagram depicting this progression).

To associate its IST with the occurrence of a particular interrupt, a device driver calls the `InterruptInitialize` function, passing the logical interrupt ID you defined in `oalintr.h` and a handle to an event object used by the kernel to signal the blocked thread when the interrupt occurs. The call to `InterruptInitialize` results in a call to `OEMInterruptEnable` to enable the physical interrupt associated with the logical interrupt ID passed in the `idInt` parameter. Your `OEMInterruptEnable` code must map the logical interrupt ID in the `idInt` parameter to your physical interrupt ID and then enable the physical interrupt in the manner required by your platform's CPU.

When the IST of a device driver completes servicing of the interrupt, the function `InterruptDone` is called, passing the logical ID of the interrupt as in the `InterruptInitialize` function. The call to `InterruptDone` causes the `OEMInterruptDone` function to be called. Like `OEMInterruptEnable`, the objective of `OEMInterruptDone` is to reenable the physical interrupt associated with the logical interrupt ID passed in the `idInt` parameter. You may find that the implementations of both functions are identical or nearly so, and thus you may call the same functions for enabling the physical interrupt. The implementation of `OEMInterruptEnable`, `OEMInterruptDone`, and `OEMInterruptDisable`, requires the following functionality:

- Map the logical interrupt ID passed to the function to a physical interrupt ID.
- Enable or disable the physical interrupt as required by the specification of each OEM function.

Nested Interrupts

One commonly held criticism of CE 2.12 and earlier versions was that the interrupt latencies were too high and were unbounded. That is, if a device were to signal its assigned IRQ, causing the associated ISR to run, the duration of time between the change in the state of the IRQ line and activation of the ISR (interrupt latency) was often too long and unpredictable (unbounded). This criticism has been addressed in CE 3.0 with many significant enhancements of the CE kernel, including the following:

- The addition of 247 more interrupt levels
- The replacement of multilevel priority boosting, when priority inversion is detected, with single-level priority boosting
- The ability of an application thread to set its own quantum (duration of the time slice granted to threads running at the same priority)
- Support for nested interrupts, allowing a running ISR to be preempted by a higher-priority ISR

In this section we will focus on nested interrupts because this feature has an impact on the implementation of certain OAL code. The other three topics in this list are covered in the Real-Time Application Development section of the CEPB 3.0 online documentation. Nested interrupts will have implications on the design and implementation of your ISR code, so it is important to understand how nested interrupts work and how to configure them in your OAL code.

To start, let's define what *nested interrupts* means in the context of CE 3.0. When a device on your platform changes the state of its assigned IRQ line, that change causes the CPU to literally interrupt execution of the currently running code in favor of the interrupt service routine (ISR). Any other ISR associated with a lower-priority IRQ that may happen to have been running at this moment in time is interrupted (or using kernel speak, *preempted*). This ability for one ISR to interrupt the execution of another, lower-priority ISR is referred to as **nested interrupts**.

This is an important feature for the overall goal of reducing the time between when the IRQ first occurs and when the associated ISR is run. This period of time, called the **interrupt**

latency, is an important measure of the overall responsiveness of an operating system. When a peripheral device generates an IRQ, the operating system must respond as quickly as possible. Failure to do so might cause a loss of data if the device was receiving data from an external source, or it might cause the system to be perceived as sluggish by a user awaiting a response to a particular action, such as the appearance of a character on the screen when a key is pressed or a graffiti character is drawn. With support for nested interrupts, CE 3.0 allows the device associated with a higher-priority IRQ to experience lower interrupt latency than is possible in CE 2.12 when a lower-priority ISR is already running. In CE 2.12, when an ISR is run, all interrupts are disabled until the ISR returns with the logical interrupt ID and the associated IST is activated.

If a given ISR can be preempted by a higher-priority ISR, you might be wondering just how you can configure ISRs that have a higher priority. The way this is accomplished differs from one CPU to the next, primarily because the internal interrupt handling mechanism for each CPU varies. In the case of an x86 processor, interrupt priorities are preprogrammed into an interrupt controller known as the programmable interrupt controller (PIC) device. In general, interrupts with a lower number have a higher priority than interrupts with a higher number have. Thus, an ISR for the serial port interrupt traditionally assigned to IRQ levels 3 and 4 may be preempted by an interrupt from IRQs 0, 1, and 2. Interrupts for IRQs 5 through 15 will be held pending in the PIC device until the higher-priority interrupt is acknowledged. Controlling interrupt priorities for x86 processors is therefore accomplished transparently to your OAL code.

For the SHx processor family, the CE kernel is in charge of determining relative interrupt priorities. An array called `IntrPrio` is exported by the SHx CE kernel and contains an entry for up to 112 interrupts. `IntrPrio` is initialized with default values for interrupts 0 through 15, with interrupt 0 at `IntrPrio[0]` being the highest-priority interrupt assigned a value of `0xF` to prevent preemption by any other interrupts (and their associated ISRs). The default value for interrupt 1 at `IntrPrio[1]` is `0xE`, indicating that interrupts with an `IntrPrio` value of `0xF`, such as interrupt 0, may preempt interrupt 1. Recall that if an interrupt is preempted, its associated ISR code will be stopped, and the ISR of the higher-priority interrupt will be started. The ISR code of the lower-priority interrupt is then resumed when the ISR for the higher-priority interrupt returns. You may change the default values assigned to the `IntrPrio` array when you're setting up your ISR code in the `OEMInit` function.

Note that for the duration of time that both interrupts are running, the CE scheduler is not running, and therefore the interrupt service threads (ISTs, described in Chapters 6 and 7) signaled by the CE kernel on the reception of a particular interrupt are prevented from running. The use of nested interrupts, though it significantly reduces interrupt latency, can increase the time for an interrupt to cause activation of the associated IST (IST latency) running in a device driver.

With this in mind, you should use nested interrupts with the utmost caution. With support for nested interrupts, it would be tempting to develop larger ISRs that completely service an interrupt without the need for a driver IST. You might do so thinking that with support for nested interrupts, your ISR will not affect overall system performance. Though you would enhance the performance of the one device serviced by your ISR, you would increase the IST latency for all other ISRs, thereby affecting the performance of all other drivers, and possibly negatively affecting overall system performance. This may be an acceptable tradeoff, depending on the device being serviced, so you should analyze your situation carefully.

Figure 5.5 depicts the effect on overall IST1 latency of the preemption of ISR1 by nested ISR2. IST1 is not unblocked until ISR1 returns with the logical interrupt ID associated with IST1. The return of ISR1, however, is delayed by the execution of ISR2, which preempts the execution of ISR1. This delay causes an overall increase in the latency of IST1 by an amount of time equal to the duration of ISR2.

OEMIOControl

The function `KernelIoControl` is called by application (user mode) code to query the value of CE kernel configuration properties and to set the values of certain configuration options. This call is passed to the OAL function `OEMIoControl` in your OAL code, requiring you to implement the specified operation and return values. The function prototype is identical to the prototype defined for the `DeviceIoControl` function, which is defined for generic access to device driver operations and appears as follows:

```
BOOL OEMIoControl ( DWORD dwIoControlCode, LPVOID lpInBuf,
DWORD nInBufSize, LPVOID lpOutBuf, DWORD nOutBufSize,
LPDWORD lpBytesReturned );
```

Each operation is defined as a unique I/O control code, passed in the `dwIoControlCode` parameter. The I/O control codes that are recommended for all configurations of the CE kernel are listed in the CEPB online documentation for the `OEMIoControl` function. An excellent example of the broad range of possible uses for this function is available in the CEPB sample OAL code for the CEPC platform.

Beyond just providing a mechanism for setting and getting kernel configuration options, `OEMIoControl` is most useful as a portal between user mode application code and kernel mode

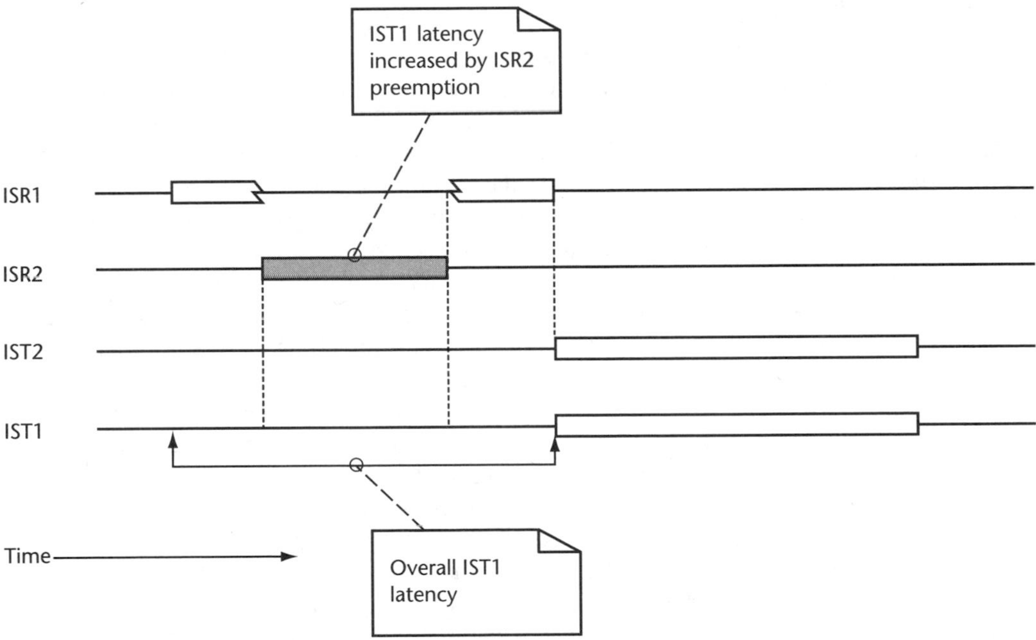

Figure 5.5 Effect of nested interrupts on IST latency

OAL code. When `OEMIoControl` is called, the system is fully preemptable, so it is safe to make CE API calls while still providing the direct hardware access available to kernel mode OAL code. This means that you could potentially extend access to hardware resources and kernel services that is available only in OAL code to application code as well. You would need to define your own I/O control codes, beyond those defined by Microsoft, and publish them in a header file available to application code for the call to `KernelIoControl`. This header file could then be included with the platform SDK provided for your custom platform and generated using the CEPB Platform **Export SDK** menu option.

OAL Development: Phase 3

The completion of phase 2 represents a major milestone in the development of your OAL code. You can now begin developing the device drivers to service those interrupts exposed as logical IDs in your `oalintr.h` file. If your platform provides an Ethernet port and you completed the *OEMEth* functions, you can begin using this high-speed connection to communicate with your custom platform, particularly when debugging your device driver code.

In phase 3 we will focus on the OAL development tasks needed to support certain optional capabilities, some of which were recently introduced in CE 3.0. We will discuss how to activate module certification in CE 3.0, to determine if a module is authenticated before it is executed. We will also discuss how to enable power management in CE 2.12 and 3.0 through the `OEMIdle` function. Finally, we will see how to save the changes made to the registry by applications, even if your platform is unable to retain the contents of RAM (through battery backup) when powering off.

Module Certification

With the introduction of CE 3.0, it is now possible for the CE kernel to authenticate a module (a file containing executable code) before loading and executing it from RAM. This capability applies to the modules that are loaded from ROM into RAM to be run, or to the applications that are later uploaded to the object store and then executed. The modules that are run directly from ROM (referred to as execute-in-place, or XIP, in the CE online documentation) will not be authenticated and are run as trusted code. Before we continue, just in case you're asking yourself why this feature is necessary, let's consider one scenario in which this feature is most useful.

Imagine for a moment that your custom platform will ultimately function as a portable device providing wireless data services. One feature offered by your device is the ability to purchase off-the-shelf software for additional features. Your concern is that by opening your platform to third-party developers, you may be unable to control the type of applications a user may run. It may be possible, in fact, for a user to inadvertently transfer an application into your device that maliciously floods the wireless network with data in a denial-of-service attack.

By enabling module certification, you could potentially eliminate these problems. You will most likely institute a testing process for verifying that an application operates within your specifications. Once an application (or device driver for that matter) has passed the test, you digitally sign the associated module (EXE, DLL, OCX, and so on). This digital signature causes a certificate to be appended to the end of the module. After the application is installed and then run by the end user, the CE kernel uses the public key embedded directly in the kernel image to verify that the module has *not* been altered since the signature was added.

OEMCertifyModuleInit and OEMCertifyModule

The OEM functions `OEMCertifyModuleInit` and `OEMCertifyModule` provide the functionality needed by the kernel to certify a module. The `OEMCertifyModuleInit` function is called once for each module that requires certification (modules that do not execute in ROM) and is used to initialize the certification process for the module named in its `lpModuleName` parameter. The function `OEMCertifyModule` is then called repeatedly with the `lpData` and `cbData` parameters until the end of the module is reached (represented by a value of 0 in the `cbData` parameter). The parameter `lpData` points to a buffer containing the actual code, while the `cbData` parameter contains the length of the buffer. Somewhere in the implementation of the `OEMInit` function, you must assign the global variables `pOEMLoadInit` and `pOEMLoadModule` the address of your `OEMCertifyModule` and `OEMCertifyModuleInit` functions. Doing so effectively activates module certification in the kernel, which is otherwise inactive in OAL development phases 1 and 2.

Note:
As of this writing, the CEPB online documentation for the `OEMCertifyModule` and `OEMCertifyModuleInit` functions incorrectly refers to the `pOEMLoadInit` and `pOEMLoadModule` variables as `pOEMCertifyModule` and `pOEMCertifyModuleInit`.

Your implementation of `OEMCertifyModule` must process each buffer using the same algorithm as that applied when the module was first signed on your development workstation. The basic objective of `OEMCertifyModule` is to independently re-create the signature for the module code referenced in the `lpData` parameter and verify that it matches the one produced on the development workstation and embedded in the module itself. Specifically which algorithm you use in `OEMCertifyModule` is strictly up to you, as long as the same one is used on the development workstation (for the initial signing).

One additional restriction is that the signature must be embedded in the module in a manner that allows it to be extracted from the data passed in the `lpData` parameter. As mentioned earlier, `OEMCertifyModule` is called repeatedly until the end of the module is reached. To locate the module's certificate, `OEMCertifyModule` would need to parse the portable executable (PE) header to find the certificate table field of the data directories list. This field would then contain an entry for the offset of the attribute certificate table, which is then used to determine the offset of one or more digital certificates in the data stream of `lpData`.

The details of the PE header format can be found on the Microsoft Web site, at http://msdn.microsoft.com/library/specs/msdn_pecoff.htm. Once the certificate data was extracted from the module, you would read the section of the certificate containing the trust level assigned to the module when initially signed on the development workstation. When the function `OEMCertifyModule` is called for the last time (`cbData` equal to 0), the return value should contain this trust level.

The trust levels that may be returned from `OEMCertifyModule` determine whether the kernel will allow the module to run and whether or not the module is trusted. If it is a trusted module (return value of `OEM_CERTIFY_TRUST`), it may operate with no restrictions, calling any available function. It may also be certified to run (`OEM_CERTIFY_RUN`) but restricted from calling certain functions (listed in the CEPB online documentation for the `OEMCertifyModule` function). The module can also be declared as generally untrustworthy with the return value OEM_CERTIFY_FALSE. This value prevents the kernel from allowing the module to run.

CEPB Tools for Implementation of OEMCertifyModuleInit and OEMCertifyModule

The CEPB provides an object module library, loadauth.lib, that contains the implementation of a series of functions prefixed with *CertifyModule.* These functions are all you need to complete your implementation of OEMCertifyModuleInit and OEMCertifyModule. The tool signfile.exe is also provided and is run from the development workstation to append a digital signature to a specified module. It is designed to use a certificate service provider to obtain a specified private key stored on the development workstation.

The implementations of OEMCertifyModuleInit and OEMCertifyModule provided in the CEPB sample OALs are based on the use of loadauth.lib. Note that these functions are named OEMLoadInit and OEMLoadModule—not OEMCertifyModuleInit and OEMCertifyModule as in the CEPB online documentation. Your implementation of the OEMCertifyModuleInit function simply forwards the call to the CertifyModuleInit function in loadauth.lib. The CertifyModule function is called repeatedly from your OEMCertifyModule function as each buffer is passed in the lpData parameter. When OEMCertifyModule is called with the final buffer (cbData equal to 0), the CertifyModuleFinal function will be called. The ppbSignData out parameter then points to the data contained in the certificate's optional attribute data, which you provided as a command-line parameter to the signfile.exe tool. This optional attribute data is typically used to contain the trust level assigned to the module, and would be used in your code to determine which trust level should be returned from the final call to OEMCertifyModule. An example of the use of signfile.exe is presented in Listing 5.6.

Listing 5.6 Sample use of the digital signing tools signfile.exe and makecert.exe

```
The following command creates a test certificate using the Cryptography API
tool makecert.exe. The key container is named CETestKey and is saved in the
store called CETestStore. The certificates created by this tool are issued by
the default test root and should not be used to sign modules ready for public
distribution. A certificate authority, such as VeriSign, must be used.

J:\dev\InetSDK\Bin\makecert -sk CETestKey -ss CETestStore

This command uses the CEPB tool signfile.exe to sign the module helloworld.exe
with the test certificate created in the previous step. The parameter -f
specifies the name of the module to sign, -k indicates the name of the key
container created in the previous step, -s indicates the optional signed
attributes that should be embedded in the module, and -a indicates the name of
the module for appending the digital signature.

J:\dev\WINCE300\PUBLIC\COMMON\OAK\BIN\I386\signfile -fHelloWorld.exe
-kCETestKey -sT -aHelloWorld.exe -pPublicKey.h
```

Listing 5.6 contains a sample of the use of the Makecert and Signfile tools on the development workstation. The tool Makecert is used to create a test certificate stored on the development workstation, and it is assigned a key container named CETestKey. Makecert is available for download from the Microsoft Web site and is included in the Internet Client SDK. The key container, CETestKey, is required by the signfile.exe parameter -k to identify the test certificate and its associated private key. The signfile.exe parameter -s contains the optional signed string data that is stored in the signature and returned in the CertifyModule-Final function. In this example, the letter T is used to indicate that the module is trusted and will cause the CEPB sample implementation of OEMCertifyModule (equivalent to OEMLoad-Module) to return the constant OEM_CERTIFY_TRUST to the CE kernel. The signfile.exe parameter -p will cause the public key be written to the specified file, publickey.h, in Listing 5.6. This file will be linked into the kernel image and will be used by the encryption algorithm in your implementation of OEMCertifyModule to authenticate the module and its digital signature. If you're using the loadauth library, the value assigned to the variable g_bSignPublicKeyBlob in publickey.h will be passed to the function InitPubKey in OEMInit.

Power Management

Power management from the perspective of the OAL is quite different from that of a device driver, which is responsible for the support of a particular device and its unique requirements. In general, CE device drivers focus on retaining the configuration of their device and, if possible, placing the device in a low power state. The retained configuration is then restored during a return to full power mode. The OAL, however, sees power management as a measure of the current activity level of the overall system. The activity level in the context of the kernel, and therefore the OAL (linked into the kernel at build time), is equivalent to the duration of time until the next thread is ready to run. If, for example, the CE scheduler indicates that no threads will be ready to run (meaning that they are sleeping, blocked, or awaiting the arrival of the time interval that will allow them to run for a specified quantum) for a period of 25 milliseconds, the system may then be placed in low power mode for the same period of time.

OEMIdle

In both CE 3.0 and CE 2.x, OEMIdle is called by the kernel when the CE scheduler has no threads ready to run. In CE 2.x, the implementation of OEMIdle simply places the CPU in a low power mode. The next interrupt generated then causes the CPU to resume on the next instruction following the one that placed it in low power mode. The interval of time before the next interrupt effectively determines the duration of time that the CPU will remain in low power mode. Therefore, in CE 2.12 this time interval never exceeds the duration of time between timer ticks because the timer interrupt is always enabled.

In CE 3.0, however, the implementation of OEMIdle has changed significantly. By examining the value of the global variable DiffMSec (described in Table 5.2), OEMIdle can calculate the total length of time before the next thread must be run. It may then reprogram the timer to interrupt after this same length of time has expired, rather than the timer's standard one-millisecond interrupt. This process significantly increases the average duration of the low power mode.

Listing 5.7 provides pseudocode for the implementation of a CE 3.0 and 2.12 OEMIdle function, based on the sample CEPB OAL source code (WINCE300\PLATFORM\ODO\KERNEL\HAL\cfwp2.c).

Listing 5.7 Pseudocode for the implementation of `OEMIdle` in CE 2.12 and 3.0

```
CE 3.0:

Get time since scheduler was run (DiffMSec)
If unprocessed ticks exist (ticksleft)
    Do not enter low power state
    Return

If profile timer (bProfileTimerRunning) is running
    Enter low power mode for standard time tick
    Return

If measuring latency (fIntrTime) or if time until next thread is ready to run
(dwSleepMin) equals 0
    Enter low power mode for standard time tick
    Update counter for total idle time
    Return

If time since scheduler was run (DiffMSec) is equal to or greater than time
until next thread is ready to run (dwSleepMin)
    Return

Subtract time since scheduler was run (DiffMsec) from time until next thread
is ready to run (dwSleepMin)

Reduce this time by platform-specific, maximum programmable timer interval

Increment and update timer variables

Set timer interval derived above

Clear any pending timer interrupt requests

Go to sleep and continue with next instruction on resume

Disable interrupts

If timer interrupt caused resume
    Update counters subtracting 1 timer interval

Else
    Update counters

Return timer interval to standard setting

Clear the timer IRQ

Return to caller (assume caller will reenable interrupts)

CE 2.12:

Go to sleep and continue with next instruction on resume
```

The CE 3.0 implementation begins by checking various global variables to confirm the need to enter a low power state. A value of greater than zero for the `ticksleft` variable indicates that timer ticks have occurred that have not yet been accounted for in the scheduler's sleep queues. These sleep queues may reference a thread that could become ready to run when these ticks are finally processed, so the low power state is aborted. If the profile timer is running or interrupt latency is being examined, the low power state is activated only for the standard timer interval, to avoid affecting the outcome of these measurements. The time since the scheduler was last run is compared to the time until the next thread is scheduled to run. If the latter value is greater, we may proceed with the low power state because there is some time remaining before the scheduler needs to be activated. To account for the time since the scheduler was last run, `OEMIdle` is used to reduce the time until the next thread is scheduled to run. The remaining code performs any preparations needed to enter a low power state. When the CPU returns from its low power state, the appropriate counters are updated and the timer is reprogrammed with its standard setting.

The implementation of CE 2.12 is quite different. Its sole purpose is to place the CPU in a low power state. The next interrupt that occurs simply causes the CPU to resume execution on the next instruction. This interrupt usually comes from the timer, which, unlike the `OEMIdle` function in CE 3.0, continues to run at its standard interval.

OEMPowerOff

The only other power management function you need to implement is `OEMPowerOff`. This function is responsible for shutting down your platform and placing it into its lowest power state so that it reacts only to an end user's pressing the power-on button. If your platform does not provide battery-backed RAM to preserve the RAM-based file system and running programs, then your objective will be to simply cause power to be terminated. No system calls are available at this point, so you are limited to writing to the appropriate registers or I/O ports to power off your platform.

The implementation of `OEMPowerOff` is a little more complicated for systems that provide battery-backed RAM. You need to place the system in its lowest power state (referred to as Suspend in the CEPB online documentation), retaining enough information so that the platform configuration can be quickly restored when the power-on button is pressed. This generally requires that certain registers be saved on the stack to preserve the state of running programs. Interrupts from peripheral devices should also be disabled to prevent a premature resume by a device that remains active. The system timer interrupt, however, will remain enabled to periodically run the scheduler and check for scheduled alarms that would cause the system to resume from Suspend. RAM will also need to be placed in a low-power refresh mode. Any other measures that must be taken to place the platform in Suspend mode must be performed in such a manner that it can be quickly returned to its previous state on resume.

Persistent Registry

The registry in CE, like its desktop counterpart, provides the central repository for configuration information. And because the registry is stored in the RAM-based CE file system, updates may be retained between power cycles. This capability does require, however, that your platform be designed with some form of battery-backed RAM. If this is not possible, an alternative is to allow the registry to be periodically written to any other form of nonvolatile storage, such as reprogrammable flash memory. The functions `WriteRegistryToOEM(DWORD dwFlags, LPBYTE lpData, DWORD cbData)` and `ReadRegistryFromOEM(DWORD dwFlags, LPBYTE lpData, DWORD cbData)` are called by the kernel to allow you to save and retrieve the registry data passed in the `lpData` parameter.

Though the names of these functions contain an *OEM* suffix instead of an *OEM* prefix, they are still considered OAL functions. Sometime during OAL initialization, perhaps in `OEMInit`, you must assign the address of each function to the global variables (exported by the kernel) `pWriteRegistryToOEM` and `pReadRegistryFromOEM`. These functions are then called by the kernel to restore the registry on power-up, overwriting the RAM-based copy of the default registry contained in the ROM image file `\WINDOWS\default.fdf`.

Both `WriteRegistryToOEM` and `ReadRegistryFromOEM` are called repeatedly until the end of the registry data is reached. In the case of `WriteRegistryToOEM`, the `lpData` parameter points to a buffer of length `cbData` provided by the kernel. Each time `WriteRegistryToOEM` is called, you write the data in `lpData` to a reserved area in some form of nonvolatile storage. If flash memory were used, an entry in `config.bib` would be required to declare the region of memory reserved for the registry backup. When the value of `cbData` is 0, the kernel is indicating that the end of the registry has been reached. At any time a return value of `FALSE` would cause the kernel to discontinue its repeated calls and indicate failure in the writing of the registry data.

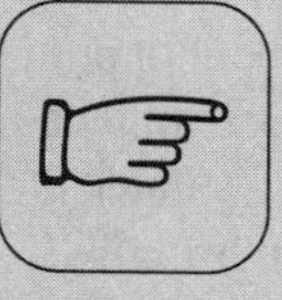

Note:
The method used to update flash memory varies by manufacturer. Most, however, have opted to support the Common Flash Interface (CFI), so it is quite possible that the same code can update flash from multiple manufacturers. One key requirement for the code that performs the update of flash memory, regardless of manufacturer, is that the code execute from RAM. The reason for this requirement is that the flash memory may not be accessed to fetch instructions for the CPU while it is being actively written. If the CE kernel (and therefore your OAL) executes from flash or ROM, it will be necessary for the `WriteRegistryToOEM` routine to be copied into RAM before it is executed.

For `ReadRegistryFromOEM`, `lpData` points to a buffer of length `cbData` allocated by the kernel. Your job is to fill this buffer, up to the maximum number of bytes specified in `cbData`. The return value indicates the actual number of bytes copied to the buffer. A return value of 0 indicates to the kernel that all registry data has been read; a value of –1 indicates failure to read additional registry data and prevents subsequent calls to this function. A failed call to `ReadRegistryFromOEM` on power-up would cause the kernel to use the copy of the default registry, which was previously copied into RAM from the ROM image file `\WINDOWS\default.fdf`.

Summary

Writing OAL code is a fundamental requirement for deploying CE on any custom platform. It serves as a low-level abstraction of your platform's capabilities that is linked directly into the CE kernel module `nk.exe`. The functionality provided by OAL code may be summarized as follows:

- It initializes the CPU to a known state before the kernel is activated (jumping to the `KernelStart` or `KernelInitialize` routine).
- It initializes the platform and its debug ports.
- It provides I/O functions for communication with a debug port.
- It provides interrupt service routines (ISRs) that map physical interrupts to logical interrupts, optionally assigning priority levels to each ISR (nested interrupts).
- It provides the functions for implementing certain optional OAL capabilities, such as module certification and the persistent registry.

6 Writing Device Drivers: Introductory Concepts

The device driver is the unsung hero of any system, large or small. It toils away, constantly active and at the beck and call of its commanding applications. It rarely, if ever, shows itself to the end user to proclaim its virtues, and in most cases it even lacks a humble about box. Without device drivers, the applications of the world that require any kind of hardware access (and that's pretty much every application ever written, if you consider access to a display device) would have to be rewritten for each type of platform supported. Enter the device drivers, promising to relieve the application writer from learning the intricacies of any particular device, while allowing applications to be written that empower the user to get some real work done.

In this chapter we will begin our exploration of what is likely to represent the largest effort in the integration of CE on your custom platform: device driver development. If you have a peripheral device that is not completely supported by an existing CEPB sample driver, you will need to develop a driver of your own or adapt an existing sample driver. We will focus on what is needed to develop most types of drivers and give you the tools to plumb the depths of CEPB within your particular area of interest.

Note:
Unless otherwise specified, any reference to the term *CEPB* refers to both CEPB 2.12 and CEPB 3.0.

You may notice as you read ahead that this chapter is missing a discussion on the important topic of device driver debugging. Considering the broad nature of this subject, we have made it the focus of an entire chapter (Chapter 9). This chapter, however, provides a more theoretical foundation for understanding CE from the perspective of a device driver developer, while Chapters 7 and 8 focus on how to implement the source code for various types of device drivers.

When to Write a CE Device Driver

The most common reason for writing a CE device driver is to expose the capabilities and resources of your device to CE applications. In most cases, an existing Win32 API will be used by those applications to communicate with your device, and all you will need to do is provide the underlying driver. This driver will resolve the hardware and platform differences into a low-level interface that the CE kernel and application subsystems can call.

When designing a custom platform, you will undoubtedly include certain peripheral devices, such as RS-232 COM ports or a keyboard controller. As you begin to plan your CE integration project, the effort for developing the drivers to support these devices will most likely make up the bulk of the time and engineering resources you allocate. You should begin this planning effort by taking an inventory of the peripheral devices you will need to support, keeping in mind that perhaps not every peripheral device in your inventory will require you to develop a device driver from scratch. You may be able to use one of the sample device drivers (discussed later in this chapter) provided with the CEPB either as is or with a few modifications. Taking this inventory will require that you become familiar with the CEPB (and CE device drivers in general) so that you can examine the sample source code, assessing the degree of support for your devices. This process will require the largest percentage of your planning efforts.

The CEPB online documentation contains a section titled Porting the Sample Native Drivers that does an excellent job of explaining the features of each sample native driver (described in more detail in Chapter 7) and the specific sections that must be modified for a custom platform. In this chapter, the section titled Sample Device Driver Source Code gives an overview of all sample driver source code, not limited to native drivers.

CE drivers are also not limited to the support of physical devices. You may opt to define a driver that provides application-level services, exposed through a standard API. This form of application-specific driver would leverage the driver management infrastructure provided for each type of driver. In this case, your driver would be automatically loaded and would operate as a single shared instance for all calling applications. These benefits are not unlike those of a COM object that provides services accessible to all applications that request them at runtime without, however, COM's object-oriented extensions. The application-level functions needed to load a driver are discussed in the section titled Device Driver Architecture later in this chapter.

As we shall see in Chapter 7, the form of a device driver may vary, depending largely on two primary device characteristics—namely, whether the device is considered a permanent part of the custom platform (not accessible by the end user), or whether it can be installed or inserted by the end user, as in the case of PC card devices purchased through retail channels. This brings us to defining the notion of onboard and installable devices.

Note:
For those of you who are CE veterans of the CE 1.0 vintage, the term *installable* may seem vaguely familiar. It was initially used to describe the driver models and the resulting drivers that provide support for devices that the end user can install. Terms such as *installable device driver* often caused confusion because the drivers used standard interfaces (described in Chapter 7) capable of supporting devices that were permanently attached to a custom platform or were inserted by the end user. Here, instead, we will use this term to describe the *hardware* that the driver supports, which is indirectly related to the type of the required driver.

Onboard and Installable Devices Compared

When considering the nature of the peripheral devices that you must support with your device driver, it will help to consider whether the device is an onboard device or an installable device. Before we delve into why this distinction is helpful, let's explain what is meant by these two terms.

An **onboard device** is considered a permanent fixture on your custom platform. It is most likely soldered to your board or permits installation only after all power sources have been removed. An **installable device**, however, may be routinely added to the system by the end user and is intended to function on a variety of platforms. The most common example of such a device occurs in PC card form factors, though as time progresses we will hopefully see more USB-enabled devices.

The *ways* you develop drivers for onboard and installable devices have some key differences, and we will occasionally refer to these differences in this chapter and the next. *What* you develop in terms of the driver model used for onboard and installable devices, however, does *not* always vary. For now, it is important to realize that if you are developing a driver for an installable device, your driver code should be as platform independent as possible to support separate builds for each target processor and platform. Onboard devices, however, require special kernel-level, platform-dependent modifications that must be present in the ROMable kernel image. The implications of these facts will become clear in the next few sections.

Device Driver Models

As operating systems have evolved and peripheral devices have become more complex, the associated device drivers have become equally complex. To simplify the work required for writing these device drivers, in the last few years developers have defined device drivers in the context of many separate layers. Typically, each layer provides a defined interface to a certain group of services that progressively processes incoming and outgoing device data. This means that the developer can provide support for a particular device by simply modifying the designated layer, rather than rewriting or adapting the entire driver in one monolithic code base. The processing commonly required for a given class of device (i.e., network, display, serial, and printer devices) is carefully isolated into specific layers that, in most cases, do not require modification. Windows Driver Model (WDM, as of this writing available only on the desktop Windows operating systems), Network Device Interface Specification (NDIS), and DirectX are examples of standards for device driver layering.

Each layering standard imposes a certain requirement on both the design and the functional requirements of your driver. To fit in, as it were, and successfully make use of the services of the surrounding layers, your driver must conform to a particular model. The NDIS driver model for example, wraps the driver into an upper and lower edge interface to provide packet translation services. The NDIS driver need only focus on transmitting and receiving of data from the network adapter, without concern for how packets are exchanged with any number of protocol stacks. So by defining the overall behavior of the driver as an abstraction of the network adapter interface, including the functions required for communication with the NDIS upper and lower edge interfaces, we can realize a driver model. The key point to remember is that a driver model is not limited to the definition of required functions, but also includes a description of overall behavior and the mechanism defined for its implementation.

Device Classes

Devices that share common attributes are often grouped together to form a category, or **class**. This grouping allows those common attributes to be expressed as a specialized driver interface, designed to support the I/O (input/output) requirements of the device class. All pointing devices, for example, produce similar data that describes the location referenced by the end user with a pen or mouse. This similarity may be expressed in the definition of an interface layer common to all devices in the class. This broad definition allows the calling code to remain unchanged even though the pointing device's controller hardware may vary between manufacturers. So if you are required to support a peripheral device on your custom platform, and it conforms to a defined Windows CE device class, in most cases you need to modify only the portion of the code that accesses the hardware. The rest of the code that implements the device class interface can remain unchanged, thus minimizing the porting effort. Because the CE *native* device driver model uses a layering mechanism, it is the primary driver model for the implementation of device class drivers. The Native Device Driver Model section of Chapter 7 describes this layering mechanism in more detail.

Table 6.1 lists the device classes supported by Windows CE at of the time of this writing. Only Microsoft can produce new device classes and their associated interfaces because the primary calling module of the device class interfaces—the Graphics, Windowing, and Events Subsystem (GWES)—is not provided in source code form in CEPB. It is possible, however, to create your own driver model, as we shall see in Chapter 7.

Table 6.1 Device Classes Supported by Windows CE

Device Class	Driver Interface	Windows NT/9x Portability	Comments
Generic streaming	Streaming I/O	Not portable	
Serial (COMx)	Layered	Not portable	
Network	NDIS 4.0 miniport	Windows NT/9x subset	
Printer	Printer miniport	Windows NT/9x subset	CE printer drivers are structurally similar to Win32 printer drivers.
Audio compression	Streaming I/O	Windows NT	Porting from Windows NT is supported by `acmdev.lib`.
Audio	Streaming I/O or layered	Not portable	A model device driver (MDD) layer, providing an implementation of the stream I/O interface, is provided to reduce the development effort to a platform device driver (PDD) layer. Implementation of an audio driver with a monolithic stream I/O interface is also possible.
Video	Layered	Windows NT subset	The CE video device driver interface (DDI) is a subset of

Table 6.1 *Continued.*

Device Class	Driver Interface	Windows NT/9x Portability	Comments
			Windows NT. Graphics Primitive Engine (GPE) classes are provided to facilitate the implementation of video acceleration.
PC card socket controller	Layered	Not portable	*PC card socket controller* refers to the onboard hardware managing the PC card slot(s), not the PC cards themselves.
Touch panel	Layered	Not portable	
Mouse	Layered	Not portable	
Keyboard	Layered and monolithic	Not portable	*Keyboard* refers to sample keyboard in both a layered and a monolithic form.
Battery	Monolithic	Not portable	The CE specification defines a single DDI layer for battery drivers and is therefore monolithic.
LED	Monolithic	Not portable	The CE specification defines a single DDI layer for LED drivers and is therefore monolithic.
Storage card (block device)	Streaming I/O	Not portable	
Unknown	WDM	Unknown	As of this writing, WDM driver support was still in development.

Device Driver Architecture

Almost every operating system supports the existence of device drivers, each in a slightly different manner. Windows NT, for example, provides a sophisticated mechanism of I/O request packets that allows the manner in which data is processed to be determined dynamically in terms of which drivers are involved and their respective order. With the introduction of the Windows Driver Model (WDM), Windows 9x also supports I/O request packets, in addition to its antecedent virtual device drivers (VxDs). VxDs provide an x86-specific method of dynamically extending the Windows 9x kernel through the use of a device driver declaration block that defines the VxDs' entry points. Of course, there's a lot more to Windows 9x/NT drivers than what we've mentioned here only briefly, as evidenced by the proliferation of books on these subjects, but the important thing to remember is that the unique aspects of an operating system dedicated to device drivers make up its device driver architecture.

The device driver architecture for Windows CE is equally unique. Windows DLLs are used for the dynamic loading of device drivers upon installation and identification (enumeration) of a device. In other cases, object module libraries are used to statically link the required device driver code directly into the kernel image at build time. Each mechanism is used in the definition of four different types of drivers (driver models), each of which will be discussed in Chapter 7.

Note:
Windows DLLs have been around since the introduction of Windows in the fall of 1985. Though the capabilities of DLLs have been enhanced over the years, the basic concept remains the same. DLLs are independent modules that contain executable code and symbols selectively exported to other modules. The DLL exports may be referenced by the linker through a separate import library module, deferring linkage and resolution of the associated symbols to runtime. DLLs exist in contrast to object module libraries, which require that the symbols of the target module be resolved by copying of the relevant code or type information directly into the target module.

Another unique aspect of Windows CE that has contributed to the flexibility of its driver architecture is that all Windows CE drivers run in user mode (see Hint 6.1 for a brief description of user mode and kernel mode). The architecture of most operating systems requires that device drivers run in kernel mode. The traditional wisdom has always been that the kernel mode provides direct access to device resources without the inherent overhead of user mode. With the increase in processor performance and the size of the processors's internal translation lookaside buffer (TLB, used to reduce the overhead of memory accesses in user mode), this extra overhead in some processors has been reduced to a single instruction cycle.

Hint 6.1 Definition of kernel and user modes

With the introduction of virtual memory, it became possible to tell the processor that specified address ranges have certain attributes. Separate address ranges could be reserved for use by the operating system and application code. In this way the operating system is protected from untrusted application code, affording it more stability. Access to the addresses reserved for the operating system requires that the processor be in a mode we refer to as **kernel mode** (also referred to as ring zero and privileged mode by some processor manufacturers), whereas access to the addresses reserved for applications is allowed in either kernel mode or user mode. **User mode** is the mode the processor is in when executing application code.

There are also many advantages to running user mode drivers. Perhaps the greatest is that the kernel is effectively protected from what we device driver developers do incorrectly. The likelihood that the kernel could be corrupted by a driver crash, potentially causing corruption of the object store or inability to restart the kernel, or any other imaginable disaster, is therefore significantly reduced. Another distinct advantage is that drivers may access all the wonderful resources that are available to application developers. That is, application interfaces such as COM and MFC could, in theory, be used for driver development (see the USB Device Driver Model section of Chapter 7 for more information on the use of application interfaces for driver development). Your driver can also call the Win32 API to interact with the end user, perhaps providing extended configuration options or prompting for additional information. Perhaps the most useful capability secured by user mode drivers, however, is the use of the same debugging tools available to application developers in the CEPB IDEs.

Note:
You may be wondering why we have, in effect, tried to sell you on user mode drivers. If you are like us, we were originally quite skeptical, fearing that user mode would prevent us from gaining the access and control to which we had become accustomed in writing drivers for Windows 9x/NT. Our skepticism has since been replaced with genuine enthusiasm, as we have realized that far from imposing unwanted obstacles, user mode has liberated us to consider driver designs otherwise impossible in kernel mode. If you are a skeptic, perhaps you, too, will reconsider.

Figure 6.1 contains a kind of family portrait of the four different driver models supported by CE. As in any family, each driver model is slightly different from its siblings and specializes in servicing particular device classes. Each driver is represented as a vertical stack of rectangles just below a wide, light gray rectangle corresponding to the primary module responsible for the management—or *parenting,* to extend the metaphor—of the driver.

In Figure 6.1, each rectangle in the vertical stack represents a defined layer in the driver's design, and the dark gray rectangles correspond to an interface defined for the particular driver model. The lower rectangles correspond to interfaces providing access (directly, or indirectly through another driver) to the physical device resources. The rectangle in the center, with large italicized type, contains the name used to collectively refer to the driver model and its respective interfaces. The stream-interface driver, for example, appearing on the far left, contains a lower rectangle labeled *Card and Socket Services.* The card and socket services driver provides a mechanism that allows the enumeration and configuration of a PC card for later access when the stream-interface driver is called by an application (via the device manager). If the stream-interface driver supports a non-PC card device, other mechanisms exist for accessing your device's physical resources.

We will discuss each of the driver models in detail in Chapter 7, so keep Figure 6.1 in mind if you need to review the big picture. For now, let's just summarize each driver model individually. The stream-interface device driver model is used most commonly to support installable devices and is managed by the device manager. Native drivers are usually managed by the Graphics, Windowing, and Events Subsystem (GWES) module. Note, however, that native drivers can also be managed by the device manager if their upper interface uses the mechanism of the stream-interface model. In this case, the native driver is acting as a kind of driver hybrid that fulfills the interface requirements of both the stream-interface driver and the native driver models.

The NDIS miniport driver model conforms to the NDIS 4.0 specification and specializes in the support of network interface devices. It is managed by a separate NDIS driver that provides the services for the upper and lower interfaces; this driver is often referred to as the NDIS wrapper. It is interesting to note that the NDIS wrapper uses the stream-interface device driver model and is in turn managed by the device manager.

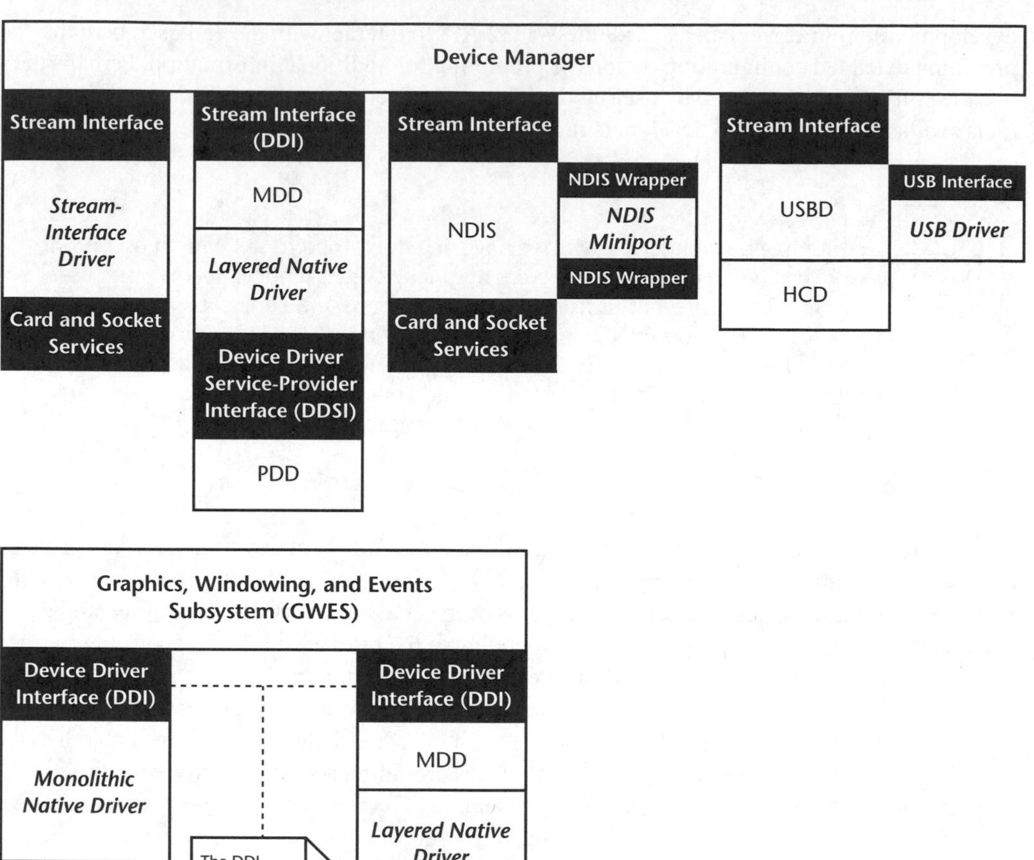

Figure 6.1 Block diagram of the device driver architecture

Like NDIS miniport drivers, USB drivers (or USB client drivers, using the rubric of the USB standard) are managed by a separate USBD module and specialize in the support of devices that transmit and receive data through the USB. The USBD module loads each registered USB client driver until one is found that indicates support for a newly connected device. The interface defined for USB client drivers is actually quite simple, as you will learn in Chapter 8, and it relies on a more passive model in which the individual USB client drivers call back into the USBD module to request access to physical device resources. Like the NDIS driver that implements the NDIS wrapper and manages NDIS miniport drivers, the USBD module is a stream-interface driver managed by the device manager.

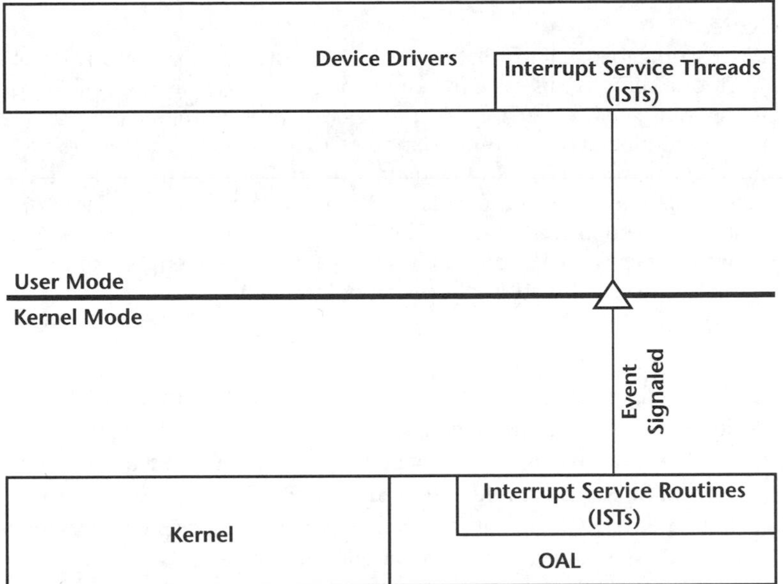

Figure 6.2 Block diagram of device driver interrupt processing

Figure 6.2 provides a high-level view of interrupt processing in CE device drivers. Note that the interrupt is first processed in the kernel mode OAL module (discussed in Chapter 5), which then signals an event object to notify the user mode driver code of a pending interrupt. Execution then resumes in the driver's high-priority interrupt service thread (IST), previously blocked on the unsignaled event, and the interrupt is processed. This will be explored more fully in Chapter 8.

Microsoft Products Required for Driver Development

As you may have noticed by now, the primary tool referenced throughout this chapter is the Windows CE Platform Builder (CEPB). This product is required when you're adapting Windows CE to custom platforms that require drivers for onboard devices, but it is not required when you're developing drivers that support an installable device. In the latter case, the only product required is the Windows CE Toolkit for Visual C++ (CETK) or eMbedded Visual C++ (eMVC, successor to the CETK). Let us explain.

Whenever a new standard platform is defined by Microsoft (i.e., Handheld PC, Palm-size PC, Handheld PC Pro, AutoPC, Pocket PC, and others as time progresses), a platform SDK is released, generally in beta form, followed shortly thereafter by a production release. These products are offered on the Microsoft Web site with, as you might imagine, a separate platform SDK provided for each platform. Each platform SDK is installed as an add-on to the CETK and eMVC and does not require the purchase of the CEPB.

Note:
It is possible to install the Platform SDK without having previously installed the CETK or eMVC. In this case, the emulator is the only available build target and is only marginally useful for driver development. Communication with the supported peripheral device (either onboard or installable) is usually required for driver development, but the emulator does not provide this support. It is capable of debugging only the code used to implement the logical interface required of your driver's model. The CE emulator is a useful tool for Win32, application-level emulation, but it is not yet capable of emulating the unique features of a target platform or peripheral device.

Despite the explicit reference to the SDK, in some cases the Platform SDK also provides the DDK for the associated platform (the Handheld PC Platform SDK, for example, does this). This DDK may be used to develop drivers for installable devices used on the particular platform addressed by the Platform SDK. You would still need to purchase the CETK or eMVC, which provides the target compilers for specific processors, but you would be able to develop your driver without the more substantial investment required for the CEPB.

When developing drivers for most onboard devices, however, you still need the CEPB. The reason is that most onboard devices require initialization when the kernel is loaded and/or must be included in the ROM image of a custom build of the CE kernel—all of which require the CEPB. This will make more sense when we begin to discuss the native device driver model in Chapter 7.

Sample Device Driver Source Code

The most difficult part of developing CE drivers often is knowing where to start. The sample source code provided in the CEPB makes a great beginning. Knowing what sort of sample source code is available and how to begin using it is essential to jump-start the development process. Tables 6.2, 6.3, and 6.4 list the sample drivers available in both the Windows CE 2.00 Platform SDK (PSDK) and the CEPB. The key difference between the PSDK and the CEPB samples is that the PSDK drivers support only installable devices, whereas the CEPB sample drivers support both installable and onboard devices. In a few cases, sample source code is provided for the same installable device in both the PSDK and the CEPB, as in the NE2000 sample driver. Though the files for this sample driver bear the same name in each case, they are slightly different, one difference being that the PSDK's NE2000 build files may be processed under the Visual C++ IDE. If your driver does support an installable device and two sets of sample source code are available, it is wise to check both.

Let's continue by surveying the CEPB sample source code in Tables 6.2, 6.3, and 6.4. All CEPB sample source code can be divided into two major groups: the platform-dependent drivers in the `.\PLATFORM\<Platform Name>\DRIVERS` directory tree, and the platform-independent drivers in the `.\PUBLIC\COMMON\OAK\DRIVERS` directory tree. The platform-dependent drivers, as the name implies, provide support for a specific peripheral device in a way that is unique to a custom platform. The `.\PLATFORM\<Platform Name>\DRIVERS` sample source code contains only the portion of the complete driver that is dedicated to the platform dependencies, while the .\PUBLIC\COMMON\OAK\DRIVERS sample source code contains the platform-independent portion. This separation accounts for the appearance of the identical subdirectory names in both directory trees. This mechanism of separation is responsible for what is referred to as the native device driver model and is discussed in detail in Chapter 7.

You generally begin with one of the drivers in the .\PLATFORM\<Platform Name>\DRIVERS directory tree, if your custom platform offers the same peripheral device. You examine the code for anything that might vary from your platform, such as inline assembly language (obviously processor dependent) and variations in platform resource assignments (IRQ lines, base port addresses, memory-mapped I/O ranges, DMA buffer addresses, and so on). In many cases the platform-independent code in the .\PUBLIC\COMMON\OAK\DRIVERS directory tree requires little or no modification.

Take the PCMCIA driver, for example. The PCMCIA directory under the .\PUBLIC\COMMON\OAK\DRIVERS directory tree contains an implementation of the card services API used for enumeration and configuration of a PC card, which is considered an installable device. The PCMCIA directory under the .\PLATFORM\ODO\DRIVERS directory tree, however, contains the sample code that communicates with the PC card socket controller, which is considered an onboard device. Though sample source code is provided for both, you generally limit your changes to the PC card socket controller driver because it will most likely vary from the implementation provided for the Odo platform.

Many of the drivers listed in Table 6.3 from the .\PUBLIC\COMMON\OAK\DRIVERS directory tree are built with an object module library (drivers with the *.lib* extension in the "Driver" column) target binary. These drivers make up a set of functions that are linked with the build of specified drivers. In most cases these functions represent the implementation of an API for a device class defined by Microsoft, or for customization of a particular operating system module, such as the calibration user interface or the out-of-memory user interface.

Note:
The Sources file used to build drivers that link in platform-independent object module libraries contains a macro called SOURCELIBS. If the name of an object module library is associated with this macro, the macro links the entire library rather than only those object modules corresponding to unresolved symbols, as is commonly the case.

In the latter case you would modify the implementation of the library code itself, which is automatically linked into another module during the build of the CE kernel image. In the former case you would typically modify the sample code in the .\PLATFORM\<Platform Name>\DRIVERS directory tree and link in the library module containing the implementation of the required device class APIs. Other object module libraries, such as those under the .\PUBLIC\COMMON\OAK\DRIVERS\ETHDBG directory tree are simply used as repositories of common utility functions that simplify the implementation of certain drivers. In this case the code would not be used unless appropriate for the supported device and is unlikely to require modification.

In Table 6.3 you will find certain modules built with an EXE target binary. Ceramdrv.exe, for example, is used to test the driver ramdisk.dll that exists under the same parent directory. This module and others like it should prove useful in testing your own customized driver. Other directories, such as .\PUBLIC\COMMON\OAK\DRIVERS\TEST\PCMCIA and .\PUBLIC\

COMMON\OAK\DRIVERS\NETSAMP, contain a suite of modules used for testing the PC card socket drivers and the CE networking communications infrastructure.

Unless otherwise noted, each sample described in Tables 6.2, 6.3, and 6.4 is available in both CEPB 2.12 and CEPB 3.0. If a particular driver is implemented with support for only the Odo or CEPC platforms, this is also noted.

Table 6.2 Sample Device Driver Resources in the CEPB Platform Directory Tree

Parent Directory	Subdirectory	Driver	Description
.\PLATFORM\ <Platform Name>\DRIVERS	ceddk	pc_ddk.dll (CEPC platform)	A customized version of ceddk.dll for PC platforms. These routines represent a collection of valuable utility functions compatible with the NT kernel mode support routines.
	com_card (CEPB 3.0)	com_card.dll (CEPC platform)	A PC card driver with support for COM port devices, based on the enhanced serial port MDD layer provided in CEPB 3.0.
	com16550 (CEPB 3.0)	com16550.dll (CEPC platform)	A *stream-interface device driver* with support for an onboard COM port device based on a 16550 UART. This driver also supports the enhanced serial port MDD layer provided in CEPB 3.0. The object module library ser16550.lib (found in the CEPB public directory tree) is used to simplify access to the UART hardware.
	display	<various>.dll, depending on display type	Display drivers modified for the designated platform. Windows CE display drivers conform to a subset of the Windows NT display driver interface (DDI). A set of C++ classes called the Graphics Primitive Engine (GPE) is provided to facilitate hardware acceleration in the implementation of the DDI functions. See Appendix D for details on writing CE display drivers.
	drvlib	drvlib.lib (Odo/OdoDUB platforms)	An object module library that acts as the repository for shared driver code in the Odo and OdoDUB platforms. As of this writing, source code is provided for manipulating the registers of the touch panel and audio device on the Odo and OdoDUB platforms. Source code is also provided for the implementation of a sleep function that does not require a system call. This is particularly useful when a delay period is required and system calls are unavailable because the kernel mode is active.
	irmac	nscirda.dll (CEPC platform)	A sample NDIS miniport driver that provides support for an IrDA adapter card based on the PC87108, PC87308, and PC87338 chip sets.

Table 6.2 *Continued.*

Parent Directory	Subdirectory	Driver	Description
	kbdmouse	<various>.dll, depending on keyboard layout (CEPC platform)	A sample *native device driver* that implements support for both a keyboard and a PS/2 mouse on a PC. This driver implements the device driver service-provider interface (DDSI) functions in the PDD layer defined for keyboard drivers.
	keybd2	<various>.dll, depending on keyboard layout (Odo/OdoDUB platforms)	A sample *native device driver* that implements support for a proprietary keyboard device on the Odo CE development platform. This driver also implements the DDSI functions in the PDD layer defined for the keyboard drivers.
	mouse	sermouse.dll (CEPC platform)	A sample serial mouse driver implemented through the *stream-interface device driver model.* This driver uses the stream-interface driver model primarily to get the driver loaded and does not expose an application's interface in the form of a device file name.
	pcmcia	pcmcia.dll	A sample *native device driver* that supports PC card socket controllers for various platforms. This driver implements the DDSI functions defined for PC card socket drivers in the platform device driver (PDD) layer.
	serial	serial.dll (Odo/OdoDUB platforms)	A sample *native device driver* that supports an RS-232 UART device. See the description below for the serial.pdd driver.
	serial.pdd	serial.dll (CEPC platform)	A sample *native device driver* that supports an RS-232 UART device. This code implements the DDSI functions in the PDD layer defined for serial devices and links in the source code library that provides the implementation of the MDD layer for serial devices. It is interesting to note that the MDD layer for this type of driver uses the *stream-interface device driver model* in the implementation of its DDI functions.
	serial_sl11 (CEPB 3.0)	sl11_ser.dll (CEPC platform)	A sample USB function controller driver (a USB driver for a peripheral device that connects to another device, typically a PC, that acts as the USB host), that supports the ScanLogic Corporation's SL11 USB function controller chip set.
	touchp	touch.dll (Odo/OdoDUB platforms)	A sample *native device driver* that supports a touch panel controller. This code implements the DDSI functions in the PDD layer defined

(continued)

Table 6.2 *Continued.*

Parent Directory	Subdirectory	Driver	Description
			for touch panel controllers. The implementation of the functions in the MDD layer is linked in as a source code library.
	wavclick	wavclick.dll (Odo/OdoDUB platforms)	A specialized driver that conforms to no predefined driver model, providing support for a dedicated key click sound device. This allows the device that is processing audio files (WAV files) to function even when the keyboard or touch panel is in use.
	wavdev	wavdev.dll	A sample *native device driver* that supports an audio controller for playback of WAV files. This code implements the DDSI functions in the PDD layer defined for audio controllers and links in a source code library for implementation of the DDI functions in the MDD layer. The MDD layer uses the *stream-interface device driver model.*
.\PLATFORM\ <Platform Name>\DRIVERS\ USB	ohcd	ohci.dll (CEPC platform)	A sample *native device driver* that supports a USB host controller conforming to the open host controller interface (OHCI). This code implements the DDSI functions in the PDD layer defined for USB host controllers. The implementation of the functions in the MDD layer is linked in through a source code library. Like the serial drivers, the implementation of the MDD layer uses the *stream-interface device driver model.*
	uhcd (CEPB 3.0)	uhci.dll (CEPC platform)	Same as for ohcd (above), with support for host controllers that conform to the universal host controller interface (UHCI).

Table 6.3 Sample Device Driver Resources in the CEPB Public Directory Tree

Parent Directory	Subdirectory	Driver	Description
.\PUBLIC\ COMMON\OAK\ DRIVERS	atadisk	atadisk.dll	A sample *stream-interface device driver* providing support for ATA /ATAPI (Advanced Technology Attachment Peripheral Interface) disk drive interface provided as an installable PC card.
	bulltlp3 (CEPB 3.0)	bulltlp3.lib	A sample smart card reader driver for a Bull TLP3 reader device.
	calibrui	calibrui.lib	A sample implementation of the functions that provide a touch screen calibration GUI.

Table 6.3 *Continued.*

Parent Directory	Subdirectory	Driver	Description
	`com_mdd2` (CEPB 3.0)	`com_mdd2.lib`	An object module library containing the implementation of a COM port driver MDD layer (device-independent, upper layer, discussed in Chapter 7), with enhanced performance characteristics, over the equivalent library in CEPB 2.12.
	`dualio`	`dualio.dll`	A sample *stream-interface device driver* providing support for a dual serial port, PC card device.
	`fatui`	`fatui.lib`	A module that processes the event messages produced by the `fatfs` component. This module may be modified to customize how these events are processed and whether they are exposed to the end user.
	`keybd`	`keybdmdd.lib`	An implementation of the DDI functions for a keyboard *native device driver,* linked in by the platform-specific PDD layer of this same driver.
	`netui`	`netui.dll`	Source code for the control panel applet used in network configuration.
	`oomui`	`oomui.lib`	Source code for the out-of-memory user interface, automatically displayed during low memory conditions by the GWES module. `Oomui.lib` is linked in during the build of `gwes.exe`.
	`parallel`	`parallel.dll`	Sample source code for the stream-interface, parallel port driver. This driver is designed according to the PDD/MDD layered architecture.
	`pcmcia`	`cardserv.lib`	Source code for the MDD layer of the card and socket services driver PC card. This module is linked in as a source code library during the build of the PDD layer source code in the `.\PLATFORM\<Platform Name>\DRIVERS\PCMCIA` directory.
	`pscr` (CEPB 3.0)	`pscr.dll`	Sample smart card reader driver for a type smart PC card. This driver conforms to the *stream-interface driver model* described in Chapter 7.
	`samptspi` (CEPB 3.0)	`samptspi.dll`	Sample telephony service provider driver, required for compliance with TAPI (Telephony API) 2.0. This driver provides a

(continued)

Table 6.3 *Continued.*

Parent Directory	Subdirectory	Driver	Description
			device-independent software interface that is used to convert TAPI service requests into access to the telephony device.
	ser_card	ser_card.lib	Sample source code for an object module library that may be used in the implementation of the PDD layer functions (DDSI) for a PC card COM port device.
	ser_card2 (CEPB 3.0)	ser_card2.lib	Same as the ser_card sample COM port driver above, but with the changes required to act as the PDD layer for the com_mdd2 (above) enhanced MDD layer.
	ser_usb (CEPB 3.0)	usbser.dll	Sample source code for the Socket USB Synch Card. This device allows a USB cable to be attached to a compact flash card. The driver exposes the card as a type of PC card that provides serial data through the serial MDD driver com_mdd2.lib library (see above). Because this device acts as a USB peripheral device (USB function) attached to a USB-enabled host, the received USB data is parsed directly and is passed up through the serial MDD DDSI interface (described in Chapter 7). This driver may also be used as an example of a USB function controller driver.
	ser16550	ser16550.lib	Sample source code for an object module library that may be used in the implementation of the PDD layer functions (DDSI) for a 16550 UART–based serial device. This object module library is linked through a TARGETLIB entry in the build of the dualio and com16550 sample serial *stream-interface device driver.*
	serial	com_mdd.lib	Sample source code for the implementation of the MDD layer functions (DDI) defined for a *stream-interface,* serial port driver. This module is generally linked through a SOURCELIB entry in the build of the platform-specific PDD layer functions (DDSI) of the serial port driver.
	smclib (CEPB 3.0)	smclib.lib	Source code for the smart card reader helper library used in the implementation of the sample smart card reader drivers (pscr, bulltlp3, and stcusb).

Table 6.3 *Continued.*

Parent Directory	Subdirectory	Driver	Description
	snmptestmib	snmp_ snmptestmib. dll	Source code for the test Management Information Base (MIB), acting as a Simple Network Management Protocol (SNMP) extension agent.
	sramdisk	sramdisk.dll	Sample source code of a block device driver (type of *stream-interface device driver*) for an SRAM (static RAM) PC card device.
	startui	startui.lib	Sample source code demonstrating the customization of the screen that is automatically displayed when the platform resumes from a Suspend state.
	tch_cal	tch_cal.lib	Sample source code demonstrating the customization of the touch screen, calibration user interface, automatically displayed during a cold boot (system startup with initialization of all hardware and software subsystems, including the object store).
	touchp	tchmdd.lib	Implementation of the MDD layer functions (DDI) required for the touch panel *native device driver.* This module is linked through a SOURCELIB entry in the build of the PDD layer functions in the .\PLATFORM\<Platform Name>\DRIVERS\TOUCHP directory.
	trueffs	trueffs.dll	Sample source code for the True Flash File System customization function flRegisterComponents, used to control the registration of the socket interface, memory technology devices (MTDs), and translation layers. The module tffscore.lib is linked through a SOURCELIB entry in the build of the trueffs.dll *stream-interface,* block device driver.
	wavedev	wavemdd.lib	Sample source code for implementation of the MDD layer functions (DDI) required for an audio driver. The audio driver uses the mechanisms of the stream interface for the implementation of MDD layer functions.
	waveui	waveui.lib	Sample source code for customization of the Audio Control Manager (ACM) filter and format selection user interface.
.\PUBLIC\ COMMON\OAK\ DRIVERS\ACM	acmdwrap	acmdwrap.lib	A layer mapping the *stream-interface device driver model* to the Windows NT Audio Compression Manager (ACM) driver interface.

(continued)

Table 6.3 *Continued.*

Parent Directory	Subdirectory	Driver	Description
	cegsm (CEPB 2.12), gsm610 (CEPB 3.0)	cegsm.lib	A sample ACM codec driver implementing the audio codec GSM (Global System for Mobile telecommunication) 6.10. The acmdwrap.lib source code library is linked in for implementation of the stream interface to the ACM mapping layer.
	msfilter	msfilter.lib	A sample ACM filter driver. See the description above for the cegsm driver.
	pcmconv	pcmconv.dll	A sample ACM codec driver. See the description above for the cegsm driver.
.\PUBLIC\ COMMON\OAK\ DRIVERS\ CEDDK	ddk_bus	ddk_bus.lib	The default implementation of certain NT kernel mode support routines. This library is generally linked in only when no other platform-specific implementation is available.
	ddk_io	ddk_io.lib	See the description above for the ddk_bus module.
	ddk_map	ddk_map.lib	See the description above for the ddk_bus module.
	dll	ceddk.dll	See the description above for the ddk_bus module.
.\PUBLIC\ COMMON\OAK\ DRIVERS\ CEDDK\TEST	isaenum	isaenum.exe	A module for testing the implementation of ceddk.dll on a platform with an ISA bus.
	pcienum	pcienum.exe	A module for testing the implementation of the ceddk.dll on a platform with a PCI (Peripheral Component Interconnect) bus.
.\PUBLIC\ COMMON\OAK\ DRIVERS\ DISPLAY	emul	emul.lib	A module implementing the emulation library used by display drivers, linked in as a source code library.
	wrap2bpp	wrap2bpp.lib	A module containing an implementation of the Graphics Primitive Engine (GPE) classes for displays with color resolution of two bits per pixel.
	wrap2dr (CEPB 2.12)	wrap2dr.lib	A dirty rectangle version of wrap2bpp.lib.
.\PUBLIC\ COMMON\OAK\ DRIVERS\ETHDBG	eboot	eboot.lib	A collection of modules implementing the functionality (TFTP and DHCP) needed to download a CE ROM image from the development workstation over an Ethernet connection. The development workstation must be running

Table 6.3 *Continued.*

Parent Directory	Subdirectory	Driver	Description
			Eshell, CESH, and optionally Eterm to receive debug messages.
	edbgsamp	edbgsamp.exe	A module that may be compiled to run on either the development workstation or a target CE device to demonstrate the use of Ethernet debug functions.
	ne2000	ne2kdbg.lib	A collection of modules that access the physical resources of an NE2000 network interface card (NIC). These functions are generally used in the development of a boot loader that must download a CE ROM image without the benefit of a networking infrastructure such as NDIS.
	smc9000	smc9000.lib	A collection of modules that access the physical resources of an SMC9000 NIC. See the description above for the `ne2kdbg.lib` module.
.\PUBLIC\COMMON\OAK\DRIVERS\IRMAC	irsir	irsirlib.lib	A collection of modules used in the implementation of an NDIS driver supporting an IrDA device.
	utils	irmacutl.lib	A collection of utility functions for translation from the NDIS to the IrDA packet format, used by the `irsirlib.lib` module described above.
.\PUBLIC\COMMON\OAK\DRIVERS\KEYBD2	ist	keybdist.lib	An implementation of the DDI functions for a keyboard *native device driver,* in addition to the interrupt server thread (IST). This module and those that follow in this parent directory are linked by the platform-specific PDD layer source code in the `.\PLATFORM\<Platform Name>\DRIVERS` directory tree.
	svkremap	svkremap.lib	A stubbed implementation of the functions used to remap certain physical keystrokes to logical keystrokes (consisting of *VK_* virtual key codes) and to track the state of modifier keys such as **Shift**, **Caps Lock**, and **Alt**. This function is fully implemented in the platform-specific layer for the sample Japanese keyboard driver.
	vkremap	vkremap.lib	An implementation of the functions described for the `svkremap` module above.
	vktochar	vktochar.lib	A minimal implementation of the functions used to remap keystrokes to Unicode characters.

(continued)

Table 6.3 *Continued.*

Parent Directory	Subdirectory	Driver	Description
.\PUBLIC\COMMON\OAK\DRIVERS\NETCARD	ne2000	ne2000.dll	Sample source code for an NE2000-compliant, network adapter driver PC card.
	proxim	proxim.dll	Sample source code to support the Proxim wireless LAN adapter PC card.
	xircom.ce2	xircce2.dll	Sample source code to support a Xircom LAN adapter PC card.
.\PUBLIC\COMMON\OAK\DRIVERS\NETSAMP	ipconfig (CEPB 3.0)	ipconfig.lib	Sample source code to query the IP settings currently in effect.
	ping	ping.exe	Source code for the standard PING utility application executed from the CE command line on the development workstation. Note that this module is a stand-alone application, even though it is located in the driver directory tree.
	rasdial	rasdial.exe	Source code for a command-line utility application used to establish a dial-up connection and exercise the network drivers. Note that this module is a stand-alone application, even though it is located in the driver directory tree.
	rasentry	rasentry.exe	Source code for a command-line application that reads a specially formatted text file to make a specified entry in the Remote Access Services (RAS) phonebook.
	route	route.exe	Source code for a command-line application that allows the network routing tables to be manipulated.
.\PUBLIC\COMMON\OAK\DRIVERS\PRINTER	pcl	pcl.dll	Sample source code for a printer driver that conforms to a subset of the desktop printer driver model.
	prnerr	prnerr.dll	Sample source code for the printer status module implementing the `ReportPrinterStatus` function.
	prnport	prnport.lib	Sample source code for the port monitor functions used by printer drivers. This driver abstracts the physical access to the printer in the same manner as the PDD/MDD layering. It is linked through a `TARGETLIB` entry in the build of printer drivers. See sample printer driver `pcl.dll` (above) for an example.
.\PUBLIC\COMMON\OAK\DRIVERS\RAMDISK	driver	ramdisk.dll	Sample block device driver (a type of *stream-interface device driver*) that uses RAM to create an external object store.

Table 6.3 *Continued.*

Parent Directory	Subdirectory	Driver	Description
	loader	ceramdrv.exe	Test program for `ramdisk.dll`. This program registers, loads, and opens a file in the object store created by the `ramdisk.dll` block device driver.
.\PUBLIC\COMMON\OAK\DRIVERS\TEST\PCMCIA	attrdump	attrdump.dll	*Stream-interface device driver* used by the Attrtest program to display the contents of attribute memory on an installed PC card device. The sample code is hard-coded to read the attribute memory of function 0 of a PC card at socket 0.
	attrtest	attrtest.exe	Utility program to register and load the `attrdump.dll` *stream-interface device driver* and initiate the display of the attribute memory on an installed PC card device.
	devtuple	devtuple.dll	*Stream-interface device driver* used by the `tupletst.exe` program to parse and display the tuple data of an inserted PC card device. (*Tuple* is PC card lingo for "data structure.")
	tupletst	tupletst.exe	Utility program to register and load the `devtuple.dll` *stream-interface device driver* that displays the contents of an inserted PC card's tuple data.
.\PUBLIC\COMMON\OAK\DRIVERS\USB	common	lock.c	Source code for a group of functions providing synchronization for multiple threads that read and write data. If `EnterWriteBlock` is called, the write thread blocks until no other read or write threads are active. If `EnterReadBlock` is called, the read thread blocks until no other write threads are active. Multiple read threads may be active, however.
	usbd	usbd.dll	Source code for implementation of the USBDI (USB driver interface) functions used by USB client drivers to allocate a USB pipe.
.\PUBLIC\COMMON\OAK\DRIVERS\USB\CLASS	hid	usbhid.dll	Sample source code for the implementation of a driver conforming to the *USB device driver model* and providing support for Human Interface Device (HID)–class USB devices.
.\PUBLIC\COMMON\OAK\DRIVERS\USB\CLIENTS	mouse (CEPB 2.12)	usbmouse.dll	Sample source code for the implementation of a driver conforming to the *USB device driver model* with specific support for a USB mouse.

(continued)

Table 6.3 *Continued.*

Parent Directory	Subdirectory	Driver	Description
	stcusb (CEPB 3.0)	stcusb.dll	Sample source code for a client driver conforming to the *USB device driver model,* with support for an SCM Microsystems USB smart card reader. It may also be used as an example of the use of the smart card reader helper library to implement a reader driver.
.\PUBLIC\COMMON\OAK\DRIVERS\USB\HCD	ohcd	ohcdmdd.lib	Sample source code for implementation of the MDD layer functions (DDI) in the USB host controller driver. This driver supports controllers that conform to the open host controller interface (OHCI).
	uhcd (CEPB 3.0)	uhcdmdd.lib	Same as for ohcd above, with support for controllers that conform to the universal host controller interface (UHCI).

Table 6.4 Sample Device Driver Resources in the Windows CE 2.00 Platform SDK

Parent Directory	Subdirectory	Driver	Description
.\WCE200\MS HPC\SAMPLES\DDK\ACM	acmdwrap	acmdwrap.lib	*Stream-interface device driver* source code linked in for the build of the cegsm.dll ACM driver. This module translates the *stream-interface device driver* entry points into calls to the equivalent ACM functions.
	cegsm	cegsm.dll	Sample source code for a driver conforming to the Audio Control Manager (ACM) driver model, acting as a codec for GSM 6.10-encoded audio data.
.\WCE200\MS HPC\SAMPLES\DDK\NETCARD	ne2000	ne2000.dll	Sample *NDIS device driver* source code, with support for an NE2000-compliant PC card device.
.\WCE200\MS HPC\SAMPLES\DDK\PCMCIA	16550	16550mod.dll	Sample *stream-interface device driver* with support for a PC card modem. The modem is expected to have a 16550 UART interface.
	pager	pagercomm.exe, newscard.dll	Support for the Motorola NewsCard pager PC card device is provided in the newscard.dll sample *stream-interface device driver.* The pagercomm.exe module is used for testing the driver.
	ramcard	ramcard.dll, writetst.exe, readtest.exe	The sample *stream-interface device driver* ramcard.dll demonstrates the reading and writing of data to an SRAM PC card device. The modules writetst.exe and readtest.exe provide write and read testing

Table 6.4 Sample Device Driver Resources in the Windows CE 2.00 Platform SDK

Parent Directory	Subdirectory	Driver	Description
			of the `ramcard.dll` *stream-interface device driver.*
	`test`	`testapp.exe`, `cardtest.dll`	The sample *stream-interface device driver* `cardtest.dll` accesses an inserted PC card and tests memory, attribute, and tuples. The module `testapp.exe` may be called from the command line (CE remote shell) to initiate each test.
`.\WCE200\MS HPC\SAMPLES\ DDK\SERIAL`	`gps`	`gps.exe`	Sample source code to open a global positioning satellite receiver PC card device and read the received location data. The received data is displayed in the remote debugger, running on the development workstation.
	`tty`	`tty.exe`	Application (provided in source code form) demonstrating basic access to a COM port device. Received data is displayed in a window, and typed characters are sent to the COM port.

Summary

This concludes the first of the four chapters dedicated to CE device driver development. In this chapter we laid the foundation for your growing understanding of the design and development of CE drivers. We discussed some of the basic concepts that are common to driver development for all embedded operating systems but that are particularly useful in CE driver development. We also covered, in some detail, the wide range of available CEPB sample source code, so you should have some idea of what's available to jump-start your driver development efforts.

The most important thing to take away from this chapter is an understanding of the overall architecture of CE drivers. This knowledge will give you a context for understanding what's to come and will make it easier for you to understand why certain drivers and driver models are designed as they are. If this chapter generated more questions than answers, we encourage you to stick with it because the next three chapters will gradually build greater understanding, hopefully answering more questions than they create.

7 Writing Device Drivers: Driver Models

In this chapter we will explore the particulars of various CE driver models. We will describe the architecture from which each driver model is derived and how it is supported by other CE modules. We will present examples of the entry points (functions) required for each driver model, focusing especially on the functionality expected for each. Many implementation practices that are associated with accessing your device's physical resources and are required for the implementation of an entry point are *not* covered in this chapter. However, these practices will be covered in Chapter 8.

We begin with an exploration of the stream-interface device driver model that forms the basic staple of CE driver development. This model supports a broad variety of devices and may be accessed from applications through the standard Win32 file I/O (input/output) interface. We continue with the native device driver model used to support devices that conform to Microsoft-defined device classes. Finally, we turn to the USB and NDIS device driver models, which are derived from the mechanisms provided by the stream-interface device driver model.

In some cases—for example, NDIS drivers (acting as the low-level interface to a network adapter)—the device driver is very similar to its desktop counterpart. We will discuss these types of drivers only from the point of view of how they differ from the desktop standard, the intent being to give you a jump-start on porting existing device driver source code.

Stream-Interface Device Driver Model

The most commonly used driver model in CE is the stream-interface device driver model, so named because of its basic file I/O interface. Stream-interface drivers are used primarily to support installable devices that may be added to the CE platform by the end user. They may also be used, however, to provide a driver that is dynamically loaded at system startup, to support a device that is *not* dynamically identified and enumerated. The stream-interface model also supports drivers that are loaded upon request by an application (described in more detail in the next few sections).

As mentioned in Chapter 6, the stream-interface model is one of many device driver models supported by the CEPB. Of the four models introduced in this chapter, it is interesting that the stream-interface model is often used directly or indirectly as a mechanism to implement the other device driver models, with the exception of certain native drivers that are contained in an object module library. The reason is that the stream-interface model is the only one with support for dynamic loading of its associated driver. By creating other driver models using the mechanisms of the stream-interface driver model, you can support specialized device classes that inherit this model's dynamic capabilities.

For example, what is known as the NDIS wrapper, the basis of the NDIS device driver model, is implemented as a stream-interface driver called `ndis.dll`. Certain registry keys that are used to load an NDIS driver of a given name appear as a stream-interface driver with the name `ndis.dll`. The actual NDIS miniport driver is referenced in another registry key and is loaded directly by `ndis.dll`. The entry points required for compliance with the NDIS device driver model are present in the miniport driver; those required for compliance with the stream-interface driver model are implemented in the stream-interface driver `ndis.dll`. The USB device driver model is architecturally similar, with the USB host controller driver (HCD) functioning as a stream-interface driver that initiates the loading of USB drivers that comply with the USB driver model.

Device Manager and Driver Control Programs

The Device Manager (DM) is dedicated to the care and feeding of stream-interface drivers. As we explore the architecture of other CE driver models, you will notice that each one has its own modules that perform functions analogous to the stream-interface model's DM. We refer to the modules that provide this class of functionality as driver control programs (DCPs).

The DM, the first DCP that we will explore, lives in its own process slot (see Chapters 1 and 8 for more information on process slots) and loads stream-interface drivers as standard CE DLL modules, mapped into the address space of the DM executable. The DM is also responsible for unloading the stream-interface driver when the device is removed or the platform is powered up from Suspend mode and the devices are re-enumerated. Figure 7.1 diagrams the relationship between the stream-interface driver and the calling application that needs to read and write to a particular device. As the figure shows, the stream-interface driver is not mapped into the address space of the calling application, as are DLL modules that are called directly by an application. Instead, the standard Win32 file I/O calls (`CreateFile`, `WriteFile`, `ReadFile`, and so on) provide basic read and write access to the device, and the module `coredll.dll` performs the necessary context switch to the process space of the DM.

When your device driver must simultaneously support more than one device, it is important to realize that the application calls are being routed to one DLL instance, requiring that you take care to protect your global variables from simultaneous access by multiple callers. You may also need to maintain separate variable space on the heap for each device being serviced. We will see how this arrangement affects the implementation of the initialization entry points of a stream-interface driver in the section on required entry points later in the discussion of this model.

When to Write a Stream-Interface Driver

Before we delve into the details of how to write a stream-interface driver, let's consider whether this is the model that best characterizes the interface to your device. In many cases the choice is quite easy because you're adapting an existing sample driver to accommodate the unique fea-

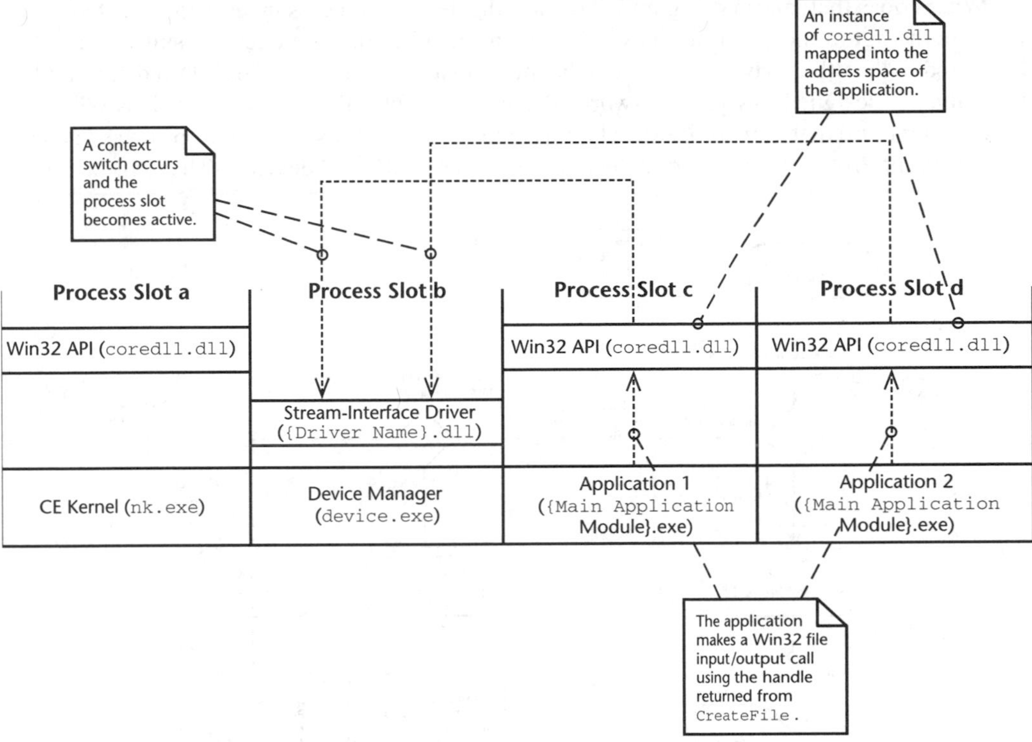

Figure 7.1 Context switch from an application to the Device Manager

tures of your device. If your device is already listed back in Table 6.1, you need only check the "Driver Interface" column for the term *streaming I/O*. If not, then you must ask yourself if the file I/O stream interface can be adapted to allow applications to request services from your device using the Win32 file I/O calls such as `ReadFile` and `WriteFile`.

Another way to evaluate the available driver models is to consider whether your device is onboard or installable. If it is an installable device, the native device driver model may not be appropriate because that model generally assumes that the device is present at system startup and does not support device insertion and removal. Other device driver models, such as the NDIS and USB driver models, may also be considered for support of installable devices and will be explored later in this chapter. If your device is an onboard device, you might consider the native driver model, assuming that the device can be mapped to the capabilities of an existing device class.

Note:
Some native device drivers use the stream interface as a mechanism for providing an application interface based on the Win32 file I/O interface. Such a native driver could be used to support installable devices. The sample COM port driver provided in the CEPB is an example of a driver that is commonly considered a native driver but uses the mechanisms of the stream-interface driver model.

Where does that leave us? Figure 7.2 depicts the decision process in terms of an activity diagram. As the figure shows, in most cases the stream-interface driver model will suit your needs. Compared to the other driver models, it is the most device independent. The NDIS driver model is specifically designed to support network adapters and application interfaces such as Winsock and would require that your device data be formatted as a packet by a transport protocol such as Point-to-Point Protocol (PPP, used in the interface to serial RS-232 devices). The USB driver

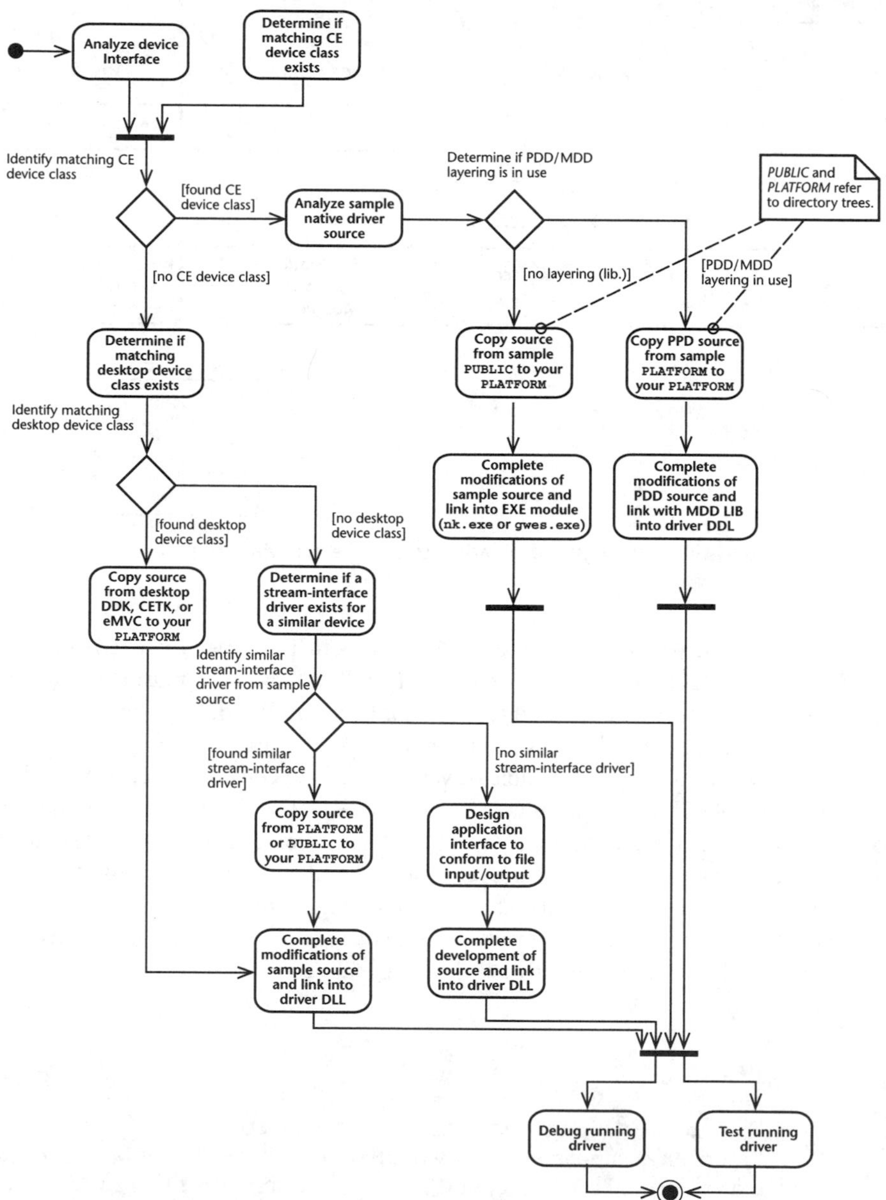

Figure 7.2 Activity diagram for driver model evaluation

model requires, among other things, that your device be connected to a USB port. As mentioned earlier, the native driver model supports specific device classes, and if your device is not functionally similar to one of the supported classes, this option is unavailable. That leaves a custom driver model, for which you would have to define your own required entry points and application interface. The section in this chapter on the USB device driver model describes one example of how a custom driver model is created.

Registry Entries

If your driver supports a physical device, either the onboard or the installable variety, you will mostly likely want it to be loaded automatically. For an onboard device the driver should load when the system is powered on, and for an installable device the driver should load when the device is enumerated by the Device Manager. In this section we will describe the registry keys available to load a stream-interface driver. In the later Load Sequence section we will see how these registry entries are used by the DM during system startup. (Refer to Hint 7.1 for a definition of the terms *registry key, subkey,* and *value.*)

Hint 7.1 Definition of a registry key, subkey, and value

A **registry key** is the parent key in which actual values may be located in the registry. It works like a path name, referring to a particular folder in a file system that contains a group of individually named files. The **subkey** refers to the name of the value contained in a particular registry key. To extend the file system metaphor, the subkey corresponds to the name of a file within a particular folder. Each subkey then contains its own **value**, much as a file contains data that may be analyzed by a program that opens the file.

HKEY_LOCAL_MACHINE\Drivers\BuiltIn

The `BuiltIn` key is used by the DM to load the drivers that support onboard devices—thus the name *BuiltIn.* Another way to view this key, however, is as a mechanism for loading a stream-interface driver that is associated with a device or system resources that are not actually enumerated by the DM (or another driver) during system startup (warm or cold boot). In other words, the `BuiltIn` key acts as a sophisticated replacement for the venerable `autoexec.bat` file used by the DOS operating system to run programs before the system is accessible to the end user. From this perspective, the `BuiltIn` key can be extended to support the loading of stream-interface drivers that act as another type of DCP and do not actually access physical device resources.

If ever you need to provide an application-level API that conforms to the file I/O model of the stream interface, the `BuiltIn` key can be used to save the calling application from the chore of manually loading the associated stream-interface driver (see the Application-Initiated Loading section later in this chapter for more information on how an application may manually load a stream-interface driver). Refer to the CEPB online documentation for a detailed discussion of the subkeys defined for the `BuiltIn` key.

In most cases, however, the `BuiltIn` key is simply used to support an onboard device. The entries are made in the `platform.reg` file that is included in the build of a custom CE kernel image. This file, described in more detail in Chapters 10 and 11, contains a list of the platform-dependent registry entries used to populate the registry during a cold boot. The list of entries is necessary because memory is initialized during a cold boot, eliminating the `BuiltIn` registry key and all other registry keys in RAM.

The CEPB 2.12 online documentation gives the impression that adding entries to the `platform.reg` file is the only way to add to the `BuiltIn` key. It is quite possible, however, to add another key under the `BuiltIn` key during the installation of a driver into the object store (perhaps using the Application Manager) while the platform is still powered on. The next time the user power-cycles your platform, either through a warm or cold boot, your driver will be loaded.

With the introduction of CE 3.0, the OEM has the option of enabling module certification. This certification requires that a module (from an application or driver) be considered *trusted* before certain registry keys, including those under the `Drivers` registry key, can be modified. To become trusted, the module binary must be digitally signed by the process described in Chapter 5. Modules present in the ROM image (referenced in the `MODULES` section of the `platform.bib` file) are automatically trusted.

HKEY_LOCAL_MACHINE\Drivers\PCMCIA

The `PCMCIA` registry key is used by the DM to collect all related registry keys used for the enumeration and installation of PC card, stream-interface drivers. Because PC card devices can be installed by the end user, the registry entries used to load such drivers are a bit more complicated. The DM collaborates with another driver, which provides an implementation of card and socket services (`pcmcia.dll`), to detect inserted PC cards, identify the card type and vendor, and load the associated stream-interface driver. Again we will defer to the CEPB online documentation for a detailed discussion of the subkeys defined for each key presented.

The `HKEY_LOCAL_MACHINE\Drivers\PCMCIA\<Plug-and-Play ID>` registry key is where the registry entries reside for the stream-interface drivers that are associated with specific PC cards identified by the value of their Plug and Play (PnP) ID. The DM uses the PnP ID from the Card Information Structure to form the name of this key. The subkeys define the name and load characteristics of the stream-interface driver.

HKEY_LOCAL_MACHINE\Drivers\PCMCIA\Detect

If the registry key formed with the PnP ID cannot be found, the DM uses the stream-interface drivers listed under the `Detect` key to find an appropriate stream-interface driver. Each key is named with a numeric identifier. The lowest-numbered key is processed first, and the corresponding stream-interface driver is loaded. The detection function named in the `Entry` subkey is then called. If the detection function returns a character string, the PC card was identified and can be handled by the stream-interface driver referenced in the registry key of the returned character string. The DM uses this character string to form a registry key by appending it to the `HKEY_LOCAL_MACHINE\Drivers\PCMCIA` key. This process effectively provides a mechanism for creating generic PC card drivers capable of supporting a specific class of devices, without being limited to PC cards that contain only a designated PnP ID.

If the detection function returns `NULL`, the DM processes the next highest numeric key under the `HKEY_LOCAL_MACHINE\Drivers\PCMCIA\Detect` registry key, causing the associated stream-interface driver to be loaded and its detection function to be called.

This process continues until a detection function returns a valid character string, or until all registry keys have been processed. If your PC card stream-interface driver supports a generic class of PC card devices and provides a detection function, it is important to consider the value of your driver's numeric key. If multiple generic drivers for the same class of PC cards exist and the driver referenced by the key with the lowest numeric value returns a valid character string, the detection function of the other generic driver will never be called. The rule to apply in selecting your numeric key requires you to consider the level of *intrusiveness* of your detection function. Probing the card for specific information that allows it to identify certain characteristics would be considered a highly intrusive detection function capable of identifying its supported devices with a high degree of accuracy. In this case the numeric value should be low to ensure that this detection function is called before all others. Higher numeric keys are therefore reserved for less intrusive detection functions that use fewer qualifying characteristics to identify the supported device. In this way the driver most able to support the PC card of a specific device class is loaded first, beginning with a driver capable of supporting the actual PnP ID and progressing to one capable of supporting a broad device class.

Listing 7.1 provides a sample implementation of a PC card stream-interface driver's detection function. Note the use of the `DevType` parameter to quickly determine if the PC card belongs to a supported device class. If the next statement, which probes the card for specific characteristics, returns `TRUE`, the character string *ATADisk* is returned. This string causes the DM to load the generic PC card driver at the registry key `HKEY_LOCAL_MACHINE\Drivers\PCMCIA\ATADisk`.

Listing 7.1 Sample detection function (excerpted from the `ATADisk` sample driver)

```
LPTSTR
DetectATADisk(
    CARD_SOCKET_HANDLE hSock,
    UCHAR DevType,
    LPTSTR DevKey,
    DWORD  DevKeyLen
    )
{
    if (DevType == PCCARD_TYPE_FIXED_DISK)
    {
        if (ATADetect(hSock) == TRUE)
        {
            _tcscpy(DevKey, TEXT("ATADisk"));
            return DevKey;
        }
    }
    return NULL;
}
```

Device File Names

You may recall from the days when the DOS command line ruled the user interface that external devices could be accessed through special three-character names. If, for example, you wanted to direct the contents of a file to a printer attached to the first of two parallel ports, you could type the command "copy file.txt LPT1:". If the printer was attached to an RS-232 serial port, the same command could be applied with a destination file name of *COM1:*. The destination files `LPT1: and COM1:` are examples of reserved file names that the file system would automatically associate with an external device attached to a port and were therefore known as **device file names**. The first three characters described the communication protocol used between the host and the attached peripheral, and the numeric index that followed distinguished a particular port from multiple identical ports.

The Win32 API supports a slightly different convention. Application developers may initiate communication with a device driver by using a special naming syntax that allows the device driver to be addressed by its file name, preceded by the characters "\\.\". CE has modified this syntax slightly for stream-interface drivers by borrowing from the device file name convention of the DOS command line. You must select a three-character device file name for your stream-interface driver, including a single-digit numeric index. This information is then placed in certain registry keys that are read by the DM on system startup (refer to the next section, Load Sequence, for more information on the DM system startup sequence). These registry entries must be made at the time the driver is installed, or they must be manually entered into the default registry (present in the files with a *.reg* extension and used when building a custom CE kernel) for an onboard device.

In the next few paragraphs we will limit our discussion to those stream-interface registry entries required to define the device file name. The other registry entries associated with stream-interface drivers were discussed earlier in this section.

The values of two registry subkeys—`Prefix` and `Index`—define the device file name for stream-interface drivers (see Table 7.1). `Prefix` consists of the first three characters in the device file name. It need not be unique; in fact, it may be one of many registry entries for other stream-interface drivers, all with the same three-character value. `Index` is used as the numeric index of the device file name. Though it appears in the device file name as a character, its data type in the registry is `DWORD`.

A third registry subkey that may be used to define the device file name is `Order`. The driver with the lowest value for the `Order` subkey is loaded first. If the DM encounters entries for other stream-interface drivers with the same value for the `Order` subkey, it loads the drivers by the order of their occurrence in the registry. Thus, you can effectively control where your driver is loaded relative to all other stream-interface drivers, or relative to a particular group of stream-interface drivers all using the same `Order` value.

Note that the `Index` subkey is optional. If it is not included, the DM will assign an index based on the load order of all other stream-interface drivers with the same value for the subkey `Prefix`. If, for example, on an HP 620LX your driver was being loaded for an onboard device and you were using the prefix *COM* without defining a value for the `Index` subkey, the DM would automatically assign an index value of 2. Let's see how this happens.

The registry entries under the `HKEY_LOCAL_MACHINE\Drivers\BuiltIn` key for the `Serial`, `Serial2`, and `IrCOMM` devices (see Figure 7.4) all have the prefix *COM*. The `Serial` key does not have an `Index` subkey, but it does have an `Order` subkey with a value of 0. Because no other drivers are using this value, the driver associated with the `Serial` key is loaded first and receives an index of 1, with a device file name of *COM1:*. Index values are assigned in sequence beginning with 1 and going up to 9, after which the value of 0 is assigned.

The next driver loaded with the prefix *COM* is `IrCOMM`, which is using an `Index` subkey value of 3. The result is a device file name of *COM3:*. The next driver loaded is `Serial2`, which is using an `Index` subkey value of 4, producing a device file name of *COM4:*. In this example, the index value of 2 was assigned to your driver because the `Index` subkey was not in use and was the next lowest value in the series of device file names with the assigned indexes of 1, 3, and 4 (COM1:, COM3:, and COM4:).

Table 7.1 Device File Name Registry Keys

Subkey	Key	Type	Example	Description
`Prefix`	`HKEY_LOCAL_MACHINE\Drivers\BuiltIn\<Driver Name>`	String	`HKLM\Drivers\BuiltIn\Modem\Prefix = "COM"`	This driver is loaded on a cold boot to support an onboard modem and is accessed with the name *COM<index>:* when `CreateFile` is being called.
	`HKEY_LOCAL_MACHINE\Drivers\PCMCIA\<PnPID>`	String	`HKLM\Drivers\PCMCIA\PROXIM-LAN_PC_CARD-E8F2\Prefix = "NDS"`	This driver is loaded when a Proxim PC card LAN adapter with an ID of PROXIM-LAN_PC_CARD-E8F2 is inserted and is accessed with the name *NDS<index>:* when `CreateFile` is being called.
	`HKEY_LOCAL_MACHINE\Drivers\PCMCIA\<Driver Class Name>`	String	`HKLM\Drivers\PCMCIA\LS120\Prefix = "DSK"`	This driver is loaded and its detection function called if no other matching entry with a PnP ID is found and no other detection function returns `TRUE`. The driver is accessed with the name *DSK<Index>:* when `CreateFile` is being called.
`Index`	`HKEY_LOCAL_MACHINE\Drivers\BuiltIn\<Driver Name>`	DWORD	`HKLM\Drivers\BuiltIn\Modem\Index = 6`	Using the value of the `Prefix` subkey presented above for the same driver, the device file name becomes *COM6*. The function `CreateFile` would therefore be called with "COM6:".
	`HKEY_LOCAL_MACHINE\Drivers\PCMCIA\<PnPID>`	DWORD	`HKLM\Drivers\PCMCIA\PROXIM-LAN_PC_CARD-E8F2\Index = 1`	Using the value of the `Prefix` subkey presented above for the same driver, the device file name becomes *NDS1*. The function `CreateFile` would therefore be called with "NDS1:".
	`HKEY_LOCAL_MACHINE\Drivers\PCMCIA\<Driver Class Name>`	DWORD	`<not present> (HKLM\Drivers\PCMCIA\LS120\<Index> not present)`	Using the value of the `Prefix` subkey presented above for the same driver, the exact device file name is unknown. An application requiring access to this device would be required to examine each `Key` subkey under the `HKLM\Drivers\Active` key to obtain the

(continued)

Table 7.1 *Continued.*

Subkey	Key	Type	Example	Description
				device file name in the `Name` subkey (under the same registry key as the `Key` subkey).
`Order`	`HKEY_LOCAL_MACHINE\Drivers\BuiltIn\<Driver Name>`	`DWORD`	`HKLM\Drivers\BuiltIn\Modem\Order = 6`	This driver would be loaded after all other drivers under the `BuiltIn` key with `Order` subkey values of less than 6 (values 0–5). It is important to remember that some drivers may have the same `Order` subkey value and may also be less than 6, meaning that the maximum number of drivers that may be loaded before this one could exceed 6 (6 possible values less than 6).
	`HKEY_LOCAL_MACHINE\Drivers\PCMCIA\<PnPID>`	`DWORD`	`<not present> (HKLM\Drivers\PCMCIA\PROXIM-LAN_PC_CARD-E8F2\<Order> not present)`	This subkey is ignored for PC card (PCMCIA) devices.
	`HKEY_LOCAL_MACHINE\Drivers\PCMCIA\<Driver Class Name>`	`DWORD`	`{not present} (HKLM\Drivers\PCMCIA\LS120\<Order> not present)`	This subkey is ignored for PC card (PCMCIA) devices.

In addition to being used in the Win32 function `CreateFile` to initiate access to the stream-interface driver, the device file name is used to determine the names of a stream-interface driver's callable functions (also referred to in this chapter as entry points). The three characters of the device file name are used as a prefix to the function names defined for stream-interface drivers. The DM then uses the `GetProcAddress` function to dynamically determine the address of each entry point in the driver. If, for example, the DM was about to load a stream-interface driver with a device file name of *COM2:*, the name of the stream-interface initialization function would be prefixed with the characters *COM* to produce a function name of *COM_Init.* A pointer to this function name would then be passed in the `lpProcName` parameter of the `GetProcAddress` function.

One advantage of this use of the device file name to derive the entry point names is the ability to provide multiple stream-interface drivers within a single DLL module. In this case, multiple registry entries would be needed for each stream-interface driver represented in the DLL. The value of the `Dll` subkey (discussed in the next section) would contain the name of the DLL module and would be the same for each entry. Allowing multiple drivers to reside in a single DLL module would be useful if your device contained multiple functions or modes of operations (a PC card with both a modem and a network interface, for example) that appeared to the end user as separate devices. This single driver would effectively provide each device function with the visibility of a distinct logical device, each with a separate device file name.

Load Sequence

Let's take the next step in gaining an understanding of stream-interface device driver design and discuss specifically how the DM uses the registry entries explored thus far, when the system is first activated. Upon a warm boot or cold boot (discussed in Chapter 4), the DM inspects certain registry entries and begins the load sequence for each driver. Figure 7.3 depicts the load sequence used by the DM and how each registry key is used to control this process.

The `HKEY_LOCAL_MACHINE/Drivers` key contains the keys used by the DM and other types of DCPs. Beginning with the `HKEY_LOCAL_MACHINE/Drivers/BuiltIn` key, the DM inspects each key it finds under the `BuiltIn` key and loads the driver named in the Dll subkey by using the `RegisterDevice` function. Calling the `RegisterDevice` function locks the DLL in memory so that it will not be swapped out of working RAM, to prevent paging activity that might otherwise delay the response to an interrupt request from the device.

Immediately after the driver is loaded, the DM calls the stream-interface initialization function. The name of this function is formed by addition of the value of the `Prefix` subkey to the string *_Init*. For example, if the `Prefix` subkey of the `HKEY_LOCAL_MACHINE\Drivers\BuiltIn\Serial` key contains the string *COM,* the string *_Init* is added to the string *COM* to produce the function name *COM_Init.*

If the initialization is successful, the DM attempts to load the numeric value of the `Ioctl` subkey if present. This value is passed in the `dwCode` parameter of the stream-interface function `COM_IoControl` (the function name formed in the same manner as the initialization function). The call to `COM_IoControl` gives your driver a chance to perform any required secondary initialization, as is common for block stream-interface device drivers (a specific type of stream-interface driver generally used to provide access to storage media) that must load a file system driver. See the driver in the `.\PUBLIC\COMMON\OAK\DRIVERS\ATADISK` directory for an example of the use of this secondary initialization.

If the initialization sequence completes successfully, meaning that all initialization functions return a success code, the DM then makes an entry in the `HKEY_LOCAL_MACHINE/Drivers/Active` key to record certain attributes of the loaded driver. These attributes include the name of the `HKEY_LOCAL_MACHINE\Drivers` registry key associated with the loaded driver, the device handle returned from the call to `RegisterDevice`, and the device file name (discussed earlier in this chapter), equivalent to the value of the `Prefix` subkey. The device file name (described in the previous section) is used by applications in the `lpFileName` parameter of the `CreateFile` function to initiate access to the stream-interface driver.

After the drivers for the `BuiltIn` key are loaded, the keys used by other DCPs are processed. The `HKEY_LOCAL_MACHINE/Drivers/PCMCIA` key is processed if a PC card is present in the socket. The card and socket services driver (`pcmcia.dll`) is used by the DM to extract the Plug and Play (PnP) ID from the PC card. If a registry key matching this ID is found

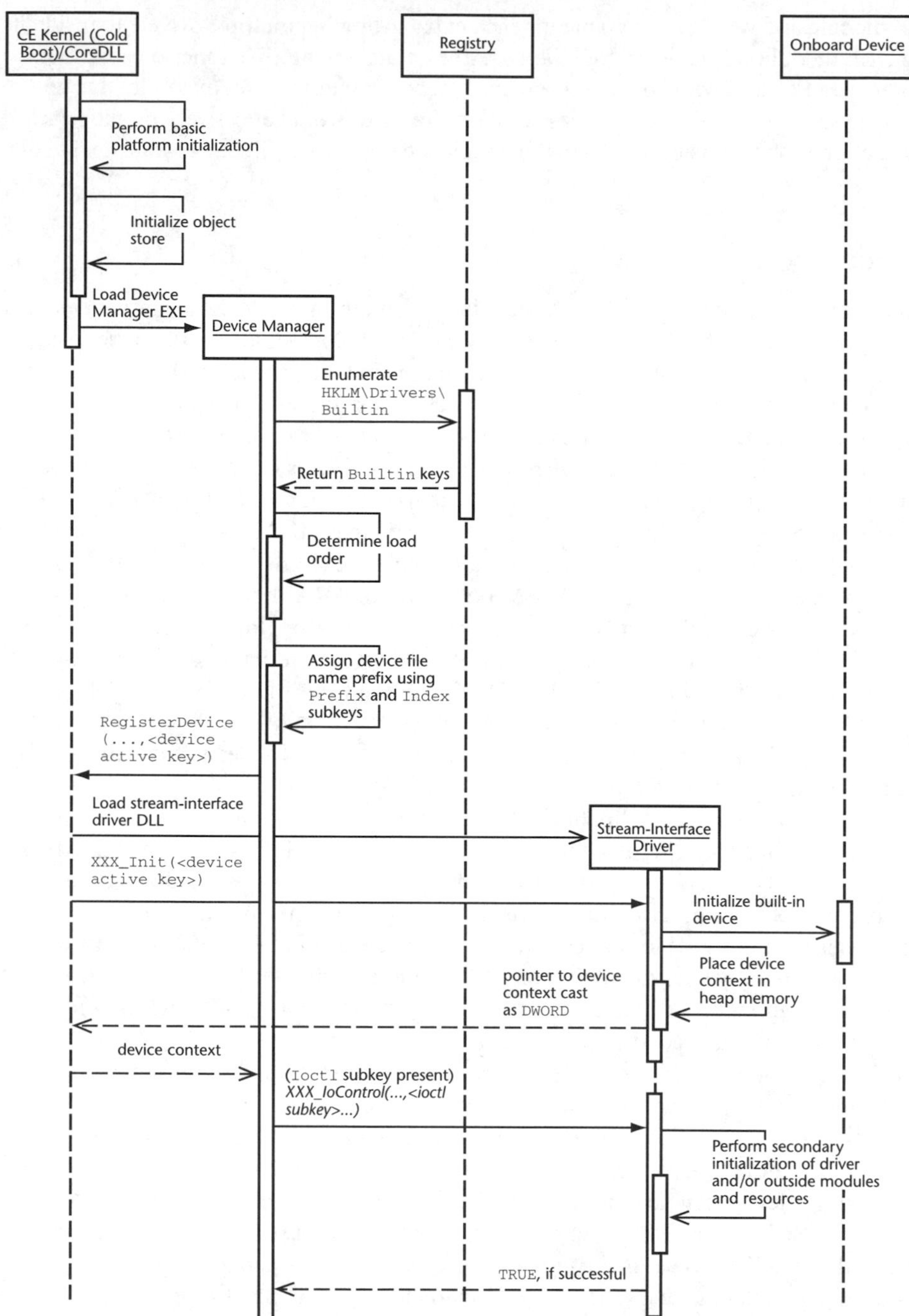

Figure 7.3 Sequence diagram of a sample Device Manager load sequence

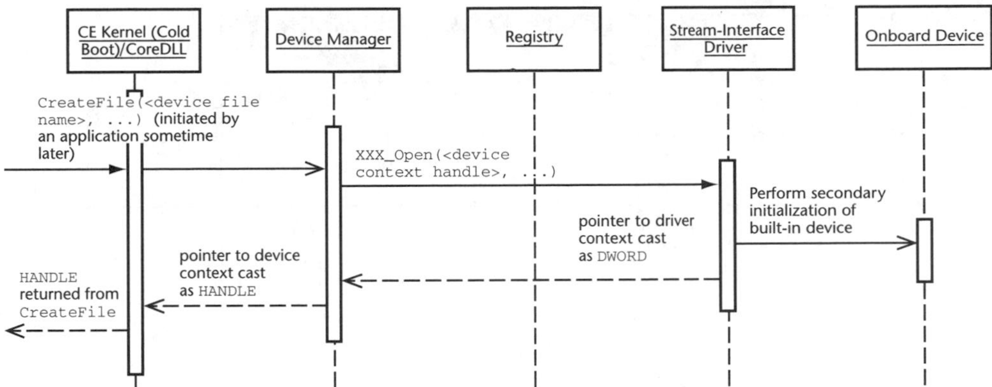

Figure 7.3 *Continued.*

under HKEY_LOCAL_MACHINE/Drivers/PCMCIA, the driver named in the Dll subkey is loaded in the same way a standard stream-interface driver is loaded.

If no matching key is found, the numeric keys appearing under the HKEY_LOCAL_MACHINE/Drivers/PCMCIA/Detect key are used to find a driver that supports the PC card as a particular class of device, rather than through a matching PnP ID. Each key is examined in sequence from lowest to highest numeric value. The driver named in the Dll subkey is loaded, and the function named in the Entry subkey (known as a detection function) is called. If the return value is NULL, the driver is unloaded and the next driver is loaded in the sequence and its particular detection function called. This process continues until a non-NULL value pointing to the character string of the driver's HKEY_LOCAL_MACHINE/Drivers/PCMCIA registry key is returned. If all keys in the sequence are exhausted and all detection functions return NULL, the DM prompts the user for the name of the driver to load for the installed PC card.

It is interesting that the DM has special knowledge of the interface to pcmcia.dll and calls certain APIs during system initialization that are not used by stream-interface drivers or applications. A case in point is the CardSystemInit function that is called by the DM to inform the pcmcia.dll module that a critical phase in the boot sequence is complete and that the PC card socket may be accessed. The DM's knowledge of this function typifies the high degree of coupling between it and pcmcia.dll.

Now that we have explored how the DM uses the registry for stream-interface driver loading and initialization, let's examine the contents of the registry on an actual Handheld PC device (HP 620LX). Figure 7.4 contains the image of the CE Remote Registry Editor tool when used to browse the contents of the Handheld PC's registry. There are six numeric entries under the HKEY_LOCAL_MACHINE\Drivers\Active key, indicating that there are currently six active stream-interface drivers. Various keys appear under the HKEY_LOCAL_MACHINE\Drivers\BuiltIn key, each one representing a different stream-interface driver that will be loaded to support onboard devices.

Each numeric key under the Active key corresponds to a successfully loaded stream-interface driver represented by a BuiltIn key. If you were to examine the contents of each numeric

Figure 7.4 Typical stream-interface registry entries for a Handheld PC device

key under the `Active` key, you would find a corresponding entry for each `BuiltIn` key, with the exception of the `AFD` module. We must assume that this stream-interface driver did not remain loaded, either because of an error or, more likely, because it was needed only during system startup to complete some form of required initialization and could be unloaded upon completion.

The `HKEY_LOCAL_MACHINE\Drivers\PCMCIA` key contains the keys that correspond to all of the PC card stream-interface drivers that are associated with PC cards from specific manufacturers. The one that stands out in the crowd of PnP IDs that contain manufacturers' names, is the `ATADisk` key, which clearly does not refer to any particular manufacturer's PC card. We can assume that this key refers to a PC card driver that supports the device class of ATA PC card adapters and is therefore a device class stream-interface driver. If you were to examine the contents of the `HKEY_LOCAL_MACHINE\Drivers\PCMCIA\Detect\50` key you would find that the `Dll` subkey contains the value of `atadisk.dll`, which is the same as the `Dll` subkey under `HKEY_LOCAL_MACHINE\Drivers\PCMCIA\ATADisk`. This indicates that the same driver is being used in the detection of PC cards of the ATA device class when a matching manufacturer-specific driver is not present in the `HKEY_LOCAL_MACHINE\Drivers\PCMCIA` key, thus confirming our assumption that this driver is a device class stream-interface driver.

> ***Note:***
> The detection function for a particular PC card device class is not required to exist in the same DLL as that used for the stream-interface driver. In most cases, however, it makes sense for them to coexist because the logic to interpret the PC card Card Information Structure (CIS) will exist in the stream-interface driver DLL and will also be needed by the detection function.

Power Cycling

It is important to consider how the DM loads and unloads drivers when a platform, such as a standard Handheld PC platform, is powered off, either by the end user or automatically to save power. In the Required Entry Points section later in this discussion we will describe the mechanism used to notify the stream-interface driver that the platform is being power-cycled.

Typically, when a standard CE platform is powered off, it enters a low-power state that retains the contents of working RAM (Suspend mode) while powering off the processor and its peripherals. This means that all previously loaded drivers will also remain in RAM, unlike the the more common desktop driver models, which require drivers to be reloaded whenever the PC is powered on. Stream-interface drivers that support onboard devices and are automatically loaded by the DM through an entry in the `HKEY_LOCAL_MACHINE/Drivers/BuiltIn` key remain loaded when the platform enters Suspend mode unless they are explicitly unloaded through the `DeregisterDevice` function. When the platform returns to full power, the onboard devices are in an uninitialized state and may need to be independently powered on, depending on the capabilities of the device. This means that the driver must be able to reconfigure the device, even though it has already been loaded. Fortunately, as we will soon see in the section on the `XXX_PowerUp` and `XXX_PowerDown` stream-interface driver entry points, the DM lets your driver know when reconfiguration of the supported device is needed. (*XXX* corresponds to the device file name prefix.)

Stream-interface drivers that support installable devices such as PC cards are processed differently. When the platform enters Suspend mode, they remain loaded, like stream-interface drivers for onboard devices, but they are unloaded and then immediately reloaded when the platform returns to a full power state. This happens as the installable devices are re-enumerated. Existing drivers for installable devices are gracefully unloaded by the `XXX_Deinit` stream-interface entry point (discussed later in this chapter), and then reloaded for each enumerated device. From the point of view of the driver, this is the first time it is loaded, causing the device to be completely reinitialized.

In the case of the drivers named under the `HKEY_LOCAL_MACHINE/Drivers/BuiltIn` key, the `XXX_PowerUp` and `XXX_PowerDown` entry points must be implemented to recognize the restoration of power and reinitialize the supported device. Installable devices, however, may leave the implementation of `XXX_PowerUp` and `XXX_PowerDown` empty and simply return because the reloading of the driver (as already described) causes the supported device to be reinitalized. In the latter case, for compliance with the stream-interface driver model the entry points must still be present, even though they only return.

Required Entry Points

It is time to put some proverbial meat on the bones of the conceptual stream-interface driver skeleton. The **required entry points** are the exported functions that you must implement in your stream-interface driver to comply with the stream-interface model. These functions are called by the DM in the load sequence of your driver, as a direct result of certain application-level Win32 API calls.

In this section we will focus on how each entry point (function) is used both by the DM and indirectly by the calling application. We will also explore how these entry points can be used to service multiple **logical devices** (devices that exist only as device file names and have no physical attributes) or multiple **physical devices** (devices that possess physical attributes on the target platform and are accessed by the driver to perform I/O operations). Source code excerpts from various sample drivers provided in the CEPB will also be presented as examples of a typical implementation of each entry point. In some cases, sequence diagrams are presented to demonstrate the usage of a particular entry point. We will *not* define each parameter or return value for the entry points because this information is thoroughly documented in the CEPB online documentation.

One of the most common applications of the stream-interface driver model is to support PC card devices. PC card devices are by their very nature installable, and the dynamic nature of the stream-interface model supports this attribute well. To obtain device-level access to the PC card, you will need to learn how to use certain functions implemented in a separate DLL module (`pcmcia.dll`). These functions comply with the PC card and socket services standard and should appear familiar if you have ever written driver software for PC cards. As we move along in our discussion of each stream-interface entry point, the PC card and socket services functions that are most applicable to each stream-interface entry point will also be discussed.

DWORD XXX_Init(DWORD dwContext);

The sample RAM disk driver located in the CEPB directory `.\PUBLIC\COMMON\OAK\DRIVERS\RAMDISK` provides an excellent example of the implementation of `XXX_Init`. It relies on the availability of onboard RAM, acquired by a call to `LocalAlloc`, and does not access any other physical resources. This makes it an ideal example of a stream-interface driver because the focus is the implementation of the stream-interface entry points instead of the API's needed for device access.

The sample SRAM disk driver located in the CEPB directory `.\PUBLIC\COMMON\OAK\DRIVERS\SRAMDISK` is very similar to the `RAMDISK` driver. The primary difference is the location of the memory used for the RAM disk, which resides on a PC card. The fact that the memory is located on a PC card allows us to focus on the use of the card and socket services APIs for access to the PC card because the stream-interface entry point functionality is largely unchanged between the `SRAMDISK` driver and the `RAMDISK` driver. We will borrow from these two examples extensively in our exploration of the stream-interface entry points.

The entry point `XXX_Init`, which is shown in Listing 7.2, is called by the DM just after the function `RegisterDevice` is called. `RegisterDevice` is called either by an application in preparation for access to a particular device (discussed in more detail later, in the Application-Initiated Loading section) or by the DM. The DM calls the `RegisterDevice` function (depicted in Figure 7.3) during processing of the `HKEY_LOCAL_MACHINE\Drivers\BuiltIn` registry key (for onboard devices). It is also called just after an installable device (USB, PC card device, and so on) has been enumerated and its corresponding stream-interface driver identified (this process of enumeration was previously described in the Device File Names section). The DM uses the PC card driver (`pcmcia.dll`) to detect and enumerate inserted PC card devices.

Listing 7.2 The `XXX_Init` entry point from the CEPB directory `.\PUBLIC\COMMON\OAK\DRIVERS\RAMDISK`

```
DWORD
DSK_Init(
    DWORD dwContext
    )
```

```
{
    PDISK pDisk;
    DWORD dwSize;
    LPWSTR ActivePath = (LPWSTR) dwContext;

    // DEBUGMSG is used for the transmission of printf-style debug
    // messages and is explained in more detail in Chapter 9.  JYW
    DEBUGMSG(ZONE_INIT, (TEXT("RAMDISK: DSK_Init entered\r\n")));
    ...
    pDisk = CreateDiskObject();
    if (pDisk == NULL) {
        RETAILMSG(1,(TEXT("RAMDISK: LocalAlloc(PDISK) failed %d\r\n"),
                  GetLastError()));
        return 0;
    }
    ...
    if (pDisk->d_DiskCardState == STATE_INITING) {
        DEBUGMSG(ZONE_INIT,
                (TEXT("RAMDISK: RAMInit returning 0x%x\r\n"), pDisk));
        return (DWORD) pDisk;
    }

    DEBUGMSG(ZONE_FUNCTION, (TEXT("-RAMInit (failure)\r\n")));
    CloseDisk(pDisk);
    return 0;
}
```

The first thing that catches the eye in Listing 7.2 is the liberal use of the `DEBUGMSG` and `RETAILMSG` macros. These two macros are essential for real-time debugging of any CE code—application-level or driver-level—and serve to transmit `printf`-style debug messages to the remote debugger running on the development workstation. Their usage is explained in more detail in the Zone Debugging section of Chapter 9, which includes a method for redirecting the message output to a local application window running on the target device.

In the excerpt of the `RAMDISK` sample driver presented in Listing 7.2, `XXX_Init` is used primarily to allocate the memory required for the `DISK` structure, which is temporarily stored in the `pDisk` stack variable. This value is returned to the DM, which will pass it to the `XXX_Open` entry point in the `hDeviceContext` parameter. Generally this entry point is called only once, when the device is first enumerated and the driver is registered (`RegisterDevice`). It is typically used to allocate any global memory that would be required by all instances of the driver (support for multiple driver instances is explored in more detail in the next section, on the `XXX_Open` entry point).

If, however, the driver is associated with multiple device file names, the `XXX_Init` entry point is called repeatedly, through repeated calls to the `RegisterDevice` function. This might be the case, for example, if the supported device were available in different configurations—one onboard configuration in which the device is a permanent part of a custom platform, and an installable configuration in which the device is available on a PC card. Let's assume that your objective is to support both device configurations simultaneously, so that even while the onboard configuration is active, the end user may insert the installable configuration on a PC card. Your driver would provide access to both device configurations, each associated with a different device file name. We will subsequently refer to this capability as support for **multiple device instances**.

Providing support for multiple device instances requires that your driver successfully process multiple calls to the `XXX_Init` entry point—once for each supported device instance. Each time it is called, you need to allocate a separate block of memory to contain the global device data for each device instance. Listing 7.3 contains a relevant excerpt of the code from the sample RAM disk driver in the `.\PUBLIC\COMMON\OAK\DRIVERS\RAMDISK` directory.

Listing 7.3 Support for multiple device instances from the CEPB directory `.\PUBLIC\COMMON\OAK\DRIVERS\RAMDISK`

```
PDISK
CreateDiskObject(VOID)
{
...
    pDisk = LocalAlloc(LPTR, sizeof(DISK));
    if (pDisk != NULL) {
        ...
        InitializeCriticalSection(&(pDisk->d_DiskCardCrit));
        pDisk->d_DiskCardState = STATE_INITING;
        EnterCriticalSection(&v_DiskCrit);
        pDisk->d_next = v_DiskList;
        v_DiskList = pDisk;
        LeaveCriticalSection(&v_DiskCrit);
    }
...
}
```

The `CreateDiskObject` function is called from the `DSK_Init` function that was provided in Listing 7.2. After the memory is allocated by a call to `LocalAlloc`, the members of the structure `DISK` (used to contain the global device instance data) are initialized. Note that the critical section, shared by all device instances, is entered and the pointer to the previously allocated `DISK` structure in the global variable `v_DiskList` is linked in through the `d_next` member of the `DISK` structure just allocated. This linking allows other functions in the driver to walk the list and access the global data for all device instances.

If your driver is limited to the support of only one device, and therefore one device instance, you may have observed that you can more easily declare this structure static, eliminating the need for the call to the `CreateDiskObject` function that uses `LocalAlloc` to allocate the needed memory dynamically. The downside to the static approach is the resulting increase in the size of the data sections produced by the linker, which in turn results in an overall increase in the size of the DLL binary image. This DLL eventually is written to the object store during installation, occupying some amount of RAM, or to ROM when included in the build of a new kernel image. If the device associated with this driver is never installed, this extra memory consumes RAM or ROM needlessly. Considering that both are precious commodities on CE devices, it is best to be a good driver citizen and dynamically allocate such data structures even when only one device instance is supported.

For PC cards, and more generally for installable devices, the implementation of the XXX_Init entry point can be more complicated. This complexity depends primarily on whether your device will be accessed immediately upon enumeration and subsequent registration. If access is deferred until an application initiates access to the driver (through the CreateFile function), XXX_Init will be very similar to that for onboard devices and will be limited to the initialization of internal data structures and any required kernel services. The XXX_Open entry point then assumes the responsibility for the selection and activation of a configuration from those represented in the Card Information Structure (CIS). If, however, the device must be accessed immediately, it will be necessary to perform nearly all required initialization in XXX_Init, leaving the XXX_Open to simply record the existence of an application that is initiating access to the device.

The PC card functions (defined in the PC card standard as *card services*) that must be called for device configuration are prefixed with *Card* and are well documented in the Device Driver Reference section of the CEPB online documentation. The data structures (referred to as **tuples** in the PC card literature) returned by a call to certain card services functions are not well documented in the CEPB online documentation, however, and you will need to purchase the PC card standards documents from the PC card association (see Appendix C for contact information) or a book on PC card system architecture (for example, Anderson 1995). Figure 7.5 depicts the calling sequence for PC card configuration, performed in XXX_Init. As described earlier, when access is initiated by a calling application, this sequence can be deferred to XXX_Open.

You will notice that in most of the CEPB sample PC card drivers, the card and socket services module (pcmcia.dll) is loaded with LoadLibrary and GetProcAddress to allow a graceful recovery if the platform does not provide these functions. This solution is better than the alternative dynalink error that appears when the pcmcia.dll module is not present and the functions of the DLL are linked through an import library.

BOOL XXX_IoControl(DWORD hOpenContext, DWORD dwCode, PBYTE pBufIn, DWORD dwLenIn, PBYTE pBufOut, DWORD dwLenOut, PDWORD pdwActualOut);

The XXX_IoControl entry point is called in direct response to an application-level call to the DeviceIoControl function. With the exception of the lpOverlapped parameter, the prototype for the DeviceIoControl function is nearly identical to that of the XXX_IoControl entry point. This entry point and the associated application function are used as a kind of catchall function for calling the functionality in a stream-interface driver that may not map to the existing entry points associated with Win32 file I/O functions, such as ReadFile and WriteFile.

Control codes are passed by the caller in the dwCode parameter and are used to identify the requested operation. As the driver developer, you must provide a header file that identifies each control code as a series of constants. The macro CTL_CODE is provided to assist in this process and may be used to define a bit-mapped control code that contains additional information on the type of the access, how the pBufIn and pBufOut parameters are used, the device type, and the function code. Function codes from 0 to 2047 are reserved by Microsoft, leaving function codes 2048 to 4095 for use in your driver.

It is not uncommon for the pBufIn and pBufOut parameters to be used to point to a structure defined in your driver's header file along with the DeviceIoControl codes. If this structure contains pointers, they must be mapped to the process space of the caller before they are

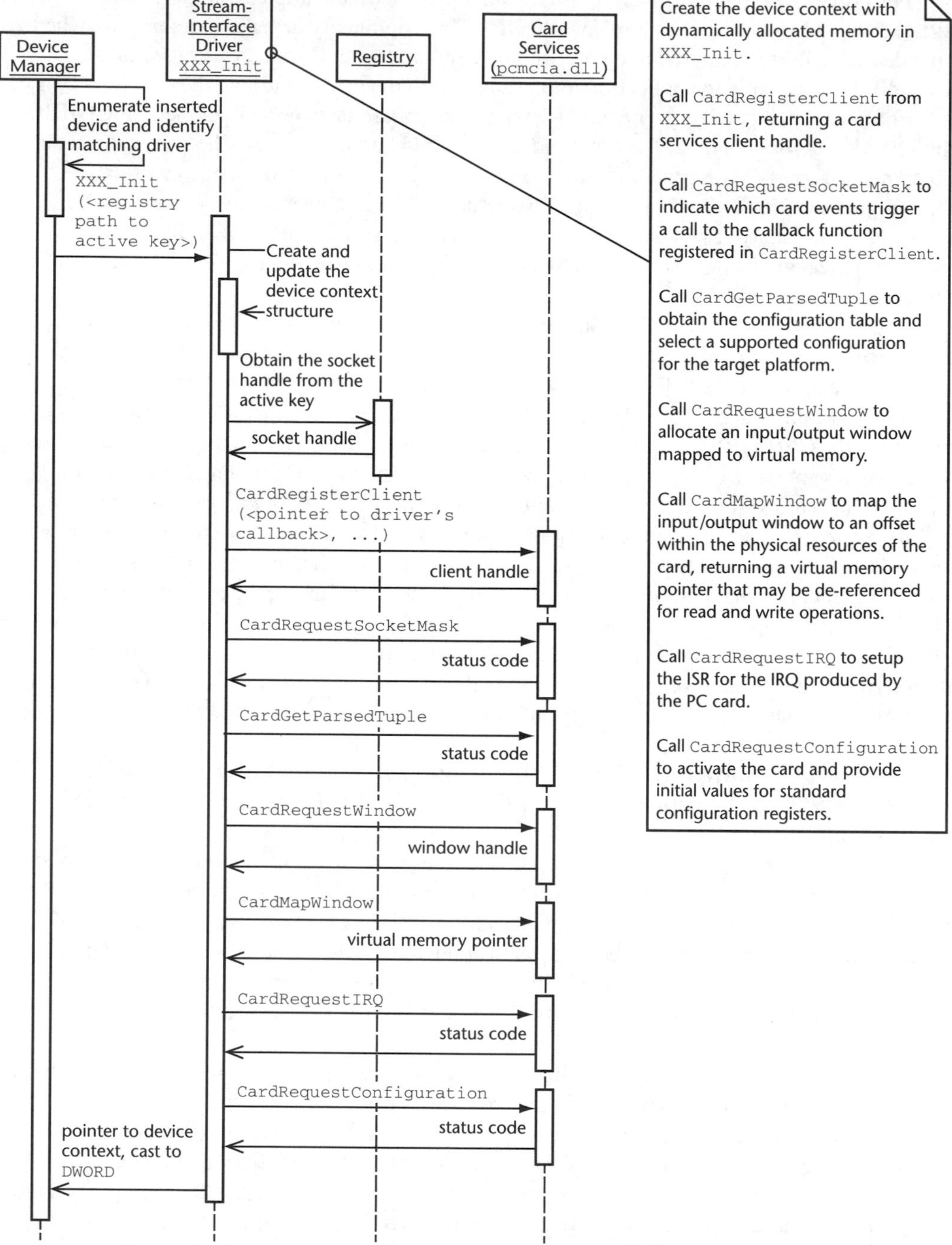

Figure 7.5 Sequence diagram of PC card configuration in `XXX_Init`

de-referenced by your driver. Listing 7.4 provides an example of the use of the `MapPtrToProcess` function excerpted from the `RAMDISK` sample driver in the `.\PUBLIC\COMMON\OAK\DRIVERS\RAMDISK\DRIVER` directory.

Listing 7.4 Using `MapPtrToProcess` to access a pointer in `pBufIn`

```
DWORD
DoDiskIO(
    PDISK pDisk,
    DWORD Opcode,
    PSG_REQ pSgr
    )
{

    ...

    num_sg = pSgr->sr_num_sg;
    pSg = &(pSgr->sr_sglist[0]);
    bytes_this_sg = pSg->sb_len;
    pBuf = MapPtrToProcess((LPVOID)pSg->sb_buf, GetCallerProcess());

    ...

}   // DoDiskIO
```

The `pBufIn` parameter of the RAM disk's `XXX_IoControl` entry point is passed to the `DoDiskIO` function in the `pSgr` parameter. The `pSg` variable contains an offset into the `pSgr` buffer and is used to obtain the pointer to another buffer that is saved in the `pBuf` variable. The `pSg` variable does not need to be mapped because it points to a memory location within the buffer referenced by the `pSgr` variable. The `sb_buf` variable, however, is mapped because it points to a memory location contained in the caller's address space. Refer to the Managing Buffer Pointers section of Chapter 8 for more details on the use of the `MapPtrToProcess` function and on how memory is mapped between processes.

The `XXX_IoControl` entry point is also used by the Device Manager for secondary initialization of the driver. For drivers automatically loaded by the DM through either the `BuiltIn` or the `PCMCIA` registry key (discussed in more detail earlier in this chapter), the value of the `Ctrl` subkey is passed to the `XXX_IoControl` entry point after all stream-interface drivers have been initialized through their respective `XXX_Init` entry points. One possible use of this capability is to initiate the loading of any other modules needed by your driver, including other stream-interface drivers. For drivers loaded during system startup, this is a valuable feature because it provides a way to delay the calling or loading of CE services that may not be available until later in the system initialization sequence.

DWORD XXX_Open(DWORD hDeviceContext, DWORD AccessCode, DWORD ShareMode);

The `XXX_Open` entry point is called by the DM in direct response to a call to the function `CreateFile` by an application. `CreateFile` is called by applications with the device file name of your driver in the parameter list. This call initiates access to your device driver, whose device file name would have been previously registered with the `RegisterDevice` function.

The hDeviceContext parameter is automatically passed to the XXX_Open entry point and is the same value that was returned in the previous call to the XXX_Init entry point. As noted earlier in the section on the XXX_Init entry point, XXX_Open represents a handle to the particular physical device currently associated with the driver. The return value from the XXX_Open entry point represents another kind of handle that we shall say references the *driver* instance (as opposed to the *device* instance introduced earlier, in the section on the XXX_Init entry point). This handle effectively allows multiple applications to access the same device instance, calling CreateFile repeatedly with the same device file name prefix. The RAMDISK sample driver (CEPB directory .\PUBLIC\COMMON\OAK\DRIVERS\SRAMDISK) simply updates a reference count that is used later in the XXX_Close entry point to determine if globally allocated resources associated with the device instance may be deallocated. This is a useful feature for the RAM disk because it is a shared storage resource that must offer simultaneous access to multiple applications calling the CreateFile function.

It may not be appropriate for your device, however, to allow unrestricted accesses by multiple applications. Perhaps your device is state driven and requires complex I/O requests to be sent in multiple parts, making access by a second application problematic. In this case you would simply check a reference count in your implementation of XXX_Open and return a NULL value if it had already been opened by another application. Perhaps access by multiple applications is acceptable, but only if one of those applications has write access while all others are restricted to read access. You can assign access rights in this way by examining the value of the AccessCode parameter in the XXX_Open entry point. If this were the first application to access the driver, a fact that is verified by a reference counting variable, you would allow both write and read access (represented by the GENERIC_WRITE and GENERIC_READ constants). If subsequent calls to XXX_Open requested write access in the AccessCode parameter, you would reject the requested access by returning a NULL value.

The ShareMode parameter provides the same sort of access restrictions as those just discussed, but in this case the restrictions are controlled by the application. The value passed in this parameter by one application allows subsequent requests made by other applications (attempting access to the same device instance) to be restricted to either read or write access. Because it is rarely used by application developers, the functionality associated with this parameter is left unimplemented for most of the CEPB sample device drivers.

In most cases the XXX_Open entry point is used to complete the initialization begun in the XXX_Init entry point. As noted earlier in the discussion of the XXX_Init entry point, if the initialization of the device can be deferred to the point at which access by a calling application is initiated with a call to CreateFile, then XXX_Open will be required to do most of the initialization work. This form of deferred initialization has the advantage of also deferring power consumption by the device until it is really needed by a calling application. The model device driver (MDD, discussed in the Native Device Driver Model section later in this chapter) layer of the CEPB sample serial driver (located in the .\PUBLIC\COMMON\OAK\DRIVERS\SERIAL directory) is one example of such a practice. The call to the platform device driver layer function HWOpen, as depicted in Listing 7.5, maps the device's I/O resources into memory and results in calls to card services functions if the COM device resides on a PC card. The HWOpen function also powers the peripheral device because it needs to be responsive to calling applications.

Listing 7.5 Example of deferred initialization in the CEPB sample serial driver (MDD layer)

```
HANDLE
COM_Open(
        HANDLE  pHead,          // @parm Handle returned by COM_Init.
        DWORD   AccessCode,     // @parm access code.
        DWORD   ShareMode       // @parm share mode - Not used in this driver.
        )
{
    PHW_INDEP_INFO  pSerialHead = (PHW_INDEP_INFO)pHead;

    ...

    if ( ! pSerialHead->OpenCnt )
    {

        ...

        if ( !pHWObj->pFuncTbl->HWOpen(pSerialHead->pHWHead) ) {
            DEBUGMSG (ZONE_OPEN|ZONE_ERROR, (TEXT("HW Open failed.\r\n")));
            goto OpenFail;
        }

        ...

        RxResetFifo (pSerialHead);
    }
    ++(pSerialHead->OpenCnt);

    return (pOpenHead);

    ...

}
```

void XXX_PowerDown(DWORD hDeviceContext) and void XXX_PowerUp(DWORD hDeviceContext)

The `XXX_PowerDown` entry point, as the name implies, is called when the platform is about to enter Suspend mode (a low-power mode that maintains the contents of RAM while removing power from the CPU and peripheral devices). As the name of the `XXX_PowerDown` entry point implies, it is called by the DM to inform the driver that the platform is about to be powered down. Your driver may react by simply updating the device context structure with this information, or you may choose to power down the supported device if it provides this capability. `XXX_PowerUp` is called when the platform is returning from Suspend mode to a full power mode to inform the driver of the possible need to reinitialize its supported device.

The file `.\PUBLIC\COMMON\OAK\DRIVERS\SERIAL\mdd.c`, used in the sample RS-232 COM port driver, is a typical example of an implementation of the `XXX_PowerDown` and `XXX_PowerUp` entry points for an onboard device. The `XXX_PowerDown` entry point calls the platform-dependent `HWPowerOff` function (implemented in the file `.\ODO\DRIVERS\SERIAL\p2io.c`) to disable interrupts and power-off the RS-232 device. The `XXX_PowerUp` entry point restores the configuration information previously saved in the driver context structure by the `XXX_Open` entry point.

Because the RS-232 COM port driver supports an onboard device, its stream-interface driver is automatically loaded when the platform is cold<\h>-booted (refer to Chapter 4 for a definition of cold booting for CE platforms). As previously discussed in the Load Sequence section, stream-interface drivers for onboard devices remain loaded when the platform is entering and returning from Suspend mode. So if the device had been initialized and opened by a calling application (through the `CreateFile` and `OpenFile` Win32 functions), it would be necessary to retain this configuration information in the device or driver context data structures.

Listing 7.6 contains an excerpt of the `XXX_PowerUp` and `XXX_PowerDown` entry points for the platform device driver (PDD) layer of the RS-232 COM port driver in the `.\PUBLIC\COMMON\OAK\DRIVERS\SERIAL\mdd.c` directory.

Listing 7.6 Sample implementation of `XXX_PowerDown` and `XXX_PowerUp` (excerpted from `.\PUBLIC\COMMON\OAK\DRIVERS\SERIAL\mdd.c`)

```
BOOL
COM_PowerUp(
            HANDLE      pHead       /*@parm Handle to device. */
            )
{
    PHW_INDEP_INFO  pHWIHead     = (PHW_INDEP_INFO)pHead;
    PHWOBJ          pHWObj;

    pHWObj  =  (PHWOBJ)pHWIHead->pHWObj;

    return  (pHWObj->pFuncTbl->HWPowerOn(pHWIHead->pHWHead));
}

BOOL
COM_PowerDown(
            HANDLE      pHead       /*@parm Handle to device. */
            )
{
    PHW_INDEP_INFO            pHWIHead     = (PHW_INDEP_INFO)pHead;

    if ( pHWIHead ) {
        PHWOBJ  pHWObj  =  (PHWOBJ)pHWIHead->pHWObj;
        return  (pHWObj->pFuncTbl->HWPowerOff(pHWIHead->pHWHead));
    } else {
        return  (1);
    }
}

// Excerpted from the CEPB sample source .\PLATFORM\ODO\DRIVERS\SERIAL\P2IO.C:
BOOL
HWPowerOn(PVOID pHead)
{
    PP2_IO_SER_INFO pHWHead = (PP2_IO_SER_INFO)pHead;

    ...

    pHWHead->bInPowerHandler = TRUE;

    ...
```

```
    P2SerialSetLineControl(pHWHead);
    SetUARTBaud( pHWHead, pHWHead->BaudRate);

    // Power up:
    ENABLE_BITS(pHWHead->pCsrB, SERB_SERIAL_POWER);
    ENABLE_BITS(pHWHead->pCsrB, SERB_NOT_SERIAL_RESET);

    // Unmask interrupts:
    ENABLE_BITS(pHWHead->pCpuMr,
                pHWHead->bIR ? IR_INTR : PRODUCT_SER_INTR);
    // Enable RX interrupts:
    ENABLE_BITS(pHWHead->pCsrB, SERB_RX_EN);

    // Set a flag to indicate to the calling application that a return from
    // Suspend has been detected and simulate an interrupt to cause the flag
    // to be processed.
    pHWHead->fPowerOff = 1;
    SetInterruptEvent (SYSINTR_SERIAL);
    SetInterruptEvent (SYSINTR_IR);

    pHWHead->bInPowerHandler = FALSE;
    return (retval);
}
```

When the platform is returning to full-power state, the `COM_PowerUp` entry point is called, and the configuration information saved in the driver context structure `pHWIHead->pHWHead` is passed to the PDD layer function `HWPowerOn`. This function restores the device to the state that was active at the moment `COM_PowerDown` was called. It also sets a flag in the device context structure `pHWIHead` and calls the `SetInterruptEvent` function to generate an interrupt that causes this flag to be processed in the interrupt service thread (IST). `SetInterruptEvent` is one of the few CE APIs that may be called from within the `XXX_PowerUp` and `XXX_PowerDown` entry points because the kernel is in a nonpreemptable mode when these entry points are called.

For stream-interface drivers that support onboard devices, the handle(s) obtained by the calling applications through the `CreateFile` function remain valid even after a power cycle. Thus, the application (and therefore the end user) may be unaware of the change in power state.

The implementation of `XXX_PowerDown` for the ATA disk driver is significantly simpler than that required for most onboard devices. It simply changes the value of the state variable `d_DiskCardState` in an array of device context structures. Because this driver is associated with an installable PC card device, it is processed differently by the DM than the previous stream-interface driver for the onboard RS-232 COM port was processed. When returning to full power state, the DM initiates the re-enumeration of installed PC card devices, resulting in the unloading and reloading of PC card drivers that were present when Suspend mode was entered. Consequently, for PC card stream-interface drivers, there is no difference between a return from Suspend mode and the insertion of the PC card by the end user. The implementation of the `XXX_PowerUp` entry point in the ATA disk driver reflects this fact by leaving this function empty. Refer to the earlier section on power cycling for a more detailed account of how the DM handles power state changes for stream-interface drivers that support installable devices.

DWORD XXX_Seek(DWORD hOpenContext, long Amount, WORD Type)

If you look for an example of the XXX_Seek entry point in the CEPB sample source code, about all you will find are stub functions (functions that simply return from the call without taking any action). XXX_Seek exists to allow the calling application to request that an internal data pointer be relocated to the offset designated in the Amount parameter through a call to the Win32 function SetFilePointer. Most devices lack an internal representation for a data pointer, so this function remains largely unused, as demonstrated by all of the sample code that simply returns an error code. SetFilePointer is present mainly to complete the file I/O model of the stream interface.

If your device maintains some form of persistent data, SetFilePointer may be of use. It's up to you to formulate an abstraction for access to your device's data that supports a seeking operation. If your device is a PC card, one option might be to provide access to the raw data contained in the Card Information Stucture (CIS). You could provide predefined offsets in a header file made available to applications, which are then used in the call to SetFilePointer to access certain tuples in the CIS. Your driver would call a card services function, passing the offset in the Amount parameter (from the XXX_Seek entry point).

If you do not intend to support this function, at a minimum you must include a stub function that returns an error code of –1. You should also consider calling the SetLastError function to allow additional information to be obtained beyond the specified error code of –1. After receiving the error code in the SetFilePointer return value, the application would immediately call GetLastError to obtain the value you set with the SetLastError function. The CEPB online documentation for SetLastError contains more information on the allowable numeric values for the error code.

DWORD XXX_Read(DWORD hOpenContext, LPVOID pBuffer, DWORD Count) and DWORD XXX_Write(DWORD hOpenContext, LPCVOID pSourceBytes, DWORD NumberOfBytes)

The XXX_Read and XXX_Write entry points are called when an application calls the Win32 ReadFile and WriteFile functions. The value of the hOpenContext parameter is returned from a call to CreateFile (with the device file name in the lpFileName parameter). ReadFile is called by an application to retrieve input data received by your device, which your driver code must copy into the pBuffer parameter. Similarly, WriteFile is called for output data that must by transmitted by your device.

Both the XXX_Read and the XXX_Write entry points are the real workhorses of your driver, and they will probably be the focus of the majority of your development efforts. Both entry points are synchronous, meaning that you may not return to the calling application until all your work is done. In general, this restriction simplifies the implementation of both entry points but adds additional overhead for buffer copies and delays continued execution of the application, which remains blocked until your driver returns. In the section titled Device Input/Output Buffering in Chapter 5 we explored an alternative implementation of the read and write functionality, which is asynchronous. In the next few paragraphs we will generalize the technical requirements of these entry points and present sample code excerpted from the RS-232 serial driver in the CEPB directories .\PUBLIC\COMMON\OAK\DRIVERS\SERIAL and .\PLATFORM\ODO\DRIVERS\SERIAL.

To send and receive data from your driver's supported hardware, you will most likely require a mechanism for processing the device's interrupts in the form of an interrupt service routine (ISR). In stream-interface drivers, the ISR exists in a separate thread and may process your device's interrupts at any time, even during execution of the XXX_Read and XXX_Write entry point code. When your code creates the IST, generally in the `XXX_Init` entry point, it is assigned a higher priority, causing any other running driver code, such as the `XXX_Read` and `XXX_Write` entry points, to be preempted when the IST becomes runnable. This preemption requires your driver code to use certain Win32 synchronization functions to prevent the reading or writing of a buffer while being simultaneously accessed by the IST. The state chart in Figure 7.6 depicts how

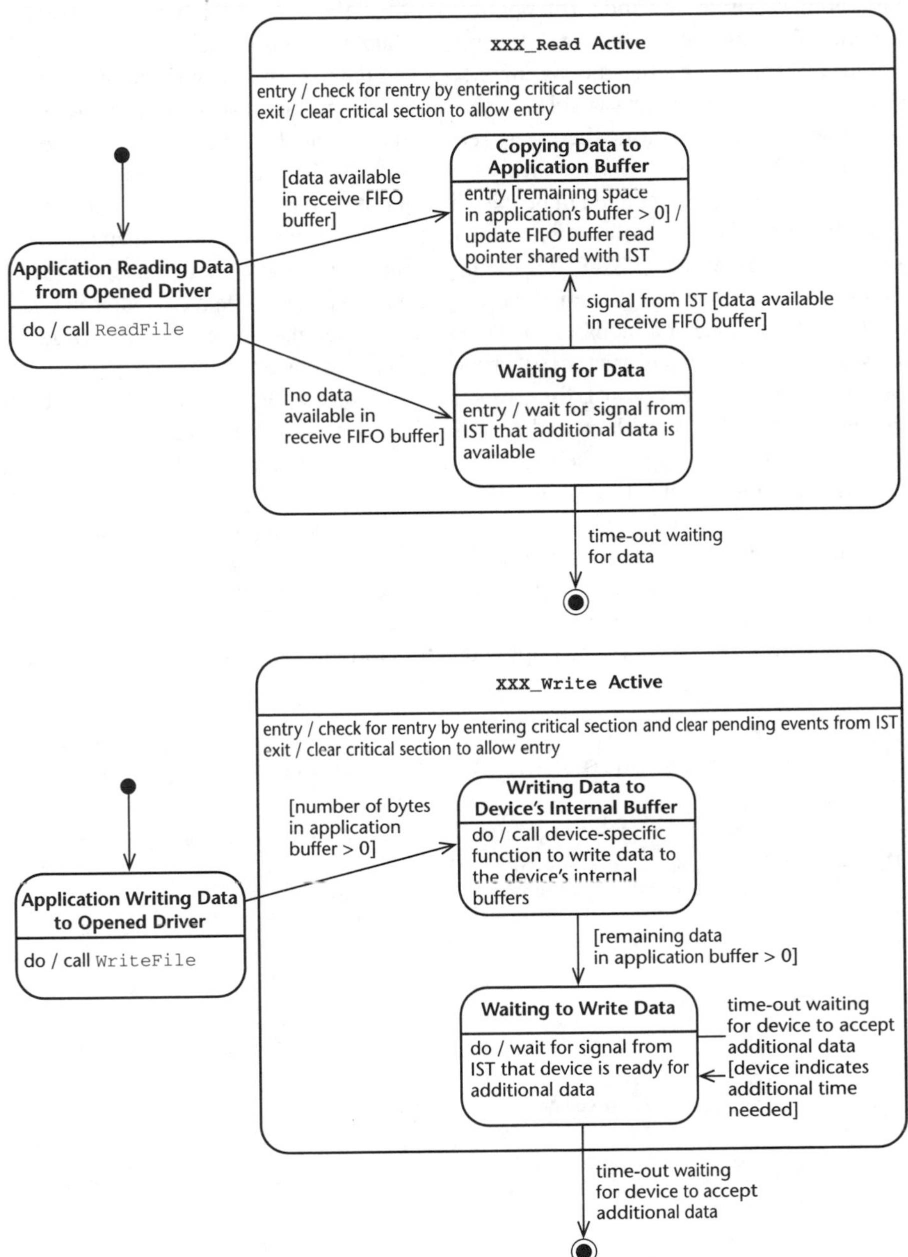

Figure 7.6 State chart for the implementation of `XXX_Read` and `XXX_Write`

this is accomplished. For more information on how to implement an IST, refer to the Processing Interrupts section of Chapter 8.

In general terms, the XXX_Read entry point that you write for your device needs to synchronize with the IST for shared access to a receive buffer used to collect data retrieved from the device. You would most likely use the driver context structure allocated for each application in the XXX_Open entry point (returned to the application in the Win32 API CreateFile as a *file handle*) to maintain separate read and write pointers in a circular queue acting as the receive buffer. The read pointer would reference the location of data not yet provided to a calling application and would be updated exclusively by the XXX_Read entry point, to avoid conflict with the IST that accesses different member variables of the same driver context structure. The write pointer would reference the location where data retrieved from the device is copied into the receive buffer, and would be updated exclusively by the IST. Because the receive buffer is a circular queue, you would, of course, need to be certain that both the read and write pointers wrapped to the beginning of the queue when incremented beyond the end of the queue.

If no data is available when the XXX_Read entry point is first entered, a mechanism must be employed to allow you to wait a particular period of time for the data to be received. You could certainly opt to poll the value of a member variable until its value became sufficiently large, but this practice would consume unnecessary CPU time and battery power. The WaitForSingleObject and WaitForMultipleObject functions are perfect for this task without requiring polling. Another member variable would be defined in the device structure to contain an event handle used by the IST to signal the XXX_Read entry point that data is available. If no data is currently available in the receive buffer, or if the quantity of data is less than that requested by the calling application in the Count parameter, XXX_Read blocks using one of the *WaitFor* functions. When more data is retrieved from the device, the IST signals the event using the SetEvent Win32 API and XXX_Read becomes runnable, copying the newly retrieved data into the calling application's buffer (passed to XXX_Read in the pBuffer parameter).

Listing 7.7 contains an excerpt of the implementation of the COM_Read entry point in the .\PUBLIC\COMMON\OAK\DRIVERS\SERIAL\mdd.c file.

Listing 7.7 Sample implementation of XXX_Read (excerpted from COM_Read)

```
ULONG
COM_Read(
        HANDLE    pHead,            //@parm [IN]     Handle returned by COM_Open.
        PUCHAR    pTargetBuffer,    //@parm [IN,OUT] Pointer to valid memory.
        ULONG     BufferLength      //@parm [IN]     Size in bytes of
pTargetBuffer.
        )
{
...

    // Practice safe threading.
    EnterCriticalSection(&(pSerialHead->ReceiveCritSec1));

...
```

```
    while ( BufferLength )
    {
        if ( RxBytesAvail(pSerialHead) )
        {
...
            // Copy the data over.
            // This copies only the continous portion; it will cause a loop
            // if the receive data spans the end of the buffer.
            Len = MIN(RxBytesAvail(pSerialHead),
                      RxLength(pSerialHead)-RxRead(pSerialHead));
            Len = MIN(Len, BufferLength);
            DEBUGMSG (ZONE_USR_READ, (TEXT("About to copy %d bytes\r\n"),
                      Len));
            memcpy (pTargetBuffer, RxBuffRead(pSerialHead), Len);
...
            // Update FIFO buffer info.
            RxRead(pSerialHead) += Len;
            RxRead(pSerialHead) %= RxLength(pSerialHead);

            // Update all the pointers.
            BufferLength -= Len;
            pTargetBuffer += Len;
            BytesRead += Len;
            RxLeaveCS(pSerialHead);
        }
        else
        {
            pSerialHead->fAbortRead = 0;
            if ( WAIT_TIMEOUT == WaitForSingleObject (pSerialHead->hReadEvent,
                 Timeout) )
           {
                // Time-out
                break;
            }
...
            if ( !pSerialHead->OpenCnt ) {
                DEBUGMSG(ZONE_USR_READ|ZONE_ERROR,
                        (TEXT("COM_Read - device was closed\n\r")));
              SetLastError(ERROR_INVALID_HANDLE);
              break;
            }
        }
    }
...
    LeaveCriticalSection(&(pSerialHead->ReceiveCritSec1));
}
```

`EnterCriticalSection` is used to prevent reentry by applications that are sharing access to the same physical RS-232 port. This means that if a calling application running in a process (or thread) A has called `ReadFile` on a particular RS-232 port, and another application running in process (or thread) B also calls `ReadFile` on the same RS-232 port, the call to `EnterCriticalSection` will cause B to stop running until the call to `COM_Read` (through `ReadFile`) returns in A, thus protecting `COM_Read` from reentry. If your driver did not support multiple device or driver instances, this would not be necessary. Instead you would have returned an error code to the process (or thread) B in the `COM_Open` entry point, which would prevent subsequent calls to `COM_Read` and `COM_Write`.

The `while` loop that comes next continues until the value of the `BufferLength` variable, passed in the parameter to the `COM_Read` entry point, is zero or another unexpected condition occurs. Data is retrieved from a buffer pointer contained in a member variable of the `pSerialHead` structure, along with the number of bytes in this buffer. When the IST is made runnable by an interrupt from the UART hardware, it retrieves the write offset into the receive buffer using the `RxBuffWrite` macro. After the data is retrieved from the device and copied to the buffer, the `RxBytesAvailable` member variable is incremented by the number of bytes read from the device. So when the `COM_Read` entry point is executed, it determines if data has already been retrieved by the IST by checking the value of `RxBytesAvailable`. If it is positive, the data is simply copied to the calling applications buffer, passed in the `pTargetBuffer` parameter of the `COM_Read` entry point.

If no data has yet been retrieved by the IST (i.e., the value of `RxBytesAvailable` is 0), the `WaitForSingleObject` function is called with a time-out parameter (`Timeout`). This will cause the calling application to block (a state in which the thread is no longer runnable and is consequently no longer scheduled for execution by the kernel) until either the time-out period has expired or the event object in the `hReadEvent` member variable is signaled. The latter condition occurs when the IST has determined that the UART has generated an interrupt as the result of a receive event and copies data into the receive buffer. Listing 7.8 contains an excerpt of the COM driver IST that signals the `hReadEvent` event object.

Listing 7.8 Excerpt of the COM driver IST signaling the retrieval of additional data from the device

```
...

if ( RxDataAvail )
{
    // Signal COM_Read that bytes are available.
    SetEvent(pSerialHead->hReadEvent);
    EvaluateEventFlag(pSerialHead, EV_RXCHAR);
}

...
```

In some ways the implementation of `XXX_Write` is easier than that of `XXX_Read`. When the application calls `WriteFile`, the `XXX_Write` entry point is called with a pointer to the applications buffer in the `pSourceBytes` parameter and its length in the `NumberOfBytes` parameter. Your objective is to send the data to the device for transmission. You need not maintain a circular queue (and its associated pointers) for buffering data collected by the IST. You simply need to get the data transmitted within a calculated time-out period, returning to the calling application when all of the data has been sent to the device or the time-out period has expired. As you will see in the sample implementation of the `XXX_Write` entry point, it may be necessary to wait until the hardware is ready to transmit more data by synchronizing with the IST. The IST receives an interrupt from the device to indicate readiness to transmit additional data, and a designated event object is set. Let's dive into the details by examining the sample code.

Listing 7.9 contains an excerpt of the implementation of the `COM_Write` entry point in the `.\PUBLIC\COMMON\OAK\DRIVERS\SERIAL\mdd.c` file. It is conceptually similar to `COM_Read`, with the notable exception of the code for handling flow control, which is omitted in Listing 7.9 for simplicity. We begin by calling `WaitForSingleObject` with the handle of the transmit event in the `hTransmitEvent` member variable of the device structure. Because the value of the `dwMilliseconds` parameter is 0, this call simply clears the event object in case it was set by the IST before `COM_Write` was called. `EnterCriticalSection` is called to prevent reentry by other calling applications.

We then enter an infinite loop, which will be exited when all of the data has been sent to the device or when the time-out period has expired. The value of the `NumberOfBytes` variable is decremented by the `HWPutBytes` function (supplied by the OEM in the PDD layer of this driver), by the value returned in the `BytesWritten` parameter. The return value from the `HWPutBytes` function indicates the number of milliseconds of delay needed before the `HWPutBytes` function is called in the next pass through the loop.

This delay would occur if the UART had been flowed off or needed additional time to physically transmit the data. This return value is saved in the `PutRet` variable and is used to calculate the value of the `Timeout` variable passed to the `WaitForSingleObject` function. This function then waits until the IST signals that the hardware is ready to transmit additional data, or until the time-out period has expired. The IST uses the `SetEvent` function to signal the event contained in the `hTransmitEvent` member variable. If the return value from `WaitForSingleObject` indicates that the a time-out has occurred (the time period in the `Timeout` variable has expired), the loop exits, unless the return value from the previous call to `HWPutBytes` indicated that a delay was needed by the UART before the transmission of additional data.

Listing 7.9 Sample implementation of `XXX_Write` (excerpted from the CEPB sample serial driver)

```
ULONG
COM_Write(HANDLE pHead,          /*@parm [IN]   Handle returned by COM_Open.*/
          PUCHAR pSourceBytes,   /*@parm [IN]   Pointer to bytes to be
                                                written.*/
          ULONG  NumberOfBytes   /*@parm [IN]   Number of bytes to be written.
                                 */
          )
{

    ...

    // Clear any pending event.
    WaitForSingleObject(pSerialHead->hTransmitEvent,0);
```

```
...
/* Lock out other threads from messing with these pointers.
 */
EnterCriticalSection(&(pSerialHead->TransmitCritSec1));

...

while ( 1 )
{

    ...

    if ( NumberOfBytes )
    {
        // Don't call PutBytes if we are flowed off.
        if ( !pSerialHead->StopXmit )
        {
            PutRet = pFuncTbl->HWPutBytes(pHWHead, pSourceBytes,
                                    NumberOfBytes, &BytesWritten);
        }
        else
        {
            ...
        }

    }
    else
    {
        break;
    }

    ...

    if ( BytesWritten )
    {
        ...

        NumberOfBytes -= BytesWritten;

        ...
    }

    // If data still left, wait until the Dispatch thread has
    // signaled that a transmit event has occurred and try again.
    if ( NumberOfBytes )
    {
        ...
        if ( PutRet )
        {
            // If HWPutBytes returns TRUE, then we need
            // to call back (after a PDD-specified interval) to
            // see if the flow control condition has
            // been removed.
```

```
                Timeout = (Timeout > PutRet) ? PutRet : Timeout;
            }
            ...

            WaitReturn = WaitForSingleObject(pSerialHead->hTransmitEvent,
                                                Timeout);

            ...

            if ( WaitReturn == WAIT_TIMEOUT )
            {
                // If we were told to wait by the PDD, then loop again
                // otherwise it is a write time-out.
                if ( ! PutRet )
               {
                    break;
                }
            }
        }
        ...
    }

    LeaveCriticalSection(&(pSerialHead->TransmitCritSec1));

    ...

    return (TotalWritten);
}
```

BOOL XXX_Close(DWORD hOpenContext)

The `XXX_Close` entry point undoes the actions of the `XXX_Open` entry point. `XXX_Close`'s actions include deallocating any dynamically allocated resources such as memory, threads, and event objects. If your driver supports more than one simultaneous calling application, through the use of multiple device and/or driver instances, you need only deallocate the resources associated with the `hOpenContext` parameter. It may also be necessary to ensure that any synchronization objects, such as those created with the Win32 `CreateEvent` function, are signaled to free any blocked threads.

As we will soon see in our sample implementation of the `COM_Close` entry point, some resources may be allocated only for the first calling application, or allocated when the driver is first loaded by the DM in the `XXX_Init` entry point. These resources, shared by all applications and closely associated with the support of the physical hardware, may need to remain allocated even after execution of the `XXX_Close` entry point. The function `CreateEvent`, for example, may have been used (after a particular device was enumerated by DM and the stream-interface driver was loaded) to allocate the event objects required by the IST to signal the `XXX_Read` and `XXX_Write` entry points. Because the event objects communicate hardware state, they are shared by all calling applications and therefore must *not* be deallocated in `XXX_Close`. As we will see in the next section, the deallocation of such resources is the responsibility of the `XXX_Deinit` entry point.

The sample implementation of the XXX_Close entry point in Listing 7.10 begins by examining the value of the OpenCnt member variable of the pSerialHead structure, allocated in COM_Init for each supported serial device. If the value is above zero, meaning that at least one application is using the serial device associated with pSerialHead, it is decremented by one to signify usage by one less application. This variable is checked again at the end of COM_Close for a value of zero, which would signify that this particular serial device is no longer used by any applications. If it is equal to zero, the function HWClose (defined in the PDD layer of the sample COM driver) is called to shut down and remove power from the serial device hardware. If the dispatch thread, the name used to refer to the IST for the serial device, were allocated in the MDD layer (signified by the THREAD_AT_OPEN constant), it would be deallocated by a call to the StopDispatchThread function.

Depending on how the calling application is designed, the COM_Close entry point could be called from one thread, while the COM_Write or COM_Read entry points are called from another thread. By calling the COM_Close entry point, the application indicates that its access to the serial device will be discontinued, invalidating any pending activity in the COM_Write or COM_Read entry point. The event objects, used by the IST to indicate a change in the state of the serial device, must be signaled to unblock any pending calls to COM_Write or COM_Read and allow their return to the calling application. This is accomplished through the StructUsers member variable, which tracks the number of times that COM_Read, COM_Write, and COM_IoControl have been entered. Each pass through the for loop causes the hReadEvent and hWriteEvent event handles to be signaled. This continues until either two seconds have elapsed, or there are no other callers of these entry points by this particular application (StructUsers equal to 0).

Listing 7.10 Sample implementation of XXX_Close (excerpted from the CEPB sample serial driver)

```
BOOL
COM_Close(PHW_OPEN_INFO pOpenHead)
{
    PHW_INDEP_INFO  pSerialHead = pOpenHead->pSerialHead;

    ...

    if ( pSerialHead->OpenCnt )
    {
        --(pSerialHead->OpenCnt);

        ...

        if ( pHWObj && (pHWObj->BindFlags & THREAD_IN_MDD) &&
             pSerialHead->pDispatchThread )
        {
            SetThreadPriority(pSerialHead->pDispatchThread,
                              THREAD_PRIORITY_NORMAL);
        }

        for ( i = 0; i < 20 && pOpenHead->StructUsers; i++ )
        {
```

```
            ...

            // Free any pending COM_Read and COM_Write functions.
            if ( pOpenHead->AccessCode & (GENERIC_READ | GENERIC_WRITE) )
            {
                SetEvent(pSerialHead->hReadEvent);
                SetEvent(pSerialHead->hTransmitEvent);
            }

            // Sleep, let threads finish.
            Sleep(100);
        }

        ...

        // If we are closing the last open handle, then close PDD also.
        if ( !pSerialHead->OpenCnt )
        {
            if ( pHWObj )
                pHWObj->pFuncTbl->HWClose(pSerialHead->pHWHead);

            // And if thread was spun in open, kill it now.
            if ( pSerialHead->pHWObj->BindFlags & THREAD_AT_OPEN )
            {
                StopDispatchThread( pSerialHead );
            }
        }

        ...

    }
    return (TRUE);
}
```

BOOL XXX_Deinit(DWORD hDeviceContext)

The call to the `XXX_Deinit` entry point is initiated by the DM just before the DM unloads the driver from memory. `XXX_Deinit` is called most commonly for stream-interface drivers that support installable devices. In the case of a PC card device, when device removal is detected by the socket driver, an event is passed to the DM that results in a call to the `DeregisterDevice` function. This function then calls the `XXX_Deinit` entry point. If an application had manually initiated the loading of a driver through a call to `RegisterDevice`, it would also need to call `DeregisterDevice` (resulting in a call to the `XXX_Deinit` entry point) when the driver was no longer required.

Conceptually this entry point is similar to the `XXX_Close` entry point, in that both deallocate operating system resources, possibly deactivating the supported device. The differences are best understood if you think of the intentions of the callers for each entry point. In the case of `XXX_Close`, an application is calling `CloseFile` (resulting in a call to `XXX_Close`) to indicate that access to the device is no longer required and that any operating system resources may be deallocated. The `XXX_Deinit` entry point is called in response to a call to `DeregisterDevice` when the device itself has been removed or deactivated and the driver is no longer needed. So any resources allocated for support of the particular device referenced in the `hDeviceContext` parameter must be deallocated by `XXX_Deinit`.

In Listing 7.11 we will examine an excerpt of the `COM_Deinit` entry point (available in the CEPB directory `.\PUBLIC\COMMON\OAK\DRIVERS\SERIAL`) for a serial device.

Listing 7.11 Sample implementation of `XXX_Deinit` (excerpted from the CEPB sample serial driver)

```
BOOL
COM_Deinit(PHW_INDEP_INFO pSerialHead)
{

    ...

    // If we have an interrupt handler thread, kill it.
    if ( pSerialHead->pHWObj->BindFlags & THREAD_IN_MDD )
    {
        StopDispatchThread( pSerialHead );
    }

    if ( pSerialHead->OpenCnt )
    {

        ...
        pEntry = pSerialHead->OpenList.Flink;
        while ( pEntry != &pSerialHead->OpenList )
        {
            pOpenHead = CONTAINING_RECORD( pEntry, HW_OPEN_INFO, llist );
            pEntry = pEntry->Flink;  // advance to next
            COM_Close(pOpenHead);
        }
    }

    // Free our resources.
    if ( pSerialHead->hSerialEvent )
        CloseHandle(pSerialHead->hSerialEvent);

    ...

    DeleteCriticalSection(&(pSerialHead->ReceiveCritSec1));

    ...

    if ( pSerialHead->RxBufferInfo.RxCharBuffer )
        LocalFree(pSerialHead->RxBufferInfo.RxCharBuffer);

    // Now, call hardware-specific deinit function.
    if ( pSerialHead->pHWObj && pSerialHead->pHWObj->pFuncTbl )
    {
        pSerialHead->pHWObj->pFuncTbl->HWDeinit(pSerialHead->pHWHead);
    }

    LocalFree(pSerialHead);

    return (TRUE);
}
```

The implementation in Listing 7.11 begins by determining if the interrupt service thread (IST) was created in the MDD layer (the layer where the `COM_Deinit` entry point resides) of the serial driver. If it was, the IST is terminated and its resources deallocated by a call to the function `StopDispatchThread`. This function was also called in the `COM_Close` entry point sample source code, but only for the last application accessing the device.

The `if` statement that follows checks the `OpenCnt` member variable to determine if any applications remain that still have access to this particular serial device. In most cases, the applications accessing the device would have called `CloseFile` (resulting in a call to `COM_Close`) to terminate access before the device was removed and the driver unloaded. If the device is a PC card, however, it may be removed at any time, causing the DM to receive an event from the socket driver. The result is a call to `DeregisterDevice` to unload the driver. It is quite possible that at this moment applications are still accessing the device and still have the handle, or driver structure, returned from `COM_Open`. The `while` loop in the sample code gets around this problem by retrieving the driver structure assigned to each application that accesses this particular serial device. The `COM_Close` entry point is then called on behalf of the application to deallocate the application-specific (nonshared) resources maintained in the driver structure. Any calls to the `COM_Write` and `COM_Read` entry points that may be blocked waiting for the IST to signal that the device is ready to send and receive more data are then unblocked.

The remaining sample code closes the resources that were dynamically allocated in `COM_Init` when the driver was first loaded. All of the event handles are closed (as depicted partially in Listing 7.11), critical section objects are deleted, and allocated memory is deallocated. The PDD function `HWDeinit` (defined for layered serial drivers) is also called, to provide the opportunity for further, device-specific shutdown, such as deactivation of the device hardware to reduce the overall power consumption of the platform.

Application-Initiated Loading

Stream-interface drivers, in addition to being loaded by the Device Manager, may be loaded directly by applications or by other stream-interface drivers. The `CreateFile` function can be used only to open access to the driver after it has already been loaded and initialized by the DM (through the `XXX_Init` entry point). If a driver is designed to support an installable device that cannot be detected by the DM upon insertion or system startup, it is the responsibility of the application to initiate the load sequence of the driver on behalf of the DM. Two functions—`RegisterDevice` and `DeregisterDevice`—accomplish this task.

HANDLE RegisterDevice(LPCWSTR lpszType, DWORD dwIndex, LPCWSTR lpszLib, DWORD dwInfo) and BOOL DeregisterDevice(Handle hDevice)

Listing 7.12 contains an excerpt of the PC card *tuple test* utility located in the `.\PUBLIC\COMMON\OAK\DRIVERS\TEST\PCMCIA\TUPLETST` directory, demonstrating the use of the `RegisterDevice` and `DeregisterDevice` functions. The `lpszType` parameter contains a pointer to the driver's device file name prefix and will be used to determine the name of the stream-interface driver's required entry points. The `dwIndex` parameter is the device identifier index that distinguishes drivers with the same device file name. It is the responsibility of the application to select a value for `dwIndex` that is not in use by other drivers with the same device file name. In most cases the application does not know which indexes have already been used, so the `RegisterDevice` function should be called repeatedly until a valid handle is returned.

The `lpszLib` parameter contains the name of the DLL module for the stream-interface driver. The next parameter, `dwInfo`, is used to pass an unspecified `DWORD` value to the `XXX_Init` entry point. If your driver requires that this parameter be used by the application to pass a pointer to one of its buffers (casting the value to `DWORD`), see the Managing Buffer Pointers section in Chapter 8 for information on how to map the pointer to the address space of your driver.

The function `DeregisterDevice` must be used by the application after access to the driver is no longer required, perhaps as the application is being unloaded. The call to this function would be preceded by a call to the `CloseFile` function to close the handle previously allocated with a call to the `CreateFile` function, as depicted in Listing 7.12. The handle returned from the call to `RegisterDevice` is passed in the `hDevice` parameter of `DeregisterDevice`.

Listing 7.12 Sample code demonstrating the `RegisterDevice` and `DeregisterDevice` functions

```
...

TestDevice = RegisterDevice(TEXT("PCM"), 1, TEXT("devtuple.dll"), 0);

if (TestDevice == 0) {
    NKDbgPrintfW(TEXT("TupleTst: RegisterDevice(devtuple.dll) failed %d\r\n"),
        GetLastError());
    return;
}

hTestDevice = CreateFile(
            TEXT("PCM1:"),
            GENERIC_READ|GENERIC_WRITE,
            0,
            NULL,
            OPEN_EXISTING,
            0,
            NULL);
...

CloseHandle(hTestDevice);
DeregisterDevice(TestDevice);

...
```

Native Device Driver Model

The word *native* is often used in the high-tech world to refer to technology that is well known or is an integral part of another technology. In the context of the native device driver model, the term *native* is consistent with this definition and generally refers to drivers for well-known devices (or device classes) with a consistent I/O model. CE supports certain device classes (listed in Table 6.1), each of which is supported with its own sample native driver and specialized driver interface. In this way the native device driver model differs from the stream-interface device driver model, which provides a single interface to support a broad variety of devices.

Most of the device classes supported by the native device driver model include devices that would most often occur as onboard devices in the design of a custom platform, though certainly nothing dictates that this must always be so. Consistent with this focus on onboard devices, the native device driver model generally requires that the driver be loaded on system startup, though nothing enforces this condition. For these reasons, this section will generally be of most interest to those of you developing a custom platform that includes onboard devices of a particular device class, possibly supported by a sample native device driver.

Though the native device driver model requires that you become familiar with a different interface for each device class, the good news is that you are not required to implement as much of your driver's code. Because the native device driver model is used to support well-known devices, it is possible to separate the interfaces for each device class into two distinct layers: one that supports the platform-independent I/O of the device class, and another that supports the platform-dependent, physical I/O of the device class. These layers are referred to as the **model device driver** (**MDD**) layer and the **platform device driver** (**PDD**) layers, respectively. Generally your changes will focus on the PDD layer, where you will modify existing sample code to accommodate the physical interface to your custom platform's onboard device. In the next section we will explore the intricacies of each layer.

Native Device Driver Model Architecture

It had long been a problem for device manufacturers that each new device required the development of a completely new device driver. Then along came the notion that device drivers could be internally structured into different layers, much as operating system and protocol stacks had been for many years. In Windows desktop operating systems (perhaps first appearing with the introduction of the printer miniport driver), this concept produced an architecture defined by the existence of a class driver and a miniport driver. The **class driver** contains the functionality common to all devices belonging to a particular device class; the **miniport driver** contains the functionality needed to address the manufacturer-specific aspects of the physical device I/O. This model has successfully achieved a significant reduction in the overall effort required to produce a driver because it focuses on creating an abstraction of the device interface and its capabilities (the miniport driver). The remaining effort required to write the code needed for support of the operating system interface is then provided by the operating system vendor as a class driver.

The native device driver model borrows heavily from the class/miniport driver architecture. The class and miniport drivers, as we have described them, roughly correspond to the MDD and PDD layers, respectively. The MDD layer, which implements the device driver interface (DDI), is provided by Microsoft and should not require modification. You are responsible for writing the PDD layer and implementing the interface, known as the device driver service-provider interface (DDSI), defined for your particular device class. The DDI functions of the MDD layer are called by operating system components, which in turn call the DDSI functions in your PDD layer. Figure 7.7 depicts this architecture.

As you can see in Figure 7.7, unlike the stream-interface drivers, which are always called by the Device Manager, native drivers may be called either by the Graphics, Windowing, and Events Subsystem (GWES) or by the Device Manager (DM). When called by GWES, the DDI functions are called directly. When called by the DM, however, the DDI functions may be called directly or they may be called indirectly through one of the functions defined for the stream-interface device driver model.

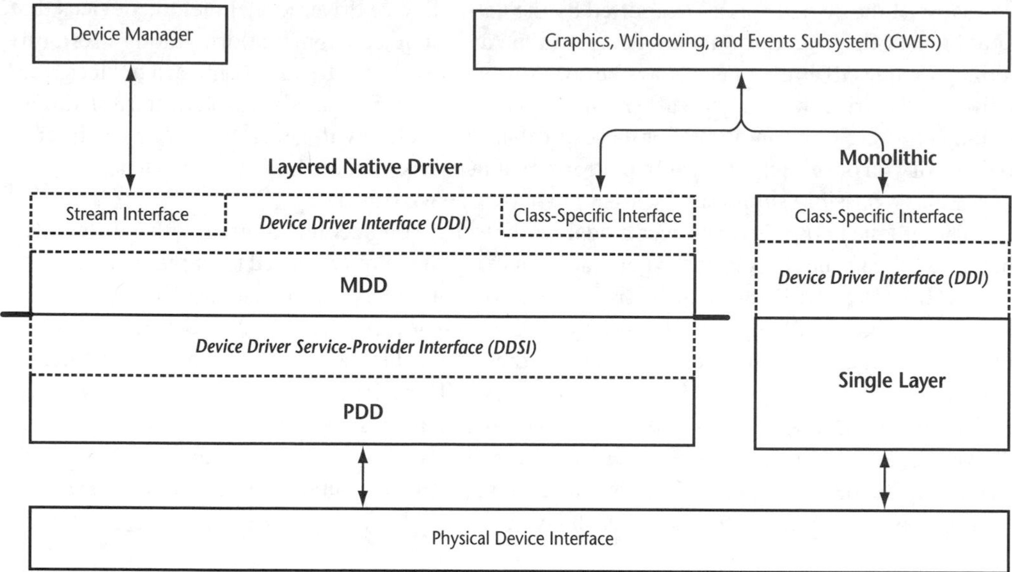

Figure 7.7 Block diagram of the native device driver model

This may sound a bit confusing, and you maybe questioning how a native driver belonging to a Microsoft-defined device class can be called by the Device Manager, which is designed to service drivers of the more generic stream-interface driver model. Could you then say that this native driver, which can be called by the DM through stream-interface functions, is also a stream-interface driver? Not really, and here's the reason:

There is nothing sacrosanct about any of the driver models we have explored in this chapter. One driver model may be defined through the interface mechanisms of another driver model. Is the new driver model defined in this manner any less of a driver model? In the spirit of effective software reuse, it is merely inheriting from the capabilities of an underlying driver model, which is providing the necessary functional enhancements, and with a clear definition of the resulting interface, a new driver model is born. This is the case with native drivers that use the mechanism of stream-interface functions as the basis of the definition of the DDI functions for that particular native driver and its associated device class. Keep this in mind as you read Hint 7.2, which defines what makes a driver a native driver, as based on the native device driver model.

Hint 7.2 Definition of a native device driver

Simply stated, a driver qualifies as a *native* driver and therefore complies with the native device driver model if it possesses a device class–specific interface, defined by Microsoft. How this device class–specific interface is implemented varies for each device class.

Most native drivers conform to the definition in Hint 7.2 by using the MDD and PDD layers. Usually the CEPB provides the MDD layer in source code form, allowing you complete control over the DDSI functions provided in the PDD layer. You can even go so far as to combine the MDD and PDD layers, eliminating the DDSI functions, to create a *monolithic* native driver. The

CEPB online documentation mentions that one reason for doing so would be to minimize the overhead of the DDSI function calls. It cautions, however, that creating a monolothic driver would lock you out of any of Microsoft's future MDD layer enhancements for your particular device class.

So, is a monolithic native driver still considered a native driver? Yes, because the only requirement for a driver that conforms to the native driver model is that its interface be defined for a specific device class. Even though the internal architecture of the monolithic native driver does not include separate MDD and PDD layers, its single-layer architecture still defines a DDI interface for the associated device class. This configuration therefore complies with the definition of a native device driver as stated in Hint 7.2.

Table 7.2 lists all of the device classes (as of CEPB 3.0) supported by the native device driver model. Note that if the identity of the DDI caller is the Device Manager, the DDI is

Table 7.2 Native Device Driver Interface Matrix

Device Class	DDI Caller	Architecture	Target Module	MDD Path	MDD Source
Serial (COMx)	Device Manager	Layered	DLL	`.\PUBLIC\COMMON\OAK\DRIVERS\SERIAL`	Yes
Parallel port	Device Manager	Layered	DLL	`.\PUBLIC\COMMON\OAK\DRIVERS\PARALLEL`	Yes
Video	GWES or Device Manager (in the case of a PC card video adapter)	Layered	DLL	`.\PUBLIC\COMMON\OAK\DRIVERS\DISPLAY`	Yes
PC card socket controller	Device Manager and other drivers	Layered	DLL	`.\PUBLIC\COMMON\OAK\PCMCIA`	Yes
USB host controller	Device Manager	Layered	DLL	`.\PUBLIC\COMMON\OAK\USB\HCD`	Yes
Touch panel	GWES	Layered	DLL	`.\PUBLIC\COMMON\OAK\DRIVERS\TOUCHP`	yes
Mouse	Passive (calls GWES through `mouse_event` function)	Monolithic	DLL	Not applicable (see sample platform drivers for source code)	Not applicable
Keyboard	GWES	Layered	DLL	`.\PUBLIC\COMMON\OAK\DRIVERS\KEYBD` and `.\PUBLIC\COMMON\OAK\DRIVERS\KEYBD2` (for general library functions)	Yes
Battery	GWES	Monolithic	LIB	Not applicable (see sample platform drivers in the `.\PLATFORM\ODO\GWE` directory)	Not applicable
LED	GWES	Monolithic	LIB	Not applicable (see sample platform drivers in the `.\PLATFORM\ODO\GWE` directory)	Not applicable

implemented through the interface mechanism of the stream-interface device driver model. In addition, if the target module is an object module library (LIB), then it is a driver that does not exist as a separate identifiable module (DLL, for example) in the ROM image, but is instead linked directly into the GWES module. If the driver's internal architecture is layered, you will find that the CEPB online documentation defines a device-independent MDD layer and a device-dependent PDD layer, each with its own respective interfaces, DDI and DDSI. If it is monolithic, then only one layer exists, defined with a single DDI interface.

Required Entry Points

Unlike the required entry points for the stream-interface driver model, those for the native driver model vary with each supported device class. The Porting Sample Native Device Drivers section of the CEPB online documentation describes both the DDI and DDSI *functions* (equivalent to the term *entry points* in this context) for each device class. If your custom platform contains a device that complies with one of these device classes, you will need to study the associated functions. Pay particular attention to the DDSI functions of the device class because these are implemented in the PDD layer and will be the focus of your implementation efforts.

For example, if your custom platform provided a PC card socket controller, you would need to implement the DDSI functions (in the PDD layer) for the PC card socket driver. As you can see if you look back at Table 6.1, sample PDD layer code is provided for the PC card socket driver on various platforms. As is the case for all native drivers, you would begin your development efforts by identifying the sample PC card socket driver PDD code in the `.\PLATFORM\{ODO|CEPC}\DRIVERS` directory that most closely matches the requirements of your platform, and then copying it to your `.\PLATFORM\<Your Platform Name>\DRIVERS` directory tree (containing your platform's drivers). Refer to Chapter 10 for more information on the structure of the `.\PLATFORM\<Platform Name>` directory tree.

If you compare the size of the narrative in this section on required entry points to that of the corresponding section for the stream-interface device driver model earlier in this chapter, you will notice that this section is significantly smaller. The reason is certainly not that native drivers are easier to implement, but rather that they require you to build a certain degree of expertise in the device class and its associated DDSI functions (entry points). Because we are trying to avoid focusing on any one device in this chapter, we will not go any further in our exploration of a native driver's entry points. We will, however, continue to explore the areas of native driver development that are common to all device classes.

Automatic Loading

The mechanisms for loading native drivers are as varied as the specialized interfaces associated with each native driver. In this section we will explore the registry entries required for each of the native drivers defined in the CEPB online documentation (keyboard, touch panel, mouse, battery, PC card and USB controllers, display). We will not, however, discuss the many subkeys specific to each type of native driver or device class. In most cases the CEPB online documentation does a pretty good job of describing the keys defined for each native driver. Occasionally you will need to examine the source code directly to determine just how a particular key is used. As is true of the registry keys described for all driver models, you may define any additional keys to extend the configuration options of your native driver.

Touch Panel, Mouse, and Keyboard Drivers

The HKEY_LOCAL_MACHINE\Hardware\DeviceMap key is currently defined to load any one of three native drivers—the touch panel, mouse, and/or keyboard native drivers—using the Touch, Mouse, and Keybd keys, respectively. The subkey DriverName is optional and is used by the driver control program (DCP) GWES to identify the name of the DLL module containing the native driver. If this subkey is not present, GWES simply loads the default DLL module name, which is the name of the key with the extension *.dll* appended.

An example of these registry entries appear in the .\PLATFORM\CEPC\FILE\platform.reg file, which is excerpted in Listing 7.13. The default DLL module name is overridden in the DriverName subkey because a single driver, kbdmouse.dll, provides the functionality for both the mouse and the keyboard native drivers.

Listing 7.13 Sample registry entries for the multifunction keyboard/mouse native driver

```
...
[HKEY_LOCAL_MACHINE\Hardware\DeviceMap\Mouse]
        "DriverName"="kbdmouse.dll"
[HKEY_LOCAL_MACHINE\Hardware\DeviceMap\Keybd]
        "DriverName"="kbdmouse.dll"
        "CalVKey"=dword:0
        "ContLessVKey"=dword:0
        "ContMoreVKey"=dword:0
        "TaskManVKey"=dword:2E
...
```

Battery and LED Drivers

The battery and LED native drivers may be loaded without the use of any registry entries. Because these native drivers are built as object module libraries and linked in (through the SOURCELIB entry in the Sources file, which is discussed shortly, in the section titled Building a Native Device Driver) with the gwes.exe module. When you do not require battery or LED support, stub functions are linked in to prevent an error in the link process. So, effectively the DDI functions of these native drivers are always present and need not be loaded through the use of registry keys.

Display Driver

Unlike the registry entries required for other native drivers, those for the display device class do not require a registry entry to be loaded. Instead, the module with the name ddi.dll is automatically loaded as the display driver. This module name can be overridden through the use of the [HKEY_LOCAL_MACHINE\System\GDI\Drivers] key and its corresponding subkey, Display=<Your display driver module name>.

The use of the module name *ddi.dll* is evident in the platform.bib file provided with the CEPB sample platforms. Each reference to the module ddi.dll is surrounded by if statements for each supported display device. When the platform is built, an environment variable is defined with the name of the default display as it appears after the if statement. The DLL module for the particular display device then appears as ddi.dll in the final ROM image. Refer to Chapter 4 for more information on how BIB files affect the content of ROM image files.

If additional registry entries are needed to describe the available options or current state of the display driver, they should be located under the `HKEY_LOCAL_MACHINE\Drivers\Display` registry key. The structure and content of these entries are really up to you, though the CEPB online documentation does specify one requirement to allow Pocket PowerPoint to use a secondary display adapter. The subkeys under the registry key(s) `HKEY_LOCAL_MACHINE\Drivers\Display\Active\<Name of the secondary display adapter(s)>` define certain characteristics of the secondary display adapter and are described in the Registry Keys for Removable Display Adapters section of the CEPB online documentation.

For more information on the development of a CE display driver, refer to Appendix D.

PCMCIA Socket Controller Driver

Just as GWES automatically loads a display driver named `ddi.dll`, the Device Manager automatically loads the native driver `pcmcia.dll` as the PC card socket controller driver. There is currently no method to override this behavior, so you must make certain that the DLL module for this native driver is `pcmcia.dll` in the `platform.bib` file.

Serial Port and USB Host Controller Drivers

The serial port driver is a bit different from most native drivers—so much so that you might ask if it really belongs with the other native drivers in the Porting the Sample Native Device Driver section of the CEPB online documentation. It is designed with the MDD/PDD layering mechanism commonly used in native drivers. The DDI functions of the MDD layer, however, are implemented through the entry points defined for the stream-interface driver model. Because the DDI interface of the serial port driver is not specific to the serial port device class, we will contradict the CEPB online documentation and declare this driver to be one that conforms to the stream-interface device driver model.

Note:

Please do not consider the declaration of the serial port driver as one that conforms to the stream-interface device driver model (contrary to the CEPB online documentation) an earth-shattering discovery, because it is really more important that you understand the requirements of each driver model and the mechanisms that support them rather than the associated semantics. The only reason for making this point is to eliminate any confusion you might experience as you increase your overall understanding of CE device drivers.

The registry keys required to load serial port drivers are, as you might expect, identical to those of stream-interface drivers. If your serial port driver supports an onboard serial port, then you will use the `HKEY_LOCAL_MACHINE\Drivers\BuiltIn` key to cause the driver to be loaded when your custom platform is powered on. If the supported serial port is an installable device, you will need to use the registry entries required by the insertion mechanism in use (either PC card or USB). Refer to the earlier discussion of the stream-interface device driver model for more information on how to write stream-interface drivers for installable devices.

Like the serial port driver, the USB host controller driver is loaded by the Device Manager. As you inspect the MDD source code in the `.\PUBLIC\COMMON\OAK\DRIVERS\USB\HCD\OHCD` directory, you will notice that certain DDI functions are implemented through stream-interface functions with a device file name of *HCD*. Even though stream-interface functions are present, we will not contradict the CEPB online documentation this time by declaring this driver to be a stream-interface driver. This is really a matter of semantics, but it is important to your understanding of the native driver model, so we will explore this point a bit further.

Unlike the serial port driver, the DDI functions for the USB HCD are specialized for the device class of USB host controllers and therefore satisfy our central definition of a native device driver in Hint 7.2. The services provided by stream-interface functions and the DM are used by the USB HCD native driver as a mechanism to get the HCD loaded and to receive power-down and power-up notifications.

The `HKEY_LOCAL_MACHINE\Drivers\BuiltIn\OHCI` registry key is used to load the USB HCD on system startup. The `OHCI` key is used to describe the type of the USB host controller interface supported, and it should be changed if your implementation of this driver supports a different type of USB host controller interface.

Building a Native Device Driver

Building a native device driver requires a `Sources` file that is more complex than the ones for other types of drivers. In this section we will focus on those aspects of the `Sources` file that are of particular importance when you're building a native driver. Refer to Chapter 10 for an explanation of how the `Sources` file fits into the overall build process.

When you build a native driver, you are often using code provided in a directory tree separate from the one for the native driver itself. This code generally constitutes the MDD layer and exists as an object module library that is linked, in its entirety, into your driver. This means that the linker effectively copies the entire contents of the LIB file into your native driver, without using an unresolved symbol in your code to identify which object modules must be extracted from the LIB file. Using object module libraries in this manner provides a mechanism for simultaneously referencing a group of object modules without specifying them individually on the linker command line. Later in this section we will see which macro within the `Sources` file causes this form of LIB file linkage.

Let's quickly examine the `Sources` file in the `.\PLATFORM\ODO\DRIVERS\PCMCIA` directory, which is provided in Listing 7.14 for reference.

Listing 7.14 `Sources` file for building the PC card socket controller native driver

```
!if "$(ODO_NOPCMCIA)" != "1"
TARGETNAME=pcmcia
!endif

RELEASETYPE=PLATFORM
TARGETTYPE=DYNLINK
TARGETLIBS=$(_COMMONSDKROOT)\lib\$(_CPUINDPATH)\coredll.lib \
           $(_COMMONOAKROOT)\target\$(_CPUINDPATH)\usa\pcmcia.res
SOURCELIBS=$(_COMMONOAKROOT)\lib\$(_CPUINDPATH)\cardserv.lib
PREPROCESSDEFFILE=1
DEFFILE=$(_COMMONOAKROOT)\inc\pcmcia.def
DLLENTRY=DllEntry
INCLUDES=..\..\inc
SOURCES= \
```

```
init.c   \
memory.c \
socket.c \
window.c
```

The TARGETNAME macro specifies the name of the executable module; the TARGETTYPE macro specifies that the type of the executable module is a dynamic link library, or DLL. The RELEASETYPE macro indicates that the destination directory of the build is PLATFORM\ <Platform Name>\TARGET\<Processor Family>\<Processor Identification>\CE\ <Type of Build {Retail|Debug}>. Later, when buildrel.bat (in the .\PUBLIC\ COMMON\OAK\MISC directory) is called by the CEPB IDE, the file pcmcia.dll is automatically copied to the release directory (.\PUBLIC\<Platform Name>\RELDIR\<Processor Identification>_{Retail|Debug} in CEPB 3.0, .\PUBLIC\<Platform Name>\RELEASE\<Processor Identification>_Release in CEPB 2.12).

The TARGETLIBS macro specifies object module libraries and import libraries (those used to reference the exported functions of a DLL). The SOURCELIBS macro specifies modules that are linked not by unresolved symbols, but instead by the inclusion of all of the object modules contained in the LIB file in the final executable module, pcmcia.dll. This is generally how the platform-independent MDD code supplied in the CEBP finds its way into native drivers. The MDD code for the pcmcia.dll module is contained in the cardserv.lib module, located in the .\PUBLIC\COMMON\OAK\LIB\<Processor Family>\<Processor Identification> \CE\<Type of Build {Retail|Debug}> directory. The contents of the COMMON directory are generally reserved for platform-independent code.

The PREPROCESSDEFFILE macro is used in combination with the DEFFILE macro to specify that a particular DEF file must be "preprocessed" by the target compiler before it is used in the linking of the DLL module. This preprocessing simply means that a single DEF file that references other DEF files through the use of #include statements can be regenerated into a single DEF file with no #include statements. Such preprocessing is required by the linker, which is apparently unable to process DEF files containing #include statements. In our example, preprocessing is not required because pcmcia.def does not use #include statements, but it is important to understand in case it is needed in your own DEF files.

The remaining macros in Listing 7.14 are somewhat self-explanatory and occur in all types of Sources files for both drivers and applications (TARGETTYPE=PROGRAM). The DLLENTRY macro simply names the function that is called when the DLL module is loaded and unloaded. The INCLUDES macro lists the directories that contain additional header files referenced by the source files listed in the SOURCES macro. You do not need to use the INCLUDES macro if you are referencing only the standard include files under the .\PUBLIC\COMMON directory tree. Because we are building a driver that contains platform-specific code, a special include directory was defined in this example at .\PLATFORM\ODO\INC. You will notice that all of the sample platforms provided with the CEPB use this directory as the common location for collecting all platform-dependent header files.

The directory named in the INCLUDES macro is referenced with a relative path name of ..\..\inc. This is considered good practice to allow a successful build even if the root directory of the developer's installation of the CEPB varies from what you use in your installation. If you need to reference multiple directories, each relative path name must be separated by a semicolon. Finally, the SOURCES macro uses the standard backslash ("\") line continuation character (also used by C compilers) to allow the macro to be defined on multiple lines. The last line, however, must not contain a backslash.

The build of the battery and LED drivers is quite different from that of other native drivers. Both drivers are built as object module libraries that are eventually linked directly into the `gwes.exe` module. In fact, you won't find these drivers in the same directory with most of the other native drivers in the CEPB sample source code. The `.\PLATFORM\<Platform Name>\GWE` directory contains the source code for both the battery and the LED drivers, along with the `Sources` file that produces object module libraries linked into `gwes.exe` through the `SOURCELIBS` macro just discussed.

Listing 7.15 contains a copy of the `Sources` file used to build the battery driver. The `RELEASETYPE` value is equal to `PLATFORM` as you would expect, since the destination of the target LIB file is in the platform directory tree. The value of `TARGETTYPE` is `LIBRARY` to cause the creation of the object module library. After the object module libraries for both the battery and LED driver are built, the `Sources` file in the `.\PLATFORM\ODO\GWE\ALL` directory combines them into yet another object module library, called `gwe_drv.lib`. In the last stage of the `gwes.exe` build, the `Sources` file in the `.\PLATFORM\ODO\GWE\BUILDEXE` directory causes `gwe_drv.lib` to be linked into `gwes.exe` through the `SOURCELIBS` macro. Because of the dependencies between the build targets of each subdirectory, the order of their build is controlled by the `Dirs` file in the `.\PLATFORM\ODO\GWE` subdirectory.

Listing 7.15 `Sources` file for building the battery driver

```
!if "$(ODO_NOBATTERY)" != "1"
RELEASETYPE=PLATFORM
TARGETNAME=battery
TARGETTYPE=LIBRARY
INCLUDES=$(_COMMONOAKROOT)\inc
SOURCES=battery.c
!endif
```

USB Device Driver Model

Unlike the NDIS driver model, which will be discussed next, the USB driver model bears little resemblance to its desktop counterpart. USB drivers under Windows 98 are developed by use of the layered architecture of the Windows Driver Model (WDM). You will notice, however, many similarities with the mechanisms of the stream-interface driver model, which is used quite heavily in the implementation of this driver model.

In this section we will be exploring what it takes to produce a basic USB driver that complies with the requirements of the USB driver model. We will begin by examining the architecture of the USB driver control program (DCP), which abstracts the services of the USB host controller, enumerates newly inserted devices, and administers the loading and unloading of USB drivers that match the capabilities of the USB device. The architecture is of particular interest because it is an excellent example of how the mechanisms of one driver model can be used in the implementation of another driver model (or DCP).

Unfortunately, we will not be exploring the realm of USB I/O and its various forms of pipe constructs, used to dynamically request access to the bus. A sizable number of functions are provided in the USB driver interface layer (USBD or USBDI) for such access, and they will require that you gain some understanding of the USB and its classes of peripheral devices. Additional references are provided in the Bibliography at the end of this book.

USB Device Driver Model Architecture

Unlike stream-interface drivers that are maintained by the Device Manager (DM), USB drivers are maintained by a USBD module. The USBD module is a driver control program (DCP, a concept introduced earlier in this chapter), and as such, one of its primary duties is to load your USB driver when the device it supports is detected on the bus (the USB serial bus). Certain registry entries are needed to support this process and are explained later in this section. When your driver needs to conduct I/O with its supported device, it uses the API exported by the USBD module to allocate a USB pipe (a logical construct with associated attributes defining the characteristics of the data transfer).

As DCPs go, the USBD module is very different from the DM, which is concerned primarily with the loading and unloading of its stream-interface drivers. The reason for this difference is that the DM is not designed to support drivers for any one particular bus or device type, and therefore does not provide an API for device I/O. It is the responsibility of the stream-interface driver to figure out how it will conduct I/O with its device. If your driver supported a PC card device, for example, you would use the card services API provided by the `PCMCIA` module (`pcmcia.dll`) to perform operations such as mapping the card's I/O space and requesting notification when it generates an interrupt.

The DM does, however, provide a stream-interface driver with something that the USBD module does not: an application interface based on the standard Win32 file I/O functions, which are mapped to the *XXX_* entry points required of all stream-interface drivers. So, if applications needed to send and receive data through your stream-interface driver's supported device, they would simply call `CreateFile` to obtain a file handle to your driver, `WriteFile` to send data to the device, and `ReadFile` to receive data from the device. All of this might sound familiar if you have read the section on stream-interface drivers earlier in the chapter.

The USBD module, though it does provide an API for I/O access with your USB device, does not provide an application interface. This means that if you need to expose your device's data to calling applications, you will need to produce your own API, by borrowing from the mechanisms of other driver models. If, however, your supported USB device conforms to a device class (defined by Microsoft), your device's data will be exposed through the APIs associated with that device class. The sample USB mouse driver provided in the CEPB is an example of just such a driver that uses the GWES function `mouse_event` to expose its data, without the need for specialized functions accessible to applications. Later, in the section titled Providing Application Services, we will describe the process for creating a specialized application interface to a USB driver.

Figure 7.8 depicts the relationship of the USBD module to the Device Manager and its client drivers (drivers compliant with the USB device driver model). The USBD module uses the stream interface as a mechanism for being loaded in the address space of the DM. This is a fine example of how a stream-interface driver can be written as a driver control program (the USBD module) to support the creation of driver models for other types of I/O buses used by peripheral devices. If,

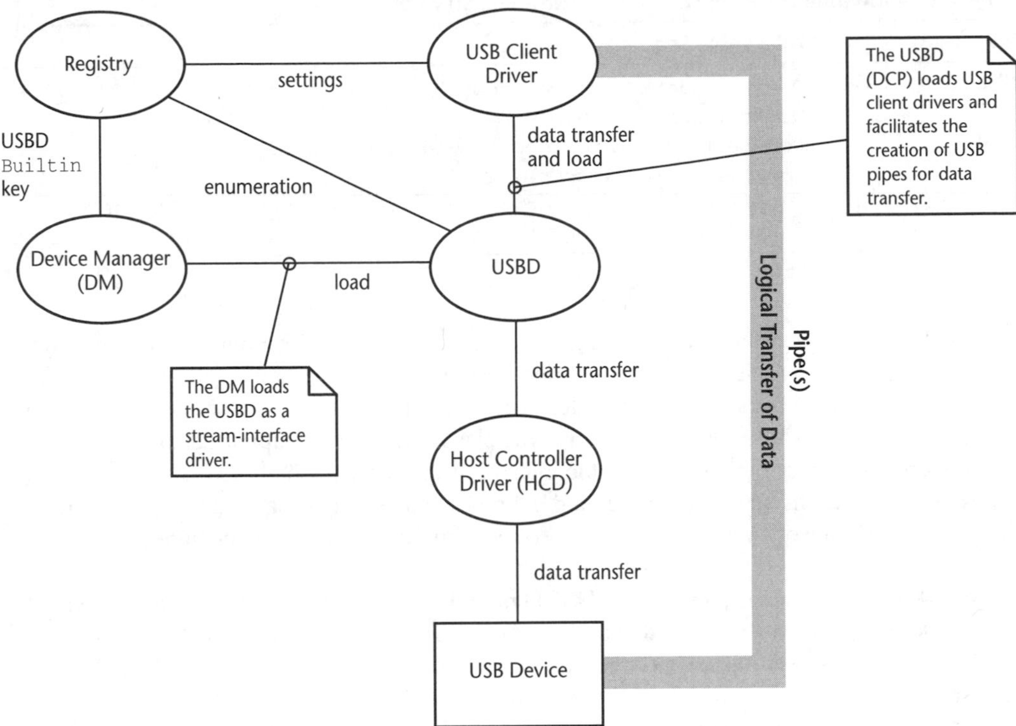

Figure 7.8 Collaboration diagram of the USB device driver architecture

for example, your custom platform provided an IEEE 1394 bus (FireWire), in the absence of support by Microsoft, the same design would most likely serve your needs and would allow your drivers to also run in the address space of the DM. Having all drivers coexist in the same address space conserves the limited CE process slot resources and allows the same instance of the driver DLL module to be shared by applications and other drivers in the DM address space.

Automatic Loading

The registry keys defined for USB drivers provide a highly flexible mechanism for associating a USB driver with a USB device. Using this mechanism, you can indicate that a driver supports a broad class of devices. You can limit the scope of your driver by indicating that only devices offering a particular interface within the specified class are supported. You can also indicate that your driver supports only USB devices from a certain vendor, product ID, and release number, or any combination thereof. All of these possibilities may be combined and are considered by the USBD module according to a hierarchical rule that we will explore shortly.

The registry keys required for USB drivers are divided into three separate groups, with each group acting as a subkey of the previous group. The template for the registry key is as follows:

```
HKEY_LOCAL_MACHINE\Drivers\USB\LoadClients\<Group1_ID>\<Group2_ID>\
<Group3_ID>\<Client Driver ID String>
```

Table 7.3 Allowable Forms of Each USB `Group` Registry Key

Key	Allowable Forms
Group1_ID	DeviceVendorID, DeviceVendorID_DeviceProductID, DeviceVendorID_DeviceProductID_DeviceReleaseNumber
Group2_ID	DeviceClassCode, DeviceClassCode_DeviceSubclassCode, DeviceClass-Code_DeviceSubclassCode_DeviceProtocolCode
Group3_ID	InterfaceClassCode, InterfaceClassCode_InterfaceSubclassCode, InterfaceClassCode_InterfaceSubclassCode_InterfaceProtocolCode

The key for each group, called `Group`, corresponds to information contained in the device descriptor and is used to describe the supported device. Each `Group` key is further divided into three separate data items, separated by underscores. `Group1` contains vendor-specific information, Group2 contains information describing the class of the device supported, and Group3 contains information describing the type of the interface supported. Each group contains numeric values, drawn from the actual values defined by the USB standard, separated by underscores. The allowable forms of each `Group` key, excerpted from the CEPB online documentation, appear in Table 7.3.

When a USB device is inserted, the USBD module collects the information contained in the device descriptors (data structures that reside on the USB device to describe its capabilities, which collectively are comparable to the Card Information Structure on PC card devices). Each USB subkey under the registry key `HKEY_LOCAL_MACHINE\Drivers\USB\LoadClients` is examined for a match beginning with the `Group1_ID` key. If a key contains a value of `default`, it is ignored and the next `Group` key is checked for a potential match. When a key does match, the remaining keys are checked for a match, unless they contain an entry of `default`. If the registry entries for two separate USB drivers match the inserted device, the one with the more general of the allowable forms appearing in Table 7.3 is selected.

So, for example, let's consider the sample USB registry entries in Listing 7.16.

Listing 7.16 Sample USB driver registry entries (without the client driver identifier string)

```
Example 1:

HKEY_LOCAL_MACHINE\Drivers\USB\LoadClients\Default\Default\3_1_2\Generic_
Sample_Mouse_Driver

HKEY_LOCAL_MACHINE\Drivers\USB\LoadClients\Default\Default\3\Generic_HID_
Driver

Example 2:

HKEY_LOCAL_MACHINE\Drivers\USB\LoadClients\158_230A_1.0\Default\Default\ACME_
Old_Sample_Mouse_Driver

HKEY_LOCAL_MACHINE\Drivers\USB\LoadClients\158_230A\Default\Default\ACME_New_
Sample_Mouse_Driver
```

```
Example 3:

HKEY_LOCAL_MACHINE\Drivers\USB\LoadClients\Default\2\2_2_1\ACME_Sample_Modem_
Driver

HKEY_LOCAL_MACHINE\Drivers\USB\LoadClients\Default\2\10_0_144\ACME_Sample_
Modem_Driver

Example 4:

HKEY_LOCAL_MACHINE\Drivers\USB\LoadClients\Default\2\2_2_1\ACME_Sample_Combo_
Modem_Ethernet_Driver

Example 5:

HKEY_LOCAL_MACHINE\Drivers\USB\LoadClients\Default\Default\Default\USB_Driver_
Monitor
```

In example 1, a USB mouse driver is inserted and the device descriptors are read from the device by the USBD module. The values are compared to the `Group3` keys present in the registry. The `Group1` and `Group2` keys are ignored because the value of each is `default`. The interface class code of both `Group3` keys is 3, corresponding to the Human Interface Device (HID) interface class. The HID interface class code is considered a match for the USB mouse and the `Dll` subkey of the `Generic_HID_Driver` key is used to obtain the name of the DLL module to load. The generic sample mouse driver (referenced in the `Generic_Sample_Mouse_Driver key`) is not loaded because it is considered a less general form of both `Group3` keys. The rule applied by the USBD module requires that the more general key be considered a superior match. If, however, this driver were to return `FALSE` from the `USBDeviceAttach` entry point, the driver referenced by the other registry key would be loaded.

In example 2, both `Group2` and `Group3` keys contain `default`, indicating that both drivers will function only with a USB mouse provided by vendor number 158 (the first numeric value in the `Group1` key). Both `Group1` keys contain a product ID of 230A, but the second entry does not contain a numeric value for the device release number. The lack of a release number implies that the associated driver for the second entry will work with all devices regardless of the release number and is therefore selected as the superior match by the USBD module, according to the rule that the more general key must be selected.

In example 3, the same driver, `ACME_Sample_Modem_Driver`, appears in both registry entries. In the first entry, the `Group2` key contains a value of 2, indicating support for devices that belong to the Communications Device Class, without regard for the device subclass or device protocol values. The `Group3` keys for each entry specify support for a different interface class. The first indicates support for devices that conform to the Communication Interface Class (numeric value 2) with an interface subclass of the Abstract Control Model (numeric value of 2, indicating support for a legacy modem with onboard data protocols and call control) and an interface protocol of V.25ter (numeric value of 1, indicating support for basic AT commands). The second entry indicates support for a related Data Interface Class (numeric value 10) with an interface protocol of V.42bis (numeric value of 144). The interface subclass value is 0 because it is unused in the USB Communications Device Class standard document. If two devices, each with a supported interface, were inserted, the same driver would be loaded by the USBD module for each supported interface. This means that a single instance of this driver must be able to support two logical devices, present on the same or separate physical devices.

The registry entry in example 4 supports the same type of modem as in example 3, with one key difference: The other interface classes that this modem is likely to provide are not directly referenced with a separate registry entry. Thus, in the implementation of this driver's `USBDeviceAttach` function, the driver must determine if the other interfaces that it may support are present (using the USBD `FindInterface` function). If an interface known to this driver is identified, the driver may either internally support the interface(s) or manually load other drivers providing such support (using the USBD `LoadGenericInterfaceDriver` function).

Example 5 uses the `default` value for each group ID, causing it to be loaded by the USBD module for every device that is inserted. This ID is useful if you're developing a driver that requires notification whenever a new device is inserted, perhaps for the implementation of some kind of USB monitoring application that display's bus status in a tray icon. In the implementation of the `USBDeviceAttach` function, you need to be careful to return `FALSE`, to ensure that the USBD module continues searching for other drivers with actual support for the device.

Required Entry Points

The prototypes needed for the required entry points are provided in the `usbdi.h` file, located in the `.\PUBLIC\COMMON\DDK\INC` directory. Two other header files must also be included in your USB driver source files—namely, `usb100.h` and `usbtypes.h`, located in the same directory. You may notice as you examine these header files more carefully that they contain prototypes for a large number of functions, beyond the entry points required for a USB driver. Most of these functions are implemented in the USBD module; others must be implemented in your USB driver and passed to other USBD functions as function pointers. We will not discuss these functions in any great detail in this section, but will merely mention them as they appear in the sample implementations of each entry point. For more complete information on the use of all USBD functions, refer to the CEPB online documentation.

Like most CE drivers, USB drivers are built as DLL modules with certain exported functions serving as the required entry points. Compliance with the USB driver model requires only three entry points, owing primarily to the lack of an application-level interface, unlike the *XXX_* entry points for stream-interface drivers. These three functions are `USBDeviceAttach`, `USBInstallDriver`, and `USBUnInstallDriver`.

Note:
Nearly all CE drivers are linked to form DLL modules, the notable exceptions being certain native drivers that are linked as object module libraries to an EXE module (e.g., `gwes.exe`).

When a new device is detected, the USBD module enumerates the device and attempts to find a matching driver—a complex process that was described earlier in this section on the USB device driver model. If the USBD module decides your driver is a potential match, the function

USBDeviceAttach is called. If the USBD module is unable to find a matching driver, a dialog box is displayed prompting the end user for the name of a DLL module. The USBInstallDriver function for the driver just entered is then called, providing the opportunity to write the required registry entries. If a TRUE value is returned, the USBD module then re-enumerates the inserted device and once again seeks a matching driver. The USBUnInstallDriver is called only when the driver is being completely deleted from the system, perhaps during the execution of an uninstallation sequence. If the USB driver is included in the build of a new CE kernel, the USBInstallDriver and USBUnInstallDriver functions will never be called because the required registry entries are manually entered in the platform.reg file along with the driver DLL in the platform.bib file (refer to Chapter 10 for more information on REG and BIB files). In the next few sections we will dive into some sample code for the implementation of these functions.

BOOL USBDeviceAttach(USB_HANDLE hDevice, LPCUSB_FUNCS lpUsbFuncs, LPCUSB_INTERFACE lpInterface, LPCWSTR szUniqueDriverId, LPBOOL fAcceptControl, LPCUSB_DRIVER_SETTINGS lpDriverSettings, DWORD dwUnused)

Listing 7.17 contains an excerpt of an implementation of the USBDeviceAttach function in the sample USB mouse driver located in the CEPB directory .\PUBLIC\COMMON\OAK\DRIVERS\USB\CLIENTS\MOUSE. The USBDeviceAttach entry point is the most important of the three required entry points and is called only when the USBD module has examined the registry entries associated with your driver and has determined that they match the characteristics of the inserted device. The fAcceptControl parameter and the return value from this function are responsible for verifying that this driver is a match for the inserted device. Because of the detailed nature of the registry entries that describe the type of device your driver will accept, in most cases you will return TRUE, indicating acceptance of the device. These registry entries were examined in great detail in the Automatic Loading section of this discussion.

Listing 7.17 Sample implementation of the USBDeviceAttach entry point

```
...

*fAcceptControl = FALSE;

// This driver should be loaded only for mouse devices; let's check
// the interface settings just to be sure.
if (lpInterface == NULL)
    return FALSE;

CMouse * pMouse = new CMouse(hDevice, lpUsbFuncs, lpInterface);

if (pMouse == NULL)
    return FALSE;

if (!pMouse->Initialize())
{
    delete pMouse;
    return FALSE;
}
```

```
    (*lpUsbFuncs->lpRegisterNotificationRoutine)(hDevice,
                                    USBDeviceNotifications, pMouse);
    *fAcceptControl = TRUE;
    return TRUE;
}
```

The sample code in Listing 7.17 shows the parameter `fAcceptControl` being dereferenced and initialized to a value of `FALSE`. If all goes well in the subsequent initialization steps, this value is replaced with `TRUE`, and the function returns also with a `TRUE` value.

The `hDevice` parameter should be retained for future reference in other functions. It is used later in Listing 7.17 to call the USBD function `RegisterNotificationRoutine` with the address of our sample driver's notification function (used in this example only to process the `USB_CLOSE_DEVICE` message). The address of the `RegisterNotificationRoutine` function is obtained from the `lpUsbFuncs` parameter, which points to a large structure containing the addresses of the entire collection of functions exported by the USBD module. The `lpUsbFuncs` parameter should also be retained for future reference. In Listing 7.17 these values, including the `lpInterface` parameter, are saved in the member variables of the `CMouse` object.

The value of the parameter `lpInterface` contains a pointer to a structure that contains among other things, a pointer to the `USB_INTERFACE_DESCRIPTOR` structure retrieved directly from the inserted USB device. The registry entries for the sample USB mouse driver describe the exact characteristics of the USB interface it will support. The USBD module automatically compares these values to the same values retrieved from the device and stored in the `USB_INTERFACE_DESCRIPTOR` structure. Therefore, the value of the `lpInterface` parameter is non-`NULL` only if the matching driver was registered with the numeric values of its supported interface (making the driver an interface driver). The sample code in Listing 7.17 knows that the driver was registered as an interface driver and verifies this fact by checking for a `NULL` value, returning an error if the value is `TRUE`.

Every USB driver must be registered with a unique identifier string. This value is passed to the `USBDeviceAttach` function in the `szUniqueDriverId` parameter and is not used in the Listing 7.17 sample code because it is already hard-coded. If any driver-specific configuration values were used by the USB mouse driver, this value could be passed to the `OpenClientRegistryKey` function to obtain an `HKEY` handle used for reading the registry values. The CEPB online documentation warns that the location of driver-specific registry entries could change in future versions of CE, and that we should refrain from opening the registry key directly by using the `OpenClientRegistryKey` function.

The fields of the `DRIVER_SETTINGS` structure referenced by the `lpDriverSettings` parameter contain the values of the group IDs described earlier, in the section of this discussion titled Automatic Loading. The structure generally is used in the implementation of the `USBDeviceAttach` function to verify that your driver is loaded as a vendor, class, or interface driver as defined by the presence of the nondefault group IDs registered for your driver. This is particularly important if your driver can handle multiple interface classes and is represented with a separate registry entry for each. Using the contents of the `lpDriverSetings` parameter, you can determine under which registry entry, and therefore which interface class, the driver is loaded. This is not important in Listing 7.17 because the USB mouse driver is registered as an interface driver able to support only one interface.

BOOL USBInstallDriver(LPCWSTR szDriverLibFile) and BOOL USBUnInstallDriver(void)

The `USBInstallDriver` entry point is called only when the USBD module needs to manually load your driver. This would be the case only if your driver were present on the target platform but were not yet registered, and if the registry entries of other drivers did not provide a match or did not accept control of the device (by returning `FALSE` in the `USBDeviceAttach` entry point). The primary purpose of this entry point is to make the required registry entries that will allow the USBD to automatically load the driver as a match for the inserted device.

Listing 7.18 contains an excerpt of an implementation of the `USBInstallDriver` function provided in the CEPB sample USB mouse driver. The code begins by obtaining an instance handle to the USBD module, later used in retrieving the address of its `RegisterClientDriverId` and `RegisterClientSettings` functions. If the USBD module were not present, this function would simply return `FALSE`, which would be a clear indication that USB support was not available on this platform. The fields of the `USB_DRIVER_SETTINGS` structure are then initialized. The values assigned correspond to the group IDs described in the earlier Automatic Loading section (depicted in example 1 of Listing 7.16) and will produce all three group ID registry keys appearing under the `HKEY_LOCAL_MACHINE\Drivers\USB\LoadClients` registry key. If the three numeric values that make up a group ID contain the `USB_NO_INFO` constant, it is translated to a group ID of `default`. The values in Listing 7.18 would produce the registry entry appearing in example 1 of Listing 7.16.

Listing 7.18 Sample implementation of the `USBInstallDriver` entry point

```
...

HINSTANCE hInst = LoadLibrary(L"USBD.DLL");

if(hInst)
{
    LPREGISTER_CLIENT_DRIVER_ID pRegisterId = (LPREGISTER_CLIENT_DRIVER_ID)
            GetProcAddress(hInst, gcszRegisterClientDriverId);

    LPREGISTER_CLIENT_SETTINGS pRegisterSettings =
            (LPREGISTER_CLIENT_SETTINGS) GetProcAddress(hInst,
            gcszRegisterClientSettings);

    if(pRegisterId && pRegisterSettings)
    {
        USB_DRIVER_SETTINGS DriverSettings;

        DriverSettings.dwCount = sizeof(DriverSettings);

        DriverSettings.dwVendorId = USB_NO_INFO;
        DriverSettings.dwProductId = USB_NO_INFO;
        DriverSettings.dwReleaseNumber = USB_NO_INFO;

        DriverSettings.dwDeviceClass = USB_NO_INFO;
        DriverSettings.dwDeviceSubClass = USB_NO_INFO;
        DriverSettings.dwDeviceProtocol = USB_NO_INFO;
```

```
        DriverSettings.dwInterfaceClass = 0x03;     // HID
        DriverSettings.dwInterfaceSubClass = 0x01; // boot device
        DriverSettings.dwInterfaceProtocol = 0x02; // mouse

        fRet = (*pRegisterId)(gcszMouseDriverId);

        if(fRet)
        {
            fRet = (*pRegisterSettings)(szDriverLibFile,
                   gcszMouseDriverId, NULL, &DriverSettings);
            ...

        }
    }
}
...
```

The functions RegisterClientDriverId and RegisterClientSettings (called through the function pointers pRegisterId and pRegisterSettings) are used to write the actual registry entries. The function RegisterClientDriverId is used to write the client driver identifier string contained in the global variable gcszMouseDriverId. The function RegisterClientSettings writes the LoadClients registry keys as specified in USB_DRIVER_SETTINGS. Note that these registry entries are not being written directly through the use of Win32 *Reg* functions (RegCreateKeyEx, RegDeleteKey, RegCloseKey, and so on). Besides the fact that the RegisterClientSettings function saves you from writing the tedious code associated with making registry entries, it has the added advantage of providing a layer of abstraction for access to the registry. Microsoft may then modify the registry key structure for future USB drivers without requiring you to modify the existing USB driver code.

Providing Application Services

As mentioned earlier, the USB device driver model contains no provision to support an application interface. This would become a problem, for example, if your driver supported a USB modem because you would want to expose your driver's data through the standard Win32 COM port functions. The key to solving this problem is recognizing that all CE drivers are merely user mode DLLs and may therefore be accessed by applications in one of two ways.

One way is to expose your driver's custom application interface using the same mechanisms employed by the DLL modules of other driver models. The mechanism of the stream interface could be used to allow access by applications through the Win32 file I/O interface (CreateFile, WriteFile, ReadFile, and so on). Such access would require that your USB driver implement the required stream-interface entry points (XXX_Open, XXX_Write, XXX_Read, and so on) either in the same DLL or in a separate DLL. If implemented in a separate DLL, the stream-interface driver would use the LoadLibrary and GetProcAddress functions to obtain the address of the private functions that you define in your USB client driver for sending and receiving data between the stream-interface driver and the USB client driver.

The stream-interface entry points could also be implemented in the same DLL module used by the USB driver. This would require two sets of registry entries for each driver model—one for the USBD module to load the driver when the matching USB device was inserted, and the other to allow the Device Manager to load the driver on system startup (using the `HKEY_LOCAL_MACHINE\Drivers\BuiltIn` registry keys). The same DLL instance would be used in both cases, so your implementation would need to be aware of the status of the USB device and could not assume that the device was active simply because the driver was loaded. You would, of course, inherit the other technical requirements for writing a stream-interface driver, all of which must coexist with those of the USB driver.

Another method exists that would rely on the application to call `LoadLibrary` and `GetProcAddress` to obtain the address of each function defined for the USB driver application interface. Though this method seems comparable to that used by the USB driver when obtaining the address of functions in the USBD DLL module, the result is quite different. When `LoadLibrary` is called from an application, the USB driver DLL is mapped to the address space of the calling application, causing a separate instance (separate copy of the data sections) of the DLL to be loaded. Because the USB driver relies on the exported functions of the USBD DLL module, another instance of this DLL would also be mapped to the application's address space when the USB driver called `LoadLibrary`. This additional DLL instance would surely cause a failure because the USBD module, which utilizes a stream interface to be loaded and unloaded, would not have been properly initialized by the DM.

Note:
A two-part article titled Using COM for Device Driver Development in Windows CE v2.0 (Maillet 1998, 1999) addresses many of the issues caused by separate instances of a driver DLL through the use of shared data sections. We highly recommend this article for an innovative view of how a driver's application interface may be exposed.

NDIS Device Driver Model

The Network Device Interface Specification (NDIS) is perhaps one of Microsoft's oldest driver models, surviving the evolution of the Windows desktop from its earliest days. With its most recent revision (version 5.0), NDIS will continue to be supported in Windows 2000. This continued support is understandable because the network interface card (NIC) device is the basis of staying connected to the ubiquitous Internet and is generally one of the first peripherals that most platform designers (and users) consider when selecting from the broad array of interface options (IrDA, USB, PC card, RS-232, and so on) to include on a custom platform.

Windows CE provides support for a subset of the NDIS 4.0 standard and is perhaps the most complete of CE's support of various desktop device driver models. If you have existing NDIS source code, plan on using it as the basis of the your CE NDIS driver. Depending on the extent of the processor- and platform-specific code in your desktop NDIS driver, you may even wish to consider maintaining the same source code base for the CE driver by adding a CE target operating system to your build process. This decision will require that you determine which aspects of the NDIS 4.0 standard used by your driver are *not* supported in the target CE release being considered for either a custom or a standard platform.

In this section we will not describe how to write an NDIS driver. The NDIS driver model, often referred to as the NDIS wrapper, is quite extensive and provides a complete API to insulate the driver from any contact with the outside operating system. One could even say that a proper treatment of the subject would require a separate chapter dedicated to NDIS, possibly even a separate book. In any case, we will assume that you are already an NDIS driver expert and are more concerned with determining how the implementation of NDIS on CE is different from its desktop counterpart. To that end, we will focus on the architecture and required registry entries. For any other information relating to NDIS, refer to the CEPB online documentation (or Windows CE DDK online documentation).

NDIS Device Driver Model Architecture

The architecture of the NDIS driver model is analogous in many ways to the architecture of the USB driver model. Both architectures use a driver control program (DCP), implemented as a stream-interface driver, to administer their respective client drivers. The module `usbd.dll` administers USB client drivers, while the module `ndis.dll` administers NDIS miniport drivers. Both driver models provide a separate collection of functions abstracting the transfer of data and all physical access to the supported device. The USBD module provides a list of functions called the USB driver interface (USBDI), and the NDIS module provides an even more comprehensive list of functions collectively referred to as the NDIS wrapper.

Figure 7.9 contains a diagram that is borrowed directly from the USB Device Driver Model section (see Figure 7.8). Note that the NDIS driver model is implemented in the stream-interface driver `ndis.dll` and is responsible for the loading and unloading of its drivers (miniport drivers). If the miniport driver provides support for a PC card device, it must also be registered as a

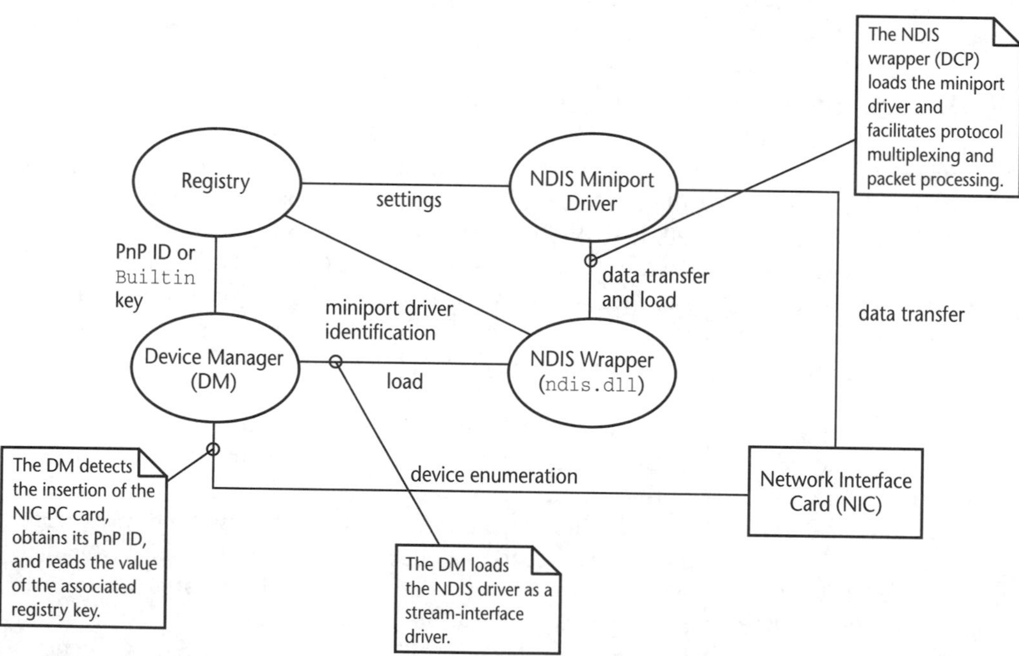

Figure 7.9 Collaboration diagram of the NDIS device driver architecture

stream-interface driver. If you were to examine the Device Manager (DM) registry entries for such a miniport, you would find that the `ndis.dll` module appears as the value of the `Dll` subkey. This means that when the PC card device is enumerated, the `ndis.dll` module is loaded (or reinitialized in the case of multiple PC cards) and is passed the registry key of the miniport driver in the `NDS_Init` entry point of `ndis.dll`. The name of the miniport driver is then extracted from the value of the `Miniport` subkey and is loaded by the NDIS module. The initialization sequence of the miniport driver conforms to the NDIS standard and performs any of the additional work needed to connect the miniport to the transport drivers (TCP/IP). If the NDIS module receives event notifications (power notifications) from the DM, they are mapped to the equivalent NDIS notifications and forwarded to the miniport driver. In the next section we will explore the registry entries required for drivers that support onboard or installable network adapters.

Automatic Loading

The registry entries required for NDIS drivers may be divided into two groups: those that represent attributes of the NDIS driver itself, and those that are used to load the NDIS driver. Listing 7.19 contains the registry entries for the sample NE2000 driver provided in the CEPB. Both groups of registry entries are represented.

Listing 7.19 Sample registry entries for an NE2000 LAN adapter

```
; The following registry entries are required for both an onboard and an
; installable NE2000 network adapter:

[HKEY_LOCAL_MACHINE\Comm\NE2000]
   "DisplayName"=LOC_FRIENDLYNE2000COMPAT
   "Group"="NDIS"
   "ImagePath"="ne2000.dll"

[HKEY_LOCAL_MACHINE\Comm\NE2000\Linkage]
   "Route"=multi_sz:"NE20001"

[HKEY_LOCAL_MACHINE\Comm\NE20001]
   "DisplayName"=LOC_FRIENDLYNE2000COMPAT
   "Group"="NDIS"
   "ImagePath"="ne2000.dll"

[HKEY_LOCAL_MACHINE\Comm\NE20001\Parms]
   "BusNumber"=dword:0
   "BusType"=dword:8
   "InterruptNumber"=dword:03
   "IoBaseAddress"=dword:0300
   "Transceiver"=dword:3
   "CardType"=dword:1

; The following registry entries are required for an onboard NE2000 network
adapter.
; This entry is generally placed in platform.reg:
```

```
[HKEY_LOCAL_MACHINE\Comm\Tcpip\Linkage]
    "Bind"=multi_sz:"ppp","ne2000"

; The following registry entries are required for a generic, installable
; (PCMCIA) NE2000 network adapter:

[HKEY_LOCAL_MACHINE\Drivers\PCMCIA\Detect\60]
    "Dll"="NE2000.DLL"
    "Entry"="DetectNE2000"

[HKEY_LOCAL_MACHINE\Drivers\PCMCIA\NE2000]
    "Dll"="ndis.dll"
    "Prefix"="NDS"
    "Miniport"="NE2000"
```

The first registry entry presented in Listing 7.19 exists under the `Comm` key and is required for all NDIS drivers. The `DisplayName` subkey contains the readable name of the driver. In this example a constant is used for localization of the string assigned to this subkey. The `Group` subkey is always assigned the string value *NDIS* to signify the driver model in use by the driver. The `ImagePath` subkey contains the path name for the driver DLL module, in this case `ne2000.dll`.

The next key, `Linkage`, also required for all NDIS drivers, contains a single subkey, `Route`, which contains the strings used to name each miniport instance. The miniport instance represents a given set of registry entries that characterize one potential configuration supported by the driver. Each miniport instance must have a key of the same name under the `HKEY_LOCAL_MACHINE\Comm` key. If your driver can support a variety of hardware configurations, each one should be represented with a separate miniport instance, assigned to the `Route` subkey. In this example only a single miniport instance is used, and it is named `NE20001`.

The `HKEY_LOCAL_MACHINE\Comm\NE20001` key contains another set of subkeys for the miniport instance `NE20001`, named in the `Route` subkey under the `Linkage` key. The subkeys `DisplayName`, `Group`, and `ImagePath` have already been discussed. The `Parms` key contains the device configuration values supported by this miniport instance. The subkeys that appear under the `Parms` key are not predefined and may be used as you see fit to describe the characteristics of the supported network adapter. The subkeys used in this example describe the hardware resources required and are named for the resources they describe.

The next group of entries are used to load the driver. Up to this point we have described only the driver and its configuration requirements. The `HKEY_LOCAL_MACHINE\Comm\Tcpip\Linkage` key is used only for drivers that support onboard devices and that must be loaded at system startup. The subkey `Bind` contains a list of strings, each of which refers to the name of a `HKEY_LOCAL_MACHINE\Comm` key corresponding to an NDIS driver that must be loaded and bound to the protocol stack.

If your supported network adapter is an installable device (PC card), you must use the driver loading mechanism defined for its associated bus technology. The registry entries in the example in Listing 7.19 will cause the NE2000 DLL module to be loaded each time a PC card device is inserted. The detection function in the NDIS driver will be called, and if the inserted device is supported, the name of the `HKEY_LOCAL_MACHINE\Drivers\PCMCIA` key is returned in the

DevKey parameter of the detection function. This key is then referenced and the driver named in the Dll subkey is loaded as a stream-interface driver.

Note that the HKEY_LOCAL_MACHINE\Drivers\PCMCIA\NE2000 key in Listing 7.19 contains a DLL module named ndis.dll, not the actual name of the NDIS driver. The ndis.dll module (the module implementing the NDIS wrapper and the NDIS driver model) exports the required stream-interface entry points and is loaded as the primary driver to support the inserted PC card device. The value of the Miniport subkey is then used to determine the name of the NDIS driver that must be loaded by the ndis.dll module. This is yet another example of how the stream-interface mechanism of the DM can be leveraged in the implementation of other driver models.

Building the Device Driver

At some point in the development process you will want to build your driver. The process you use will vary with the tool being used and the type of platform targeted for your device. If you are developing a driver for an installable device designed to work with standard CE platforms (Handheld PC, Palm-size PC, and Handheld PC Pro), you should use eMbedded Visual C++ (eMVC) or Windows CE Toolkit for Visual C++ (CETK) to build your driver. You could still use CEPB, but you would not have access to the platform SDK (PSDK) that is made available by Microsoft for each standard platform. The use of the PSDK is important because it provides an abstraction of the platform's capabilities in the context of header files and library modules that limit access only to those APIs available on the particular standard platform.

If your driver's supported device is intended only for a custom platform, you should use the CEPB to build your driver. The CEPB provides a graphical build environment that allows you to interactively configure and build a custom CE kernel. When building a driver, however, you must still produce certain files manually that will integrate the build of the driver into the overall build of the kernel.

In this section we will first list the steps required for building a driver that is to be included in the build of a CE kernel image for a custom platform. Next we will briefly discuss how the eMVC may be used to build drivers for installable devices designed to operate on standard CE platforms.

Building from the Command Line with the Platform Builder

Each step will focus on the files that must be manually modified to make your driver a part of the overall build of the CE kernel image when executed from the command line. We will not, however, discuss the many options available for customization and configuration of the CE kernel when you're using the CEPB. Refer to Chapter 3 for more information on these CEPB capabilities.

1. The first step in this process is to decide where in the CEPB source tree your driver's source code will be located. If your driver is platform or peripheral dependent (meaning that it provides a service requiring the presence of a certain feature built into the CPU or onboard peripheral), then your code will be located

under the PLATFORM directory tree. Otherwise it will be located under the PUBLIC directory tree.

If, for example, you were developing a driver named MYDRIVER for a custom platform, the source code would be located in the directory $(_PLATFORMROOT)\$(_TGTPLAT)\DRIVERS\MYDRIVER. If necessary, create the MYDRIVER subdirectory. The dollar signs appearing in the path name denote Windows NT environment variables that you create using the batch file wince.bat or during the installation of CEPB. Next, modify the Dirs file located in the $(_PLATFORMROOT)\$(_TGTPLAT)\DRIVERS directory, by adding the directory MYDRIVER (created in step 1) to the DIRS macro appearing in the Dirs file. Be certain to include a backslash at the end of the line if MYDRIVER is not the last directory name assigned to DIRS.

2. Copy the file makefile from any source directory under DRIVERS into the MYDRIVER subdirectory. You will rarely need to modify this file, so in most cases simply copying it is acceptable.

3. Create a file called Sources in the MYDRIVER subdirectory. This file must define a value for various macros that will be used by the CEPB build tool build.exe to control how the driver is built and where the resulting executable will appear. A sample Sources file for MYDRIVER appears in Listing 7.20.

Listing 7.20 Sample Sources file for the driver MYDRIVER

```
TARGETNAME=MYDRIVER
SOURCES= \
    API.cpp \
    IO.cpp
INCLUDES=..\..\inc; \
    $(_COMMONDDKROOT)\inc; \
    $(_COMMONOAKROOT)\inc
RELEASETYPE=PLATFORM
TARGETLIBS= \
   $(_COMMONSDKROOT)\lib\$(_CPUINDPATH)\coredll.lib
SOURCELIBS=
   $(_COMMONOAKROOT)\lib\$(_CPUINDPATH)\MyCompanyUtils.lib
TARGETTYPE=DYNLINK
DLLENTRY=MyDriverDllEntry
```

The TARGETNAME macro defines the root file name for the executable generated by the build process. The SOURCES macro lists the source files in the MYDRIVER subdirectory. The INCLUDES macro provides a list of the directories to search when locating include files referenced in the MYDRIVER source files. The macro RELEASETYPE determines the destination path name for the executable. The value PLATFORM for the RELEASETYPE macro is used for drivers designed to operate on custom platforms. It implies that the source resides in the $(_PLATFORMROOT)\$(_TGTPLAT)\DRIVERS directory and causes the executable to be copied into the $(_TARGETPLATROOT)\TARGET\$(_CPUINDPATH) directory. The macro TARGETLIBS refers to import or static libraries, which are generally provided by Microsoft as SDK components.

The macro SOURCELIBS refers only to static libraries that will be linked in their entirety. The linking process in which unresolved symbols are matched to an object module in the library file is not performed. The source library for the MDD layer of a layered device driver, for example, is a possible value for the SOURCELIBS macro.

The TARGETTYPE macro determines the form of the executable (EXE, DLL, static LIB.). The value DYNLINK for the TARGETTYPE macro in the MYDRIVER example (Listing 7.20) automatically generates both a DLL and an import library. The value for the DLLENTRY macro is the name of the function acting as the primary entry point of the MYDRIVER DLL and is applicable only if the TARGETTYPE macro equals DYNLINK. Many other options exist for the Sources file than what is listed here. Refer to the CEPB online documentation for a more comprehensive list.

4. To get the Romimage builder tool to include the MYDRIVER executable, the file platform.bib located in the $(_TARGETPLATROOT)\FILES directory must be modified. A sample modification of the platform.bib file appears in Listing 7.21.

Listing 7.21 Sample platform.bib entry for the driver MYDRIVER

```
. . .
    IF MYPLATFORM_NOMYDRIVER !
        mydriver.dll      $(_FLATRELEASEDIR)\mydriver.dll                    NK   SH
    ENDIF
. . .
```

In Listing 7.21, the file mydriver.dll will be included in the ROM image only if the environment variable MYPLATFORM_NOMYDRIVER is *not* defined. The syntax of this notation is unique to a build tool called Cefilter that preprocesses all BIB files, producing a single, combined BIB file: ce.bib. Only those lines in a BIB file where the conditional evaluates to TRUE will appear in ce.bib. The letters *NK,* which appear after the file name, refer to the memory area in the ROM image where MYDRIVER will be located. The file config.bib, located in the $(_TARGETPLATROOT)\FILES directory, defines the address range of the NK memory area, in addition to any other memory areas. These include memory areas that are predefined and those that are unique to your custom platform. The next pair of letters determines the file attributes of the mydriver.dll file in the CE file system. In this example the file attributes are S (for *system*) and H (for *hidden*).

5 To complete this step, you need to run the build in the MYDRIVER source directory. How this is accomplished depends on the organization of the overall build for your custom platform. For this example we have simply modified the batch file blddemo.bat located in $(_PROJECTOAKROOT)\MISC. These modifications appear in Listing 7.22.

Listing 7.22 Sample modifications to `blddemo.bat` for building `mydriver.dll`

```
. . .
    PUSHD %_PLATFORMROOT%\%_TGTPLAT%\DRIVERS\MYDRIVER
    BUILD -cfs
    if not exist build.err goto ELSE_10
           echo !!!! Build in %_PLATFORMROOT%\%_TGTPLAT%\DRIVERS\MYDRIVER had
errors.
        pause
    :ELSE_10
    POPD
. . .
```

6. Now you are ready to run the build and witness the effect of all the changes in the previous steps. You can accomplish this most easily through the CEPB IDE. You could also load a command shell with all of the many environment variables properly defined. Executing the batch file `wince.bat` with the CPU type, CPU, target operating system, target project, and target platform as parameters accomplishes this task. An easier method for defining the environment variables is simply to copy one of the icons appearing in the CEPB program group, modifying the parameter list as appropriate. In either case, at the command prompt type "BLDDEMO" as directed by `wince.bat`, and away you go! If everything goes well, a file containing the totality of your CE ROM image, called `nk.bin`, will be generated in either the `$(_FLATRELEASEDIR)` directory or the `.\PUBLIC\<Platform Name>\RELEASE\<CPU Family>_Release` directory, depending on whether the build is executed manually from the command shell or from the CEPB IDE. The file `nk.bin` may be uploaded to your target platform and subsequently started by the target's boot loader. Refer to Chapter 9 for more information on uploading and debugging device drivers.

Building with the Platform Builder IDE

Preparing to build your driver from the Platform Builder IDE requires far fewer steps than the command-line build described in the previous section. A command-line build requires you to modify various files (`Dirs`, `Sources`, `platform.bib`, and `blddemo.bat`) to control the build when executed from the command line. The CEPB IDE, however, can also be used to build your driver, while eliminating the manual modification of all but one file, `platform.bib`, described in step 4 of the previous section. The section titled Building a Device Driver for Debugging: Method 2 in Chapter 9 discusses how to use the CEPB IDE to set up a driver project to produce your driver's DLL module and include it in the build of the CE kernel image.

Building with eMbedded Visual C++

eMbedded Visual C++ (eMVC) or the Windows CE Toolkit for Visual C++ (CETK) may be used to build drivers for installable devices designed to support standard CE platforms. The process is identical to that for a standard CE DLL. You begin by defining a new project using the WCE Dynamic-Link Library Project Wizard. As a result, a dialog box appears, asking you to select the kind of DLL desired: **An empty Windows CE DLL Project**, **A simple Windows CE DLL project**, or **A DLL that exports some symbols**. Any of these options produces a DLL capable of acting as a driver for an installable device, including the stream-interface, NDIS, and USB drivers—basically any driver for a standard CE platform that occurs in the form of a DLL.

There will be some limitations on the features of the driver model you may implement. The reason for these limitations is that the CETK and eMVC should be used to build drivers only for standard CE platforms. This means that you would not be able to develop an IST for a stream-interface driver because you do not have access to the `oalintr.h` file, which defines the logical interrupt IDs returned by the platform ISR(s). You would, however, be able to develop code that processes an interrupt using the card services API (used to access PC card devices), or in the context of another driver model, such as the NDIS driver model. (The NDIS wrapper also uses card services to internally map an NDIS miniport driver's interrupt handler to the interrupt processing provided by the card services function `CardRequestIRQ`.) This is possible because the APIs themselves are using their own internal ISTs to map to a callback function passed in by your driver. The card services API `CardRequestIRQ` is one example of such an API.

One word of caution: If you develop your driver using the MFC library or any other library that requires the presence of an external DLL, you must be certain that this DLL is included in your final deliverable or is already present on the standard CE platform. One common symptom of failing to do this is that the driver silently refuses to load. If you're accustomed to programming applications for Windows desktop operating systems, you may also be accustomed to seeing a dialog box appear under such circumstances announcing that your application is missing a required DLL module, along with the name of the missing module. This dialog box does not appear with CE drivers, and the lack of reported error condition—either by the driver itself, which simply is never loaded, or by CE—can be the cause of much frustration. This is a less common problem when you're developing drivers for custom platforms because you may have been involved in formulating the build of the custom CE kernel to ensure that all required libraries were present.

Device Driver Installation

If you are developing a driver for an installable device on a standard CE platform, you have one extra task that you do not have on custom platforms. Namely, you must consider how your driver will be presented to the end user (downloaded or bundled with the installable device), and how it will be subsequently transferred to the user's standard CE device. In this section we will focus on the point in the installation process that begins after the end user has completed a preliminary installation of the driver to his or her PC's hard disk.

Application Manager

With the introduction of CE Services 2.2, a separate application for the end user's desktop PC was provided called the Application Manager. Its purpose is to support the installation of CE applications on standard platforms, but it works equally well for the installation of drivers. The applications (or drivers) are installed from the installation media to the hard disk of the desktop PC and later uploaded to the standard platform. The Application Manager then keeps track of the applications already installed on this particular device and maintains the application's files on the desktop PC for uninstallation from the standard platform and later reinstallation.

Perhaps the most important capability of the Application Manager, however, is its ability to identify the type of the standard platform and its associated CPU, and then match this information to the correct executable. This capability allows you to produce multiple builds of your driver, each targeted to a different standard platform. The Application Manager then does the work of identifying the configuration of the end user's particular standard platform and uploads only the executable that matches this configuration. This greatly simplifies the complexity of the installation program provided on the installation media for the driver, which must copy only the targeted executables to the end user's hard disk. It also relieves the end user from the error-prone process of visually identifying the configuration of his or her own standard platform by responding to an on-screen prompt that contains a long list of supported devices.

Note:
Experience has shown that you can save yourself many hours of manual setup if you begin developing the Application Manager INI and INF files (explored later in this discussion) early in your development schedule. It is not uncommon in driver development to occasionally require the hard reset and clearing of non-volatile RAM on the target platform. In this case the driver will require complete reinstallation, including the registry entries in the target platform's registry. Considering that such reinstallation is likely to be repeated many times throughout the development process, the Application Manager can become a valuable tool in automating the process for quick setup of target platforms used for driver development and testing.

Cabwiz.exe CAB Files

Cabinet (CAB) files have been used by Microsoft for years as a means of distributing software deliverables in one large compressed file. The CAB file structure has more recently been extended to support the distribution of ActiveX objects referenced by a Web page and includes the ability to deliver targeted ActiveX objects with separate executable images for each supported processor. Because this capability is quite close to the requirements for distributing software (both applications and drivers) on the many available configurations of CE devices, it is the file format supported by both the Application Manager and the `wceload.exe` installation utility (which runs directly on CE devices). In this section we will explore what you need to know to create the CAB file containing multiple copies of your driver executable, with each target compiled for a different processor.

The basis for the creation of a CAB file is the CAB Wizard (`cabwiz.exe`), and the method for communicating with the CAB Wizard is the INF file. If you are familiar with the creation of INF files for the installation of drivers on Windows desktops, the general syntax will seem familiar. We will not probe the details of all available INF entries, or *sections,* as they are referred to in the CEPB online documentation. Instead, we will define a common installation scenario and describe the details of each section and its associated labels. For a more comprehensive listing of all supported sections and labels, refer to the CEPB online documentation.

In this scenario we need to install an ATAPI (Advanced Technology Attachment Peripheral Interface) stream-interface driver with the file name `ls120.dll`. This driver provides support for LS-120 drives through an ATAPI PC card adapter. Because of limited resources, this driver is certified for operation on a limited number of CE platforms with certain target CPUs. So in this scenario, even though a build of the driver is provided for an SH4 processor, a Jupiter (Handheld PC Pro) standard platform with this same CPU will not be supported. A `readme.txt` file is provided and must be copied to the desktop window of the CE device, where it is most visible. Certain registry entries are required to ensure that the driver is automatically loaded when the supported PC card (ADPI [Analog & Digital Peripherals, Inc.] ATAPI PC card adapter) is inserted. Let's define the contents of a sample INF that will allow the CAB Wizard to produce the CAB files supporting these requirements.

All CAB files are separated into defined sections whose names are enclosed by square brackets. Each section generally contains a series of labels that are assigned numeric or string values (in quotation marks). The names of these sections and their associated labels are predefined and are documented in the CEPB online documentation. The sections and labels need not appear in any particular order, but they generally appear in the INF according to their similarity. The first group of sections (section group 1) consists of sections dedicated to identifying the target operating system and the string assignments that may be used in defining the values of other labels. The second group (section group 2), describes the type of support provided for standard CE platforms in terms of the platform name and CPU type, including the names of the executable images and data files associated with each. The third group (section group 3) defines the registry entries that will be automatically added to the platform's registry during installation of the CAB file.

Listing 7.23 contains an excerpt of the `ls120.inf` file that satisfies the requirements of our scenario for section group 1.

Listing 7.23 Sample CAB Wizard INF file: Section group 1

```
...

; ---------------------------------------------------------------------------

; Ls120.inf file used to generate the CAB file using the CAB Wizard
(cabwiz.exe).
; ---------------------------------------------------------------------------

[Version]
Signature = "$Windows NT$"
Provider = "ADPI"
CESignature = "$Windows CE$"

; This section contains the string assignments for setup information likely to
change
; between development environments.
[Strings]
SourceDirectory = "G:\Dev\LS120"

; This section is used for string substitution throughout this file.
[CEStrings]
AppName = "LS120 Driver"
InstallDir = %CE2%

...
```

The section [Version] contains two labels, Signature and CESignature, that are the same for all INF files. Simply copy these into your own driver's INF file. The Provider label contains your company name, which will be used as the first part of the name of the driver when it is combined with the value of label AppName in the [CEStrings] section. We use the [Strings] section to assign a character string value to a label that is used later in the INF file by placing the percent symbol ("%") before and after the label for the desired string. The label SourceDirectory contains the path of the root directory where the driver files are located and will need to be changed for your driver, generally to the project directory containing your driver's source code.

The [CEStrings] section, unlike the [Strings] section, must contain two particular labels. One required label is AppName, which contains the name of the application or driver contained in the CAB files. This label will be prefixed by the Provider string and displayed by the Application Manager to the end user in a list box of available applications for devices that conform to the configurations specified later in the INF file. In our example, the rather mundane but descriptive name *LS120 Driver* is used.

The other label required in the [CEStrings] section is InstallDir. It contains the name of the primary directory on the target standard platform where the executable image is located. This label would be used later as %InstallDir% to specify the destination of individual files in the CAB file, usually acting as the prefix to a subdirectory appropriate for the particular file.

Listing 7.24 contains an example of what is perhaps the most important group of sections for the installation of a device driver.

Listing 7.24 Sample CAB Wizard INF file: Section group 2

```
...

; This section provides platform-specific information that identifies the target
; supported by the executable images contained in each CAB file.
[CEDevice]
UnsupportedPlatforms = "Palm PC"
VersionMin           = 2.0
VersionMax           = 2.11

[CEDevice.SH3]
ProcessorType           = 10003         ;HITACHI_SH3
UnsupportedPlatforms    = "Jupiter"

[CEDevice.SH4]
ProcessorType           = 10005         ;HITACHI_SH4
UnsupportedPlatforms    = "Jupiter"

[CEDevice.MIPS]
ProcessorType           = 4000      ; MIPS_R4000
UnsupportedPlatforms    = "Jupiter"

[CEDevice.ARM]
ProcessorType           = 2577          ;STRONGARM
VersionMin              = 2.11
VersionMax              = 2.11
UnsupportedPlatforms    = "HPC"

...
```

The [CEDevice] section is used to define the common aspects of all supported or unsupported standard platforms. The label UnsupportedPlatforms in Listing 7.24 contains the name of the standard platform, *Palm PC,* which is not supported in any of the target builds. This value is not associated with any particular target CPU, so it refers to all platforms designated as *Palm PC,* regardless of the CPU type of that platform. Subsequent [CEDevice.<name of the supported CPU>] sections that contain the name of the supported CPU after the period may also contain the label UnsupportedPlatforms. This use of the UnsupportedPlatforms label refers only to the platform of the designated type, with the CPU type as named after the period in the section name. We will see an example of this use of the UnsupportedPlatforms label shortly.

Only certain reserved values may be assigned to the UnsupportedPlatforms label. Each defined value describes a different standard CE platform; the values are listed in Table 7.4. As more standard platforms appear on the scene, Microsoft will undoubtedly update this list.

The next two labels, VersionMin and VersionMax, define the versions of CE that, by default, are supported by targeted builds described in subsequent sections. So in Listing 7.24 the LS-120 driver supports versions 2.0 through 2.11 (2.0, 2.1, and 2.11), unless otherwise specified for a particular CPU in a subsequent section.

The next few sections appear with the name of the CPU after the period. Each of these sections acts as a CPU-specific description of the configuration more generally described in section [CEDevice] (without the CPU name appended). The name of the CPU appearing after the period in the section name may be whatever you deem appropriate. The same name, however, must be used consistently after the period in the names of other sections, as we will soon see. The ProcessorType label is where the actual processor type is associated with your defined processor name appearing after the period in the section name. These numeric values are defined in the header file winnt.h located in the .\VC98\INCLUDE\ directory and are provided in Table 7.5 for reference.

In the example in Listing 7.24, four processor-specific sections are defined. The first one—[CEDevice.SH3]—includes a ProcessorType label and is assigned the numeric value defined for the Hitachi SH3 processor. The *SH3* suffix appended to *CEDevice* will be used again when we

Table 7.4 Standard Platform Identifiers Used in the UnsupportedPlatforms Label

Standard Platform Description	Reserved String Assigned to UnsupportedPlatforms (CAB Wizard INF File)	Applicable CE Version
Handheld PC running Windows CE 1.0	Not supported by Application Manager	Not supported by Application Manager
Handheld PC running Windows CE 2.0	"HPC"	2.0
Handheld PC running Microsoft Windows CE, Handheld PC Pro, version 3.0	"Jupiter"	2.11
Palm-size PC, monochrome	"Palm PC"	2.1
Palm-size PC, color	"Palm PC"	2.11

Table 7.5 Processor IDs Used in the `ProcessorType` Label

Processor Description	Numeric Identifier
Hitachi SH3	10003
Hitachi SH3E	10004
Hitachi SH4	10005
Motorola 821	821
Generic SHx (SH3)	103
Generic SHx (SH4)	104
StrongARM	2577
ARM 720	1824
ARM 820	2080
ARM 920	2336
ARM 7TDMI	70001
MIPS R4000 (including R4101 and R3910)	4000

need to describe a particular CAB file as processor specific. The `UnsupportedPlatforms` label indicates that Jupiter platforms (Handheld PC Pro devices) containing an SH3 processor are not supported. This label effectively provides a processor-specific addition to the list of unsupported platforms that first appeared in the `[CEDevice]` section. Thus far, we have said that we do not support all Palm-size PC devices or Jupiter devices with an SH3 processor. With regard to the SH3 processor, this statement implies that the only supported platform is the Handheld PC.

The processor-specific sections continue until we reach the section `[CEDevice.ARM]`, which defines the processor associated with the suffix *ARM,* appearing after the period. The labels `VersionMin` and `VersionMax` are included to indicate that the only version of CE supported for this particular processor is version 2.11. This provides additional restrictions beyond those defined in the non-processor-specific section, `[CEDevice]`. The `UnsupportedPlatforms` label is used to indicated that in addition to the Palm-size PC platform specified in the `[CEDevice]` section, Handheld PC platforms with StrongARM processors are also not supported. Effectively, if the platform has a StrongARM processor, it is supported only if it is a Handheld PC Pro device running CE version 2.11. The fact that the `VersionMax` and `VersionMin` labels are identical indicates that only CE version 2.11 is supported.

The last group of sections, presented in Listing 7.25, provides the details on the files to be installed on the target standard platform. It is important to be aware that in this section group, more than any of the others, the definitions of particular labels can be nested. That is, the value of a particular label can be used in the selection of another label, whose value in turn can cause the selection of yet another label.

Listing 7.25 Sample CAB Wizard INF file: Section group 3

```
...

[DefaultInstall]
AddReg=LS120RegistryEntries.All
Copyfiles=Files.Readme, Files.Driver

[Files.Readme]
Readme.txt,,,0x00000001

[Files.Driver]
LS120.dll,,,0x20000001

[SourceDisksFiles]
Readme.txt = 1
LS120.dll = 2

[SourceDisksNames]
1 = ,"Readme.txt Last Minute Updates",,"%SourceDirectory%"

[SourceDisksNames.SH3]
2 = ,"SH3 LS120 Driver Files",,"%SourceDirectory%\WCESH3Rel"

[SourceDisksNames.SH4]
2 = ,"SH4 LS120 Driver Files",,"%SourceDirectory%"\WCESH4Rel"

[SourceDisksNames.ARM]
2 = ,"ARM LS120 Driver Files",,"%SourceDirectory%"\WCEARMRel"

[SourceDisksNames.MIPS]
2 = ,"MIPS LS120 Driver Files",,"%SourceDirectory%"\WCEMIPSRel"

[DestinationDirs]
Files.Driver = 0,%CE2%
Files.Readme = 0,%CE3%

; This section updates the target device registry with the following values.
[LS120RegistryEntries.All]
HKLM,Drivers\PCMCIA\Detect\15,Dll,0x00000000,"LS120.DLL"
HKLM,Drivers\PCMCIA\Detect\15,Entry,0x00000000,"DetectATADisk"
HKLM,Drivers\PCMCIA\LS120,Dll,0x00000000,"LS120.DLL"
HKLM,Drivers\PCMCIA\LS120,Prefix,0x00000000,"DSK"
HKLM,Drivers\PCMCIA\LS120,Ioctl,0x00010001,4
HKLM,Drivers\PCMCIA\LS120,FSD,0x00000000,"FATFS.DLL"

...
```

The first section appearing in Listing 7.25 is `[DefaultInstall]`. This is the section where the files to be installed and their locations on the desktop PC, including the associated registry entries, are defined. The value of the label `AddReg` (`LS120RegistryEntries.All`) defines the name of the section that contains the registry entries added to the target platform's registry during the installation process. The value of the subsequent label, `CopyFiles`, defines the names of the sections that contain the files to be installed onto the target platform, in this case `Files.Readme` and `Files.Driver`.

It would also have been possible for the `[DefaultInstall]` section name to be specified with one of the processor-specific suffixes defined in section group 2 of Listing 7.24, as in `[DefaultInstall.SH3]`. This would have allowed the definition of separate labels for each processor type, causing a different set of registry entries and files to be copied for each target platform. In the example in Listing 7.25, we accomplish the same objective using the processor-specific suffix in the `[SourceDisksFiles]` section instead. This section will be explored in more detail shortly.

The next two sections—`[Files.Readme]` and `[Files.Driver]`—define the names of the files on the desktop PC and the corresponding names of the target platform files. `Readme.txt` is a file that is copied to the target platform without being renamed (because the second parameter, after the first comma, is blank) and produces an end user warning if it is skipped. The value of `0x00000001` causes this warning and is documented along with all other defined flags in the CEPB online documentation section titled Creating an INF File for the CAB Wizard. The file `ls120.dll`, as named in the `[Files.Driver]` section, is also copied to the target without being renamed. The flag value of `0x20000001` consists of two OR'd values: `0x20000000` and `0x00000001`. The latter value we just discussed; the former value indicates that the file should not be copied if the target platform contains a file of the same name, but with a newer date.

The `[SourceDisksFiles]` section associates the file names specified in the previous sections with the location on the development workstation's hard disk and is used by the CAB Wizard to locate the files as they are compressed and added to the CAB file. Each file to be installed on the target platform is named in this section as a label and is equated to one of the numeric values defined in the next section.

The `[SourceDisksNames]` section defines each of the numeric values used in the previous section in terms of a textual description of the files and their location in the directory `%SourceDirectory%` named at the end of the label value. The first section name, `[SourceDisksNames]`, does not contain a processor-specific suffix (e.g., *SH3*) and is therefore the same for all processor types. The next sections, `[SourceDisksNames.<processor-specific suffix>]`, appear once for each processor-specific suffix previously defined in Listing 7.24 and define the location of the file and its textual description for each particular processor. These sections allow you to build targeted versions of your driver and locate each executable image in a different subdirectory. The processor-specific information is stored in each CAB file generated by the CAB Wizard and will be accessed by the Application Manager in determining which CAB file should be decompressed and copied to the matching target platform.

The `[DestinationDirs]` section defines the location of the files contained in each section referenced in the `CopyFiles` label at the top of Listing 7.25. The files associated with the `Files.Driver` label (referring to the previous section of the same name) are located on the target platform in the directory associated with the reserved string *%CE2%* (`\WINDOWS`). A complete list of all reserved strings used for directory names is contained in the Creating an INF File for the CAB Wizard section of the CEPB online documentation. The files associated with the `Files.Readme` label are located in the `%CE3%` directory `\WINDOWS\DESKTOP`.

The next section, `[LS120RegistryEntries.All]`, first appeared as a value for the `AddReg` label under the `[DefaultInstall]` section. It contains a list of the registry entries to be added to the registry on the target platform. Rather than containing labels, this section has just a list of all required registry entries, formatted as registry_root_string, subkey, [<value_name>], flags, value[,<value>]. The first registry entry, for example, occurs under the HKEY_LOCAL_MACHINE root key (abbreviated *HKLM* in Listing 7.25) and uses a key name of Drivers\PCMCIA\Detect\15, with a subkey of Dll. The value associated with the subkey is ls120.dll and contains the name of the driver executable image in our example. The value of flags in the next four entries is 0x00000000 to specify a registry value of type REG_SZ. The value of flags in the fifth entry is 0x00010001, which specifies a registry value of type REG_DWORD.

After you have completed the development of your INF file, you will still need to run the CAB Wizard (cabwiz.exe) to generate the CAB files. The command-line syntax for cabwiz.exe is

```
cabwiz.exe "inf_file" [/dest <dest_directory>] [/err <error_file>] [/cpu
<cpu_type> [<cpu_type>]]
```

In our sample INF file, the following command line was used:

```
"G:\Tools\Windows CE Tools\WCE200\MS HPC\support\appinst\bin\Cabwiz.exe"
"G:\dev\LS120\LS120.inf" /dest "G:\dev\LS120" /cpu SH3 SH4 MIPS ARM
```

Note that each processor-specific suffix defined in the INF file is specified at the end of the command line. The names of the CPUs used here (SH3, SH4, MIPS, and ARM) are consistent with the names defined in Listing 7.24, and none are reserved names of any particular syntax. The CPU type of SH3 at the end of the command line could just as easily have been MYPLATFORM_SH3, as long as it was defined as such with a section name of [CEDevice.MYPLATFORM_SH3].

In this example, four separate CAB files are generated with the naming convention LS120.<processor-specific suffix>.CAB. The name *LS120* is automatically selected by the CAB Wizard to match the name of the INF file. The four files generated are therefore ls120.sh3.cab, ls120.sh4.cab, ls120.mips.cab, and ls120.arm.cab.

Now that the processor- and platform-specific CAB files have been generated by the CAB Wizard, the next step is to upload them to the target platform. A variety of methods for uploading are possible. The method requiring the least development effort requires the end user to drag the icon of the CAB files already installed on his or her desktop PC's hard disk to the Explorer window displaying the file system of the user's standard platform. You could also automate the installation from a Web page, executing the target platform installation program wceload.exe from within the HTML source. The most common method, however, is to register your CAB files with the Application Manager provided in CE Services 2.2 and ActiveSync. Doing so allows you to use the features automatically provided with the Application Manager and described earlier in the Application Manager section of this chapter. In the next section we will explore how this is accomplished.

Ceappmgr.exe INI Files

To register your CAB files, you must use a program called ceappmgr.exe. The command-line syntax for ceappmgr.exe is

```
CEAppMgr.exe [/report] "<CEAppMgr_ini_filename>" ["<CEAppMgr_ini_filename>"]
```

In our sample INF file, the following command line was used:

```
"D:\Program Files\Windows CE Services\CeAppMgr.exe" /report
"G:\Dev\LS120\setup.ini"
```

The `ceappmgr.exe` program would usually be run from within an installation program located on the installation media downloaded by the end user or provided with the end user's newly purchased device. The program is run after you have copied the CAB files to the end user's hard disk, generally under the `.\WINDOWS CE SERVICES\{<Driver Name>|<Company Name>}` directory for CE Services 2.2 or the `.\MICROSOFT ACTIVESYNC\{<Driver Name>|<Company Name>}` directory for ActiveSync, where the *{<Driver Name>|<Company Name>}* subdirectory represents a meaningful name associated with your driver. The `/report` parameter is not used in the execution of this program from within an end user installation program; it is used only when you're diagnosing problems in the registration of your CAB files by `ceappmgr.exe`.

Listing 7.26 contains a sample INI file for registering the CAB files generated by the sample INF file presented in the previous section. The first section, `[CEAppManager]`, contains two labels. `Version` is assigned a value representing the version of the Application Manager that this INI file supports. `Component` is assigned the name of the section associated with the driver to be installed. In our example, this section name is *LS120Driver.*

The section name `[LS120Driver]` contains the labels that describe how the driver should be displayed to the end user in the Application Manager's list of registered applications, and the names of the CAB files to be registered. The label `IconFile` contains the file name `ls120.ico`, which will be used as the icon representing the driver in the Application Manager's application list. The label `IconIndex` identifies which icon to use in a resource file containing multiple icons. In our example, this value is zero because the file name defined by the `IconFile` label contains only one icon. The `Description` label contains the text string displayed in the application list. The `CabFiles` label contains the names of the CAB files generated by the `cabwiz.exe` program and its INF file, described in the previous section.

Listing 7.26 Sample Application Manager (`ceappmgr.exe`) INI file

```
[CEAppManager]
Version=1.0
Component=LS120Driver

[LS120Driver]
IconFile = LS120.ICO
IconIndex = 0
Description  = ADPI LS120 driver
CabFiles=LS120.SH3.CAB,LS120.SH4.CAB,LS120.ARM.CAB,LS120.MIPS.CAB
```

User Requested

Another option in the installation of your driver on both standard and custom platforms is to let the Device Manager perform the installation. This will work only if the driver has already been copied to the desired directory on the target device. It could perhaps be of use as a backup installation option, in the event your driver becomes separated from the installation application and is copied by the end user to another device. This type of installation would allow the end user to type the name of the driver when prompted by the DM (or for that matter any other driver control program) for the name of a driver to support the recently enumerated device.

To allow the DM to install the driver, you must export the function `Install_Driver` in your driver's DLL. Currently this function is called only by the DM, which implies that only stream-interface drivers and NDIS drivers (both loaded by the DM) may be installed in this manner. The `Install_Driver` function must make any additional files required and create any needed registry entries. If a `TRUE` value is returned, the DM re-enumerates the device, looking for a matching driver. At this point your driver would be loaded because of the registry entries made by the `Install_Driver` function that now associate this driver with the enumerated device.

Listing 7.27 contains an excerpt of the `wince.c` `Install_Driver` code provided in the CEPB sample NE2000 driver (located in the `.\PUBLIC\COMMON\OAK\DRIVERS\NETCARD\NE2000` directory).

Listing 7.27 Sample implementation of the `Install_Driver` function

```
LPWSTR
Install_Driver(
    LPWSTR lpPnpId,
    LPWSTR lpRegPath,
    DWORD  cRegPathSize
    )
{
    ...

    //
    // Format RegPath as "Drivers\\PCMCIA\\<PnpId>".
    //
    wcscpy(lpRegPath, (TEXT("Drivers\\PCMCIA\\")));
    wcscat(lpRegPath, lpPnpId);

    if (!AddKeyValues(lpRegPath, PcmKeyValues)) {
        goto wid_fail1;
    }

    for (i = 0; i < (sizeof(KeyNames)/sizeof(LPWSTR)); i++) {
        if (!AddKeyValues(KeyNames[i], Values[i])) {
            goto wid_fail;
        }
    }

    ...

    //
    // Return "Drivers\\PCMCIA\\NE2000".
    //
    wcscpy(lpRegPath, KeyNames[0]);
    return lpRegPath;

    ...

}
```

The parameter `lpPnpId` contains the Plug and Play (PnP) ID extracted from the Card Information Structure (within PC cards only) by the DM. The first few lines of code append this PnP ID to the registry key that will be written to the registry of the target platform later in the code. This key will associate the driver with this specific device by its PnP ID and allow automatic installation with no end user prompts on the next power cycle or insertion of the device. This particular sample driver also provides a detection function (not depicted in Listing 7.27) to allow the driver to be loaded whenever a device is detected that does not have a specific registry entry associated with its PnP ID. This function would no longer be called for this particular device after successful execution of `Install_Driver`.

The `for` loop that comes next systematically writes all other required registry keys hard-coded in the `KeyNames` global variable, along with the values hard-coded in the `Values` global variable, to the target platform's registry. If this process is completed successfully, the more generic registry key referencing this driver is returned instead of the PnP ID key, even though they both contain the same values.

Keep in mind that the detection function of a class driver (stream-interface driver) is called before the `Install_Driver` function can be called. So if you copy your driver to the target platform expecting to see a dialog box that will allow you to type the name of your driver, it may not appear. Such a scenario would be possible if your device were recognized by a class driver that then returned `TRUE` when its detection function was called to indicate that it would support your device. The `TRUE` value would prevent the DM from displaying the dialog box, which would be displayed only after the registry was scanned for a matching PnP ID key and each registered detection function was called and returned `FALSE` (indicating that the device is not supported). Detection functions are discussed in the Stream-Interface Device Driver Model section earlier in this chapter.

Summary

In this chapter we covered four of the most frequently used CE device driver models. First we discovered that the stream-interface device driver model is quite generic and can be extended to support any device that can be abstracted to the Win32 file I/O application interface. Then, in the Native Device Driver Model section, we saw that native drivers are class specific and have a layered architecture. By using one of the sample native drivers provided in the CEPB, we need only modify the platform device driver (PDD) layer to support our custom device. The USB device driver model was discussed next, and we discovered that, unlike the other driver models, it does not directly support an application interface. You may implement your USB client drivers to include the implementation of the stream interface—assuming, that is, that your application interface may be abstracted as a file I/O interface. Finally, we briefly examined the NDIS device driver model that exists as a close approximation to the same driver model on Windows desktop operating systems.

We also discussed how to build your driver using the `Sources` file. This file is automatically included by a generic makefile in the CEPB and may be used to define certain macros that control the make process. We also learned that for standard platforms, the CETK or eMVC may be used to build your driver.

In the final section of this chapter we discussed the requirements for installing your driver on both custom and standard platforms. We also expended considerable effort probing the benefits of the Application Manager to achieve a target independent installation. Through the use of the Application Manager, we are able to upload only the driver that matches the end user's standard platform configuration, allowing the use of a single CAB file containing multiple target builds.

8 Writing Device Drivers: Implementation Practices

The central focus of most drivers is to access their supported devices. In CE you cannot simply de-reference the port addresses or memory-mapped I/O (input/output) regions without first taking certain steps. CE is a protected-mode operating system; consequently, you must first map the physical memory to the address space of your driver. Certain functions may be called to map a virtual memory address to the desired physical address, with caching disabled.

Likewise, if you need to receive an interrupt from your device, you cannot simply install your interrupt vector or ISR (interrupt service routine) into the area of memory reserved by your processor for such functions. You must call certain functions that register a Win32 event object with a logical interrupt ID (associated with the physical interrupt). This event object is then signaled when the interrupt is detected by the CE kernel, allowing your driver to block on the event until an interrupt is ready for processing.

This chapter will focus on how the physical resources of your device, of the kind just described, may be accessed. We will also discuss other development practices common to CE driver development to equip you for what may lie ahead in your own driver development. An example of many of these practices can be found in the source code for the Driver Mapper debugging tool, which is presented in Chapter 9.

What you get from this chapter will depend in large part on your understanding of the material presented in Chapters 6 and 7, so if you have not yet read these chapters, you may want to do so now before you jump into this one.

Processing Interrupts

If you can remember back to the days of DOS device drivers, you might remember how the interrupt from the device was hooked by direct modification of an entry in an interrupt vector table. Your code was the first to run after the device interrupt, and you were responsible for maintaining the state of the CPU at the time of the interrupt by restoring any registers to their original values before returning from the interrupt. You were also responsible for chaining to the other interrupt handlers that might be present when your interrupt handler was installed. All of this changed when protected-mode operating systems, such as Windows CE, appeared on the scene.

CE processes all incoming interrupts in its exception handler, ultimately activating an interrupt service thread (IST) that resides in your driver. We will discuss how to implement an IST a little later, but for now let's explore the flow of control from the exception handler in kernel mode on up to your driver's IST running in user mode. Figure 8.1 is a sequence diagram that traces the flow of control from the occurrence of an interrupt to the IST in your device driver.

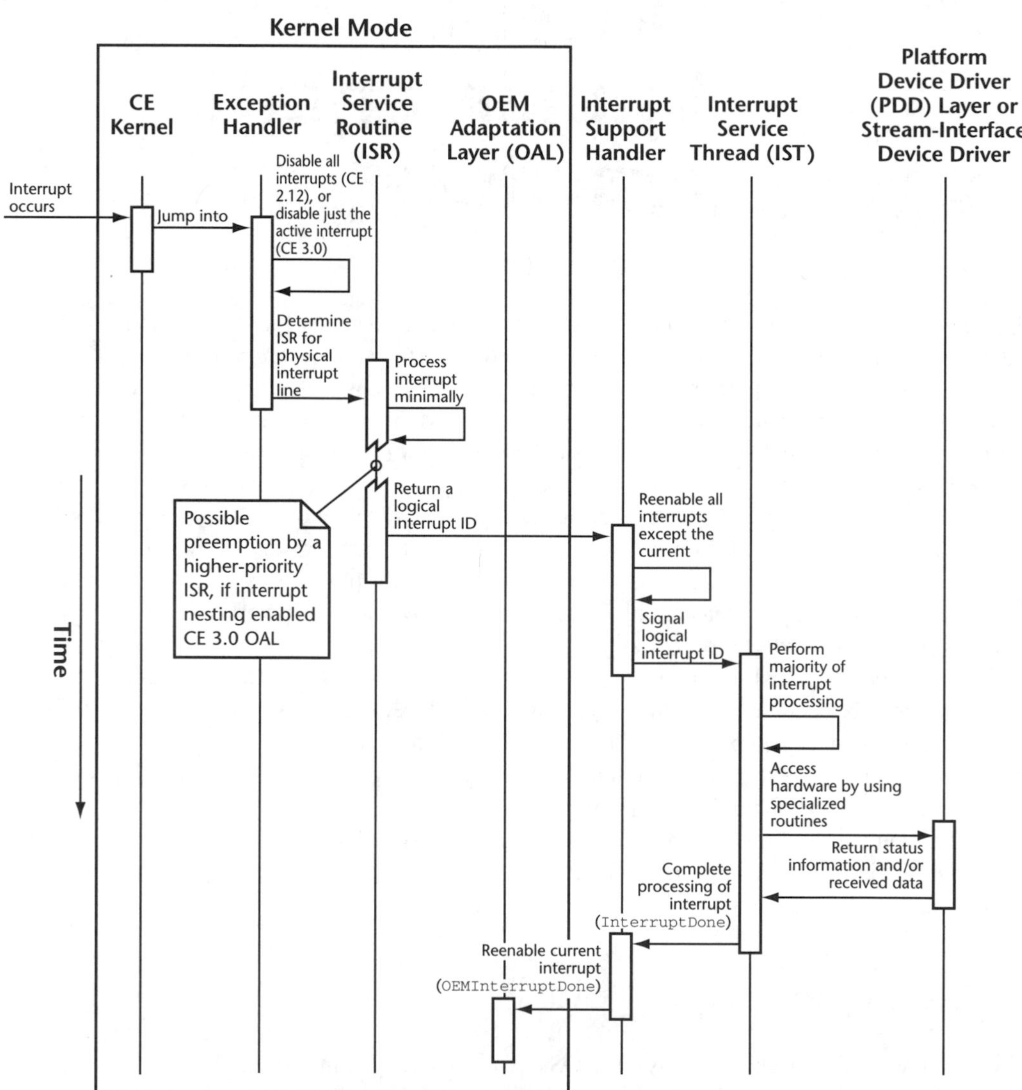

Figure 8.1 Sequence diagram of an interrupt in Windows CE

The interrupt occurs in the device, which causes the Windows CE exception handler (a module supplied only by Microsoft) to be activated. The exception handler then determines the address of the ISR associated with the physical interrupt line and jumps to this code. Interrupts in the CE 2.12 kernel are disabled at this point, so it is important for the ISR to be as simple as possible to minimize latency. With the exception of the currently active interrupt, all interrupts in the CE 3.0 kernel, however, are still enabled, thus allowing interrupt processing to be *nested.* By nesting interrupts, CE 3.0 provides a more deterministic interrupt latency that does not vary with the duration of ISR processing.

Note:
In actuality, whether interrupts are reenabled in an ISR depends on how the OAL was written for your particular platform. OAL developers can configure interrupt processing in the kernel so that ISR processing cannot be preempted (also referred to as *nested*), allowing interrupts to be processed in the same manner as in the CE 2.12 kernel.

The objective of an ISR in CE is to return a logical interrupt ID. For ISRs associated with multiple physical interrupts, it is also necessary to identify which physical interrupt occurred and return the associated logical interrupt ID. The values of the logical IDs are contained in the OAL header file `oalintr.h`, located in the `.\PLATFORM\<Platform Name>\INC` directory. We will mention this file again when we discuss how to develop an IST, in the next section. For more information on ISR development, refer to Chapter 5.

Once the ISR has returned the logical ID, the interrupt support handler (analogous to the exception handler in its association of physical interrupts with ISRs) must associate the logical ID with a particular IST and its event object. The event object is used by the interrupt support handler to signal the IST running in user mode. In CE 2.12, it is now safe for the kernel mode portion of the interrupt processing to accept other interrupts. All interrupts, *except the particular interrupt that just caused the IST to be signaled* (the device interrupt itself), are then reenabled. Up to this point in CE 2.12, the overall system was subject to interrupt latency. Now, however, only the device interrupt continues to be vulnerable to latency.

The flow of control for interrupt processing in CE 3.0 ISRs is basically the same, with one notable exception: In CE 3.0, interrupts are reenabled in the exception handler *before* the ISR is called. This means that the ISR may be preempted by another, higher-priority interrupt and its associated ISR. This potential preemption is noted in Figure 8.1 as a break in the activation rectangle of the ISR.

Once the IST is scheduled by the CE kernel, the real work of servicing the interrupt begins. The IST is where data is retrieved from and written to the device, advancing any internal pointers that track the accumulation of data in your driver's internal buffers. You can also signal other drivers' threads that might be awaiting the arrival of new data, so that they may return the data to their calling application. If your driver was designed according to the PDD and MDD layering model presented in the Native Device Driver Model section of Chapter 7, the IST would reside in the MDD layer and would call upon predefined routines in the PDD layer for hardware access.

As depicted in Figure 8.1, when the IST is finished servicing the interrupt, it calls the `InterruptDone` function to notify the interrupt support handler that the processing of the interrupt has been completed. This notification causes the device interrupt to be reenabled (in both CE 2.12 and CE 3.0 kernels), allowing another interrupt from this device to be processed. Up to this point the IST could not be reentered if the device generated an interrupt while the previous one was still being processed.

The Interrupt Service Thread

Now that we have described how ISTs work, in this section we will describe how to develop IST code. ISTs are the mechanism provided by Windows CE to directly associate your driver code with a device's interrupt. The IST exists as a standard, user mode, Win32 thread and is generally created by your driver code during its initialization (by `XXX_Init` for a stream-interface driver) or when the device is opened by an application (by `XXX_Open` for a stream-interface driver). ISTs differ from Windows CE interrupt service routines (ISRs, described more fully in Chapter 5) in that the job of the ISR is to identify the device's interrupt by returning a predefined logical ID (contained in `oalintr.h`), whereas the IST does all the work to service the device, retrieving and writing data as needed.

Note:
Let's consider where ISTs are commonly used in CE driver development. If you are developing a driver that employs a layered design, as is true for most native drivers, chances are that the IST exists in the MDD layer. In this case, the device-specific code you're writing in the PDD layer will provide access to the device hardware that the IST in the MDD layer will call to retrieve and send data. If you are writing a driver based on a non-stream-interface driver model, such as the NDIS driver model, or a driver that uses a CE-supported data bus, such as PC card and USB, you may need to use the APIs defined in the driver model as the means for being notified of the device interrupt, or any other kind of device-related event for that matter. ISTs are most applicable when you're developing a monolithic, stream-interface driver. Keep this in mind as we jump into the details of some sample source for a typical IST.

Listing 8.1 presents the source code for an IST called `MyDeviceFunctionIST`. This function acts as the thread start routine in a prior call to the Win32 function `CreateThread`.

Listing 8.1 Sample IST for the logical interrupt `SYSINTR_MYDEVICE_FUNCTION1`

```
// ----------------------------------------------------------------------
// This function provides a sample implementation of an interrupt service
// thread for the logical interrupt ID SYSINTR_MYDEVICE_FUNCTION1. Assume
// that this function is initially activated by a call to CreateThread from
// the main function of MyDriver.
// ----------------------------------------------------------------------
DWORD MyDeviceFunctionIST(LPVOID pVarg)
{
```

```
    HANDLE hevInterrupt;  // event signaling a received interrupt
    // Begin by elevating the priority of this thread to be
    // certain that it preempts the execution of application
    // threads.
    SetThreadPriority(GetCurrentThread(), THREAD_PRIORITY_HIGHEST);

    // Create an unnamed event for use by the interrupt support
    // handler to signal this thread that an interrupt has been received.
    if ((hevInterrupt = CreateEvent(NULL, FALSE, FALSE, NULL)) == NULL)
    {
        return (ERROR_INVALID_HANDLE);
    }

    // Inform the interrupt support handler of the event handle
    // associated with the logical interrupt ID SYSINTR_MYDEVICE_FUNCTION1.
    if ( !InterruptInitialize(SYSINTR_MYDEVICE_FUNCTION1, hevInterrupt, NULL,
                              0))
    {
        return (ERROR_GEN_FAILURE);
    }

    // Remain in this loop indefinitely, and assume that this driver will
    // always be loaded.
    while (TRUE)
    {
        // Wait for the interrupt support handler to indicate that an
        // interrupt has been received by the ISR.
        WaitForSingleObject(hevInterrupt, INFINITE);

        // We are now ready to access Function1 of MyDevice. The next few
        // lines of code, for example, might read MyDevice registers or
        // data from a predefined port address.
        .
        .
        .
        // All processing related to this interrupt is complete.  Inform
        // the interrupt support handler so that the physical interrupt
        // associated with the logical interrupt ID will be reenabled.
        InterruptDone(SYSINTR_MYDEVICE_FUNCTION1);
    }

    return (ERROR_SUCCESS);
}
```

We begin by setting the thread priority to `THREAD_PRIORITY_HIGHEST` through a call to `SetThreadPriority`. Calling this function allows the thread to preempt most running application threads, reducing the overall latency in servicing the device. Keep in mind that if other application threads or ISTs are running at the same priority, you must wait until their quantum (time slice) has expired or they are blocked while awaiting the availability of a system resource.

When the IST's quantum has expired, it may then be preempted to allow other threads at the same priority to run. To avoid this preemption, CE 2.1x allows you to set the thread priority to `THREAD_PRIORITY_TIME_CRITICAL`. This setting allows the thread to run to completion, when it yields control through a blocking call, as in the call to `WaitForSingleObject` used in waiting for the next interrupt. The downside of this approach is that it increases the overall latency of other ISTs in the system, so use this capability with the utmost care.

In CE 3.0, the 8 priority levels provided in CE 2.12 were expanded to include an additional 247 priority levels. Together, all these levels provide a much finer degree of control when you're assigning priorities to ISTs, allowing you to avoid the use of a run-to-completion thread priority (as in CE 2.12), which affects overall IST latency. Priority levels are divided into four different ranges:

1. Levels 0 through 96 are reserved for high-prority real-time tasks and could potentially be assigned to an IST to reduce its latency and avoid preemption by other threads.

2. Levels 97 through 152 are generally assigned to the main thread (the thread assigned to the DLL when it is loaded) of a device driver. The Real-Time Priority System section of the CEPB 3.0 online documentation lists the default priority assignments for various drivers.

3. Levels 153 through 247 are reserved for threads that must run at a priority higher than that reserved for application threads, but that must not preempt the threads of a device driver.

4. Levels 248 through 255 are reserved for non-real-time threads and are generally used by applications.

While we're on the subject of latency, we should discuss one more major contributor to interrupt latency in CE 2.1x. If it becomes necessary for your IST to wait for a resource to become available, perhaps using the `WaitForSingleObject` function, it is wise to verify that the resource cannot also be held by a lower-priority thread. To avoid the priority inversion that would result in such a case, the CE 2.1x kernel temporarily boosts the priority of the lower-priority thread, to be certain it can run long enough to release the resource that is causing the IST to block. In addition, in CE 2.1x, if the same lower-priority thread happens to be blocked on a resource held by another lower-priority thread, the priority of the other thread will also be boosted. This process continues for each lower-priority thread that may be causing another lower-priority thread to block. The priority levels are eventually restored when the IST receives the resource that was causing it to block.

Note:
Priority inversion is a condition in which a higher-priority thread is indefinitely blocked while waiting for a resource held by a lower-priority thread. The thread scheduler does not allow the lower-priority thread to run, because of the existence of the higher-priority thread. But because the higher-priority thread is waiting for a resource held by the lower-priority thread, now unable to run, the higher-priority thread also becomes unrunnable. Both threads remain in this state unless the thread scheduler is able to detect this deadlock condition and take action to temporarily boost the priority of the lower-priority thread. Boosting its priority allows the lower-priority thread to run, thus releasing the resources for which the higher-priority thread is waiting.

The impact on IST latency of this form of *chained* priority boosting in CE 2.12 is undetermined. Considering the value of deterministic behavior in a real-time system, CE 3.0 provides priority boosting down to only one level. Thus, the higher-priority threads remain blocked, and the lower-priority threads (causing the higher-priority threads to block) run according to the standard scheduling algorithm. When the resource used by the lower-priority threads is finally freed, the higher-priority threads are unblocked and are ready to run.

The next line of source code after the call to `SetThreadPriority` in Listing 8.1 creates an event object that subsequently will be passed to the interrupt support handler through the `InterruptInitialize` function. The `InterruptInitialize` function is called with the event object handle `hevInterrupt` and the constant `SYSINTR_MYDEVICE_FUNCTION1`, representing the logical ID of the interrupt to be serviced. This logical ID is platform specific and must be supplied by the hardware vendor, generally through some form of Windows CE board support package (BSP) that is installed in the CEPB source tree. In general, the BSP would include a file called `oalintr.h`, located in the `.\PLATFORM\<Platform Name>\INC\` directory.

At this point everything is set up to receive notification of the interrupt specified by the logical ID `SYSINTR_MYDEVICE_FUNCTION1`. We enter an infinite loop that immediately calls the `WaitForSingleObject` function to wait for the event object `hevInterrupt` to become signaled by the interrupt support handler. Because a time-out parameter of `INFINITE` is being used, we will not return from this call until the event is signaled.

When the physical interrupt associated with the logical interrupt ID `SYSINTR_MYDEVICE_FUNCTION1` finally occurs, the event is signaled and execution continues from the next line of code after the call to `WaitForSingleObject`. This is where most of the work is done to process the interrupt, which would most likely include access to the device's physical resources, such as onboard memory for the reading and writing of data. Because CE drivers run in user mode, you cannot access these physical resources directly without first obtaining a virtual memory address that is mapped to the address of the physical resource. We will defer discussion of how to obtain this virtual address to the next section, Accessing the Physical Resources of Your Device.

When the processing of the interrupt is complete and the IST is ready for the next interrupt from its device, the function `InterruptDone` is called. This function informs the interrupt support handler that it may reenable the physical interrupt (associated with the logical ID `SYSINTR_MYDEVICE_FUNCTION1`). In the example in Listing 8.1, the `InterruptDone` function is called when all required processing is complete. It is also possible to call this function earlier, in the `while` loop. This approach would allow the physical interrupt to be reenabled sooner, but would still not cause the IST to be reentered. It would just cause the event object to be signaled sooner so that when the `WaitForSingleObject` function was called, the return would be immediate.

If the ISR in the OAL for your platform is written to generate different logical interrupts for a given physical interrupt, depending on the physical state of the platform, the result is a kind of interrupt multiplexing. In this case it is particularly important to call `InterruptDone` as soon as possible in the implementation of your IST to clear the multiplexed, physical interrupt and avoid any latency in the activation of the ISTs written to service the other logical interrupt IDs, yet to be signaled.

Accessing the Physical Resources of Your Device

When writing an IST (as described in the previous section), at some point you will undoubtedly require access to the physical resources of your device, perhaps including the device's registers, I/O ports, or memory regions for memory-mapped I/O or DMA transfers (collectively referred to as physical resources). Because CE is a protected-mode operating system, you will need to obtain a virtual address that is mapped to the physical address of your device's resources. Specifically how this is accomplished is the subject of this section.

Before we begin our discussion of how to obtain a virtual address mapped to a particular physical address, let's explore how the value of the physical address is determined. The processors supported by CE provide a 4GB, 32-bit (2^{32} virtual address space. Most processors (the notable exception being x86 processors) are limited to a 29-bit physical address space of 512MB (2^{29}). Consequently, the virtual address space above 2GB (0x80000000) is generally reserved as a kind of **shadow memory**, accessible only in privileged (kernel) mode. This upper 2GB of address space is generally divided into four adjacent regions of 512MB, each shadowing the physical memory address that is derived by the upper three bits of the virtual address being cleared. The processor may then generate the appropriate physical addresses automatically, without resorting to an expensive address translation lookup using its internal translation look-aside buffer. The important thing to remember about each of these regions is that they access physical memory by using different caching options, the most important option for device drivers being cached or uncached access. Caching options have important implications for the access to physical resources in your device driver.

The address of your device's physical resources must lie within the 512MB physical address range. This address may only be accessed through an address in one of the 512MB regions shadowing the physical address range. You must be certain that you have selected the region with the uncached access because device I/O is required. So, for example, if one of the registers on your device were assigned to the physical address 0x10000000 on an SHx processor, you would need to add this to the value of 0xA0000000, for a physical address in shadow memory of 0xB0000000. The 512MB region on the SHx between 0xA0000000 and 0xC0000000 is reserved for uncached memory accesses. As you will soon see, any function requesting a physical address must use the form of the address in the appropriate shadow memory region. So in the SHx example just presented, we would use the shadow memory address of 0xB0000000, not the true physical address of 0x10000000 that lies within the 29-bit physical address space. Let's take a look at some sample code in which the shadow memory address is required. As we do so, it is important to remember that CE considers the shadow memory address an alias for the true physical address and does not differentiate between the two.

Listing 8.2 contains an excerpt of the CEPB sample serial driver. This driver uses a layered MDD/PDD architecture, and as you might imagine, the sample code in Listing 8.2 is executed in the platform device driver (PDD, discussed in Chapter 7) layer of the serial driver, and is located in the p2io.c file in the .\PLATFORM\<Platform Name>\DRIVERS\SERIAL directory.

Listing 8.2 Sample code mapping a virtual address for uncached access to a designated physical address (shadow memory address)

```
//
// Excerpt from the file .\PLATFORM\<Platform Name>\INC\p2.h
//
    #define DMA_BUFFER_BASE              0xAC000000
    #define DMA_PHYSICAL_BASE            DMA_BUFFER_BASE

//
// Excerpt from the file .\PLATFORM\<Platform Name>\DRIVERS\SERIAL\serfw.h
//
    ...

    #define     BUFFERSIZE       2048

    #define     HW_RX_BUFFER     DMA_BUFFER_BASE + 0x4000
    #define     IR_RX_BUFFER     (HW_RX_BUFFER + 4 * BUFFERSIZE)

    ...

//
// Excerpt from the file .\PLATFORM\<Platform Name>\DRIVERS\SERIAL\p2io.c
//
    ...
    pHWHead->PhysRxStart = bIR ? IR_RX_BUFFER : HW_RX_BUFFER;

    ...

    ReceiveRingBuffer = (PUCHAR)VirtualAlloc(0,
                                             4 * BUFFERSIZE,
                                             MEM_RESERVE,
                                             PAGE_NOACCESS);

    ...

    CopyReturn = VirtualCopy((LPVOID)ReceiveRingBuffer,
                             (LPVOID)pHWHead->PhysRxStart,
                             4 * BUFFERSIZE,
                             PAGE_READWRITE | PAGE_NOCACHE);
    ...
```

The constants `IR_RX_BUFFER` and `HW_RX_BUFFER`, which define the physical address we will be mapping, are defined in the two files `p2.h` and `serfw.h`, excerpted in Listing 8.2. The value of the shadow memory region beginning at `0xA000000` has already been added to the physical address of the DMA buffer at `0xC000000`, producing a shadow memory address of `0xAC000000`. This value is then added to an offset of `0x4000` for a resulting shadow memory address of `0xAC004000` assigned to the constant `HW_RX_BUFFER`. We will not use this address until the call to `VirtualCopy`, however.

Mapping the shadow memory address (which is interchangeable with the term *physical address* in CE) of `0xAC004000` described here is a two-step process. First, the function `VirtualAlloc` is called to reserve an address in the virtual address space of the driver. The first parameter, `lpAddress`, is generally unused in most CE driver code and is passed as a `NULL` value to allow the automatic assignment of an available virtual address. The `dwSize` parameter is the size of the virtual address range to be reserved. The next parameter, `flAllocationType`, indicates how the virtual address range will be processed. The most commonly used parameter in driver development, `MEM_RESERVE`, is used simply to reserve the address range without actually allocating any physical memory. The last parameter, `flProtect`, specifies the access protection for the virtual address range allocated. In the example in Listing 8.2, we use the value `PAGE_NOACCESS` to prevent all access to the address range because it has not yet been mapped to physical memory.

The call to `VirtualCopy`, which is the second of the two steps in this process, associates the virtual address range allocated in the call to `VirtualAlloc`, with the physical memory specified. The `lpvDest` parameter contains the return value of the previous call to `VirtualAlloc` and represents the starting memory address that may be used for subsequent access to the physical memory (synonymous with shadow memory). The variable `ReceiveRingBuffer` is used in our example because it contains the return value of `VirtualAlloc`. The `lpvSrc` parameter is used to pass the address of the physical memory that is to be associated with the virtual address range in the previous parameter. In our example, this address is derived as an offset into the uncached, 512MB shadow memory region and is contained in a member variable of `pHWHead`. The `cbSize` parameter must be an even multiple of the page size for the target CPU, a value that may be obtained programmatically by a call to `GetSystemInfo`. Our example simply multiplies the 2K buffer by a value of 4 to match the size of the virtual address range allocated in the previous step.

The `fdwProtect` parameter offers the same access protection options as the `flProtect` parameter in the `VirtualAlloc` function (the exception being the addition of the `PAGE_PHYSICAL` option in the `VirtualCopy` function). Because we are committing the virtual memory region to physical memory, we use additional access protection options beyond those that were specified in the call to `VirtualAlloc`. The device hardware will be accessed directly, so we use `PAGE_NOCACHE` to ensure that data is read and written directly from hardware and not from the CPU's internal cache memory. The `PAGE_READWRITE` option is used to override the `PAGE_NOACCESS` option used in the `VirtualAlloc` function to allow data to be sent to and retrieved from the device.

You will find as you study the CEPB sample driver code that in some instances the `PAGE_PHYSICAL` option is OR'd with the `PAGE_READWRITE` and `PAGE_NOCACHE` options. The CEPB documentation indicates that this option is needed when you're mapping a physical address beyond 512MB (`0x1FFFFFFF`), but there is ample evidence of physical addresses beyond this value that are mapped without the `PAGE_PHYSICAL` option. It is possible that this option was introduced in later versions of CE and is not yet fully implemented in all of the CEPB sample code. For this reason, we recommend that you include this option in the development of all new driver source code.

For x86-based platforms, the physical address passed to the `VirtualCopy` function in the `lpvSrc` parameter must always be OR'd with the address `0x80000000`. This requirement exists even if the physical address to the I/O of your device is well below this address. So, for example, on a CEPC platform the registers for COM1 are located at `0x3F8` to `0x400`, which when OR'd with `0x80000000`, must be passed to the `VirtualCopy` function as `0x800003F8` in the `lpvSrc` parameter. A value of 8 is passed in the `cbSize` parameter for the length of the I/O region.

Another option exists for mapping physical memory to your driver's virtual address space. The function `MmMapIoSpace` combines the functionality of both `VirtualAlloc` and `VirtualCopy` into one function. It is compatible with the Windows NT kernel mode support routine of the same name and will save you a few lines of code. The source code for the `MmMapIoSpace` function is provided in the `ddk_map.c` file located in the `.\PUBLIC\COMMON\OAK\DRIVERS\CEDDK\` directory.

The only reason not to use this function, in favor of the more cumbersome two-step approach, might be to obtain an extra degree of control over the access protection options passed to the `VirtualCopy` function. Say, for example, that your device provided a register with read-only access, meaning that it was used only to report the value of a particular device state that could not be altered by the host platform (your driver). Let's assume also that the same physical address associated with the read-only register was also used for a different, write-only register. In each case a different virtual address could be mapped to the same physical address, one with access protection set to `PAGE_READONLY` for the read-only register, and the other set to `PAGE_READWRITE` for the write-only register. By setting the access protection for the read-only register to `PAGE_READONLY`, you would prevent inadvertent writes to this register that would otherwise alter the contents of the write-only register at the same physical address.

If you are mapping physical memory for use by your driver's IST, you should do so somewhere during the initialization of your driver. This memory can remain mapped as long it is required by your driver. When access to the physical memory is no longer required, most likely when the driver is unloaded, you will need to call the `VirtualFree` function if `VirtualAlloc` and `VirtualCopy` were used as previously described in this section. If `MmMapIoSpace` was used, then `MmUnmapIoSpace` should be used instead.

Platform-Independent Input/Output

Once you have successfully mapped the physical memory to the virtual address space of your driver, additional functions are provided to support basic I/O. These functions are prefixed with *READ_PORT, WRITE_PORT, READ_REGISTER,* or *WRITE_REGISTER.* Each variation of the function supports the reading and writing of 8-bit, 16-bit, and 32-bit values to a specific address, or to a specific starting address when you're reading and writing a buffer. The source code for each function is provided in the CEPB, and it varies slightly for each processor, with the most notable difference in the x86 code.

Though you could certainly get by without these functions, particularly since it is clear that there is no real magic in their implementation, it makes sense to use them. If you faithfully apply them throughout your code, it is possible to have one version of your driver that may simultaneously support multiple platforms and processors, without lots of `#ifdef` statements that might make your code hard to read and maintain.

Making sure that these functions are available to your driver requires taking certain steps. If you are developing a custom platform, you will need to be certain that the `ceddk.dll` module is included in your build of the CE kernel, a process discussed in Chapter 10. During implementation of the OEM Abstraction Layer (OAL), the CEDDK functions from a CEPB sample platform would have been copied to the platform source tree for your custom platform and modified as needed. The header file for the these functions is `ceddk.h`, located in the `.\PUBLIC\COMMON\DDK\INC` directory.

If you are developing a driver for an installable device intended for a standard CE platform, these functions are available only in version 2.0 and earlier versions of the CETK Platform SDK. The header file, `ntcompat.h`, is available in the directories `.\WCE\INCLUDE\WCE100` and `.\WCE200\MS HPC\INCLUDE` for the version of the CETK supporting CE 1.00 and 2.00, respectively. Newer versions of the Platform SDK for the Handheld PC Pro and Palm-size PC did not provide a header file for these and other device driver–related functions. Refer to Hint 8.1 for more information on how to gain access to device driver functions on the Handheld Pro and Palm-size PC Platform SDKs.The CEDDK module also provides functions prefixed with *Hal* that are intended for platforms equipped with one or more I/O buses and are compatible with Windows NT kernel mode support routines of the same name. These functions are really intended for the CEPC platform, and they are used to enumerate and configure your device on the designated bus (Peripheral Component Interconnect [PCI], ISA, and so on). They will mostly likely be useful only if your custom platform is PC based.

Hint 8.1 Locating device driver functions in the Handheld PC Pro and Palm-size PC Platform SDKs

The release of the Platform SDK for the Palm-size PC (CE 2.01), Handheld PC Pro (CE 2.11), and Pocket PC (CE 3.0) standard platforms did not include support for driver development. However, such support was included in the Handheld PC Platform SDK and was demonstrated with sample drivers in the directories `.\WCE200\MS HPC\SAMPLES\DDK` and `.WCE\DDK`, depending on the release of the CETK installed. Even if you own the CEPB, you do not have the import libraries needed for the standard platform, but only those for platforms that are provided as samples (such as Odo and CEPC) and, of course, those you create using CEPB.

A workaround for this problem is to use the Win32 function `LoadLibrary` in combination with `GetProcAddress` to obtain the address to the functions needed. You need to copy the function prototype from one of the header files in the Handheld PC Platform SDK (PSDK) and identify which library from the PSDK contains the function in question. If the call to LoadLibrary fails, you must conclude that the vendor of your particular standard platform either does not support this DLL or has moved the implementation of the function into a different DLL. The subsequent call to GetProcAddress could also fail, indicating that the function is not provided in this particular DLL. In either case, your driver should fail gracefully and notify the end user that it is not functional on this particular platform.

To help identify the DLL that has the needed function, you could use the Dumpbin command-line utility with the `/EXPORTS` option. You could begin by listing the exports within the import libraries provided in the Handheld PC (CE 2.0) PSDK, until you found a match. After making a code change in your driver to load the associated DLL, you would then test your driver to determine if the function could be found in the same DLL on the Handheld PC Pro, Palm-size PC, or Pocket PC target platform. You could also copy selected DLLs from the target platform (using a CE services or ActiveSync connection) to the development workstation. The same Dumpbin utility could be used on these modules to list the available exports directly.

If you are lucky enough to own the CEPB, this same process could be applied to the many DLL modules produced during a CE kernel build with the predefined MAXALL configuration. Refer to Chapter 3 for more information on bulding the CE kernel with the CEPB. Ultimately, however, you must run your driver on the target platform to verify that the needed function is in the DLL loaded.

Managing Buffer Pointers

Chances are that if your driver provides some form of I/O, you will need to pass data between your driver and its calling application. If you are writing a stream-interface driver, the calling application most likely will pass its pointer to a buffer via the `ReadFile` and `WriteFile` calls. The same is true for a driver that conforms to a non-stream-interface driver model that merely exposes a stream interface as a mechanism for supporting the Win32 `CreateFile`, `ReadFile`, and `WriteFile` application interfaces (see the section on the USB device driver model in Chapter 7 for an example of such a driver). The `ReadFile` call would be used by the application (resulting in a call to your stream-interface driver's `XXX_Read` entry point) to pass a pointer to a buffer that your driver could use to return received data. Similarly, the application would call `WriteFile` (resulting in a call to your stream-interface driver's `XXX_Write` entry point) to provide the pointer to a buffer containing data that needs to be processed by your driver and its supported device. It would also be possible for the application to use the `DeviceIoControl` function (resulting in a call to your stream-interface driver's `XXX_IoControl` entry point) for both read and write pointers to be passed simultaneously to your driver.

As long as the pointers directly reference the memory to be read from or written to by your driver, everything should work fine. Problems emerge when you use buffer pointers in either of two scenarios: (1) to pass a reference to a structure containing member variables, some of which contain buffer pointers; and (2) to access shared memory, where buffer pointers are accessed from independent threads managed by the driver. The latter scenario is commonly used in the implementation of asynchronous I/O. Let's begin by discussing the first scenario.

If you haven't read Chapter 1, the next few paragraphs may be a bit confusing. So before we go further, let's review some of the relevant concepts.

All CE processes run in one of 32 distinct process slots, each with their own unique address space. Process slot 0 is reserved for active (running) processes and is used to map in any one of the 31 other process slots when one of them becomes active. Any pointers in an active application (running as the active process in slot 0) are also mapped into slot 0. This means that this pointer will point to the correct data only when the process slot of the application is active and is mapped into slot 0. When a different process becomes active, the address of this pointer will no longer point to the correct data. We know from our discussion of stream-interface drivers in Chapter 7 that they run in the process slot of the Device Manager (DM), not the process slot of the calling application. So, when a pointer shows up as a parameter in the call to a stream-interface driver's `XXX_Read`, `XXX_Write`, or `XXX_IoControl` entry point, why does it point to the correct data? Let's begin to answer this question.

Because each process slot represents a unique 32MB address space, the upper seven bits of a pointer correspond to the process slot ID. When an application calls the Win32 `ReadFile`, `WriteFile`, or `DeviceIoControl` function, the upper seven bits of the address are automatically fixed up to reference the process slot where the application permanently resides in virtual memory, not slot 0, which is remapped during a context switch between active processes. However, if this pointer references a structure with member variables containing other pointers, this automatic fix-up will not occur for any of the member variables. This is understandable because the content of your structure is unknown to CE. The function `MapPtrToProcess`, is designed to address this problem (no pun intended).

The function `MapPtrToProcess` accepts two parameters: The first one is the pointer you wish to map, and the second is the ID of the process where the pointer is located. The name of the function may be confusing at first because it implies that the second parameter represents the ID of the process requiring access to the pointer, in this case the process ID of the driver. Just consider the slot ID in the upper seven bits, and remember that what is really meant is that this function will modify the pointer so that it refers to the process slot where the address is located in virtual memory.

As an example of the use of this function, let's assume that your driver requires a structure that contains member variables pointing to a series of buffers dynamically allocated by the calling application. For the purpose of this discussion, assume that the structure is similar to that presented in Listing 8.3.

Listing 8.3 Sample structure passed to a stream-interface driver in `DeviceIoControl`

```
typedef struct _MYDRIVERSDATA
{
        UINT uStructLength;         // length of this structure, new fields at end
        UINT uBuffer1Length;        // length of data referenced by pBuffer1
        UINT uBuffer2Length;        // length of data referenced by pBuffer2
        PVOID pBuffer1;             // points to data allocated by caller
        PVOID pBuffer2;             // points to data allocated by caller
        .
        .
        .
} MYDRIVERSDATA, *PMYDRIVERSDATA;
```

The calling application would initialize the value of `pBuffer1` and `pBuffer2` with the following code:

```
MyDriversData.pBuffer1 = MapPtrToProcess(pCallerBuffer1, GetCurrentProcess());
MyDriversData.pBuffer2 = MapPtrToProcess(pCallerBuffer2, GetCurrentProcess());
```

The call to `GetCurrentProcess` provides a pseudohandle to the process slot of the calling application. Because we are using `MapPtrToProcess` to map the pointer to the process slot of the application, `GetCurrentProcess` is just what we need. Another option would allow you to relieve the calling application of this burden by calling `MapPtrToProcess` in your driver using the following code:

```
MyDriversData.pBuffer1 = MapPtrToProcess(pCallerBuffer1, GetCallerProcess());
MyDriversData.pBuffer2 = MapPtrToProcess(pCallerBuffer2, GetCallerProcess());
```

Note:
The term *pseudohandle* is used to distinguish this handle from one that would require deallocation when no longer needed. A pseudohandle simply identifies a particular resource and generally is not used as are most handles: for some form of table lookup.

The call to `GetCallerProcess` still returns the required pseudohandle for the process slot of the calling application. If we had used `GetCurrentProcess` the buffer pointer would have been incorrectly mapped to the address space of the DM's process slot because it is called from your driver and is the currently active process.

Sharing Memory between Drivers and Applications

If you are writing a driver that conforms to a non-stream-interface driver model, buffer pointers may be processed in a manner different from the one just discussed. In the NDIS driver model, for example, the NDIS wrapper (a type of driver control program) provides buffer pointers through a sophisticated mechanism that supports segmentation and reassembly of packet data. The NDIS wrapper also provides the added capability of support for asynchronous I/O, where your driver may accept control of a buffer pointer (pointer to a packet of data in this context), return from the call by the NDIS wrapper, and then later notify the wrapper when the transmission or reception sequence is complete. For an I/O-intensive device, such as a network interface card (NIC), this capability significantly reduces the likelihood that the driver becomes a bottleneck in overall system performance.

If you happen to be writing a stream-interface driver and your device is not as I/O intensive as a NIC, the synchronous I/O (not returning to the calling application until the requested I/O is complete) provided by the `ReadFile`, `WriteFile`, and `DeviceIoControl` functions might be adequate. If, however, you decide to provide support for asynchronous I/O, similar to that provided by the NDIS wrapper, let's say, you will need to provide a custom application interface into your stream-interface driver. As currently defined, Windows CE does not support the Win32 overlapped I/O (a synonym for asynchronous I/O) extensions to the `ReadFile`, `WriteFile`, and `DeviceIoControl` functions. So you will need to design your driver to read and write from the supported device using threads. The buffer pointers provided by the calling application through your custom API will be accessed by these threads to send and receive data from the device, while the application continues satisfying the requests of the end user. The only problem with this plan is that your driver's threads cannot directly access these buffer pointers. Such access requires that certain steps be taken, which we will explore in the next few paragraphs.

Before we get into the details, you might be asking yourself why we are even discussing this topic. It is tempting to simply pass the value of the pointer to a child thread in the `lpParameter` argument of the `CreateThread` function or copy its value into a global variable. Both alternatives would cause an access violation exception, however, when the pointer was de-referenced. Using the handy `MapPtrToProcess` function presented in the previous section also will not work because your driver's thread does not have permission from the CE kernel to access buffer pointers mapped to the address space of outside process slots. This may sound confusing because the pointer returned from `MapPtrToProcess` works just fine when accessed from within a stream-interface driver's entry point, indirectly called by an application also in an outside process slot. The piece of this puzzle that we are missing is what happens when the application makes a call to a Win32 function, like `ReadFile`, that results in the activation of the DM's process slot associated with the driver.

At some point in the initial processing of the Win32 `ReadFile` call made by the application, the DM process slot is made active (most likely by the `coredll.dll` module). At this point the DM process is granted sufficient permissions to access not only the address space of its own process slot, but also that of the calling application. It is modification of the permissions associated with the DM process slot that is missing when the driver's thread becomes runnable. When the pointer, correctly mapped to an outside process slot (a process slot that does not belong to the DM) through `MapPtrToProcess`, is de-referenced, an exception occurs because permission has not been granted to access the particular process slot associated with the application. Now that we have a good grounding on what's happening, let's take a look at some code demonstrating two different methods for resolving this problem.

Each method uses different APIs to achieve the same result: shared access to memory allocated by one process in another process. The first method uses a memory-mapped file to obtain read access to the memory region described by a predefined file name. After a series of Win32 APIs is called, a pointer is obtained that may be used for read or write access to the file. This file could then be used to contain data to be sent to the device, written by the caller, or data retrieved from the device, written by the driver.

Considering that files in Windows CE are generally stored in the object store that resides in RAM, you may be wondering why we bother with a *memory*-mapped file, remapping to memory what is already in memory. Without memory mapping, the process requiring read access would need to provide a buffer in the `lpBuffer` parameter, which would be used by `ReadFile` to make a copy of the requested data. This extra step violates one of the objectives of asynchronous I/O: to avoid the overhead associated with the copying from the buffer of one process to the other process. Memory mapping, however, produces a pointer that may be de-referenced for direct access to the file data without buffer copies.

Listing 8.4 contains sample code for a driver thread that requires access to the calling application's buffer. Once the buffer pointer has been successfully mapped, the data referenced is copied to flash memory, though this code is omitted for brevity.

Listing 8.4 Sample code for passing data to a driver thread using a memory-mapped file

```
DWORD MyDriverThread(LPVOID pTempFileName)
{
    LPTSTR pszTempFileName = (LPTSTR)pTempFileName;
    ASSERT(pszTempFileName != NULL);

    // Open the existing file name provided in the pTempFileName parameter
    // of this thread.
    HANDLE hFileFlashBuffer =
        CreateFileForMapping(pszTempFileName, GENERIC_READ, FILE_SHARE_READ,
        NULL, OPEN_EXISTING, FILE_ATTRIBUTE_NORMAL | FILE_FLAG_RANDOM_ACCESS,
        NULL);
    ASSERT(hFileFlashBuffer != INVALID_HANDLE_VALUE);

    // Create a mapping object from the file handle just created.
    HANDLE hMapFlashBuffer =
        CreateFileMapping(hFileFlashBuffer, NULL, PAGE_READONLY, 0, 0, NULL);
    ASSERT(hMapFlashBuffer != INVALID_HANDLE_VALUE);

    // Now use this mapping object to obtain a pointer into the file, within
    // the address space of this thread.
    LPVOID pData =
        MapViewOfFile(hMapFlashBuffer, FILE_MAP_READ, 0, 0, 0);
    ASSERT(pData != NULL);
```

```
    // The data referenced by the address in pData is now available for
    // read-only access by the driver's thread.  Additional code accessing
    // this data would normally follow.
...

    // Shut down all of the resources allocated.
    VERIFY(UnmapViewOfFile(pData));

    // Close the mapping object, but do NOT close the file handle.
    // Experience has shown that this handle is closed automatically when
    // the mapping object is closed.  Any attempt to close the file handle
    // will cause an exception.
    VERIFY(CloseHandle(hMapFlashBuffer));

    return (ERROR_SUCCESS);
}
```

The parameter `pTempFileName` passed to the thread start routine `MyDriverThread` contains the name of the predefined file specified in your driver interface. The `CreateFileForMapping` function is used to obtain the file handle that is passed as a parameter in the calls to subsequent functions in this example. We use the value `OPEN_EXISTING` in the `dwCreationDisposition` parameter because we are expecting to read the memory already written to by another process. To this end we are requesting read-only access (`GENERIC_READ`), which also ensures that this code should work in CE versions 2.0 and beyond. Think of the `CreateFileForMapping` function as a special version of the Win32 `CreateFile` function with the extensions to support memory-mapped files.

The next function called is `CreateFileMapping`, which does the work of specifying certain boundaries on the virtual memory region reserved for mapping the file and any access restrictions. The first parameter is the file handle returned from the previous call, to `CreateFileForMapping`. A reserved value of `0xFFFFFFFF` can also be passed in this parameter. This reserved value would be used if you simply needed a region of shared memory not associated with a named file in the file system. The last parameter, `lpName`, would be used to name the mapping object produced by `CreateFileMapping`, and it would be used by the outside process requiring access to the memory-mapped file. When the outside process calls the `CreateFileMapping` function, it passes this name in the `lpName` parameter and the existing mapping object is returned. If the outside process happens to use an incorrect name in the `lpName` parameter, it receives the handle to a new mapping object, so it is important to call the `GetLastErrors` function, which returns `ERROR_ALREADY_EXISTS` in confirmation that the mapping object is shared. A named file is used in this example, however, just in case we need to check for the existence of the file and examine its contents during debugging. A named file also has the advantage of ensuring that the outside process has already created the file that will be mapped for shared memory access. Any chance that we might accidentally obtain a new mapping object by an incorrect name in the `lpName` parameter is eliminated because the `dwCreationDisposition` parameter in the `CreateFileForMapping` function was called with the `OPEN_EXISTING` parameter.

In the next function, called `MapViewOfFile`, the system resources are finally allocated and the virtual memory needed to map the file is committed to our process's address space. The return value corresponds to the beginning of the address space allocated and may be de-referenced just like any other buffer pointer. This first parameter is the handle of the file-mapping object returned in the previous function call, to `CreateFileMapping`. Because we need read access to only the shared memory, we use the `FILE_MAP_READ` value in the `dwDesiredAccess` parameter. The virtual memory allocated will be protected from any other access, and will generate an access violation if we accidentally write to the address range referenced in the `pData` variable. The next three parameters are zero because we need to read the entire mapped file (synonymous with shared memory in this context).

The `MapViewOfFile` function is interesting because it provides the flexibility to map selected portions of shared memory, through the `dwFileOffsetHigh`, `dwFileOffsetLow`, and `dwNumberOfBytesToMap` parameters. Using the `dwDesiredAccess` parameter, you can create self-imposed limits on how you access the shared memory, in the event that the outside process creating the memory-mapped file provides both read and write access (available in CE 2.1x). Collectively, these parameters can be used in a practice of defensive programming that is most effective in finding bugs and preventing those that might occur in future code changes.

Let's assume for example that you needed a memory-mapped file to establish a large shared memory area to collect data retrieved from the device. When your driver receives an interrupt, you need to copy the data from the device's onboard memory to the shared memory-mapped file. So, if the shared memory were structured as a circular queue, the `MapViewOfFile` function could be used to limit access to the region of the queue already read by the application, leaving the unread data protected from write access. Refer to the CEPB online documentation for more information on the use of the `MapViewOfFile` function.

Before the thread exits, the previously allocated resources must be freed. The function `UnmapViewOfFile` is used to remove the mapping of the file associated with the address first returned from the `MapViewOfFile` function. This code uses the original address returned in the `MapViewOfFile` function and not the one that might have been used to access other bytes, offset from the beginning of the shared memory region. If `MapViewOfFile` had been called to map only a portion of the total memory-mapped file defined in the `CreateFileMapping` function, you would call `UnmapViewOfFile` to unmap the region of memory no longer needed and `MapViewOfFile` to map the next region of memory requiring access.

Note:

Until the release of Windows CE 2.10, it was not possible to request file mapping with write access. If you are not certain which version of CE your driver will be running on, you may wish to consider assigning the processes that require write access the responsibility for creating the original file (using the Win32 `CreateFile` function). One possible implementation would require that the driver create the file used to contain data retrieved from the device. Another file would be created by the calling application for data to be sent to the device. Your driver would map the file provided by the application to read the data to be sent to the device. Data retrieved from the device would be written to the other file (created by your driver) by the Win32 `WriteFile` call.

A buffer copy is created with the call to the `WriteFile` function in both the application and the driver, so this approach should be considered a less efficient alternative. Later in this section we will consider the advantages and disadvantages of each approach.

The second method we will explore requires the use of functions undocumented prior to the release of CE 2.11. It is based on two functions—`GetCurrentPermissions` and `SetProcPermissions`—both of which provide a powerful mechanism for gaining broad access to the entire address space (process slot) of the calling application. `GetCurrentPermissions` is used to obtain the value of the current thread's permission bit mask, loosely referred to in the CEPB sample code as the **thread access key**. When you are ready to de-reference a pointer to a buffer in the calling application's address space, the function `SetProcPermissions` is called with the thread access key of the calling application. The thread access key of the calling application would have been obtained in an entry point of your driver that was activated as a direct effect of a particular application-level API, such as `XXX_Open` in the case of a stream-interface driver.

To be certain that you don't place the application that your driver is intended to serve in a vulnerable state, you must remember to restore the thread access key associated with the driver thread as soon as possible. So, when the access to the buffer pointer is complete, the function `SetProcPermissions` is used to restore the thread access key to its original value, previously saved somewhere in the beginning of the thread start function. We have a strong opinion about the wisdom of using the `SetCurrentPermissions` and `GetCurrentPermissions` functions, which we will present in the next section, Shared Memory Approaches Compared.

Listing 8.5 contains sample code demonstrating access to the buffer pointer passed to the thread start function `MyDriverThread`. `GetCurrentPermissions` is called somewhere at the top of the thread, before the address (contained in the parameter `pBuffer`) to the calling application's address space is de-referenced. `GetCurrentPermissions` captures the thread access key of the thread before it is altered to match that of the calling application. The call to `SetProcPermissions` occurs next, with the value of the calling applications thread access key contained in the global variable `g_dwCallersAccessKey`. This variable would have been initialized elsewhere in the code, perhaps in the `XXX_Open` entry point called as a direct effect of the application-level function, `CreateFile`. An entry point such as `XXX_Init` could not have been used because this function is called when the DM loads the driver, which is not yet associated with an application.

When the thread has finished transferring data from the device's onboard FIFO buffer, `SetProcPermissions` is called with the value contained in `dwThreadsAccessKey` to restore the current thread's permissions mask to its original value. This function should be called immediately after the access to the `pBuffer` pointer is complete, to minimize the exposure of the calling application's address space to unintended access produced by a runaway pointer in your driver.

Listing 8.5 Sample code for passing data to a driver thread using thread access keys

```
DWORD MyDriverThread(LPVOID pBuffer)
{
    // Assume that the value of pBuffer passed to this thread start
    // function has already been mapped to the process slot of the calling
    // application through the MapPtrToProcess function, discussed in a
    // previous section.

    ...
```

```
    // Save the internal permissions mask of this thread for later
    // restoration, after the pointer has been de-referenced.
    dwThreadsAccessKey = GetCurrentPermissions();

    // The internal permissions mask of the calling process was
    // previously obtained in one of the driver's entry points
    // and was saved in the global variable g_dwCallersAccessKey.
    // Set the permissions mask of the this thread to allow the
    // pointer passed by the caller to be de-referenced.
    SetProcPermissions(g_dwCallersAccessKey);

    // Assume for now that g_pFifoBuffer has been previously
    // nitialized to an address that is mapped to the physical
    // memory of the device's onboard FIFO memory using VirtualAlloc
    // and VirtualCopy, or MmMapIoSpace (discussed in the section
    // titled Accessing the Physical Resources of Your Device).
    LPVOID pFifoBuffer = g_pFifoBuffer;

    for ( UINT uFifoBytesRemaining = FIFO_MAX_LENGTH;
          uFifoBytesRemaining;
          —uFifoBytesRemaining)
    {
        *pBuffer++ = *pFifoBuffer++;

        ...
    }

    // Restore the permissions mask of this thread to those of its former
    // state.
    SetProcPermissions(dwThreadsAccessKey);

    ...

    return (ERROR_SUCCESS);
}
```

Shared Memory Approaches Compared

The use of memory-mapped files requires a bit more effort than the comparable use of the SetProcPermissions and GetProcPermissions functions. It takes more time to become accustomed to the complex calling sequence that is also required of the calling application to obtain access to the memory-mapped files. The names of the memory-mapped files, or where to retrieve these names (from the registry most likely), need to be defined in some form of interface specification for your driver to ensure that the calling application and your driver use the same name. Even with this extra effort, we strongly encourage the use of memory-mapped files over SetProcPermissions and GetProcPermissions. Let's explore this provocative statement further.

Simply stated, SetProcPermissions and GetProcPermissions definitely have their place, but in the implementation of a driver interface supporting shared memory they represent a "loaded gun." The pointer to the calling application's buffer, passed to the driver and later accessed in a driver thread, cannot be validated. This means that if the pointer is non-NULL but references the wrong address in the address space of the calling application, the driver inadvertently reads or writes data that could potentially cause either the driver or the application to crash. Even if the pointer is valid, nothing controls how your driver uses this pointer, and it could inadvertently read or write past the end of the shared memory region, causing unpredictable results.

Compare this scenario to the memory-mapped file alternative. When the `CreateFileForMapping` function is called, a valid handle will be returned only if the file name was valid. It is unlikely that an incorrect file name will result in access to the wrong memory region (or the wrong file). Chances are that the call will just fail and the error will be immediately identified. When the mapping object is created through a call to the `CreateFileMapping` function, the size of the mapped memory region can be specified through the `dwMaximumSizeHigh` and `dwMaximumSizeLow` parameters. The type of access can also be specified through the `flProtect` parameter, preventing unintentional writes to the shared memory by a misbehaving application or driver. It is also possible to define upper and lower boundaries for access to a portion of the shared memory region, through the `dwFileOffsetHigh` and `dwFileOffsetLow` parameters in the `MapViewOfFile` function. Crossing these boundaries would cause an access violation, thus protecting the unsuspecting memory that surrounds your shared memory region. So with all the protections afforded—size, boundary, and access—why would you ever risk possible memory corruption by using `SetProcPermissions` in the implementation of shared memory? One reason might be to avoid requiring the calling application to create the files that must later be mapped by the driver. If the object store were not included in the build, the use of the memory-mapped files would not be possible. In most cases, however, the use of memory-mapped files is the superior approach to shared memory.

API Readiness

As you know from Chapter 6, CE device drivers run in user mode. Thus, you can call the same Win32 APIs that are available to applications, or any other function exported in a DLL. If you avail yourself of this useful capability, you will need to take a few precautions in calling these functions when your driver is being loaded.

If your driver is loaded early in the CE startup sequence, the module containing the implementation of the function you are calling may not yet be loaded. The result would be an exception that would cause the loading of your driver to be aborted and subsequently unloaded from memory. There is a function made available in CE 2.01, called `IsAPIReady`, that is designed to verify the availability of a specified group of APIs, or services. This function returns `FALSE` if the associated module has not yet been loaded. If a function in your driver depends on a particular API, you could fail the call to your driver by returning an error code, or you could poll the return value of `IsAPIReady` until it returns `TRUE`, indicating that the desired function is now available. Listing 8.6 contains an excerpt of the `GetClientDriverName` function in the `usbddrv.cpp` file (contained in the `.\PUBLIC\COMMON\OAK\DRIVERS\USB\USBD` directory) for polling the return value of the `IsAPIReady` function.

Listing 8.6 Sample code for polling the `IsAPIReady` function used during driver initialization

```
static BOOL
GetClientDriverName(LPWSTR szDriverName)
{
    ...

    // In case we're booting, wait for the window manager to come up.
    while (! IsAPIReady(SH_WMGR))
    {
        DEBUGMSG(ZONE_LOADER,(TEXT("USBD:GetClientDriverName, waiting for \
                 WMGR...\r\n")));
        Sleep(1000);
    }

    ...

    return TRUE;
}
```

Summary

By now you should have a pretty good idea of how to write a CE driver. In this chapter we focused on common practices in the implementation of CE drivers, including how to write an interrupt service thread (IST) for processing interrupts from your driver's supported device. We also discussed what is needed to access your device's physical resources and how to access memory across processes, between the address space of the Device Manager (DM) and a calling application.

If your driver is loaded during system startup, you will need to be careful to call only those functions in outside modules that have already been loaded and initialized. To this end, we discussed how to verify that certain groups of APIs are ready for access.

In the next chapter we will conclude our coverage of CE driver development by walking through various debug scenarios using the CEPB. The topics in this discussion will include setup of the development workstation and the target platform, remote debugging and command-line tools, and coding techniques to support the unique challenges of debugging real-time code. We will also present the Driver Mapper debugging tool (provided in source code form on this book's CD, or on the Web site), which may be used to remotely debug drivers operating on a standard platform that is not equipped to communicate with the CEPB kernel mode debugger.

9 Debugging Device Drivers

Device drivers are often some of the earliest modules of software written on a new platform. The driver may have been written before the platform or the kernel itself was completely functional. A partially functional platform or kernel may prevent the use of an interactive debugger relegating the developer to "debugger-less" approaches. It is not uncommon to find device driver developers poking and prodding their code with small experimental source changes, hoping to gain some insight from the observed results.

Fortunately, the Windows CE Platform Builder (CEPB) provides many driver debugging tools, supporting a variety of interfaces to the target platform. With the Driver Mapper tool, it is even possible to use the Visual C++ Windows CE Toolkit (CETK or eMVC) for driver debugging. We will start our exploration of CE driver debugging with a general overview of the relevant available tools.

Note:
The Visual C++ Windows CE Toolkit (CETK) is an add-on product for Visual C++ 5.0 and 6.0. It allows applications to be developed for standard and custom platforms (for custom platforms, the Export SDK tool in CEPB must be used) based on CE kernel versions 2.12 or earlier. The supported standard platforms include the Handheld PC, Handheld PC Pro, and Palm-size PC. The eMbedded Visual C++ product (eMVC) was introduced with the release of the CE 3.0 kernel and is a stand-alone product also dedicated to application development for standard and custom platforms. The same standard platforms, with the exception of the Handheld PC, are supported in eMVC. The key difference is that eMVC supports application development for products based on CE kernel version 3.0 or earlier, with the exception of Handheld PC standard platforms as noted. If you plan on developing applications for the Pocket PC standard platform, eMVC will be required because the Pocket PC is based on the CE 3.0

kernel. Otherwise, which product you use may depend simply on when you purchased your CE application development tools.

For the sake of our discussion, all references to eMVC, unless otherwise noted, also apply to CETK.

Background

The CETK and CEPB both provide remote and local debugging capabilities. In this section we will define the concepts of remote and local debugging in a Windows CE context, and we will consider the relative merits of each for resolving various types of bugs. For the sake of our discussion, the term *debugger* refers to the tool being used to analyze and control the execution of a particular software module, or *debuggee.*

Remote Debugging

In some ways, remote debugging is like trying to control a distant satellite orbiting another planet in the solar system. By its very nature, the satellite is an autonomous device, and you are forced to work with tools running on a local host computer to achieve some degree of control over your satellite. Eventually you learn to tolerate a delay in the response to your commands because they require time for transport and interpretation by the remote satellite. As with the true satellite, **remote debugging** attempts to achieve control of a remote device through some form of data transport—that is, serial cable, parallel cable, or Ethernet cable. There are no real limitations on the kind of transport that can be used, and it is not uncommon to find dial-up connections being used.

The debugger running on the development workstation (local host computer), not unlike the tools used for controlling the satellite, provides a virtualized representation of the state of the remote device and its running program(s). The goal of the debugger is to provide as much information and control of the remote device as possible, allowing you to feel as if the device were running inside your development workstation. To create this impression, a small "monitor" program generally runs on the remote device, to communicate with the debugger running on the development workstation. Figure 9.1 depicts the commands and data passed between the debugger and the remote device using the data transport. The monitor program interprets the command and can provide control of designated programs, the operating system under which the programs are running, and/or the hardware that constitutes the remote device.

To accomplish this control, the monitor program must function as unobtrusively as possible, lest it become a factor in the very problem it's trying to help resolve. This means that the monitor program itself must occupy as little memory as possible on the remote device. Some processors are able to provide a kind of hardware debug assist, to achieve the control needed by the monitor program. Such hardware-assisted debugging allows the monitor program not only to consume less memory, but to function with less impact on the operation of the program being debugged. You could set breakpoints, for example, by simply loading a register with the address of the instruction, rather than inserting a new instruction in the program code at the location of the breakpoint, to activate the debugger. Some processors go one step further in their support of

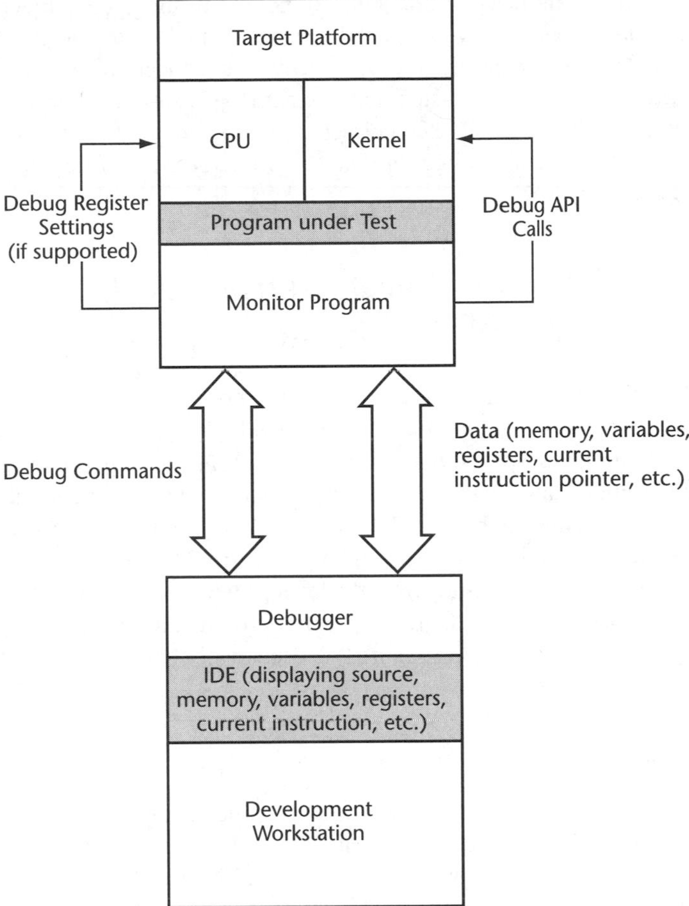

Figure 9.1 Block diagram of a remote monitor program

hardware-assisted debugging and allow the monitor program to be removed from the remote device. This is discussed in more detail in the Hardware-Level Debugging section a little later in this chapter.

Local Debugging

Let's quickly define local debugging in the context of this chapter, just for the sake of completeness. As the name implies, **local debugging** does not require a connection to a remote device through which debugging commands and responses are exchanged. Both the program being debugged and the debugger run on the same device, in this case the development workstation. When using the CE emulator, for example, you are performing local debugging because the CE program being debugged is running under the emulator, on the same computer as the debugger itself.

Local debugging has the obvious advantage of not requiring that the target binary be uploaded to the remote device every time a code change is made to the program being debugged. Because there is no need to control the program through a connection to the remote device, all debugging operations, such as single-stepping, are noticeably faster. When you are writing device drivers, you will mostly likely need direct access to onboard or installable hardware, and you will not be able to use local debugging. The CE emulator is therefore of limited value in writing CE device drivers.

Log-Level, Application-Level, Kernel-Level, and Hardware-Level Debugging

So far in this chapter, we have discussed two different types of debugging—remote and local—and attempted to define the characteristics of each type. In this section we will define an aspect of each type of debugging as a particular debugging *level.* The debugging levels further define the capabilities of remote and local debugging, with each level providing progressively more control of the executable module being debugged (the debuggee) and its target platform. We will begin with a description of the debugging level that provides the least amount of control—log-level debugging—and progress down to the level providing the most control—hardware-level debugging. We will define the degree of support provided for each level in both the remote and local debugging configurations. In Figure 9.2, each level of debugging is depicted in terms of the degree of control it provides.

Log-Level Debugging

Log-level debugging provides services that allow trace messages to be logged to a file located on either the target platform or the development workstation. The driver source code must be modified to call the function that logs the trace message. This function call may affect the performance of the driver to some degree, but it has the distinct advantage of operating without a connection to an external debugging tool.

One scenario for log-level debugging is to ship the retail build of the driver with the calls to the logging function present but disabled. They can then be enabled when a problem is identified to gather detailed information on the inner workings of the driver as it functions on the platform experiencing the problem. Log-level debugging allows a more complete characterization of the problem than an end user description can, and with clear documentation of which source code was executed.

Application-Level Debugging

This level of debugging is perhaps the one most commonly available and it provides more control than log-level debugging. Most development environments, regardless of language or operating system, provide some means of controlling the application under development. The Windows CE toolkits for both Visual C++ and Visual Basic (CETK, or eMVC, and eMVB) provide an integrated application debugger.

Before we go further, let's clarify the meaning of the term *control.* In this context, *control* refers to the number of entities (both software and hardware) that may be controlled by the

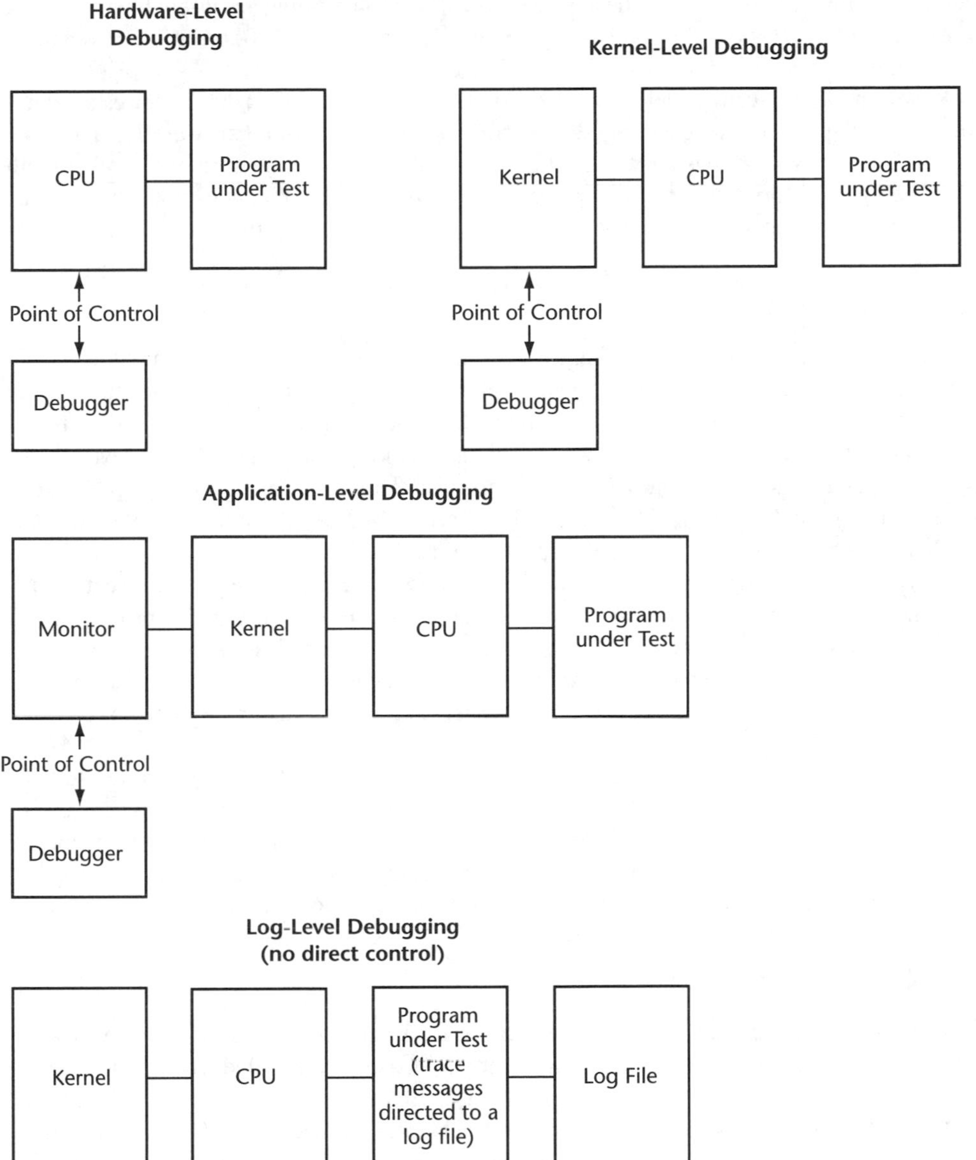

Figure 9.2 Block diagram of debugging levels

debugger. An **application-level debugger** therefore controls only the execution of the application. Other applications, in addition to the operating system kernel and processor, are unaffected.

This means that in CE, when a breakpoint is hit on a particular line of source code, only the debuggee containing that line is suspended. Other applications or processes with which the debuggee may communicate continue to run. So let's assume you're writing a device driver that is required to respond to an application's request within a given time-out period. When a breakpoint set in your driver hits, the application will continue to run and probably will time out while waiting for a response as you study your code in the debugger. To the application, the driver simply appears unresponsive.

Resolving a time-critical debug scenario such as the one just described requires a form of debugging that provides a higher degree of control, such as kernel- or hardware-level debugging. In the next two sections we will explore both of these debugging options. Another method of debugging that works well in time-critical debug scenarios, but that does not actually require a debugger, was discussed in the previous section, Log-Level Debugging.

Kernel-Level Debugging

As its name implies, **kernel-level debugging** requires the kernel to communicate directly with the debugger and allows control over all applications running on the target platform. When the debugger is running on a remote workstation, the kernel contains a module(s) that communicates directly with the remote debugger to exchange commands and data. Kernel-level debugging is provided only in the Windows CE Platform Builder (CEPB) product through the use of a specialized module, known as KDSTUB, and is included in the build of the kernel image. Chapter 5 discusses kernel-level debugging support in more detail.

If kernel-level debugging were used in the scenario discussed in the previous section, not only would the debuggee containing the breakpoint be suspended, but all other processes and threads would be suspended as well. This is clearly a better alternative for time-critical code because all other dependent modules and threads remain synchronized to the execution of the debuggee. CE supports both application- and kernel-level debugging and will be discussed throughout this chapter.

Where kernel-level debugging falls short is in the debugging of the kernel code itself. This is important if you are writing the OAL code for support of your custom platform because it is linked directly into the CE kernel. To debug OAL code, which includes the boot-level code that initializes the processor and later jumps to the kernel entry point, you need a greater degree of control. Hardware-level debugging, the subject of the next section, provides that level of control.

Hardware-Level Debugging

Hardware-level debugging provides a specialized interface between the remote device and the development workstation. Two of the more common interfaces are called Background Debug Mode (BDM) and Joint Test Access Group (JTAG, IEEE standard 1149.1) boundary scan. The BDM and JTAG interfaces are available on various high-end processors and require that the board of the remote device be specifically designed to support the attachment of a specialized BDM or JTAG cable.

The debugger, running on the development workstation, uses this interface to communicate directly with the processor and command the same debugging operations otherwise provided by a monitor program. In most cases, the development workstation contains an ISA (Industry Standard Architecture) or PCI (Peripheral Component Interconnect) adapter card, or an external adapter device connected to an existing port (parallel, serial, or USB). This adapter is used to communicate with the target via the signaling defined by the debug interface. In some cases, these interfaces provide advanced debugging capabilities that back in the "old days" required

CE Version Memo
With the introduction of CEPB 3.0, hardware-level debugging is now supported. The vendor for your debugging interface adapter must provide a specialized driver that implements an interface called EXDI. CEPB will call this software interface to control the target platform for the requested debug operation.

large external devices such as an emulator or a logic analyzer. The ability to set a breakpoint or access a particular memory region (or register) is one example of such an advanced capability.

Driver (DLL) Debugging

As you learned in Chapter 6, most types of device drivers for CE exist as dynamic link libraries (DLLs). CE DLLs follow the conventions of Win32 DLLs and must be associated with an EXE module. In most cases, this module is the Device Manager (`device.exe`), whose primary responsibility is the loading and unloading of device drivers both at system startup and upon device insertion (for PC card and USB devices). In addition, like Win32 DLLs, CE DLLs have a primary entry point that you identify to the linker, typically named `DllMain`. Both of these facts present additional challenges for the debugging of CE drivers with the eMVC application-level debugger.

Note:
Many other authors (and Microsoft itself) have examined the topic of the building and development of Win32 DLLs in great detail. Therefore, we will not be rediscovering this information here. If you need a source code example, however, refer to the sample driver discussed in the Driver Mapper section.

When the CE kernel begins to map your DLL into the process space of its associated EXE module, the primary entry point is called with the `DLL_PROCESS_ATTACH` argument to get things started. If at this point your code returns `TRUE`, indicating successful initialization, the DLL is officially loaded and available to its calling EXE module. Until this happens, the CE kernel reports that your DLL is not yet loaded when queried by the remote debugger, even though it clearly must have been loaded in order to call the `DllMain` function. When you're using the application-level debugger in the CETK, this means that you will not be able to set breakpoints in your `DLL_PROCESS_ATTACH` code. The kernel-level debugger provided with the CEPB, however, will allow debugging of the `DLL_PROCESS_ATTACH` code. Upon return from `DllMain` (called with the `DLL_PROCESS_ATTACH` argument), the DLL appears loaded to the application-level debugger, so all other calls to `DllMain` may be debugged. In the Driver Mapper section presented later in this chapter, we will discuss how you can circumvent this problem by mapping the driver into its own process space.

As was just mentioned, a CE driver is associated with the EXE module `device.exe` (the Device Manager), which runs in its own process space. At system startup, `device.exe` is loaded and begins navigating the registry to determine which other drivers must also be loaded (refer to Chapters 6 through 8 for more information on the role of `device.exe` in the CE architecture). If the driver supports an installable device (a device that may be inserted by the end user), it will not be loaded until device insertion, at which time `device.exe` will enumerate the inserted device and find the matching driver. In either case, drivers are loaded into the address space of `device.exe` as individual threads.

Running as a DLL loaded by `device.exe` is not a problem when you're using the CEPB kernel-level debugger, but it is a problem when you're using the eMVC application-level debugger to debug drivers that support installable devices. The root of the problem is in the inability of the eMVC debugger to attach to running DLLs. For example, let's assume that your driver is designed to run on a standard platform and is loaded at the moment of device insertion. When you start the eMVC and attempt to debug your driver DLL, you are prompted for the name of the associated EXE module and its location on your workstation's hard disk. Entering this information causes the EXE module to be run on the standard platform, in an attempt to load your DLL debuggee.

Unfortunately, this process does not work on standard platforms, where your DLL is loaded by `device.exe`, which is already running. So what's a CE developer who is developing for standard platforms to do? Throughout this chapter we will discuss various alternatives for developing a driver for an installable device targeted to a standard platform. For now, we will mention these alternatives briefly and refer to the sections in this chapter where they are discussed in more detail.

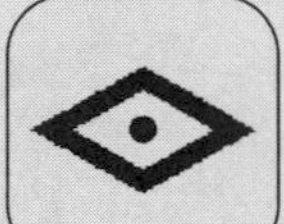

Note:
It is unlikely that you would use the CETK debugger on a standard platform to debug a driver that supports an onboard (noninstallable) device. Driver development for an onboard device implies that your device exists on a custom platform and that you rebuild the kernel image to include your driver in ROM or flash memory. Because rebuilding the kernel image requires the CEPB, we will assume that you would normally use the kernel-level debugger provided in the CEPB for debugging a driver that supports an onboard device rather than the CETK application-level debugger.

One alternative is to use the Log Tracer tool (provided in source code form at this book's Web site or on the enclosed CD), which is described later in the chapter. Log Tracer provides a replacement for the `DEBUGMSG` macros normally used to send `printf`-style debug messages to your remote development workstation. It operates independently of the remote debugger by writing the debug messages to a log file on the target platform.

Driver Mapper (also provided in source code form at this book's Web site or on the enclosed CD) is another alternative. It provides a solution slightly more intrusive then Log Tracer, but it has the advantage of allowing the remote debugger to debug all but the `DLL_PROCESS_ATTACH` code. Using Driver Mapper effectively maps the address space of the driver (associated with the `device.exe` process) to the address space of a stub EXE module. Driver Mapper is discussed later in the chapter.

If you have purchased the CEPB, you can use a PC as your target platform to enable kernel-level debugging of your driver. You add your driver to the build of the CEPC kernel by modifying certain BIB files. The configuration requirements of the CEPC platform are very specific, however, and you may find that configuring an unused PC to meet these requirements is quite challenging. The PC drivers provided for the CEPC platform support a limited selection of peripheral devices, such as the USB, LAN NIC, and PC card onboard devices, and you might need to hunt around for a supplier of this supported hardware (see Appendix C for a list of available CEPC vendors).

Breakpoint and Single-Stepping Issues

At some point you might find yourself single-stepping through your code, either to determine what code is executed after running a suspect function, or possibly to validate the execution of newly minted code. If we assume that you are using the eMVC integrated debugger and a standard platform for the development of your driver, we can also assume that as long as you are using Driver Mapper (which will be discussed in detail later in this chapter), single-stepping will work as expected. If, however, you have created a debug kernel image containing your driver, single-stepping through your code could pose a problem.

When the Romimage tool incorporates your driver into the kernel image, it, like all of the other drivers referenced in the BIB files, is set up to run at a particular location in ROM or flash memory. When you later choose to write this kernel image to ROM or flash memory, you will find that it is not possible to set a breakpoint for single-stepping through your code. This will be true even though you correctly built a debug kernel image with the stub code necessary to communicate with the kernel debugger running on the development workstation.

The reason is that the code pages, now running in place out of read-only memory (ROM or flash), cannot be modified by the stub code when a breakpoint is set from within the CEPB kernel debugger. These modifications are necessary to halt the execution of your driver code and are standard practice for most processor-independent debuggers. If your custom platform is based on a processor that contains special debug registers, then modifying the code to cause a breakpoint or single step (a series of successive breakpoints) is unnecessary. Single-stepping through code in ROM or flash memory should not be problem for processors so equipped. As of this writing, however, the kernel debugger stub code for x86 processors is the only one that takes advantage of this feature.

In most cases, being unable to single-step through code running from ROM or flash memory should not present too severe a limitation. If you simply build your debug kernel images to run out of RAM (by changing the address of the `RAMIMAGE` entry in the `platform.bib` file), you will be able to single-step with impunity. This is one reason for including support for enough extra RAM on your custom platform to equal the amount of ROM or flash memory.

One other problem you might encounter occurs when your driver code makes protected server library (PSL) calls. PSLs are hybrids between stand-alone processes and DLLs, and they provide a low-overhead mechanism for a client-server separation of application or driver code and the Win32 library. When you attempt to single-step *into* a Win32 PSL call, you will find that it functions just like a step *over* and puts you at the next line of source code, rather than displaying the assembly language listing of the called Win32 function.

Another problem occurs if you set a breakpoint in a function that is later called back by a function that resides in a PSL, and then attempt to display a call stack from your development workstation. The call stack will contain only a single entry. One way around this problem is to set a breakpoint just after the call to the Win32 function that causes the callback and use the `Go` command from within the callback. Don't use the step-out debugger command because the address of the caller of your function (the Win32 code itself) is considered invalid, so this command will behave as though you selected the `Go` command.

We have covered CE debugging capabilities in general and discussed some of the problems you might encounter. Next we will dive into the details, beginning with a discussion of debugger transports.

Debugger Transports

As we have already mentioned, CE debugging requires a means of communication between the target CE system running your driver and the debugger running on the development workstation. This communication can be achieved through different communication media, which are collectively referred to as **debugger transports**. Nothing affects the performance of your debugger more than the speed of the debugger transport. When single-stepping, for example, you will notice an immediate difference between the use of an Ethernet cable and an RS-232 cable connecting the CETK debugger to a custom platform. The delay from one line of source code to another is less noticeable when you're using the Ethernet cable.

Each single step requires certain overhead in the form of data and commands exchanged between the CETK debugger and the custom platform, so the faster the transport, the faster you may single-step, giving the Ethernet transport a decided advantage. If you have other debug windows open, such as a memory or variable window, additional overhead is required to update these windows between single steps, thus increasing the delay. In subsections that follow, we will discuss each of the debugger transports supported by the CETK and CEPB debuggers, including how they are activated and configured.

Platform Builder Remote Connections

The CEPB kernel debugger communicates with a target platform using a serial port, an Ethernet connection, an EXDI driver, or shared memory. When you're using a serial port, a null modem cable is connected between the development workstation and the serial port of your target platform. Debugger commands and responses are sent over the serial cable at a maximum of 115.2 Kbps, along with debug messages sent by the debug message macros, such as `DEBUGMSG` (which is discussed in the Zone Debugging section later in this chapter). The OAL functions `OEMInitDebugSerial`, `OEMWriteDebugByte`, `OEMWriteDebugString`, and `OEMReadDebugByte` are linked directly into the kernel and are used to communicate with the debugger.

Note:
Although it is possible for the CEPB kernel debugger to communicate with a CE kernel running on a standard platform, in this section we assume that the kernel debugger is connected to a custom platform. The term *target platform* is used, however, to imply that either platform type is supported.

Before the kernel can use the serial port, however, it must be loaded onto the target platform, into either RAM or flash memory. The kernel is loaded via a separate port, which is later used to maintain a CE command shell on the development workstation while the kernel debugger is active. This port typically exists as a bidirectional parallel port because it provides high data rates and allows rapid uploads of large kernel images from the development workstation to the target platform. The program that runs on the development workstation, acting as a kind of file server for the kernel image on the target platform, is called `cesh.exe` (CESH, for *CE Shell,* was discussed in detail in Chapter 3). This tool and its various options will be described further in the Debugging Use Cases section later in this chapter. The pin assignments of the parallel port cable do not conform to current standards for printer cables, and they provide a null cable connection. A specification for the pin assignments is contained in the CEPB online document entitled Parallel Port Interface Reference (see also Table 3.3).

Figure 9.3 depicts a typical remote connection between the kernel debugger and the development workstation using a serial port and a parallel port. The advantage of using a serial and parallel port combination as the interface to the development workstation is the relative simplicity of the supporting software running on the target system. When you bring up a custom platform for the first time, the board is gradually brought to life with the activation of individual subsystems. In this case it is often necessary to have debugging capability that relies on a minimum of functionality to allow the debugger to be used in debugging the boot loader and the hardware.

In this regard, the serial and parallel ports are often better options than an Ethernet port for connecting to the development workstation (refer to Chapters 4 and 5 for more information on the development of the boot loader and OAL software to support debugger connections). If reliable Ethernet hardware becomes available, you will find it a more attractive option than the

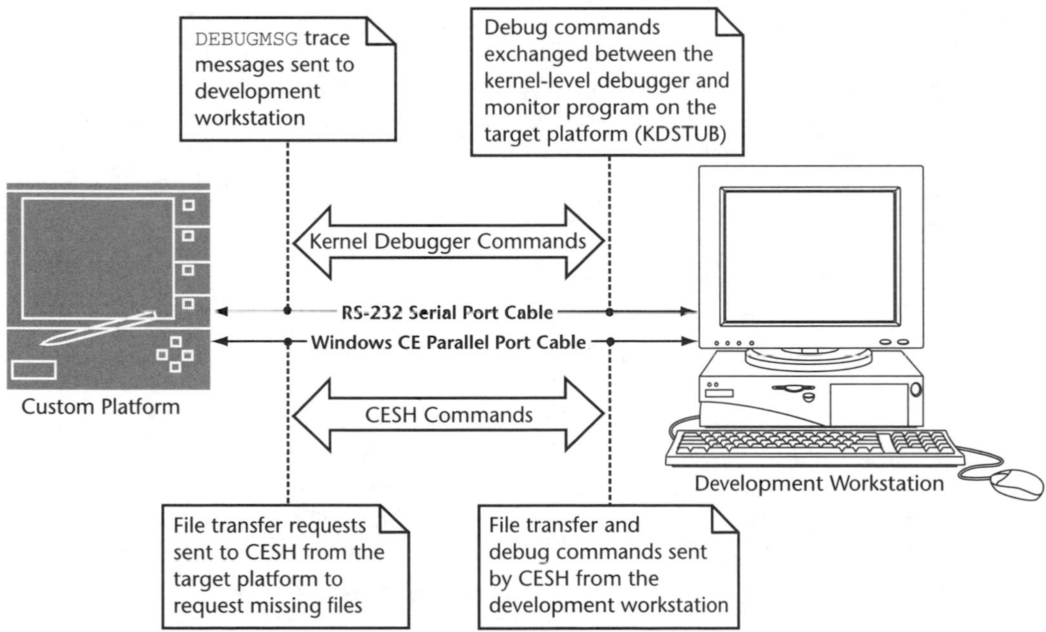

Figure 9.3 Kernel debugger serial port configuration

serial and parallel ports. Figure 9.4 depicts the configuration of a custom platform connected to a development workstation through a single Ethernet port.

The most notable difference between the serial and parallel port combination and the Ethernet port, when used for debugging, is the fact that a single cable can simultaneously support multiple debug services. Your development workstation is more likely to have a connection to a LAN than an available serial and parallel connection. Though the Ethernet connection is more difficult to configure, as you will soon see, it operates far more consistently on the development workstations of different manufacturers. Bidirectional parallel ports must often be configured by your workstation's BIOS, and often the implementation on older workstations is incompatible with that of newer workstations. In addition, the Ethernet connection is faster than the bidirectional parallel port and is not limited to the 20-foot maximum length of the parallel port cable. You can connect to your custom platform from literally anywhere an Internet connection exists. In the section titled Custom Platform Ethernet Debugging Configuration: Use Case 1 later in this chapter, we will discuss how an Ethernet kernel debugger connection is configured and how this connection may be used to communicate with your own debug tools running on the target platform.

Platform Manager

The Platform Manager is a tool provided in eMVC for configuring the connection to remote devices used for application-level debugging. If you are using a standard platform to debug your driver (perhaps using the utility discussed in the Driver Mapper section later in this chapter), the Platform Manager will allow you to describe the type of transport protocol your standard platform supports, grouped by device type (*H/PC Ver. 2.00, H/PC Pro 2.11, Palm-size PC 2.01, Pocket PC 3.0,* and so on). The Platform Manager can also be used to configure the connection to custom platforms if you include this support in your kernel image. The inclusion of Platform Manager support in the build of a kernel image for a custom platform is covered later in this section.

In Figure 9.5, the Platform Manager dialog box, accessible under the **Tools | Configure Platform Manager** menu option, displays the list of platforms currently recognized. New plat-

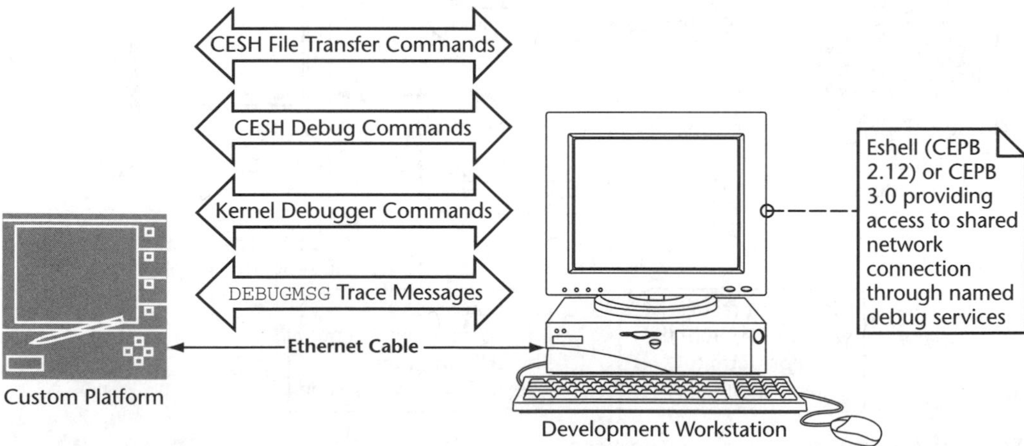

Figure 9.4 Kernel debugger Ethernet configuration

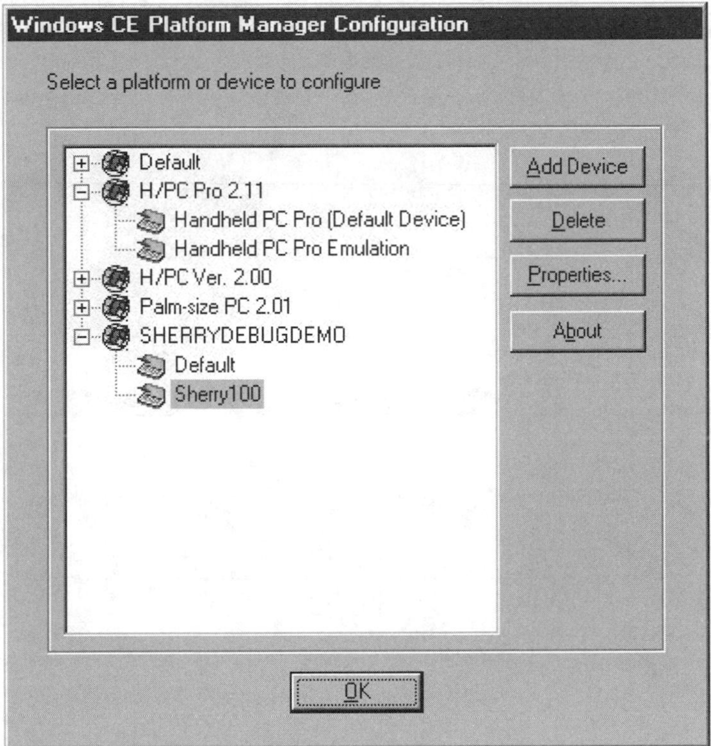

Figure 9.5 Platform Manager Configuration dialog box

forms are added through the installation of additional platform SDKs. Microsoft generally provides the platform SDKs (PSDKs) for standard platforms, and makes them freely available for download from its Web site. Not depicted are the AutoPC and Pocket PC platforms, both of which have an associated PSDK.

The names of the known devices for each platform type appear indented under the platform name. As displayed in Figure 9.5, there are two Handheld PC Pro 2.11 devices, one associated with the emulator for the Handheld PC Pro platform (included in the installation of the Handheld PC PSDK) and the other associated with a generic Handheld PC Pro "default device." If a particular device is selected, the **Properties...** button may be pressed to produce a list of the supported transports. (More information on the Sherry platform is available in Appendix C.) The platform appearing in Figure 9.5 called SHERRYDEBUGDEMO is a custom platform that was installed from a PSDK generated through the **Platform | Export SDK** menu option in the CEPB. If the **Properties** button were pressed for the SHERRYDEBUGDEMO platform (or device in this context) called Sherry100, it would display a list of supported debugger transports, as depicted in Figure 9.6.

Each of the transports listed in Figure 9.6 requires a separate supporting software component on the target device. The optional components under the **Platform Manager** folder in the

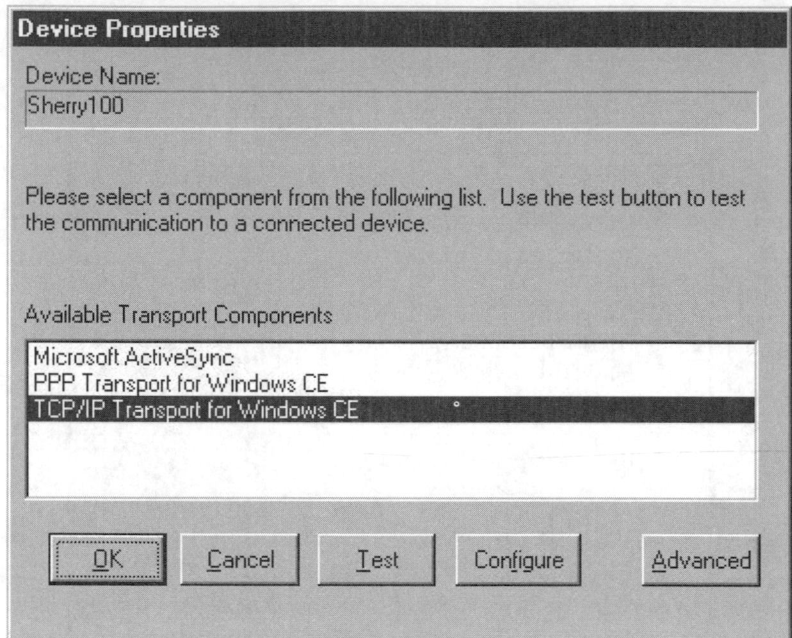

Figure 9.6 Platform Manager **Device Properties** dialog box

CEPB **Catalog** window (discussed in more detail in Chapter 3) were included in the build of the Sherry platform's kernel image by simply being dragged from the **Catalog** window to the **Component View** window for the Sherry board's CEPB project (SHERRYDEBUGDEMO). A **Catalog** window for the Sherry platform is provided in Figure 9.7.

Each component appearing under **transport** in Figure 9.7 corresponds to the target platform DLL that supports communication with the eMVC application-level debugger running on the development workstation. These transports would also be listed in the Platform Manager's **Properties** dialog box for the custom device (displayed for the Sherry100 device in Figure 9.6). As the names imply, `pm_ppp` is the target device component that supports communication using PPP (a Mac layer protocol), `pm_tcpip` supports communication using TCP/IP, and `pm_cesrv` supports communication using CE services. All three of these target device software components are included in the standard installation of CEPB. Additional DLLs that run on the development workstation (COM components) are needed for each of these transports and are automatically included in the standard eMVC installations.

You may also define a custom transport for your platform that enables the use of the eMVC application-level debugger. The APIs for the transport DLLs that reside on both the development workstation and the target are defined in the Exporting a Software Development Kit section of the CEPB online documentation, along with a description of how to generate the development workstation and target device projects using the WCE Transport Layer Wizard. Both projects are generated under CEPB, but the one for the development workstation uses a specialized interface known as the Component Object Model (COM) and may be built only through the use of Visual C++ (the IDE on which the CETK, not eMVC, is based). When gener-

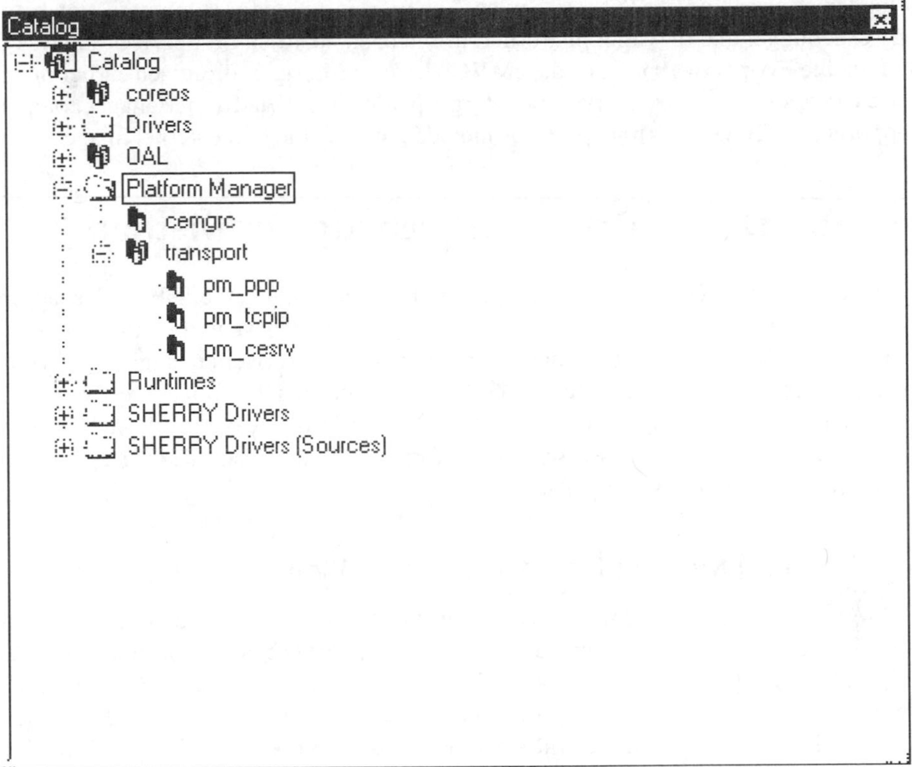

Figure 9.7 Catalog view showing Platform Manager components

ating your custom platform's PSDK (using CEPB), you are prompted for the location of the COM components so that they can be added to your PSDK's installation.

In Figure 9.8, a typical CETK application-level debugger configuration is depicted. Driver Mapper (discussed later in the chapter) is used to allow debugging of a stream-interface driver

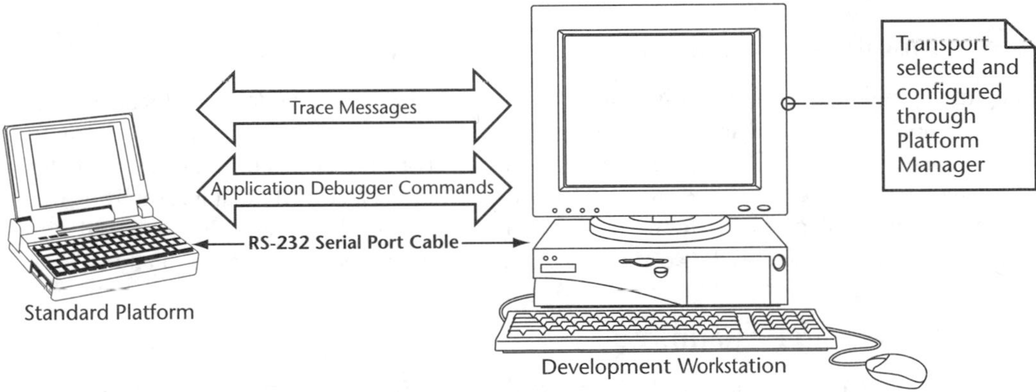

Figure 9.8 Platform Manager serial port configuration

that is loaded on insertion of a PC card device. The transport used for communication between the eMVC debugger and the target platform (custom or standard) is CE Services and was selected via the **Properties** option of the eMVC Platform Manager (discussed earlier in this section). We can assume that for this particular target platform, the Platform Manager component that supports the CE Services transport was included in the build of the kernel image.

Building a Device Driver for Debugging: Method 1

Before you can use the CEPB kernel debugger for driver debugging, the IDE work space must include both a platform and a device driver project. In this section we will focus on those aspects of the IDE work space configuration that are essential to device driver debugging. We will assume that you have successfully created a platform project and that you are ready to begin debugging a device driver, either one developed from scratch or one being adapted from an existing driver provided in the CEPB sample platforms. Let's first examine the steps required to debug a driver provided in a sample platform.

Step 1: Selecting Modules from the Catalog Window

The **Catalog** window (displayed through the **View | Catalog** menu option), as the name implies, shows a catalog of the modules provided by the board support package (BSP) that you selected when creating a new platform with the WCE Platform Wizard (activated through the **File | New | Platforms** menu option). After the platform is automatically generated, you drag the modules (typically device drivers) from the **Catalog** window to the **Component View** window, viewable in **Platform View** display mode. If you are debugging a sample driver supplied in your BSP, you may drag it from the **Catalog** window to the **Component View** window to include it in the build of the ROM image.

Another option is to treat the sample driver as your own driver by building it as a distinct project (discussed later in this section). The term *project* in this context is differentiated from *platform.* Whereas *project* refers to the source files required for the build of a single module, *platform* refers to the collective build of all modules, including the final generation of the ROM image file, `nk.bin`.

Step 2: Modifying Platform.bib

Using the **Parameter View** dialog box of the **Platform View** display mode, you indicate which modules should be included in the ROM image by editing the `platform.bib` file. For a sample driver, the entries in the `platform.bib` file should already be present. You simply need to determine which environment variable is associated with your driver and verify that it is set by using the **Environment** tab of the **Platform Settings** dialog box. This file is eventually combined with other BIB files and is used by the `romimage.exe` build tool that is automatically run by CEPB.

Step 3: Modifying Platform.reg

You must also examine the file `platform.reg` to determine which environment variable is associated with the registry entries required for the sample driver, and verify that this value is set using the

Environment tab. Like the BIB files, this file is combined with other REG files and is processed by the `regcomp.exe` build tool. Chapter 3 describes the internals of the build process in more detail.

Step 4: Setting Up a Stub Project

Having modified the `platform.bib` and `platform.reg` files, you are just about ready to debug a sample driver. The final step requires that you set up at least one project using the **File | New | Projects** tab. For our purposes it does not matter what type of project you set up because the sample driver will be built through the use of a `Sources` file in the directory containing the driver's source files. As you will see shortly in the Debugging Use Cases section, the CEPB IDE will not allow you to start the kernel debugger without at least one project configured.

Thus far, you have performed the steps necessary to build the sample driver whenever the build of the platform is initiated. Certainly these steps must be completed by the time you're ready to include the final version of the driver in the release build of your ROM image. Completing these steps also enables the use of the kernel debugger to establish breakpoints and debug your driver's source code (explored in the Debugging Use Cases section). You may find, however, that regenerating the ROM image each time you modify the source code of the sample driver is time-consuming. Not only must you wait for the ROM image itself (`nk.bin`) to be generated on your development workstation, but you must also upload it to the memory (flash or RAM) of your target platform. However, a faster alternative—one that allows you to simply build the driver itself and reboot the target platform when you want the new version to be loaded—is explored in the next section.

Building a Device Driver for Debugging: Method 2

Figure 9.9 shows the relationship between the driver executable and the ROM image file. The ROM image contains all the modules required by the custom platform, with the exception of the driver under development. When the CE kernel attempts to load the driver and determines that it is not present in the RAM or ROM memory regions of the object store, it attempts to load the driver into RAM using the CE Shell (CESH) build tool. If the driver exists in the CEPB release directory on your development workstation (the directory used by CEPB to collect all modules that would later be combined into the ROM image file, `nk.bin`), it is transported to the target platform over the active CESH transport (parallel, serial, or Ethernet).

CESH is a tool we will learn more about in the Debugging Use Cases section of this chapter. For this method of building a device driver, however, its capabilities as an extension to the CE file system are used to allow the driver executable to reside on the development workstation. Between successive code changes you need only rebuild the driver and restart your platform, to initiate the transfer of the driver from the development workstation to the target platform. In the next few sections we will present modifications of the method 1 steps for method 2.

Step 1: Removing Modules from the Catalog Window

Let's assume that you're using a driver provided in a BSP and that you have selected this driver for inclusion in your ROM image by dragging the component from the **Catalog** window to the **Component View** window. In this step you must delete the component from the **Component**

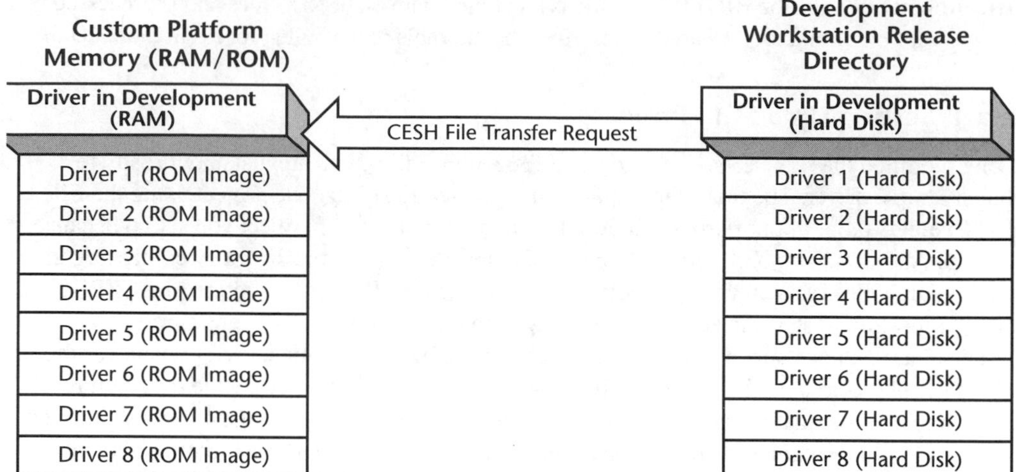

Figure 9.9 Using the CESH virtual file system to support debugging of a device driver

View window because it will instead become a part of your platform's work space through the addition of a new project. If your driver was developed from scratch, you may have already established a project, so in this case this step does not apply.

Step 2: Creating a Driver Project

In this step we will create a driver project from an existing driver provided in the BSP for our platform. We will focus on how the build of the driver, as established by the BSP, can be adapted to the build process that occurs in a driver project.

First, select the menu option **Files | New | Projects** and choose the **WCE Dynamic-Link Library** Project Wizard entry in the list box. This selection causes a project to be generated for a DLL executable module that will build the source for our driver. A dialog box then appears, asking you to identify the type of DLL you wish to generate. For now, just select the simplest DLL type, though any of the options presented would be acceptable.

Step 3: Adding the Driver Source Modules to the Project

When the wizard generated the project, it automatically added it to the work space for your platform. What it did not do was add the source files from the BSP sample driver. To determine the source files required by the sample driver, open the `Sources` file (described in more detail in Chapter 10), located in the directory `.\PLATFORM\<Platform Name>\DRIVERS\<Driver Name>`. Each of the source files for the driver is assigned to the macro `SOURCES` asd should be added to the driver project created in step 2. If a DEF file appears in the source directory, it, too, should be added to the driver project.

You may also need to add the path names associated with the macros `INCLUDES`, `TARGETLIBS`, and `SOURCELIBS` to the driver project. Begin by adding the path name assigned to the `INCLUDES` macro to the list of include file path names available in the **Project | Settings** menu option. The TARGETLIBS and SOURCELIBS macros may have already been included as a default library list for the driver project. If undefined symbol errors appear when the driver project is built, try adding the libraries associated with these macros to the driver project (also available through the **Project | Settings** menu option).

In most cases the values of the other macros in the Sources file need not be transferred to the driver project. If you encounter build errors not explained by a missing library or include file, you may want to attempt a series of builds successively defining each of these macros until all build errors have been resolved.

Step 4: Modifying the DLL Entry

Another macro in the Sources file, named DLLENTRY, defines the name of the function called by the DLL startup code. The function that is called by the startup code and is automatically linked with the DLL project established in step 2, however, must be DllMain. If you find that the function associated with the DLLENTRY macro is different, you must change it in the driver's sample source code to DllMain.

If you overlooked this step, you might expect to see a build error or a warning message generated during the loading of the driver and then sent to the debugger running on the development workstation. In fact, however, your driver just silently fails to load, leading you to believe that no attempt was made to load it. You might even find yourself checking for an incorrect registry entry in the file platform.reg. To avoid such frustration, always remember that when you're using a project to build the sample driver source code provided with a BSP, the name of the startup function should be DllMain.

Step 5: Modifying Platform.bib

An entry in platform.bib ensures that the module will be included in the ROM image. Because it is our intent to download the executable module on demand using CESH, we must remove the entry in platform.bib for the sample driver. One option is simply to comment out the lines that reference the driver executable.

An excerpt of a platform.bib file for the driver mousecom.dll is provided in Listing 9.1.

Listing 9.1 Adding an environment variable to the executable module entry in platform.bib

```
...
IF SHERRY_MOUSECOM_CESH!
IF SHERRY_MOUSECOM
       mousecom.dll     $(_FLATRELEASEDIR)\mousecom.dll              NK        SH
ENDIF
ENDIF

IF SHERRY_SERIAL
       serial.dll       $(_FLATRELEASEDIR)\serial.dll                NK        SH
ENDIF
```

```
IF SHERRY_KEYBOARD
        keybddr.dll       $(_FLATRELEASEDIR)\keybddr.dll                NK        SH
ENDIF
...
```

Note that the reference to the module `mousecom.dll` is enclosed in an `IF` statement. This prevents the inclusion of `mousecom.dll` during the Sysgen phase of the build process (refer to Chapter 10 for more information on this phase) unless the `SHERRY_MOUSECOM` environment variable was defined. In this example we have added another environment variable, `SHERRY_MOUSECOM_CESH!`, allowing the inclusion of `mousecom.dll` only if `SHERRY_MOUSECOM` is defined *and* `SHERRY_MOUSECOM_CESH` is *not* defined. So, by simply adding the environment variable `SHERRY_MOUSECOM_CESH` to the **Platform | Settings | Environment** dialog box, we remove the module `mousecom.dll` from the ROM image. When you are finished debugging this module, you can add it back to the ROM image (undoubtedly a requirement for your release build) by removing this environment variable through **Platform | Settings | Environment**.

Step 6: Modifying Platform.reg

In method 1, we needed to verify that an entry was present in the `platform.reg` file for the sample BSP driver. Without a registry entry, it would not be possible for the Device Manager (`device.exe`) to associate a particular driver with an onboard or installable device. Therefore, the driver would not be loaded during system startup (or device insertion). The same requirement exists for method 2 as well. Even though the executable module is not included in the ROM image for method 2, its registry entries are still required to cause the loading of the driver, and the subsequent transfer from CESH to the RAM of the target platform.

Now when the platform or the project is built, the driver's executable module is copied to the directory associated with the environment variable `_FLATRELEASEDIR`. When the Device Manager attempts to load the driver, the CE file system will find that it is not present in the local object store and request the file from CESH. CESH will then upload to the target platform the recently rebuilt driver from the release directory (copied here during the build process) on the development workstation.

Debugging Use Cases

Thus far in our discussion of CE device driver debugging, we have covered some basic debugging concepts and the steps required to build a device driver using CEPB. This discussion included a description of the tools used to connect to a remote device from both the eMVC (providing application-level debugging) and the CEPB (providing kernel-level debugging). What we need now are a few actual debugging use cases in which we begin to apply what we have learned about CE debugging transports. Along the way we will discuss the use of additional tools required for connecting a custom platform to CEPB's kernel-level debugger.

Each use case will focus on a different configuration for connecting the target device to the debugger. The first two use cases will focus on how to establish a debugging session between the CEPB kernel debugger and a custom platform. Use case 1 will include a typical Ethernet configuration for connecting a custom platform to the kernel debugger. The various tools that run on the development workstation (under CEPB 2.12 and 3.0) to allow a single Ethernet connection to be shared by multiple debugging tools will also be presented. Use case 2 will discuss debug configurations for custom platforms that require a combination of a serial and a parallel port or two serial ports.

In use case 3 we will focus on the use of the eMVC for driver debugging on standard platforms. We will introduce two tools, Driver Mapper and Log Tracer, that help overcome the inability of the eMVC application debugger to debug a dynamically loaded device driver. Though the capability for standard platforms to provide support for CEPB kernel-level debugging in a retail build is feasible, to date few if any standard platforms offer this capability.

Custom Platform Ethernet Debugging Configuration: Use Case 1

In this use case we will assume that your custom platform provides an Ethernet port and optionally a serial port. The Ethernet port will be used to connect our custom platform to the kernel debugger on the development workstation. The serial port will be used to communicate with the custom platform's boot loader (refer to Chapter 4 for more information) to configure how the CE kernel will be started. In this use case the custom platform will need to be configured with an IP address, so a terminal emulation application (HyperTerminal, for example) will be used to enter the IP address from the development workstation.

If all that was needed to configure the custom platform were the IP address, it would also have been possible for the boot loader to automatically obtain an IP address from a DHCP (Dynamic Host Configuration Protocol) server. In this use case, however, a DHCP server is not available, so the IP address must be entered manually through HyperTerminal over a serial port communicating with the boot loader. Figure 9.10 shows the connections between the custom

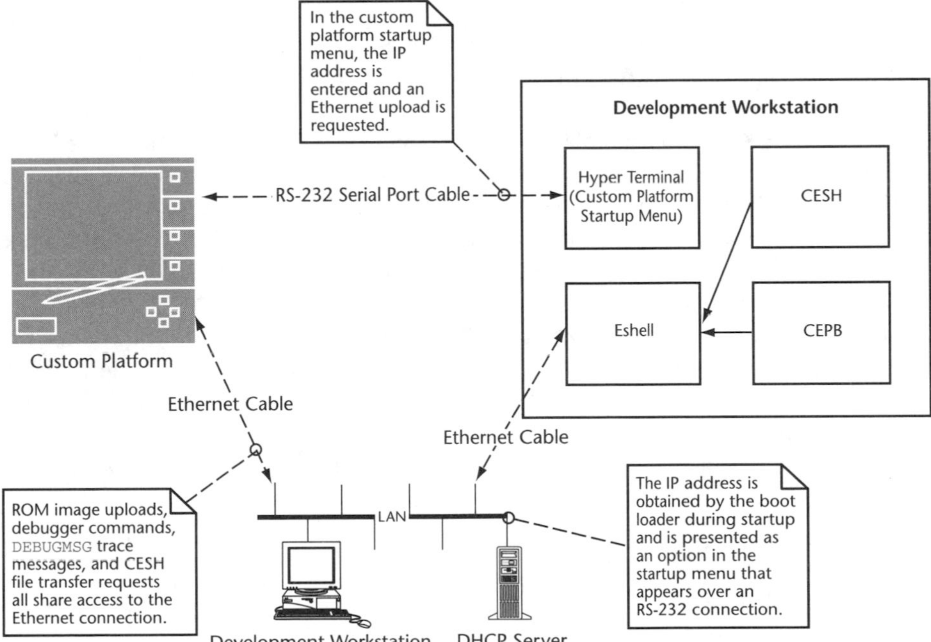

Figure 9.10 Use Case 1: Ethernet kernel debugging configuration

platform and the development workstation. Note the serial cable (null modem) used for communication with the boot loader.

The custom platform we will demonstrate in this use case is called a Sherry board and is used as a reference platform for the SH3 processor. It provides three serial ports (one of which is typically used for a connection to an external mouse), one parallel port, and one Ethernet port, and it will be used in the kernel debugging use cases presented in this chapter. Information on where this platform can be purchased is available in Appendix C.

The Ethernet connection between the development workstation and the Sherry board was made with a "crossover" 10Base-T cable, allowing a direct connection to the custom platform from the Ethernet adapter on the development workstation. Because a crossover cable was used, the Ethernet connection was able to exist independently of the corporate LAN, and without the need for a network hub. The serial cable is a "null modem" serial cable, to support the direct connection of two Data Terminal Equipment (DTE; custom platform and development workstation) devices. (The pin configuration of a standard serial cable assumes a connection to an external device [modem, printer, and so on] on one end and a host PC on the other.) The development workstation in this configuration is a Pentium II laptop running at 450MHz, with a 10GB hard disk and 256MB of RAM.

Note:
The primary development workstation in all these use cases was a Pentium II laptop. We have found that the compromises required when you use a laptop for development are insignificant, compared to the advantages of total mobility in the development of software for a mobile device on a mobile workstation.

Step 1: Configuring Eshell for the Ethernet Connection

Before you can get the kernel debugger to communicate with your custom platform over Ethernet, you must first get your custom platform to be detected by CEPB and its associated tools. This is accomplished in CEPB 2.12 by a stand-alone tool called Eshell that acts as a kind of proxy server for the connection with the target platform. In CEPB 3.0, however, a newer version of Eshell provides a superset of the functionality provided by the CEPB 2.12 Eshell. The key difference is that the use of Eshell in CEPB 3.0 is optional because its functionality is also provided as an integrated option of the CEPB 3.0 IDE.

From this point forward, as we describe the steps for each use case, we will begin with a discussion of how they are performed in CEPB 2.12 and then contrast this with how the same steps are performed in CEPB 3.0. In most cases, you will be concerned with only one or the other, but it is important that you read both descriptions. If you are using CEPB 3.0, you will undoubtedly benefit from an understanding of the way things were done in CEPB 2.12, to explain the implicit decisions made in Microsoft's development of CEPB 3.0.

Note:
A simple example of the benefit of some knowledge of CEPB 2.12, for those focused exclusively on the use of CEPB 3.0, is in the name of the executable `eshell.exe`. In CEPB 3.0, the more complete name of this tool is *Windows CE Debug Shell.* One might wonder why it was not simply called `ceshell.exe`, especially since it supports target platforms with either Ethernet or serial/parallel port configurations. The name `eshell.exe` was most likely retained for continuity because the version of `eshell.exe` provided in CEPB 3.0 is a direct descendant of the `eshell.exe` provided in CEPB 2.12.

CEPB 2.12

The best way to understand the role of Eshell in a connection to your target platform is to imagine it as an Internet Domain Name System (DNS) for CE custom platforms. Its primary responsibility is to associate a platform name that you define with a connection (and its configuration) to a particular custom platform. Then, all CEPB 2.12 debug tools running on the development workstation that need to communicate over Ethernet do so using the functions of the Ethernet debug services API described in the CEPB online documentation (valid for CEPB 2.12 and 3.0). This platform name is then used in the parameter list of certain Ethernet debug services functions. As you will soon see, the platform name is also passed on the command line of certain CEPB 2.12 debug tools to cause the use of an Ethernet connection, rather than the default serial or parallel port connection, for remote device communication.

To get Eshell to recognize your custom platform, you must first get it to appear in the **Controlled Devices** list that is accessed through the Eshell menu option **Tools | Manage Device List,** depicted in Figure 9.11. To do so, in general you simply activate the custom platform and then select the **Manage Device List** dialog box from Eshell. The designated name for your platform should appear in the **Non Controlled Devices** list box, from which you can add it to the **Controlled Devices** list box by selecting it and clicking the center button (see Figure 9.11).

Precisely what happens when the name of your custom platform magically appears in the list box, as just described, is discussed more fully in Chapter 4. Suffice it to say that the boot loader on your custom platform must be specifically provisioned to communicate with Eshell using a special protocol. In CEPB 2.12, the source code for this protocol is its only documentation and is located in the `.\PUBLIC\COMMON\OAK\DRIVERS\ETHDBG\EBOOT` directory. The object module library `eboot.lib` is built from this source code and contains the implementation of a series of functions prefixed with *Eboot.*

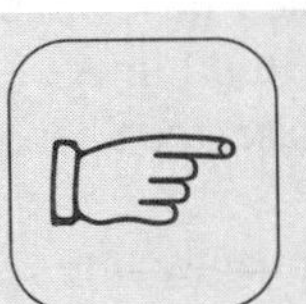

Note:
The Eshell protocol, specifically the `BOOTME` packet, is documented in part in the CEPB 3.0 online documentation.

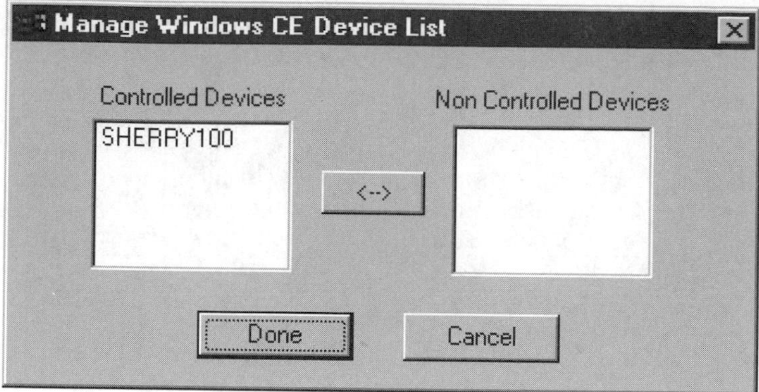

Figure 9.11 CEPB 2.12 Eshell **Manage Device List** dialog box

After your boot loader has configured its onboard NIC and obtained an IP address, either through a boot loader terminal interface (as in the Sherry board, which uses a serial port to communicate with HyperTerminal) or through a DHCP server, the function `EbootSendBootme` is called. This function causes a specially formatted `BOOTME` packet to be broadcast (sent to IP address 255.255.255.255), and if Eshell is loaded at this moment, the name of your custom platform (included in the `BOOTME` packet) will appear in the list.

As already described, the Sherry board's boot loader sends a startup menu to the development workstation, through its serial port. If your boot loader, like the Sherry boot loader, supports both Ethernet and serial port/parallel port debugging, you will also need a method to indicate to the boot loader that Ethernet debugging is desired, before your platform can be detected by Eshell according to the sequence just described. A sample boot loader startup menu for the Sherry board demonstrated in this use case is provided in Figure 9.12. This startup menu appears when a particular button is pressed in combination with the reset button. Simply pressing the **E** key selects the Ethernet debugging option. As prompted by the boot loader, pressing the **Enter** key then selects the default IP address saved in EEPROM because a DHCP server is not available.

At this point, Eshell is ready to communicate with your custom platform using its specialized protocol (supported in your boot loader by linking in the `eboot.lib` object module library provided in CEPB). Once your custom platform is selected as a controlled device, the device name is automatically retained by Eshell, and the name reappears when Eshell is reloaded. One additional step is required, however, before a ROM image can be uploaded to your device. You must provide the location of the CEPB ROM image file to be uploaded, through the **File | Select Image File…** option. Other options are also available to control how the selected ROM image file is processed when the presence of a controlled device is detected (in this use case, the Sherry board itself).

If you are using CEPB to build various configurations of a ROM image, you may want to select the **Download Only On Command** option in the **Options** menu. This option allows you to change the release directory of the ROM image before the download is initiated. Otherwise, if Eshell is already loaded when you restart your custom platform, the ROM image last selected is automatically uploaded, rather than the newly built ROM image in a different release directory.

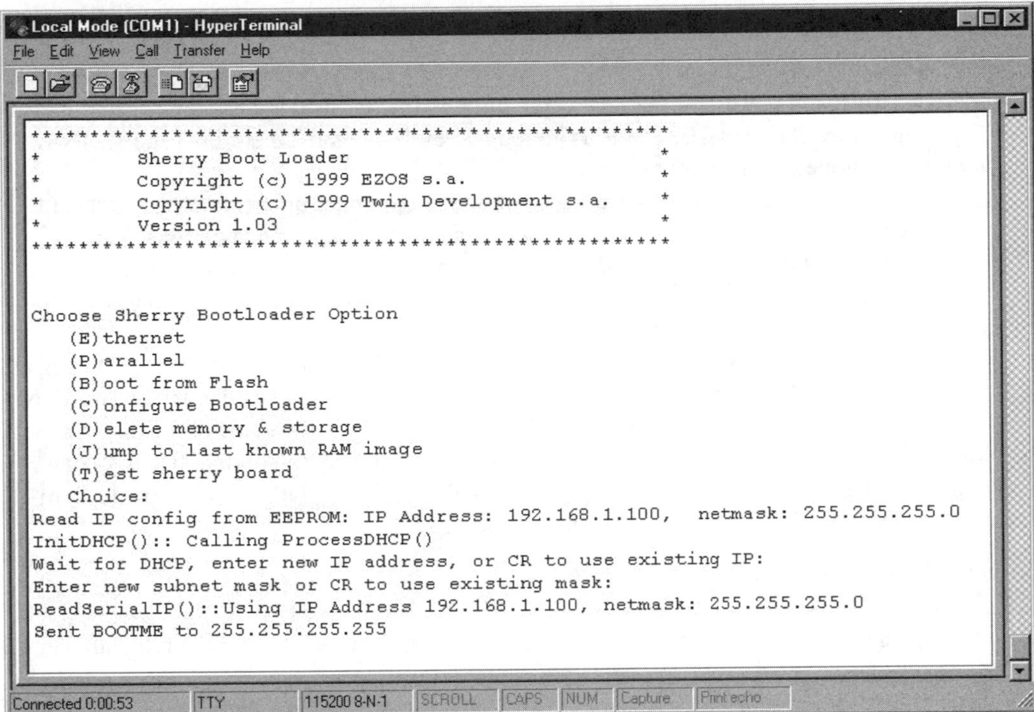

Figure 9.12 Sample boot loader startup menu

Once the location of the ROM image file (`nk.bin`) in the release directory has been selected, you need to reboot your custom platform to generate another `BOOTME` packet. The first `BOOTME` packet, generated when the Ethernet option was selected from the Sherry board's boot loader menu, was used to add the platform name *Sherry100* to the list of controlled devices. On the next reboot, when the `BOOTME` packet is sent from the Sherry board, Eshell immediately recognizes the platform.

CEPB 3.0

In CEPB 3.0, the role of Eshell has changed significantly. It no longer acts as a proxy for Ethernet connections to the target platform. The CEPB 3.0 IDE is able to request Ethernet debug services independently, including the upload of the kernel image to the target platform. This capability makes the use of Eshell in CEPB 3.0 for Ethernet debugging optional. If you wish to access the CE command line (*CESH* in the Ethernet debug service, *PPSH* in CEPB 2.12) through your Ethernet connection, but as a stand-alone application (separate from the CEPB 3.0 IDE), this is where the CEPB 3.0 version of Eshell comes in handy. The CEPB 3.0 Eshell registers for both the CESH and DBGMSG Ethernet debug services, and provides a split-window view of the output from each debug service. We will discuss how to configure the CEPB 3.0 Eshell for Ethernet debug services later in this section.

In CEPB 2.12, the DBGMSG Ethernet debug service is provided by a stand-alone application called `ceterm.exe` (described later in this chapter), while the CESH (or PPSH in CEPB

2.12) debug service is provided by another application, called cesh.exe. Only the DBGMSG Ethernet debug service is integrated with the CEPB 2.12 IDE, so cesh.exe must be used for a CE command shell over Ethernet. When attempting to use cesh.exe or ceterm.exe for Ethernet debug services in CEPB 3.0, however, you will find that the use of the -e<platform name> parameter available in CEPB 2.12 is no longer valid. You must therefore use Eshell to obtain all stand-alone Ethernet debug services.

Cesh.exe and ceterm.exe in CEPB 3.0 continue to provide support for serial and parallel ports. In CEPB 3.0, the com{1|2|3|<n>]} command-line option may be used to cause CESH to use a serial port instead of the default parallel port. This option is also available in cesh.exe for CEPB 2.12, though it is not documented in the pop-up documentation window that appears for the command-line option -?.

When you load Eshell, you will always be prompted for the name of your target platform, as depicted in Figure 9.13. If at this point you reset your target platform, its name will be added to the list box when the BOOTME packet is received. You may also type the name of the platform so that when it is later reset, a connection will be formed automatically (an option that was not available in the CEPB 2.12 version of Eshell). You may specify the platform name on the command line to bypass this dialog box, using the following syntax:

```
Eshell [<platform name>]
```

The first time a particular platform name is entered, you will be prompted for the full path name of the kernel image file (nk.bin) for upload to the target platform.

After you press the **OK** button, the main Eshell window appears as depicted in Figure 9.19, but without all the messages. These messages are produced later, after the kernel image is uploaded to the target platform and is then activated by the boot loader (discussed later, in step 4). The top pane provides the same services as CESH, in an editable, scrollable window. The bottom pane contains the messages associated with the DBGMSG Ethernet debug service and provides the same services as Ceterm. The **DOWNLOAD** and **CLEAN** indications appearing in the lower right corner describe how the kernel image is processed on reset of the target platform. In this case, *DOWNLOAD* indicates that the kernel image is always uploaded to the target whenever it is reset, and *CLEAN* indicates the clearing of any file system that may remain in RAM since the last time the kernel was active.

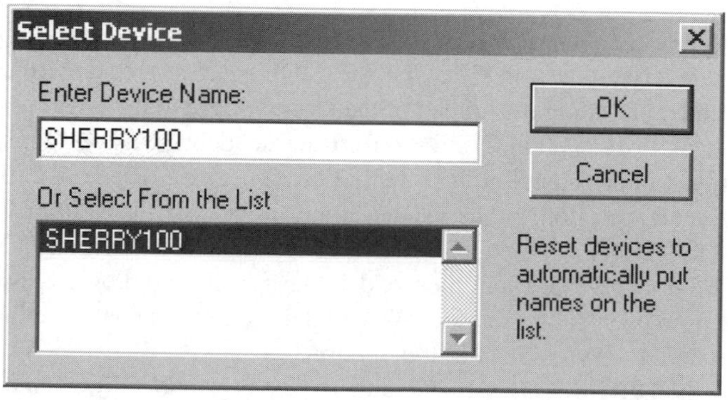

Figure 9.13 CEPB 3.0 **Select Device** dialog box

In this use case we have opted to use the **Options | Download on reset** menu option, indicated by the appearance of **DOWNLOAD** in the lower right corner of the window. This option causes the kernel image to be automatically uploaded to the target as soon as the `BOOTME` packet is received. The CEPB 3.0 version of Eshell does not provide an equivalent to the CEPB 2.12 **Download Only On Command** option, so we need to be careful when switching to a kernel image located in a different release directory. To avoid an inadvertent upload of the wrong kernel image, we must select the release directory of any other kernel image files (by selecting **File | Select Image)** before resetting the target platform.

One other aspect of the CEPB 3.0 version of Eshell that you should be aware of is its support of certain advanced settings accessible through the **Options** menu. By selecting **Download Only**, one of the options depicted in Figure 9.14, you can make the CEPB 3.0 version of Eshell function more like its CEPB 2.12 predecessor, without CESH and Ceterm integration. The connection to the target platform would be used only to upload the kernel image. CESH and Ceterm Ethernet debugging services would not be requested. Using this same dialog box, you can cause parallel and serial connections to be used for CESH and Ceterm debug services, as will be demonstrated in the next use case 2.

Step 2: Configuring the Ethernet Connection in CE Platform Builder

Assuming everything went well in configuring Eshell to communicate with your custom platform, you must perform an analogous process for CEPB. In CEPB 2.12, the configuration of the Ethernet connection to the target platform is limited to kernel debug services, whereas in CEPB 3.0 the Ethernet connection may be configured for CE Shell (CESH) and Ceterm (DBGMSG) debug services as well. For this use case we have opted to use only the kernel debug services provided in CEPB 3.0 so that we may demonstrate the use of Eshell. As mentioned in step 1, however, the use of Eshell for Ethernet debugging is optional.

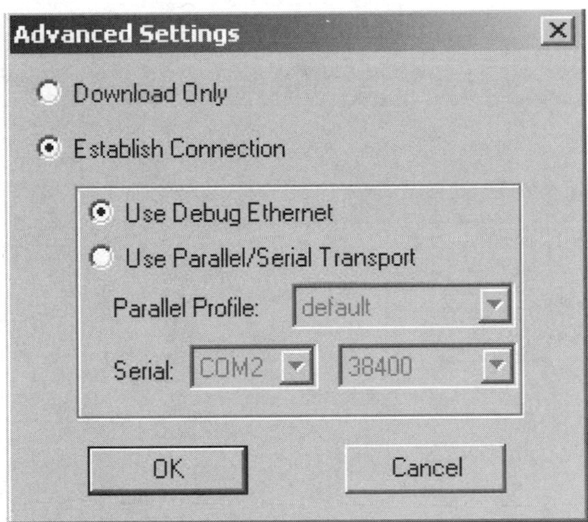

Figure 9.14 CEPB 3.0 Eshell **Advanced Settings** dialog box

CEPB 2.12

In CEPB 2.12, the kernel debugger Ethernet connection is configured through the **Build | Debugger Remote Connection** menu option. A dialog box appears with a separate list box for the connection type, limited to one selection: **Kernel Debugger Port**. Pressing the **Settings...** button causes the dialog box in Figure 9.15 to appear. In this use case the **Network (UDP)** option should be selected and the name of your custom platform (as it appears in Eshell's list of controlled devices; see Figure 9.11) entered in the adjacent edit field.

CEPB 3.0

In CEPB 3.0, the Ethernet connection to the remote target is configured through the **Target | Configure Remote Services** option. In Figure 9.16, the **Services** tab of the resulting dialog box is depicted. The type of transport may be selected for each debug service supported by CEPB 3.0. The first combobox allows the transport to be selected for both the CESH and Ceterm debug services. For this use case, the option **None** was selected because Eshell is being used to provide these services. This same combobox also contains **Ethernet** and **Parallel and Serial** options. If the **Parallel and Serial** option were selected, the parallel port would be used for the CESH service and the serial port for the Ceterm service. The **Parallel** and **Serial** tabs appearing in the dialog box provide certain configuration options unique to the type of transport. The **Ethernet** tab, however, provides the platform name of the remote target for the Ethernet connection, and is depicted in Figure 9.17.

When the the **Ethernet** tab is displayed, we reset our target platform. The `BOOTME` packet is then broadcast on the Ethernet network, causing the platform name *Sherry100* to appear (see Figure 9.17), the same as that provided in the configuration of Eshell in the previous step. We then press the center button to add the platform name to the **Current Device** list. Pressing the **Add Device** button allows you to type the platform name, thus avoiding the need to reset the target just to cause the `BOOTME` packet to be sent.

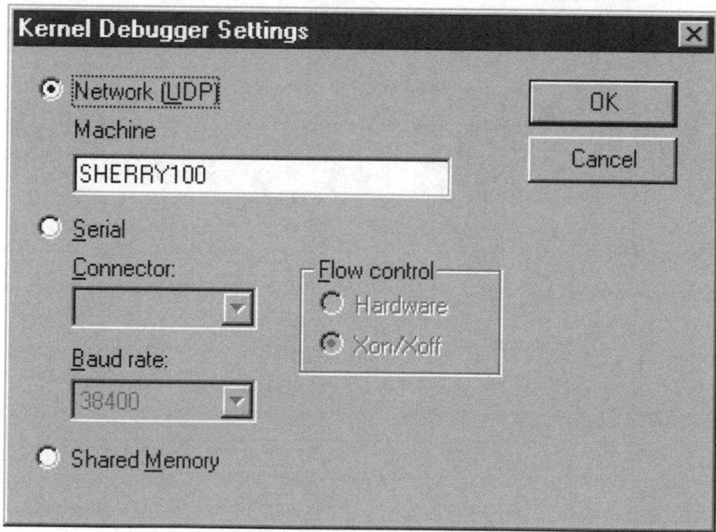

Figure 9.15 Kernel Debugger Settings dialog box

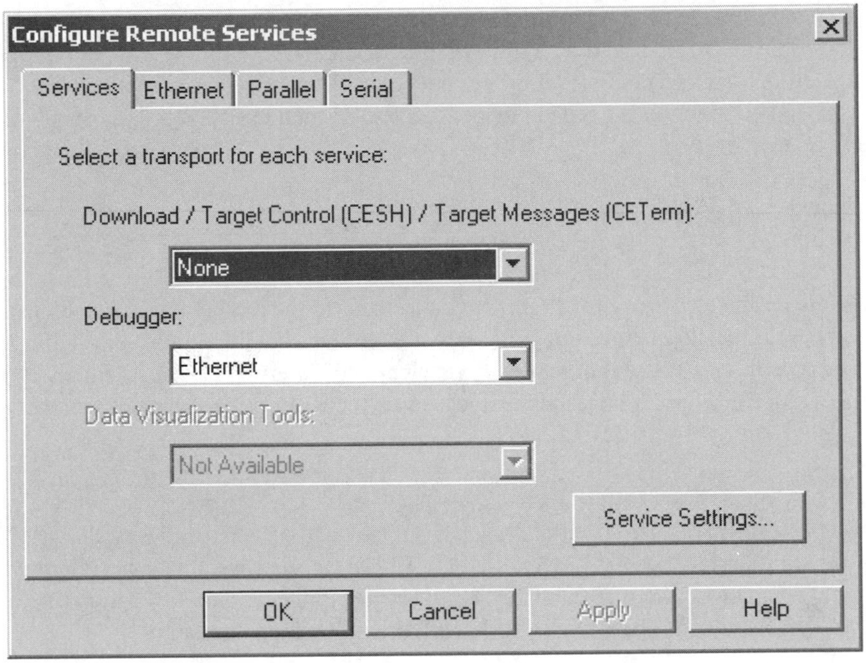

Figure 9.16 **Services** tab of the **Configure Remote Services** dialog box

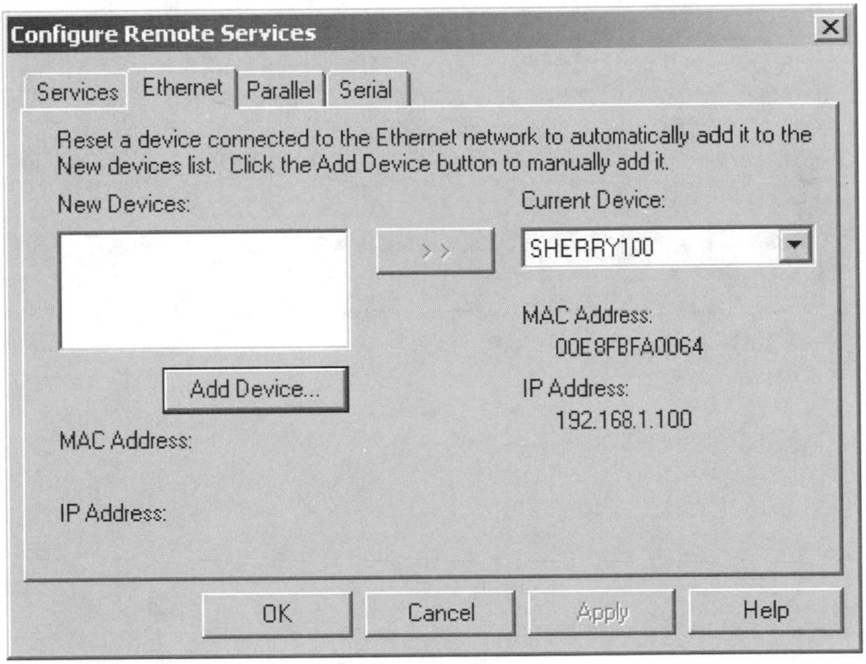

Figure 9.17 **Ethernet** tab of the **Configure Remote Services** dialog box

In comparing the CEPB 3.0 IDE with that of CEPB 2.12, you may have noticed that an extra step is required to indicate the platform name. In CEPB 2.12, this step is not necessary because Eshell is used as a proxy for the Ethernet connection to the target platform. In CEPB 3.0, the Ethernet connection is formed independently of Eshell in CEPB 3.0, so the platform name must be reentered.

Step 3: Loading CESH

As you might recall, in step 1, when Eshell was loaded for CEPB 3.0 and CEPB 2.12, it provided markedly different capabilities for each version. Eshell in CEPB 2.12 provides download services while acting as a proxy for Ethernet connections to the remote target. Eshell in CEPB 3.0 provides the same capabilities but goes further by integrating the stand-alone debug applications CESH (CESH or PPSH Ethernet debug service) and Ceterm (DBGMSG Ethernet debug service). Considering that CESH debug services are effectively loaded when Eshell is loaded, this step is not required for CEPB 3.0.

CEPB 2.12

By now we have identified the target platform as a controlled device using Eshell (and CEPB 3.0), and we are ready to load the CE Shell tool (CESH). Because we are using Ethernet for debugging, we want to make sure that CESH requests its connection to the custom platform by registering with Eshell. To do so, start CESH with the following command:

```
CESH -e {<Platform Name in the Eshell Device List>}
```

The name of your custom platform as it appeared in step 2 is entered in place of the curly braces. If this option were not used, CESH (the version in CEPB 2.12) would attempt to use your development workstation's parallel port to connect to the custom platform.

In Figure 9.18, Eshell is displayed just after CESH has been loaded. The Eshell output window contains a message indicating that a client application has registered for a particular type of debug service called *PPSH* (the name is a holdover from the predecessor to CESH, called `ppsh.exe`, which was changed to *CESH* in CEPB 3.0). When CESH is loaded with the `-e`

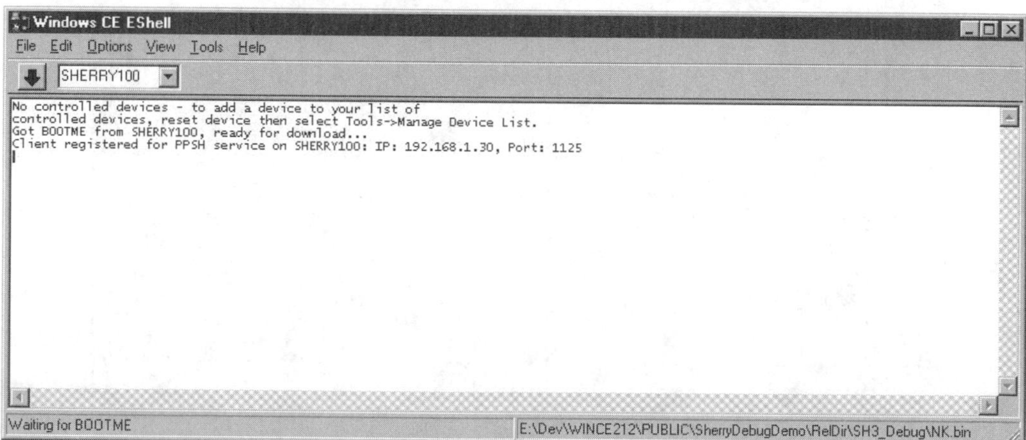

Figure 9.18 Eshell after CESH registration

command-line option, it uses the Ethernet debug services function `EdbgRegisterClient` (documented in the CEPB online documentation) to request the PPSH debug service. The debug service names *KDBG* and *DBGMSG* are reserved. KDBG is used by the kernel debugger, and DBGMSG is used by applications to receive debug messages sent by the `OutputDebugString` function when called on the target platform. You will see this debug service name appear in the Eshell output window as we perform the next few steps in this use case. Refer to Hint 9.1 for information on how to create your own applications that use the Ethernet debug services.

Hint 9.1 Custom debug service names

It is possible to write your own debug applications that use the shared Ethernet debug connection to the target platform for communication between the development workstation and target platform. You must first define a unique service name. Then the `OEMIoControl` function in the OAL on the target platform (discussed in more detail in Chapter 5) must be modified to recognize the EDBG I/O control (IOCTL) codes. The debug applications running on both the target platform and the development workstation will request Ethernet debug services using the `EdbgRegisterClient` function with the unique service name, and can then begin communicating using their own predefined protocol. The complete set of Ethernet debug service functions (each prefixed with *Edbg*) is documented in the CEPB online documentation.

Step 4: Uploading the ROM Image to the Target Platform

Now that CESH is loaded for both CEPB 2.12 (as depicted in Figure 9.18) and CEPB 3.0 through Eshell (as depicted in Figure 9.19), we are ready to begin the actual upload of the ROM image file, `nk.bin`. It is important to remember to load CESH or the CEPB 3.0 version of Eshell before attempting an upload because it provides the virtual file system from which modules not included in the ROM image may be uploaded to the target platform (see the section titled Building a Device Driver for Debugging: Method 2 earlier in this chapter for more information on the use of CESH as an extension of the CE object store).

Note:
In this use case, it is more accurate to use the term *upload* to refer to the transfer of the ROM image file, `nk.bin`, from the development workstation to the target platform (Sherry100). Unfortunately, the distinction between uploading and downloading is not made in any of the CEPB tools or documentation. To avoid confusion, just remember that *upload* refers to the transfer of a file from the location of reference (development workstation) to another location (target platform), while *download* refers to the transfer of a file from a remote location (the target platform) to the location of reference (the development workstation). In other words, when the development workstation transfers a ROM image file to the target platform, this process is considered an upload, and when the development workstation receives a file from the target platform, it is considered a download.

CEPB 2.12

In the CEPB 2.12 section of step 1, the menu option **Download Only On Command** was selected to prevent the automatic upload of the ROM image to the target platform when a `BOOTME` packet is received from a controlled device (in this use case, the platform named Sherry100). Therefore, to initiate the upload, it is necessary to press the arrow button in the CEPB 2.12 version of Eshell.

Once the upload of the ROM image was completed, the boot loader immediately jumped to the entry point of the CE kernel. Because we selected the debug build of the ROM image along with the Eshell option **Options | Always Wait For Ethernet Services**, the boot sequence was halted until the DBGMSG and KDBG services were loaded in the next step.

CEPB 3.0

Upon reset of the target platform, the upload of the kernel image is automatically initiated. This action is the result of the **Options | Download on reset** option having been enabled in step 1. The top pane of the Eshell main window, containing the CESH debug service, appears as depicted in Figure 9.19 just after the upload is complete. The boot loader immediately jumps to the CE kernel entry point and begins the startup sequence that produces the messages appearing in the bottom pane (Ceterm debug service).

Note that unlike the CEPB 2.12 version of Eshell, the kernel startup sequence was not delayed until additional Ethernet debug services were requested. Considering that both Ceterm

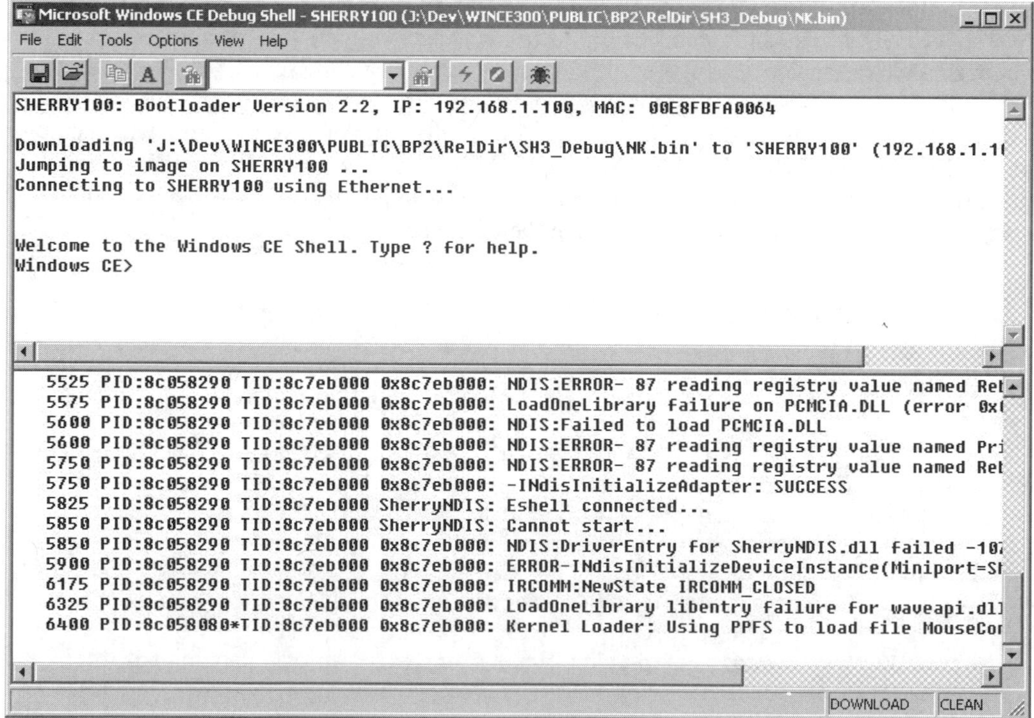

Figure 9.19 CEPB 3.0 Eshell main window

and CESH debug services are integrated in the CEBP 3.0 version of Eshell, these debug services are automatically connected, so no delay is needed. The KDBG Ethernet debugging service, however, is provided separately in the CEPB IDE. If the KDSTUB module was linked into your kernel image (through the **Platform | Settings | General | Enable Kernel Debugging** option), the kernel startup sequence will not continue until KDSTUB detects a connection request from the kernel debugger on the development workstation. In the next step we will explore the options available in CEPB 3.0 for starting the kernel debugger.

Step 5: Starting the Kernel Debugger

Assuming that you have configured the Ethernet connection to the target platform and have also established both a platform and a driver project (as described earlier in this chapter), then you are ready to activate the kernel debugger built-in to the CEPB IDE. The process for doing so differs slightly between CEPB 2.12 and CEPB 3.0.

CEPB 2.12

Simply selecting the **Build | Start Debug | Go** menu option for CEPB 2.12 causes the kernel debugger to register its services with Eshell and begin communicating with the CE kernel. If this is the first time you have attempted debugging your device driver, you will be prompted for the name of the local (development workstation) and remote (target platform) executable modules. You may respond by selecting the executable module of your driver located in the release directory on your local hard disk. Your response to the remote executable module prompt could include the path name of the location of your driver on the target platform, most likely the directory `\WINDOWS`. In reality, it will not matter how you respond to either of these prompts because your driver is automatically loaded during system startup. These prompts are more useful when the executable module being debugged needs to be loaded by the kernel debugger, most likely the case when the executable is an application EXE module rather than a driver DLL module.

The CEPB IDE depicted in the lower left corner of Figure 9.20 is shown with a breakpoint hit denoted by the arrow in the center of a solid dot. This breakpoint was set on the first line of code in the main entry point of the Sherry board's mouse driver and was hit when the driver was loaded by the Device Manager. The registry entries for this driver indicated that it should be loaded during system startup, and the DM dutifully complied.

In the upper right corner of Figure 9.20 is the output window of Eshell. Note the messages in this window indicating that two clients have registered for Ethernet debug services called DBGMSG and KDBG. When the kernel debugger was activated, it registered for both of these services. The DBGMSG service is used to capture the character strings passed to the debug function `OutputDebugString` and displayed in the **Debug** tab of the IDE's **Output** window. The KDBG service is used by the kernel debugger to query and control the CE kernel for debugging operations such as setting breakpoints, querying registers, and evaluating variables.

The HyperTerminal window in Figure 9.20 (lower right) appears with a series of debug messages generated by the kernel during kernel startup. You might be wondering why these messages appear over the serial port when the kernel debugger has already registered for the DBGMSG service. The messages in the HyperTerminal window originate from the `EdbgOutputDebugString` function that is commonly used in the Ethernet code to implement the debug services in the boot loader and the OAL. Because the Ethernet interface in the CE kernel is not operational until late in the boot sequence, the `EdbgOutputDebugString` function is provided to direct strings through the serial port. The name of this function seems to imply that

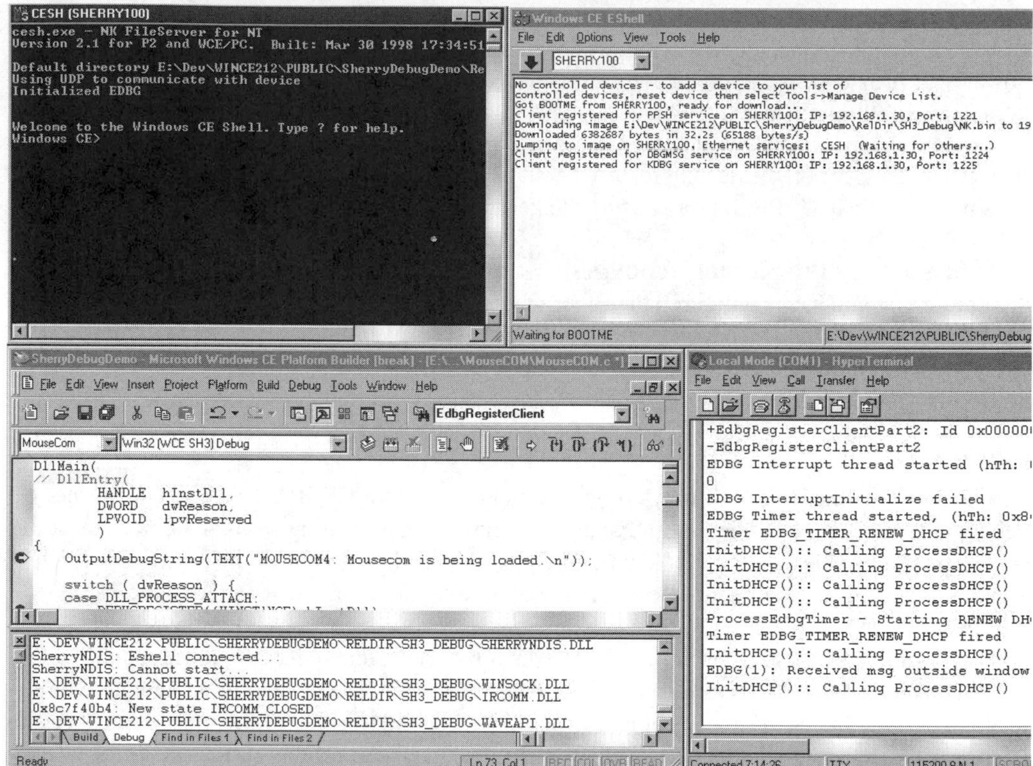

Figure 9.20 CEPB 2.12 kernel debugger desktop view

the output will be directed through the Ethernet interface, so do not let this misleading name confuse you.

One thing to keep in mind when you are single-stepping through your code using the kernel debugger is that the performance of the debugger is best when a minimum of debug windows are open. Each time you single-step in CEPB 2.12, the kernel debugger must update each open debug window with current information (in CEPB 3.0, discussed in the next section, it is possible to disable the automatic update of open debug windows). So, if a debug window containing variables or memory were displayed, the value of each variable and each memory region would need to be retrieved between each breakpoint or single step. This overhead is most noticeable when you're attempting to single-step through the code rapidly and you encounter wait times as high as a few seconds between steps.

CEPB 3.0

After the upload of the kernel to the target platform in the previous step, the KDSTUB module (linked into the kernel when the **Platform | Settings | General | Enable Kernel Debugging** option was selected) waits for a connection with the kernel debugger running on your development workstation. Selecting the **Target | Start | Debugger** option in the CEPB 3.0 IDE completes the connection, and the boot sequence continues. This process may also be accomplished automatically by the CEPB 3.0 version of Eshell. When the upload process is complete, Eshell loads the CEPB IDE and activates the kernel debugger. If you prefer manual activation of the kernel debugger, you can disable this option by selecting the Eshell **Options | Do not auto-start Kernel Debugger**.

When the kernel debugger is automatically activated by the CEPB 3.0 version of Eshell, a separate work space, called *nk.opt,* is created. The window configuration and breakpoint assignments are saved in the work space and are automatically restored the next time the kernel debugger is automatically activated.

Figure 9.21 depicts the view of the desktop after the kernel image has been uploaded to the target platform by Eshell, and the kernel debugger activated. The top pane of the Eshell window (upper right corner) contains the **Windows CE>** prompt, allowing you to type CE Shell commands to query the status of the kernel, check on loaded processes and threads, and manually cause a module included in the kernel image (or in the release directory of the development workstation) on the target platform to be loaded. Debug messages generated by the Win32 function `OutputDebugString`, the `DEBUGMSG` macro, or the function pointer `lpWriteDebugStringFunc` (for debug message output in OAL code) appear in the lower pane of the Eshell window (lower right corner).

The window on the left in Figure 9.21 contains the CEPB 3.0 IDE, after a breakpoint that was set in the `DllMain` function of the `mousecom.dll` driver (for the Sherry platform) has hit. The small window in the upper right corner of this CEPB IDE window contains a list of processes active at the time the breakpoint hit. You can automatically refresh this list, as in other

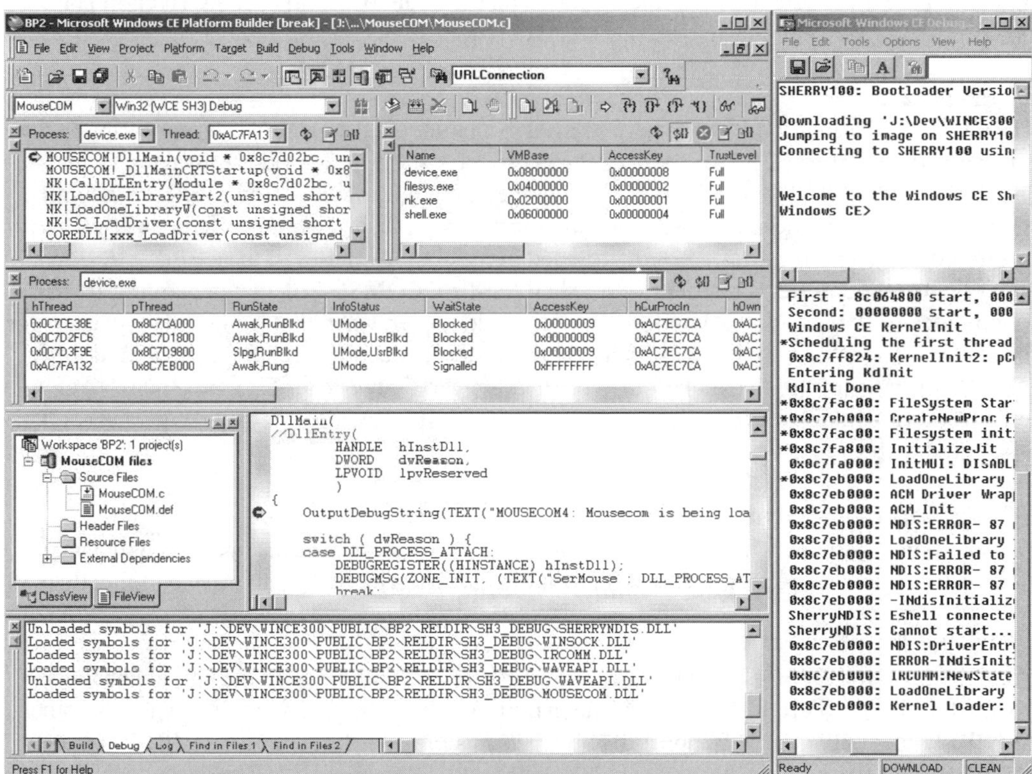

Figure 9.21 CEPB 3.0 kernel debugger desktop view

windows, by pressing the button containing the curly braces and arrows. Pressing this button causes the contents of the window to be updated when the next breakpoint hits, or as you single-step through your code. Of course, these updates add to the overhead of single-stepping, requiring a noticeable delay between each step, so you may prefer to leave this option disabled. You can also manually refresh the contents of such windows after a breakpoint hits, by pressing the button to the left, containing the two arrows. Pressing this button would allow you to single-step more rapidly, updating only those windows with information that is of interest.

The other windows display information on the status of the `device.exe` process. Double-clicking on the `device.exe` process entry in the upper right window causes a list of threads associated with this process to appear just below. Double-clicking once again on the last thread listed in this window causes another window to appear in the upper left that contains the stack trace for the MouseCOM driver source code displayed below.

Using these debug windows in combination, you can obtain information not only on the code being debugged, but also on the overall state of the system as each line of code is executed. In the section titled Tracking Processes and Threads later in this chapter, we provide an example of how a particular bug was identified and isolated with this information.

Step 6: Loading Ceterm

Ceterm, provided in both CEPB 2.12 and CEPB 3.0, is a stand-alone tool that runs on the development workstation and receives debug messages sent by the target platform. In CEPB 3.0, however, Ceterm is able to communicate only with the target platform over a serial port connection. In this use case, it is therefore considered only for use in CEPB 2.12.

CEPB 2.12

The CEPB 2.12 version of Ceterm may be used to capture the debug messages appearing in the output window of the CEPB 2.12 IDE. Ceterm provides additional options for saving its message buffer to a file, or for continuously saving incoming messages to a log file. Each incoming message may also be time-stamped, allowing them to be collected over a long time period and examined later. These are features not provided in the output window of the CEPB 2.12 IDE.

When loaded, Ceterm registers with Eshell for the DBGMSG Ethernet debugging service, as indicated in Eshell's output window. The kernel debugger, when first loaded, also registers for the DBGMSG service. By loading Ceterm after the kernel debugger is started, you effectively override the previous registration of the kernel debugger. Only one tool at a time may be registered for a particular service, with the tool registering last receiving access to the packets of data associated with the service.

Step 7: Shutting Down the Debugger

At some point, perhaps when you are ready to make a corrective code change, you will want to shut down the kernel debugger. CEPB 2.12 and 3.0 have slightly different ways of doing this.

CEPB 2.12

In CEPB 2.12, the **Debug | Stop Debugging** menu option is used to stop the kernel debugger. You just need to be certain to select this menu option *before* you reset the target platform; otherwise the kernel debugger will appear to lock up as it attempts to communicate with the target platform using the previously registered KDBG Ethernet debug service. The kernel debugger calls either the `EdbgSend` or the `EdbgRecv` function to communicate with the target platform to facilitate an orderly termination of the connection to the CE kernel. These functions then block indefinitely while waiting for a response from the target platform that has since been reset. For some reason, the time-out parameter available in both of these functions either is not being used, or is not functioning correctly in CEPB version 2.12.

CEPB 3.0

In CEPB 3.0, you can deactivate (or disconnect) the kernel debugger by selecting the **Target | Stop | Debugger** menu option. This option causes the kernel debugger service to be disconnected from the target, while the CESH and Ceterm debugging services continue to run. As of this writing, however, you can start the CESH and Ceterm debugging services without first starting the kernel debugging service (refer to Hint 9.2 for more information on the use of CEPB IDE integrated debugging services).

Hint 9.2 Using the CEPB 3.0 IDE without Eshell

The CEPB 3.0 IDE represents the total integration of all CE debugging tools, including Eshell, Ceterm, and CESH. It is therefore possible to conduct a kernel debugging session without the use of Eshell (with its integrated implementation of Ceterm and CESH) or the stand-alone implementations of CESH and Ceterm. This is not true in CEPB 2.12 and represents a major improvement in the ease of use for CE kernel-level debugging.

The functions of CESH are provided in three menu options located in the CEPB IDE **Target** menu. The **Advanced Commands (CESH)** option displays a dialog box that allows you to type the CESH command to be issued. The results of this command are then displayed in the **Debug** pane of the **Output** window (at the bottom of the screen in Figure 9.21). The **Run Program** option provides a list of all available programs in the kernel image, including a command-line field to allow the name and/or parameters of the program to be specified. When the **Run** button is pressed, the program is loaded from the ROM image, if present, or from the release directory of the development workstation. The **Debug Zones** option provides a list of all loaded modules (EXEs and DLLs) and their defined debug zones (discussed later, in the section titled Zone Debugging). You may selectively enable and disable a debug zone by clicking the check box that appears next to each named zone. This latter option represents a major improvement over the command-line CESH interface, which also allows debug zones to be enabled and disabled. The commands are often difficult to remember and are time-consuming to type with the CESH command-line interface.

The other menu options that represent the further integration of debug functionality with CEPB IDE are those dedicated to uploading the kernel image and resetting the target platform. If you select the **Target | Download Image** option, CEPB will wait until the `BOOTME` packet is received from the target platform and then begin the upload process. You may also warm-boot the target by selecting the **Jump to Image** option to jump to the kernel entry point, or cold-boot it by selecting the **Reset Device** option. If you want the kernel image to be uploaded automatically once the reset is complete, you may select the option **Reset Device | Reset on Download**.

There are a few disadvantages to the use of the CEPB 3.0 IDE to replace Eshell functionality. For one, as of this writing, it lacks the ability to automatically write to a specified file the output of the message window containing the messages generated through the Ceterm debug service (**Debug** tab of the **Output** window in CEPB 3.0, and bottom pane of the Eshell window). You must also load the entire CEPB IDE to achieve an interface to your platform. Eshell is a small program, requiring only the files `eshell.exe` and `edbg.dll` to provide both a command-line interface and a debug message window. You may also produce a build that does not have kernel debugging enabled (KDSTUB), but that is still considered a debug build. Whereas Eshell could provide the command-line interface to such a build, the CEPB 3.0 IDE services require that KDSTUB be present in your kernel image.

The CEPB 2.12 problem associated with the deactivation of kernel debugging services after the target has been reset (mentioned in the preceding CEPB 2.12 section), is resolved in CEPB 3.0. If the target platform is reset, subsequent deactivation of CEPB 3.0 debug services will not cause the IDE to block.

Custom Platform Serial/Parallel Port Debugging Configuration: Use Case 2

An Ethernet connection clearly provides the highest-performance kernel-debugging environment, significantly reducing the time required to upload a newly built kernel image to your custom platform, as well as providing a more responsive interface between the CE kernel and the kernel debugger. These advantages help make you more efficient by reducing the minimum time for the typical code change/build/debug development cycle. That being said, the Ethernet debugging configuration presented in use case 1 is clearly a more attractive option than the serial/parallel port configuration presented in this use case. However, there are distinct advantages to serial/parallel port configuration that you should consider, particularly for untested, newly minted, custom platforms.

The complexity of the Ethernet hardware means that both the boot loader (covered in Chapter 4) and the OAL (covered in Chapter 5) are more difficult to develop. In the development of a custom platform, the boot loader not only supports the transfer of the CE ROM image file, `nk.bin`, to the memory (RAM or flash) of your custom platform; it also acts as the first software to be run on a platform based on an untested design, often produced by an equally untested manufacturing process. By necessity, this testing burden falls to the boot loader. Anything that can be done to simplify the hardware interface that is required to communicate with the development workstation reduces the number of subsystems on your custom platform that must be operational. It may also reduce the development time required for the boot loader and get those prototype custom platforms into the hands of the other members of the software engineering team that much sooner.

As depicted in Figure 9.3, a bidirectional parallel port is used by CESH to upload the CE ROM image to the custom platform. The hardware interface to the parallel port is far simpler than that of an Ethernet controller that must support access to a shared transport medium, and thus helps fulfill the objective of boot loader simplification.

In CEPB 3.0, CESH is provided as a stand-alone, command-line application and as an integrated function of Eshell. The stand-alone version supports both serial and bidirectional parallel interfaces to the target platform, while the CESH debug service in Eshell supports bidirectional parallel port, serial, and Ethernet (as presented in use case 1) interfaces. In CEPB 2.12, CESH is offered only as a stand-alone command-line application, with support for bidirectional parallel port, serial, and Ethernet interfaces. In all cases, regardless of the interface used, CESH acts as an extension to the CE object store by providing a virtual file system. When a module is not found in the ROM image, the CE kernel automatically downloads it from the release directory by using the CESH debug service.

After the CE kernel is successfully uploaded, the boot loader is directed to jump to the entry point of the CE kernel. A serial port (separate from the one used by CESH if a serial port interface is in use) is then used by the CE kernel to communicate with the kernel debugger running on the development workstation. Debug messages are sent only to the CEPB output window and may not be redirected to any other tools, such as Ceterm (as in the previous use case). Because the serial port runs at a maximum of 115.2 Kbps, debugger operations through it can be a bit sluggish, as you will soon see.

The narrative presenting the steps for this use case will occasionally reference the steps presented in use case 1. If you have not already done so, you may find it beneficial to study use case 1, even if your custom platform does not support an Ethernet debugging configuration.

Step 1: Configuring the Parallel Port

The CESH debug service, when configured to operate on a bidirectional parallel port, is the CE development tool that causes perhaps the most frustration. Once the development workstation's bidirectional parallel port is properly configured to work with CESH and the ROM image is successfully uploaded to the target platform, CESH soon becomes your debugging stalwart, providing rapid uploads of the ROM image, a virtual file system, and a remote CE command-line interface. Getting to this point, however, requires the configuration of your development workstation NT drivers and BIOS settings. In the next few subsections we will discuss this process in some detail. Later you may wish to refer back to this section if you find that you're having difficulty getting the CESH parallel port connection to function on other development workstations.

Development Workstation BIOS Configuration

Most PCs sold within the last few years provide built-in parallel ports that function in different communication modes using the same physical port. The development workstation that was used for writing this chapter, for example, supports standard and bidirectional EPP 1.7, EPP 1.9, and ECP modes. Each of these modes uses the pins of the parallel port slightly differently and requires a supporting cable. The standard mode supports data transfer in one direction and is typically used to support a connection to older peripheral devices, such as printers. When using the parallel port, however, CESH performs data transfer in both directions and requires that you configure the parallel port using one of the BIOS settings that support bidirectional data transfer.

CESH Custom Cable

CESH also requires that you use a specially configured cable with custom pin assignments. The pin assignments are documented in the Parallel Port Interface Reference section of the CEPB 2.12 online documentation and in the Customizing a Parallel Cable section of the CEPB 3.0 online documentation. Because this cable does not conform to a public standard, you will need to either craft it by hand, using a jumper block or break-out box, or purchase it from a custom cable vendor. See Refer to the CEPB online documentation for the name of a cable supplier providing CESH-compliant cables.

Development Workstation Driver Configuration

Because CESH requires a custom pin configuration, it also requires the use of a custom device driver on your development workstation. The name of the driver is ppshell and should appear in the list of installed devices when you're using the NT 4.0 Devices control panel applet. Enabling ppshell for Windows 2000 is described in the Using Cesh.exe with a Parallel Port Connection section of the CEPB 3.0 online documentation. This driver is automatically installed during the installation of CEPB, and if you responded positively when prompted, the default parallel port drivers—parvdm, parallel, and parport—should appear disabled in the NT 4.0 list of installed devices, or set for manual load in the specified Windows 2000 registry settings. You may want to confirm this if you're having problems getting CESH to load.

Note:
Using the System control applet in NT 4.0 or Windows 2000, you can define an alternative hardware profile. This profile may then be associated with the changes made to the load status of the standard parallel port drivers. If, for example, you find that your parallel port is used by applications other than CESH, you may want to create another Windows CE debugging profile in which the standard parallel port drivers (parvdm, parport, and parallel) are disabled and the CESH parallel port driver (ppshell) is enabled. In your default hardware profile, you would then disable the CESH parallel port driver and enable the standard parallel port drivers. When restarting NT 4.0 or Windows 2000, you would be prompted with a menu allowing you to select the desired hardware profile.

System Environment Configuration

The stand-alone, command-line version of CESH requires the `_FLATRELEASEDIR` environment variable to be set to the location of the binary modules used to generate the ROM image file, `nk.bin`. This directory is used to locate both the file `nk.bin` and any of the modules needed by the CESH file server. Quite probably the default value for this environment variable is incorrect if you have recently created a new platform using the WCE Platform Wizard (available in **File | New | Platforms**). You should also verify that the `PATH` environment variable includes the directory where `cesh.exe` is located so that a full path name is not necessary when CESH is being executed from the command prompt.

Loading CESH

If all of the steps outlined to this point were completed, you would need to activate the CESH debug service, a process that varies slightly for CEPB 2.12 and CEPB 3.0.

CEPB 2.12

In CEPB 2.12, CESH is provided only as a stand-alone, command-line tool. It supports the parallel port, serial, and Ethernet (as described in use case 1) interfaces to the target platform. The serial interface would be useful if your target platform did not possess a bidirectional parallel port interface, though the duration of the ROM image upload would be significantly longer. This serial interface would need to be separate from the one on the target platform that is used by the kernel debugger in this use case.

To load CESH for this use case, use the following command:

```
CESH [-p <CESH configuration saved in the registry>]
```

The `-p` option is necessary only if the default CESH configuration is not used. Upon the installation of CEPB 2.12, one alternate CESH configuration is provided, called CEPC. It is typically used when CESH is being connected to a CEPC target platform, but we have found that it works more successfully with custom platforms than the default configuration does. The best thing to do is experiment with both configurations to determine which one works better.

CEPB 3.0

In CEPB 3.0, the CESH debug service is provided in three different tools. The command-line CESH is still available as it was in CEPB 2.12, and it supports both a serial and a parallel interface to the target platform. Eshell and the CEPB 3.0 IDE support the bidirectional parallel port and Ethernet interfaces to the target, but not the serial interface as in the command-line CESH.

Loading the command-line CESH for this use case requires the same command as described in the preceding subsection for CEPB 2.12. You may also opt to use the CESH debug services included in the CEPB 3.0 version of Eshell. The CESH debug service provided in Eshell is automatically activated when it is loaded. The CESH debug service in the CEPB 3.0 IDE is activated when the upload of the ROM image is initiated through the **Target | Download Image** option. If the CESH debug service in Eshell is used, you will be able to use only the kernel debugger service provided in the CEPB 3.0 IDE because the CESH and Ceterm services are claimed by Eshell when it is loaded.

Step 2: Configuring the Serial Port in CE Platform Builder

In this use case the kernel debugger uses the serial port for communication with the target platform, and the CEPB IDE needs to be appropriately configured.

CEPB 2.12

In CEPB 2.12, the serial port is configured through the dialog box accessed by the **Build | Debugger Remote Connection | Settings** menu option (see Figure 9.15). You must select the connector (COM port), baud rate (used synonymously in this context with the term *bit rate*), and flow control to match what is expected by the target platform.

CEPB 3.0

In CEPB 3.0, the **Target | Configure Remote Services | Debugger** option (depicted in Figure 9.16) must be set to serial, and the **Serial** tab of the same dialog box to the appropriate COM port, bit rate (used synonymously in this context with the term *bit rate*), and flow control. If you are using Eshell to provide the Ceterm debug service, the serial port and baud rate (bit rate) will need to be selected through the **Use Parallel/Serial Transport** option of the dialog box accessed through the **Options | Advanced Settings** menu option (depicted in Figure 9.14).

Step 3: Uploading the ROM Image to the Target Platform

To get CESH to upload the ROM image to the target platform, we will need to configure the platform's boot loader to use the parallel port over any other port that it may also support for ROM image upload (Ethernet or serial port). In this use case, as in use case 1, the Sherry board is used, which provides a boot loader menu, as depicted in Figure 9.12. Selecting the parallel port option causes the boot loader to transmit the boot packet. If the CESH debug service is in the mode in which it listens for this boot packet, the upload process will begin. Placing the CESH debug service into this mode is slightly different for CEPB 2.12 and CEPB 3.0.

CEPB 2.12

In CEPB 2.12, if CESH (the command-line tool) is loaded, the upload starts and a progress bar in the command prompt window displays the percentage of the upload that has been completed. CESH is automatically placed in listen mode when it is first loaded. To abort the listen mode, press **Ctrl-C**, causing CESH to unload and return to the command prompt.

CEPB 3.0

To initiate the CESH debug service listen mode in the CEPB 3.0 IDE, select the **Target | Download Image** option. In Eshell, the listen mode is automatically activated if the **Use Parallel/Serial Transport** option was selected in the dialog box accessed through the **Options | Advanced Settings** menu option.

Note:

We have found that the parallel port support provided by CESH often works, but with varying degrees of success, depending on the parallel port provided in the development workstation. One thing you might try to get it working is to tinker with the settings provided in the CESH `HKEY_LOCAL_MACHINE\SYSTEM\CurrentControlSet\Services\ppsh\<config name>` registry entry. The Cesh.exe Registry Entries section of the CEPB 2.12 and 3.0 online documentation lists the defined registry entries.

Another, perhaps less frustrating option is to purchase an after-market parallel port adapter card. We have found that the probability of success across platforms is much higher when such cards are used. They generally provide a range of configuration options exceeding that provided in most parallel port BIOS configurations.

Step 4: Starting the Kernel Debugger

After CESH has completely uploaded the ROM image to the target platform, the boot loader jumps to the CE kernel entry point. If you produced a debug build, the CE kernel then attempts to communicate with the kernel debugger on the development workstation. In this use case, an RS-232 serial connection, configured for a baud rate (bit rate) of 115.2 Kbps, is used. Early in its startup sequence, the CE kernel waits for a response from the kernel debugger before continuing. Starting the kernel debugger in CEPB 2.12 and CEPB 3.0 is explained in the two paragraphs that follow.

CEPB 2.12

As in use case 1, we start the kernel debugger simply by selecting the **Build | Start Debug | Go** menu option.

CEPB 3.0

In the CEPB 3.0 IDE, we start the kernel debugger by selecting the **Target | Start | Debugger** option.

Step 5: Shutting Down the Debugger

In CEPB 2.12, we shut down the debugger by selecting the **Debug | Stop Debugging** menu option, as in the previous use case 1. In CEPB 3.0, selecting the **Target | Stop | Debugger** option shuts down the kernel debugger.

Alternative Configurations

Considering the availability of three different debug transports (Ethernet, serial, and parallel) to the target platform, we certainly could have considered other use cases in the previous section. Rather than explore all the various combinations of debug transports, in this section we will explore the mechanism that may be used to map certain debug services to designated debug transports.

By default, the CE kernel calls the functions `OEMWriteDebugByte`, `OEMWriteDebugString`, and `OEMReadDebugByte` to send debug messages and to communicate with the kernel debugger on the development workstation. In contrast, the functions `OEMParallelPortGetByte`, `OEMParallelPortGetStatus`, and `OEMParallelPortSendByte` are used to communicate with CESH. You are expected to provide an implementation of these functions in the OAL (described in Chapter 5), which is linked directly into the CE kernel.

If your OAL code determines that the debug services should be configured differently, it calls the `SetKernelCommDev` function early in the CE kernel startup sequence to map any one of the three debug services (`KERNEL_SVC_DBGMSG`, `KERNEL_SVC_PPSH`, or `KERNEL_SVC_KDBG`) to a designated transport (`KERNEL_COMM_SERIAL`, `KERNEL_COMM_PARALLEL`, or `KERNEL_COMM_ETHER`). Not all services can be mapped to all available transports, however. The `KERNEL_SVC_KDBG` service, for example, cannot be mapped to the `KERNEL_COMM_PARALLEL` transport. This restriction is confirmed by the lack of any supporting parallel port option in the **Kernel Debugger Settings** dialog box depicted in Figure 9.15. Refer to the CEPB online documentation on `SetKernelCommDev` for more information on unsupported combinations.

One combination of transports not specifically supported by `SetKernelCommDev` in CEPB 2.12 and 3.0 is two serial ports—one for communication with the kernel debugger, and the other for communication with CESH. Considering that a spare serial port can sometimes be easier to procure than a parallel port, this configuration may prove quite useful, so we will consider how one might work around the limitation against this combination in `SetKernelCommDev`.

As already mentioned, the default debugger transport configuration uses the functions that carry the prefix *OEMParallel* to communicate with CESH. It is clear from the names of these functions that they were originally intended for communication with parallel port hardware. Because you are expected to supply the implementation of these functions in the OAL, you control the type of hardware that will be used. As long as your implementation of these functions is consistent with the specification provided in the CEPB online documentation, you can just as well have them communicate with serial port hardware on your custom platform. To do so, you would have to load the command-line CESH on the development workstation using the `COMx` command-line option (where the *x* corresponds to the number of an available serial port):

```
CESH COM<number of a serial port available on the development workstation>
```

This command causes CESH to use the specified serial port rather than the default parallel port.

Note:
The dialog box that **appears** when you type "CESH -?" in CEPB 3.0 indicates that the `COMx` parameter should be preceded by a hyphen. However, this is incorrect. No hyphen is required.

The CESH debug services provided in the CEPB 2.12 IDE and the CEPB 3.0 version of Eshell do not allow a serial port to be selected. You are therefore limited to the use of command-line CESH when running CESH debug services over a serial port.

Standard Platform Serial Port Debugging Configuration: Use Case 3

If you are charged with the responsibility of writing a driver to support an installable device, you will probably need to test and certify your driver on standard platforms. If a problem arises on a particular platform, you will probably attempt to debug the problem on that same platform. In some cases, you may even find yourself using a standard platform for developing your driver. In either case, the use of a standard platform for driver development and debugging requires the use of the application-level debugger included in the eMVC. In this section we will focus on how to use the eMVC application-level debugger.

Driver Mapper

The eMVC application-level debugger, as discussed earlier in the chapter, is able to control the execution of only individual EXE modules and their associated DLLs. Considering that most types of CE drivers exist as a DLL module with an associated EXE (in most cases implemented by the Device Manager in the `device.exe` module), the eMVC application-level debugger would need access to run the EXE module to load its supported driver. In the case of the Device Manager, running `device.exe` would be problematic because it is already loaded at system startup, before most drivers are loaded. The Driver Mapper utility presented in this section is designed to resolve this problem.

Before we get started, you may want to reference the Driver Mapper source code as we discuss its operation and design. It is available on this book's accompanying CD and on this book's Web site. Check the Web site for any updates to the source code that may not have been available when the CD was produced.

Design of Driver Mapper

The basic job of Driver Mapper is to map the entry points of a stream-interface driver and the services it must access (such as the PCMCIA card services DLL, `pcmcia.dll`) to an outside process that may be controlled by the eMVC application debugger. Doing so allows your stream-interface driver to be controlled and debugged by the eMVC debugger because it is running in the Driver Mapper process space (`drvmap.exe` created specifically to contain your driver.

Driver Mapper consists of four separate executable modules: `drvmap.exe`, `apimap.dll`, `drvstub.dll`, and `logtrace.dll`. The last module contains a replacement for the implementation of the `DEBUGMSG` macro, which is commonly used for sending trace statements to the development workstation. Instead of sending the trace statements to a development workstation through a serial or Ethernet port, the implementation in `logtrace.dll` sends them to a file on the target platform (a standard platform in the case of Driver Mapper). When you're trying to diagnose a problem related to the real-time execution of the driver, on a platform without the benefit of a development workstation connection, this capability can be very handy. The Log-Trace module may be used separately in the development of your own drivers, and is discussed in more detail in the section titled Log Tracer later in this chapter.

Note:
`Logtrace.dll` is based on a function originally written and provided in source code form by Phil McGahan.

Figure 9.22 contains a block diagram for the design of Driver Mapper. The DrvMap module functions as a kind of function router, translating messages received into function calls directed to your driver. It obtains the address of each of your driver's stream-interface entry points when the **Apply** button is pressed and initializes the APIMap module. You may think of DrvMap as a kind of replacement for the Device Manager.

The DrvStub module acts as a replacement for your driver and is named in the registry entries where the name of your stream-interface driver would normally appear (discussed in more detail in the next few paragraphs). The APIMap module exports the same functions as those provided by the `pcmcia.dll` module, along with a few other utility functions that act as

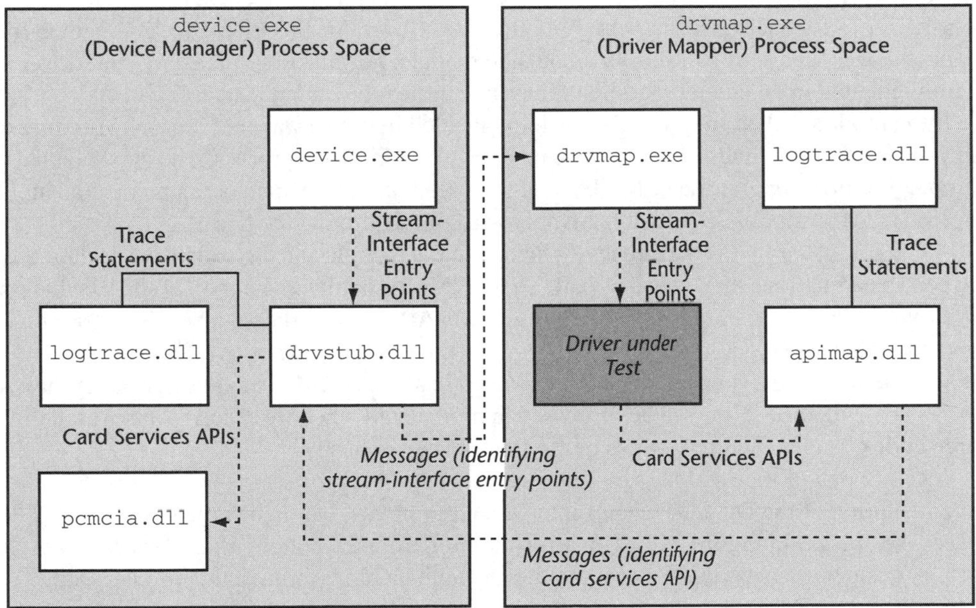

Figure 9.22 Block diagram for the design of Driver Mapper

extensions and replacements to certain CE functions, which are described shortly, in the section titled Driver Source Code and Registry Changes.

Let's consider how the driver for an ATA flash card, inserted into a PC card slot, works when using Driver Mapper. When the card is first inserted, the Device Manager examines the registry for a driver with a registry entry in `HKEY_LOCAL_MACHINE\Drivers\PCMCIA\<Plug-and-Play ID>` that matches the Plug and Play ID of the card inserted. If none is found, the Device Manager loads each of the drivers listed in the `HKLM\Drivers\PCMCIA\Detect` key for a generic driver that might support the device class of ATA flash cards. This process is discussed in more detail in Chapter 7.

Eventually the Device Manager comes to the registry entry for the DrvStub stream-interface driver, acting as a replacement for the ATADisk entry under the `HKLM\Drivers\PCMCIA\Detect` key. The DrvStub's detection function, `DRV_Detect`, is called. The DrvStub module then attempts to establish communication with the DrvMap module, which should already be loaded. If it is able to do so, DrvStub exchanges the window handles and access keys and sends a message to the DrvMap module using the `SendMessage` function. (Because nearly all types of CE drivers run in user mode, it is possible to call the `SendMessage` function, even though it is more typically associated with applications providing a user interface.) If the name of the mapped driver module, in this case `atadisk.dll`, has already been entered and successfully loaded by use of the DrvMap **Apply** button (depicted in Figure 9.23), this message is converted into the corresponding call to the detection function in the mapped driver, `atadisk.dll`. The return value from the call to this function is then returned to the DrvStub module as the return value from the `SendMessage` function. The DrvStub module, in turn, returns this value to the calling Device Manager.

This is the general pattern for all the remaining stream-interface driver entry points. DrvStub, as the name implies, provides an implementation stub for each entry point and contains a corresponding call to `SendMessage`. A designated message ID is passed to `SendMessage` for each particular entry point called. Generally, this is an effective method for mapping driver functions called *from* an outside module. For functions called *by* your driver that are implemented in an outside module, things are a little more complicated.

If the module called by your driver is implemented in such a way that it may be running in only one process at a time, it must also be mapped to the DrvMap process. The most notable example of this occurs for the PCMCIA card services functions, which are implemented in the `pcmcia.dll` module. Typically, drivers use a combination of the `LoadLibrary` and `GetProcAddress` functions to retrieve a handle to the module and the address of each of the card services functions they intend to call. The APIMap module is designed to address this issue and provides an implementation of the card services APIs (and certain other APIs whose functions must be stubbed out in some way). However, this implementation is effective only if you are able to modify your driver's source code to load the APIMap module instead of the `pcmcia.dll` module. This will be discussed in more detail when we describe the overall driver source code changes required for use of the Driver Mapper utility.

A call to one of the APIMap functions triggers the same process as that described for the implementation of the DrvStub stream-interface entry points, but in the reverse direction. This process is depicted in Figure 9.22 as an arrow coming from the bottom of the *Driver under Test* block. A designated message ID is sent to the DrvStub module (through the `SendMessage` function), and the corresponding function is called from the DrvStub process space. In some cases, the function provided in the APIMap module exists to modify the functionality of a standard API (refer to the next subsection for a list of these types of functions). In this case, the modified function is implemented in the APIMap module and may include a call to the original API instead of to the `SendMessage` function.

Driver Source Code and Registry Changes

To use Driver Mapper for standard platform debugging with the eMVC application debugger, you must make certain modifications to your driver source code. In this section we will list each of the changes, using the source code of Driver Mapper itself as an example.

If your driver is based on one of the samples provided in the CEPB or was developed from the template DLL generated by the WCE Dynamic-Link Library Project Wizard (accessed from the **File | New | Projects** menu option), certain source changes and practices must be followed to ensure that your driver can be built by eMVC and successfully loaded by the Device Manager on a standard platform:

- Rename (if necessary) your driver's main routine to *DllMain*. The CEPB command-line build of the CE kernel image allows the use of the `Sources` file (discussed in Chapter 10) to specify build parameters for a particular module. The `DLLENTRY` macro may be used in the `Sources` file to name the function used as your driver's main routine. The default startup code linked in by the eMVC, however, expects your driver's main routine to be named `DllMain`.

- You may optionally replace the DEF file used for specifying the names of exported and imported functions, with the storage-class specifier `__declspec({dllexport|dllimport})`. You will often see this specifier associated with a macro such as `APICALL` or `EXPORT`, as in the Driver Mapper DrvStub source code.

- Zone debugging, discussed later in this chapter, is not supported by the eMVC application debugger. The `DBGPARAM` structure is therefore not defined. If your driver source code is based on a CEPB example, you will need to comment out the definition of the associated `DBGPARAM` variable in order for your source code to compile. The `DEBUGMSG` macro, discussed later in the Zone Debugging section, may remain if the `trace.h` file is included. `Trace.h` includes the definition of a replacement `DEBGUGMSG` macro that calls a function in the `logtrace.dll` module and adds the trace messages to the log file specified in the `TraceStart` function. The `TraceStart` function is typically called somewhere in your driver's `DllMain` main routine. A `DEBUGZONE` macro must also be created. The Driver Mapper DrvStub source code simply defines this macro as follows:

```
#define DEBUGZONE(x)     1
```

In addition to the changes just listed, you will need to replace certain function calls with Driver Mapper equivalents, implemented in the `apimap.dll` module. The functions that must be replaced are indicated in the following list:

- If your driver calls the PCMCIA card services functions implemented in the `pcmcia.dll` module, chances are it calls these functions by using function pointers obtained with the `LoadLibrary` and `GetProcAddress` functions. The `LoadLibrary` function would be called with the name of the `pcmcia.dll` module. The return value from this function would be passed to the `GetProcAddress` function along with the name of each card services function requiring a function pointer.

Because `pcmcia.dll` may be called only from the Device Manager process, Driver Mapper provides an implementation of each card services function in the `apimap.dll` module. The `apimap.dll` card services functions send a message to the DrvStub module to allow the call to be routed to `pcmcia.dll` (as described earlier in this section). To load the `apimap.dll` module, you must modify the call to the `LoadLibrary` function to load this module instead of `pcmcia.dll`:

```
// Driver Mapper: Modified to map the PCMCIA card services functions
// to the Device Manager process.
v_hPcmciaDll = LoadLibrary(TEXT("APIMap.DLL"));
//    v_hPcmciaDll = LoadLibrary(TEXT("PCMCIA.DLL"));
```

- The `LoadFSD` function is typically called by stream-interface drivers that act as a file system's (`fatfs.dll`, for example) block device driver. Like the PCMCIA card services functions, `LoadFSD` must be called from the Device Manager process. The `MapLoadFSD` function is provided in the `apimap.dll` module to cause a message to be sent to the DrvStub module, where the actual `LoadFSD` function is called. The `MapLoadFSD` function must be used in place of the `LoadFSD` function. The import library generated during the build of the `apimap.dll` module must also be linked with your driver to associate the `MapLoadFSD` function with `apimap.dll`.
- The `GetCallerProcess` function, as the name implies, is called to obtain the handle to the process space of the caller of your driver's entry point. It is often used as a parameter in the call to `MapPtrToProcess` when you are de-referencing a pointer to an address in the caller's process space. If this function is called in your driver, it will return the handle to the `drvmap.exe` process space, which is the caller (acting as a Device Manager replacement) to each of your driver's entry points. Because this is *not* the handle of the original caller, the `apimap.dll` module provides the `MapGetCallerProcess` function to be used as a replacement for the `GetCallerProcess` function in your driver's source.

The Driver Mapper module `drvstub.dll` acts as a stand-in for your driver and is directly loaded by the Device Manager. The registry entries normally used by your driver must be modified to reference the `drvstub.dll` module instead of your own driver's DLL module. The device file name prefix registry key must also be modified to refer to the device file name of the `drvstub.dll` module. Sample registry changes required for using Driver Mapper to debug the CEPB sample driver ATADisk, are provided in Listing 9.2.

Listing 9.2 Driver Mapper registry entries for ATADisk

```
Registry entries for the ATADisk CEPB sample driver before and after
modification to allow debugging with Driver Mapper:

Before Modifications:

[HKEY_LOCAL_MACHINE\Drivers\PCMCIA\Detect\50]
"Dll"="ATADISK.DLL"
"Entry"="DetectATADisk"

[HKEY_LOCAL_MACHINE\Drivers\PCMCIA\ATADisk]
"Dll"="ATADISK.DLL"
"Prefix"="DSK"
"Ioctl"=dword:00000004
"FSD"="FATFS.DLL"

After Modifications:

[HKEY_LOCAL_MACHINE\Drivers\PCMCIA\Detect\50]
"Dll"="DrvStub.dll"
"Entry"="DRV_Detect"

The following entry replaces the above [HKEY_LOCAL_MACHINE\Drivers\PCMCIA\
ATADisk]
entry:

[HKEY_LOCAL_MACHINE\Drivers\PCMCIA\DrvStub]
"Prefix"="DRV"
"Dll"="DrvStub.dll"
"Ioctl"=dword:00000004
"FSD"="FATFS.DLL"
```

Operation of Driver Mapper

Before we start learning how to use Driver Mapper, here are the assumptions made regarding your use of this utility:

- You have installed the Driver Mapper source code and you have successfully built Driver Mapper and its supporting modules (`drvstub.exe`, `logtrace.dll`, `drvstub.dll`, and `apimap.dll`) for your standard platform.
- You are attempting to debug a stream-interface driver that optionally uses PCMCIA card services. USB drivers, though not strictly considered stream-interface drivers, are indirectly maintained by the Device Manager but are not currently supported by Driver Mapper. (See the next subsection, Limitations of Driver Mapper, for more information on what driver types are supported by Driver Mapper.)
- You have made the required changes to your driver's source and registry entries that were documented a little earlier in the Driver Source Code and Registry Changes section. One way to simplify the use of Driver Mapper is to add your own driver's eMVC project to that of Driver Mapper. Doing so

allows any source code changes made to either Driver Mapper or your driver to be automatically uploaded to the standard platform after each project build.

The first step in using the Driver Mapper utility is to associate the `drvmap.exe` module with your driver's eMVC project. The dialog box accessed by the option **Project | Settings | Debug | General** provides a field called **Local executable path and file name** (**Executable For Debug Session** in the CETK). You may use this field to enter the name of the EXE module that loads your driver's DLL module. You should enter the fully qualified path name of the Driver Mapper EXE module (`drvmap.exe`) from the perspective of your development workstation. The actual path name depends on the type of the processor used on your standard platform and on where you have chosen to locate and build the Driver Mapper project.

When you are ready to begin debugging your driver, select the eMVC menu option **Build | Start Debug**, thus causing the `drvmap.exe` module to be uploaded (if not already present) to the standard platform and executed. The user interface displayed in Figure 9.23 then appears. It is implemented as a single dialog box through a basic MFC (Microsoft Foundation Classes) Single Document Interface model, and requires the DLLs `mfcce20.dll` and `olece20.dll` modules (`mfcce20d.dll` and `olece20d.dll` if you run the debug build of Driver Mapper) to be present in the `\WINDOWS` directory of the standard platform. If you receive an error when first running `drvmap.exe`, check that both of these DLLs are present.

The fields on this screen contain the information needed by Driver Mapper to load your driver. The fully qualified path name of your driver's DLL module on the standard platform is entered in the **Driver:** field. If your driver is located in the standard platform's `\WINDOWS` directory, you may enter the DLL module name without a path name. The three-character prefix associated with your driver's stream-interface entry points is entered in the **DFN Prefix:** field (where *DFN* stands for *device file name*). The detection function is the name of the function provided by your driver and called by the Device Manager to determine if your driver will support a device that lacks a matching `HKLM\Drivers\PCMCIA\<PnP ID>` registry entry. The device file name prefix and detection functions are discussed in more detail in Chapter 7.

After the data required for each field has been entered, with the last field remaining blank, if your driver does not provide a detection function you may press the **Apply** button. Doing so causes the values to be written to the registry so that they may be retrieved the next time

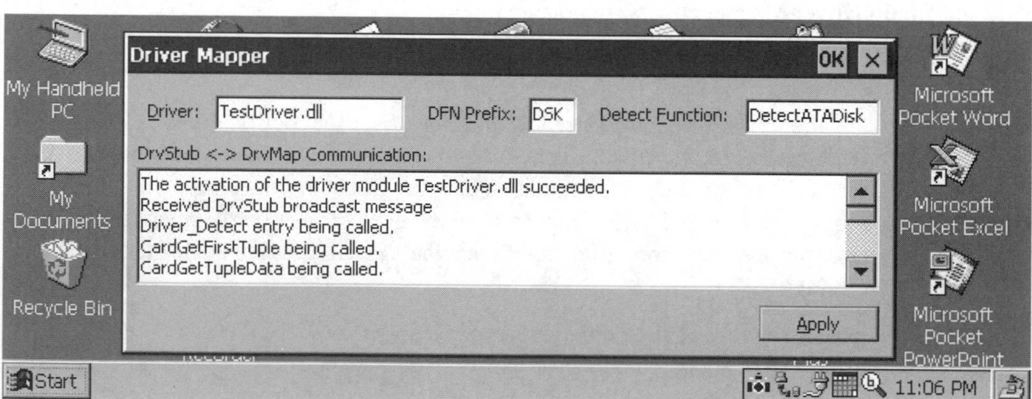

Figure 9.23 Driver Mapper user interface

drvmap.exe is loaded. It also causes your driver to be loaded and the address of each of its entry points to be retrieved (via the GetProcAddress function). If the load is successful, you will see a message similar to the one that appears at the top of the Driver Mapper list box depicted in Figure 9.23.

As drvmap.exe receives messages from drvstub.dll indicating that a certain entry point has been called, the corresponding entry points will be called in your driver. In addition, as your driver calls functions in the apimap.dll module (discussed earlier, in the section titled Design of Driver Mapper), corresponding messages will be sent to the drvstub.dll module. These messages will cause the appearance of additional log messages in the Driver Mapper list box. The messages appearing in Figure 9.23 were generated when Driver Mapper was used to debug the sample CEPB atadisk.dll driver, rebuilt as testdriver.dll.

Limitations of Driver Mapper

Driver Mapper is a valuable utility for debugging certain types of stream-interface drivers on standard platforms. Because it must be loaded *before* your driver is loaded, however, it is limited to debugging drivers that are loaded after system startup. A common example of the types of stream-interface drivers that are supported are those that support installable devices such as a PC card (PCMCIA) device. In contrast, if you were writing a stream-interface driver that was loaded during system startup to support an onboard device, Driver Mapper would not work. This is an unlikely occurrence, however, because drivers that support onboard devices are generally included in the build of a custom kernel image and could be debugged by the CEPB kernel debugger instead of by Driver Mapper.

Driver Mapper functions by mapping calls to your driver to the process space of the Driver Mapper EXE module, drvmap.exe. Calls flowing in the opposite direction that originate in the driver are mapped to the process space of the Device Manager module, device.exe, through the apimap.dll module. Currently, the only driver interface supported is that defined for stream-interface drivers through the DrvStub module. You could add support for other driver models and their respective interfaces by creating other DrvStub-like modules. Each DrvStub-like module would need to provide a stub implementation for each of the functions required by the driver model. The result would be new messages (defined in the messageids.h file) to be sent to the drvmap.exe module, which would need to be specially modified to process these newly defined messages.

The APIMap module provides a stub implementation of the card services API used for access and configuration of PC card devices. No other APIs, most notably those used by USB drivers (USBDI), are currently supported. To provide support for drivers calling USBDI functions, you would need to add stub implementations of each USBDI function to the APIMap module, along with messages for each function. You would then need to modify the DrvStub module to receive these messages and execute the associated function call to the USBD module.

Driver Mapper Technology

Now that you are aware of the limitations of the Driver Mapper utility in debugging certain types of drivers, you may be inclined to extend the current source code to overcome these limitations, or perhaps you have conceived a useful extension to the capabilities provided by the existing source code. To this end, this section provides a description of selected Driver Mapper source modules. We will focus particularly on those modules that demonstrate a development practice that may be of general use in CE driver development. The development practices are as follows:

- How to establish interprocess communication using Windows message queues
- How to pass pointers to memory in one process that may be accessed in another process
- How to remap virtual memory associated with a particular physical address if access to the same physical memory is required in a different process
- How to use the `__declspec(dllexport)` directive along with `extern "C"` to eliminate the use of DEF files

In the spirit of the open-source licensing under which this utility is published, we encourage you to make your changes to the Driver Mapper source code available to your fellow CE driver developers. This book's Web site provides the latest Driver Mapper source code and describes a mechanism for readers to contribute enhancements that may be downloaded by other readers. Refer to the Web site for notifications of Driver Mapper bug fixes and enhancements. Table 9.1 contains a functional description of selected source files (other source files contain code commonly used in MFC or DLL modules), with particular focus on how each file may be used as a demonstration of certain techniques that may be useful for CE driver development in general.

Table 9.1 Selected Driver Mapper Source Files

Module	Source File	Description
`drvmap.exe`	`drvmapdlg.cpp`	This file contains the MFC classes for processing user interface and mapping messages. The MFC message pump is used to associate the `OnStubMessage` function with the `WM_STUB_CALL` message sent by the `drvstub.dll` module to the `drvmap.exe` module when the stream-interface entry points are being mapped to the DrvMap process space. This file is notable for its use of the `SetProcPermissions` function to obtain access to the structures pointed to in the LPARAM parameter of the `OnStubMessage` message-handling function. `OnStubMessage` processes messages sent by the DrvStub module and results in a call to a corresponding method of the `CStreamInterfaceDriver` object.
	`streaminterface driver.cpp`	This file contains an implementation of the object whose purpose is to provide a general abstraction of the driver being debugged. The `Initialize` method loads the driver DLL module and retains the pointers to each of the driver's entry points, obtained through the `GetProcAddress` function. The methods prefixed with *XXX* are then called from the `OnStubMessage` function. These methods then de-reference the corresponding pointer to call the mapped driver's entry point.
`apimap.dll`	`apimap.cpp`	This file contains the DLL startup function, as well as an initialization function called by `drvmap.exe` to pass the window handle and the permission mask (obtained through the `GetCurrentPermissions` function) of the DrvStub

Table 9.1 *Continued.*

Module	Source File	Description
		module. The `TraceStart` function, implemented in the `logtrace.dll` module, is used to begin logging the `DEBUGMSG` strings to a specified file. Using `DEBUGMSG` in this way is particularly useful when you're debugging real-time operations that may not be single-stepped without time-outs occurring. The `logtrace.dll` module may be used separately from Driver Mapper and is discussed later, in the Log Tracer section.
	`kernelmap.cpp`	This file contains the implementation of certain standard CE functions that must be modified to successfully map the driver being debugged. The two functions `MapLoadFSD` and `MapGetCallerProcess` replace the equivalent CE functions `LoadFSD` and `GetCallerProcess`, respectively. The implementation of `MapLoadFSD` sends a message to the DrvStub module, causing it to call `LoadFSD` from within the process space of the `device.exe` module (Device Manager). `MapGetCallerProcess` returns the process ID of the DrvStub module even when the actual caller of the mapped driver's entry point is the DrvMap module.
	`pcmciamap.cpp`	This file contains the implementation of the card services functions used by PC card stream-interface drivers. Each function simply sends a message to the DrvStub module, causing it to call the corresponding function in the `pcmcia.dll` module. The `MapPtrToProcess` function is used to alter the pointer to the parameter block passed in the `LPARAM` parameter of the `SendMessage` function. As of this writing, this function returns the same address passed to it with the upper four bits set to the process slot where the address is contained. The file also contains the implementation of the `LocalCardMapWindow` function, used to map the same physical memory address as that passed to the card services function `CardMapWindow`. This additional mapping is necessary because the physical address mapped by `CardMapWindow` is valid only in the process space of the `pcmcia.dll` module (the same process space as that of the Device Manager).
`drvstub.dll`	`drvstub.cpp`	This file contains an implementation of each entry point required for stream-interface drivers. If communication has been established with the DrvMap module, a message is sent to cause the corresponding function in the mapped driver to be called. The `EXPORT` macro (which equates to `__declspec(dllexport)`) is used instead of an `EXPORT` section in a DEF file to enable each entry point to be callable by outside modules. The `MessageQueueThread` function, also contained in this file, is used as the thread start routine for

(continued)

Table 9.1 *Continued.*

Module	Source File	Description
		the message queue used to receive messages sent from DrvMap or APIMap.
	mapcalls.cpp	This file contains an implementation of the OnMapCall function called from the MessageQueueThread function implemented in the drvstub.cpp module and is used to map certain functions from the mapped driver to the process space of the Device Manager. The OnMapCall function translates the message sent, to a corresponding function call, and is typically used to cause card services functions to be called.

Tracking Processes and Threads

At some point in your debugging efforts you may find that your driver has entered an unknown state, perhaps becoming unresponsive to the device it supports. Fortunately, CE is a preemptive multitasking operating system, so when this occurs the CE kernel continues to run and is able to continue communicating with the debug tools running on your development workstation. The debugging tools we will focus on in this section allow you to peer into the execution of your driver to assess its operational state. We will begin by presenting a hypothetical driver bug that will serve as the context of our exploration of three different debugging tools: the CESH command -gi, the **Process Info** and **Remote Process Viewer** dialog boxes in CEPB 2.12, and the **Processes** and **Threads** windows in CEPB 3.0.

Let's assume for now that you are writing a mouse driver that will function as a stream-interface driver called mousecom.dll. The device file name prefix of this particular driver is *SRM;* that is, the function names for each stream-interface driver entry point begin with *SRM.* When the driver is initialized by the Device Manager (device.exe), the entry point SRM_Init is called. The implementation of SRM_Init initializes access to a serial port, either COM1 or COM2, depending on where the serial mouse is connected. It is interesting that the serial port in SRM_Init is initialized in the same way that an application (possible because stream-interface drivers run in user mode) would initialize access to a serial port: through a call to the CreateFile function. This call ultimately causes another driver to be called and is a typical example of how one driver in CE may freely access another driver.

Upon successful initialization of the serial port, the SRM_Init entry point creates a thread called ReadThread, which is used to read data sent by a serial mouse. An excerpt of the ReadThread start routine is contained in Listing 9.3. So as not to waste CPU cycles polling the serial port for received data, the WaitCommEvent function is used to allow the thread to block until the serial driver signals that data has been received. So if everything is working well, this thread should remain blocked until the mouse is moved, causing it to generate data. In our hypothetical bug, something has gone awry and the mouse pointer moves only a few pixels before becoming stuck in one position on the screen.

Listing 9.3 Excerpt of the MouseCOM thread function `ReadThread`

```
...

    DEBUGMSG(ZONE_READTHREAD, (TEXT("MOUSECOM: Thread handle: 0x%X\n"),
             GetCurrentThreadId()));

    //
    // We can exit the thread by setting g_fStopThread.
    //
    while ( !g_fStopThread ) {
        //
        // We spend most of our time waiting for a serial event here.
        //
        WaitCommEvent (g_hSerial, &fdwCommMask, 0);

        if ( fdwCommMask & EV_RXCHAR ) {
            //
            // We've woken up because a real character is arriving.
            //
            DEBUGMSG(ZONE_READTHREAD,
                     (TEXT("SerMouse : ReadThread : Char ready\r\n")));

            do {
                //
                // Continue to read the serial port while data is available.
                //
                bSuccess = ReadFile(g_hSerial, &serialBytes, 3, &dwBytesRead,
                                    NULL);
...
            } while ( (!g_fStopThread) && dwBytesRead && bSuccess );
...
```

Before diving into the source code for the MouseCOM driver, using the CESH command `-gi` in both CEPB 2.12 and CEPB 3.0, you can assess the overall state of the driver. In Figure 9.24, a copy of the output from this command from the command-line CESH in CEPB 2.12 is presented (there is one slight difference with the CEPB 3.0 command-line CESH, which we will note as we proceed with the analysis). The process you would initially focus on is `P03`, the one that corresponds to the Device Manager, `device.exe`. Reading from left to right, we can see that `device.exe` has been assigned a process handle of `0x0C7F4096` and an access key of `0x00000008`. We will use the process handle when we examine the threads appearing as `T` under `P03`, to determine which process is mapped as active (mapped to slot 0) when the thread is running. The access key is a bit-mapped value that indicates which process slot address space a particular process or thread has permission to access. For `P03`, bit 3 is set in the access key and will be OR'd into the access keys of each of the threads owned by `P03`.

The `dwVMBase` value of `0x08000000` is the base virtual address where the process was loaded and is the offset used to determine the actual virtual memory address for variables that are assigned an offset at compile time. The `CurZone` value is another bit-mapped value, where each bit set corresponds to an active debug zone defined in the source code for the process. In this case, no debug zones are active for the Device Manager, but as we will soon see, the debug zones for many of the modules listed at the bottom of Figure 9.24 are in fact active.

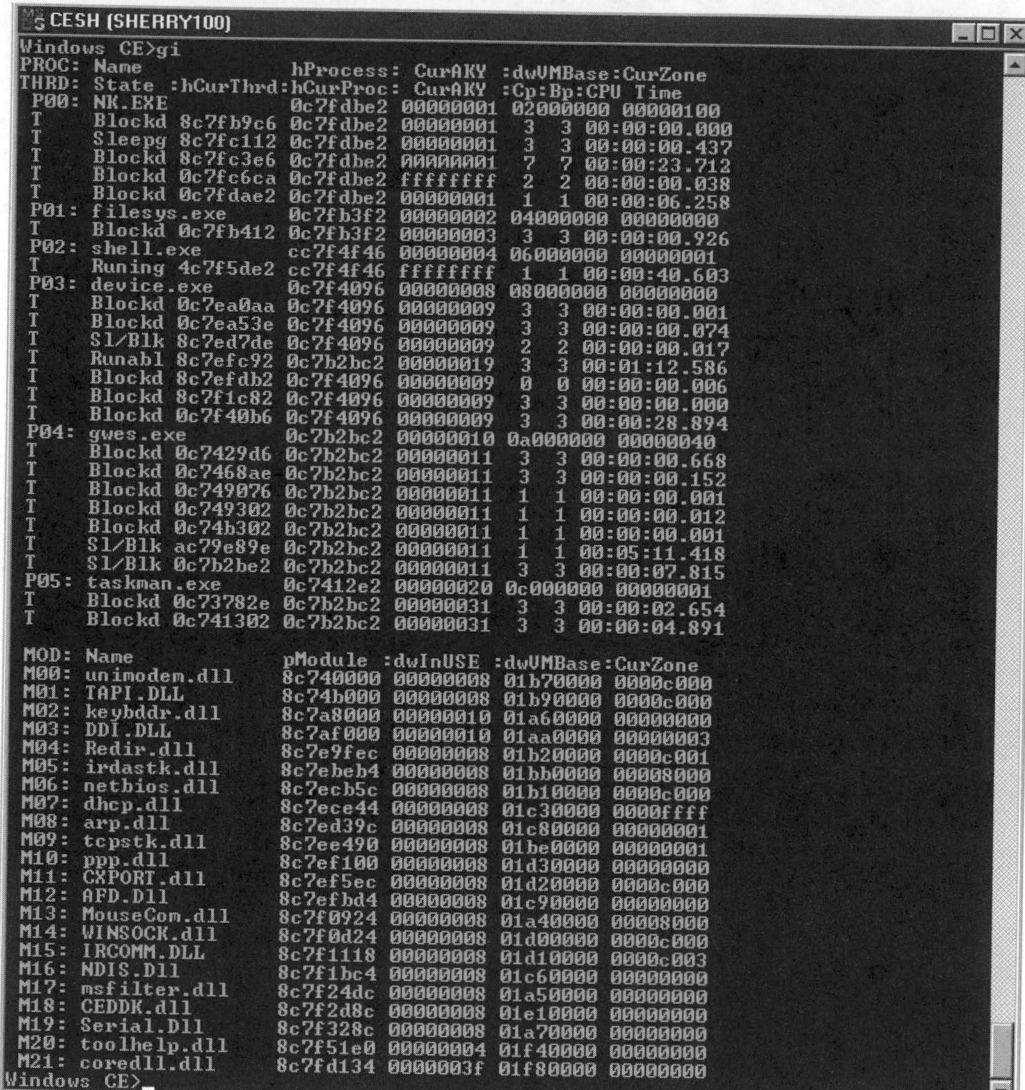

```
CESH (SHERRY100)
Windows CE>gi
PROC: Name           hProcess: CurAKY  :dwVMBase:CurZone
THRD: State :hCurThrd:hCurProc: CurAKY  :Cp:Bp:CPU Time
 P00: NK.EXE          0c7fdbe2 00000001 02000000 00000100
 T    Blockd 8c7fb9c6 0c7fdbe2 00000001  3  3 00:00:00.000
 T    Sleepg 8c7fc112 0c7fdbe2 00000001  3  3 00:00:00.437
 T    Blockd 8c7fc3e6 0c7fdbe2 00000001  7  7 00:00:23.712
 T    Blockd 0c7fc6ca 0c7fdbe2 ffffffff  2  2 00:00:00.038
 T    Blockd 0c7fdae2 0c7fdbe2 00000001  1  1 00:00:06.258
 P01: filesys.exe     0c7fb3f2 00000002 04000000 00000000
 T    Blockd 0c7fb412 0c7fb3f2 00000003  3  3 00:00:00.926
 P02: shell.exe       cc7f4f46 00000004 06000000 00000001
 T    Runing 4c7f5de2 cc7f4f46 ffffffff  1  1 00:00:40.603
 P03: device.exe      0c7f4096 00000008 08000000 00000000
 T    Blockd 0c7ea0aa 0c7f4096 00000009  3  3 00:00:00.001
 T    Blockd 0c7ea53e 0c7f4096 00000009  3  3 00:00:00.074
 T    Sl/Blk 8c7ed7de 0c7f4096 00000009  2  2 00:00:00.017
 T    Runabl 8c7efc92 0c7b2bc2 00000019  3  3 00:01:12.586
 T    Blockd 8c7efdb2 0c7f4096 00000009  0  0 00:00:00.006
 T    Blockd 8c7f1c82 0c7f4096 00000009  3  3 00:00:00.000
 T    Blockd 0c7f40b6 0c7f4096 00000009  3  3 00:00:28.894
 P04: gwes.exe        0c7b2bc2 00000010 0a000000 00000040
 T    Blockd 0c7429d6 0c7b2bc2 00000011  3  3 00:00:00.668
 T    Blockd 0c7468ae 0c7b2bc2 00000011  3  3 00:00:00.152
 T    Blockd 0c749076 0c7b2bc2 00000011  1  1 00:00:00.001
 T    Blockd 0c749302 0c7b2bc2 00000011  1  1 00:00:00.012
 T    Blockd 0c74b302 0c7b2bc2 00000011  1  1 00:00:00.001
 T    Sl/Blk ac79e89e 0c7b2bc2 00000011  1  1 00:05:11.418
 T    Sl/Blk 0c7b2be2 0c7b2bc2 00000011  3  3 00:00:07.815
 P05: taskman.exe     0c7412e2 00000020 0c000000 00000001
 T    Blockd 0c73782e 0c7b2bc2 00000031  3  3 00:00:02.654
 T    Blockd 0c741302 0c7b2bc2 00000031  3  3 00:00:04.891

 MOD: Name            pModule :dwInUSE :dwVMBase:CurZone
 M00: unimodem.dll    8c740000 00000008 01b70000 0000c000
 M01: TAPI.DLL        8c74b000 00000008 01b90000 0000c000
 M02: keybddr.dll     8c7a8000 00000010 01a60000 00000000
 M03: DDI.DLL         8c7af000 00000010 01aa0000 00000003
 M04: Redir.dll       8c7e9fec 00000008 01b20000 0000c001
 M05: irdastk.dll     8c7ebeb4 00000008 01bb0000 00008000
 M06: netbios.dll     8c7ecb5c 00000008 01b10000 0000c000
 M07: dhcp.dll        8c7ece44 00000008 01c30000 0000ffff
 M08: arp.dll         8c7ed39c 00000008 01c80000 00000001
 M09: tcpstk.dll      8c7ee490 00000008 01be0000 00000001
 M10: ppp.dll         8c7ef100 00000008 01d30000 00000000
 M11: CXPORT.dll      8c7ef5ec 00000008 01d20000 0000c000
 M12: AFD.Dll         8c7efbd4 00000008 01c90000 00000000
 M13: MouseCom.dll    8c7f0924 00000008 01a40000 00008000
 M14: WINSOCK.dll     8c7f0d24 00000008 01d00000 0000c000
 M15: IRCOMM.DLL      8c7f1118 00000008 01d10000 0000c003
 M16: NDIS.Dll        8c7f1bc4 00000008 01c60000 00000000
 M17: msfilter.dll    8c7f24dc 00000008 01a50000 00000000
 M18: CEDDK.dll       8c7f2d8c 00000008 01e10000 00000000
 M19: Serial.Dll      8c7f328c 00000008 01a70000 00000000
 M20: toolhelp.dll    8c7f51e0 00000004 01f40000 00000000
 M21: coredll.dll     8c7fd134 0000003f 01f80000 00000000
Windows CE>_
```

Figure 9.24 CESH `-gi` command for assessing the overall system state

It is important to note, before we begin examining the `T` entries appearing under the `P03` entry, that each `T` entry for the Device Manager generally corresponds to a loaded device driver. Each stream-interface driver is loaded as a separate DLL module that runs in its own separate thread. These threads, or drivers, may cause additional drivers to be loaded, producing additional threads, all of which would be collected under `P03`. The key to assessing the overall state of your driver is knowing which thread(s) to focus on under the Device Manager process (`P03` in this case).

Each `T` entry is uniquely identified with a thread handle in the `hCurThrd` column. The best way to correlate this handle with the thread(s) associated with your driver is to use the macro `DEBUGMSG` to print the value of the thread's handle somewhere in each thread's startup function, making certain that the zone (debug zones are described shortly, in the section titled Zone Debugging) used in DEBUGMSG is active. The following line of source code is typical and would cause the thread handle to appear in the kernel debugger's output window (or in the window of the application registered with Eshell for the DBGMSG service). A debug zone value of TRUE is used to ensure that this output appears unconditionally in the output window.

```
DEBUGMSG(TRUE, (TEXT("MOUSECOM: Thread handle: 0x%X\n"), GetCurrentThreadId()));
```

The primary thread on which the MouseCOM driver is loaded corresponds to the last T entry in Figure 9.24, with a thread handle of 0x0C7F40B6, under the P03 Device Manager process. Sometime during the initialization of this driver (for complete source code, refer to the sample code in .\PLATFORM\CEPC\DRIVERS\MOUSE\SERMOUSE), a thread is created with a startup function called ReadThread, which was excerpted in Listing 9.3. This thread has a handle of 0x8C7EFC92 and is the fourth entry in the group under P03.

In the next few paragraphs we will examine these two lines of the CESH -gi output. The first thing we notice is that the read thread is considered runnable (denoted by *Runabl* on Figure 9.24); refer to the document Debugging Processes and Threads in the CEPB 2.12 online documentation or Threads Window in the CEPB 3.0 online documentation for more information. This fact alone should be enough to cause suspicion because by design, the thread should be blocked, waiting for additional input from the serial port driver (providing data from the mouse). Our suspicions are confirmed by the unreasonably large value in the CPU time column. From this information alone, we can be certain that there is a problem in the implementation of ReadThread.

By looking at the value in the hCurProc column for this same thread, we can also determine where it was spending its time when the CESH -gi command was executed. The value of 0x0C7B2BC2 is interesting because it is not the value of the process handle for P03. It is, however, the value of the process handle for P04, gwes.exe (the Graphics, Windowing, and Events Subsystem). This means that this thread is currently mapped into the process slot for P04, implying that it has not yet returned from a call to one of the many functions implemented in GWES (see Chapter 1 for a discussion of protected server libraries, such as GWES, that act as hybrid DLL/EXE modules for the implementation of Microsoft-supported APIs). This mapping is further confirmed by the fact that the current value of the access key in the CurAKY column is 0x00000019, indicating that process slots 0, 3, and 4 all have access to the memory of the thread. We can see that slot 4 is actually where GWES resides, which makes sense because a call to a GWES function requires the access key of the calling thread to be OR'd with GWES's access key to allow it access to the thread's address space.

By now you might be ready to study your source code and set some breakpoints in ReadThread to determine what code is actually being run. To facilitate exploration of another tool that provides output similar to that of the CESH -gi command, let's assume that you will opt to extract further information by using the **Process Info** dialog box in CEPB 2.12 or the **Processes** and **Threads** windows of the CEPB 3.0 IDE. The next two sections discuss how these integrated tools are used in CEPB 2.12 and 3.0.

CEPB 2.12

The **Process Info** dialog box of CEPB 2.12 provides a symbolic stack trace for each selected thread. Thus, knowing both the name of the process responsible for loading our driver (`device.exe`) and the handle of the thread in question, we might be able to determine which GWES function was being called. Of course, this determination depends on whether the GWES function was being called at the moment the **Process Info** dialog box was displayed.

Figure 9.25 contains an image of the **Process Info** dialog box displayed shortly after execution of the CESH `-gi` command. You can access this dialog box by selecting the CEPB 2.12 **Debug | Process** menu option. This option appears only when the kernel is halted, which occurs when it hits a breakpoint or executes the CESH `break` command. In Figure 9.25 the thread ID selected is `0x8C7EFCB0`. This does *not* match the thread ID provided by the `DEBUGMSG` statement previously mentioned. It is not clear why these values are different. They are, however, consistently different by an amount of `0x1E` after the upper three bits of the thread ID value are set. In our case, the following **Process Info** thread ID would result:

CESH `-gi` Thread ID		**Mask**		**Offset**		**Process Info Thread ID**
`0x8C7EFC92`	|	`0xE0000000`	|	`0x1E`	=	`0x8C7EFCB0`

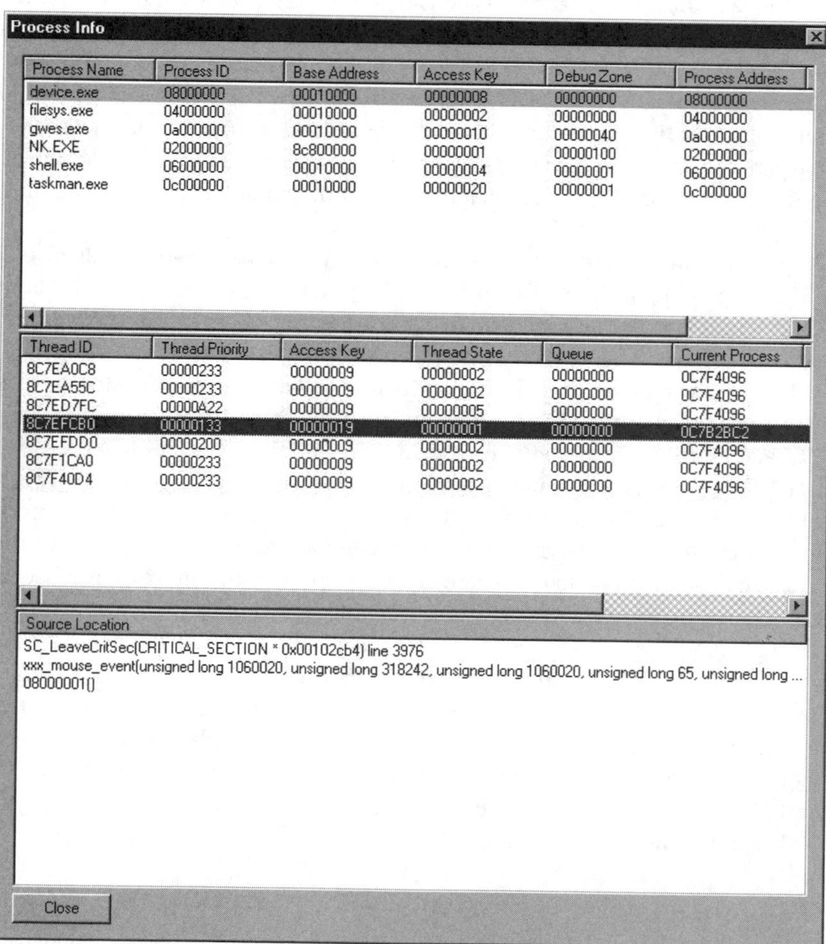

Figure 9.25 Process Info dialog box displaying the `ReadThread` symbolic stack trace

An alternative method for determining the **Process Info** thread ID is simply to use the value that automatically precedes each debug message appearing in the output window of the kernel debugger. This approach works as long as you have at least one debug message in the thread's startup function.

After selecting the list box entry for the newly derived thread ID of `0x8C7EFCB0`, the symbolic stack trace at the bottom of Figure 9.25 appears. Note that the `xxx_mouse_event` function was called. This call is a direct result of a call to the GWES function `mouse_event`, which is used in the `ReadThread` function to pass mouse coordinates collected from the serial port (through the serial port stream-interface driver) to GWES, which in turn animates the mouse cursor by moving it across the screen. So, we may now surmise that when the first set of mouse coordinates is generated, the GWES function `mouse_event` is called repeatedly. This repeated call significantly narrows the scope of the debugging effort in the `ReadThread` startup function.

CEPB 3.0

Let's assume that in our exploration of the **Processes** and **Threads** windows in the CEPB 3.0 IDE, we find the same debug scenario as that presented in the previous section. The **Process Info** dialog box in CEPB 2.12 is now more fully integrated with the CEPB 3.0 IDE, appearing as two separately docked windows (originally depicted in Figure 9.21, second window from the left, at the top of the screen, and the window just below it). You can display the **Processes** window by selecting the **Target | Processes** menu option. By pressing the button at the top of this window that shows two blue arrows, you can refresh the contents of the window with a list of the currently loaded processes. Like the **Process Info** dialog box in CEPB 2.12, this information is available only when the kernel has been halted by a breakpoint (or an unhandled exception).

As in CEPB 2.12, we double-click on the `device.exe` entry of the **Processes** window. (In this scenario, we can assume that the Device Manager is responsible for loading the MouseCOM driver, and that its module name is `device.exe`.) As a result, the **Threads** window, also depicted in Figure 9.21 (second window down from the top on the left-hand side), appears. Unlike the **Process Info** dialog box in CEPB 2.12 allows us to do, we are able to match the thread ID provided by the `DEBUGMSG` macro (and the output of the CESH command `-gi`) with a particular entry listed in the **Threads** window without performing any calculations on the value. Double-clicking on this entry produces a stack trace window containing the same entries as those at the bottom of the **Process Info** dialog box in CEPB 2.12.

Zone Debugging

When attempting to characterize a real-time problem with your driver, you may need to consider using trace statements over setting breakpoints and single-stepping with the application- or kernel-level debugger. Trace statements have the advantage of allowing the time-bounded operations of your driver to proceed unaffected, except by the overhead required to transmit the actual trace statement to the development workstation. A typical situation in which trace statements are most useful occurs when your code is required to respond to the notification of another driver or the device itself within a defined time period. If a breakpoint were set in the code processing this notification, the response returned to the notifying hardware or software would undoubtedly be too late.

Fortunately, CEPB provides a mechanism for receiving trace statements from the custom platform over the serial or Ethernet debugger connections. Debug messages are generally sent over a serial connection when you're configuring your custom kernel image for debugging, as described earlier, in the section titled Custom Platform Serial/Parallel Port Debugging Configuration: Use Case 2. Likewise, they are sent via an Ethernet connection when configured for Ethernet debugging, as described in the section titled Custom Platform Ethernet Debugging Configuration: Use Case 1.

The `DEBUGMSG` macro is used to send a character string to the development workstation and requires two parameters. The first parameter contains a zone index that associates the character string with a particular category of debug messages. The second parameter contains the actual trace message within parentheses and may also contain `printf`-formatted specifiers along with their associated values. A typical `DEBUGMSG` macro is presented in Listing 9.4.

Listing 9.4 `DEBUGMSG` macro syntax

```
DEBUGMSG(<zone list>,<printf-formatted trace message>);

Example:

DEBUGMSG(ZONE_PCMCIA | ZONE_INIT | ZONE_ERROR,
        (TEXT("ATADISK: CardRequestWindow(hATARegAlt) failed %d\r\n"),
       GetLastError()));

Remarks:

The first parameter of this DEBUGMSG macro contains a list of zones (appearing
as OR'd constants) that, if enabled, would allow the trace message in the
second parameter to be transmitted to the development workstation. The trace
message in the second parameter is a printf-formatted character string that
displays the return value of the GetLastError function.
```

A maximum of 16 zone indexes may be defined and must appear as constants in one of your driver's header files via the `DEBUGZONE` macro. Typically, separate constants would be defined to identify error severity levels and the type of source code described by the message. The `DEBUGZONE` macro contains a statement that creates a mask from your zone index that is logically AND'd with a member of the `DBGPARAM` structure, discussed in the next paragraph. This mask allows `DEBUGMSG` macros to be described with multiple zone indexes, logically OR'd together, as depicted in Listing 9.4. A typical set of zone indexes used in the implementation of the ATADisk sample driver is shown here:

```
#define ZONE_ERROR       DEBUGZONE(0)
#define ZONE_WARNING     DEBUGZONE(1)
#define ZONE_FUNCTION    DEBUGZONE(2)
#define ZONE_INIT        DEBUGZONE(3)
#define ZONE_PCMCIA      DEBUGZONE(4)
#define ZONE_IO          DEBUGZONE(5)
```

The `DBGPARAM` structure is declared in the `dbgapi.h` header file. It must be defined in one of your driver's source files as the global variable `dpCurSettings`. The first member of this structure contains the name of the driver. The next member contains an array of character strings naming each of the zone indexes you have defined for your driver. The position of each string determines which index it describes, with the first string describing zone index 0. The sample DBGPARAM structure presented below contains a string naming each ZONE_ constant presented above. The last member contains a zone mask used to determine which of the 16 possible zone indexes are enabled when the driver is first loaded.

```
DBGPARAM dpCurSettings =
{
    TEXT("ATA Disk"),
    {
        TEXT("Errors"),
        TEXT("Warnings"),
        TEXT("Functions"),
        TEXT("Initialization"),
        TEXT("PCMCIA"),
        TEXT("Disk I/O"),
        TEXT("Undefined"),
        TEXT("Undefined"),
        TEXT("Undefined"),
        TEXT("Undefined"),
        TEXT("Undefined"),
        TEXT("Undefined"),
        TEXT("Undefined"),
        TEXT("Undefined"),
        TEXT("Undefined"),
        TEXT("Undefined")
    },
    0xFFFF
};
```

In order for the trace message passed in the second DEBUGMSG macro parameter to be sent to the development workstation, at least one of the zone indexes contained in the first DEBUGMSG macro parameter must be enabled. By changing the value of the zone mask in the DBGPARAM structure, you can selectively enable and disable trace messages, depending on the type of problem being debugged. This capability provides compile-time control of trace messages. Using CESH, you can also change this value at runtime (as discussed later in this section).

Somewhere in your driver's code you must also pass the DBGPARAM structure to the CE kernel using the DEBUGREGISTER macro. This macro is typically called in the main entry point of your driver's DLL (DllMain, for example) and must be passed the value of your driver's instance handle (which is passed to the main entry point). The DEBUGREGISTER macro assumes that the dpCurSettings variable has been defined somewhere in your code, and it calls the RegisterDbgZones function, passing the instance handle and the value of dpCurrSettings.

By using CESH, you can alter the value of the zone mask in the DBGPARAM structure at runtime from your development workstation. The command in question is zo. It has the following syntax:

```
zo [p | m] <Index> [<Zone>. [on | off][<ZoneIndex>]]
```

The p parameter indicates that the subsequent Index parameter is a process index; the m parameter indicates that it is a module index. The Zone parameter that follows contains the new zone mask and replaces the value hard-coded within the DBGPARAM structure definition. The

ZoneIndex parameter may be used instead of the Zone parameter to enable and disable the specified zone index. ZoneIndex is functionally equivalent to Zone but allows you to more conveniently refer to the zone index rather than calculating the corresponding zone mask.

Figure 9.26 contains an image of the CESH command line for enabling the zone index defined in the MouseCOM sample driver as the constant ZONE_FUNCTION. Note that the first step requires the value of the module index to be determined by the CESH command gi mod. In this case the value of the MouseCOM module has an index of 4. The zo m 4 command causes the names of each zone index to be displayed, and the index of the ZONE_FUNCTION zone is determined to be 13. Both the zone and the module index values are then used in the next command, zo m 4 on 13, which enables the ZONE_FUNCTION zone and allows the trace messages associated with this zone to be received by the development workstation.

CEPB 3.0

As you may have noticed, enabling and disabling a zone using CESH can be a bit time-consuming, considering that as many as three commands must be entered. Fortunately, CEPB 3.0 now provides a graphical option for enabling and disabling debug zones. Selecting the **Target | Debug Zones** menu option displays the dialog box depicted in Figure 9.27. The list box on the left of the dialog box provides a list of loaded modules. Selecting the module in question pro-

```
CESH (SHERRY100)
Windows CE>gi mod
 MOD: Name                pModule :dwInUSE :dwVMBase:CurZone
 M00: unimodem.dll        8c7a9c00 00000008 01b70000 0000c000
 M01: TAPI.DLL            8c752800 00000008 01b90000 0000c000
 M02: keybddr.dll         8c7a1800 00000010 01a60000 00000000
 M03: DDI.DLL             8c7adc00 00000010 01aa0000 00000003
 M04: Redir.dll           8c7ea20c 00000008 01b20000 0000c001
 M05: irdastk.dll         8c7ec0d4 00000008 01bb0000 00008000
 M06: netbios.dll         8c7ecd7c 00000008 01b10000 0000c000
 M07: dhcp.dll            8c7ed064 00000008 01c30000 0000ffff
 M08: arp.dll             8c7ed5bc 00000008 01c80000 00000001
 M09: tcpstk.dll          8c7ee6b0 00000008 01be0000 00000001
 M10: ppp.dll             8c7ef30c 00000008 01d30000 00000000
 M11: CXPORT.dll          8c7ef7f8 00000008 01d20000 0000c000
 M12: AFD.Dll             8c7efcd4 00000008 01c90000 00000000
 M13: MouseCom.dll        8c7f0924 00000008 01a40000 00008000
 M14: WINSOCK.dll         8c7f0d24 00000008 01d00000 0000c000
 M15: IRCOMM.DLL          8c7f1118 00000008 01d10000 0000c003
 M16: NDIS.Dll            8c7f1bc4 00000008 01c60000 00000000
 M17: msfilter.dll        8c7f24dc 00000008 01a50000 00000000
 M18: CEDDK.dll           8c7f2d8c 00000008 01e10000 00000000
 M19: Serial.Dll          8c7f316c 00000008 01a70000 00000000
 M20: toolhelp.dll        8c7f51e0 00000004 01f40000 00000000
 M21: coredll.dll         8c7fd134 0000003f 01f80000 00000000
Windows CE>zo m 13
Registered Name:SerMouse    CurZone:00008000
Zone Names - Prefixed with bit number and * if currently on
 0 Data                 : 1 ReadThread          : 2 2              : 3 3
 4 4                    : 5 5                   : 6 6              : 7 7
 8 8                    : 9 9                   :10 10             :11 Values
12 Init                 :13 Function            :14 Warning        :15*Error
Windows CE>zo m 13 on 13
Registered Name:SerMouse    CurZone:0000A000
Zone Names - Prefixed with bit number and * if currently on
 0 Data                 : 1 ReadThread          : 2 2              : 3 3
 4 4                    : 5 5                   : 6 6              : 7 7
 8 8                    : 9 9                   :10 10             :11 Values
12 Init                 :13*Function            :14 Warning        :15*Error
Windows CE>_
```

Figure 9.26 CESH zo command example

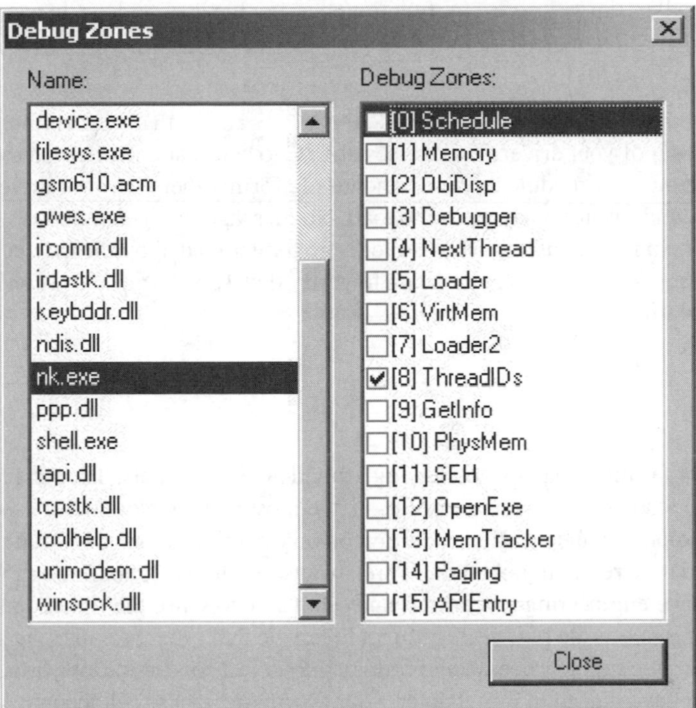

Figure 9.27 CEPB 3.0 debug zone graphical interface

duces the list on the right, which contains all debug zones defined for the selected module. Debug zones currently enabled appear checked. To enable additional debug zones, you simply check the zone desired.

Log Tracer

If you are developing your driver on a standard platform, or you are unable to connect to a development workstation from your custom platform, you will be unable to receive the trace messages passed to the `DEBUGMSG` macro. To overcome this limitation, we have developed a utility called Log Tracer (used in the development of Driver Mapper) to replace the `DEBUGMSG` macro with a call to a function in `logtrace.dll`. This function time-stamps the trace message and writes it to a log file on the target platform for later viewing. The source code for `logtrace.dll` is available on this book's CD and Web site.

To use Log Tracer, you must make the following changes to your driver source code:

- Add the include file `trace.h` to all of your source files where `DEBUGMSG` is used. This addition will cause the `DEBUGMSG` macro to be redefined with a call to the `Trace` function implemented in the `logtrace.dll` module.

- Add a call to the `TraceStart` function, passing the desired log file name, somewhere in your driver's initialization function (in your driver's main entry point, `DllMain`).
- Modify the project settings to include the `logtracer.lib` import library in the linking of your driver. This causes eMVC to automatically upload the `logtrace.dll` module to your standard platform; otherwise your driver will silently and mysteriously refuse to load. No messages are generated for such an error, so if you find that your driver is no longer loaded by the Device Manager (`device.exe`), be certain to verify that `logtrace.dll` is on the target platform.

Summary

Debugging is about far more than just collecting a small arsenal of tools. Though having the right tool can often lead to a more rapid resolution, the most valuable tool of all is between your ears. We have personally witnessed the resolution of very complex bugs just through the skilled application of deductive reasoning. And there are always developers who, through years of experience, regularly have engineering revelations and seem able to sense the right course of action. In either case, debugging is the part of the project life cycle that often provides the greatest challenges, defying the scheduling process and producing the most frustration. We hope that with the knowledge you have gained in this chapter, your debugging tasks will become more predictable and fulfilling. For the purposes of review, each topic covered in this chapter is summarized here.

Beginning with a discussion of available debugging technologies in use industrywide, we defined log-level, application-level, kernel-level, and hardware-level debugging. We discussed the advantages and disadvantages of each debugger transport, particularly as it relates to newly developed, untested hardware platforms. After the discussion of these topics, you were ready to begin some actual debugging, so we prepared by building a sample driver for debugging using the CEPB IDE. We then began a step-by-step presentation of specifically how to use both the CEPB and eMVC for debugging the sample ATADisk driver. The Driver Mapper and Log Tracer tools were presented as one option that would allow the use of a standard platform and the eMVC for driver debugging. We also explored the use of CESH, for tracking processes and threads at runtime, in addition to enabling and disabling debug zones.

10

The Windows CE Build Process

Chapter 3 introduced Platform Builder and building custom versions of Windows CE. Behind the highly productive IDE, a set of powerful build tools perform all the hard work. Understanding these tools and how they work opens the way to understanding how Windows CE puts itself together. Unfortunately, the build process is not always smooth sailing. It can be fraught with errors, the cause of which can be the organization of components and modules, their subsequent compilation, or, during the final stages, the process of putting together the image on the basis of directives specified in a multitude of configuration files. Understanding this build process then becomes a critical aspect of mastering Platform Builder.

In this chapter we will take an internal tour of the Windows CE build process. We will describe each tool and its position in the sequence of events that builds Windows CE. In effect, we will build Windows CE from the command line, much as the IDE does.

Components and Modules Revisited

Let's further explore the concept of a module. The operating system kernel is an obvious one. However, even the kernel is further partitioned into components. For example, a small version of the kernel can be constructed with a minimal feature set. Features can be added that will grow the kernel in both size and functionality. The Windows CE Platform Builder contains a project called `MINKERN` that constructs a minimal kernel. Let's look at the components included in such a minimal kernel. Table 10.1 lists components and modules in the `MINKERN` configuration. When you scan this table, remember that each component exports a set of APIs related to the features they contain. By including a certain component, you get its functionality and the related Win32 API.

Table 10.1 Components and Modules Included in the `MINKERN` Configuration

System File	Type	Contents
`coredll`	Module	System services.
`filesys`	Module	Windows CE file system.
`nk`	Module	The kernel module. It is responsible for memory, process, and file management.
`coreloc`	Component	Localization.
`coremain`	Component	Base functionality for `coredll.dll`. This includes file and system time functions and some thread-related functionality.
`fsheap`	Component	System heap support. Required only for RAM-based file systems.
`fsmain`	Component	Base functionality for file system.
`fsreg`	Component	ROM-based system registry.
`fsysrom`	Component	ROM-based file system.
`lmem`	Component	Local heap and memory allocation.
`pmstub`	Component	Post message stub component.
`thunks`	Component	Kernel and Win32 thunks.

Several components can be linked to form a module. A **module** is an executable or library file that performs a set of well-defined operations and exports a well-defined API. The division of a module into components is based on areas of functionality, albeit historically restricted by how the code was written. Microsoft has done its best to separate the modules into components in such a way that OEMs can select only the functionality they need for their platform. Some objects, like the kernel (`nk.exe`), cannot be broken down further into components and exist only as modules.

Note that there is no GUI support in the `MINKERN` configuration. Also missing are communications and networking. Windows CE allows you to add components according to the functionality you need. For Point-to-Point Protocol (PPP) for example, you would add the `ppp` component to Windows CE. A component called `tcpip` would enable TCP/IP support.

By nature, the Windows CE build process is quite flexible, but this flexibility comes at a price: Because the build process is complex, Windows CE builds are prone to errors. When adapting Windows CE for your hardware, you will end up making changes to the build process. Much goes on under the hood when you add a single component to Windows CE. We'll take a guided tour of the Windows CE build to gain a thorough understanding of the process.

The Directory Structure of Platform Builder

The directory structure of Platform Builder is shown in Table 10.2.

Table 10.2 Platform Builder Directory Structure

Directory	Subdirectory		Contents[a]
DDTK			Files for testing device drivers (see Chapter 12).
OTHERS			Runtime support for various Microsoft development environments.
	ADOCE		Files required to support ActiveX Data Objects for CE on a device.
	ATL		Files required to support and develop applications with Active Template Library for CE.
	MFC		Files required to support and develop applications with Microsoft Foundation Classes.
	PLATMGR		Files required to support Platform Manager communication on the device side.
	TOOLS		Tools used to add runtime support to a build. This is done via a tool called pbmerge.exe that merges BIB files (which are discussed in depth later in this chapter).
	VBRT		Runtime support for Visual Basic.
PLATFORM			Root directory for all platforms (_PLATFORMROOT).
	CEPC		Sample CEPC platform (_TARGETPLATROOT).
		DRIVERS	Source code for platform-specific device drivers.
		EBOOT	Source code and integration files for a PC Ethernet boot loader.
		FILES	Platform-specific initialization information for registry, database, localization, and CE image.
		GWE	Root directory for modules that are linked with the Graphics, Windowing, and Events Subsystem.
		INC	Repository for platform-specific header files.
		KERNEL	Code that is specific to the Hardware Abstraction Layer and the kernel.
		LOADCEPC	Source code for the utility run on the CEPC to download a binary image from the development workstation.
		LIB	Platform-specific libraries stored in processor-dependent paths.

(continued)

Table 10.2 *Continued.*

Directory	Subdirectory			Contents[a]
		PPFSTOOL		Source code for a parallel port download utility used to transfer an image to a target platform over a parallel port. This source can be customized for different platforms to incorporate any difference in the parallel port hardware.
		TARGET		Platform-specific executables stored in processor-dependent paths.
		TEST		An application to test PC video performance.
	ODO			Sample Odo platform.
	ODODUB			Sample Odo platform to demonstrate the CE dial-up boot loader.
PUBLIC				Root directory for all projects (_PUBLICROOT).
	COMMON			Microsoft-supplied modules and components common to all platforms and projects.
		CESYSGEN		Files used to build system modules from selected components.
		DDK		Platform-independent header files for device drivers.
		SDK		Platform- and project-independent header files and libraries for applications.
		OAK		OEM Adaptation Kit—files used by the OEM to adapt Microsoft-supplied content to a custom platform.
			BIN	Utilities used to build CE.
			DRIVERS	Device drivers bundled with CE (supplied by Microsoft or third-party vendors).
			FILES	Common initialization information for registry, database, localization, and CE image.
			INC	CE header files that are modified later by component availability.
			LIB	CE libraries that may be built according to the components selected in the build.
			MISC	Utilities (mostly batch files) used in the CE build process.
			TARGET	Prebuilt Windows CE modules and components.
	MINKERNS			Sample project with minimal kernel support (_PROJECTROOT).

Table 10.2 *Continued.*

Directory	Subdirectory		Contents[a]
	OAK		Files that may be modifed by the OEM to customize the CE build (_PROJECTOAKROOT).
		FILES	Project-specific initialization information for registry, database, localization, and image.
		MISC	Cesysgen.bat file that specifies components and modules to include in the image.
	CESYSGEN		Repository for intermediate files during the build.
		DDK	Headers and libraries to be used by device drivers for the custom platform being built.
		SDK	Headers and libraries to be used by applications for the custom platform being built.
		OAK	Intermediate storage for files modified by the OEM.
SDK			SDK for the target created by the ETK (_SDKROOT).
	BIN		Compilers and tools used to build the operating system.

[a] Paths in the Platform Builder tree that are stored in environment variables for reuse in an installation-independent fashion are given in parentheses.

Underneath its IDE, Platform Builder uses a combination of a project and a platform to create a **target**. Different projects can be combined with platforms without restriction as long as the combination makes sense for a particular target. For example, the MINKERN project and the CEPC platform together refer to a target. In this case, the target is an 80486 PC running a minimal Windows CE kernel. The CEPC platform can also be combined with another project, like the sample MAXALL project, that includes a major set of available Windows CE components in the operating system. The MAXALL target includes GUI and communications support. Since the CEPC platform has drivers for a display and a network card, it can now use the operating system support for GUI and communications. We built such a platform, called Adam, in Chapter 3.

Because a platform is a combination of the processor and related peripherals, a change in processor should merit a change in platform. For a highly integrated processor, this is most likely true, because the types of peripherals connected to the processor change when the processor changes. However, Windows CE stores its platform-dependent files in directories that are processor specific. Thus, in theory a platform can support multiple processors.

The directory called COMMON under the PUBLIC directory bears special mention. This directory contains platform- and project-independent files that are supplied by Microsoft or a third-party vendor. Files under this directory are considered to come bundled with Windows CE. For example, you will find a model device driver for audio, a PCMCIA device driver, and an IEEE 1284 parallel port driver in this directory. These drivers are generic and are supplied by

Microsoft. You will also find the driver for the RangeLAN2 wireless PCMCIA card (supplied by Proxim) under this directory tree. Support for widely used or strategic third-party products can also be found under PUBLIC\COMMON.

If you are not a system integrator reselling an enhanced Platform Builder to customers, avoid modifying any files under this directory. Avoiding modification will decrease the complexity of upgrading to future versions of Windows CE.

When building for the CEPC-MINKERN target, the libraries and modules that are built are deposited into a directory under MINKERN called CESYSGEN. This directory is an intermediate repository for files. The files are then copied into in the \WINCE\RELEASE directory, also denoted by the environment variable _FLATRELEASEDIR. A final binary image of Windows CE that can be uploaded into ROM or RAM is constructed from these output files.

Setting Up the Build Process

The Windows CE build process uses a variety of tools to build a binary image. These tools are a combination of executables and batch files. They communicate with each other through environment variables. You can pass information from one tool to another by setting the value of a particular variable.

To set up the environment correctly for the build, we invoke a batch file called wince.bat with the following parameters:

```
Wince.bat TgtCpuType TgtCpu Os Project Platform
```

This file will set up the basic environment variables used by the Windows CE build tools. It tweaks some standard environment variables, such as PATH, LIB, and INCLUDE, and then defines a handful of new variables that point to certain directories in the Platform Builder tree. By using these variables to refer to the directories, the build tools remain independent of the structure of the directory. If the directory tree of the Platform Builder changes in the future, the tools will continue to function properly.

The arguments passed to wince.bat define environment variables that convey information about the target (Table 10.3).

Table 10.3 Options for Wince.bat

Option	Value	Example
TgtCpuType	Family of processors to which the target's processor belongs	X86, PPC
TgtCpu	Target processor type	I486, PPC821
Os	Operating system	Always set to CE
Project	Name of project	MINKERN
Platform	Name of hardware platform	CEPC

How Wince.bat Works

`Wince.bat` primes the Windows CE build process by perfoming the following tasks:

1. `Wince.bat` sets a variable called `_HOSTCPUTYPE` according to the processor type on the host. A Windows NT system variable called `PROCESSOR_ARCHITECTURE` is used according to Table 10.4.

Table 10.4 Determining Host Architecture

PROCESSOR_ARCHITECTURE	HOSTCPUTYPE
mips	mips
NULL	i386
ppc	ppc
x86	i386

2. `Wince.bat` uses the `_HOSTCPUTYPE` variable to construct a processor-dependent path at a later stage.
3. `Wince.bat` sets the variable `_FLATRELEASEDIR`, which holds the value of the Windows CE release directory, to `%_WINCEROOT%\RELEASE`.
4. `Wince.bat` locates and runs a utility called `setdrive.exe` from the `%_WINCEROOT%\PUBLIC\COMMON\OAK\BIN\%_HOSTCPUTYPE%` directory with the following parameters:

   ```
   Setdrive %_WINCEROOT% _WINCEDRIVE
   ```

   Setdrive extracts the drive letter from its first argument (in our example, `C:\WINCE`) and creates a batch file called `setdrv.bat` with the following line in it:

   ```
   @set _WINCEDRIVE=C:
   ```

   Recall that `_WINCEDRIVE` is the second argument passed to the Setdrive utility. The file `setdrv.bat` is then executed. In effect, Setdrive defines its second argument as a new environment variable and sets it to the drive letter extracted from its first argument. `_WINCEDRIVE` now holds the drive letter in which the Windows CE installation resides.
5. `Wince.bat` calls Setdrive repeatedly to set up environment variables as in Table 10.5.

Table 10.5 Environment Variables Set Up by Setdrive

Variable	Value
`_WINCEDRIVE`	Drive on which Windows CE is installed
`_SDKDRIVE`	Drive on which the SDK is installed
`_PUBLICDRIVE`	Drive where the `PUBLIC` directory is created
`_PLATFORMDRIVE`	Drive where the `PLATFORM` directory is created
`_PRIVATEDRIVE`	Drive where the `PRIVATE` directory is created

6. `Wince.bat` adds the directories listed in Table 10.6 to the `PATH` variable
7. `Wince.bat` constructs a list of valid arguments that can be passed to it (Table 10.7). Each list is used to initialize an environment variable.

Table 10.6 Directories Added to the `PATH` Variable by `Wince.bat`

Directory	Contents
`%_PUBLICROOT%\COMMON\OAK\BIN\%_HOSTCPUTYPE`	Tools for building and debugging
`%_PUBLICROOT%\COMMON\OAK\MISC`	Batch files for building
`$_WINCEROOT%\DEVELOPR\%USERNAME%`	Any private utilities used by the developer

Table 10.7 Valid Arguments for `Wince.bat`

Variable	Value
`__VALIDCPUTYPE`	`ARM`, `MIPS`, `PPC`, `SHx`, or `x86`
`__VALIDCPU`	`R3000`, `R4100`, `R4111`, `R4200`, `R4300`, `PPC821`, `SH3`, `SH4`, `i486`, `SA1100`, or `ARM720`
`__VALIDOS`	`NT`, `NTANSI`, or `CE`
`__VALIDPROJ`	`(NULL)`
`__VALIDPLAT`	`NOPLAT`, `DESKTOP`, or `DESKTOP_SDK`

8. If the `-h` option is passed, `wince.bat` displays its command-line usage and exits.
9. `Wince.bat` checks whether the batch file is being run twice from the same command prompt. If it is, it exits with an error. A variable called `_WINCECALLED` is used to check this condition. This check ensures that variables set to customize the Windows CE build process are not reset to their default values.
10. `Wince.bat` sets up internal variables to the values of the arguments passed to the batch file (Table 10.8).

Table 10.8 Environment Variables for `Wince.bat` Arguments

Variable	Value
_TGTCPUTYPE	cputype
_TGTCPU	cpu
_TGTOS	os
_TGTPROJ	project
_TGTPLAT	platform

11. `Wince.bat` checks the value of `_TGTCPUTYPE` against the list of valid CPU types in the `__VALIDCPUTYPE` variables. If the `cputype` is not valid, it displays an error message and exits.
12. `Wince.bat` validates the value of `_TGTCPU` against the value of `__VALIDCPU`.
13. `Wince.bat` validates the value of `_TGTOS` against the value of `__VALIDOS`.
14. `Wince.bat` sets the `_WINCECALLED` variable to 1 to indicate that this batch file has been called.
15. `Wince.bat` sets some environment variables to the values shown in Table 10.9.

Table 10.9 Environment Variables Used by the Build

Variable	Value
_PROJECTROOT	_PUBLICROOT_TGTPROJ
_PROJECTSDKROOT	_PROJECTROOT\SDK
_PROJECTOAKROOT	_PROJECTROOT\OAK
_PROJECTDDKROOT	_PROJECTROOT\DDK
_TARGETPLATROOT	_PLATFORMROOT_TGTPLAT

16. `Wince.bat` defines the directory where the Make environment can be found. This directory holds a central makefile that is used to centralize rules for building the entire source code in the Platform Builder. The directory `_PUBLICROOT\COMMON\OAK\MISC` is stored in a variable called `_MAKEENVROOT`.
17. `Wince.bat` adds the SDK bin directory `%_SDROOT%\BIN` to the `PATH` variable. This directory contains the processor-specific compiler, assembler, linker, and related utilities.
18. `Wince.bat` trashes any values set up for the `INCLUDE` and `LIB` variables. The build process expects that library and include paths that must be searched will be specified by the `/I` and `/LIB` directives to the compiler and linker, respectively. These directives lengthen the command line for the compiler and linker but create build files that are easy to understand and maintain.

19. `Wince.bat` sets defaults for the `build.exe` utility used to compile and link the source code in the Windows CE installation. The options for `build.exe` that are set as defaults are shown in Table 10.10.

Table 10.10 Options Passed to `Build.exe`

Option	Usage
`-e`	Generates log files. The Build utility logs errors in `build.err`, warnings in `build.wrn`, and commands and messages in `build.log`.
`-nmake -I`	Passes the `-i` option to the Nmake utility. Build calls Nmake to build the source code. The `-i` option instructs Nmake to ignore commands that fail. This option allows the Build utility to run to completion and log all events in the respective files.
`-w`	Shows warnings on the screen.

20. `Wince.bat` sets up environment variables that specify how to create a custom build of Windows CE (Table 10.11).

Table 10.11 Environment Variables That Modify the Build

Variable	Value	Usage
`BUILD_OPTIONS`	`NULL`	Contains options passed to the Build utility.
`COUNTRY`	`USA`	Sets language to U.S. English.
`WINCECOD`	`1`	Creates assembler listings of source code when compiling.
`WINCEDEBUG`	`retail`	Builds a retail version of CE with no debugging information.
`WINCEEMULATION`	`NULL`	Unknown.
`WINCEMAP`	`1`	Generates map files, which you can use to look up addresses when you're tracking exceptions.
`WINCEOEM`	`NULL`	Indicates that this build is not being used by an OEM.
`WINCEREL`	`NULL`	Used during incremental development. When set to 1, any module that is built successfully is automatically copied into the CE release directory (denoted by `_FLATRELEASEDIR`).

21. `Wince.bat` calls a project-specific batch file if it exists. The developer can create project-specific batch file called `%_TGTPROJ%.bat` can be created in the `%_PROJECTROOT%` directory that sets variables to customize the Windows CE build process.

22. `Wince.bat` calls a platform-specific batch file if it exists. The developer can create a platform-specific batch file called `%_TGTPLAT%.bat` can be created in the `%_TARGETPLATROOT%` directory that sets variables to customize the platform being built.

23. `Wince.bat` executes the Platform Builder environment file `%_WINCEROOT%\PUBLIC\COMMON\OAK\MISC\etkenv.bat`. This file adds the `BIN` directories from the Windows CE Toolkit for Visual C++ to the `PATH` variable.

24. `Wince.bat` looks for and executes a batch file, `%_WINCEROOT%\DEVELOPR\%USERNAME%\setenv.bat`. This file can be set up by the developer to perform any customized build steps. For example, the developer may establish paths in the `INCLUDE` and `LIB` variables used by the compiler and linker to search for header files and libraries, respectively. Any additional arguments passed to the `wince.bat` file are passed unchanged to the `setenv.bat` file, thus creating an opportunity for the developer to write a generic `setenv.bat` file whose behavior can be modified according to the arguments passed.

25. `Wince.bat` creates the Windows CE release directory, denoted by `%_FLATRELEASEDIR%`.

26. `Wince.bat` creates the following build information (BIF) files:

    - `%_TGTPROJ%.bif`
    - `%_TGTPLAT%.bif`
    - `%_TGTCPU%.bif`
    - `%_TGTOS%.bif`

    These files are used to perform two release checks:

    1. **Release check 1.** If any of one or more (but not all) of the BIF files do not exist, set the value of `WINCEREL` to `NULL` to prevent any modules from being automatically copied into the release directory. The reason for doing this is that if no BIF files have been created properly, the build process has not completed successfully, implying that the release directory has not been populated correctly and cannot be used to release individual modules.
    2. **Release check 2.** Check the BIF files to make sure that the platform directory is being used by the same project that used it previously. If another project is being used with the same platform directory, the project modules must be cleaned up and overwritten with those from the new project. Thus, a clean build is performed the next time the developer attempts to build Windows CE.

27. `Wince.bat` discards any internal environment variables it has used.

Once `wince.bat` has been run successfully, the command prompt is ready to build a Windows CE image. The Platform Builder installation creates shortcuts to open a command prompt and run `wince.bat` with the appropriate parameters.

Building a Project

Before we begin to build an image, we need some way to tell the build tools which components—both system components and components developed by OEMs—to include in the image. The information again is supplied in the form of environment variables. For the `MINKERN` project, these environment variables are set or reset in the project-specific batch file `minkern.bat` in `_PROJECTROOT`. Recall that `wince.bat` runs a project-specific batch file during its execution. That batch file is `minkern.bat`. The environment variables set by `minkern.bat` are listed in Table 10.12.

Once these variables have been defined, all that remains is to execute a batch file called `blddemo.bat`. This file is usually found in the `_PUBLICROOT\COMMON\OAK\MISC` directory, although each project can choose to override it by creating its own `blddemo.bat` file and placing it in the `_PROJECTROOT\OAK\MISC` directory. An activity diagram of `blddemo.bat` files is shown in Figure 10.1.

Note that `blddemo.bat` invokes four utilities: Sysgen, Build, Buildrel, and Makeimg. The first two are invoked indirectly through a batch file called `cebuild.bat`. We will examine each utility in turn on our tour of the build process. By understanding the inner workings of each utility, we will be able to unlock the internals of the entire process.

Table 10.12 Environment Variables Set by `Minkern.bat`

Variable	Value	Meaning
MINKERN_NODATABASE	NULL	Add database support
MINKERN_NOPASSWORD	NULL	Add password security
MINKERN_NORAMFS	NULL	Add RAM-based file system
MINKERN_NOTOOLHELP	NULL	Add ToolHelp module for viewing system processes and threads
ODO_NOAUDIO	1	No audio support
ODO_NOBATTERY	1	No battery support
ODO_NODISPLAY	1	No display support
ODO_NOGWES	1	No GUI support
ODO_NOKEYBD	1	No keyboard support
ODO_NONLED	1	No LED support
ODO_NOPCMCIA	1	No PCMCIA support
ODO_NOSERIAL	1	No serial port support
ODO_NOSERMODEM	1	No serial modem support
ODO_NOTOUCH	1	No touch panel support

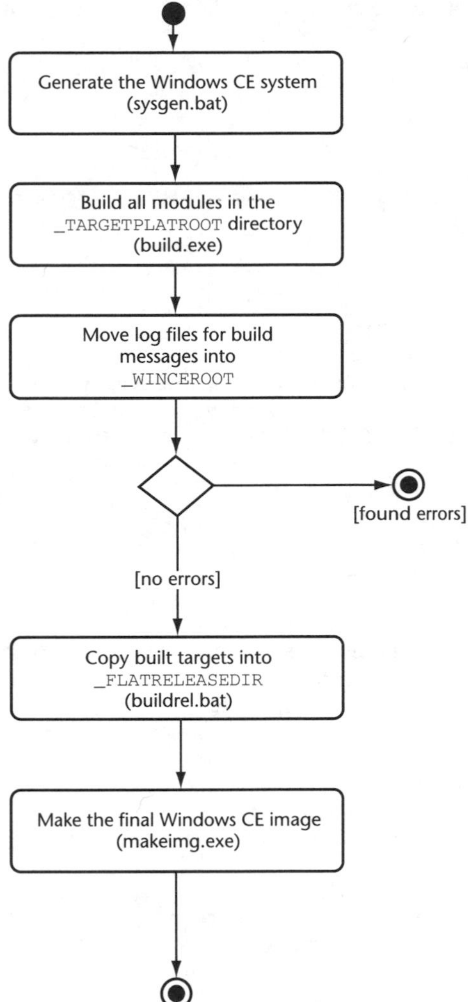

Figure 10.1 Activity diagram of `blddemo.bat`

Generating the Windows CE System: Sysgen.bat

The process of selecting components that go into making Windows CE is called **generating the system**. As mentioned earlier, third-party drivers are included in this definition. `Sysgen.bat` is the utility that generates the system. Throughout this chapter we will refer to the modules and components that ship from Microsoft with the Platform Builder as "system" modules and components.

Let's take a closer look at how the environment variables set by `minkern.bat` are used. `Sysgen.bat` executes a file called `cesysgen.bat` in the `_PROJECTROOT\Oak\Misc` directory. The file `cesysgen.bat` is where the modules and components that will constitute the custom version of Windows CE are configured. The file is modified by the system integrator during adaptation.

The `cesysgen.bat` file supplied with the `MINKERN` project is shown in Listing 10.1.

Listing 10.1 `Cesysgen.bat` **for the** `MINKERN` **project**

```
****************************************************************
REM
REM Coredll, Filesys
REM ****************************************************************
REM // required modules
set CE_MODULES=coredll filesys nk
REM // required coredll components.
set COREDLL_COMPONENTS=coremain coreloc lmem thunks
if "%MINKERN_NOFMTMSG%"=="1" goto endif_00
       set COREDLL_COMPONENTS=%COREDLL_COMPONENTS% fmtmsg
:endif_00
REM // Configure to have a RAM FS or not
set FILESYS_COMPONENTS=fsysrom
if "%MINKERN_NORAMFS%"=="1" goto endif_05
       set FILESYS_COMPONENTS=fsysram
:endif_05
REM // other essential FS components for boot: heap, registry
set FILESYS_COMPONENTS=%FILESYS_COMPONENTS% fsreg fsheap fsmain pmstub
REM // Include database if desired
if "%MINKERN_NODATABASE%"=="1" goto endif_10
       set FILESYS_COMPONENTS=%FILESYS_COMPONENTS% fsdbase
:endif_10
REM // Include password API's
if "%MINKERN_NOPASSWORD%"=="1" goto endif_15
       set FILESYS_COMPONENTS=%FILESYS_COMPONENTS% fspass
:endif_15
REM // Adds toolhelp API
if "%MINKERN_NOTOOLHELP%"=="1" goto endif_20
       set CE_MODULES=%CE_MODULES% toolhelp
:endif_20
REM // Helpful for debugging: remove before shipping
set CE_MODULES=%CE_MODULES% shell
REM // Sample applications
set CE_MODULES=%CE_MODULES% hello
```

`Cesysgen.bat` defines two types of environment variables. One, called `CE_MODULES`, contains a list of modules that must be included in the build. For example, the line

```
CE_MODULES=coredll filesys nk
```

is used to include the core API (`coredll`), file system (`filesys`), and kernel (`nk`) modules.

The second type of variable, which has a *_COMPONENTS* suffix, lists the names of the components that must be included in a module. The module name itself is the initial string in the environment variable. For example, the line

```
set COREDLL_COMPONENTS=coremain coreloc lmem thunks
```

is used to include the base functionality (coremain), localization (coreloc), memory allocation (lmem), and kernel thunk (thunks) components in the core module (coredll).

Conditionals can be added to cesysgen.bat—for example,

```
if "%MINKERN_NODATABASE%"=="1" goto endif_10
      set FILESYS_COMPONENTS=%FILESYS_COMPONENTS% fsdbase
:endif_10
```

These statements add the components that enable file system database support (fsdbase) to the existing list of components that make up the file system module. However, the assignment is performed only if the environment variable MINKERN_NODATABASE is *not* defined to a value of 1. Recall that we set this variable to NULL in the minkern.bat file. Thus, when cesysgen.bat is executed, the fsdbase component will be added to the list of file system components. The customized Windows CE image will thus contain database support.

After executing cesysgen.bat, sysgen.bat transfers its attention to the task of building modules using the selected components. To perform this operation, it enlists the help of the Nmake utility. Nmake.exe operates on script files called makefiles. The makefile that is used by sysgen.bat to create system modules is found in the _PUBLICROOT\COMMON\CESYSGEN directory. The makefile contains instructions for combining the components into modules. (See Appendix B for a primer on Nmake and makefiles.) If Nmake completes without errors, it populates the _PUBLICROOT\COMMON\OAK\LIB directory with system libraries and the _PUBLICROOT\COMMON\OAK\TARGET with system DLLs and executables. All the components are localized and stored in a processor-dependent path. For the CEPC target (CPU family: x86, CPU type: i486), the files are stored in _PUBLICROOT\COMMON\OAK\TARGET\X86\I486\CE\RETAIL. The final directory in the path signifies the type of build and can be set to Debug if modules are built with debug information. When constructing this processor-dependent path, all utilities use the environment variables liberally. The path is constructed as follows: %_PUBLICROOT%\COMMON\OAK\TARGET\%_TGTCPUTYPE%\%_TGTCPU%\%_TGTOS%\%WINCEDEBUG%.

The attentive reader may well ask, "What about variables like ODO_NOSERIAL? They don't seem to be in the cesysgen.bat file!" We'll address that very valid concern as we motor through the build process.

Windows CE Initialization Files

It's time to take a little detour and introduce the initialization files. These files are used by the build process to initialize the image, registry, database, and RAM.

Binary Image Builder Files

A Binary Image Builder file, which fittingly carries the *.bib* extension, is used to specify how the final Windows CE image will be built. BIB files specify the name and location of modules that must be included in the image. They are divided into several sections:

- The MEMORY section defines the memory layout on the CE device.
- The CONFIG section configures how the CE image is built.

- The MODULES section lists the modules that must be included in the image.
- The FILES section lists the data files that should be added to the image.

The format for entries in the MODULES section is

```
ModuleName SourcePath MemoryRegion FileAttributes
```

This directive copies the file from SourcePath in the release directory to ModuleName in the CE image and places it in the region of memory denoted by MemoryRegion. The file in the image is given the attributes denoted by FileAttributes.

As an example, consider the following directive:

```
testtime.dll      $(_FLATRELEASEDIR)\testtime.dll      NK   SH
```

This directive loads the module testtime.dll from the release directory into the NK region of memory and gives the file S (system file) and H (hidden) attributes. Recall that NK is a memory region defined in the MEMORY section of the BIB file. If testtime.dll had any resources that we wanted to compress, we could assign it the R file attribute. Alternatively, the C attribute compresses the entire file. If you have ROM that allows you to execute in place (XIP ROM), you should specify no compression. If your ROM does not support XIP, you can specify compression. A compressed module will be decompressed in RAM *before* execution. Windows CE supports on-demand paging. Whenever a page is required from a file, it is decompressed and loaded. This optimization keeps pages that are never required from being decompressed and improves overall load time.

You can compress any module or file except the file system (filesys.exe) and kernel (nk.exe). Compression can have a significant impact on the ROM and RAM requirements of a target. If you have 2MB of compressed modules in ROM and your compression ratio is on average 2:1, you will need at least 4MB of RAM to uncompress all the modules. Additional RAM will be required for application data and buffers. In this simplistic scenario, you could opt for 2MB of ROM and 8MB of RAM for your target. If you have XIP ROM on your target and do not compress any modules, you might be able to configure 4MB of ROM and 4MB of RAM. This is a design decision that must be made during hardware and software design. The tradeoff could have a significant impact on the cost of the device. Sizing your operating system requirements early in the integration process will provide critical input into such decisions.

The FILES section lists data files that should be added to the image. The format for a directive in this section is identical to that used in the MODULES section. However, the R and C file attributes are not permitted with this directive. Data files have no resources to compress, and the entire file is compressed by default. An additional attribute, U, is provided to mark uncompressed files. If a particular data file is likely to be used heavily, it should be marked uncompressed so that it doesn't require decompression every time it is used.

Four BIB files are associated with a build. The file _TARGETPLATROOT\Files\config.bib is used to specify configuration information for ROM and RAM. _TARGETPLATROOT\Files\platform.bib contains MODULES and FILES sections for platform-dependent modules and data files that must be loaded into the image. Platform-independent modules and data files are listed in their respective sections in the file _PROJECTROOT\OAK\FILES\project.bib. The directives that include the system modules can be found in the file _PUBLICROOT\COMMON\OAK\FILES\common.bib. All these files contain conditionals that can be used to filter out some directives. Environment variables are used to trigger these conditionals. As such, you can modify the value of certain environment variables to leave out or include certain modules from the build image. To ease future maintenance, system integrators should avoid modifying the common.bib file.

Registry Initialization

When Windows CE boots, the filesys module initializes the Windows registry. The initial values that are written to the registry on power-up can be specified by the system integrator in files that carry the *.reg* extension. Registry files have the following syntax:

```
[Key\Subkey]
        "ValueName"="String value"
        "ValueName"=DataType:Value
```

Registry entries are used by applications for persistent storage. Windows CE, unlike its desktop brethren, implements the registry entirely in RAM. If the device is completely powered down, the contents of RAM will be lost and the device will lose all its settings. On devices like the Handheld PC, power is never really turned off when the **Off** button is pressed. A small charge is used to keep the contents of RAM refreshed. This feature works very nicely with the instant-on feature of CE devices. Because the RAM is never powered down, all loaded applications remain fully functional and in the same state when the device is "turned on." Some versions of Windows CE—a.k.a., the Windows-based terminal toolkit—provide for a way to save the registry to flash memory or other persistent storage because such devices are required to power down completely. The presence of the registry in Windows CE is not negotiable. The fsreg component that provides registry support is required because the system relies on registry entries for initialization.

Many of the registry entries that are specified in REG files provide startup information required by the system. For instance, the system module device makes heavy use of such registry information. Another important piece of information found in the registry files is instruction on which programs to launch at startup (for an example, see Listing 10.2).

Listing 10.2 Launch information in a sample registry file

```
[HKEY_LOCAL_MACHINE\init]
        "Launch10"="shell.exe"
        "Launch20"="device.exe"
        "Launch30"="gwes.exe"
        "Depend30"=hex:14,00
        "Launch50"="taskman.exe"
        "Depend50"=hex:14,00, 1e,00
```

The init subkey under HKEY_LOCAL_MACHINE contains entries with the Launch keyword. Launch entries are of the form

```
"LaunchID"="Program.exe"
```

The kernel will launch program.exe at startup on processing a Launch entry. *ID* stands for a number that is the launch identifier. To improve the overall response time of the startup process, the kernel launches each such program in a separate thread, without trying to coordinate them.

This brings up the interesting problem of starting a process that communicates with another one. Such communication requires the kernel to launch a particular process after another process has been launched. The registry provides a mechanism to model such a situation. A list of dependent processes can be specified in the form

```
"DependID"=LaunchID1, LaunchID2
```

This entry specifies the dependent list for the `LaunchID` entry. Matching identifiers associate a `Depend` entry with its `Launch` entry. A sequence of `Launch` identifiers is used to identify the dependent processes. Upon processing this entry in the registry, the kernel launches the processes `LaunchID1` and `LaunchID2` before attempting to launch the process associated with `LaunchID`. Single or multiple dependent processes may be specified.

In Listing 10.2, `shell.exe` and `device.exe` are launched concurrently in separate threads by the kernel. `Gwes.exe` depends on `device.exe` (hex 14 = decimal 20) and is launched only after `device.exe`. It is important to understand that the kernel simply waits to launch `gwes.exe` until after `device.exe` has been *launched.* In other words, it is entirely likely that `device.exe` might not be fully initialized and in a state in which `gwes.exe` can start using its services. An internal handshaking mechanism is usually provided between modules in such cases. If you use the registry entries to launch modules that depend on each other, you will need to establish such a handshaking mechanism between those modules. However, the registry dependency does ensure that when a call is made by a module, the called module is loaded and able to respond to the request.

Three different registry files are used to specify registry entries according to context. The file `_TARGETPLATROOT\FILES\platform.reg` contains platform-dependent registry entries. `_PROJECTROOT\OAK\FILES\project.reg` contains registry entries that configure the target in a platform-independent way, and `_PUBLICROOT\COMMON\OAK\FILES\common.reg` contains registry entries relevant to system modules. To ease future maintenance, system integrators should avoid modifying the `common.reg` file.

Registry keys can be chained across these files. The `HKEY_LOCAL_MACHINE\Init` key can be specified in `common.reg` as well as `project.reg`. These files are merged toward the end of the build process, and these entries are consolidated in a single output file. As such, `project.reg` could contain the following entries in addition to those in `common.reg`:

```
[HKEY_LOCAL_MACHINE\init]
        "Launch70"="myprog.exe"
        "Depend70"=hex:14,00, 1e,00
```

The entries `Launch70` and `Depend70` specify that `myprog.exe` must be launched after `device.exe` (hex 14 = decimal 20) and `gwes.exe` (hex 1e = decimal 30) have both been launched. The identifier in the `Depend` entry refers to a `Launch` entry created in `common.reg`.

RAM Initialization

RAM in Windows CE is sectioned into a region allocated for loading modules (program memory) and a region for storing data (storage memory). **Program memory** contains program files that are loaded directly into RAM from ROM during execution. This transfer to RAM typically involves some decompression for modules compressed in ROM. Dynamically allocated buffers and stack space come from this region. **Storage memory**, also referred to as the object store, holds the file system, database, and registry. It contains the files installed on a Handheld PC *after market.* files created by the user are also stored in this region. If your device doesn't require a file system, you can minimize the RAM allocated for storage memory.

RAM initialization files have a *.dat* extension and specify the directory layout in storage memory. In addition, files that need to be copied from ROM into these directories can be named. The syntax of directives consists of four keywords:

1. `root:-Directory("name")` creates a directory specified by `name` under the root directory.
2. `root:-Permdir("name")` creates a nonmovable directory specified by `name` under the root directory.
3. `Directory("\path"):-Directory("name")` creates a subdirectory specified by `name` under the directory specified by `\path`.
4. `Directory("\path"):-File("file", "sourcefile")` copies the file specified by `sourcefile` and gives it the name specified by `file` in the directory specified by `\path`.

The files for RAM initialization are `_TARGETPLATROOT\FILES\project.dat` for project-specific initialization, `_PROJECTROOT\OAK\FILES\project.dat` for platform-independent initialization, and `_PUBLICROOT\COMMON\OAK\FILES\common.dat` for system-related initialization. To ease future maintenance, system integrators should avoid modifying the `common.dat` file.

Database Initialization

The Windows CE object store can contain databases for structured storage. The databases with which your object store is initialized are specified in files with the *.db* extension. The `Database` directive is used to define a new database:

```
Database: "name" : databaseID : numericalSortingOrder : [propertyID : flags:…]
End Database
```

The newly defined database is specified by the variable `name` with a unique identifier equal to thc valuc of `databaseID`. If the database contains multiple indices, the number of indices must be specified in `numericalSortingOrder`. The sort order for each index is defined as a `propertyID:flags` pair. The parameter `propertyID` identifies the property identifier of a field in a database record that is used as the sorting index. Possible values for flags that specify sorting order are 1 (descending), 2 (case insensitive), 4 (unknown properties first), and 0 (ascending and case sensitive, with unknown properties last). The flag is a bitmap, so values can be combined. If the database has multiple indices, each index must be followed by a `propertyID:flags` pair that identifies the index and its sorting order.

A record is defined by the following directive with the `Database...End Database` directive:

```
Record:
Field: propertyID : value
End
```

A record is defined as having a field that has a unique identifier of `propertyID` and data equal to `value`. The value of this record can be a string or a number.

A sample database called Bulls1998, which holds information about the 1998 NBA championship–winning Chicago Bulls, can be defined as shown in the following code segment. The index is the player number, which has a property identifier of 40000000:

```
Database: \\Bulls1998 : 800 : 1 : 40000000 : 0
        Record
        Field: 40000000: 23
        Field: 40000001: "Michael Jordan"
        End
        Record
        Field: 40000000: 91
        Field: 40000001: "Dennis Rodman"
        End
        Record
        Field: 40000000: 9
        Field: 40000001: "Ron Harper"
        End
        Record
        Field: 40000000: 7
        Field: 40000001: "Tony Kukoc"
        End
End Database
```

Databases are defined in `_TARGETPLATROOT\FILES\platform.db`, `_PROJECTROOT\OAK\FILES\project.db`, and `_PUBLICROOT\COMMON\OAK\FILES\common.db`. To ease future maintenance, system integrators should avoid modifying the `common.db` file.

The CE Component Filter

Our little detour into the realm of initialization files is at an end, so let's continue with our task of generating a Windows CE system.

One of the more interesting activities carried out by the Nmake utility when called by `sysgen.bat` is the invocation of another utility, known as the component filter. The **component filter** is the utility called `cefilter.exe`. Cefilter's main purpose is to prune header files and CE initialization files according to the components selected for the build. To appreciate the benefits of Cefilter's work, consider the way in which header files are used.

Device drivers and applications include header files in order to use constants or data structures defined in the header file. An application may create a window and hence use a handle to a window (`HWND`). Since the `MINKERN` project doesn't have any GUI support, the application trying to create a window will crash. This is late in the game to realize that the application must be modified so that it doesn't use any windows. Cefilter runs through all the Windows CE header files and removes content related to modules that are not part of the build. If a project does not include support for GUI, Cefilter removes all constants and data structures related to GUI support from the header files. The application will now refuse to compile, warning you that a discrepancy exists between features expected by your application and features provided by the version of Windows CE being built.

Cefilter trims all the files listed in Table 10.13.

Table 10.13 Files Processed by Cefilter

Source File(s)	Type of File	Destination
_PUBLICROOT\COMMON\OAK\FILES\common.bib	Binary Image Builder	_PROJECTROOT\CESYSGEN\OAK\FILES
_PUBLICROOT\COMMON\OAK\FILES\common.reg	Registry initialization	_PROJECTROOT\CESYSGEN\OAK\FILES
_PUBLICROOT\COMMON\OAK\FILES\common.db	Database initialization	_PROJECTROOT\CESYSGEN\OAK\FILES
_PUBLICROOT\COMMON\OAK\FILES\common.dat	RAM initialization	_PROJECTROOT\CESYSGEN\OAK\FILES
_PUBLICROOT\COMMON\SDK\INC*.h	Header files	_PROJECTROOT\CESYSGEN\SDK\INC
_PUBLICROOT\COMMON\OAK\INC*.h	Header files	_PROJECTROOT\CESYSGEN\OAK\INC
_PUBLICROOT\COMMON\DDK\INC*.h	Header files	_PROJECTROOT\CESYSGEN\DDK\INC

To understand how Cefilter trims header files, look at the code sample in Listing 10.3, which is taken from the `winbase.h` file.

Listing 10.3 Excerpt from `winbase.h`, filtering the `lmem` component in the `coredll` module

```
// @CESYSGEN IF COREDLL_LMEM

/* Why does Win32 not use the LSB flag ? */
#define LMEM_FIXED          0x0000
#define LMEM_MOVEABLE       0x0002
#define LMEM_NOCOMPACT      0x0010      /**** Used for Moveable Memory  ***/
#define LMEM_NODISCARD      0x0020      /**** Ignored *****/
#define LMEM_ZEROINIT       0x0040
#define LMEM_MODIFY         0x0080      /*** Used only in LocalReAlloc() **/
#define LMEM_DISCARDABLE    0x0F00      /**** Ignored ****/
#define LMEM_VALID_FLAGS    0x0F72
#define LMEM_INVALID_HANDLE 0x8000

#define LHND                (LMEM_MOVEABLE | LMEM_ZEROINIT)
#define LPTR                (LMEM_FIXED | LMEM_ZEROINIT)

#define NONZEROLHND         (LMEM_MOVEABLE)
#define NONZEROLPTR         (LMEM_FIXED)

/* Flags returned by LocalFlags (in addition to LMEM_DISCARDABLE) */
#define LMEM_DISCARDED      0x4000
#define LMEM_LOCKCOUNT      0x00FF
// @CESYSGEN ENDIF
```

Note that constant definitions are bounded by the `@CESYSGEN` tag. Cefilter looks for this tag when reading the header file. The tag is usually followed by a statement of type `IF <moduleM>_<componentC>`. The conditional is used to wrap all lines of code that are specific to the component `componentC` included in module `moduleM`. The first `@CESYSGEN` tag in the listing tells Cefilter to check whether the `lmem` *component* is included in the `coredll` *module*. Cefilter will translate this request and check whether the string *lmem* is part of the value of the environment variable `COREDLL_COMPONENTS`.

Recall how `cesysgen.bat` listed the components that were included in the `coredll` component:

```
set COREDLL_COMPONENTS=coremain coreloc lmem thunks
```

Because the `lmem` component was included in the `coredll` component, Cefilter includes the definitions between the beginning and ending `@CESYSGEN` tags. The new version of `winbase.h` will thus contain the definitions with the `@CESYSGEN` tags removed.

Let's look at another excerpt from the `winbase.h` file (see Listing 10.4).

Listing 10.4 Excerpt from `winbase.h`, filtering the `fmtmsg` component from the `coredll` module

```
// @CESYSGEN IF COREDLL_FMTMSG

WINBASEAPI
DWORD
WINAPI
FormatMessageA(
    DWORD dwFlags,
    LPCVOID lpSource,
    DWORD dwMessageId,
    DWORD dwLanguageId,
    LPSTR lpBuffer,
    DWORD nSize,
    va_list *Arguments
    );

#ifndef COREDLL
WINBASEAPI
#endif
DWORD
WINAPI
FormatMessageW(
    DWORD dwFlags,
    LPCVOID lpSource,
    DWORD dwMessageId,
    DWORD dwLanguageId,
    LPWSTR lpBuffer,
    DWORD nSize,
    va_list *Arguments
    );
```

```
#ifdef UNICODE
#define FormatMessage  FormatMessageW
#else
#define FormatMessage  FormatMessageA
#endif // !UNICODE

// @CESYSGEN ENDIF
```

In this case, when processing the header file, Cefilter will recognize the `@CESYSGEN` tag and will evaluate the condition `IF COREDLL_FMTMSG`. Because the `fmtmsg` component (for formatted messages) was not included in the `coredll` module by `cesysgen.bat`, the test will fail and Cefilter will remove the lines between the beginning and ending tags from the header file. Any application or device driver that attempts to use the `FormatMessage` data structure will fail to compile, thus warning the developer of the lack of underlying support in the operating system.

Cefilter uses the same technique to trim BIB files. BIB files specify which modules to include in the Windows CE image. As such, they deal with modules and not components. The tag syntax that Cefilter looks for is a little different for BIB files. Examine Listing 10.5, which shows an excerpt from the `common.bib` file.

Listing 10.5 Excerpt from `common.bib`

```
; @CESYSGEN IF CE_MODULES_FILESYS
   filesys.exe      $(_FLATRELEASEDIR)\filesys.exe             NK   SH
; @CESYSGEN ENDIF
; @CESYSGEN IF CE_MODULES_GWES
   gwes.exe         $(_FLATRELEASEDIR)\gwes.exe                NK   SH
 @CESYSGEN ENDIF
```

The syntax immediately following the `@CESYSGEN` tag is of the form `CE_MODULES_<modulename>`. The first conditional in the listing (`CE_MODULES_FILESYS`) looks for the existence of the `filesys` module in the build. To check its existence, Cefilter looks for the string *filesys* as the value of the `CE_MODULES` environment variable. According to the value of `CE_MODULES` set in `cesysgen.bat`, the *filesys* string will be found and Cefilter will keep the following line in the resulting file. This line is a directive to include `filesys.exe` from the Windows CE release directory (`_FLATRELEASEDIR`) in the image.

The next conditional (`CE_MODULES_GWES`) forces a check for the existence of the GWES module in the build. Since the GWES module is not part of our build, Cefilter will fail to locate a *GWES* string in the value of the `CE_MODULES` variable, thus removing the following line from the output file. This line would have included `gwes.exe` from the release directory in the binary image. An activity diagram of how Cefilter works is shown in Figure 10.2.

Cefilter also parses and filters initialization files like `common.reg`, `common.db`, and `common.dat` in the same way. These files are placed in the intermediate repository `_PROJECTROOT\CESYSGEN\OAK\FILES`.

If `sysgen.bat` fails for some reason, Cefilter doesn't get a chance to run. In this case the required header files will not be filtered and copied over to the `_PROJECTROOT\CESYSGEN` directory tree. Any subsequent attempts to compile source code will result in errors stating that

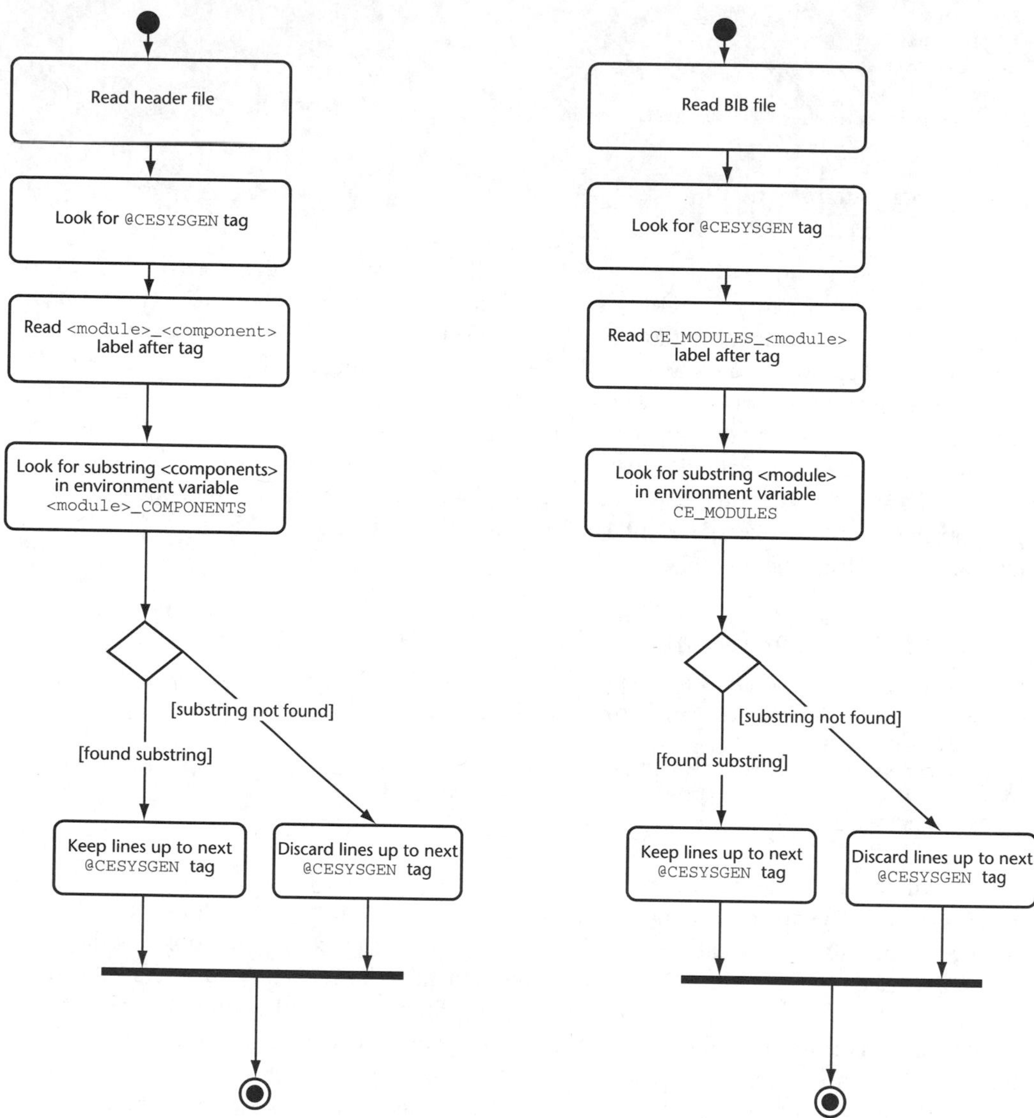

Figure 10.2 Activity diagram of `cefilter.exe`

required header files (like `windows.h`) cannot be found. This type of error is indicative of a botched attempt at generating the system. `Sysgen.bat` logs errors in a file called `build.log` in the `_WINCEROOT` directory. By examining this log, you will be able to determine the cause of failure and correct it before attempting to compile your source code. The Windows CE system *must* be generated successfully for subsequent source code to be compiled and linked properly.

How Sysgen.bat Works

We've looked at the operation of sysgen.bat. The following list details the activities performed by this utility:

- Usage: Sysgen [-h] [-b] [-c] [<targets>]
  - If the -h option is passed, sysgen.bat displays the command-line usage and exits.
  - If the -b option is passed, sysgen.bat sets the variable __BATCHMODE to 1.
  - If the -c option is passed, sysgen.bat sets the variable __CLEANMODE to 1.

- If not in batch mode:
  1. Sysgen.bat calls setlocal to localize environment changes within the batch file only.
  2. Sysgen.bat deletes the log files created by the Build utility (build.log, build.wrn, build.err).
  3. If _TGTOS is not set to CE, sysgen.bat exits with an error.
  4. Sysgen.bat displays the *Starting sysgen phase* message.
  5. Sysgen.bat calls cesysgen.bat from the directory %_PROJECTROOT%\OAK\MISC. Cesysgen defines environment variables that are used to modify the build process.
  6. Sysgen.bat sets the list of languages that Windows CE supports in a variable called _LANGIDLIST. If a variable called CE_LANGUAGES is set, it is used to initialize the value of _LANGIDLIST. If the variable is set to NULL, _LANGIDLIST is set by a search of the Windows CE installation for the supported languages.

     The directory %_WINCEROOT%\PUBLIC\COMMON\OAK\LIB\%_TGTCPUTYPE%\%_TGTCPU%\%_TGTOS%\%WINCEDEBUG% holds the processor-dependent library modules for Windows CE. Localized resource files used by these libraries are stored in language-specific directories in this directory. A directory name is a three-letter abbreviation that denotes the language it supports. We look into each subdirectory for the file that holds resources for the core library, coreres.res. If this file is found, the name of the subdirectory is appended to _LANGIDLIST as an available language. The variable is set by a file called bldlist.bat, which is called by sysgen.bat for each language. _LANGIDLIST is used by the makefile called by sysgen.bat later.
  7. Sysgen.bat appends replacement components to default Windows CE components by adding variables set in cesysgen.bat.
  8. The *_REPLACE* variables contain a list of components that are specified as user-defined replacements for standard system components supplied by Microsoft: COREDLL_COMPONENTS = COREDLL_COMPONENTS + COREDLL_REPLACE_COMPONENTS + COREDLL_REPLACE.
  9. Sysgen.bat calls Nmake with the sysgen target for the makefile in the %_PUBLICROOT%\COMMON\CESYSGEN directory. The log for this process is saved in the %_WINCEROOT%\build.log file.

10. Sysgen.bat checks for any errors during the Make process. If Nmake produced errors, sysgen.bat displays them unless you're in batch mode, in which case it simply appends an error message to %_WINCEROOT%\build.err. The QBUILDERROR variable is set to sysgen. Although not consistently used, this variable has the purposc of helping to identify the stage at which the build produced an error.
11. Sysgen.bat ends the localization of environment variables.
12. Sysgen.bat deletes any local variables used by the batch file.

Building OEM Source Code: Build.exe

Having generated a system, we are now in a position to start compiling internal source code. The MINKERN project compiles source code in the _TARGETPLATROOT directory tree. You can also compile any source you may have in the _PROJECTROOT tree, and projects that are complex and contain platform-independent modules are likely to do so.

Source code is built by build.exe, which utilizes a file called Sources. This file contains a list of source files and the format and location of the final output. We'll dive into the specifics of the Sources file later. If Build finds a Sources file, it will attempt to build the source code according to the instructions provided. Build has the ability to process directories recursively, looking for source code to build. This is a handy feature because you can start Build in a top-level directory, and the utility will build all the source code in that directory tree. A file called Dirs is used to guide Build into various directories. The Dirs file that can be found in the _PLATFORMROOT\CEPC\DRIVERS directory is shown in Listing 10.6.

Listing 10.6 Dirs file from _PLATFORMROOT\CEPC\DRIVERS

```
DIRS= \
     ceddk \
     wavedev \
     serial.pdd \
     kbdmouse \
     pcmcia \
     display \
     usb \
     mouse \
     irmac
```

The DIRS= statement contains a list of directories that Build can expect to find in its current directory. Build peeks into each of these directories and looks either for another Dirs file for further directories to process or for a Sources file for instructions on how to build the module in the given directory. The activity diagram in Figure 10.3 in captures the behavior of Build.

Let's delve a little bit deeper into how the Sources file operates. The Sources file contains multiple equate statements that define macros processed by a makefile. Instead of writing a complete makefile for building your source, you can simply define these macros in your Sources file. Build does the work of creating a makefile from the Sources file. We'll start with a sample before we peel away the layers of the onion. Listing 10.7 shows the Sources file for a fictitious program that displays controls for manipulating audio.

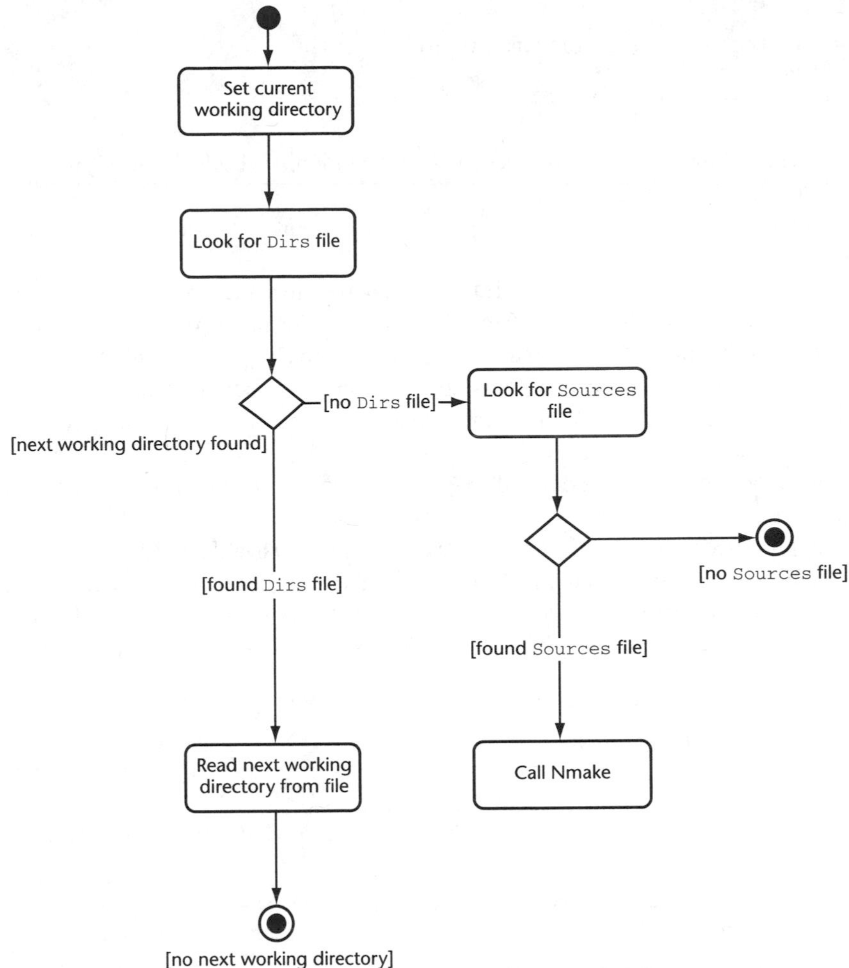

Figure 10.3 Activity diagram of `build.exe`

Listing 10.7 `Sources` file for a sample audio control program

```
#----------------------------------------------------------------------
# Sample Audio Control Program Sources file
# © Aspi Havewala/Jim WIlson 1999
#----------------------------------------------------------------------
INCLUDES=
RELEASETYPE=PLATFORM
SOURCELIBS= \
   $(_COMMONOAKROOT)\lib\$(_CPUINDPATH)\audiomdd.lib
SOURCES= \
    audiocontrol.c
```

```
TARGETLIBS= \
   $(_COMMONSDKROOT)\lib\$(_CPUINDPATH)\coredll.lib
TARGETNAME=AudioControl
TARGETTYPE=PROGRAM
```

The macros used in the `Sources` file specify how the module is built. Table 10.14 explains the purpose of each macro in the sample file.

Additional macros that fine-tune the build process are supported by the `Sources` file (see Table 10.15).

In addition to macros that modify the build, some macros are set up to abstract path names. You can use the macros listed in Table 10.16 to refer to directories in the Windows CE tree.

Note that the macros for the CPU-independent path and the CPU-dependent path are set to the same value. The Windows CE build process does not inherently support processor-independent modules. Any values you set for these macros in the `Sources` file are overwritten when Build executes.

How and where are these macros defined? We must delve into the operations of Build to answer this question.

When Build processes a `Sources` file, it reads the `SOURCES` variable and analyzes each source file in the list. It then creates a dependency list, which it caches on the hard disk in a file called `build.dat` that is stored in the `_TARGETPLATROOT` directory. This cache is checked against any changed files on subsequent builds. If a file has changed since the last time the cache

Table 10.14 Macros Used in the `Sources` File

Macro	Value	Value in Listing 10.7
`CDEFINES`	List of flags to be passed to the processor-specific compiler	No additional compiler flags required.
`INCLUDES`	Any directories that may contain header files used by the source code	Set to `NULL`, but can include any directory path with header files.
`RELEASETYPE`	Destination of the release directory	`PLATFORM`. Copies targets into the platform-specific repositories.
`SOURCELIBS`	Platform-dependent static libraries to be linked with source code	`Audiomdd.lib` (link with the audio model device driver for calls to control the audio hardware).
`SOURCES`	List of source files to be compiled and linked	`Audiocontrol.c` (this file is compiled and linked).
`TARGETLIBS`	Libraries that must be linked with the compiled source code	Link with `coredll.lib`.
`TARGETNAME`	Name of the final target being built	`Audiocontrol` (will build `audiocontrol.exe`).
`TARGETTYPE`	Type of target module being built	`PROGRAM` (will build the audio control target as an EXE file). Can also be `LIBRARY` (for a LIB file) or `DYNLINK` (for a DLL file).

Table 10.15 Macros Supported by the `Sources` File

Macro	Usage
COPYRES	Copies a resource file to the release directory.
CPPBROWSE	Copies a browser database for the source code.
DEFFILE	Specifies the export (DEF) file name.
DLLBASE	Specifies the base address for loading a DLL.
DLLENTRY	Specifies the entry point for a DLL module.
EXEBASE	Specifies the base address for loading the executable.
LDEFSTACK	Specifies a maximum stack size (`LDEFSTACKSIZE=/STACK:262144` sets a maximum stack size of 256K). The default is 64K.
PRECOMPILED_INCLUDE	Specifies the header file to be precompiled.
PRECOMPILED_PCH	Gives the name of the precompiled header file.
PREPROCESSDEFFILE	Uses the compiler (with the `/EP` flag) to preprocess the export (DEF) file before compiling. This allows conditionals to be specified in the DEF file.
RESFILE	Copies a resource file named in the macro to the release directory. The file is renamed to `$(TARGETNAME).def` in the release directory.
SYNCHRONIZE_BLOCK	Builds the current directory before building any other directories.
SYNCHRONIZE_DRAIN	Builds all previous directories in `Dirs` files before building the `Sources` file in the current directory.
TARGETTHREADMODEL	Specifies the threading model: `ST` for single thread or `MT` for multithreaded.
WINCE_VERBOSE_LINK	Displays linker progress.
WINCELINKERDEBUG	Specifies linker flags that override those that create debug information and disable incremental linking.
WINCEMEMTRACK	Enables code in the module that allows the kernel to track the memory allocated.
WINCEOEM	When set, adds the `_OEMINCPATH` in the include path. If not set, `_ISVINCPATH` is added to the include path. Only platform-dependent modules must set this macro to 1.
WINCEPROFILE	Enables profiling code in the module.
WINCEPROJ	Specifies the scope of the project. Can be set to `COMMON` if your module will be used across projects or `CURRENT` if your module is used only within the current project.

WINCETARGETFILE0	Specifies the path and file name of the export (DEF) file. This macro is used by the central makefile to include `makefile.inc` from the current directory. This makefile should define a target that will copy the DEF file to an intermediate directory. For example, the target
	`$(_PROJECTOAKROOT)\LIB\$(_CPUINDPATH)\`
	`myprog.def:$(_OBJDIR)\$(TARGETNAME).def`
	`  copy $? $@`

(continued)

Table 10.15 *Continued.*

Macro	Usage
	will copy myprog.def to the processor-independent directory. WINCETARGETFILE0 is set in this case to $(_PROJECTOAKROOT)\LIB\$(_CPUINDPATH)\myprog.def and is inserted as a dependent of the All target. This dependency, in turn, fires the target set up by makefile.inc. This macro can be used to copy any file into an intermediate directory.
WINCETARGETFILES	Operates like WINCETARGETFILE0, but the dependency is checked after WINCETARGETFILE0 is processed.

was built, that portion of the cache is regenerated and the file is recompiled. This is a substantial optimization for large projects in which several files may remain unchanged, resulting in a static dependency list.

Build then calls a helper file called srcgen.bat to generate a couple of environment variables that will hold include paths for two different types of Platform Builder users. One type of user, the independent software vendor (ISV) is serviced by a variable called _ISVINCPATH. The original equipment manufacturer (OEM) has a path set up in the variable _OEMINCPATH. The names and values of these variables are stored in a file called sources.gen that is saved in the _TARGETPLATROOT directory. Different include paths exist for these uses because OEMs are expected to work with platform-dependent code. ISVs, on the other hand, are expected to create platform-independent applications. The include path for OEMs contains header files that are platform dependent. Shortly, we'll see how sources.gen is used.

To generate the include paths, Srcgen uses another helper file, called srcgen1.bat, that generates these include paths. Srcgen examines a variable defined in wince.bat called _DEPTREES. _DEPTREES contains a list of directories that your project depends on. A dependent directory is a directory that may contain files or libraries that your project will require. The targets and libraries in these directories must be built before your project is built. For the MINKERN project, _DEPTREES is set to the value winceos Minkern. The tree winceos contains the operating system modules that your project depends on but that aren't available in the Platform Builder. It is thus treated as a special case by srcgen1.bat when the include path is being generated. Table 10.17 shows how the include path is constructed according to the value of the _DEPTREES variable.

Table 10.16 Macros for the Windows CE Directory Tree

Macro	Directory
_COMMONDDKROOT	$(_COMMONPUBROOT)\DDK
_COMMONOAKROOT	$(_COMMONPUBROOT)\OAK
_COMMONPUBROOT	$(_PROJECTROOT)\CESYSGEN
_COMMONSDKROOT	$(_COMMONPUBROOT)\SDK
_CPUDEPPATH	$(_TGTCPUTYPE)\$(_TGTCPU)\$(_TGTOS)\$(WINCEDEBUG)
_CPUINDPATH	$(_TGTCPUTYPE)\$(_TGTCPU)\$(_TGTOS)\$(WINCEDEBUG)
__PROJROOT	$(_PROJECTROOT)

Table 10.17 Include Paths for OEMs and ISVs

Dependent Tree	Variable	Include Path Added
Minkern	_ISVINCPATH	_PROJECTROOT\SDK\INC
	_OEMINCPATH	_PROJECTROOT\SDK\INC
		_PROJECTROOT\OAK\INC
		_PROJECTROOT\DDK\INC
Winceos	_ISVINCPATH	_PROJECTROOT\CESYSGEN\SDK\INC
	_OEMINCPATH	_PROJECTROOT\CESYSGEN\SDK\INC
		_PROJECTROOT\CESYSGEN\OAK\INC
		_PROJECTROOT\CESYSGEN\DDK\INC

The generated `sources.gen` file is shown in Listing 10.8.

Listing 10.8 `Sources.gen`

```
_ISVINCPATH=F:\Dev\WINCE\public\Minkern\sdk\inc;F:\Dev\WINCE\public\Minkern\
cesysgen\sdk\inc;
_OEMINCPATH=F:\Dev\WINCE\public\Minkern\oak\inc;F:\Dev\WINCE\public\Minkern\
sdk\inc;F:\Dev\WINCE\public\Minkern\ddk\inc;F:\Dev\WINCE\public\Minkern\
cesysgen\oak\inc;F:\Dev\WINCE\public\Minkern\cesysgen\sdk\inc;F:\Dev\WINCE\
public\Minkern\cesysgen\ddk\inc;
```

Once the dependency list is generated, Build calls Nmake. Nmake shoulders the responsibility of compiling and linking the source. Nmake operates on a makefile. Every `Sources` file is accompanied by a makefile that contains the following single line:

```
!INCLUDE $(_MAKEENVROOT)\makefile.def
```

Recall that the `_MAKEENVROOT` variable was set by `wince.bat` to the directory that holds the common Make rules for building modules. `Makefile.def` is a complex makefile that defines a set of common rules and macros that in turn dictate how the source code in Platform Builder is built. These common sets of rules include definitions of compiler and linker flags and specifications for how different targets must be built.

The makefile includes the `Sources` file from the directory that contains the source code. This arrangement has the effect of plugging the `Sources` file directly into the makefile that is being processed. In effect, when you write a `Sources` file, you are writing a small portion of the makefile that is used to build your source. The makefile also includes the `sources.gen` file, which sets up the include paths for ISVs and OEMs. Some complex directory paths are also stored in makefile macros to simplify addressing directories and files. Processor-specific tools like compilers, linkers, and assemblers are selected for building the source. Finally, rules for building different targets, such as executables, libraries, DLLs, and so on, are defined for the different processors supported by Windows CE.

Table 10.18 Release Types Permitted in the Sources File

Value of RELEASETYPE	Output Directory
CUSTOM	Directory value stored in TARGETPATH qualified by the processor-based path
DDK	_PUBLICROOT\OAK_TGTCPUTYPE_TGTCPU_TGTOS\WINCEDEBUG
LOCAL	.\OBJ_TGTCPUTYPE_TGTCPU_TGTOS\WINCEDEBUG
PLATFORM	_TARGETPLATROOT\Target_TGTCPUTYPE_TGTCPU_TGTOS\WINCEDEBUG
SDK	_PUBLICROOT\OAK_TGTCPUTYPE_TGTCPU_TGTOS\WINCEDEBUG

Centralizing these Make rules is an excellent idea. It allows developers to reuse the significant effort required to write this makefile. Moreover, it isolates developers from the complexity of having to understand makefile syntax. A definite disadvantage is that although the Sources file is adequate for most building tasks, customized build steps are difficult to integrate into this model. Makefiles require that all macro definitions be made before rules are defined. Because the Sources file is included in the macro definition section of makefile.def, rules cannot be set up in the Sources file. This restriction precludes your setting up a custom build step. Your best bet is to modify the makefile that accompanies the Sources file and add your custom build step as a rule after the centralized makefile has been included:

```
!INCLUDE $(_MAKEENVROOT)\makefile.def
# … Add rules for custom build step here
```

Again, remember that you can define only rules at this stage. All macro definitions must be made in Sources only.

Build collects modules in predefined directories. These directories are defined in makefile.def according to the value of the RELEASETYPE macro (Table 10.18).

Building the Release: Buildrel.bat

It's time to build the release. This step in the process involves collecting all the built modules into a release directory, normally set to _WINCEROOT\RELEASE. Recall that wince.bat defined a convenient environment variable called _FLATRELEASEDIR for us.

Buildrel.bat is the tool that is chartered for performing this task. This is a simple batch file, and a quick look at the salient operations it performs will give you a good idea of what files are copied and in what order:

1. Usage: BuildRel.bat [-u] [-f] [<build_root>]
   - If the -h option is passed, buildrel.bat displays the command-line usage and exits.
   - If the -u option is passed, buildrel.bat sets a variable called ____BLDRELNOCLEAN. If this variable is set, all the files in the release directory (_FLATRELEASEDIR) are deleted before any fresh copies are created.

- If the -f option is passed, buildrel.bat sets a variable called __BLDRELNOBIN. When set, this variable instructs the batch file to skip copying target modules. This option is used when the developer has been using the WINCEREL option to automatically copy individual modules after each individual build.

2. Buildrel.bat calls the batch file bldrel1.bat to perform the copying.
3. Buildrel.bat copies the subdirectories listed in Table 10.19 from the _PROJECTROOT\CESYSGEN\OAK directory.

Table 10.19 Directories Copied by Buildrel.bat

Source	Target	Types of Files
TARGETS	_FLATRELEASEDIR	Project-dependent target modules
FILES	_FLATRELEASEDIR	Registry, database, localization, and binary image initialization files
JAVA	_FLATRELEASEDIR\JAVA	Java classes
TOKENS	_FLATRELEASEDIR\TOKENS	Tokens
INTLTRNS	_FLATRELEASEDIR\INTLTRNS	Localized strings

Recall the _PROJECTROOT\CESYSGEN directory holds intermediate files from the build performed in the _PUBLICROOT\COMMON directory that holds Microsoft-supplied files common to all projects and platforms. This includes Windows CE system modules.

4. Buildrel.bat repeats the copying of subdirectories for the root directory _PROJECTROOT\OAK, resulting in in the copy of all project-specific intermediate files into the release directory.
5. For the root directory, _TARGETPLATROOT, buildrel.bat copies the subdirectories listed in Table 10.20, resulting in the copy of all platform-specific intermediate files to the release directory, including components like the HAL, GWES, and platform-specific drivers.

Table 10.20 Files Copied by Buildrel.bat

Source	Target	Types of Files
TARGETS	_FLATRELEASEDIR	Platform-dependent target modules
FILES	_FLATRELEASEDIR	Platform-specific registry, database, localization, and binary image initialization files

Buildrel.bat never fails, and when it is finished, the _FLATRELEASEDIR holds all the files required to build the Windows CE image. All we need to do is build the image. Although doing so means invoking a single command called makeimg.exe, much goes on under the hood that merits understanding.

Making the Windows CE Image: Makeimg.exe

The utility Makeimg is used to bring together all the information required in creating the image of the operating system. Makeimg calls several helper utilities, and we will examine the work done by each in this section. Along the way we will make some digressions to explain activities performed by the utility. Figure 10.4 shows an activity diagram of Makeimg.

Among the first tasks performed by Makeimg is the creation of a table of National Language Support (NLS) locales. A locale is the set of features in a user's environment that depend on the country and language being utilized. Locales are used to configure a user's machine with conventions like currency, date and time formats, and keyboard layout. In Windows, the locale is specified by a locale identifier. A locale identifier is a user-defined double-word data type called `LCID` that consists of a language identifier and an identifier for sorting conventions for that language.

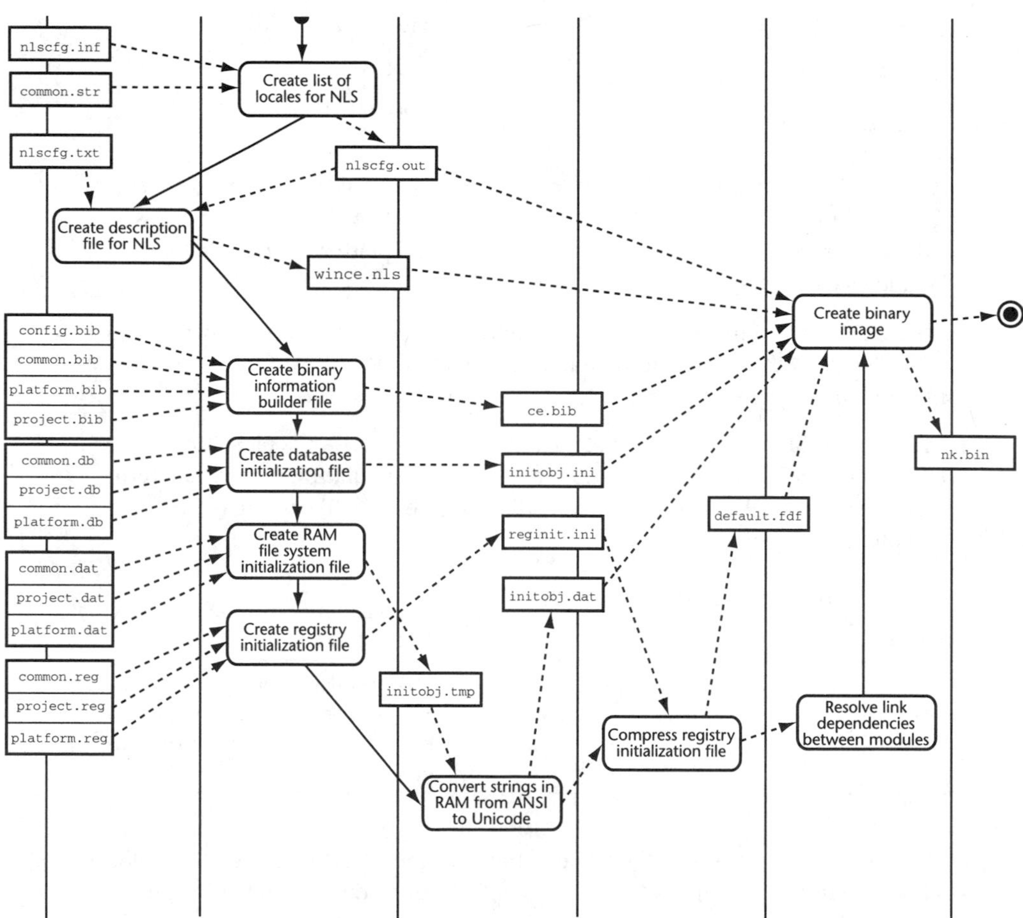

Figure 10.4 Activity diagram of `makeimg.exe`

Locale IDs are listed in the file `nlscfg.inf`, which is found in the `_PUBLICROOT\COMMON\OAK\FILES` directory. This file is preprocessed by a utility called `fmerge.exe` using a string replacement file called `common.str` to form the final locale table that is loaded by the operating system. The `common.str` file contains C preprocessor-like constant definitions. The file is located in the `_PUBLICROOT\COMMON\OAK\FILES\INTLTRNS\USA` directory. The last three letters of the path represent the language used by the operating system. Windows CE supports several languages—for example, Japanese, German, French, Italian, Spanish, Brazilian Portuguese, Dutch, and Swedish. If the target language is different from those supported by Windows CE, you can add your own custom locale. `Common.str` holds additional locales to be added to the locale table. The constant `LOC_INCLUDELOCALES` in the file contains a list of custom locales. When you wish to localize the operating system in additional languages, you add your custom locale to this constant. When the locale table is constructed in the file `nlscfg.out`, your custom locale is added to it.

Windows CE Localization

We'll make our first digression in this discussion to spend some more time on localization. Windows provides support for localization by separating the program code from the display text. The display text and intimately related information (such as the dimensions of the window that can display the text) are stored in a resource file. Resource files have *.res* extensions, and in Windows CE the resource files related to the modules of the operating system are stored in directories under `_PUBLICROOT\COMMON\OAK\LIB\_TGTCPUTYPE\_TGTCPU\_TGTOS\WINCEDEBUG\<language>`. The `<language>` directory carries a three-letter name that corresponds to the language being specified for the operating system. We specify the language by setting the `COUNTRY` environment variable on the command line. Files for U.S. English are treated differently for historical reasons. They do not require their own language-specific subdirectory.

The language identifiers are listed in Table 10.21.

Table 10.21 Language Identifiers

Language	Identifier
Chinese (People's Republic of China)	CHS
Chinese (Taiwan)	CHT
Spanish (Spain)	ESP
French	FRA
German	GER
Italian	ITA
Japanese	JPN
Dutch (Netherlands)	NLD
Portuguese	PTB
Swedish	SVE
U.S. English	USA

During generation of the system, these resource files are copied into the CESYSGEN directory under the project directory. The exact directory in which they are stored is _PROJECTROOT\CESYSGEN\OAK\TARGET_TGTCPUTYPE_TGTCPU_TGTOS\WINCEDEBUG\<language>. Buildrel.bat deposits these files into the _FLATRELEASE\<language> directory during the building of the release. Makeimg later calls on the services of a tool called res2exe.exe, which takes the correct resource file according to the language and inserts it into the corresponding code module, thus completing the localization of the module.

The code module and the resource file are required to have the same name with different extensions. For example, the resource file for the core services module coredll.dll must be called coredll.res. How does Makeimg know which modules require resource binding? It finds this information in a file called common.loc, which contains a list of such modules. This file is generated by the master makefile, makefile.def, during generation of the system. The makefile builds modules according to the components selected. The list of modules to localize is constructed at the same time. Makefile.def contains hard-coded information about which included modules require localization (and thus have a corresponding resource file).

The only two modules used by MINKERN that require localization are the core system services module and the file system module. Thus, for MINKERN the file common.loc contains the following lines:

```
coredll

filesys
```

By deferring the binding of resources to code in this way, the build process allows for custom localization of the operating system.

Further localization is packaged via our recent acquaintance, the string replacement file common.str. Recall that this file contains constants. These constants can be used in any of the initialization files, such as BIB, registry initialization (REG), database initialization (DB), and RAM file-system initialization (DAT) files for string replacement. For example, the following constant in common.str:

```
#define LOC_FRIENDLYHAYESCOMPAT "Hayes Compatible on COM1:"
```

is used to replace the constant with the string in the following section of the common.reg file:

```
[HKEY_LOCAL_MACHINE\ExtModems\HayesCompat]
   "Port"="COM1:"
   "DeviceType"=dword:1
   "FriendlyName"=LOC_FRIENDLYHAYESCOMPAT
```

The last line in the section is rewritten as follows:

```
"FriendlyName"="Hayes Compatible on COM1:"
```

Use of the string replacement file allows the creation of initialization files that are language independent. The correct language strings are simply inserted during the localization phase by Makeimg. A special construct in the string replacement file also allows the substitution of numbers in the initialization files. The construct is the tilde character (~). The following constant in common.str:

```
#define LOC_LCID ~"409"
```

is used to replace the constant by the number in the following section of common.reg:

```
[HKEY_LOCAL_MACHINE\nls]
      "DefaultLCID" = dword:LOC_LCID
```

The final line of the section is rewritten as follows:

```
      "DefaultLCID" = dword:409
```

In effect, the tilde character causes the encapsulating quotation marks to be discarded.

You can turn off the entire localization phase of Makeimg by setting an environment variable called IMGNOLOC to 1. The default value leaves this variable undefined, thus causing Makeimg to perform localization.

If you are developing for a particular language other than U.S. English, you may have some resource files translated into the language for which you are localizing, but not all. In this situation, developers simply use the available resource file for the initial language until the translations are done. For example, the U.S. English resource file is used until its translated counterpart is available. A potential problem with this approach, however, is that you may forget to replace one such file in your localized directory.

When localization is turned on, Makeimg uses whatever language-specific resource files it can locate. If it cannot find one (presumably because it is not available yet), it uses the resource file for U.S. English, which is assumed to always exist. If you are missing resource files for some modules, Makeimg won't complain and you can continue developing. When the release date of your product is drawing near, you should define the environment variable called IMGSTRICTLOC to 1. This feature, called **strict localization**, will cause Makeimg to fail if it cannot find the language-specific resource file for a module in its rightful place. If one of your files hasn't come in from the translation department yet, you will be prevented from building the final binary image.

Localizing Project- and Platform-Specific Modules

The resource-binding phase for system modules is also used to bind resources for platform- and project-specific modules.

When creating code for modules, localized items must be moved to a resource file. According to convention, the resource files must have the same name as the module itself. All resource files must be placed in the _PUBLICROOT\COMMON\OAK\LIB_TGTCPUTYPE_TGTCPU_TGTOS\WINCEDEBUG\<language> directory except U.S. English resource files, which go in the _PUBLICROOT\COMMON\OAK\LIBS_TGTCPUTYPE_TGTCPU_TGTOS\WINCEDEBUG directory.

All the platform- and project-specific modules that require localization must be added to platform.loc and project.loc files in the _TARGETPLATROOT\Files and _PROJECTROOT\OAK\FILES directories, respectively. When Makeimg binds resources to modules, it will process these files and run Res2res on the specified modules as well.

A string replacement file can be set up for the platform and project in the _TARGETPLATROOT\OAK\FILES\INTLTRNS\<language> and _PROJECTROOT\OAK\FILES\INTLTRNS\<language> directories, respectively. These files can be used as described earlier to create language-independent initialization files. All string replacement files are merged by Makeimg, which looks for them using the FindFirstFile and FindNextFile functions with the **.str wild card.*

Because these functions operate alphabetically, the string replacement files in the COMMON subdirectory in _PUBLICROOT are located first. The platform- and project-specific files are found later. This order is significant because when merging files, Makeimg replaces duplicate entries with the last one it finds. The implication here is that settings in the operating system string replacement file, common.str, can be replaced by settings in your platform- or project-specific string replacement file.

Merging Initialization Files

The next phase in creating the image requires the merging of initialization files—namely, the BIB, REG, DB, DAT, and NLS files. The Fmerge utility is used to merge the files. The BIB files merged are common.bib, config.bib, project.bib, and platform.bib. Fmerge creates an output file called ce.bib that contains the information from all of the input BIB files. When performing the merge, Fmerge also filters out information on the basis of the environment variables set up for the build. The platform.bib file, for instance, contains the following lines describing modules that must be included in the image:

```
IF IMGNOCEDDK !
   ceddk.dll      $(_FLATRELEASEDIR)\pc_ddk.dll                    NK   SH
ENDIF

  ...
IF ODO_NOAUDIO !
   wavedev.dll    $(_FLATRELEASEDIR)\wavedev.dll                   NK   SH
ENDIF
```

The conditionals surrounding the directives tell Fmerge to include them only if the constants following the conditionals are not defined. If IMGNOCEDDK is *not* defined, the following line must be included. Similarly if ODO_NOAUDIO is *not* defined, the following line must be included. Recall that in minkern.bat, we did not define IMGNOCEDDK but did set ODO_NOAUDIO to 1. Ce.bib will thus contain the following line:

```
ceddk.dll         $(_FLATRELEASEDIR)\pc_ddk.dll                    NK   SH
```

Similar filtering is performed on project.bib. The environment variables used to define modules and components for the operating systems are lists, as opposed to binary settings like ODO_NOAUDIO. The conditionals are thus specified differently for common.bib, which contains directives to include operating system modules and components (see Listing 10.9).

Listing 10.9 Conditionals in `common.bib`

```
MODULES
;  Name           Path                                          Memory Type
;  -------------  --------------------------------------------  -----------
IF IMGNODEBUGGER
   nk.exe         $(_FLATRELEASEDIR)\nknodbg.exe                 NK   SH
ENDIF
IF IMGNODEBUGGER !
   nk.exe         $(_FLATRELEASEDIR)\nk.exe                      NK   SH
ENDIF
```

When processing BIB files, Fmerge looks for conditionals on the basis of environment variables, which are of the form `IF <env_var>`. Recall that Cefilter also processes this file looking for the keyword `;@CESYSGEN`. Cefilter does not recognize conditionals that do not begin with a semicolon, leaving these for Fmerge.

In the code sample shown in Listing 10.9, the conditional `IF IMGNODEBUGGER` is an instruction to include the lines following up to the closing keyword `ENDIF` if the environment variable `IMGNODEBUGGER` has been defined. In the `minkern.bat` file, `IMGNODEBUGGER` is not defined. Thus, the following line is skipped. This line would have included the kernel file without debugging support. The next conditional uses the exclamation character (!). This tells Fmerge to include the lines up to the closing conditional if `IMGNODEBUGGER` is *not* defined. Here this is the case, so the following line, which adds the kernel with debug support in the image, is included in the output file `ce.bib`.

Note that the BIB file that is processed by Fmerge has been deposited in `_PUBLICROOT\CESYSGEN\OAK\FILES` by the Cefilter utility. After processing the file, Cefilter leaves the `;@CESYSGEN` keywords in the file. The result can be a useful debugging aid. By searching through `ce.bib`, you can determine if your image is including all the modules and components as expected. An empty conditional is an indicator that a module or component is missing from `cesysgen.bat`. Because each such line, including its closing conditional (`; @CESYSGEN ENDIF`) is preceded by a semicolon, Fmerge treats it as a comment and ignores the line.

When parsing the BIB files, Fmerge merges files in the following order: `config.bib`, `common.bib`, `platform.bib`, and `project.bib`. Sections within the BIB files are grouped together.

Fmerge filters and merges other types of files in a similar way, always filtering on the basis of environment variables. Table 10.22 enumerates all such files.

The merged registry file, along with the database and RAM file-system initialization files, is loaded in the image. The registry file is compressed first by a utility called `regcomp.exe`. The utility names the compressed output `default.fdf`. The RAM file-system initialization file `initobj.tmp` contains folder and file names in ANSI. A tool called Txt2ucde converts all the ANSI strings in the file to Unicode and creates an output file called `initobj.dat`.

The initialization files themselves are included in the image by directives in `ce.bib`, as shown in Listing 10.10. The lines are added only when certain environment variables are defined. It is left as an exercise to the reader to understand how the environment variables are being used in this excerpt.

Table 10.22 Files Merged by Fmerge

Files	Type	Output
nlscfg.inf and common.str	NLS files	nlscfg.out
config.bib, common.bib, platform.bib, and project.bib	Binary Image Builder files	ce.bib
common.db, platform.db, and project.db	Database initialization files	initobj.ini
common.dat, platform.dat, and project.dat	RAM file-system initialization files	initobj.tmp
common.reg, platform.reg, and project.reg	Registry initialization files	reginit.ini

Listing 10.10 Excerpt from ce.bib

```
FILES

; @CESYSGEN IF COREDLL_CORELOC
   wince.nls       $(_FLATRELEASEDIR)\wince.nls                         NK  SH
; @CESYSGEN ENDIF
; @CESYSGEN IF FILESYS_FSYSRAM
   initobj.dat      $(_FLATRELEASEDIR)\initobj.dat     NK  SH
; @CESYSGEN ENDIF
; @CESYSGEN IF FILESYS_FSREG
   default.fdf      $(_FLATRELEASEDIR)\default.fdf     NK  SH
; @CESYSGEN ENDIF
; @CESYSGEN IF FILESYS_FSDBASE
   initdb.ini       $(_FLATRELEASEDIR)\initdb.ini      NK  SH
 @CESYSGEN ENDIF
```

Creating the Final Image

The final step in building the Windows CE image is performed by romimage.exe. The syntax for using this utility is as follows:

```
Romimage [<inputfile>] [-o <directory>]
```

The -o option specifies an output directory for the image. Makeimg calls this utility with ce.bib as an input file. Romimage builds the image by including the modules and files specified in ce.bib. The MEMORY section of ce.bib contains the name that Romimage will use for the image. For MINKERN, this line is

```
NK       80200000  00900000  RAMIMAGE
```

The final image is named nk.bin. Before creating the image, Romimage performs an important step: It resolves link dependencies between all modules in ce.bib. When you're building an operating system made up of components, it is possible to leave out some required components. A global sanity check must be performed verifying that all the components and modules in the image have all the APIs and components expected. For example, an application included in your BIB file might create a window, thus using services defined in the GWES module. When matching the imports required by this application, Romimage would be unable to find corresponding exports that were part of the GWES module, which would have been left out. An error would be produced with a message that the final image will not run properly on the target. The result of this hard error is that no image is created at all. You must resolve all such link errors before you produce an image. Romimage includes the name of the module that requires the import and the name of the module that must provide the export. This is usually enough information for you to figure out the genesis of the error.

If Romimage completes successfully, the image is built and can be found in the directory `_FLATRELEASEDIR`.

The dependencies between tools and resulting files are depicted in Figure 10.5.

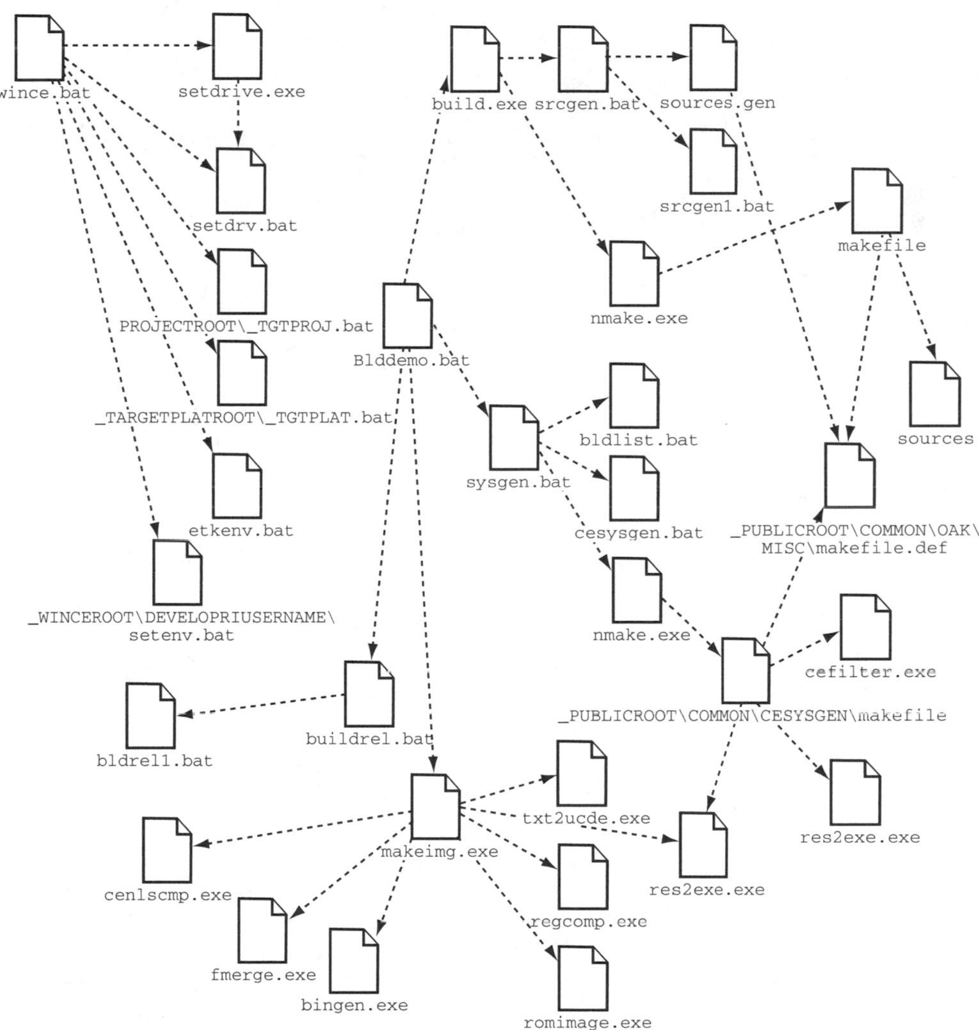

Figure 10.5 Component diagram of Build tools

Summary

Windows CE has been designed to run on a variety of different devices where space and processor speed is at a premium. The build process is very flexible, in keeping with the adaptable nature of the operating system. It consists of several utilities that perform the build. These utilities communicate with each other via environment variables. A centralized makefile builds all source code. The process supports multiple processors and hardware platforms.

Microsoft has subdivided Windows CE into components by area of functionality. This growing list of components provides a store of functionality from which the system integrator can make selections. Components that ship from Microsoft can be customized and integrated with modules developed by the system integrator to produce a single Windows CE image. Applications and data can also be integrated into the build.

11 Building a Sample Windows CE Project

Now that we have examined the plumbing of the build process, let's discuss what it takes to create your own project and build it. We'll create a hypothetical target that will run Windows CE. Typically, you would design a product on the basis of market research and brainstorming and then decide which operating system will run on it, but this is a book on Windows CE, so we'll have to bypass that part of the process.

Brewster: A Coffee Maker for the Millennium

Our hypothetical target device will be a coffee maker. Our coffee machine does more than just brew coffee. It roasts and grinds beans according to several different blends, and it filters premium coffee. Let's call our coffee machine Brewster. This name will have to stand until the marketing department starts to earn its pay.

Brewster really shines in the communications department. It is capable of wirelessly synchronizing with a Handheld PC and downloading appointments (or at least a subset). Each morning, Brewster checks your appointments and brews your favorite blend of coffee a couple of hours before your first scheduled appointment. A couple of hours after your last appointment of the day, Brewster prepares a slightly different cup of coffee (your favorite evening selection perhaps). How does Brewster know to use a two-hour window before and after appointments? Why, that's your commute time, or at least that's what your car told Brewster during their last synching session.

This scenario is not unlike projected reality at many corporations in the embedded appliances space today. In a communications-intensive world where appliances learn how to communicate along with humans, Brewster will find a niche. Armed with this mission statement, we set about the task of creating a target build.

After a series of long meetings during which the immediate need for a Brewster-like product is deeply felt, the hardware architecture of the device is hammered out. While the board is being designed, the software development team decides to forge ahead. A highly convenient platform for early prototyping for Windows CE is the CEPC platform. The CEPC platform contains a Hardware Abstraction Layer and drivers that enable Windows CE to run on an x86 PC. The best way to start a project is to study the sample projects that ship with Platform Builder and choose one that most closely resembles the one you are about to embark on. Solely for purposes of demonstration, we will pick the `MAXALL` project as our base project. `MAXALL` is a sample project that includes several interesting CE components and modules. As its name suggests, `MAXALL` creates a bloated Windows CE image. But for purposes of illustration, it fits the bill nicely precisely because it is so large. Table 11.1 lists the components included by the `MAXALL` project.

Since `MAXALL` is our base project, we start by copying the `MAXALL` directory under `_WINCEROOT\PUBLIC` and renaming it `WEBSTER` under the same directory. The next step is to initialize the Windows CE build environment by calling `wince.bat` with the appropriate parameters. In our case, `wince.bat` must be invoked with the parameters listed in Table 11.2.

Table 11.1 Components Included by `MAXALL`

Module	Components
Kernel	Memory, process, and file management
Core DLL	Localization, local heap and memory allocation, serial port, kernel/Win32 thunks, messaging, user input, windowing, GDI, serial and TAPI support, cryptography wave API, Input Method Manager (IMM) core, console API support, shell API support, Software Input Panel support
file system	RAM-only file system, database, registry, password support, FAT file system (ATA disk, SRAM disk)
GWES messaging and user input support	Power management, notification LEDs, GDI, TrueType and raster fonts, text drawing, palette, printing, touch panel calibration user interface, network user interface, wave API, pulse code modulation (PCM) manager, IMM, window manager, dialog manager, startup user interface, out-of-memory user interface, console, notification API, common controls, common dialogs, handwriting, Software Input Panel
Serial communications	IrDA support, PC card serial
Networking	Winsock SSL and security, TCP/IP, IrDA, NDIS, DHCP, SLIP/PPP, RAS, WNet/SMB (Server Message Block) redirector, Internet protocol, FTP, TAPI , NDIS sample drivers, USB sample driver
Native drivers	Display, keyboard, battery, notification LED, touch screen, audio
Stream-interface drivers	Unimodem, serial, PCMCIA
Add-on technologies COM	OLE
Windows CE Shell components	Desktop manager, task manager, command line, communications applications
Debugging	Windows CE Debug Shell, ToolHelp

Table 11.2 Parameter Values for `Wince.bat`

Parameter	Value
Cputype	x86
Cpu	i486
Os	CE
Platform	CEPC
Project	Webster

Running `wince.bat` with these parameters at a command prompt initializes the Windows CE build environment. You can set up a desktop shortcut to the Windows NT command prompt `cmd.exe` and pass it `wince.bat`, with all its parameters, using the `/k` option. The `/k` option instructs `cmd.exe` to execute the command string following the option and then start a command shell:

```
cmd.exe /k C:\WINCE\public\common\oak\misc\wince.bat x86 i486 CE Brewster CEPC
```

Running the `set` command at the command prompt reveals the environment variables set up by `wince.bat`:

```
C:\WINCE>set
BUILD_DEFAULT=-e -w -nmake -i
COUNTRY=USA
IMGNODEBUGGER=1
IMGNODFLTDDK=1
IMGUSB=1
Path=C:\Program Files\DevStudio\SharedIDE\..\wce\bin;D:\Program
Files\DevStudio\SharedIDE\..\vc\bin;C:\WINCE\sdk\bin\i386;C:\WINCE\public\
common\oak\Bin\i386;C:\WINCE\private\bin\i386;C:\WINCE\private\bat;C:\WINCE\
public\common\oak\misc;C:\WINCE\developr\ahavewala;C:\WTSRV\system32;C:\
WTSRV;C:\program
files\devstudio\sharedide\bin\ide;C:\programfiles\devstudio\sharedide\bin;C:\
program files\devstudio\vc\bin;C:\WINDOWS;C:\WINDOWS\COMMAND
WINCECOD=1
WINCEDEBUG=retail
WINCEMAP=1
_CURSLMTREE=Brewster
_DEPTREES=winceos Brewster
_FLATRELEASEDIR=C:\WINCE\release
_MAKEENVROOT=C:\WINCE\public\common\oak\misc
_PLATFORMDRIVE=C:
_PLATFORMROOT=C:\WINCE\platform
_PREWINCEPATH=C:\WTSRV\system32;C:\WTSRV;C:\program files\devstudio\sharedide\
bin\ide;C:\program files\devstudio\sharedide\bin;C:\program files\devstudio\vc\
bin;C:\WINDOWS;C:\WINDOWS\COMMAND
_PRIVATEDRIVE=C:
_PRIVATEROOT=C:\WINCE\private
_PROJECTDDKROOT=C:\WINCE\public\Brewster\ddk
_PROJECTOAKROOT=C:\WINCE\public\Brewster\oak
_PROJECTROOT=C:\WINCE\public\Brewster
_PROJECTSDKROOT=C:\WINCE\public\Brewster\sdk
```

```
_PUBLICDRIVE=C:
_PUBLICROOT=C:\WINCE\public
_SDKDRIVE=C:
_SDKROOT=C:\WINCE\sdk
_TARGETPLATROOT=C:\WINCE\platform\CEPC
_TGTCPU=i486
_TGTCPUTYPE=x86
_TGTOS=CE
_TGTPLAT=CEPC
_TGTPROJ=Brewster
_WINCECALLED=1
_WINCEDRIVE=C:
_WINCEEXTERNAL=1
_WINCEROOT=C:\WINCE
```

With this as our environment, we can build our project. Before we begin to customize Webster, we can build it just like `MAXALL`. We do this by invoking the `blddemo.bat` file. This batch file calls all the relevant utilities required to perform the entire build. Being a batch file doesn't lend itself well to the grind of building projects. For one, different parts of the process cannot be run from `blddemo.bat` in a modular fashion. If the building of your platform fails, you cannot simply restart that part of the build process. By translating `blddemo.bat` into a makefile, we can create a modular build process that provides a single interface for performing the many tasks involved in creating a Windows CE build.

The Brewster Makefile

Figure 11.1 shows the organization of the makefiles that are used to build Brewster. The master makefile (`makefile`) includes helper makefiles. The helper makefiles are split up by area of functionality. The idea behind having helper makefiles is to abstract functionality that can be tailored according to a project's unique settings, thereby creating reusable helpers that can be customized easily for other projects.

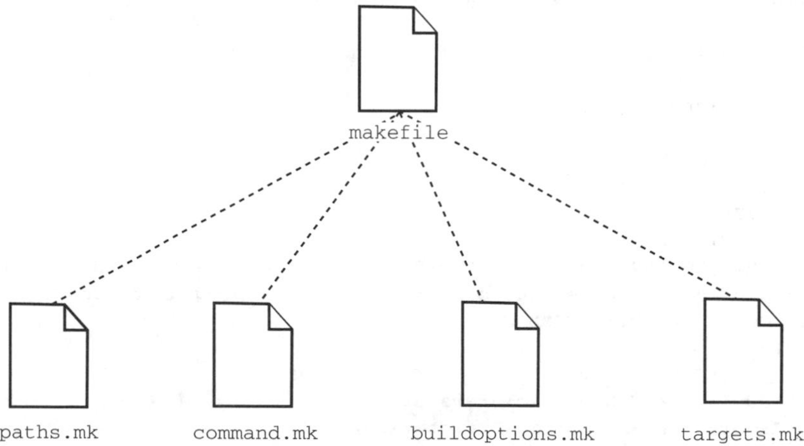

Figure 11.1 Makefile organization of Brewster

The Master Makefile

The master makefile (Listing 11.1) allows the integrator to build the Windows CE image using a series of targets. A list of targets defined in the master makefile is shown in Table 11.3.

Listing 11.1 Master makefile for Brewster

```
###############################################################################
#
# Master makefile for building Windows CE images.
# (c) Jim Wilson and Aspi Havewala 2001
#
###############################################################################

!include <>Paths.mk>
!include <Command.mk>
!include <BuildOptions.mk>

all: SetupEnvironment BuildSystem2 BuildPlatform2 BuildProject2 BuildRelease2
MakeImage2

SetupEnvironment:
$(SETENV) WINCEREL=$(WINCEREL)
        $(SETENV) WINCEMAP=$(WINCEMAP)
        $(SETENV) WINCECOD=$(WINCECOD)
        $(SETENV) WINCEDEBUG=$(WINCEDEBUG)
        $(SETENV) COUNTRY=$(COUNTRY)
        $(SETENV) IMGATAPI=$(IMGATAPI)
        $(SETENV) IMGTINYFSRAM=$(IMGTINYFSRAM)
        $(SETENV) IMGNODEBUGGER=$(IMGNODEBUGGER)
        $(SETENV) IMGNODRIVERS=$(IMGNODRIVERS)
        $(SETENV) IMGFLASH=$(IMGFLASH)
 $(SETENV) IMG_NOCURSOR=$(IMG_NOCURSOR)
        $(SETENV) IMGUSB=$(IMGUSB)
        $(SETENV) IMGNOCOMM=$(IMGNOCOMM)
        $(SETENV) IMGNOCONSOLE=$(IMGNOCONSOLE)
        $(SETENV) IMGNOCTLPNL=$(IMGNOCTLPNL)
        $(SETENV) IMGNOFILES=$(IMGNOFILES)
        $(SETENV) IMGNOCEDDK=$(IMGNOCEDDK)
        $(SETENV) IMGNOETHER=$(IMGNOETHER)
        $(SETENV) IMGNOJAVA=$(IMGNOJAVA)
        $(SETENV) IMGNOREDIR=$(IMGNOREDIR)
        $(SETENV) IMGNOOLE32=$(IMGNOOLE32)
        $(SETENV) IMGNOSECURITY=$(IMGNOSECURITY)
        $(SETENV) IMGNOSIR=$(IMGNOSIR)
        $(SETENV) IMGNOTXTSHELL=$(IMGNOTXTSHELL)
        $(SETENV) IMGNSCFIR=$(IMGNSCFIR)
        $(SETENV) IMGNOSHELL=$(IMGNOSHELL)
        $(SETENV) IMGNOPCMCIA=$(IMGNOPCMCIA)

        $(SETENV) ODO_NOPCMCIA=$(ODO_NOPCMCIA)
        $(SETENV) ODO_NOIRDA=$(ODO_NOIRDA)
        $(SETENV) ODO_NOBATTERY=$(ODO_NOBATTERY)
        $(SETENV) ODO_NONLED=$(ODO_NONLED)
```

```
        $(SETENV) ODO_NOSERIAL=$(ODO_NOSERIAL)
        $(SETENV) ODO_NOAUDIO=$(ODO_NOAUDIO)
        $(SETENV) ODO_NOKEYBD=$(ODO_NOKEYBD)
        $(SETENV) ODO_NODISPLAY=$(ODO_NODISPLAY)

        $(SETENV) CEPC_SERMOUSE=$(CEPC_SERMOUSE)
        $(SETENV) CEPC_PARALLEL=$(CEPC_PARALLEL)
        $(SETENV) CEPC_DDI_VGA8BPP=$(CEPC_DDI_VGA8BPP)
        $(SETENV) CEPC_DDI_CT655X=$(CEPC_DDI_CT655X)
        $(SETENV) CEPC_DDI_S3VIRGE=$(CEPC_DDI_S3VIRGE)

        $(SETENV) IMG_FATFS=$(IMG_FATFS)
        $(SETENV) IMG_UNIMODEM=$(IMG_UNIMODEM)
        $(SETENV) IMG_TAPI=$(IMG_TAPI)
        $(SETENV) IMG_ETHERLINK3=$(IMG_ETHERLINK3)
        $(SETENV) IMG_NE2000=$(IMG_NE2000)
        $(SETENV) IMG_PROXIM=$(IMG_PROXIM)
        $(SETENV) IMG_XIRCOM2=$(IMG_XIRCOM2)
        $(SETENV) IMG_PPP=$(IMG_PPP)
        $(SETENV) IMG_IRDA=$(IMG_IRDA)
        $(SETENV) IMG_SIP=$(IMG_SIP)
        $(SETENV) IMG_PRINT=$(IMG_PRINT)
        $(SETENV) IMG_TOOLHELP=$(IMG_TOOLHELP)
        $(SETENV) IMG_IMESAMPLE=$(IMG_IMESAMPLE)
        $(SETENV) IMG_COMMAPPS=$(IMG_COMMAPPS)
        $(SETENV) IMG_HWX=$(IMG_HWX)
        $(SETENV) IMG_TCP=$(IMG_TCP)
        $(SETENV) IMG_DUALIO=$(IMG_DUALIO)
        $(SETENV) IMG_NOTIFYAPI=$(IMG_NOTIFYAPI)
        $(SETENV) IMG_COMMONDIALOGS=$(IMG_COMMONDIALOGS)
        $(SETENV) IMG_COMMONCONTROLS=$(IMG_COMMONCONTROLS)
        $(SETENV) IMG_TASKMANAGER=$(IMG_TASKMANAGER)
        $(SETENV) IMG_IMM=$(IMG_IMM)

        $(SETENV) _ECHOON=$(VERBOSE)
        $(SETENV) _FLATRELEASEDIR=$(_FLATRELEASEDIR)

        $(IFF) not exist $(_FLATRELEASEDIR) mkdir $(_FLATRELEASEDIR)

        $(DISPLAY) "CPU      : $(_TGTCPU)"
        $(DISPLAY) "CPUType  : $(_TGTCPUTYPE)"
        $(DISPLAY) "OS       : $(_TGTOS)"
        $(DISPLAY) "Platform : $(_TGTPLAT)"
        $(DISPLAY) "Project  : $(_TGTPROJ)"
!   if "$(DEBUG)"=="1"
        $(DISPLAY) "Build    : Debug"
!   else
        $(DISPLAY) "Build    : Retail"
!   endif

BuildSystem: SetupEnvironment BuildSystem2
BuildSystem2:
        @-Sysgen.bat $(SYSGEN_FLAGS)
```

```
BuildPlatform: SetupEnvironment BuildPlatform2
BuildPlatform2:
	$(CHANGEDIR) $(_TARGETPLATROOT)
	$(BUILD_CMD) $(BUILD_FLAGS)
	$(CHANGEDIR) $(_PROJECTROOT)

BuildProject: SetupEnvironment BuildProject2
BuildProject2:
	$(CHANGEDIR) $(_PROJECTROOT)\Oak
	$(IFF) exist Dirs $(BUILD_CMD) $(BUILD_FLAGS)
	$(CHANGEDIR) $(_PROJECTROOT)

BuildRelease: SetupEnvironment BuildRelease2
BuildRelease2:
	$(CMDECHO)BuildRel $(BUILDREL_FLAGS)

MakeImage: SetupEnvironment MakeImage2
MakeImage2:
	$(CMDECHO)MakeImg

BuildBootLoader: SetupEnvironment BuildBootLoader2
BuildBootLoader2:
	$(CHANGEDIR) $(_TARGETPLATROOT)\Boot
	$(BUILD_CMD) $(BUILD_FLAGS)
	$(CHANGEDIR) $(_PROJECTROOT)

Clean:
	$(IFF) exist $(_FLATRELEASEDIR) $(RMDIR2) $(_FLATRELEASEDIR) /s /q
	$(IFF) exist $(_PROJECTROOT)\cesysgen\*.* $(RMDIR2) $(_PROJECTROOT)\
cesysgen /s /q
	$(IFF) exist $(_PROJECTROOT)\target\*.* $(RMDIR2) $(_PROJECTROOT)\
target /s /q
	$(IFF) exist $(_TARGETPLATROOT)\target\*.* $(RMDIR2)
$(_TARGETPLATROOT)\target /s /q
	$(IFF) exist $(_FLATRELEASEDIR)\*.bif $(DELETE2) $(_FLATRELEASEDIR)\
*.bif

Run:
	$(CHANGEDIR) $(_FLATRELEASEDIR)
	$(CESH) $(CESH_OPTIONS) Nk.bin
	$(CHANGEDIR) $(_PROJECTROOT)

Usage:
	$(DISPLAY) "nmake [Target] [Options]"
	$(DISPLAY) "Targets"
	$(DISPLAY) "    All:            Builds CE image from scratch"
	$(DISPLAY) "    BuildSystem:    Builds Windows CE system"
	$(DISPLAY) "    BuildPlatform:  Builds all drivers in the
$(_TARGETPLATROOT) directory"
	$(DISPLAY) "    BuildProject:   Builds all modules in the
$(_PROJECTROOT) directory"
	$(DISPLAY) "    BuildRelease:   Copies all built files into the release
directory"
```

```
        $(DISPLAY) "    MakeImage:        Creates the Windows CE OS image"
        $(DISPLAY) "    BuildBootLoader:Builds the bootloader"
        $(DISPLAY) "    Clean:            Deletes all intermediate and output
files from the build"
        $(DISPLAY) "    Run:              Uploads the image to the target
platform"
        $(DISPLAY) "Options"
        $(DISPLAY) "    CLEAN=0/1:        Builds everything from scratch if 1"
        $(DISPLAY) "    DEBUG=0/1:        Creates a debug build if 1"
        $(DISPLAY) "    VERBOSE=0/1:      Displays all commands executed by this
makefile if 1"

!include <>targets.mk>
```

Table 11.3 Makefile Targets

Target	Usage
`BuildBootloader`	Builds the boot loader for the target.
`BuildPlatform`	Builds all platform-dependent modules.
`BuildProject`	Builds all platform-independent modules.
`BuildRelease`	Copies all built modules into the release directory.
`BuildSystem`	Generates the Windows CE system.
`Clean`	Deletes all previously built modules and images.
`MakeImage`	Creates the Windows CE image.
`Run`	Uploads the image to the target.
`Usage`	Displays instructions for using the makefile.

Since Nmake allows the execution of specific targets in a makefile, the master makefile allows developers to restart the build process at any of its stages. Nmake also accepts a list of targets, which it executes from the makefile in order of priority from left to right. This is an extremely valuable tool when errors occur at interim stages of the build. If a platform-specific module fails to build, you can use the makefile to test this part of the build, with the command

```
Nmake BuildPlatform
```

Once the problem is resolved, you can restart the build process with the command

```
Nmake BuildProject BuildRelease MakeImage
```

The makefile runs through all the steps of the build process using the `All` target:

```
all: SetupEnvironment BuildSystem2 BuildPlatform2 BuildProject2 BuildRelease2
MakeImage2
```

The default target `All` depends on multiple targets, each of which performs a task in the overall Windows CE build process. The first target, `SetupEnvironment`, has no dependents and translates the macros defined in `buildoptions.mk` into environment variables that will be understood by the various Microsoft build utilities. The next target, `BuildSystem2`, generates the system. It is simply a wrapper around the `sysgen.bat` utility.

Because the makefile allows the developer to run portions of the build process, the environment must be set up before each step. `SetupEnvironment` must be called each time. Every target in the makefile that can be called by the system integrator and that runs a section of the build process has the `SetupEnvironment` target as its dependent. This arrangement ensures that macros are translated into environment variables before the target is executed. A secondary version of each such step is provided with the suffix *2* attached to each target. These secondary targets perform the same tasks as their counterparts, but they assume that `SetupEnvironment` has already been executed. For example, the target `BuildSystem` depends on `SetupEnvironment`, but `BuildSystem2` does not. Thus, `BuildSystem2` can be chained in the `All` target. This optimization prevents the `SetupEnvironment` target from being executed for each target in the build when the targets are being executed in sequence.

The environment variables defined in the makefile are deleted automatically when Nmake exits. This approach is cleaner than setting the variables in a separate batch file. When build options are being changed, the batch file requires editing and execution. On the other hand, you can quickly change the environment variable in the makefile by simply changing the macro on the command line:

```
Nmake IMGUSB=
```

This command will remove USB support from the image.

The feature comes in handy when you're switching between debug and retail versions of the build. You can perform a debug build by invoking Nmake with the following command:

```
Nmake DEBUG=1
```

Switching to the retail build involves calling Nmake with the following argument:

```
Nmake DEBUG=0
```

Similarly you perform a clean build by calling Nmake with the `CLEAN` argument set to 1. The `VERBOSE` option is used in a similar fashion to display all the commands executed by the build process, an invaluable debugging tool when the build fails inexplicably.

During incremental development, a particular device driver or application needs to be debugged. Building all the modules in Windows CE for debug will create a large binary file. Besides the performance penalty incurred when you're running the operating system, applications, and device drivers in debug mode, additional time is wasted in uploading a large image to your target. In debug mode, all modules emit traces to the Windows CE kernel debugger, so you will have to sort through hundreds of trace messages to filter out those that belong to the module being debugged. You can alleviate this problem somewhat by using the CESH command `gi` to filter certain types of traces from a module or filter out all traces from a module entirely.

However, what is required is a way of mixing and matching debug and retail components in a single build. The master makefile supports this approach inherently. All release components, whether debug or retail, are collected in the same release directory. A full retail build is required first. This must be followed by use of the makefile to build an individual module with the debug flag. Once this module is built, the `BuildRelease` and `MakeImage` targets in the makefile must be called, and the final image will contain a cocktail of retail modules mixed with the debug build of the module being debugged.

The Helper Makefile Paths.mk

This helper makefile (Listing 11.2) defines environment variables that identify any additional directory paths.

Listing 11.2 `Paths.mk` for Brewster

```
################################################################################
#
# Makefile that defines directory paths important to the build process.
# (c) Aspi Havewala 2001
#
################################################################################

_FLATRELEASEDIR = $(_WINCEROOT)\Release\$(_TGTPLAT)_$(_TGTPROJ)
```

As the last line of Listing 11.2 shows, the `_FLATRELEASEDIR` variable, which identifies the release directory, is redefined in this file.

The suffix *$(_TGTPLAT)_$(_TGTPROJ)* is added to the original value set up in `_FLATRELEASEDIR`. The Windows CE build process defines a single release directory for all projects. If you're working on more than one project, the entire release directory has to be deleted and the project must be rebuilt again. You can avoid this rigmarole by changing the release directory on a per project basis. By combining the platform and project names and appending the combined name to the release directory, you can create a unique path for each project. For the Webster project, the release directory is defined as `C:\WINCE\RELEASE\CEPC_WEBSTER`.

The Helper Makefile Command.mk

The master makefile calls on a variety of utilities to perform the build. The names of these utilities are abstracted into a helper makefile called `command.mk` (Listing 11.3).

Listing 11.3 `Command.mk` for Brewster

```
################################################################################
#
# Makefile that defines shell commands.
# (c) Jim Wilson and Aspi Havewala 2001
#
################################################################################

!if "$(VERBOSE)"=="1"
CMDECHO =
_ECHOON = 1
```

```
!else
CMDECHO = @
_ECHOON =
!endif

IFF = $(CMDECHO)if
XCOPY = $(CMDECHO)xcopy
COPY = $(CMDECHO)copy
CHANGEATTRIB = $(CMDECHO)attrib
DISPLAY = $(CMDECHO)echo
DISPLAY2 = echo
BUILD_CMD = Build
CHANGEDIR = $(CMDECHO)cd
SETENV = $(CMDECHO)set
RMDIR = $(CMDECHO)rmdir
RMDIR2 = rmdir
DELETE = $(CMDECHO)del
DELETE2 = del
SENDTO = >
APPENDTO = >>
```

This helper file also supports the `VERBOSE` option for the master makefile. The `VERBOSE` flag can be passed to the master makefile in the following way:

```
Nmake VERBOSE=1
```

With this flag set, the master makefile displays every command executed by the build process. `Command.mk` simply adds the character "@" as a prefix to each command if the `VERBOSE` flag is not set. This character prevents a command from being displayed as it is executed. The macro `_ECHOON` is also set to 1 if the `VERBOSE` option is specified. This macro is translated into an environment variable by the master makefile and is used by the build utilities to display their contents.

The Helper Makefile Buildoptions.mk

This helper file (Listing 11.4) is assigned the task of setting the values of macros corresponding to the environment variables that will modify the build process.

Listing 11.4 `Buildoptions.mk` for Brewster

```
#############################################################################
#
# Makefile that defines flags used to control the Windows CE build process.
# (c) Jim Wilson and Aspi Havewala 2001
#
#############################################################################

COUNTRY=USA
WINCEREL=1
```

```
WINCEMAP=1
WINCECOD=1

IMGATAPI=
IMGNOCOMM=
IMGNOCONSOLE=
IMGNOCTLPNL=
IMGNOETHER=
IMGNOCEDDK=
IMGNODRIVERS=
IMGNOFILES=
IMGNOJAVA=
IMGNOOLE32=
IMGNOREDIR=
IMGNOPCMCIA=
IMGNOSECURITY=
IMGNOSIR=
IMGNOTXTSHELL=
IMGNSCFIR=
IMGNOSHELL=
IMGTINYFSRAM=1
IMGUSB=1
IMGFLASH=$(FLASH)
MG_NOCURSOR=
ODO_NOPCMCIA=
ODO_NOIRDA=1
ODO_NOBATTERY=
ODO_NONLED=
ODO_NOTOUCH=
ODO_NOSERIAL=
ODO_NODISPLAY=
ODO_NOKEYBD=
ODO_NOAUDIO=

# CEPC platform variables
CEPC_SERMOUSE=
CEPC_PARALLEL=1

# Display drivers. One of the following 3 must be set to 1
CEPC_DDI_VGA8BPP=
CEPC_DDI_CT655X=
CEPC_DDI_S3VIRGE=1

IMG_FATFS=1
IMG_UNIMODEM=1
IMG_TAPI=1
IMG_ETHERLINK3=
IMG_NE2000=
IMG_PROXIM=
IMG_XIRCOM2=
IMG_PPP=1
IMG_IRDA=1
IMG_SIP=1
IMG_PRINT=1
```

```
IMG_TOOLHELP=1
IMG_IMESAMPLE=1
IMG_COMMAPPS=
IMG_HWX=1
IMG_TCP=1
IMG_DUALIO=1
IMG_NOTIFYAPI=1
IMG_COMMONDIALOGS=1
IMG_COMMONCONTROLS=1
IMG_TASKMANAGER=1
IMG_IMM=1

!if "$(DEBUG)"=="1"
WINCEDEBUG=debug
IMGNODEBUGGER=

!else

WINCEDEBUG=retail
IMGNODEBUGGER=1

!endif

!if "$(CLEAN)"=="1"
BUILD_FLAGS = -cf
BUILDREL_FLAGS = -c
SYSGEN FLAGS = -c
!else
BUILD_FLAGS = -f
!endif

CESH = Ppsh
CESH_OPTIONS = -p cepc
```

The master makefile translates these macros into environment variables. All macros set by the helper file are listed in Table 11.4.

Table 11.4 Macros Set to Modify the Build Process

Macro	Value	Meaning
CEPC_DDI_CT655X	NULL	Exclude Chips & Technologies CT655x-compatible display driver.
CEPC_DDI_S3VIRGE	1	Include S3 ViRGE–compatible display driver.
CEPC_DDI_VGA8BPP	NULL	Exclude eight-bits-per-pixel VGA display driver.
CEPC_DISKONCHIP	NULL	Include True flash file System driver.
CEPC_PARALLEL	1	Include parallel port driver.
CEPC_SERMOUSE	NULL	Exclude serial mouse driver.

(continued)

Table 11.4 *Continued.*

Macro	Value	Meaning
CEPC_USB_USE_EXISTING	NULL	Make sure USB host controller IRQ assigned by BIOS matches value in registry.
COUNTRY	USA	Country for localization.
IMG_COMMAPPS	NULL	Exclude communications applications.
IMG_COMMONCONTROLS	1	Add common control support.
IMG_COMMONDIALOGS	1	Add common dialog support.
IMG_DUALIO	1	Include Socket Dual Serial I/O (input/output).
IMG_FATFS	1	Include FAT file system.
IMG_HWX	1	Include handwriting support.
IMG_IMESAMPLE	1	Include sample for Input Method Editor (IME).
IMG_IMM	1	Include Input Method Manager (IMM).
IMG_IRDA	1	Include infrared support.
IMG_NE2000	NULL	Remove NE2000-compatible network driver support.
IMG_NOCURSOR	NULL	Don't exclude cursor support.
IMG_NOTIFYAPI	1	Include notification API.
IMG_PPP	1	Include Point-to-Point Protocol (PPP).
IMG_PRINT	1	Add print support.
IMG_SIP	1	Include Software Input Panel.
IMG_TAPI	1	Include Telephony API.
IMG_TASKMANAGER	1	
IMG_TCP	1	Include TCP/IP stack.
IMG_TOOLHELP	1	Include debugging support via ToolHelp.
IMG_UNIMODEM	1	Add Unimodem driver.
IMGATAPI	NULL	Include hard disk and CD file system.
IMGCOM2	NULL	Serial port on COM2.
IMGCOM3	NULL	Serial port on COM3.
IMGFLASH	1	Configure memory addresses to flash memory.
IMGNOCEDDK	NULL	Include hardware abstraction API.
IMGNOCOMM	NULL	Don't exclude communication components.
IMGNOCONSOLE	NULL	Don't exclude console.
IMGNOCTLPNL	NULL	Don't exclude Windows CE control panel.
IMGNODEBUGGER	1 or 0	Add or remove kernel debugger from image.
IMGNODRIVERS	NULL	Image will contain device drivers.
IMGNOETHER	NULL	Include Internet support.

Table 11.4 *Continued.*

Macro	Value	Meaning
IMGNOFILES	NULL	Don't exclude WAV files for system sound.
IMGNOJAVA	NULL	Don't exclude Java support.
IMGNOOLE32	NULL	Don't exclude OLE support.
IMGNOPCMCIA	NULL	Include PC card services.
IMGNOREDIR	NULL	Don't exclude network redirector.
IMGNOSECURITY	NULL	Don't exclude security components.
IMGNOSHELL	NULL	Don't exclude shell.
IMGNOSIR	NULL	Don't exclude infrared support.
IMGNOTXTSHELL	NULL	Don't exclude text shell.
IMGNSCFIR	NULL	Don't exclude Fast Infrared.
IMGTINYFSRAM	1	Allocate a smaller percentage of RAM for the file system.
IMGUSB	1	Include USB.
ODO_NOAUDIO	NULL	No audio support included.
ODO_NOBATTERY	NULL	Don't exclude battery driver.
ODO_NODISPLAY	NULL	No display driver required.
ODO_NOIRDA	NULL	Don't exclude infrared driver.
ODO_NOKEYBD	NULL	No keyboard driver included.
ODO_NONLED	NULL	Don't exclude LED driver.
ODO_NOPCMCIA	NULL	Don't exclude PC card driver.
ODO_NOSERIAL	NULL	Don't exclude serial port driver.
ODO_NOTOUCH	NULL	Don't exclude touch panel driver.
WINCECOD	1	Create assembly listings from compiled source.
WINCEDEBUG	retail or debug	Create debug or retail build of CE.
WINCEMAP	1	Create map files during the link process.
WINCEREL	1	Copy individually built drivers into the release directory.

The Helper Makefile Targets.mk

During incremental development of integration components, drivers, and applications, a system integrator may need to build individual modules. Targets that build individual modules are collected in this helper makefile (Listing 11.5). These targets are listed in Table 11.5.

Listing 11.5 `Targets.mk` **for Brewster**

```
##############################################################################
#
# Makefile that defines individual targets for the build process.
# (c) Jim Wilson and Aspi Havewala 2001
#
##############################################################################

# Generic target to build a driver.
BuildDriver: SetupEnvironment
    $(DISPLAY) Building $(DRIVER)
    $(CHANGEDIR) $(_TARGETPLATROOT)\DRIVERS\$(DRIVER)
    $(BUILD_CMD) $(BUILD_FLAGS)
    $(IFF) exist build.err $(DISPLAY2) Failed to build
$(_TARGETPLATROOT)\DRIVERS\$(DRIVER).
    $(CHANGEDIR) $(_WINCEROOT)

# Build CE DDK layer.
BuildCeDdk: SetupEnvironment BuildCeDdk2
BuildCeDdk2:
    $(DISPLAY) Building CeDdk
    $(CHANGEDIR) $(_TARGETPLATROOT)\DRIVERS\CeDdk
    $(BUILD_CMD) $(BUILD_FLAGS)
    $(IFF) exist build.err $(DISPLAY2) Failed to build
$(_TARGETPLATROOT)\DRIVERS\CeDdk.
    $(CHANGEDIR) $(_WINCEROOT)

# Build WDM HAL layer.
BuildWdmHal: SetupEnvironment BuildWdmHal2
BuildWdmHal2:
    $(DISPLAY) Building WDMHAL
    $(CHANGEDIR) $(_TARGETPLATROOT)\WDMHAL
    $(BUILD_CMD) $(BUILD_FLAGS)
    $(IFF) exist build.err $(DISPLAY2) Failed to build
$(_TARGETPLATROOT)\WDMHAL.
    $(CHANGEDIR) $(_WINCEROOT)

# Build kernel and HAL.
BuildKernel: SetupEnvironment BuildKernel2
BuildKernel2:
    $(DISPLAY) Building KERNEL
    $(CHANGEDIR) $(_TARGETPLATROOT)\KERNEL
    $(BUILD_CMD) $(BUILD_FLAGS)
    $(IFF) exist build.err $(DISPLAY2) Failed to build
$(_TARGETPLATROOT)\KERNEL.
!   if "$(WINCEREL)"=="1"
    $(XCOPY)
$(_TARGETPLATROOT)\Target\$(_TGTCPUTYPE)\$(_TGTCPU)\$(_TGTOS)\$(WINCEDEBUG)\$(
KERNEL_NAME).exe $(_FLATRELEASEDIR)
    $(XCOPY)
$(_TARGETPLATROOT)\Target\$(_TGTCPUTYPE)\$(_TGTCPU)\$(_TGTOS)\$(WINCEDEBUG)\$(
KERNEL_NAME).pdb $(_FLATRELEASEDIR)
!   endif
    $(CHANGEDIR) $(_WINCEROOT)
```

```
# Build serial driver.
BuildSerial: SetupEnvironment BuildSerial2
BuildSerial2:
    $(DISPLAY) Building Serial
    $(CHANGEDIR) $(_TARGETPLATROOT)\DRIVERS\Serial.pdd
    $(BUILD_CMD) $(BUILD_FLAGS)
    $(IFF) exist build.err $(DISPLAY2) Failed to build
$(_TARGETPLATROOT)\DRIVERS\Serial.pdd.
    $(CHANGEDIR) $(_WINCEROOT)

# Build USB drivers.
BuildUsb: SetupEnvironment BuildUsb2
BuildUsb2:
    $(DISPLAY) Building Usb
    $(CHANGEDIR) $(_TARGETPLATROOT)\DRIVERS\Usb
    $(BUILD_CMD) $(BUILD_FLAGS)
    $(IFF) exist build.err $(DISPLAY2) Failed to build
$(_TARGETPLATROOT)\DRIVERS\Usb.
    $(CHANGEDIR) $(_WINCEROOT)

# Build audio driver.
BuildAudio: SetupEnvironment BuildAudio2
BuildAudio2:
    $(DISPLAY) Building Audio
    $(CHANGEDIR) $(_TARGETPLATROOT)\DRIVERS\Audio
    $(BUILD_CMD) $(BUILD_FLAGS)
    $(IFF) exist build.err $(DISPLAY2) Failed to build
$(_TARGETPLATROOT)\DRIVERS\Audio.
    $(CHANGEDIR) $(_WINCEROOT)

# Build wave device driver.
BuildWaveDev: SetupEnvironment BuildWaveDev2
BuildWaveDev2:
    $(DISPLAY) Building WaveDev
    $(CHANGEDIR) $(_TARGETPLATROOT)\DRIVERS\WAVEDEV
    $(BUILD_CMD) $(BUILD_FLAGS)
    $(IFF) exist build.err $(DISPLAY2) Failed to build
$(_TARGETPLATROOT)\DRIVERS\WAVEDEV.
    $(CHANGEDIR) $(_WINCEROOT)

# Build card services driver.
BuildPcmcia: SetupEnvironment BuildPcmcia2
BuildPcmcia2:
    $(CHANGEDIR) $(_TARGETPLATROOT)\Drivers\PCMCIA
    $(BUILD_CMD) $(BUILD_FLAGS)
    $(IFF) exist build.err $(DISPLAY2) Failed to build
$(_TARGETPLATROOT)\Drivers\PCMCIA.
    $(CHANGEDIR) $(_PROJECTROOT)

# Build keyboard and mouse drivers.
BuildKbdMouse: SetupEnvironment BuildKbdMouse2
BuildKbdMouse2:
    $(CHANGEDIR) $(_TARGETPLATROOT)\Drivers\KbdMouse
    $(BUILD_CMD) $(BUILD_FLAGS)
```

```
    $(IFF) exist build.err $(DISPLAY2) Failed to build
$(_TARGETPLATROOT)\DRIVERS\KbdMouse.
    $(CHANGEDIR) $(_PROJECTROOT)

# Build all display drivers.
BuildDisplay: SetupEnvironment BuildDisplay2
BuildDisplay2:
    $(CHANGEDIR) $(_TARGETPLATROOT)\Drivers\Display
    $(BUILD_CMD) $(BUILD_FLAGS)
    $(IFF) exist build.err $(DISPLAY2) Failed to build
$(_TARGETPLATROOT)\DRIVERS\Display.
    $(CHANGEDIR) $(_PROJECTROOT)

# Build battery driver.
BuildBattery: SetupEnvironment BuildBattery2
BuildBattery2:
    $(DISPLAY) Building GWE\BATTERY
    $(CHANGEDIR) $(_TARGETPLATROOT)\GWE\BATTERY
    $(BUILD_CMD) $(BUILD_FLAGS)
    $(IFF) exist build.err $(DISPLAY2) Failed to build
$(_TARGETPLATROOT)\GWE\BATTERY.
    $(CHANGEDIR) $(_WINCEROOT)

# Build LED driver.
BuildLED: SetupEnvironment BuildLED2
BuildLED2:
    $(DISPLAY) Building GWE\NLEDDRV
    $(CHANGEDIR) $(_TARGETPLATROOT)\GWE\NLEDDRV
    $(BUILD_CMD) $(BUILD_FLAGS)
    $(IFF) exist build.err $(DISPLAY2) Failed to build
$(_TARGETPLATROOT)\GWE\NLEDDRV.
    $(CHANGEDIR) $(_WINCEROOT)

# Generic target to build GWES component.
# Define GWESCOMP to name of directory containing component.
BuildGWESComponent: SetupEnvironment
    $(DISPLAY) Building GWE\$(GWESCOMP)
    $(CHANGEDIR) $(_TARGETPLATROOT)\GWE\$(GWESCOMP)
    $(BUILD_CMD) $(BUILD_FLAGS)
    $(IFF) exist build.err $(DISPLAY2) Failed to build
$(_TARGETPLATROOT)\GWE\$(GWESCOMP).
    $(CHANGEDIR) $(_WINCEROOT)
    $(MAKE) $(MAKEFLAGS) BuildGWES

# Build intermediate GWES library.
BuildGWEAll: SetupEnvironment BuildGWEAll2
BuildGWEAll2:
    $(DISPLAY) Building GWE\ALL
    $(CHANGEDIR) $(_TARGETPLATROOT)\GWE\ALL
    $(BUILD_CMD) $(BUILD_FLAGS)
    $(IFF) exist build.err $(DISPLAY2) Failed to build
$(_TARGETPLATROOT)\GWE\ALL.
    $(CHANGEDIR) $(_WINCEROOT)
```

```
# Build GWES module with all built-in drivers.
BuildGWES: SetupEnvironment BuildGWES2
BuildGWES2: \
!   if "$(ODO_NOBATTERY)"!="1"
    BuildBattery2              \
!   endif
!   if "$(ODO_NONLED)"!="1"
    BuildLED2                  \
!   endif
    BuildGWEAll2
    $(DISPLAY) Building GWE Executable
    $(CHANGEDIR) $(_TARGETPLATROOT)\GWE\BUILDEXE
    $(BUILD_CMD) $(BUILD_FLAGS)
    $(IFF) exist build.err $(DISPLAY2) Failed to build
$(_TARGETPLATROOT)\GWE\BUILDEXE.
!   if "$(WINCEREL)"=="1"
    $(XCOPY)
$(_TARGETPLATROOT)\Target\$(_TGTCPUTYPE)\$(_TGTCPU)\$(_TGTOS)\$(WINCEDEBUG)\Gw
es.exe $(_FLATRELEASEDIR)
    $(XCOPY)
$(_TARGETPLATROOT)\Target\$(_TGTCPUTYPE)\$(_TGTCPU)\$(_TGTOS)\$(WINCEDEBUG)\Gw
es.pdb $(_FLATRELEASEDIR)
!   endif
    $(CHANGEDIR) $(_PROJECTROOT)
```

Table 11.5 Targets Specified in `Targets.mk`

Target	Usage
`BuildAudio`	Builds the audio driver.
`BuildBattery`	Builds the battery driver. The battery driver is a GWES component, and the `BuildGWES` target must be called after the driver has been built successfully.
`BuildCeDdk`	Builds the CeDDK module that exports routines to abstract bus I/O and memory mapping.
`BuildDisplay`	Builds all available display drivers.
`BuildDriver`	Generic target to build a driver. When this target is called, the macro `DRIVER` must be set to the name of the driver at the command line—that is, `Nmake BuildDriver DRIVER=Display`.
`BuildGWES`	Builds the GWES module with the device drivers linked in.
`BuildGWESComponent`	Generic target to build a GWES component. Drivers like the battery and LED driver are linked with the GWES module before being loaded into the image. This requires each GWES component to be linked with GWES upon successful compilation. This target will build the component passed in the command line macro `GWESCOMP` and then link it with the GWES module—that is, `Nmake GWESCOMP=Battery`.
`BuildKbdMouse`	Builds the keyboard and mouse drivers.
`BuildKernel`	Builds the OEM adaptations to the kernel (HAL).

(continued)

Table 11.5 *Continued.*

Target	Usage
`BuildLED`	Builds the LED driver. The LED driver is a GWES component and the `BuildGWES` target must be called after the driver has been built successfully.
`BuildPcmcia`	Builds the card services driver.
`BuildSerial`	Builds the serial port driver.
`BuildUSB`	Builds the USB drivers.
`BuildWavedev`	Builds the wave device driver.
`BuildWdmHal`	Builds the Windows Driver Model (WDM) library for drivers.

Modules under incremental development that integrators are likely to build can be added to this helper file. Makefile options like `DEBUG`, `CLEAN`, and so on apply to the individual targets as well.

Specifying System Modules and Components

One of the principal tasks in adapting Windows CE to a target platform is to specify the modules and components of the system that will go into the final image.

As we have seen before, the file where one specifies the modules and components that go into the custom version of Windows CE is the batch file `cesysgen.bat`. `Cesysgen.bat` sets environment variables to lists of components. This batch file is found in the project directory tree. It must be customized per project. Instead of deleting and adding components in `cesysgen.bat`, the batch file has been modified to look for environment variables that filter the components to be included. This approach allows the reuse of `cesysgen.bat` for other projects. Windows CE uses the same technique to create a reusable `cesysgen.bat`. As an example, consider the following lines from the Brewster project:

```
if "%ODO_NOTOUCH%"=="1" goto endif_10
    set GWE2_COMPONENTS=%GWE2_COMPONENTS% tchui calibrui
:endif_10
```

If the environment variable `ODO_NOTOUCH` is set to 1, the GWES components `tchui` and `calibrui` are not included in the image. `GWE2_COMPONENTS` contains a list of GWES components that is deciphered by Cefilter during the system build phase. Recall that Cefilter will include the components listed by this environment variable when filtering the BIB file `common.bib`.

Variables that have the *ODO_NO* prefix are used to specify platform-dependent components for the Odo platform. Variables used to filter system components have the *IMGNO* prefix. If any of these variables is defined to a value of 1, the component associated with the variable is *not* included in the final image. When you're defining new variables that select and filter components in a similar way, you can avoid this slightly unwieldy behavior by defining variables such that when they are set to 1, the components associated with are included. This approach makes the batch file considerably more readable.

In the modified sample `cesysgen.bat`, we retain the previously defined variables to avoid confusion. These variables are liberally used in the BIB and registry files for the CEPC platform. Any new variables we create will have the *IMG_* prefix. The underscore distinguishes variables created by us from those predefined by the build process. When given a value of 1, these variables cause a particular component or module to be added to the image:

```
if "%IMG_PPP%"=="1" set CE_MODULES=%CE_MODULES% ppp
```

The modified `cesysgen.bat` file can now be used in different projects. The entire file is shown in Listing 11.6.

Listing 11.6 `Cesysgen.bat` for Brewster

```
REM
REM Sample cesysgen.bat file. Modified to demonstrate how additions should be
made
REM (c) Aspi Havewala/Jim Wilson 2001
REM

REM Base components for Coredll and file system
REM ***********************************************
set CE_MODULES=coredll filesys nk
set COREDLL_COMPONENTS=coremain coreloc lmem thunks fmtmsg accel_c
set FILESYS_COMPONENTS=fsysram fsreg fsheap fsmain fspass fsdbase

REM ToolHelp for debugging
REM ***********************
if "%IMG_TOOLHELP%"=="1" set CE_MODULES=%CE_MODULES% toolhelp
REM CE Shell
REM ********
if not "%IMGNOSHELL%"=="1" set CE_MODULES=%CE_MODULES% shell

REM Base GWES components
REM ********************
set CE_MODULES=%CE_MODULES% gwes
set GWE1_COMPONENTS=wmbase gweshare gwesmain immthunk msgque loadstr
GSetWinLong
set COREDLL_COMPONENTS=%COREDLL_COMPONENTS% rectapi wmgr_c
set GWE1_COMPONENTS=%GWE1_COMPONENTS% foregnd uibase kbdui journal hotkey idle
getpower nled msgbeep

REM Base GDI components
REM ********************
set GWE2_COMPONENTS=mgbase mgbitmap mgblt mgblt2 mgdc mgdibsec mgdraw mgrgn
mgwinmgr mgpalnat
set COREDLL_COMPONENTS=%COREDLL_COMPONENTS% mgdi_c
REM Extra MGDI components + tt support + printing
REM ************************************************
set GWE2_COMPONENTS=%GWE2_COMPONENTS% mgtt mgdrwtxt mgpal mgprint mgtci
mgalias mgfe
```

```
REM Touch panel user interface
REM **************
if "%ODO_NOTOUCH%"=="1" goto endif_10
    set GWE2_COMPONENTS=%GWE2_COMPONENTS% tchui calibrui
:endif_10

REM Window manager
REM **************
if "%IMG_NOCURSOR%"=="1" set GWE3_COMPONENTS=icon cursor cursor8
if not "%IMG_NOCURSOR%"=="1" set GWE3_COMPONENTS=iconcurs mcursor mcursor8
set GWE3_COMPONENTS=%GWE3_COMPONENTS% winmgr sbcmn nclient caret clipbd timer
accel defwndproc gcache loadbmp loadimg syscolor
set GWE3_COMPONENTS=%GWE3_COMPONENTS% menu mNoTapUI cascade column moverlap
menuscrl drawmbar
set GWE4_COMPONENTS=%GWE4_COMPONENTS% dlgmgr dlgmnem msgbox msgbox28 gwectrl
btnctl stcctl
set GWE4_COMPONENTS=%GWE4_COMPONENTS% startup oomui oom startui cmbctl cdlctl
edctl imgctl lbctl scbctl
if "%COUNTRY%" == "JAPAN" set GWE4_COMPONENTS=%GWE4_COMPONENTS% edimefe
edimejpn

REM Input Method Manager
REM ********************
if "%IMG_IMM%" set COREDLL_COMPONENTS=%COREDLL_COMPONENTS% coreimm

REM Software Input Panel
REM ****************
if not "%IMG_SIP%"=="1" gotot endif_11
    set COREDLL_COMPONENTS=%COREDLL_COMPONENTS% coresip
    set CE_MODULES=%CE_MODULES% softkb
:endif_11

REM Device manager
REM **************
set CE_MODULES=%CE_MODULES% device

REM Communications components
REM ************************
if not "%IMGNOCOMM%" == "1" set CE_MODULES=%CE_MODULES% cxport winsock afd
netui
REM TCP stack
REM *********
if "%IMG_TCP%" == "1" set CE_MODULES=%CE_MODULES% tcpstk

REM PPP support
REM ***********
if "%IMG_PPP%"=="1" set CE_MODULES=%CE_MODULES% ppp

REM IrCOMM and IrDA
REM ***************
if "%IMG_IRDA%"=="1" set CE_MODULES=%CE_MODULES% ircomm irdastk
```

```
REM Internet support
REM ******************
if "%IMGNOETHER%"=="1" goto endif_12

    set CE_MODULES=%CE_MODULES% ndis arp netdetec dhcp

    if "%IMG_NE2000%"=="1" set CE_MODULES=%CE_MODULES% ne2000
    set CE_MODULES=%CE_MODULES% wininet
    set WININET_COMPONENTS=inetftp

:endif_12

REM USB
REM ***
if "%IMGUSB%"=="1" set CE_MODULES=%CE_MODULES% usbd usbmouse

REM Serial port
REM ***********
if "%ODO_NOSERIAL%"=="1" goto endif_13
    set COREDLL_COMPONENTS=%COREDLL_COMPONENTS% serdev
:endif_13

REM Telephony API
REM *************
if not "%IMG_TAPI%"=="1" goto endif_14
    REM // Tapi
    set COREDLL_COMPONENTS=%COREDLL COMPONENTS% tapilib
    set CE_MODULES=%CE_MODULES% tapi
:endif_14

REM Unimodem
REM ********
if "%IMG_UNIMODEM%"=="1" set CE_MODULES=%CE_MODULES% unimodem

REM Security modules and components
REM *******************************
if "%IMGNOSECURITY%"=="1" goto endif_16
    set CE_MODULES=%CE_MODULES% secur32 ntlmssp schannel rsabase
    set WINSOCK_COMPONENTS=sslsock
    set COREDLL_COMPONENTS=%COREDLL_COMPONENTS% cryptapi rsa32
:endif_16

REM Network redirector
REM ******************
if not "%IMGNOREDIR%"=="1" set CE_MODULES=%CE_MODULES% redir netbios

REM COM and desktop-compatible OLE
REM ******************************
if "%IMGNOOLE32"=="1" goto endif_20
    set CE_MODULES=%CE_MODULES% uuid ole32 oleaut32
    set OLE32_COMPONENTS=ole232 com docfile msf exp
:endif_20
```

```
REM FAT file system and related drivers
REM ***********************************
if not "%IMG_FATFS%"=="1" goto endif_22
    REM // FatFS support: needs PCMCIA
    set CE_MODULES=%CE_MODULES% fatfs atadisk ramdisk ceramdrv sramdisk
trueffs
:endif_22

REM Socket Dual Serial card
REM ************************
if "%IMG_DUALIO%" == "1" set CE_MODULES=%CE_MODULES% dualio

REM Wave API and PCM manager support
REM *********************************
if not "%IMG_AUDIO%"=="1" goto endif_28
    set CE_MODULES=%CE_MODULES% waveapi cegsm msfilter
    set COREDLL_COMPONENTS=%COREDLL_COMPONENTS% wavelib
    set GWE1_COMPONENTS=%GWE1_COMPONENTS% audio
:endif_28

REM Printing support
REM ****************
if "%IMG_PRINT%"=="1" set CE_MODULES=%CE_MODULES%  parallel pcl prnport prnerr

REM Handwriting recognition
REM ***********************
if not "%IMG_HWX%"=="1" goto endif_32
    REM // Handwriting recognition
    if "%COUNTRY%" == "JAPAN" set CE_MODULES=%CE_MODULES% hwxjpn
    if not "%COUNTRY%" == "JAPAN" set CE_MODULES=%CE_MODULES% hwxusa splusa
:endif_32

REM Notification APIs
REM *****************
if "%IMG_NOTIFYAPI%"=="1" set GWE1_COMPONENTS=%GWE1_COMPONENTS% notify

set GWES_COMPONENTS=gwe1 gwe2 gwe3 gwe4

REM Console support
REM ***************
if "%IMGNOCONSOLE%"=="1" goto endif_34
    set CE_MODULES=%CE_MODULES% console cmd
:endif_34

set COREDLL_COMPONENTS=%COREDLL_COMPONENTS% fmtres
set COREDLL_COMPONENTS=%COREDLL_COMPONENTS% corestrw corestra coresiow
coresioa

REM Shell API components
REM If any are chosen, shcore must also be included
REM **********************************************
if "%IMGNOSHELL%"=="1" goto endif_36
    set COREDLL_COMPONENTS=%COREDLL_COMPONENTS% shcore shortcut shexec shmisc
fileopen fileinfo
```

```
:endif_36

REM Common dialogs
REM **************
if "%IMG_COMMONDIALOGS%"=="1" set CE_MODULES=%CE_MODULES% commdlg
REM Common controls
REM ***************
if "%IMG_COMMONCONTROLS%"=="1" set CE_MODULES=%CE_MODULES% commctrl
REM Task Manager
REM ************
if "%IMG_TASKMANAGER%"=="1" set CE_MODULES=%CE_MODULES% taskman

REM Control panel support. Must have the first line if any CTLPNL applet is
used.
REM Other lines are the individual applets. Choose any/all/none as applicable
REM Portrait form-factor CPL applets have a "g" postfix
REM ************************************************************************
if "%IMGNOCTLPNL%"=="1" goto endif_50
    set CE_MODULES=%CE_MODULES% control ctlpnl
    if "%IMG_SIP%"=="1" set CE_MODULES=%CE_MODULES% sipcpl
    set CE_MODULES=%CE_MODULES% system screen passwrd
    if "%IMG_AUDIO%"=="1" set CE_MODULES=%CE_MODULES% sounds soundsg
    set CE_MODULES=%CE_MODULES% comm intl power main
    if not "%IMGNOETHER%"=="1" set CE_MODULES=%CE_MODULES% network networkg
    set CE_MODULES=%CE_MODULES% systemg screeng passwrdg commg intlg powerg
:endif_50

REM Communications apps
REM *******************
if "%IMG_COMMAPPS%"=="1" set CE_MODULES=%CE_MODULES% pegterm termctrl rnaapp
remnet

REM Sample SDK apps
REM ***************
if "%IMG_SDKSAMPLES%"=="1" set CE_MODULES=%CE_MODULES% msim testtime
```

When you're modifying `cesysgen.bat`, it is best to make your changes incrementally. It is particularly tedious to correlate errors you get when building the system with the changes made to `cesysgen.bat`. By changing a few lines at a time and incrementally testing the system build, you will be able to correlate errors with changes instantly. Modifying `cesysgen.bat` is not a task you will have to perform repeatedly; hence, the incremental approach can be justified. Start by making a copy of your project directory and build the system to make sure the copy was successful. You can do this by running the batch file associated with the copied project and then running `sysgen.bat`. If `sysgen.bat` completes without errors, you have a good working copy of an existing project. Now you may begin making changes incrementally to `cesysgen.bat`, running `sysgen.bat` between your changes. If you define a variable to create a conditional in `cesysgen.bat`, add the variable first to `buildoptions.mk` and then to the `SetupEnvironment` target in the master makefile.

If errors occur in the build process, you should examine the log file `build.log` that is placed in the `_WINCEROOT` directory. The errors generated by the system build come from the makefile that is used to build all the modules and components in the system. Testing this portion of the build process before attempting a full build is productive because making changes to `cesysgen.bat` has an impact on the system build only.

Modifying the Initialization Files

Windows CE is further customized in the initialization files. Each type of initialization is used to customize a different aspect of the operating system.

BIB files

Environment variables can be used to specify conditionals in the BIB files. Consider the following lines from the CEPC BIB file `platform.bib`:

```
; CEPC Serial Mouse Driver
IF CEPC_SERMOUSE
   sermouse.dll    $(_FLATRELEASEDIR)\sermouse.dll              NK  SH
ENDIF
```

If the `CEPC_SERMOUSE` variable is defined, the next line is retained in the BIB file. This will include the `sermouse.dll` file in the image. This conditional is processed by Fmerge when it merges BIB files into `ce.bib`. The *CEPC_* prefix in this case denotes a CEPC platform–dependent modification. Because the CEPC platform evolved from Odo, the first platform developed by Microsoft for Windows CE, the *ODO_* variables remained in the CEPC files, producing a confusing cocktail of variable-naming conventions. Rather than cleaning up these files, we will provide samples that will contain all variations of names you are likely to come across. When developing corresponding files for a project, you may choose to follow one naming convention.

Another caveat of note is that Fmerge doesn't check to see if the value of `CEPC_SERMOUSE` is set to 1. It is quite happy if the variable has simply been defined to *any* value. For uniformity, we continue defining all such variables as having the value 1. To check if a variable is *not* defined, we append the exclamation character (!) to the conditional, as in this sample:

```
IF COUNTRY=JAPAN !
    kbdmouse.dll      $(_FLATRELEASEDIR)\KbdMsEngUs1.dll             NK  SH
ENDIF
```

However, Fmerge is capable of checking the exact value assigned to a variable. This check is performed with the following syntax:

```
IF <env_var> = <value>
ENDIF
```

The BIB files for Brewster are shown in Listings 11.7 and 11.8.

Listing 11.7 Platform-specific BIB file for Brewster (`platform.bib`)

```
MODULES
;  Name             Path                                      Memory Type
;  -------------    ----------------------------------------  ----------
IF IMGTINY !
IF IMGNODRIVERS !

IF IMGNOCEDDK !
   ceddk.dll        $(_FLATRELEASEDIR)\pc_ddk.dll              NK  SH
ENDIF

; USB drivers
IF IMGUSB
   ohci.dll         $(_FLATRELEASEDIR)\ohci.dll                NK  SH
   usbd.dll         $(_FLATRELEASEDIR)\usbd.dll                NK  SH
   usbmouse.dll     $(_FLATRELEASEDIR)\usbmouse.dll            NK  SH
ENDIF

; CEPC serial mouse driver
IF CEPC_SERMOUSE
   sermouse.dll     $(_FLATRELEASEDIR)\sermouse.dll            NK  SH
ENDIF
;

; MGDI (Multiplatform Graphical Device Interface) display driver
; The default display driver is the S3 Trio64 display
; To use the 8-bits-per-pixel generic VGA, set the environment variable
; CEPC_DDI_VGA8BPP to 1.  To use the CT driver, set
; CEPC_DDI_CT655X to 1. To use the accelerated S3 ViRGE driver,
; set CEPC_DDI_S3VIRGE to 1.

IF ODO_NODISPLAY !

IF CEPC_DDI_VGA8BPP
   ddi.dll          $(_FLATRELEASEDIR)\ddi_vga8.dll            NK  SH
ENDIF
IF CEPC_DDI_CT655X
   ddi.dll          $(_FLATRELEASEDIR)\ddi_ct.dll              NK  SH
ENDIF

IF CEPC_DDI_S3VIRGE
   ddi.dll          $(_FLATRELEASEDIR)\ddi_s3v.dll             NK  SH
ENDIF

IF CEPC_DDI_S3VIRGE !
IF CEPC_DDI_CT655X !
IF CEPC_DDI_VGA8BPP !
   ddi.dll          $(_FLATRELEASEDIR)\ddi_s364.dll            NK  SH
ENDIF
ENDIF
ENDIF

ENDIF
```

```
IF ODO_NOKEYBD !
IF COUNTRY=JAPAN !
    kbdmouse.dll    $(_FLATRELEASEDIR)\KbdMsEngUs1.dll             NK   SH
ENDIF

IF COUNTRY=JAPAN
    kbdmouse.dll    $(_FLATRELEASEDIR)\KbdMsJpn2.dll               NK   SH
ENDIF

ENDIF
IF ODO_NOAUDIO !
   wavedev.dll      $(_FLATRELEASEDIR)\wavedev.dll                 NK   SH
ENDIF
IF ODO_NOSERIAL !
   serial.dll       $(_FLATRELEASEDIR)\serial.dll                  NK   SH
IF ODO_NOIRDA !
IF IMGNOSIR !
IF IMGNSCFIR !
   irsir.dll        $(_FLATRELEASEDIR)\irsir.dll                   NK   SH
ENDIF
ENDIF
ENDIF
ENDIF

IF ODO_NOIRDA !
IF IMGNSCFIR
   nscirda.dll      $(_FLATRELEASEDIR)\nscirda.dll                 NK   SH
ENDIF
ENDIF

IF ODO_NOPCMCIA !
   pcmcia.dll       $(_FLATRELEASEDIR)\pcmcia.dll                  NK   SH
ENDIF
IF IMGATAPI
   atapipci.dll     $(_FLATRELEASEDIR)\atapipci.dll                NK   SH
   cdfs.dll         $(_FLATRELEASEDIR)\cdfs.dll                    NK   SH
ENDIF

IF CEPC_PARALLEL
;  Parallel port driver
   parallel.dll     $(_FLATRELEASEDIR)\parallel.dll                NK   SH
ENDIF

ENDIF
ENDIF
```

Listing 11.8 Platform-independent BIB file for Brewster (`project.bib`)

```
MODULES
;  Name             Path                                            Memory Type
;  -------------    ----------------------------------------------  ----------
IF IMGTINY !
IF TESTTIME=TESTTIME
    testtime.dll    $(_FLATRELEASEDIR)\testtime.dll                 NK   SH
ENDIF   TESTTIME=TESTTIME
IF TESTSIP
    msim.dll        $(_FLATRELEASEDIR)\msim.dll                     NK   SH
ENDIF   TESTSIP
ENDIF

FILES
;  Name             Path                                            Memory Type
;  -------------    ----------------------------------------------  ----------
IF IMGTINY !
IF TESTTIME=TESTTIME
    rkc.txt         $(_FLATRELEASEDIR)\rkc.txt              NK   SH
ENDIF   TESTTIME=TESTTIME
ENDIF

   ; All of the system UI components (commctrl, commdlg, control panel,
applets,
   ; taskman, etc.) depend on the Tahoma font to look right. Also the console
   ; depends on the presence of a fixed-pitch font (such as Courier)
   tahoma.ttf      $(_FLATRELEASEDIR)\tahoma.ttf                  NK   SHU
   cour.ttf        $(_FLATRELEASEDIR)\cour.ttf                    NK   SHU
   arial.ttf       $(_FLATRELEASEDIR)\arial.ttf                   NK   SHU
   symbol.ttf      $(_FLATRELEASEDIR)\symbol.ttf                  NK   SHU
   times.ttf       $(_FLATRELEASEDIR)\times.ttf                   NK   SHU

IF COUNTRY=JAPAN
   impact.ttf       $(_FLATRELEASEDIR)\impact.ttf                  NK   SU
   kino.ttf         $(_FLATRELEASEDIR)\kino.ttf                    NK   SU
   mslogo.ttf       $(_FLATRELEASEDIR)\mslogo.ttf                  NK   SU
   timesbd.ttf      $(_FLATRELEASEDIR)\timesbd.ttf                 NK   SU

   msgothic.ttc     $(_FLATRELEASEDIR)\msgothic.ttc                NK   U
   test01.tte       $(_FLATRELEASEDIR)\test01.tte                  NK   U
   test02.tte       $(_FLATRELEASEDIR)\test02.tte                  NK   U
   test03.tte       $(_FLATRELEASEDIR)\test03.tte                  NK   U
   eudc.tte         $(_FLATRELEASEDIR)\eudc.tte                    NK   U
ENDIF

IF IMGTINY !
IF IMGNOFILES !
   ; These WAV files used to play system sounds (selected in the SOUND CPL
applet)
       asterisk.wav   $(_FLATRELEASEDIR)\asterisk.wav              NK S
       close.wav      $(_FLATRELEASEDIR)\close.wav                 NK S
       critical.wav   $(_FLATRELEASEDIR)\critical.wav              NK S
       default.wav    $(_FLATRELEASEDIR)\default.wav               NK S
       empty.wav      $(_FLATRELEASEDIR)\empty.wav                 NK S
```

```
        exclam.wav     $(_FLATRELEASEDIR)\exclam.wav                NK S
        infbeg.wav     $(_FLATRELEASEDIR)\infbeg.wav                NK S
        infend.wav     $(_FLATRELEASEDIR)\infend.wav                NK S
        infintr.wav    $(_FLATRELEASEDIR)\infintr.wav               NK S
        menupop.wav    $(_FLATRELEASEDIR)\menupop.wav               NK S
        menusel.wav    $(_FLATRELEASEDIR)\menusel.wav               NK S
        openprog.wav   $(_FLATRELEASEDIR)\openprog.wav              NK S
        question.wav   $(_FLATRELEASEDIR)\question.wav              NK S
        startup.wav    $(_FLATRELEASEDIR)\startup.wav               NK S
        windmax.wav    $(_FLATRELEASEDIR)\windmax.wav               NK S
        windmin.wav    $(_FLATRELEASEDIR)\windmin.wav               NK S
    ; These BMP files are used for desktop background bitmap (selected in the
SCREEN CPL applet)
        wince.bmp      $(_FLATRELEASEDIR)\wince.bmp                 NK S
ENDIF
ENDIF
```

Registry files

Registry entries that the system registry must initialize at boot are specified in the REG files.

Note that creating long names for subkeys, value names, and values in the registry uses up precious space in RAM. The benefits of readability and self-documentation of long names must be weighed against the space requirements of your target.

Again, environment variables can be used to specify conditionals in registry files. Since Fmerge processes registry files as well, the syntax is similar to the one for BIB files. In the following sample code from `platform.reg`, the entries set up the wave device driver as a CE built-in driver if the variable `ODO_NOAUDIO` has not been defined as 1:

```
IF ODO_NOAUDIO !
[HKEY_LOCAL_MACHINE\Drivers\BuiltIn\WaveDev\]
   "Prefix"="WAV"
   "Dll"="wavedev.dll"
   "Index"=dword:1
   "Order"=dword:0
   "Irq"=dword:0a
   "Dma"=dword:5
   "IoBase"=dword:220
ENDIF
```

The registry initialization files for Brewster are shown in Listings 11.9 and 11.10.

Listing 11.9 Platform-specific registry file for Brewster (`platform.reg`)

```
; Platform type: 1=DK3, 2=Perp 3=Rose
[HKEY_LOCAL_MACHINE\Platform]
   "Name"=LOC_PLATFORMNAME
   "Type"=dword:2

IF ODO_NOPCMCIA !
; Intel 82365-compatible PCMCIA socket controller resources
; Most 82365-compatible controllers use 0x3e0 and 0x3e1 (like the Simple
```

```
; Technology controller). The SCM controller uses 0x3e2 and 0x3e3
[HKEY_LOCAL_MACHINE\Drivers\PCMCIA]
   "Irq"=dword:0b
   "IoBase"=dword:03e0
   ;"IoBase"=dword:03e2 ; for SCM controller
   "IoLen"=dword:2
ENDIF

IF IMG_NE2000
; These are the registry settings for using the Kingston PCI NE2000 Ethernet
; adapter on a CEPC. "BusType=5" => PCI, InterruptNumber, and IoBaseAddress
; were obtained by running a PCI device enumerator program.
; These settings will conflict with those for PCMCIA NE2000 in that comm
settings
; with multiple instances are not yet supported (i.e., NE20001, NE20002 ...)
[HKEY_LOCAL_MACHINE\Comm\NE2000]
   "DisplayName"=LOC_DISPLAYNAME_COMM_NE2000
   "Group"="NDIS"
   "ImagePath"="ne2000.dll"

[HKEY_LOCAL_MACHINE\Comm\NE2000\Linkage]
   "Route"=multi_sz:"NE20001"

[HKEY_LOCAL_MACHINE\Comm\NE20001]
   "DisplayName"=LOC_DISPLAYNAME_COMM_NE20001
   "Group"="NDIS"
   "ImagePath"="ne2000.dll"

[HKEY_LOCAL_MACHINE\Comm\NE20001\Parms]
   "BusNumber"=dword:0
   "BusType"=dword:5
   "InterruptNumber"=dword:0f
   "IoBaseAddress"=dword:0f8e0
   "Transceiver"=dword:3
   "CardType"=dword:1

[HKEY_LOCAL_MACHINE\Comm\NE20001\Parms\TcpIp]
   "EnableDHCP"=dword:1
   ; This should be MULTI_SZ
   "DefaultGateway"=""
   ; Use zero for broadcast address? (or 255.255.255.255)
   "UseZeroBroadcast"=dword:0
   ; Thus should be MULTI_SZ, the IP address list
   "IpAddress"="0.0.0.0"
   ; This should be MULTI_SZ, the subnet masks for the above IP addresses
   "Subnetmask"="0.0.0.0"

[HKEY_LOCAL_MACHINE\Comm\Tcpip\Linkage]
   ; This should be MULTI_SZ
   ; This is the list of llip drivers to load
    "Bind"=multi_sz:"ppp","ne20001"
ENDIF
```

```
IF ODO_NOAUDIO !
[HKEY_LOCAL_MACHINE\Drivers\BuiltIn\WaveDev\]
    "Prefix"="WAV"
    "Dll"="wavedev.dll"
    "Index"=dword:1
    "Order"=dword:0
    "Irq"=dword:0a
    "Dma"=dword:5
    "IoBase"=dword:220
ENDIF

IF ODO_NOSERIAL !
[HKEY_LOCAL_MACHINE\Drivers\BuiltIn\Serial]
    "Irq"=dword:03
    "IoBase"=dword:02F8
    "IoLen"=dword:8

IF IMGCOM2
[HKEY_LOCAL_MACHINE\Drivers\BuiltIn\Serial2]
    "Irq"=dword:04
    "IoBase"=dword:03E8
    "IoLen"=dword:8
    "Tsp"="Unimodem.dll"
    "DeviceArrayIndex"=dword:1
    "Prefix"="COM"
    "Dll"="Serial.Dll"
    "Order"=dword:0
    "DeviceType"=dword:0
    "FriendlyName"=LOC_FRIENDLYNAME_SERIAL2
    "DevConfig"=hex: 10,00, 00,00, 05,00,00,00, 10,01,00,00, 00,4B,00,00,
00,00, 08, 00, 00, 00,00,00,00
ENDIF

IF IMGCOM3
[HKEY_LOCAL_MACHINE\Drivers\BuiltIn\Serial3]
    "Irq"=dword:05
    "IoBase"=dword:02E8
    "IoLen"=dword:8
    "Tsp"="Unimodem.dll"
    "DeviceArrayIndex"=dword:2
    "Prefix"="COM"
    "Dll"="Serial.Dll"
    "Order"=dword:0
    "DeviceType"=dword:0
    "FriendlyName"=LOC_FRIENDLYNAME_SERIAL3
    "DevConfig"=hex: 10,00, 00,00, 05,00,00,00, 10,01,00,00, 00,4B,00,00,
00,00, 08, 00, 00, 00,00,00,00
ENDIF

ENDIF

IF ODO_NOIRDA !
IF IMGNOSIR !
```

```
IF IMGNSCFIR !
[HKEY_LOCAL_MACHINE\Comm\IrDA\Linkage]
    "Bind"=multi_sz:"Irsir1"

[HKEY_LOCAL_MACHINE\Comm\Irsir]
   "DisplayName"=LOC_DISPLAYNAME_IRSIR
   "Group"="NDIS"
   "ImagePath"="irsir.dll"

[HKEY_LOCAL_MACHINE\Comm\Irsir\Linkage]
   "Route"=multi_sz:"Irsir1"

[HKEY_LOCAL_MACHINE\Comm\Irsir1\Parms]
   "BusNumber"=dword:0
   "BusType"=dword:0
   "Port"=dword:1
   ; 0 = Use external dongle, 1 = Use internal IR
   "IntIR"=dword:0
   ; 0 = Internal transceiver, 1 = Extended Systems JetEye dongle
   "TransceiverType"=dword:1
ENDIF
ENDIF

IF IMGNSCFIR
[HKEY_LOCAL_MACHINE\Comm\IrDA\Linkage]
   "Bind"=multi_sz:"NscIrda1"

[HKEY_LOCAL_MACHINE\Comm\NscIrda]
   "DisplayName"=LOC_DISPLAYNAME_NSCIRDA
   "Group"="NDIS"
   "ImagePath"="nscirda.dll"

[HKEY_LOCAL_MACHINE\Comm\NscIrda\Linkage]
   "Route"=multi_sz:"NscIrda1"

[HKEY_LOCAL_MACHINE\Comm\NscIrda1\Parms]
;  Supported BoardType:
;       PC87108: 0x0
;       PC87308: 0x1
;       PC87338: 0x2
;       PC87560: Not supported
   "BoardType"=dword:2

;  Supported DongleType:
;       HP:      0
;       TEMIC:   1
;       SHARP:   2
;       DELL:    3
;       PNPDONG: 4
   "DongleType"=dword:1

   "BusNumber"=dword:0
   "BusType"=dword:1
   "ConfigBase"=dword:398
```

```
    "IoBase"=dword:2e8
    "Irq"=dword:5
    "Dma"=dword:3
ENDIF
ENDIF

IF IMGUSB
; USB - OHCI driver
[HKEY_LOCAL_MACHINE\Drivers\BuiltIn\OHCI]
    "Prefix"="HCD"
    "Dll"="ohci.dll"
    "Index"=dword:1
    "Order"=dword:1
    ; Resource config information.  We don't have routines to modify
    ; PCI (Peripheral Component Interconnect) IRQ and memory base,
    ; so we specify two different config modes - if UseExistingSettings
    ; is nonzero, accept whatever resources were assigned
    ; by the BIOS, and fill in the Irq and MemBase fields dynamically.
    ; Otherwise, check settings and fail driver load if IRQ doesn't match the
    ; registry value.
IF CEPC_USB_USE_EXISTING
    "UseExistingSettings"=dword:1
ENDIF
IF CEPC_USB_USE_EXISTING !
    "UseExistingSettings"=dword:0
ENDIF
    "Irq"=dword:0F
    "MemBase"=dword:FFBFE000

; USB - mouse driver
[HKEY_LOCAL_MACHINE\Drivers\USB\LoadClients\Default\Default\3_1_2\Generic_Samp
le_Mouse_Driver]
    "DLL"="USBMOUSE.dll"

; USB - mouse driver
[HKEY_LOCAL_MACHINE\Drivers\USB\ClientDrivers\Generic_Sample_Mouse_Driver]

ENDIF

IF CEPC_PARALLEL
; Parallel port driver
[HKEY_LOCAL_MACHINE\Drivers\BuiltIn\Parallel]
    "DeviceArrayIndex"=dword:0
    "Prefix"="LPT"
    "Dll"="Parallel.Dll"
    "Order"=dword:0
    "IoBase"=dword:278
    "IoLen"=dword:C
    "DeviceType"=dword:0
    "FriendlyName"=LOC_FRIENDLYNAME_PARALLEL
    "DevConfig"=hex: 10,00, 00,00, 05,00,00,00, 10,01,00,00, 00,4B,00,00,
00,00, 08, 00, 00, 00,00,00,00
ENDIF
```

```
; Mouse driver
[HKEY_LOCAL_MACHINE\HARDWARE\DEVICEMAP\MOUSE]
        "DriverName"="kbdmouse.dll"

IF ODO_NOKEYBD !
; Keyboard driver is the same
[HKEY_LOCAL_MACHINE\HARDWARE\DEVICEMAP\KEYBD]
        "DriverName"="kbdmouse.dll"
        "CalVKey"=dword:0
        "ContLessVKey"=dword:0
        "ContMoreVKey"=dword:0
        "TaskManVKey"=dword:2E
ENDIF

; For CEPC, we don't support Suspend, so don't let it happen
[HKEY_LOCAL_MACHINE\SYSTEM\CurrentControlSet\Control\Power]
"BattPowerOff"=dword:0
"ExtPowerOff"=dword:0

IF CEPC_DISKONCHIP
[HKEY_LOCAL_MACHINE\Drivers\BuiltIn\TrueFFS]
   "Index"=dword:1
   "Dll"="TrueFFS.dll"
   "Prefix"="DSK"
   "Order"=dword:1
   "Ioctl"=dword:4
   "FSD"="FATFS.DLL"
   "WindowBase"=dword:D0000
ENDIF

IF CEPC_SERMOUSE
[HKEY_LOCAL_MACHINE\Drivers\BuiltIn\SerMouse]
   "Index"=dword:1
   "Dll"="SerMouse.dll"
    "Prefix"="SRM"
   "Order"=dword:1
   "Port"=dword:1
ENDIF

IF IMGNOCTLPNL !
; This setting converts the Stylus CPL applet into a Mouse CPL applet.
; Remove it if you have a touch screen instead of a Mouse
[HKEY_LOCAL_MACHINE\ControlPanel]
        "IsMouse"=dword:1
ENDIF
```

Listing 11.10 Platform-independent registry file for Brewster (`project.reg`)

```
;;; Add a test printer ;;;;;;;;;;;;

; Settings for 'MaxAll Test Color Printer'
[HKEY_LOCAL_MACHINE\Printers\MaxAll Test Color Printer]
    "Driver"="pcl.dll"
    "High Quality"="300"
    "Draft Quality"="75"
    "Color"="Color"

[HKEY_LOCAL_MACHINE\Ident]
    "Name"=LOC_IDENT_NAME
    "Desc"=LOC_IDENT_DESC

[HKEY_LOCAL_MACHINE\Drivers\BuiltIn\Serial]
   "Tsp"="Unimodem.dll"
   "DeviceArrayIndex"=dword:0
  "Prefix"="COM"
   "Dll"="Serial.Dll"
   "Order"=dword:0
   "DeviceType"=dword:0
   "FriendlyName"=LOC_FRIENDLY_SERIAL
   "DevConfig"=hex: 10,00, 00,00, 05,00,00,00, 10,01,00,00, 00,4B,00,00,
00,00, 08, 00, 00, 00,00,00,00

[HKEY_LOCAL_MACHINE\Drivers\BuiltIn\IrCOMM]
   "Tsp"="Unimodem.dll"
   "Dll"="IRCOMM.DLL"
   "Prefix"="COM"
   "Order"=dword:1
   "Index"=dword:3
   "DeviceType"=dword:6
   "FriendlyName"=LOC_FRIENDLY_IRCOMM
   "DevConfig"=hex: 10,00, 00,00, 02,00,00,00, 10,01,00,00, 00,4B,00,00,
00,00, 08, 00, 00, 00,00,00,00

; Default display driver
[HKEY_LOCAL_MACHINE\HARDWARE\DEVICEMAP\TOUCH]
IF _TGTPLAT=PC !
IF _TGTPLAT=CEPC !
IF _TGTPLAT=PUZZLE !
"DriverName"="touch.dll"
ENDIF
ENDIF
ENDIF
IF _TGTPLAT=PC
"DriverName"="keybddr.dll"
ENDIF
IF _TGTPLAT=PUZZLE
"DriverName"="keybddr.dll"
ENDIF
IF _TGTPLAT=CEPC
"DriverName"="keybddr.dll"
ENDIF
```

```
; Redirector settings
[HKEY_LOCAL_MACHINE\Comm\Redir]
   ; Expose \NETWORK dir for mapped resources
   "RegisterFSRoot"=dword:1

;
; Audio Compression Manager (ACM) drivers
;
[HKEY_LOCAL_MACHINE\Drivers\BuiltIn\CODEC_CEGSM]
   "Prefix"="ACM"
   "Dll"="cegsm.dll"
   "Index"=dword:1
   "Order"=dword:0

[HKEY_LOCAL_MACHINE\Drivers\BuiltIn\FILTER]
   "Prefix"="ACM"
   "Dll"="msfilter.dll"
   "Index"=dword:2
   "Order"=dword:0

; Set memory thresholds for Hibernate
[HKEY_LOCAL_MACHINE\SYSTEM\Hibernate]
        "Bytes"=dword:20000
        "Pages"=dword:28

;
; Font linking and end user-defined characters (EUDCs)
;
IF COUNTRY=USA

[HKEY_LOCAL_MACHINE\SOFTWARE\Microsoft\FontLink\SystemLink]
          "Arial"="\\Windows\\msgothic.ttc,MS PGothic"
 "Microsoft Logo"="\\Windows\\msgothic.ttc,MS PGothic"
"Times New Roman"="\\Windows\\msgothic.ttc,MS Gothic"
         "Tahoma"="\\Windows\\msgothic.ttc,MS PGothic"
    "Courier New"="\\Windows\\msgothic.ttc,MS PGothic"
         "Symbol"="\\Windows\\msgothic.ttc,MS Gothic"
        "Kino MT"="\\Windows\\msgothic.ttc,MS Gothic"

[HKEY_LOCAL_MACHINE\SOFTWARE\Microsoft\FontLink\SkipTable]
        "Tahoma"="005c,00a5,007e,0391-03c9,2026,2116,221a,25a0-25ff"

[HKEY_CURRENT_USER\EUDC]
"SystemDefaultEUDCFont"="\\Windows\\eudc.tte"
"Times New Roman"="\\Windows\\test01.tte"
"Tahoma"="\\Windows\\test03.tte"
"Arial"="\\Windows\\test02.tte"
"Impact"="\\Windows\\test02.tte"
"Courier New"="\\Windows\\test03.tte"
"Microsoft Logo"="\\Windows\\test03.tte"
"Symbol"="\\Windows\\test03.tte"

"MS PGothic"="\\Windows\\test03.tte"
"MS Gothic"="\\Windows\\test01.tte"
```

```
ENDIF COUNTRY=USA

IF COUNTRY=JAPAN
[HKEY_LOCAL_MACHINE\SOFTWARE\Microsoft\FontLink\SystemLink]
          "Arial"="\\Windows\\msgothic.ttc,,l,r ,ofSfVfbfN"
 "Microsoft Logo"="\\Windows\\dfgoteb.ttc,,c,e,o"Á'_fSfVfbfN'Ì"
"Times New Roman"="\\Windows\\msgothic.ttc,,l,r fSfVfbfN"
         "Tahoma"="\\Windows\\msgothic.ttc,,l,r ,ofSfVfbfN"
    "Courier New"="\\Windows\\msgothic.ttc,,l,r fSfVfbfN"
         "Symbol"="\\Windows\\dfgoteb.ttc,,c,e"Á'_fSfVfbfN'Ì"
        "Kino MT"="\\Windows\\dfgoteb.ttc,,c,e,o"Á'_fSfVfbfN'Ì"

[HKEY_LOCAL_MACHINE\SOFTWARE\Microsoft\FontLink\SkipTable]
        "Tahoma"="005c,00a5,007e,0391-03c9,2026,2116,221a,25a0-25ff"

[HKEY_CURRENT_USER\EUDC]
"SystemDefaultEUDCFont"="\\Windows\\eudc.tte"
"Times New Roman"="\\Windows\\test01.tte"
"Tahoma"="\\Windows\\test03.tte"
"Arial"="\\Windows\\test02.tte"
"Impact"="\\Windows\\test02.tte"
"Courier New"="\\Windows\\test03.tte"
"Microsoft Logo"="\\Windows\\test03.tte"
"Symbol"="\\Windows\\test03.tte"

",l,r ,ofSfVfbfN"="\\Windows\\test03.tte"
",l,r fSfVfbfN"="\\Windows\\test01.tte"

",c,e,o"Á'_fSfVfbfN'Ì"="\\Windows\\eudc.tte"
",c,e"Á'_fSfVfbfN'Ì"="\\Windows\\test03.tte"

",c,e,oPOP'Ì"="\\Windows\\eudc.tte"
",c,ePOP'Ì"="\\Windows\\test03.tte"
ENDIF COUNTRY=JAPAN

; SIP
[HKEY_LOCAL_MACHINE\Drivers\BuiltIn\SIP]
"Prefix"="SIP"
"Dll"="softkb.DLL"
"Order"=dword:1
"Index"=dword:0

IF TESTSIP
; SIP Input Method values
[HKEY_CURRENT_USER\ControlPanel\Sip]
"AllowChange"=dword:1
"DefaultIm"="{42429667-ae04-11d0-a4f8-00aa00a749b9}"
"DragStyle"=dword:1

; Default keyboard initial delay and autorepeat
[HKEY_CURRENT_USER\ControlPanel\Keybd]
"InitialDelay"=dword:177
"RepeatRate"=dword:8
```

```
[HKEY_CLASSES_ROOT\CLSID\{42429667-ae04-11d0-a4f8-00aa00a749b9}]
@=LOC_KEYBOARD
"KBMode"=dword:5
[HKEY_CLASSES_ROOT\CLSID\{42429667-ae04-11d0-a4f8-
00aa00a749b9}\InprocServer32]
@="\\windows\\msim.dll"
[HKEY_CLASSES_ROOT\CLSID\{42429667-ae04-11d0-a4f8-
00aa00a749b9}\IsSIPInputMethod]
@="1"
[HKEY_CLASSES_ROOT\CLSID\{42429667-ae04-11d0-a4f8-00aa00a749b9}\DefaultIcon]
@="\\windows\\msim.dll,0"

ENDIF   TESTSIP

IF COUNTRY=JAPAN
[HKEY_CURRENT_USER\Control Panel\Input Method\Hot Keys\00000030]
        "VK"=dword:19
        "KM"=dword:C001
        "Ime"=dword:e0010411

[HKEY_CURRENT_USER\Keyboard Layout\Preload\1]
        @="e0010411"

IF TESTTIME=TESTTIME
[HKEY_LOCAL_MACHINE\System\CurrentControlSet\Control\Layouts\e0010411]
        "Layout Text"="KBD e0010411"
        "Ime File"="testtime.dll"
ENDIF
ENDIF
```

Data files

Data (DAT) files map out the RAM area known as storage memory. DAT file directives set up a directory layout and copy files from ROM into the RAM area. For Brewster, we set up a couple of directories for the few sample applications that are part of the sample project. First, a directory called `PROGRAM FILES` is created (see Listing 11.11).

We use an environment variable to establish a conditional that will fire only if we have chosen to include the SDK samples in the image. A directory called `INPUT METHOD EDITOR` is created under `\PROGRAM FILES`, and two executables are copied from ROM into these directories laid out in RAM. `Msim.exe` is copied into RAM and renamed to `INPUT METHOD SAMPLE`, and `testtime.exe` is copied and renamed to `TEST TIME`. The DAT file performs similar functions to copy communication applications if they were included in the image.

Listing 11.11 RAM initialization file for Brewster (`project.dat`)

```
root:-Directory("Program Files")

IF IMG_IMESAMPLE
Directory("\Program Files"):-Directory("Input Method Editor")
Directory("\Input Method Editor"):-File("Input Method Sample",
"\Windows\msim.exe")
```

```
Directory("\Input Method Editor"):-File("Test Time", "\Windows\Testtime.exe")
ENDIF

IF IMG_COMMAPPS
Directory("\Program Files"):-Directory("Comm Apps")
Directory("\Comm Apps"):-File("Terminal", "\Windows\pegterm.exe")
Directory("\Comm Apps"):-File("Terminal Control", "\Windows\termctrl.exe")
Directory("\Comm Apps"):-File("Remote Networking", "\Windows\remnet.exe")
ENDIF
```

Database files

Database (DB) files are used to construct the database on initialization. Brewster requires a small database that contains instructions for roasting and grinding different blends. The Roasts database contains records with two fields: the name of the roast and an internal ID that identifies the temperature at which the beans must roast. The Grinds database contains records that have two fields: the type of grind and an internal setting that identifies the granularity of the ground beans. The information from these two databases is used to set up the Blends database, with records that contain roast and grind information (Listing 11.12).

Listing 11.12 Database initialization file for Brewster (`project.db`)

```
Database: "\\Roasts" : 800 : 1 : 440100000 : 0
    Record :
    Field : 440010000 : "Extra Light"
    Field : 440100000 : 1
    End
    Record :
    Field : 440010000 : "Light"
    Field : 440100000 : 2
    End
    Record :
    Field : 440010000 : "Medium"
    Field : 440100000 : 3
    End
    Record :
    Field : 440010000 : "Medium Dark"
    Field : 440100000 : 4
    End
    Record :
    Field : 440010000 : "Full Body"
    Field : 440100000 : 5
    End
    Record :
    Field : 440010000 : "Dark"
    Field : 440100000 : 6
    End
    Record :
    Field : 440010000 : "Extra Dark"
    Field : 440100000 : 7
    End
```

```
    Record :
    Field : 440010000 : "French"
    Field : 440100000 : 8
    End
    Record :
    Field : 440010000 : "Italian"
    Field : 440100000 : 9
    End
End Database

Database: "\\Grinds" : 810 : 1 : 440a00000 : 0
    Record :
    Field : 4400a0000 : "Rocky"
    Field : 440a00000 : 1
    End
    Record :
    Field : 4400a0000 : "Coarse"
    Field : 440a00000 : 2
    End
    Record :
    Field : 4400a0000 : "Granular"
    Field : 440a00000 : 3
    End
    Record :
    Field : 4400a0000 : "Smooth"
    Field : 440a00000 : 4
    End
    Record :
    Field : 4400a0000 : "Fine"
    Field : 440a00000 : 5
    End
End Database

Database: "\\Blends" : 820 : 1 : 440b00000 : 0
    Record :
    Field : 4400b0000 : "Light"
    Field : 4400a0000 : "Smooth"
    Field : 440010000 : "Breakfast"
    End
    Record :
    Field : 4400b0000 : "Dark"
    Field : 4400a0000 : "Smooth"
    Field : 440010000 : "Vienna"
    End
    Record :
    Field : 4400b0000 : "Extra Dark"
    Field : 4400a0000 : "Coarse"
    Field : 440010000 : "Dark Swirl"
    End
    Record :
    Field : 4400b0000 : "French"
    Field : 4400a0000 : "Fine"
    Field : 440010000 : "Baroda"
    End
End Database
```

Adding Source Code to Brewster

Once the directory tree for Brewster has been established and a few successful runs of the build have been performed, the build can be uploaded to a CEPC. When Brewster is running on a CEPC, you can begin prototyping some of the software that will run on the target. The obvious choice for prototyping is application software. However, as discussed in Chapter 2, you can really leverage the CEPC platform by prototyping device drivers.

The directories that are part of the Brewster project are show in Table 11.6.

Table 11.6 Brewster Directories

Directory	Contents
`C:\WINCE\PLATFORM\CEPC\DRIVERS`	Device drivers
`C:\WINCE\PLATFORM\CEPC\DRIVERS\DISPLAY\`	Display drivers
`C:\WINCE\PLATFORM\CEPC\DRIVERS\MOUSE\`	Mouse drivers
`C:\WINCE\PLATFORM\CEPC\DRIVERS\USB`	USB drivers
`C:\WINCE\PLATFORM\CEPC\DRIVERS\IRMAC`	IrDA drivers
`C:\WINCE\PLATFORM\CEPC\DRIVERS\NETCARD`	Network drivers
`C:\WINCE\PLATFORM\CEPC\DRIVERS\CEDDK\DDK_BUS`	Platform-specific code to perform bus I/O
`C:\WINCE\PLATFORM\CEPC\DRIVERS\CEDDK\DDK_MAP`	Platform-specific code to map memory
`C:\WINCE\PLATFORM\CEPC\FILES\platform.reg`	Platform-specific registry entries
`C:\WINCE\PLATFORM\CEPC\FILES\platform.db`	Platform-specific data in database
`C:\WINCE\PLATFORM\CEPC\FILES\platform.dat`	Platform-specific RAM data
`C:\WINCE\PLATFORM\CEPC\FILES\platform.loc`	Platform-specific modules to localize
`C:\WINCE\PLATFORM\CEPC\INC`	Common platform-specific include files
`C:\WINCE\PLATFORM\CEPC\GWES\BATTERY`	Battery driver (GWES component)
`C:\WINCE\PLATFORM\CEPC\GWES\NLEDDRV`	Notification LED driver (GWES component)
`C:\WINCE\PLATFORM\CEPC\KERNEL\HAL`	Hardware Abstraction Layer (HAL)
`C:\WINCE\PLATFORM\CEPC\KERNEL\HAL\X86`	HAL processor-specific code
`C:\WINCE\PLATFORM\CEPC\KERNEL\PROFILER`	Kernel-profiling code
`C:\WINCE\PLATFORM\CEPC\KERNEL\PROFILER\X86`	Processor-specific code required for profiling
`C:\WINCE\PUBLIC\BREWSTER\OAK\FILES\v.reg`	Project-specific registry entries
`C:\WINCE\PUBLIC\BREWSTER\OAK\FILES\project.db`	Project-specific data in database
`C:\WINCE\PUBLIC\BREWSTER\OAK\FILES\project.dat`	Project-specific RAM data
`C:\WINCE\PUBLIC\BREWSTER\OAK\FILES\`	System files like bitmaps, fonts, sounds, and so on
`C:\WINCE\PUBLIC\BREWSTER\OAK\MISC\cesysgen.bat`	Modules and components to include in CE
`C:\WINCE\PUBLIC\BREWSTER\OAK\SRC\`	Platform-independent code (applications)
`C:\WINCE\PUBLIC\BREWSTER\`	Makefiles to build project

The locations of these directories can be changed along with their relative positions in the directory trees. You will have to make corresponding changes to the build environment variables defined by `wince.bat`. If you change your structure at a deeper level—for example, if you change the directories where your intermediate files are collected—you will need to make corresponding modifications to the batch file utilities used to build CE.

Once the target hardware becomes available, the CEPC platform must be discarded and a new CE platform must be created for your hardware. We call our new platform Kafe and allocate the directory `_WINCEROOT\PLATFORM\KAFE` for its contents. Assume for the purpose of illustration that Kafe uses a Motorola MPC821 processor. Adjustments must be made to the build environment variables that track the platform being built. We make these adjustments by changing the platform parameter to `wince.bat`:

```
Wince.bat PPC PPC821 CE Kafe Brewster
```

Run the `set` command to make sure that your environment variables have been set up correctly. The makefiles discussed in this chapter are project and platform independent. Thus, all you need to build your new target is to invoke Nmake from the command prompt.

Summary

Our sample project illustrates all the salient aspects of the build process that need to be performed to create a custom version of Windows CE. A set of makefiles was shown to simplify and standardize the various steps in the build. The makefiles can be extended to other Windows CE projects.

12

Device Driver Test Kit

Support for automated testing is available in the Windows CE Tools suite in the form of the Device Driver Test Kit (DDTK). The DDTK contains tools that allow tests to run in an orderly repeatable fashion and provides extensible logging facilities to deliver status to a variety of output devices. We will look at these tools in detail in this chapter.

Note that the automated test tools do not provide support for manipulating user elements such as buttons, menus, fields, and so on. For this reason, the test kit is restricted to testing device drivers and their internal operation. However, nothing fundamentally prevents the DDTK from being used for other purposes. For example, you may want to test memory allocation or GDI operations, or you may want to write a test to stress window creation. Your tests do not have to be restricted to device drivers.

The tools that facilitate automated testing on CE are called Tux and Kato. Tux (which we encountered briefly in Chapter 2) is a client-server application that can be used to select and launch tests. Kato (also introduced in Chapter 2) is a tool that can be used to log test results to a variety of output media, but we'll talk more about that later.

The Tux server can be used to view and select the tests available on a target device being tested, a device that runs Windows CE. A Tux server typically runs on a Windows NT workstation, whereas the Tux client, which organizes the tests on the target machine, is a CE application. Tests are identified by a label and can be organized hierarchically like the directory structure in a file system. This hierarchy is used to group tests by functionality and eases the selection process, in which functionality must take precedence over an individual test.

The Tux server provides a graphical user interface that allows a user to manipulate the list of tests and select the ones that will run. The Tux server simply exchanges this information with the Tux client, which does all the work of communicating with the test harnesses on the target device. Because the Tux client, a console application, forms the heart of the automated testing system, we'll refer to it simply as Tux.

DDTK Tools

Figure 12.1 shows a block diagram of the automated test tools. Tux, the Tux application (or test harness), the device driver being tested, and the Kato client all run on the target CE device. Tux calls into the test harness for each test. The device driver carries out the requests required to perform the test. Results and traces are passed on to the logging client, Kato, by the test harness. Results are returned to Tux.

Tux, in turn, communicates with the Tux server, which runs typically on an NT workstation. Tux carries out requests to run specific tests from the server. The Kato server is an application produced by the user that provides trace logging. Traces can be logged to a variety of devices: a text file, a device on the network, even a paging service. By allowing the user to produce the Kato server, the logging mechanism becomes very extensible.

The important point to note here is that the server components are entirely optional. Tux can be run as a stand-alone application to execute tests on the target device, and the logging feature can be bypassed if the end result of each test is all that the user is interested in obtaining.

Tux Test Harness

A Tux test harness is simply a Windows DLL that registers with Tux and responds to its requests. The harness must be a DLL because Tux expects to load it using the Windows

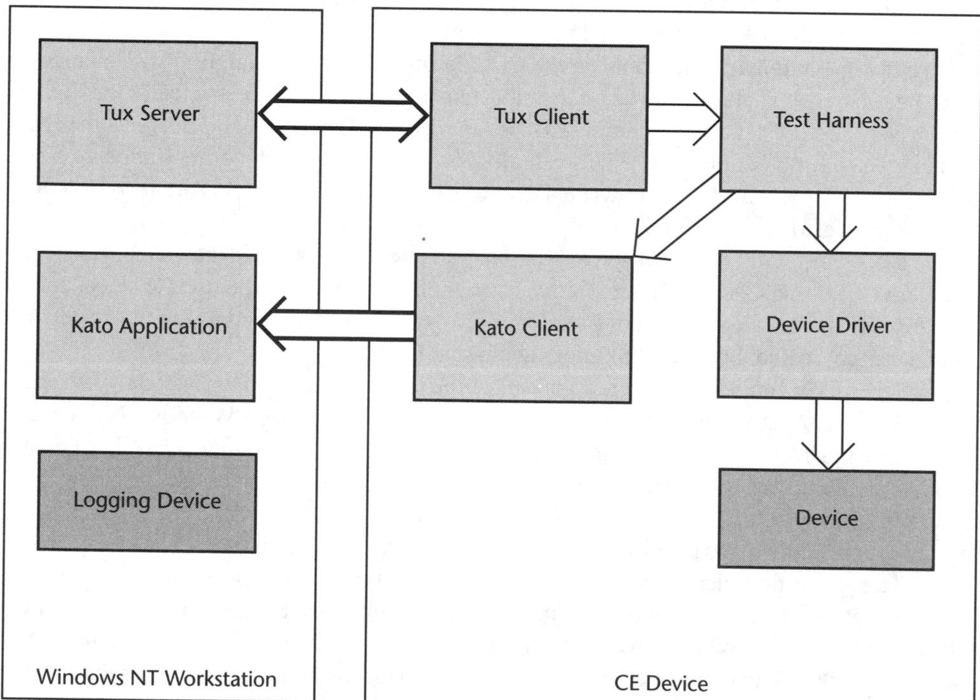

Figure 12.1 DDTK automated test tools

LoadLibrary call. The idea behind loading a DLL is that device drivers under Windows CE run in user mode and are usually DLLs. Thus, the device driver can support automated testing by registering as a Tux test harness. If the additional code is not acceptable in the retail version of the driver, a separate test harness can provide automated testing functionality by calling the device driver when necessary. The test harnesses can then be bundled into a special version of the CE build that can be utilized during testing. Care must be taken to ensure that the test harness does not enhance the functionality of the device driver. It should simply act as a test interface. If you follow this guideline, you can remove the test harness from the build without significantly altering the retail content of the build. After testing is complete, the retail version of the build can be stripped of its test harnesses, leaving behind fully tested device drivers.

Tux, Kato, and related components are available in the Device Driver Test Kit.

CE Version Memo

In Windows CE 2.0, 2.10, and 2.11, the DDTK is available as a separate downloadable ZIP file available from the Microsoft Windows CE Web site. The ZIP file can simply be uncompressed in the root directory of the Platform Builder (or ETK) installation.

In Windows CE 2.12, DDTK is available as a separate ZIP file on the Platform Builder CD. The ZIP file must be uncompressed in the root directory of the Platform Builder installation.

In this chapter we will use a Tux demo program that ships with Platform Builder. This program, called Tuxdemo, is located in the DEMO subdirectory of the DDTK root directory.

Test Scripts

This is a pertinent time to introduce the notion of what Tux calls test scripts. Tests can be selected to run either manually or via a command file. The set of tests selected to run is called a run list. A run list of tests is also referred to as a script. A **Tux script** is thus a set of tests that will be executed on the target. Scripts may contain groups of tests or individual tests. A group contains tests of related functionality. Groups are specified by the test harness. Scripts are specified by Tux via run lists that are passed from the Tux server or are constructed by the Tux client's user interface.

Test Discovery

Tux discovers tests contained in the test harness via a table of information that is passed between the two modules. Before this table can be exchanged, Tux and the test harness establish a partnership. Tux loads the test harness DLL and uses the module handle of the DLL to send it a message. This message, SPM_REGISTER, *must* be handled by the test harness. If a test harness accepts the offer to register from Tux, thus establishing a partnership, it returns the code SPR_HANDLED. During the handling of the message, the test harness also passes the table of information to Tux.

The function table is expressed as a structure in the file tux.h, which is included by every test harness. The members of the structure FUNCTION_TABLE_ENTRY (Listing 12.1) are used to provide information to Tux about a specific test contained in the test harness. The values expressed by the members are listed in Table 12.1.

Listing 12.1 Definition of FUNCTION_TABLE_ENTRY

```
typedef struct _FUNCTION_TABLE_ENTRY
{
    LPCTSTR  lpDescription;
    UINT     uDepth;
    DWORD    dwUserData;
    DWORD    dwUniqueID;
    TESTPROC lpTestProc;
} FUNCTION_TABLE_ENTRY, *LPFUNCTION_TABLE_ENTRY;
```

Table 12.1 Members of the FUNCTION_TABLE_ENTRY Structure

Member	Description
lpDescription	A string label that describes the test
uDepth	The depth in a tree hierarchy of tests
dwUserData	Any data that the test harness would like to receive when this particular test is called
dwUniqueID	Unique ID for this test
ipTestProc	A pointer to a function that is the test procedure

The test harness typically creates an array of FUNCTION_TABLE_ENTRY. Each array entry describes a test contained in the harness. The tests can be organized in a hierarchy, which can be used to group tests during selection. We set up the hierarchy by setting a value corresponding to the level within the hierarchy of each test in the member uDepth. The root level corresponds to the value 0. A value of 1 would indicate a test that is nested once in the hierarchy and is a level below the root. The array is terminated by NULL values for all members of the FUNCTION_TABLE_ENTRY structure.

This array is passed to Tux during the handling of the SPM_REGISTER message. To see how the array is passed, we must first take a quick look at the function used to send messages to the test harness.

Passing Information to the Test Harness

The test harness exports a single call, ShellProc. After loading the test harness, Tux grabs the address of this procedure from the test harness by calling GetProcAddress. ShellProc is used to send messages from Tux to the harness. The prototype for the ShellProc function is shown here:

```
#define SHELLPROCAPI INT __declspec(dllexport) WINAPI
typedef LPARAM  SPPARAM;
SHELLPROCAPI ShellProc(UINT uMessage, SPPARAM spParam)
```

The uMessage parameter passes the SPM_REGISTER message. ShellProc switches on the value of uMessage to interpret each message. The argument spParam is overloaded for each message type to pass a pointer to a context-specific structure with each message. The context-specific structure contains values that are relevant in the context of the message being processed. In the case of the SPM_REGISTER message, spParam contains a pointer to a structure of type SPS_REGISTER:

```
typedef struct _SPS_REGISTER
{
   LPFUNCTION_TABLE_ENTRY lpFunctionTable;
} SPS_REGISTER, *LPSPS_REGISTER;
```

The structure contains a single member, a pointer to one or an array of FUNCTION_TABLE_ENTRY structures. This pointer must be initialized to the function table. The test harness must allocate and manage the memory associated with this pointer. On most occasions, the test harness maintains a function table and simply initializes this pointer to the location of the table. This technique is illustrated in Listing 12.2.

Listing 12.2 Passing function information to Tux

```
#define BASE 0x00010000

// The function table that we pass to Tux
static FUNCTION_TABLE_ENTRY g_lpFTE[] = {
   TEXT("Memory Allocation Tests"          ), 0,   0,            0, NULL,
   TEXT(   "new/delete (0 Threads)"        ), 1,   0,      BASE+  1, NewDeleteTest,
   TEXT(   "new/delete (1 Thread)"         ), 1,   1,      BASE+  2, NewDeleteTest,
   TEXT(   "new/delete (100 Threads)"      ), 1, 100,      BASE+  3, NewDeleteTest,
   TEXT("Device Context Tests"             ), 0,   0,            0, NULL,
   TEXT(   "GetDC/ReleaseDC (0 Threads)"   ), 1,   0,      BASE+ 10,
GetDCReleaseDCTest,
   TEXT(   "GetDC/ReleaseDC (1 Thread)"    ), 1,   1,      BASE+ 11,
GetDCReleaseDCTest,
   TEXT(   "GetDC/ReleaseDC (100 Threads)" ), 1, 100,      BASE+ 12,
GetDCReleaseDCTest,
   TEXT("Semaphore Tests"                  ), 0,   0,            0, NULL,
   TEXT(   "Producer/Consumer (2 Threads)" ), 1,   2,      BASE+ 20,
ProducerConsumerTest,
   TEXT(   "Producer/Consumer (100 Threads)"), 1, 100,     BASE+ 21,
ProducerConsumerTest,
   TEXT("Window Tests"                     ), 0,   0,            0, NULL
   TEXT(   "Window Test (1 Thread)"        ), 1,   1,      BASE+ 30, WindowTest,
   TEXT(   "Window Test (25 Threads)"      ), 1,  25,      BASE+ 31, WindowTest,
   TEXT("Process Tests"                    ), 0,   0,            0, NULL,
   TEXT(   "Process Test (1 Thread)"       ), 1,   1,      BASE+ 40, ProcessTest,
   TEXT(   "Process Test (25 Threads)"     ), 1,  25,      BASE+ 41, ProcessTest,
```

```
    TEXT("Exception Handling"                    ), 0,   0,               0, NULL,
    TEXT(    "Access Violation"                  ), 1,   0,          BASE+ 50,
AccessViolationTest,
    TEXT("Possible Results"                      ), 0,   0,               0, NULL,
    TEXT(    "Pass"                              ), 1, TPR_PASS,    BASE+ 60, ResultTest,
    TEXT(    "Fail"                              ), 1, TPR_FAIL,    BASE+ 61, ResultTest,
    TEXT(    "Skip"                              ), 1, TPR_SKIP,    BASE+ 62, ResultTest,
    TEXT(    "Abort"                             ), 1, TPR_ABORT,   BASE+ 63, ResultTest,
    NULL,                                           0,   0,               0, NULL   // marks
end of list
};
SHELLPROCAPI ShellProc(UINT uMsg, SPPARAM spParam) {
        switch (uMsg) {
        . . .
        case SPM_REGISTER: {
                Debug(TEXT("ShellProc(SPM_REGISTER, ...) called"));
                ((LPSPS_REGISTER)spParam)->lpFunctionTable = g_lpFTE;
                 return SPR_HANDLED | SPF_UNICODE;
       }
       . . .
       }
}
```

In Listing 12.2, an array of function table entries is set up in `functionInfoTable`. Entries in the table correspond to individual tests, except for entries that are used to describe a group. Recall that the `FUNCTION_TABLE_ENTRY` member `uDepth` is used to indicate the depth of the entry in a tree hierarchy. A depth of 0 indicates the root level. The entries that constitute the next level immediately follow an entry with a given level. An entry that has entries below it in the tree hierarchy describes a group of tests. A group entry does not contain a function pointer because it does not describe a test, but merely a group of tests. Entries that are at the leaf level of the hierarchy describe tests. Such entries contain a function pointer that is aimed at the test function. Group entries also do not require a unique identifier.

In the listing, memory tests are grouped under the label *Memory Tests.* These tests are further separated into two groups: Allocation and Deletion. The group Allocation contains two tests—one that performs 10 memory allocations (ID 1) and another that performs 100 allocations (ID 2). Both entries point to the same function: `AllocateTest`. `AllocateTest` handles both tests because all that changes is essentially the number of allocations. How does `AllocateTest` know which test to perform? The answer is in the third member of each entry, which is the placeholder for the member `dwUserData` in the `FUNCTION_TABLE_ENTRY` structure. The value held in `dwUserData` is passed to the function held in the function pointer of the entry when the test is invoked by Tux. Note that the number of allocations is equated to `dwUserData` in the memory allocation test entries. The function table is terminated by a `NULL` entry.

When `ShellProc` is called with the message parameter set to `SPM_REGISTER`, the `spParam` argument is set to a pointer to an `SPS_REGISTER` structure. The solitary member of this structure is set to point to `functionInfoTable`, which is allocated statically in the test harness. The value returned from `ShellProc` is a bitmap indicating that the message was handled successfully by the test harness and that its text is in Unicode.

Once the list of functions has been obtained by Tux during registration, Tux is free to call each test in the test harness. The test harness cannot expect a certain sequence in which the tests may be invoked. It is written to accommodate any test being called in random sequence. The order in which tests are invoked depends on the selection made by the user.

The `SPM_REGISTER` message is not the only one sent by Tux to the test harness. Tux needs to communicate with the test harness to start and stop tests. Thus, other housekeeping messages need to be passed to the test harness as well.

Housekeeping Messages

Tux sends the test harness a message to indicate that it has been loaded (`SPM_LOAD_DLL`) and another to indicate that it is about to be unloaded (`SPM_UNLOAD_DLL`). These messages are designed to give the harness an opportunity to perform one-time initialization to prepare for any test functions being called.

Immediately after receiving the `SPM_LOAD_DLL` message, the harness can expect to receive the `SPM_SHELL_INFO` message. This message is used to communicate information about Tux that can be used by the harness for housekeeping.

To execute the tests that have been configured, Tux sends three sets of messages to the harness. Tux looks for a script first. On finding one, it executes the script. The script may have groups of tests. Each group will have one or more individual tests. The three sets of messages correspond to the beginning and end of the execution of a script (`SPM_START_SCRIPT`, `SPM_STOP_SCRIPT`), a group (`SPM_BEGIN_GROUP`, `SPM_END_GROUP`), and an individual test (`SPM_BEGIN_TEST`, `SPM_END_TEST`).

Tux sends the messages merely to allow the test harness to perform housekeeping (Figure 12.2). You can execute the tests directly by using the function pointer to the test passed in the function table.

On occasion, the test code being executed by the harness may cause an exception. Tux traps this exception and notifies the harness, using the `SPM_EXCEPTION` message.

Most messages that Tux sends to the harness are accompanied by a structure specific to that message, as outlined in Table 12.2. A pointer to this structure is passed in the `spParam` argument of `ShellProc`.

We've looked extensively at the interaction between Tux and a test harness. Tux sends messages related to test execution to the `ShellProc` function in the harness so that housekeeping may be performed. The actual process of launching the test is carried out separately by Tux and is more involved than just launching the function pointer in a given function table entry.

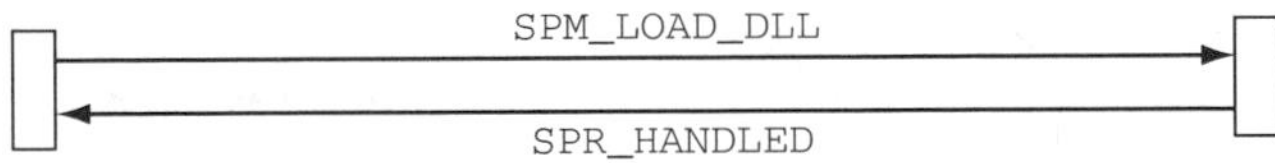

Figure 12.2 Sequence diagram of Tux and the test harness

Table 12.2 Messages Sent by Tux to a Test Harness

Message	Structure	Members	Description
SPM_LOAD_DLL	SPS_LOAD_DLL	BOOL fUnicode	Set to TRUE if the test harness passes information in Unicode strings to Tux.
SPM_SHELL_INFO	SPS_SHELL_INFO	HINSTANCE hInstance	Instance handle of Tux. This handle can be used in calls that require the instance handle of the process to be passed as an argument.
		HWND hWnd	Handle to Tux's window. Always set to NULL.
		HINSTANCE hLib	Instance handle of the test harness as loaded by Tux. This handle can safely be used in calls that require an instance handle to be passed as an argument.
		HANDLE hevmTerminate	Handle to a global event that is interpreted by Tux as a termination event, if signaled. Test harnesses can check for this event during tests, especially if the test is lengthy. If the event is set, the test harness should terminate the ongoing test in the best way possible so that Tux can clean up and terminate. Tux checks this event only after each test has completed.
		BOOL fUsingServer	Set to FALSE if Tux is being run as a stand-alone application (without a server).
		LPCTSTR szDllCmdLine	Command-line string specified by the user when the test harness is loaded. This string must be interpreted by the test harness for commands and options.
SPM_REGISTER	SPS_REGISTER	LPFUNCTION_TABLE_ENTRY lpFunctionTable	Pointer to the list of functions that the test harness can execute.
SPM_START_SCRIPT	None		
SPM_BEGIN_GROUP	None		

Table 12.2 *Continued.*

Message	Structure	Members	Description
SPM_BEGIN_TEST	SPS_BEGIN_TEST	LPFUNCTION_TABLE_ENTRY lpFTE	Pointer to the FUNCTION_TABLE_ENTRY entry in the list of functions that describes the test that is being started.
		DWORD dwRandomSeed	Random seed that is passed to the test harness. If the test being executed uses random numbers, it should use this number to seed its random sequence. If the test produces an error, Tux reports this random seed to the user. The seed can then be used to reproduce the error condition.
		DWORD dwThreadCount	Number of threads in which the test will be executed. A value of 0 causes the test to be run in Tux's process. A value of 1 creates an independent thread in which the test can run. Values greater than 1 create as many threads, each running the test in parallel. This value can be tweaked to uncover thread-specific issues where the test may be vulnerable.
SPM_END_TEST	SPS_END_TEST	LPFUNCTION_TABLE_ENTRY lpFTE	Pointer to the FUNCTION_TABLE_ENTRY entry in the list of functions that describes the test that is being started.
		DWORD dwResult	Result code for the test that was completed. The code can be one of the following: TPR_SKIP, TPR_PASS, TPR_FAIL, or TPR_ABORT. TPR_SKIP is returned if the harness responds to the SPM_BEGIN_TEST message with the code SPR_SKIP. TPR_PASS and TPR_FAIL are returned by the test harness to indicate the status of the test. TPR_ABORT is a special condition returned by the test harness if the test was executed but not completed.

(continued)

Table 12.2 *Continued.*

Message	Structure	Members	Description
		DWORD dwRandomSeed	Random seed passed to the test.
		DWORD dwThreadCount	Number of threads created to execute the completed test. This number may be different from the number of threads requested in the SPM_BEGIN_TEST message. If Tux cannot create enough threads to honor a request for multiple threads, it will allow a smaller number of threads to execute the test in parallel and report the number in this variable.
		DWORD dwExecutionTime	Number of milliseconds for the test case to execute the completion.
SPM_END_GROUP	None		
SPM_STOP_SCRIPT	None		
SPM_EXCEPTION	SPS_EXCEPTION	LPFUNCTION_TABLE_ ENTRY lpFTE	Pointer to the function table entry that corresponds to the test function being executed when the exception occurred. If an exception occurs outside of an executing test, the value of this variable is NULL.
		DWORD dwExceptionCode	Type of exception that occurred.
		EXCEPTION_POINTERS *lpExceptionPointers	Pointer to a structure that contains an exception context and any related exception records. The exception context may be changed if the test harness wants to retry the exception.
		DWORD dwExceptionFilter	Value that indicates how the exception must be handled. A value of EXCEPTION_ EXECUTE_HANDLER invokes the default handler that is resident in Tux. The exception is handled gracefully, and if possible, Tux moves on to the next test.

Table 12.2 *Continued.*

Message	Structure	Members	Description
			If the value is set to EXCEPTION_CONTINUE_SEARCH, the exception is passed to the debugger. If Tux is not running with a debugger present, it will be terminated and all loaded test harnesses and related DLLs will be unloaded. A value of EXCEPTION_CONTINUE_EXECUTION causes the exception to be retried. If the exception context returned in the EXCEPTION_POINTERS variable is altered, the exception may be rectified.

We've looked extensively at the interaction between Tux and a test harness. Tux sends messages related to test execution to the ShellProc function in the harness so that housekeeping may be performed. The actual process of launching the test is carried out separately by Tux and is more involved than just launching the function pointer in a given function table entry.

The Test Function

Any test that is exported by the test harness conforms to a given prototype:

```
#define TESTPROCAPI  INT WINAPI
TESTPROCAPI TestFunction (UINT uMessage, TPPARAM tpParam, LPFUNCTION_TABLE_ENTRY
lpFTE);
```

The test function is called with three arguments. The first parameter is a message that is passed from Tux to the test function. Only two messages can be passed to the test function, but we'll say more about that later. The argument tpParam depends on the value of uMessage. The third and final argument, lpFTE, is a pointer to the entry corresponding to TestFunction in the function table.

Executing a Test

When Tux is ready to call the test function, it calls it with the message TPM_EXECUTE. When the test function receives this message, it should execute itself and carry out the test it was written to perform. The tpParam argument for this message is a pointer to a structure of type TPS_EXECUTE:

```
typedef struct _TPS_EXECUTE
{
   DWORD dwRandomSeed;
   DWORD dwThreadCount;
   DWORD dwThreadNumber;
} TPS_EXECUTE, *LPTPS_EXECUTE;
```

The first two members of this structure are familiar friends. The `dwRandomSeed` member carries the seed that should be used by the test if it generates a random number sequence. The `dwThreadCount` member represents the number of threads that will execute independent versions of the test. We haven't come across `dwThreadNumber` before. This member represents the number of the thread that is being used to execute this test. If the user requested three threads to execute the test function, `dwThreadCount` would be 3. The test function would then be called three times with `dwThreadNumber` set first to 1, then to 2, and finally to 3.

In the case of `dwRandomSeed`, the test cannot be executed with the same random seed in multiple threads because each thread would be duplicating the same test. For a test using random numbers to succeed, each instance of the test must be seeded with a different number. However, this requirement violates the ability of the user to reproduce the test case by using a known seed. Tux handles this situation by using a known seed for the first instance of the test case. For each subsequent instance, it uses a predictable algorithm to derive a different number from the previous seed. This new number then becomes the seed for the next instance of the test.

Random seeds can be specified by the user to create repeatable runs only when using the Tux server. If the Tux client is run as a stand-alone application, there is no way to create a random seed and pass it to the run list.

It is important to understand that when a test has been designated to run in multiple threads, Tux does not start each thread in sequence. Rather, Tux creates each thread and waits for the threads to reach an idle state. Once all threads have been primed in this way, Tux begins to execute all threads simultaneously. This makes for a more rigorous test scenario using multiple threads. Tux won't return a result to the user until all threads have completed. In effect, Tux treats the multithreaded tests as a single test case, returning a single test result upon completion.

Upon completion of the test, the function must return `TPR_PASS` if the test completed successfully or `TPR_FAIL` if the test did not run to its expected completion. A return value of `TPR_ABORT` indicates that the test did not run to completion. The pass/fail status of a test is indeterminate in this case.

A test function can decide to bypass its own execution by returning the value `TPR_SKIP`. A runtime check may be performed by the test to decide if conditions are ideal for its execution. This check might look for a particular program loaded in memory that is incompatible with the test or a certain amount of free memory. If the basic conditions of the test are not met, it can skip its own execution. Recall that the shell procedure itself can decide to skip a particular test by returning the value `SPR_SKIP` during the processing of the `SPM_BEGIN_TEST` message. In this case, the test function will never be called by Tux.

Running the Test in Multiple Threads

Multithreaded execution of tests requires that the thread count for each test be specified. This information is best held in the test itself. Tux queries this information by sending a

TPM_QUERY_THREAD_COUNT message to the test harness. The tpParam argument to the test function is a structure of type TPS_QUERY_THREAD_COUNT:

```
typedef struct _TPS_QUERY_THREAD_COUNT
{
   DWORD dwThreadCount;
} TPS_QUERY_THREAD_COUNT, *LPTPS_QUERY_THREAD_COUNT;
```

The test function being called sets the dwThreadCount member of this structure to the desired value of threads that Tux should create for the function. This structure arrives with the value of dwThreadCount set to its default of 0. If the value is unchanged when the function returns service of this message, the test function will be executed in Tux's main thread.

Thus, the number of threads to execute for a test is held in the test code itself. Tux obtains this information from the test harness for each test and passes it with relevant messages to the ShellProc function that handles housekeeping tasks. Tux is also responsible for creating the threads required to honor the request. This mechanism allows the test harness to localize the thread count information in each test function. No global variables are required to cache this information.

Running Tests from Tux

Tests can be run from Tux when it is run in stand-alone mode. The command-line interface of Tux can be used to load test harnesses, list test cases, and execute specific tests. Table 12.3 lists the command-line options in Tux.

Suite Files

You can load individual test harnesses via Tux using the command-line options outlined in Table 12.3. Alternatively, you can create a command file that instructs Tux to perform a series of tests

Table 12.3 Tux Command-Line Options

Option	Description
-d testharness.dll	Load the test harness DLL.
-l	List all the tests that are contained in the loaded test harness.
-x t1, t2, t3-t5	Build a run list of tests t1, t2, and t3 through t5 contained in the loaded test harness and begin executing the run list.
-b	Break after each test harness is loaded.
-c <cmds>	Pass the string *cmds* to the test harness. This option can be used to pass an explicit command line to the test harness.
-e	Disable Tux's exception handling. Exceptions will be passed on to the system.
-s Suitefile	Execute the tests specified in a suite file (see the next section).

from one or more test harnesses. A collection of groups of tests and individual tests is called a suite. A suite can be specified in a command file that is called a **suite file**.

The format of a suite file is fairly straightforward:

```
[Section]
Key=Value
```

A section is followed by one or more keys that are equated to certain values. This file format is derived from INI files, which were the de facto method of saving persistent information in 16-bit Windows (Windows 3.x and earlier versions). A suite file supports three sections, each of which supports unique key names (see Table 12.4).

As an example, let's say we want to run our test harness, called `systemtest.dll`, and load specific tests. We will use Listing 12.2 as the function table for `systemtest.dll`. A sample suite file is shown in Listing 12.3.

Table 12.4 Suite File Format

Section	Key	Value	Description
Options			Describe how the suite file must be interpreted.
	`Iterations`	`N`	Run the entire suite file *N* number of times.
DLLs			List test harnesses to be loaded by Tux.
	D_1	`[<path>\]testharness.dll`	Load the DLL specified by `testharness.dll`. A fully qualified path is optional. D_1 is a number that starts with 1 and is incremented for successive entries. Multiple $D_1 \ldots D_n$ may be specified to load multiple test harnesses.
Tests			Specify a run list of tests from the harnesses loaded in the previous section.
	T_1	D_1, ID_1	Run the test with the unique ID ID_1 from the test harness corresponding to key D_1 in the DLLs section. The key T_1 is a number that starts with 1 and is incremented for successive entries. Multiple $T_1 \ldots T_n$ may be specified to run multiple tests. Tux starts the tests in the order they are read from the suite file. Tests from different harnesses can be run in

Listing 12.3 Sample suite file

```
# SystemSuite10.ini
[Options]
Iterations=10
[DLLs]
1=SystemTest.dll
[Tests]
1=1, 10
2=1, 12
3=1, 20
4=1, 21
```

The sample suite file instructs Tux to load the test harness `systemtest.dll` and execute tests 10, 12, 20, and 21. The tests must be repeated 10 times before Tux unloads the test harness. The suite file can be executed with the following command:

```
Tux -s SystemSuite10.ini
```

Logging Tux Test Results

The nature of an automated test scenario suggests unattended tests. In these situations, a log of activities undertaken by the tests is critical. An extensive log of how key decisions were made in the code can be used to retrace program execution in the case of test failure or an exception.

The DDTK comes with a tool called Kato that provides logging facilities for Tux. As a tool, Kato is independent of Tux and can be used separately. As with Tux, the client-server model is primary to Kato's operation, although the client can run without the server. Kato provides a C and a C++ interface. We'll focus on the latter. Hierarchical traces are allowed by Kato, with the hierarchy specified by the test performing the log. In addition, a verbosity index can be specified with each trace. The index can then be used to filter out certain traces. This feature is crucial in sorting through large log files when reconstructing a particular thread of execution in the program.

The Kato client passes its traces to the server if one is currently in operation. Multiple log streams are accepted by the server, so potentially multiple tests can simultaneously generate logs. For simplicity, we will refer to the Kato client as simply Kato. The Kato server can be extended to support different logging media or output systems. A user-supplied plug-in can be written that knows how to express a log to a given output system. This plug-in then receives the trace and communicates it to the media it supports. By default, the Kato server streams traces to the **Spy Output System**, a scrolling window.

Creating a Kato Object

To start logging traces, a test harness creates a Kato object. The logical connection created by the object with Kato in order to pass traces is called a **stream**. A test harness may have multiple streams. Each stream must be created separately by the creation of a new Kato object. A Kato object is represented by the `CKato` class. The `CKato` constructor takes an optional argument that specifies the name of the Kato object, and hence the stream:

```
CKato::CKato(LPCWSTR wszName = NULL);
```

If no argument is specified, the object doesn't acquire a name. More objects can be created and named independently from a single test harness. The following code snippet creates a Kato object with the name *Main Stream:*

```
CKato katoMain ("Main Stream");
```

Starting a Level

Once the object is created, traces can be sent to Kato via the object. Kato supports hierarchical levels that can be used to separate traces. You can start a level by calling the `BeginLevel` member of the `CKato` class:

```
INT  WINAPIV CKato::BeginLevel (DWORD dwLevelID, LPCWSTR wszFormat, ...);
```

The `dwLevelID` argument specifies a number that is used to identify a level. Level IDs start from 0 and can reach a maximum defined by the constant `KATO_MAX_LEVEL`. `KATO_MAX_LEVEL` is currently set to 31, yielding a maximum of 32 levels. The `wszFormat` argument and optional arguments that follow define a `printf`-style argument list that specifies a trace to identify the level being started. `BeginLevel` returns the new level on success and –1 on failure. The most common reason that this call fails is specification of a level ID that is greater than `KATO_MAX_LEVEL`.

The following code snippet begins a level with ID 0 and identifies it with a trace, which displays the group name of the test:

```
katoMain.BeginLevel (0, "Begin tests from group %s", szGroupName);
```

Sending Traces for Logging

Once a level has been started, traces can be sent to Kato for logging. A trace is specified with the `Log` member of the `CKato` class:

```
BOOL WINAPIV CKato::Log (DWORD dwVerbosity, LPCWSTR wszFormat, ...);
```

The first argument of this member specifies a verbosity value. A verbosity value is a number between 0 and the constant `KATO_MAX_VERBOSITY`. Verbosity values are indirectly proportional to the criticality of the trace. If the trace announces an error, the verbosity value is always set to 0. As the verbosity value increases, the trace associated with it is considered more informational. This verbosity value is used at the server to filter traces to the output system. If a user is interested only in sorting through all the errors generated by the test harness, the verbosity value of 0 can be used to filter out all other traces.

The `wszFormat` and optional arguments that follow specify the display of the trace. A trace that announces an error can be created by execution of the following line of code:

```
katoMain.Log (0, "Error %d in test %s", GetLastError (), szTestName);
```

The constant KATO_MAX_VERBOSITY is currently set to 15, allowing for a maximum of 16 verbosity levels.

Filtering Logs with Verbosity

An interesting feature supported by Kato related to verbosity values is a verbosity count. A **verbosity count** is a number that is incremented each time a particular verbosity value is sent with a trace. If a test harness sends eight traces, each with a verbosity value of 3, the verbosity count for the value 3 will be 8. If verbosity values are associated with specific conditions, the count can then be used to maintain a tally of how many times a particular condition occurred during a test. Verbosity counts are maintained separately for each level. You can obtain the verbosity count for a particular verbosity value by calling the GetVerbosityCount function:

```
INT   WINAPI CKato::GetVerbosityCount(DWORD dwVerbosity, DWORD dwLevel = -1);
```

The first argument, dwVerbosity, is the verbosity value that needs to be tallied. The second argument, dwLevel, specifies the level for which the verbosity count must be tallied. A value of –1 for dwLevel indicates the current level entered by the test harness.

Ending a Level

When a group of tests has been completed, the test harness can leave the level at which it was operating by calling the EndLevel member of CKato:

```
INT  WINAPIV CKato::EndLevel (LPCSTR szFormat, ...);
```

A call made to BeginLevel must be followed by a call to EndLevel. If EndLevel is not called, the level automatically terminates when the destructor for the CKato class is called.

Kato supports an additional type of trace function, apart from Log:

```
BOOL WINAPIV CKato::Comment (DWORD dwVerbosity, LPCSTR szFormat, ...);
```

The Comment member operates in the same fashion as Log, except that verbosity values are not tallied. These traces are meant to provide informational value and not to describe error conditions.

If a test harness has multiple threads, it can create multiple Kato objects to handle the stream from each thread. Different streams can also be created to trace different pieces of functionality within the same thread. There is also a need for a test harness to use a single stream for all its logs. In this case, the test harness has to maintain a global Kato object that is created once and reused for all streams. The Kato API KatoGetDefaultObject facilitates this type of operation without requiring an explicit global object to be created:

```
HKATO KatoGetDefaultObject (VOID);
```

This is a C function call that returns a handle to a Kato object. When used from C++ code, the handle can be safely cast to a CKato object. This CKato object is a default global object created on the first call to KatoGetDefaultObject. On subsequent calls, the same object is returned to the caller, thus synchronizing the streams used throughout the test harness. The object is deleted by the Kato libraries when the test harness is finished.

All of Kato's logs are transmitted to the Kato server via the client. Thus, a log cannot be viewed locally on the client on which it is being generated. A test harness that runs independently of a server may want to implement a window or file that captures the Kato log at the client itself, thus removing the need for a server. The Kato API provides a way of capturing the log on the client side before it makes its way to the server. This capability is provided in the form of Kato callbacks. A **Kato callback** is a function of type `LPKATOCALLBACK`:

```
BOOL CALLBACK KatoCallback(LPKATOCALLBACKSTRUCT lpkcbs);
```

The callback function accepts a Kato callback structure as its single argument. The Kato callback structure is defined as follows:

```
typedef struct _KATOCALLBACKSTRUCT {
       LPARAM  lParam;
       HKATO   hKato;
       DWORD   dwThreadID;
       DWORD   dwTickCount;
       DWORD   dwLevel;
       DWORD   dwLevelID;
       DWORD   dwVerbosity;
       LPCTSTR szLog;
} KATOCALLBACKSTRUCT, *LPKATOCALLBACKSTRUCT;
```

The parameters of the structure are explained in Table 12.5.

Table 12.5 Members of the Kato Callback Structure

Member	Description
`lparam`	Value passed by the user to `KatoSetCallback`.
`hkato`	Handle to the Kato object. This handle can safely be cast to `CKato`.
`dwThreadID`	Thread ID of the logging thread.
`dwTickCount`	Clock tick count at the time the log was generated by the logging thread.
`dwLevel`	Level specified by the logging thread.
`dwLevelID`	Level ID of the log string.
`dwVerbosity`	Verbosity level of the log string.
`szLog`	Log string that the logging thread is sending to the Kato engine.

The Tux Demo Program

Having reviewed all the various ways in which Tux and Kato functionality can be leveraged, let's put the Tux demo program, Tuxdemo, through its paces.

Tuxdemo contains several sample tests (see Table 12.6) that are useful for studying the behavior of a typical Tux test harness.

Table 12.6 Tests Performed by Tuxdemo

Group	Test	Function	Parameter	Purpose
Memory Allocation Tests				
	New/delete (0 threads)	`NewDeleteTest`	0	Allocates a buffer of random size between 1 and 2,000 bytes and deletes it. This operation is carried out 100 times. Logs an error message to Kato if the new operator fails.
	New/delete (100 threads)	`NewDeleteTest`	100	Performs the new/delete test for 100 threads simultaneously.
Device Context Tests				
	Get device context/release device context (0 threads)	`GetDCReleaseDCTest`	0	Grabs the desktop device context and checks for validity, then releases it. This operation is carried out 100 times. Logs an error message to Kato if the device context is not valid or the release fails.
	Get device context/release device context (1 thread)	`GetDCReleaseDCTest`	1	Performs the get device context/release device context test using a separate thread.
	Get device context/release device context (100 threads)	`GetDCReleaseDCTest`	100	Performs the get device context/release device context test for 100 threads simultaneously.
Semaphore Tests				
	Producer/consumer (2 threads)	`ProducerConsumerTest`	2	Performs a classic producer/consumer test. Creates an even number of

(continued)

Table 12.6 *Continued.*

Group	Test	Function	Parameter	Purpose
				threads. Even-numbered threads are producers, and odd-numbered threads are consumers. Consumer threads wait on 100,000 semaphores in a loop. Producer threads release an equal number of semaphores in a similar loop.
	Producer/consumer (100 threads)	`ProducerConsumerTest`	100	Performs the producer/consumer test for 100 threads simultaneously.
Window Tests				
	Window (1 thread)	`WindowTest`	1	Randomly creates windows of arbitrary size from among a collection of options: button, combobox, edit box, list box, scrollbar, and static box. The window is displayed and then destroyed.
	Window (25 threads)	`WindowTest`	25	Performs the window test for 25 threads simultaneously.
Process Tests				
	Process (1 thread)	`ProcessTest`	1	Launches the calculator (`calc.exe`) with a random size specification, sleeps for a random time between zero and one seconds, and then terminates the process. This operation is carried out 15 times. Because Windows CE doesn't come with a program called `calc.exe`, this test will fail (unless you change the `CreateProcess` call to execute another program or create a dummy `calc.exe` and include it in your build).
	Process (25 thread)	`ProcessTest`	25	Performs the process test for 25 threads simultaneously.

Table 12.6 *Continued.*

Group	Test	Function	Parameter	Purpose
Exception Handling				
	Access violation	`AccessViolationTest`	0	Causes an exception by attempting to assign a value to a `NULL` pointer. The resulting exception is caught in the `SPM_EXCEPTION` message handler in the `ShellProc` function.
Possible Results				
	Pass	`ResultTest`	`TPR_PASS`	Displays the value of the pass code and returns the code itself. This test is purely for informational purposes.
	Fail	`ResultTest`	`TPR_FAIL`	Displays the value of the fail code and returns the code itself. This test is purely for informational purposes.
	Skip	`ResultTest`	`TPR_SKIP`	Displays the value of the skip code and returns the code itself. This test is purely for informational purposes.
	Abort	`ResultTest`	`TPR_ABORT`	Displays the value of the abort code and returns the code itself. This test is purely for informational purposes.

Now that we've reviewed the tests performed by the Tux demo program that ships with Platform Builder, let's put the demo through its paces.

To run Tux on the target, you will need `tux.exe`, the helper DLL `tooltalk.dll`, and the test harness, `tuxdemo.dll`. The Kato engine is linked in as a library and does not require a run-time component. Recall the command-line arguments that can be passed to Tux. `Tux.exe` operates on a test harness when you pass in the name of the DLL using the `-d` argument. Invoking `tux.exe` with the `-l` argument will cause Tux to spit out all the tests listed in the test harness:

```
Tux.exe -d tuxdemo.dll -l
```

If your target has a serial port connection back to a workstation, you will see the following trace in your debugger window:

```
TUXDEMO: ShellProc(SPM_LOAD_DLL, ...) called
TUXDEMO: ShellProc(SPM_SHELL_INFO, ...) called
TUXDEMO: ShellProc(SPM_REGISTER, ...) called

tuxdemo.dll

   Memory Allocation Tests
      65537: new/delete (0 Threads)
      65538: new/delete (1 Thread)
      65539: new/delete (100 Threads)

   Device Context Tests
      65546: GetDC/ReleaseDC (0 Threads)
      65547: GetDC/ReleaseDC (1 Thread)
      65548: GetDC/ReleaseDC (100 Threads)

   Semaphore Tests
      65556: Producer/Consumer (2 Threads)
      65557: Producer/Consumer (100 Threads)

   Window Tests
      65566: Window Test (1 Thread)
      65567: Window Test (25 Threads)

   Process Tests
      65576: Process Test (1 Thread)
      65577: Process Test (25 Threads)

   Exception Handling
      65586: Access Violation

   Possible Results
      65596: Pass
      65597: Fail
      65598: Skip
      65599: Abort

TUXDEMO: ShellProc(SPM_UNLOAD_DLL, ...) called
```

Strings that carry the prefix *TUXDEMO:* are debug traces generated by Tuxdemo and are displayed in the debugger window. If you build Tuxdemo without debug information, you will not see these strings in your listing. The number listed before each test is the test identification number. To run a specific test, Tux must be passed the test number(s) prefixed with the `-x` argument.

As a sample run, we call Tux to run the window test with one thread.

```
Tux.exe -d tuxdemo.dll -x 65566 -o
```

Note the additional `-o` argument. This will force the Kato engine to direct logs to the debugger. In the absence of a Kato logging engine running on a server, you can use this option to obtain traces in your debugger or any windowing program that can establish a connection with the serial port (like HyperTerminal). Tuxdemo will generate the following trace to the debugger window:

```
TUXDEMO: ShellProc(SPM_LOAD_DLL, ...) called
TUXDEMO: ShellProc(SPM_SHELL_INFO, ...) called
TUXDEMO: ShellProc(SPM_REGISTER, ...) called

*** ================================================================
*** SUITE INFORMATION
***
*** Suite Name:        N/A (built on the fly)
*** Suite Description: N/A
*** ================================================================
*** ================================================================
*** SYSTEM INFORMATION
***
*** Date and Time:            10/31/1999  8:35 PM (Sunday)
***
*** OS Version:               2.12
*** Build Number:             9165
*** Platform ID:              3 "Windows CE"
*** Version String:           ""
***
*** Processor Type:           0x000001E6 (486) "Intel 486"
*** Processor Architecture: 0x0000     (0) "Intel"
*** Page Size:                0x00001000 (4,096)
*** Minimum App Address:      0x00010000 (65,536)
*** Maximum App Address:      0x7FFFFFFF (2,147,483,647)
*** Active Processor Mask:    0x00000001
*** Number Of Processors:     1
*** Allocation Granularity: 0x00010000 (65,536)
*** Processor Level:          0x0004     (4)
*** Processor Revision:       0x0000     (0)
*** ================================================================

*** ================================================================
*** MEMORY INFO
***
*** Memory Total:     2,797,568 bytes
*** Memory Used:      1,650,688 bytes
*** Memory Free:      1,146,880 bytes
***
*** Store Total:      2,772,736 bytes
*** Store Used:         130,504 bytes
*** Store Free:       2,642,232 bytes
*** ================================================================

TUXDEMO: ShellProc(SPM_START_SCRIPT, ...) called
TUXDEMO: ShellProc(SPM_BEGIN_GROUP, ...) called
BEGIN GROUP: TUXDEMO.DLL
*** vvvvvvvvvvvvvvvvvvvvvvvvvvvvvvvvvvvvvvvvvvvvvvvvvvvvvvvvvvvvvvvv
*** TEST STARTING
***
*** Test Name:      Window Test (1 Thread)
```

```
*** Test ID:        65566
*** Library Path:   tuxdemo.dll
*** Random Seed:    6897
*** Thread Count:   1
*** vvvvvvvvvvvvvvvvvvvvvvvvvvvvvvvvvvvvvvvvvvvvvvvvvvvvvvvvvvvvvvvvvv
TUXDEMO: ShellProc(SPM_BEGIN_TEST, ...) called
   BEGIN TEST: "Window Test (1 Thread)", Threads=1, Seed=6897
TUXDEMO: ShellProc(SPM_END_TEST, ...) called
   END TEST: "Window Test (1 Thread)", PASSED, Time=9.532
*** ^^^^^^^^^^^^^^^^^^^^^^^^^^^^^^^^^^^^^^^^^^^^^^^^^^^^^^^^^^^^^^^^^^
*** TEST COMPLETED
***
*** Test Name:      Window Test (1 Thread)
*** Test ID:        65566
*** Library Path:   tuxdemo.dll
*** Result:         Passed
*** Random Seed:    6897
*** Thread Count:   1
*** Execution Time: 0:00:09.532
*** ^^^^^^^^^^^^^^^^^^^^^^^^^^^^^^^^^^^^^^^^^^^^^^^^^^^^^^^^^^^^^^^^^^
TUXDEMO: ShellProc(SPM_END_GROUP, ...) called
END GROUP: TUXDEMO.DLL
TUXDEMO: ShellProc(SPM_STOP_SCRIPT, ...) called
*** ==================================================================
*** MEMORY INFO
***
*** Memory Total:     2,797,568 bytes
*** Memory Used:      1,650,688 bytes
*** Memory Free:      1,146,880 bytes
***
*** Store Total:      2,772,736 bytes
*** Store Used:         130,504 bytes
*** Store Free:       2,642,232 bytes
*** ==================================================================

*** ==================================================================
*** SUITE SUMMARY
***
*** Passed:          1
*** Failed:          0
*** Skipped:         0
*** Aborted:         0
*** -------- ---------
*** Total:           1
***
*** Cumulative Test Execution Time: 0:00:09.532
*** Total Tux Suite Execution Time: 0:00:09.684
*** ==================================================================
@@@@@@0
TUXDEMO: ShellProc(SPM_UNLOAD_DLL, ...) called
```

Tux initially generates system information and logs it to the Kato engine. Next, it prints out a memory footprint of the system. This exercise is carried out again after the requested tests have run. This repetition is useful when you want to ensure that your test does not leak memory.

Tux notifies you when the test starts and gives you the name and ID of the test and the random seed generated. A summary is generated after the test has finished execution. The summary includes the status returned by the test and the elapsed time. This information is displayed for each test executed in the suite. After all the tests are done executing, a suite summary is printed by Tux that shows how many tests passed or failed or were skipped or aborted. A cumulative execution time is also displayed.

Summary

We've seen how the Device Driver Test Kit can be leveraged to create test harnesses for drivers, as well as for applications running on a Windows CE platform. Logging capabilities for traces are provided by a special engine called Kato. Kato is extensible and allows the creation of sophisticated logging capabilities.

Tux supports automated testing via a suite file that can be used to specify a suite of tests to run. Furthermore, a Tux server can be used to initiate tests on more than one client simultaneously. If you plan to write utilities to test your code, you should consider creating Tux test harnesses.

Windows CE Modules and Components

The component-based nature of Windows CE means that the operating system has been split up into components that each encapsulate a particular area of functionality. These components are either poorly documented or not documented at all by Microsoft. There are components that an integrator may never insert in `cesysgen.bat`. However, a list of such components and the area of functionality each one encapsulates, as presented in this appendix, is an excellent study in how the various parts of the operating system have been divided by Microsoft. You can also use this appendix as a reference if you come across a library or executable whose contents you would like to decipher.

Component	Description
`accel`	Accelerator.
`accel_c`	Support for creating accelerator tables.
`acmdwrap`	Interface for Audio Compression Manager (ACM) driver.
`afd`	Management of the Windows CE communication protocol.
`arp`	Address Resolution Protocol.
`asform`	Unknown.
`asyncio`	Support for the `GetOverlappedResult` function to support asynchronous I/O (input/output).
`asyncmac`	Asynchronous Media Access Control (MAC) miniport driver used to support NDISWAN.
`atadisk`	ATA flash PCMCIA card device driver.
`audio`	Support for audio API.
`audiomdd`	Audio driver modem device driver layer for the built-in device driver.

`autodial`	Internet Connection Sharing (ICS).
`btnctl`	Button control.
`bulltlp3`	Bull TLP3 serial smart card reader.
`calibrui`	Support for user interface (touchpad) calibration.
`cardpdd`	Card services platform device driver (PDD) layer.
`cardserv`	Card services (PCMCIA support).
`caret`	Caret functionality.
`cascade`	Cascading menus.
`cdlctl`	Candidate list control.
`ce_awt`	Java AdvancedWindow Toolkit (AWT) library.
`ce_irda`	Java IrDA library.
`ce_local`	Java localization library.
`ce_math`	Java big integer support.
`ce_net`	Java networking library.
`ce_zip`	Java compression library.
`ceddk`	Abstracting of bus and peripheral I/O.
`cefnk`	Unknown.
`cegsm`	Audio compression support.
`cejava`	Windows CE Java support.
`cejvm`	Java virtual machine.
`ceramdrv`	RAM disk driver for creating storage cards in RAM.
`ceshell`	Sample CE shell for OEMs.
`clipbd`	Clipboard-related Windows messages, clipboard formats, and API functions.
`cmbctl`	Combobox control.
`cmd`	CE command line.
`cmdbar`	Sample for command bar buttons and capabilities.
`column`	Multicolumn support for menus.
`com`	Component Object Model (COM) base services.
`com_mdd`	Serial model device driver (MDD) for the built-in device driver.
`com_pdd`	Serial platform device driver (PDD) for the built-in device driver.
`comm`	Control panel applet for communications.
`commctrl`	Common control support.
`commdlg`	Reusable common dialogs.
`commg`	Control panel applet for communications in portrait mode (portrait mode is used to support the Palm-size PC).
`console`	Console device driver.
`control`	Control panel application.

corecrt	C runtime library (Windows 2.12 and earlier versions).
coredll	Core system service API functions. Required.
coreimm	Input Method Manager (IMM).
coreloc	National Language Support (NLS) API functions, which support localization.
coremain	Base functionality for `coredll.dll`. Required.
coresioa	Studio support.
coresip	Software Input Panel (SIP) support.
corestra	C runtime support (Windows CE 3.0 and later versions).
crypt32	Support for Cryptography API 2.0 (Windows CE 3.0 and later versions).
cryptapi	Cryptography API (Windows CE 2.12 and earlier versions).
ctlpnl	Sample control panel applet.
cursor	Cursor functionality.
cxport	Common transport utilities.
dbg	Debugger initialization support.
dbview	Sample for database functions.
dc21x4	Digital DC21X4 network interface card (NIC) driver.
ddk_bus	Bus abstraction routines used by `ceddk`.
ddk_io	I/O routines used by `ceddk`.
ddkmap	Memory mapping routines used by `ceddk`.
defwndproc	Support for the `DefWindowProc` API function.
device	Device manager, which loads and manages device drivers.
dhcp	Dynamic Host Configuration Protocol support.
dlgmem	Dialog mnemonic support.
dlgmgr	Dialog manager.
docfile	COM Structured Storage support.
docfile msfexp	OLE desktop binary-compatible storage.
drawmbar	Support for `DrawMenuBar` function.
dsif	DirectSound interface.
dsound	DirectSound.
dualio	PCMCIA serial driver interface for Socket Dual I/O PC card.
dvdif	DVD-ROM interface driver.
eboot	Support for booting processor on target from Ethernet.
edctl	Edit control.
edimechn	Chinese edit control component.
edimefe	Far East edit control component.
edimefek	Korean language Input Method Editor (IME).
edimejpn	Japanese edit control component.

elnk3	Intel Etherlink 3 NIC driver.
emul	Display emulation driver.
etcha	Sample to demonstrate drawing primitives.
ethdbg	Debugging support over Ethernet interface.
exp	OLE storage services.
fatfs	Support for the FAT file system.
fileinfo	Support for Shell function (SHGetFileInfo) to retrieve file information.
fileopen	GetOpenFileName and GetSaveFileName functions.
filesys	Support for the Windows CE file system, which exposes the object store API functions. These API functions support a ROM-based file system, a RAM-based file system, a structured storage system known as the Windows CE database, and a system registry.
fmtmsg	FormatMessage support.
foregnd	Foreground window functionality.
fpemul	Floating-point emulation support for targets that do not feature floating-point hardware.
fsdbase	Database support.
fsdmgr	File system driver (FSD) management.
fsheap	RAM file system heap support.
fsmain	Base functionality for file system.
fspass	Password functionality for file system.
fsreg	Registry API support (implemented in ROM).
fsysram	RAM-based file system.
fsysrom	ROM-based file system.
gcache	GWES initialization.
gdi_c	CreateDIBSection and EqualRgn.
gdi_s	Simple Graphical Device Interface (GDI).
generic	Sample for basic graphics and windowing capabilities.
getpower	Power management (battery) functionality.
gpe	Graphics Primitive Engine (GPE) used by display drivers.
gsetwinlong	Support for the GetWindowLong and SetWindowLong API functions.
gsm610	GSM (Global System for Mobile telecommunication) 6.10 voice-encoding standard, originally developed for digital cellular-telephone encoding.
gwectrl	Basic control functionality.
gwes	Graphics, Windowing, and Events Subsystem.
gweshare	Shared GWES functionality.
gwesmain	Core GWES functionality. Required.
gwestubs	Stub routines for modules omitted from GWES.

`hello`	Sample that outputs "hello" to the serial port. Very useful when booting CE on target without display.
`hid`	USB host controller interface driver.
`hotkey`	Hot-key support.
`httpd`	Web server.
`httpdadmn`	Support for remote Web server administration via a Web browser.
`httpdsvc`	HTTP service.
`hwxjpn`	Handwriting recognition for Japanese.
`hwxusa`	Handwriting recognition for U.S. English.
`icmplib`	Internet Control Message Protocol (ICMP) support.
`icon`	Icon drawing support.
`iconcurs`	Cursor functionality for target platforms that support mouse cursors.
`idle`	Support system idle functionality.
`ieepro`	Intel EtherExpress Pro NIC driver.
`iexplore`	Internet Explorer.
`ime`	Input Method Editor.
`imgctl`	Image control.
`immthunk`	Thunks to call IMM DLL if present.
`inetcore`	Windows Internet DLL core services.
`inetftp`	Windows Internet DLL FTP services.
`intl`	Control panel applet for regional settings.
`intlg`	Control panel applet for regional settings in portrait mode.
`ipconfig`	IP configuration utility.
`iphlpapi`	IP helper API.
`ipnat`	Support for Internet Connection Sharing (ICS).
`ircomm`	IrDA emulated serial port driver.
`irdastk`	IrDA protocol stack.
`irsir`	Implementation for infrared serial NDIS MAC driver initialization functions.
`jcls`	Java class support.
`journal`	Basic journal support.
`jscript`	JavaScript support.
`jsen`	Unknown.
`jshell`	Java shell support.
`jview`	Command-line loader for Java.
`kbdmsg`	Sample program to test keyboard.
`kbdui`	Support for keyboard user input.
`kd`	Kernel debugging support.

keybd	Keyboard support.
keybdist	Interrupt service thread (IST) for the keyboard model device driver (used as a sample).
keybdmdd	Keyboard model device driver (MDD) layer for the built-in device driver.
keybdpdd	Keyboard PDD layer for the built-in device driver.
ksguid	Unknown.
labledit	Inbox component.
lbctl	List box control.
lmem	Local heap and memory allocation functions for coredll.dll. Required.
loadbmp	Bitmap-loading functionality.
loaddbg	Unknown.
loadimg	Image-loading functionality.
loadstr	String-loading and resource-locking functionality.
locusa	U.S. English localization.
lpcd	Local procedure call driver.
lpcrt	Runtime support for local procedure call driver.
mailutil	Inbox component.
main	Control panel applet for keyboard settings.
mcursor	Cursor functionality for target platforms that support mouse cursors.
mdibsec	`DIBSection` support.
mdraw	Basic drawing support (pens, brushes, lines, rectangles, and so on).
mdrwtxt	`DrawText` API.
memtool	Tool to display kernel memory usage.
menu	Menu functionality.
menubc	Handling of menu fonts.
menuscrl	Support for scrolling menus.
mgalias	Font face name aliasing. Can be used with either raster or TrueType font engine.
mgbase	Base functionality for Multiplatform Graphical Device Interface (MGDI) components.
mgbitmap	Bitmap creation functions.
mgblt	Basic bit block transfer (Blt) functions.
mgblt2	Advanced Blt functions.
mgdc	Advanced device context functions.
mgdi_c	Device-independent bitmaps (DIBs) and compare regions.
mgdibsec	Support for the `CreateDIBSection` API function.
mgdx	DirectX support.
mgfe	Far East word-break support for `DrawText`.

Module	Description
mgjfonts	Japanese raster font support.
mgpal	Palette operations.
mgpalmin	Smallest supported default palette.
mgpalnat	Recommended default palette (matches desktop's halftone palette).
mgprint	Printing.
mgrast	Basic raster font support.
mgrast2	Advanced raster font support.
mgrgn	Regions.
mgtci	`TranslateCharsetInfo` API.
mgtt	TrueType fonts.
mgwinmgr	APIs required for GWES's window manager.
mnoover	Restriction of overlap in cascading menus.
mnotapui	Unknown.
moverlap	Resolution of overlap in cascading menus.
mqoa	Microsoft Message Queue (MSMQ) component.
msasn	Support for Cryptography API version 2.0.
msf	Support for OLE storage (in conjunction with the exp component).
msfilter	Audio Compression Manager (ACM) sample filter driver.
msgbeep	`MessageBeep` API function.
msgbox	`MsgBox` API function.
msgque	Message queue support.
msgstore	Inbox component.
msim	Microsoft Input Method (IM) support.
msmqapi	MSMQ component.
msmqd	Microsoft Message Queue (MSMQ).
msmqdm	MSMQ component.
msmqrt	MSMQ component.
mstsc	Windows Terminal Server (WTS) and Remote Desktop Protocol (RDP).
mtapui	User interface for Telephony API (TAPI).
multibox	Sample input method for Japanese handwriting input.
nclient	Nonclient window area support.
ndis	NDIS support for CE.
ne2000	NE2000-compatible NDIS driver.
ne2kdbg	Debugging routines for NE2000 network driver.
net	Support for Microsoft Message Queue (MSMQ) functionality.
netbios	NetBIOS over TCP/IP.
netui	Common controls and dialogs used by network applications.

network	Control panel applet for network settings.
networkg	Control panel applet for network settings in portrait mode.
nk	Windows CE kernel. The kernel is responsible for memory management, process management, and file management functions. It manages virtual memory, scheduling, multitasking, multithreading, and exception handling.
nkcompr	Kernel with compression support. Causes kernel to add 10K of RAM for decompression support.
nknocomp	Kernel without compression support.
nkoem	OEM-supplied functions that make up the Windows CE Hardware Abstraction Layer (HAL).
nkprof	Profile-enabled kernel library.
nled	Support for LED manipulation.
nocefnk	Unknown.
notify	User notification support via the `CeSetUserNotification` call.
ntcompat	Definitions for NDIS drivers for compatibility with NT.
ntlmssp	Windows NT LAN Manager security support provider.
ohcd	USB host controller driver for Open HCI (host controller interface).
ohcdmdd	USB host controller model device driver (MDD).
ole232	"Upper layer" OLE services.
ole32	Base OLE support.
oleaut32	Base OLE automation support.
olemain	Main OLE entry point.
oom	Out-of-memory detection and resolution functionality.
oomui	User interface for `oom` component.
parallel	Low-level parallel port driver.
passwrd	Control panel applet for changing password.
passwrdg	Control panel applet for changing password in portrait mode.
pcl	Support for printer control language (PCL) printers.
pcmconv	Conversion routines for pulse code modulation (PCM) data.
peghelp	Windows CE Help.
pegterm	Terminal connection application.
pime_files	Support for the Japanese Pocket IME.
ping	Packet Internet Groper (PING) command-line utility.
pmstub	`PostMessage` stub routine.
polygons	Sample for rendering polygons.
power	Control panel applet for power management.
powerg	Control panel applet for power management in portrait mode.
ppp	Point-to-Point Protocol driver.

prnerr	User interface for reporting printer error.
prnport	Printer transport layer.
proxim	Proxim RangeLAN2 radio card driver.
pwd_res	Pocket Word component.
pword	Pocket Word.
pwwiff	Pocket Word component.
ramdisk	RAM disk driver.
rapiserv	Remote Access Programming Interface (RAPI) server.
rasdemo	Remote Access Services (RAS) sample.
rasdial	RAS utility to establish connection.
rasentry	Utility to make telephone book entries.
rectapi	Basic rectangle manipulation support.
redir	Network redirector.
remnet	Remote network dialing application.
repllog	Support for Windows CE Services used to synchronize data between the device and a host computer.
reversi	Sample game to show Graphical Device Interface (GDI) operation.
rmonkey	Sample to show registry API. Traverses registry tree like a ...
rnaapp	Maintenance of remote networking connection.
route	Utility to configure TCP/IP routing tables.
rsa32	RSA Data Security, Inc., cryptography support.
rsabase	Basic RSA cyptographic service provider (CSP) support.
rsaenh	Enhanced RSA CSP support with key strengths of up to 128 bits.
rsrc	Executable resource support.
sbcmn	Base scroll bar functionality.
scard	Smart card PC/SC (personal computer/smart card) resource manager functionality.
scbctl	Scroll bar control.
schannel	Support for SSL/PCT (Secure Sockets Layer/Private Communication Technology) security.
schedlog	Support for hardware-assisted profiling.
screen	Control panel applet for display settings.
screeng	Control panel applet for display settings in portrait mode.
sctovk	Conversion of keyboard scan code to virtual key.
secur32	Security Support Provider Interface (SSPI).
ser_card	PCMCIA serial platform device driver layer.
ser16550	16550 UART (universal asynchronous receiver-transmitter) library functions.
serdev	Serial device Win32 functions.

shcore	Core shell functionality.
shell	Exposure of user interface elements, such as the common dialogs, command bar, desktop, shell APIs, and controls. The shell provides a familiar interface for accessing documents, launching applications, switching between tasks, browsing the file system, and managing user interactions.
shexec	Support for programmatically executing applications.
shmisc	Miscellaneous shell support.
shortcut	Support for manipulating desktop shortcuts.
simple	Sample that simply creates a window.
sipcpl	Control panel applet for Software Input Panel (SIP).
sipselect	Sample program for dynamic selection of any available input method.
smc9000	SMC Networks chip set NIC driver.
snmp	Simple Network Management Protocol (SNMP) server.
snmp_hostmib	SNMP Host Resources Management Information Base (MIB).
snmp_mibii	SNMP MIB II.
snmptestmib	Support for SNMPTESTMIB application for SNMP.
softkb	Software keyboard.
sounds	Control panel applet for volume and sound settings.
soundsg	Control panel applet for volume and sound settings in portrait mode.
spincube	Custom control library to render spinning cubes for spintest sample.
spintest	Sample demonstrating GDI and custom controls. Displays a spinning cube in four quadrants on screen.
splusa	Spell checker for U.S. English.
sramdisk	SRAM PCMCIA card device driver.
sslsock	Secure Sockets Layer (SSL).
startui	User interface for the startup or power-on screen.
startup	Startup or power-on functionality.
stcctl	Static text control.
stcusb	SCM Microsystems USB smart card reader.
stg	OLE lightweight storage.
syscolor	Support for setting and retrieving system colors.
system	Control panel applet for system settings.
systemg	Control panel applet for system settings in portrait mode.
tapi	Telephony API (TAPI) functions.
tapilib	TAPI support.
taskman	Task manager.
tch_cal	Touch panel calibration.
tchmdd	Touch panel model device driver (MDD) layer for the built-in device driver.

`tchui`	Touchpad user interface support.
`tcpstk`	TCP/UDP/IP protocol stack.
`termctrl`	Terminal control application.
`text`	Sample to demonstrate rotated TrueType output to GDI.
`thunks`	Kernel or Win32 thunks.
`timer`	Base timer functionality (`WM_TIMER` messages).
`toolhelp`	Support for ToolHelp (debugger support) API functions.
`touch`	Touch panel support.
`trueffs`	PC card linear flash driver.
`uibase`	Base user interface support.
`unimodem`	TAPI service provider for AT command modems.
`unload`	Unknown.
`usbd`	Universal Serial Bus (USB) client driver interface.
`usbhid`	USB Human Interface Device (HID) support.
`usbmouse`	USB mouse driver.
`utl98`	Support for Input Method Editor 98.
`uuid`	UUID support.
`verifier`	Java byte code verifier.
`vkremap`	Virtual key remapping for the keyboard model device driver (MDD).
`vktochar`	Character generation from virtual key codes for the keyboard MDD.
`watapi`	Windows Driver Model (WDM) driver for ATA packet interface.
`waveapi`	Support for the Audio Compression Manager (ACM), Mapper, and the Wave API Manager (WAM).
`wavelib`	Base multimedia sound support.
`wavemdd`	Audio model device driver (MDD).
`wcdrom`	Unknown.
`wdevice`	Unknown.
`wdisk`	Unknown.
`wdm`	Support for Windows Driver Model (WDM).
`wdmhal`	Support for WDM in HAL.
`wdmlib`	Advanced kernel API for device drivers.
`wininet`	Internet services.
`winmgr`	Core window management functionality.
`winscard`	PC/SC (personal computer/smart card) services for using smart cards and smart card readers.
`winsock`	Winsock services.
`wmbase`	Base window manager functionality (includes wmgr_c).

wmgr_c	Core window manager (window class and accelerator) support. Required for all windows.
wrap2bpp	Two-bits-per-pixel display driver.
wrap2dr	Two-bits-per-pixel dirty rectangle driver used to support hardware displays that are not designed to support the Microsoft Graphics Primitive Engine (GPE) classes. Displays with a nonlinear frame buffer are an example of such hardware.
wserial	Unknown.
wudfs	Unknown.
xircce2	Xircom CE-2 NIC driver.

APPENDIX

B

A Makefile Primer

The Windows CE build process makes extensive use of the Nmake tool that ships with most Microsoft software and driver development kits. Makefiles allow projects to be built incrementally. Consider a program that consists of multiple object modules. When the program is being built, each source file is compiled into its object module and then linked to produce the final program. During incremental development of the program, if a particular file is modified, only that file must be recompiled for the changes to be incorporated into the program. The remaining files that have not been touched need not be recompiled. The result is time savings proportional to the size of the project.

Nmake provides a mechanism to specify dependencies among source files, object modules, and programs. This dependency list is scanned, and the time stamp of each entry in the list is determined. Nmake then uses this information to decide which files need to be rebuilt. It is important to understand that Nmake doesn't gain time savings for the link phase of your program. A modification to a single file will require linking the entire program again. Many popular C++ compilers support a feature called **incremental linking** that links only newly built objects into the final executable. However, you can do more than just compile and link using this utility. The Microsoft makefile builds resources, creates directories, copies files, and calls other utilities to perform housekeeping tasks.

Defining Targets

The file in which dependency lists are specified is called a **makefile.** A makefile is a script that is parsed by Nmake. A dependency list consists of a **target** and its **dependents** in the following format:

```
Target: Dependent1 Dependent2
Cmd1
Cmd2
```

A target is separated from its list of dependents by the colon character. The line specifying a target and its dependents is followed by one or more commands, which are responsible for building the target. Targets and dependents can be names of files.

When parsing the makefile (called `makefile` by default), if Nmake sees a target, it checks the list of dependents first. If the target and its dependents are files, Nmake compares the time stamps on the files to see if the dependents are newer than the target. If this is the case, Nmake **builds** the target; that is, it processes the commands that follow the target definition. If the dependents have an older time stamp than the target, Nmake does not build the target.

As an example, consider a C++ program that needs to be compiled and linked:

```
Hello.exe: hello.cpp
   Cl hello.cpp
```

In this example, Nmake will look for a file called `hello.exe` and compare its time stamp to that of its source file, `hello.cpp`. If `hello.cpp` has been modified since the last time `hello.exe` was built, Nmake will invoke the C++ compiler `cl.exe`. `Cl.exe` will create a new `hello.exe` file (assuming the source code compiles and links successfully) with a new time stamp. If Nmake were to be run again, the dependent `hello.cpp` would have an older date than `hello.exe`. In this case, Nmake would not run the compiler again.

Dependents of a target can be targets themselves. Nmake examines each dependent and builds it if required, and then it builds the final target. The dependents may have more dependents themselves, so the process can be recursive. If no dependents are specified for a target, Nmake always builds the target.

A makefile can have multiple targets. Which target must Nmake build? The answer is the *first* target that Nmake sees in the makefile. However, there is an exception to this rule: If Nmake finds a target called `All`, it builds this target above all others in the makefile. The predefined target `All` is often used to list all the targets that Nmake must process in the makefile.

The following example directs Nmake to process the `hello.exe` target:

```
All: hello.exe
```

The `All` target typically doesn't have any lines following its dependency list. In other words, the `All` target isn't a physical target that is built. It serves only as a dependency list. Such dependency lists are usually set up to allow Nmake to iterate through a list of targets.

Macros

Macros are string replacement tokens and are used much like preprocessor definitions in C++. Nmake uses macros as string replacement tokens in the makefile. Macros are defined by being equated to a value. The following are examples of macros:

```
PROGRAM = hello
SOURCES = hello.cpp
CC = cl
```

To access the value of a macro, you must use the `$()` operator. Whenever Nmake sees a macro surrounded by the `$()` operator, it replaces the macro with its string value. The following code sample sets up the target for `hello.exe` using macros:

```
$(PROGRAM).exe: $(SOURCES)
        $(CC) $(SOURCES)
```

Note how this affects the reusability of the makefile. If you were to switch to building a program called `goodbye.exe`, you would simply change the value of the `PROGRAM` and `SOURCES` macros. The rest of the makefile would not require any changes. Hello, `goodbye!`

In addition to user-defined macros, Nmake defines macros corresponding to each environment variable that it inherits from the command line. Thus, you can use environment variables throughout your makefile just like macros using the `$()` operator.

Nmake also predefines some command macros that you can sprinkle in your makefile for constructing compile commands (see Table B.1).

Nmake predefines macros that can be used to refer to files within a target (see Table B.2). These macros are extremely useful because you can use them to define targets in a highly generic fashion, thus improving the reusability of your program.

Table B.1 Command Macros for Constructing Compile Commands

Macro	Value	Meaning
AFLAGS	NULL	Assembler options
AS	ml.exe	Macro assembler
CC	cl.exe	C compiler
CFLAGS	NULL	C compiler options
CPP	cl.exe	C++ compiler
CPPFLAGS	NULL	C++ compiler options
CXXFLAGS	NULL	C++ compiler options
RC	rc.exe	Resource compiler
RFLAGS	NULL	Resource compiler options

Table B.2 Predefined Macros for Referring to Files within a Target

Macro	Value	Example
`$@`	Full path name of current target	`\PROJECTS\OUTPUT\hello.exe`
`$*`	Path and base name of current target minus extension	`\PROJECTS\OUTPUT\hcllo`
`$**`	List of current target's dependents	`\PROJECTS\SOURCE\hello.cpp`
`$?`	Dependents that have a newer time stamp than the target	

If you choose to define any macros with the same name, you will override the existing definitions. As an example, we will construct a slightly more complicated code snippet and relate each of the macros to the example. `Hello.exe` is now built from two source files, `hello.cpp` and `output.cpp`:

```
\Projects\Output\Hello.exe: \Projects\Source\Hello.obj
        link \Projects\Output\Hello.obj \Projects\Output\Output.obj /
out:\Projects\Output\Hello.exe
\Projects\Output\Hello.obj: \Projects\Source\Hello.cpp
        cl /c /Fo \Projects\Source\Hello.obj \Projects\Source\Hello.cpp
\Projects\Output\Output.obj: \Projects\Source\Output.cpp
        cl /c /Fo \Projects\Source\Output.obj \Projects\Source\Output.cpp
```

There is a lot of repetition in this file that makes it lengthy and difficult to read. Using macros, we can rewrite our previous sample:

```
PROGRAM = Hello
CC = cl
LINK = link
CFLAGS = /c /Fo $
LFLAGS = /out:$
SOURCEDIR = \Projects\Source
OUTPUTDIR = \Projects\Output
OBJECTS = $(OUTPUTDIR)\Hello.obj $(OUTPUTDIR)\Output.obj
$(OUTPUTDIR)\$(PROGRAM).exe: $(OBJECTS)
        $(LINK) $(OBJECTS) $(LFLAGS)
$(OUTPUTDIR)\Hello.obj: $(SOURCEDIR)\Hello.cpp
        $(CC) $(CFLAGS) $#
$(OUTPUTDIR)\Output.obj: $(SOURCEDIR)\Output.cpp
        $(CC) $(CFLAGS) $#
```

Note that the use of command and file name macros allows us to write highly compact code for the makefile. The reusability of the makefile is also increased, as is our ability to change paths and file names of the files.

The file name macro `$@` may be modified in several says. Consider a sample target name of `C:\PROJECTS\OUTPUT\hello.exe` (see Table B.3).

Table B.3 Modifications of the the File Name Macro $

Modification	Value	Example
$(@D)	Drive and directory name of target	\PROJECTS\OUTPUT
$(@B)	Base name of target	hello
$(@F)	Base name and extension of target	hello.exe
$(@R)	Drive, directory,and base name of target	\PROJECTS\OUTPUT\hello

Microsoft uses file name macros liberally throughout its master makefile.

Makefile Preprocessing

You can specify conditional processing using preprocessor directives. These work in a similar fashion to the C++ preprocessor. Some of the directives relevant to our material are listed in Table B.4.

Table B.4 Preprocessor Directives

Directive	Usage
!ERROR [<text>]	Displays the error text if specified, and forces Nmake to exit with an error.
!IF expression[=<value>] !ELSE	If the expression is true or its value matches the optional value specified, the statements up to the first !ELSE or !ENDIF, whichever comes first, are processed.
!ENDIF	
!INCLUDE <path and file name>	Inserts the named file in the current makefile and processes it.
!MESSAGE <text>	Displays a text message and allows Nmake to continue processing.
!UNDEF	Undefines a macro from Nmake's symbol table.

Command-Line Options

The syntax for using Nmake is as follows:

```
Usage: NMAKE [<options>] [/f <makefile>] [/x <stderrfile>] [<macrodefs>]
[<targets.]
```

A list of the options is provided in Table B.5.

Table B.5 Command-Line Options

Option	Meaning
/A	Build all targets regardless of time stamps. Used to force a clean build of a project.
/B	Build if time stamps are equal. Normally the build occurs if the time stamps are newer.
/C	Do not display output messages.
/D	Display build information.
/E	Override environment variables with user-defined macros.
/HELP	Display Help.
/I	Ignore exit codes from commands. Normally Nmake fails when any one command returns an error. This option allows Nmake to finish processing all targets before exiting.
/K	Build unrelated targets on error.
/N	Display commands but do not execute. This is an excellent option when you want to verify the flow of control in your makefile without actually building anything.
/NOLOGO	Suppress copyright message.
/P	Display the steps performed by Nmake when the makefile is being processed.
/Q	Check time stamps but do not build.
/R	Ignore predefined macros.
/S	Silent mode. Do not display any commands executed from the makefile.
/T	Update time stamps but do not build. This option can be used if you want to mark all modifications in your project obsolete.
/U	Display included files.
/Y	Disable batch mode.
/?	Display usage.

The `-f` option can be used to include a makefile that has a name other than the default. This option allows you to have multiple makefiles in the same directory with different names. When invoking Nmake on a particular file, simply use the `-f` option.

The `targets` argument is of particular interest. Earlier we saw that Nmake processes the `All` target or the first target it encounters in the makefile. The `targets` flag can be used to control which target is processed by Nmake. When told to do so, Nmake processes only the target or targets listed as arguments. This technique can be used with the makefile used to generate the system. For example, if you want to build only the tools that ship with Platform Builder, you can invoke the makefile in `_PUBLICROOT\COMMON\CESYSGEN` with the specific target:

```
Nmake tools
```

This will cause Nmake to execute the `tools` target inside the makefile.

The `macrodefs` argument allows you to override or define new macros on the command line. Invoking Nmake with the following command line:

```
Nmake DEBUG=1 CLEAN=0
```

causes the macros `DEBUG` and `CLEAN` to be inserted into Nmake's symbol table and their values to be set to 1 and 0, respectively.

CE Developer Resources

Usenet Newsgroups

Usenet newsgroups are moderated or unmoderated discussion bulletin boards that focus on a particular topic (see Table C.1). Queries and responses to a newsgroup are called **posts** and can be viewed with a Network News Transfer Protocol (NNTP) newsreader. Microsoft Internet Explorer has a freeware add-on newsreader called Outlook Express. Posts that apply to a particular discussion are called a **conversation thread** and are usually grouped together by a newsreader for readability. To subscribe to a newsgroup, a news server is required. Microsoft's public news server msnews.microsoft.com is a good resource for Windows CE discussions. Deja News (www.deja.com) also maintains an archive of newsgroup discussions and indexes them for advanced search capabilities.

Table C.1 Usenet Newsgroups

Newsgroup	Topics
comp.os.ms-windows.ce	Windows CE usage and product information
microsoft.public.office.developer.automation	Automation on Windows CE
microsoft.public.windowsce	Windows CE usage and product information
microsoft.public.windowsce.app.development	Application development discussions
microsoft.public.windowsce.developer.betas	Windows CE beta discussions
microsoft.public.windowsce.embedded.vb	eMbedded Visual Basic
microsoft.public.windowsce.embedded.vc	eMbedded Visual C++
microsoft.public.windowsce.platbuilder	Windows CE Platform Builder discussion for developers
microsoft.public.windowsce.platbuilder.beta	Windows CE Platform Builder beta discussions

Publications

Dr. Dobb's Journal (www.ddj.com) features articles of interest to developers and covers Windows CE in intermittent articles. *MSDN Magazine* (http://msdn.microsoft.com/msdnmag) covers Windows systems programming and often features articles on Windows CE.

Microsoft covers various developer products in the Product News section of *Windows CE Wire,* an e-mail newsletter that tracks breaking information on Windows CE. An e-mail newsletter exclusively for developers called *Windows CE Developers News* is sent out biweekly. You can sign up for these newsletters on Microsoft's home page, at www.microsoft.com.
An online magazine published by ZATZ that caters to users of Windows CE, *Pocket PC Life Magazine,* can be found at www.windowscepower.com.

Web Sites

The number of Internet Web sites devoted to Win32 programming in general and Windows CE in particular has increased significantly. Table C.2 lists the ones that we have found most useful in gathering knowledge pertaining to development for Windows CE.

Table C.2 Web Sites Devoted to Win32 and Windows CE

Name	URL	Contents
CE Monster	www.interworld.pda.tucows.com/cesoft.html	Extensive list of software shareware and freeware programs for Windows CE.
Chris De Herrera's Windows CE Website	www.cewindows.net	Product information and an excellent FAQ for users.
Microsoft Developer Network (MSDN) online library	msdn.microsoft.com	Online documentation for developers. Although Platform Builder documentation is not available, you can find plenty of CE documentation for developing applications and device drivers for PC companions. The online nature of the library makes it the place to go for the latest documentation.
Microsoft Windows CE home page	www.microsoft.com/embedded/ce/default.asp	Latest news, product information, technical articles, and downloads. Maintained by Microsoft.
MSN Computing Central's Windows CE Forum	www.computingcentral.msn.com/topics/windowsce/default.asp	Chat rooms, forums, product information, and software downloads for CE users.
Windows CE Webring	www.webring.org/cgi-bin/webring?ring=windowsce&list	Bookmarks to numerous useful sites that feature information on Windows CE.

Mailing Lists

A **mailing list** is a simple e-mail alias that circulates e-mail among people who have signed up to be on the list. Mailing lists are created around common interests. The premier mailing list for a Windows CE developer is the windowsce-dev list. You can sign up to receive e-mail messages as members send them. Alternatively, you can opt to receive a daily digest that combines all the e-mail traffic and sends out one integrated e-mail. You can sign up for this mailing list at www.lists.hpc.com.

Windows CE System Integrators

A list of Windows CE system integrators for North America can be found at www.microsoft.com/windows/embedded/ce/partners/si-domestic.asp. The worldwide version of this list, categorized by country, can be found at www.microsoft.com/windows/embedded/ce/partners/si-world.asp.

Third-Party Tools

Third-party tools for Windows CE are listed at www.microsoft.com/windows/embedded/ce/partners/3rdtools.asp.

CEPC Vendors

CEPCs manufactured according to specification are provided by Special Computing. You can order or get more information at www.specialcomp.com/cepc/index.html.

CE Reference Platform Vendors

Table C.3 lists CE reference platforms other than the CEPC reference platform that was referred to earlier. The boards may be used to jump-start the development process by allowing you to begin building CE kernel images and debugging device drivers before prototypes for your custom platform are available. When considering the purchase of a reference platform, attempt to find a platform that most resembles the configuration of your custom platform. This will allow you to develop code requiring little or no modifications when ported to your custom platform. In many cases the processor vendor for your custom platform can provide additional references on the availability of CE reference platforms with specific support for their processor.

Table C.3 CE Reference Platforms

Platform	Description
Sherry board	This platform was used extensively in the development of certain chapters of this book. It is based on an SH3 processor and provides three serial ports, one bidirectional parallel port, a keyboard port, VGA video, and a 10Base-T RJ-11 connector. More information on the purchase of the platform and associated training services is available at www.ezos.com.
MBX board	The MBX board is based on an MPC82x PowerPC processor or MPC860 PowerPC processor. It includes a power supply, a chassis, a 10Base-T Ethernet connector, serial ports, a parallel port, a PCMCIA slot, keyboard and mouse connectors, and options for color LCD, touch screen, and function keys or PC/104-Plus SVGA. It is encased in a rugged, metal enclosure that gives this board the ability to survive the punishment of transport between engineering labs. More information is available at www.mcg.mot.com.
Odo board	The Odo board, officially known as the Hitachi D9000, is a reconfigurable development platform developed jointly by Microsoft and Hitachi. It is one of the supported sample platforms provided in Platform Builder. More information is available at www.hitachi-first.com and http://semiconductor.hitachi.com/windowsce.

ROM Emulation Tools

ROM emulation tools (see Table C.4) replace a board's memory chips with an external emulation unit and specialized cable. This allows large ROM images to be rapidly uploaded to the custom platform, without the delay associated with the reprogramming of the flash or EPROM memory chips. Through the use of a small monitor program, certain products provide various debug services, available before activation of the operating system image. Such tools are particularly useful during debugging of CE boot loader code.

Table C.4 ROM Emulation Tools

Tool	URL
PromICE	www.promice.com
IcePROM	www.incept.ie/iceprom.html

Silicon Vendors

Companies that make microprocessors or chip sets that are supported by Windows CE are listed at www.microsoft.com/windows/embedded/ce/partners/semi.asp.

PCMCIA Documentation Sources

The PCMCIA Web site (www.pc-card.com) lists books on PCMCIA that are available at www.pc-card.com/bookstore.htm. A comprehensive list of software, cards, and developer resources can be found at www.pcmcia.oaktree.com/main.cfm.

APPENDIX D

An Introduction to Writing Windows CE Display Drivers

by Jeff Spurgat
e-mail: j.spurgat@futurality.com

For many developers, writing display drivers can be an intimidating task. Windows CE, Microsoft's operating system targeted toward embedded devices, is no exception. Fortunately, Microsoft provides C++ classes that can be used to simplify the writing of display drivers. As convenient as these classes are, they can be improved to further simplify display driver development and make display drivers more portable across Windows CE devices.

Increased portability provides additional value for display drivers as Windows CE moves to different platforms with various display requirements, such as Internet appliances, video conferencing systems, and game consoles. Even within a product family, such as Handheld PCs, this portability is valuable because each generation of product adds more features and functionality and is often implemented via different display hardware.

This appendix reviews the fundamentals of graphics, display hardware, and Windows CE display driver development, including the display driver C++ classes. It then explores improvements to these C++ classes to simplify display driver development. In the end, you will have a set of improved display driver classes that should be simple enough to quickly and easily get running on any device, yet complete enough to support any additional hardware features.

Fundamentals of Graphics and Display Hardware

For those developers not familiar with the principles of graphics hardware, it is worth providing a quick overview of the fundamentals of graphics and display technology in the context of a typical Windows CE display device. Graphics hardware is composed primarily of a display controller, a frame buffer, and a digital-to-analog converter (DAC). The display controller handles access to the frame buffer by the CPU, generates the video timing for the current display mode, and fetches the display data from the frame buffer to be displayed. The frame buffer stores the display data. The DAC converts the digital display data to an analog format to be sent to the monitor. This conversion is necessary because most monitors expect analog voltage levels that represent the intensity of each color channel. Figure D.1 demonstrates the relationships among these components. Note that as a result of the high level of integration achieved in today's silicon, some manufacturers include all three components in a single chip.

Because most monitors cannot maintain the display image on their own, the display must be continuously refreshed. Standard noninterlaced displays are refreshed one line at a time in sequence. Interlaced displays, such as televisions, refresh all the even lines first, then all the odd lines, sometimes resulting in display flicker. The time after one display line is completed and before the next one is started is called the **horizontal blanking period**. The time after a complete display refresh is done until the next display refresh is started is called the **vertical blanking period**. These blanking periods are the result of monitor technology requirements. Cathode ray tubes (CRTs) used in monitors direct a beam along the face of the tube. This beam causes phosphors on the tube to emit light, which you see as the image on the surface of the display. After the beam traces a line across the tube, it needs to retrace to the beginning of the next line. While it is retracing, the beam is shut off, or blanked. The same applies for a complete display with vertical retracing and blanking.

The display itself is organized in rows and columns. Each element, or **pixel**, in the display is stored in the frame buffer, where between one and 32 bits are used per pixel. The color of a pixel is represented by the intensity of each of the red, green, and blue color channels. These intensities are represented directly by the pixel data in modes in which a pixel is 16 bits or more. When a pixel is 8 bits or less, the pixel data usually represents an index into a color lookup table (see Figure D.2). This lookup table stores the red, green, and blue intensities for each index in the palette of currently available colors. In this case, the lookup table values are passed to the DAC.

In Windows, bitmaps are used to represent graphical images. A bitmap typically contains the pixel data for the image, the dimensions and color depth of the image, and possibly the palette for the image, among other things. Information in a Windows bitmap is not directly available; rather it is abstracted and accessible only through calls to Win32 APIs. A Windows CE display driver typically sees bitmaps in a format called a **surface**. These surfaces contain the information associated with the bitmap, but in a format that is directly accessible by the display driver.

If you require additional background information before getting started on a display driver project, plenty of good video and graphics books are available to cover the basics of these topics in more detail.

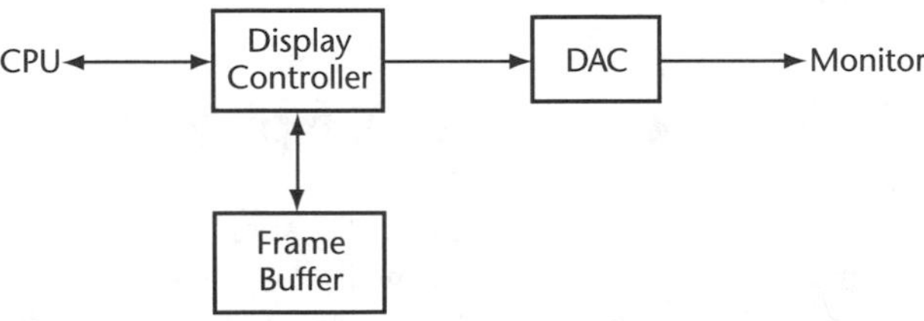

Figure D.1 Components of display hardware

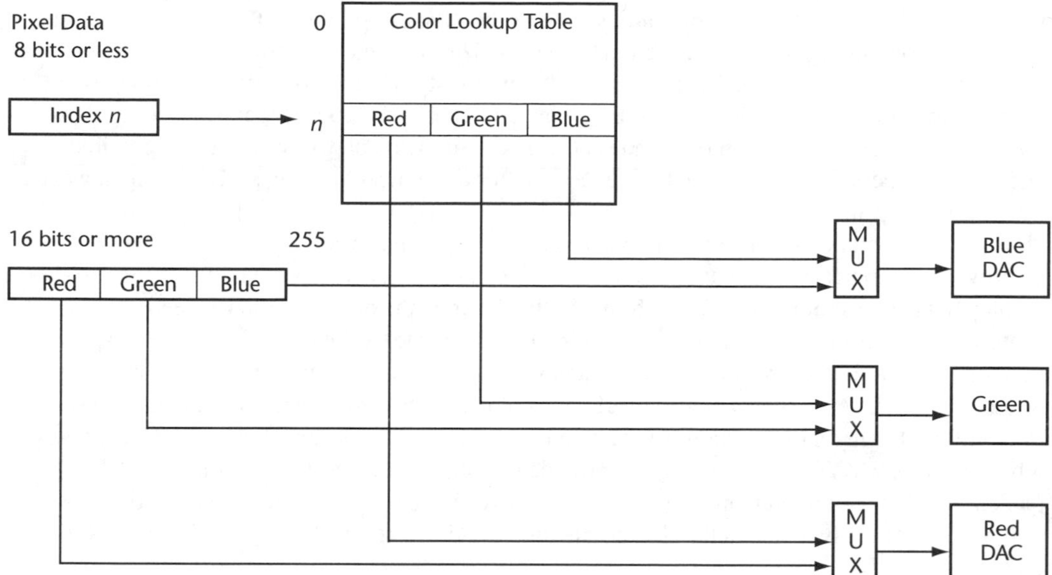

Figure D.2 Using a color lookup table

Display Driver Overview

The Graphical Device Interface (GDI) is the system component that loads and calls the display driver. It is also where bit block transfers, or blits, and drawing-related Win32 APIs are handled. In Windows CE, the GDI is contained in the Graphics, Windowing, and Events Subsystem (GWES). Interestingly, in Windows CE, GWES is an optional component, making the display driver optional as well. It is therefore possible to make Windows CE devices that are *headless*—that is, with no graphics display interface. It is important to be aware of this when you are writing other device drivers because you may not be able to depend on having access to graphical objects, such as dialog boxes, to communicate with the user.

The display driver is a native driver in Windows CE. This means that it has a custom interface that provides a standard set of functionality for display devices. In fact, this display device driver interface (DDI) is a subset of the Windows NT DDI. One of the major differences is that all Windows CE display drivers have the same level of functionality, so there is no "punting" of complex operations back to the GDI. A Windows CE display driver has only one function that it is required to export: `DrvEnableDriver`. This function is called by the GDI when the driver is loaded and is responsible for returning pointers to the other DDI functions.

Writing display drivers using the DDI directly can involve a lot of duplication of code from one display driver to the next. To greatly simplify and speed development, Microsoft has provided a set of C++ classes, called the Graphics Primitive Engine (GPE), that contain most of the base code required for any display driver. What this means for display driver developers in Windows CE is that they need to add code only for functionality that is specific to the display controller, such as initialization and mode setting, hardware cursors, and accelerated blits and line drawing.

You can really appreciate how much time these classes save if you have ever developed display drivers for other Windows operating systems. In a typical Windows CE display driver, the most time-consuming tasks usually are device initialization and mode setting. The reason is that CE does not provide video BIOS calls in which initialization and mode setting would normally be handled. The one exception is the CEPC platform, where the boot loader, Loadcepc, does make video BIOS calls to initialize and set the mode for the display device. This is possible because Loadcepc is actually a DOS application. For the typical Windows CE system, however, this is not an option.

Microsoft makes several recommendations for display hardware that are intended to improve driver performance and simplify development. The most important of these is that the display hardware should use a linear frame buffer. That is, the display memory needs to be contiguous, with this entire block of memory directly accessible by the CPU. Therefore, display memory should not be accessed through bank selection. Another important recommendation is not to use bit planes—that is, not to place each color channel or intensity component in a separate buffer. Display memory bank selection and bit planes exist as part of legacy VGA support, while most newer VGA controllers also provide support for a linear frame buffer as well as for packed pixel, or nonplanar, display modes. It is important to follow these recommendations if you wish to take advantage of the default blit and line-drawing functions provided in the C++ classes.

Graphics Primitive Engine Classes

As previously mentioned, Microsoft provides a set of C++ classes called the Graphics Primitive Engine (GPE) that simplify display driver development in Windows CE. The most important of these is the `GPE` class, which represents the display device. It is a pure virtual class, which means that other classes must be derived from it and that certain base class functions must be implemented. Because Platform Builder provides neither source code for this class nor documentation on how it is called by the DDI functions, it is useful to review the functions that require implementation:

- `NumModes` returns the number of display modes supported by the display driver.
- `GetModeInfo` returns information about a specific display mode, such as display width and height in pixels and number of bits per pixel. This function should handle the number of display modes returned by the `NumModes` function. The first mode entry in the list of supported modes is always the one selected for configuration when `SetMode` is later called.
- `SetMode` sets the display mode. This can be the most time-consuming function to write in the entire driver, especially for VGA controllers because configuration of the display device can be a fairly complex process.
- `AllocSurface` allocates a surface, which is just a block of system or video memory in which to store pixel data. The `GPESurf` class can be used to represent surfaces in system memory. To represent surfaces in video memory,

your class must be derived from `GPESurf`. The `GPESurf` class is discussed in more detail later in this appendix.

- `SetPointerShape` sets the cursor bitmap and cursor hot spot.
- `MovePointer` moves the cursor.
- `BltPrepare` is called before the blit operation is performed. It allows the driver to set up the blit hardware for performing the operation, if it is supported. It must return the actual function to be called to perform the blit operation, which can be the default blit function provided in the `GPE` class.
- `BltComplete` is called after the blit operation has been performed. It allows the driver to do any cleanup required after the blit operation, if necessary.
- `Line` is called before and after a line-drawing operation. When it is called before the line drawing is done, the function can set up the line-drawing hardware for performing the operation, if it is supported. It must return the actual function to be called to perform the line-drawing operation, which can be the default line-drawing function in the `GPE` class. When it is called after the line drawing is done, the function can do any cleanup required after the line-drawing operation, if necessary.
- `SetPalette` sets the palette. This function applies only for modes that support a palette, which is typically eight bits per pixel or less.
- `InVBlank` indicates if the display update is in the vertical blanking period. This function is useful for reducing an animation problem known as tearing, in which the display memory update is not in sync with the display refresh on the monitor.

Some other functions in the `GPE` class have default implementations that can be overridden for nondefault behavior:

- `IsPaletteSettable` returns `TRUE` if the palette can be set or `FALSE` if the palette is fixed or if the mode doesn't require a palette, such as 16-bit- or 24-bit-per-pixel modes. The default implementation checks the `Bpp` field of the `m_pMode` variable and returns `TRUE` if it equals 8, or `FALSE` otherwise.
- `GetGraphicsCaps` indicates if the display driver supports additional graphics features. The default implementation returns 0.
- `ContrastControl` receives commands related to contrast control, such as getting and setting the current contrast value. This function is useful if the display is an LCD panel. The default implementation does nothing and always returns 1.
- `PowerHandler` receives power-on and power-off notification. The function can be used to suspend or resume power to the display device. As with any other driver that receives power notifications, this function should not make

any calls that could cause the thread to block because it is the only thread running at the time it is called.

Besides these, there is a set of functions in the GPE class that are described as being required for DirectDraw Hardware Abstraction Layer (DDHAL) support. The implication is that these functions are part of the DDHAL. Since the display driver model for version 2.0 was developed well ahead of the release of DirectDraw for Windows CE, these functions were probably included as a best "guess" of the display driver requirements for DirectDraw support. As it stands, these functions are only part of the story for DirectDraw support and are not required for a standard display driver, so they will not be specifically discussed here. However, these functions do provide additional capabilities that, if properly exported, could be used by applications to bypass the GDI for improved performance.

If your display device is VGA based, you may choose to derive your device class from the `GPEVGA` class rather than `GPE`. `GPEVGA` is itself derived from `GPE`, and it is still pure virtual. It contains function implementations for `SetPalette` and `InVBlank`, using standard VGA accesses. It also contains input/output mappings to standard VGA registers. Beyond this, you will still need to implement the remaining functionality defined in the `GPE` base class.

There is a variation of the `GPE`-based driver, called a dirty rectangle driver. Its purpose is to allow a display driver based on the `GPE` class to work with a banked memory display device. An example of this is the sample driver VGA8BPP. It is a very inefficient driver from both system resource and performance standpoints and should really be used only if a linear frame buffer is not available. It works by creating a frame buffer in system memory that is the size of the display. This is very inefficient from a system memory standpoint because memory is usually a critical resource in a Windows CE device. All drawing by the GPE default drawing functions is done into this system memory frame buffer. These areas where drawing is done, or dirty rectangles, are then copied to the display memory on a bank-by-bank basis. The inefficiency here, of having to do the drawing in two steps, is obvious.

Another important class is `GPESurf`, which is used to represent surfaces located in system memory. If the driver supports the creation of surfaces in video memory, other classes will need to be derived from `GPESurf`. However, these changes are fairly minor and require mostly capturing of the `Node2D` information (see the next paragraph) and setting the flag to indicate that this surface is located in video memory.

The last class we will explore is `Node2D`. This class is used for managing video memory surfaces. An instance of a `Node2D` object is initially created that contains the pixel dimensions of the total video memory. Allocation of video memory for surfaces, including the primary display surface, is then handled through this `Node2D` instance. Within the class itself, the video memory is managed as a list of free and allocated rectangles, with all coordinates handled in pixel dimensions. The limitations of this class are that video memory surfaces cannot be created that are wider than the pixel dimensions supplied when the instance of the class was created. The video memory surfaces must also have the same color depth as the display.

Note that the GPE classes haven't changed much since version 2.0, so the information presented here should be useful and accurate across many different versions of Windows CE.

Improving the Display Driver Classes

As useful as these C++ classes are for writing display drivers in Windows CE, it is clear that additional base class functionality could be included to further simplify display driver development. The two classes to be improved upon are `GPE` and `GPESurf`. Because the source code for these classes is not provided, we need to derive classes from them in order to improve them. These new classes are called `NewGPE` and `NewGPESurf`.

A good starting point for building the `NewGPE` class is configuration and initialization. The NewGPE class is designed to require as little modification or overriding of functions as possible. The class constructor, the function `NewGPE`, provides default initialization for the variables. Currently, the only variable that would need to be changed here is `m_bIsVGADevice`, if a non-VGA device is being used. This variable is used to enable mapping of the VGA registers, as well as selection of a default VGA functionality, performed elsewhere in the driver:

```
NewGPE::NewGPE()
{
    // Flags for hardware features
    //
    m_bIsVGADevice = TRUE;      // default to VGA device
    m_bHWCursor = FALSE;        // default to software cursor
    m_b555Mode = FALSE;         // default to 5-6-5 mode for 16 bpp

    // NOTE:
    // The following data members are modified to their final values
    // by the default implementation of SetMode and shouldn't need to
    // modified here or in ModeInit.
    //
    m_pPrimarySurface = NULL;   // pointer to primary display surface
    m_nScreenWidth = 0;         // display width
    m_nScreenHeight = 0;        // display height
    m_pMode = NULL;             // pointer to information on current mode
    m_p2DVideoMemory = NULL;    // pointer to video memory manager
    m_pLAW = NULL;              // pointer to linear access window
    memset(&m_ulBitMasks[0], 0, sizeof(m_ulBitMasks)); // bit masks

    // NOTE:
    // The following data members MUST be modified to their final
    // values by the display hardware-specific function ModeInit.
    //
    m_nLAWPhysical = 0;     // physical address of the linear access
                            // window for accessing the frame buffer
    m_nLAWSize = 0;         // size of linear access window
    m_nVideoMemorySize = 0; // size of video memory, which can be different
                            // from the linear access window
    m_nVideoMemoryStart = 0;// offset within the linear access window to the
                            // start of video memory (usually 0)
    m_nScreenStride = 0;    // number of bytes per display line
}
```

To allow these functions to be hardware independent, mode information used by NumModes and GetModeInfo is taken from the variable m_gpeModeTable, a table of the supported display modes:

```
int NewGPE::NumModes()
{
    // count the number of entries in the mode table

    BOOL bDone = FALSE;
    int nIndex = 0;
    while (!bDone) {
        if (m_gpeModeTable[nIndex].Bpp==0) {
            // no more entries in the table
            bDone = TRUE;
        }
        else {
            // count entry and go to next entry
            nIndex++;
        }
    }

    return nIndex;
}

SCODE NewGPE::GetModeInfo(
                GPEMode *pMode,
                int modeNo )
{
    // make sure that the mode is valid (index is zero based)
    if ((modeNo<0) || (modeNo>=NumModes()))
        return E_INVALIDARG;

    // get data from mode table
    *pMode = m_gpeModeTable[modeNo];

    return S_OK;
}
```

The variable m_gpeModeTable needs to be initialized by the driver developer according to the modes that will be supported by the driver. It is statically defined in the source file newgpe.cpp (provided on this book's accompanying CD). However, this could be changed so that the table is instead loaded from the Windows CE registry or a configuration file when the driver is first run.

The SetMode function has been written to require no additional modification. It handles all the hardware-independent mode initialization. The first step is to verify the selected mode from the list of supported modes. Once this verification is complete, the hardware-dependent mode initialization function, ModeInit, is called. ModeInit must be overridden or modified to initialize the specific hardware and set up certain variables used elsewhere in the initialization process. These variables are as follows:

- m_nLAWPhysical specifies the physical address of the linear access window of the display device for accessing the frame buffer.

- m_nLAWSize specifies the size of the linear access window.
- m_nVideoMemorySize specifies the total amount of video memory available.
- m_nVideoMemoryStart specifies the offset (usually 0) of video memory in the linear access window.
- m_nScreenStride specifies the number of bytes per display line.
- m_bHWCursor indicates support for a hardware cursor, which is used to bypass existing software cursor support. The actual implementation for hardware cursors would still need to be included.
- m_b555Mode indicates that the 16-bit mode uses 5 bits each for red, green, and blue.
- m_bIsVGADevice indicates that the device is VGA based. This flag should be cleared in the constructor to prevent mapping of VGA registers, but at this point is still useful in bypassing default VGA implementations for SetPalette and InVBlank.

Once the hardware-specific initialization is completed in ModeInit, the SetMode function continues the hardware-independent mode initialization:

```
SCODE NewGPE::SetMode(
                int modeId,
                HPALETTE *pPaletteHandle )
{
    int nModeNum = 0;
    GPEMode gpeMode;
    // get mode entry that matches modeId
    BOOL bDone = FALSE;
    int nNumModes = NumModes();
    while (!bDone) {
        if (nModeNum>=nNumModes) {
            // failed to find matching mode entry
            bDone = TRUE;
        }
    else if ((GetModeInfo(&gpeMode, nModeNum)==S_OK) &&
        (gpeMode.modeId==modeId)) {
            // found matching mode entry
            bDone = TRUE;
        }
        else {
            // check next entry
            nModeNum++;
        }
    }
    // check if mode number is valid
    if (nModeNum>=nNumModes) {
        return E_INVALIDARG;
    }

    // pass mode info to the hardware-specific initialization
```

```
    // function
    SCODE scInit = ModeInit(&m_gpeModeTable[nModeNum]);

    if (scInit!=S_OK) {
        // something failed here, don't go any further
        return scInit;
    }
    // verify parameters that ModeInit is required to initialize
    if ((m_nLAWPhysical==0) || (m_nLAWSize==0) || (m_nVideoMemorySize==0) ||
        (m_nScreenStride==0)) {
        // ERROR: ModeInit failed to properly initialize some data
        //        members that are required. These data members need
        //        to be initialized for this function to work.
        return E_FAIL;
    }

    // continue with hardware-independent initialization
    //
    // Using the following values initialized by ModeInit:
    // * m_nLAWPhysical
    // * m_nLAWSize
    // * m_nVideoMemorySize
    // * m_nVideoMemoryStart
    // * m_nScreenStride
    // * m_bHWCursor (optional)
    // * m_b555Mode (optional)
    //
    // Initialize the remaining values:
    // * m_pMode
    // * m_nScreenWidth
    // * m_nScreenHeight
    // * m_pLAW
    // * m_p2DVideoMemory
    // * m_pPrimarySurface
    // * m_ulBitMasks
    //
    // And don't forget to initialize the palette parameter
    // pPaletteHandle.

    // initialize remaining values
    //
    m_pMode = &m_gpeModeTable[nModeNum];     // current mode
    m_nScreenWidth = m_pMode->width;         // current display width
    m_nScreenHeight = m_pMode->height;       // current display height

    // generate pointer to linear access window
    // (can't address physical memory directly, but need to
    //  create and map a pointer)
    m_pLAW = (unsigned char *) VirtualAlloc(NULL, m_nLAWSize, MEM_RESERVE,
                                                           PAGE_NOACCESS);
    BOOL bCreateLAW;
    if (m_nLAWPhysical<0x20000000) { // handle <512MB address differently
        bCreateLAW = VirtualCopy(m_pLAW, (LPVOID) (m_nLAWPhysical|0x80000000),
                                                     m_nLAWSize,
            PAGE_READWRITE|PAGE_NOCACHE);
```

```
}
else {
    bCreateLAW = VirtualCopy(m_pLAW, (LPVOID) (m_nLAWPhysical>>8),
                 m_nLAWSize,
                 PAGE_READWRITE|PAGE_NOCACHE|PAGE_PHYSICAL);
}
// check for error creating a pointer to LAW memory
if (!bCreateLAW) {
    return E_FAIL;
}

// create Node2D instance (for managing video memory)
m_p2DVideoMemory  = new Node2D(m_nScreenWidth, m_nVideoMemorySize/
                               m_nScreenStride,
                               0, 0, 32/m_pMode->Bpp);
// check for an error while creating Node2D instance
if (m_p2DVideoMemory==NULL) {
    return E_FAIL;
}

// create primary surface
SCODE scAlloc = AllocSurface(
    &m_pPrimarySurface,
    m_nScreenWidth,
    m_nScreenHeight,
    m_pMode->format,
    GPE_REQUIRE_VIDEO_MEMORY);
// check for an error while allocating primary surface
if (scAlloc!=S_OK) {
    return E_FAIL;
}

// initialize bit masks based on current bits per pixel
memset(&m_ulBitMasks[0], 0, sizeof(m_ulBitMasks));
if (m_pMode->Bpp==16) {
    // 16Bpp has two mask options
    if (m_b555Mode) {    // 5-5-5 mode
        m_ulBitMasks[0] = 0x7C00; // red
        m_ulBitMasks[1] = 0x03E0; // green
        m_ulBitMasks[2] = 0x001F; // blue
    }
    else {               // 5-6-5 mode
        m_ulBitMasks[0] = 0xF800; // red
        m_ulBitMasks[1] = 0x07E0; // green
        m_ulBitMasks[2] = 0x001F; // blue
    }
}

// create a default palette, if necessary
if (pPaletteHandle!=NULL) {
    // create palette
    switch (m_pMode->Bpp) {
    case 24:
    case 32:
        *pPaletteHandle = EngCreatePalette (PAL_BGR, 0, NULL, 0, 0, 0);
```

```
            break;
        case 16:
            *pPaletteHandle = EngCreatePalette(PAL_BITFIELDS, 0, NULL,
                                  m_ulBitMasks[0],
                                  m_ulBitMasks[1],
                                  m_ulBitMasks[2]);
            break;
        case 8:
            *pPaletteHandle = EngCreatePalette(PAL_INDEXED,256,(ULONG *)
                                               m_rgbIdentityPal,0,0,0);
            SetPalette(m_rgbIdentityPal, 0, 256); // palette needs to be set
                                                  // here
            break;
        case 4:
            *pPaletteHandle = EngCreatePalette(PAL_INDEXED,16,(ULONG *)
                                               m_rgbIdentityPal16,0,0,0);
            SetPalette(m_rgbIdentityPal16, 0, 16); // palette needs to be set
            break;
        default:
            RETAILMSG(1,
              (TEXT("NewGPE::SetMode Failed to create unknown palette type.\r\n")));
            break;
        }
    }

    return S_OK;
}
```

The m_pMode, m_nScreenWidth, and m_nScreenHeight variables, used by other functions, are set for the new display mode. Then a pointer, m_pLAW, to be used later for accessing video memory, is mapped to the physical address of the linear access window of the display device. This mapping requires calls to the VirtualAlloc and VirtualCopy functions to allow direct access to physical memory without caching. (See Chapter 8 for more information on these functions.)

Next, a Node2D object, m_p2DVideoMemory, representing all available video memory is created. This Node2D object manages video memory for the AllocSurface function, which is then called to create the primary display surface, m_pPrimarySurface. Finally, the bit mask is initialized and the default palette is set up. It may not be clear within this function, but there are really two different 16-bit display modes in common use. One mode uses 5 bits each for red, green, and blue, while the other mode uses 5 bits for red and blue and 6 bits for green. The mask values are used by the GDI to generate the correct pixel value to represent a particular color. The flag m_b555Mode is used in the driver to determine which 16-bit display mode has been set in the hardware when the mask values are being initialized. For modes other than 16-bit, this flag is ignored. Note that the bit mask created here, m_ulBitMasks, is also used by the DDI function DrvGetMasks to return pixel formatting information.

To support the creation of video memory surfaces, we must derive from the base surface class, GPESurf. Since default management of video memory is already defined within the NewGPE class through the Node2D object m_p2DVideoMemory, it makes sense to include support for the creation of video memory surfaces in our derived surface class, NewGPESurf. We do this by providing a constructor that sets the video memory flag and maintains the Node2D instance for the video memory of this surface. The destructor is then responsible for deleting the saved Node2D instance, thus freeing the video memory occupied by this surface. This is all that needs to be done for the NewGPESurf class:

```
NewGPESurf::NewGPESurf(
                int width,
                int height,
                void *pBits,
                int stride,
                EGPEFormat format,
                int offset,
                Node2D *pNode)
{
    // call general GPESurf initialization
    Init(width, height, pBits, stride, format);
    m_pNode2D = pNode;

    if (pNode!=NULL) {
        // surface in video memory, set flags and parameters
        m_fInVideoMemory = TRUE;
    }
}

NewGPESurf::~NewGPESurf()
{
    // free video memory if applicable
    if (m_fInVideoMemory && (m_pNode2D!=NULL)) {
        delete m_pNode2D;
    }
}
```

The AllocSurface function in the NewGPE class is responsible for creating system and video memory surfaces. It uses m_p2DVideoMemory, the Node2D object previously created in the SetMode function, for allocating video memory. We then create the surface itself using our derived NewGPESurf class. As previously noted, video memory surfaces can be created only in the same pixel format that the current display mode has because of limitations in Node2D. We create system memory surfaces using the base GPESurf class:

```
SCODE NewGPE::AllocSurface(
                GPESurf **ppSurf,
                int width,
                int height,
                EGPEFormat format,
                int surfaceFlags )
{
    SCODE scRet = S_OK;
    *ppSurf = NULL;

    // check that parameters are valid:
    //   video memory surface must have same pixel format as display
    if (surfaceFlags & GPE_REQUIRE_VIDEO_MEMORY) {
        // video memory surface must have same pixel format as display
        if (format!=m_pMode->format)
```

```
        return E_INVALIDARG;
    }

    // check if video memory surface requested
    if ((surfaceFlags & GPE_REQUIRE_VIDEO_MEMORY) ||
        ((surfaceFlags & GPE_PREFER_VIDEO_MEMORY) &&
        (format==m_pMode->format))) {
        // try allocating out of video memory
        Node2D *pNode = m_p2DVideoMemory->Alloc(width, height);

        if (pNode!=NULL) {
            // get offset into video memory
            DWORD dwOffset = (m_nScreenStride * pNode->Top()) +
                ((pNode->Left() * EGPEFormatToBpp[format]) / 8);

            // now create a surface for the allocated video memory
            *ppSurf = new NewGPESurf(
                width,
                height,
                m_pLAW + dwOffset,
                m_nScreenStride,
                format,
                dwOffset,
                pNode);
            if (*ppSurf!=NULL) {
                // video memory surface allocated successfully
                return S_OK;
            }

            // failed creating surface for video memory
            delete pNode; // free video memory
        }

        // if we got here, then unable to allocate out of video memory
        if (surfaceFlags & GPE_REQUIRE_VIDEO_MEMORY)
            return E_OUTOFMEMORY; // fail because surface requires video memory
    }

    // Allocate surface from system memory if not in video memory
    *ppSurf = new GPESurf(width, height, format);
    if (*ppSurf!=NULL) {
        // make sure system memory allocated
        if ((*ppSurf)->Buffer()!=NULL) {
            // system memory surface allocated successfully
            return S_OK;
        }

        // system memory surface allocation failed
        delete *ppSurf;
        // just fall through to fail
    }

    // if we got here, then something in the previous code failed
    return E_OUTOFMEMORY;
}
```

The most straightforward places to provide default implementations are the line-drawing and blit functions. For `BltPrepare`, all that needs to be done is to specify the default GPE blit function. For `BltComplete`, nothing needs to be done:

```
SCODE NewGPE::BltPrepare( GPEBltParms *pBltParms )
{
        // use the default blit function
        pBltParms->pBlt = EmulatedBlt;

        return S_OK;
}

SCODE NewGPE::BltComplete( GPEBltParms *pBltParms )
{
        // don't need to do anything here
        return S_OK;
}
```

As with `BltPrepare`, the function `Line` can simply specify the default GPE line-drawing function:

```
SCODE NewGPE::Line(
                GPELineParms *pLineParms,
                EGPEPhase phase /* = gpeSingle */ )
{
        // use the default line function
        pLineParms->pLine = EmulatedLine;

        return S_OK;
}
```

For display devices that handle cursors in hardware, the cursor functions `SetPointerShape` and `MovePointer` need to be changed or overridden to include this support. Because this functionality is not available in all display hardware or is available only in certain display modes, software cursor support is provided here in the base class implementation of these functions. Refer to the source file `cursor.cpp`, provided on this book's accompanying CD, for more details on software cursor support. Note that software cursor management requires changes in other sections of the driver as well. Searching the provided source files for the variable `m_bHWCursor`, the flag for selecting a software or hardware cursor, will highlight these additional changes.

For `SetPalette` and `InVBlank`, the VGA implementations are well defined, and they are even provided in the `GPEVGA` class. Therefore, default VGA support is included in the `NewGPE` class as well. For non-VGA display devices, support will have to be added to these functions. For reference, see the implementation of these functions in the source file `misc.ppp` (also on this book's CD).

As you have seen, the `NewGPE` class requires only the `ModeInit` function to be modified or overridden when you're using a VGA display device that supports a linear frame buffer. For non-VGA display devices, the only additional functions that need to be modified are `SetPalette` and `InVBlank`. In addition, for any display device type, the `m_gpeModeTable` variable needs to be initialized with the modes supported by the driver. It would be difficult to make display driver development any simpler than this.

Summary

The Windows CE display driver model and the Microsoft-provided C++ classes are a good starting point for display driver development. The improvements made here to these C++ classes can further simplify this development process, while still allowing for the same level of flexibility that was provided in the original classes. In addition, these changes should make the classes more portable as you go from project to project. However, keep in mind that this discussion is by no means comprehensive in its coverage of display driver–related development in Windows CE, and that there are plenty of other topics you will need to explore.

Notes on the Code:
The source files for the `NewGPE` and `NewGPESurf` classes are provided on this book's accompanying CD and were originally developed with CD Platform Builder 2.12. Any differences that may exist among different versions of CE were not taken into consideration, except where noted.

Bibliography

Anderson, Don. 1995. *PCMCIA System Architecture: 16-Bit PC Cards,* 2nd Ed. Addison-Wesley, Reading, MA.

Brown, Ralf, and Jim Kyle. 1995. *Uninterrupted Interrupts: A Programmer's CD-ROM Reference to Network APIs and to BIOS, DOS, Third-Party Calls.* Addison-Wesley, Reading, MA.

Brown, William J., Raphael C. Malveau, Hays W. McCormick, and Thomas J. Mowbray. 1998. *Anti-patterns: Refactoring Software, Architectures, and Projects in Crisis.* Wiley, New York.

Douglass, Bruce Powel. 2000. *Real-Time UML: Developing Efficient Objects for Embedded Systems,* 2nd Ed. Addison-Wesley, Reading, MA.

Gamma, Erich, Richard Helm, Ralph Johnson, and John Vlissides. 1995. *Design Patterns: Elements of Reusable Object-Oriented Software.* Addison-Wesley, Reading, MA.

Hyde, John. 1999. *USB Design by Example: A Practical Guide to Building I/O Devices.* Wiley, New York.

Maillet, Steve. 1998. "Using COM for Device Driver Development in Windows CE v2.0, Part 1: Basic Principles of COM Programming." *Windows CE Tech Journal* 1 (4) (http://www.cetj.com).

Maillet, Steve. 1999. "Using COM for Device Driver Development, Part 2: Device-Driver Implementation." *Windows CE Tech Journal* 2 (1) (http://www.cetj.com).

Phoenix Technologies Ltd. 1991. *System BIOS for IBM PCs, Compatibles, and EISA Computers: The Complete Guide to ROM-Based System Software,* 2nd Ed. Addison-Wesley, Reading, MA.

Spurgat, Jeff. 1999. "Power On Notification for Applications." *Windows CE Tech Journal* 2 (3) (http://www.cetj.com).

Index

H

I

P

CD-ROM Warranty

Addison-Wesley warrants the enclosed disc to be free of defects in materials and faulty workmanship under normal use for a period of ninety days after purchase. If a defect is discovered in the disc during this warranty period, a replacement disc can be obtained at no charge by sending the defective disc, postage prepaid, with proof of purchase to:

Editorial Department
Addison-Wesley Professional
Pearson Technology Group
75 Arlington Street, Suite 300
Boston, MA 02116
Email: AWPro@awl.com

Addison-Wesley makes no warranty or representation, either expressed or implied, with respect to this software, its quality, performance, merchantability, or fitness for a particular purpose. In no event will Addison Wesley, its distributors, or dealers be liable for direct, indirect, special, incidental, or consequential damages arising out of the use or inability to use the software. The exclusion of implied warranties is not permitted in some states. Therefore, the above exclusion may not apply to you. This warranty provides you with specific legal rights. There may be other rights that you may have that vary from state to state. The contents of this CD-ROM are intended for personal use only.

More information and updates are available at:
http://www.awl.com/cseng/titles/ 0-201- 61636-X